Rolando Dromundo

State-Building in the Middle of a Geopolitical Struggle:

The cases of Ukraine, Moldava and Pridnestrovia

With a Prologue by Nicolai N. Petro

Rolando Dromundo

STATE-BUILDING IN THE MIDDLE OF A GEOPOLITICAL STRUGGLE:

The cases of Ukraine, Moldava and Pridnestrovia

With a Prologue by Nicolai N. Petro

ibidem-Verlag
Stuttgart

Bibliografische Information der Deutschen Nationalbibliothek
Die Deutsche Nationalbibliothek verzeichnet diese Publikation in der Deutschen Nationalbibliografie; detaillierte bibliografische Daten sind im Internet über http://dnb.d-nb.de abrufbar.

Bibliographic information published by the Deutsche Nationalbibliothek
Die Deutsche Nationalbibliothek lists this publication in the Deutsche Nationalbibliografie; detailed bibliographic data are available in the Internet at http://dnb.d-nb.de.

Cover picture: kirill_makarov/Shutterstock.com

∞

Gedruckt auf alterungsbeständigem, säurefreien Papier
Printed on acid-free paper

ISBN-13: 978-3-8382-1172-5

© *ibidem*-Verlag
Stuttgart 2018

Alle Rechte vorbehalten

Das Werk einschließlich aller seiner Teile ist urheberrechtlich geschützt. Jede Verwertung außerhalb der engen Grenzen des Urheberrechtsgesetzes ist ohne Zustimmung des Verlages unzulässig und strafbar. Dies gilt insbesondere für Vervielfältigungen, Übersetzungen, Mikroverfilmungen und elektronische Speicherformen sowie die Einspeicherung und Verarbeitung in elektronischen Systemen.

All rights reserved. No part of this publication may be reproduced, stored in or introduced into a retrieval system, or transmitted, in any form, or by any means (electronic, mechanical, photocopying, recording or otherwise) without the prior written permission of the publisher. Any person who does any unauthorized act in relation to this publication may be liable to criminal prosecution and civil claims for damages.

Printed in the EU

Contents

Acknowledgements 7

Prologue 11

Introduction... 15

    1   Some theoretical considerations 25
    2   Geopolitics of Capital or Geopolitics of states under
        the logic of Capital?...25
    3   About geopolitics and Carl Schmitt.................................... 29
    4   About strategy and geostrategy 42
    5   Identities in post-Soviet societies...................................... 48

1 Geopolitical Issues Between Russia and the West 63

    1.1 The first post-Soviet years: A stateless Russia 69
    1.2 Rebuilding a Russian state 88
        1.2.1 Renaissance of a foreign policy... 97
            1.2.1.1 Gazprom and the new Russian energy politics (and policy)....... 101
            1.2.1.2 From the Commonwealth of Independent States
            *   to the Eurasian Union...111*
    1.3 United States' strategic interests in Eurasia
        after the Cold War.. 123
        1.3.1 NATO's enlargement towards Eastern Europe 127
        1.3.2 The 'colour revolutions'..131
    1.4 The EU and Eastern Europe 138
        1.4.1 EU policy towards Eastern Europe:
               The 2004, 2007 and 2013 enlargements................................. 144
        1.4.2 EU Eastern Partnership 149
        1.4.3 Can the European Union build a common
               and sovereign policy towards Russia? 151
    1.5 Conclusions 156

2 Ukraine..161

    2.1 Historical background 163
    2.2 The Soviet years 174
        2.2.1 Ukraine within the USSR..177
        2.2.2 Different attitudes towards independence 191
    2.3 Kravchuk: Trying to build a state in the middle of chaos ...196
    2.4 Kuchma: The emergence of the oligarchs 206

    2.5 Yushchenko: The myth of a revolution............................ 220
    2.6 Yanukovych: The Donbas clan stakes
        their hold on power... 260
        2.6.1 Pro Russians or pro oligarchs? 262
        2.6.2 The Ukrainian crisis, 2013–2014 277
    2.7 Crimea 305
    2.8 What next? 318

**3 Moldova and the Pridnestrovian Moldovan Republic,
Historically Justified or Geopolitical Inventions? 337**
    3.1 Historical background and the idea
        of the Great Romania...337
    3.2 The Moldovan Soviet Socialist Republic 355
    3.3 The Republic of Moldova, a failed state from its origins . 363
        3.3.1 The war after the Soviet fall 363
        3.3.2 The fragile Republic of Moldova 369
        3.3.3 Gagauzia and Taraclia 378
        3.3.4 The weak and changing foreign policy of Moldova.............. 385
    3.4 Pridnestrovia, more sovereign than Moldova? 400
        3.4.1 The inner politics of Pridnestrovia:
            The 'benefits' of the lack of recognition 400
        3.4.2 The foreign policy of Pridnestrovia....................................... 410
    3.5 The geopolitical role of the region 423

4 Conclusions 427
    4.1 Future clashes between Russia and the West...................427
        4.1.1 The evolution of the relation between
            the United States and Russia 427
        4.1.2 Could the EU develop an independent stance
            from the United States?...432
    4.2 Buffer states or failed states?.. 439
        4.2.1 Ukraine 441
        4.2.2 Moldova 454
        4.2.3 Pridnestrovia 460
    4.3 Is it possible to build a state in the middle
        of a geopolitical struggle? 463

Bibliography 469
    Electronic Sources.. 480
    Videos 517

Acknowledgements

This work is the consequence of my PhD research and it represents an effort that involves so many contributions. In that sense, to notice where does it start would be difficult but certainly it involves people from different hemispheres and therefore the need to use different languages.

Во всяком случае, моя главная благодарность это Кате за то, что она была важной мотивацией в этой работе и за то, что она всегда поддерживала меня продолжать мою академическую карьеру.

En la lista de agradecimientos me parece fundamental la contribución que representó CONACYT. Esa reminiscencia de lo que fue el Estado mexicano, que ha permitido a numerosos connacionales estudiar en el extranjero y que sin su apoyo hubiera sido imposible esta investigación. En este punto agradecería igualmente a mis hermanos Daniel y Erick por haber sido una ayuda importante en las complejidades administrativas requeridas por esta institución.

Igualmente en México doy un gran agradecimiento en su conjunto a la Universidad Nacional Autónoma de México (UNAM). Entre mis viajes a casi 70 países aún no encuentro una institución académica que la iguale en su vasta complejidad, inclusión, diversidad, masividad, heterogeneidad y que mantenga hoy en dia el caracter de una universidad pública, laica, gratuita y autónoma. Y ese sentido, como egresado de la Facultad de Ciencias Políticas y Sociales de esta institución, mi más sincero agradecimiento a una de las influencias acedémicas más importante en mi vida, Gerardo Avalos Tenorio. Su capacidad crítica y gran disciplina académica fueron un ejemplo en muchos sentidos y por eso le agradezco al igual que por ser una valiosa amistad.

A su vez, quisiera agradecer al amigo y profesor emérito Octavio Rodríguez Araujo, por transmitirme al menos un poco su actitud irreverente ante el mundo. Otro agredecimiento sería para Jacobo Alaves, quien me transmitió siempre con humor su pasión y conocimiento sobre muchas problemáticas de América Latina y momentos fundamentales de la historia de México.

Entre las valiosas amistades a quienes agradecer quisiera incluir a Fidel Irving, con quien mantuvimos a distancia numerosas discusiones sobre diversas cuestiones de política y geopolítica las cuales me llevaron a reflexionar sobre varios puntos de este libro. Otro agradecimiento también a Armando Carballal con quien compartimos las virtudes y desavenencias de TELESUR y quien durante numerosas charlas me permitió ampliar la perspectiva de nuestros temas.

In Italia, sarebbe obbligatorio ringraziare prima di tutto la professoressa Elena Dundovich chi ha avuto la dedicazione e pazienza di seguirmi durante la mia ricerca dottorale inoltre trasmettere sempre una gran gioia e buon umore davanti alla vita. Vorrei ugualmente ringraziare lo sforzo di Grazia Ricci che con la sua gran umanità e disponibilità è una parte fondamentale del funzionamento del dottorato. La sua presenza nel dipartimento rappresentò un cambio unico, il quale ringraziamo tutti quelli che siamo stati coinvolti in questo programma negli ultimi anni.

Ugualmente vorrei ringraziare tutti i colleghi del dottorato con chi ho condiviso il percorso. In primo posto menzionerei ad Azzurra (la mia dottoranda preferita) ed Enrico, chi inoltre a essere grandi amici entrambi sono stati un sostegno importante durante momenti difficili. Ugualmente ringrazio a Mariangela chi è stato il mio primo contatto e sostegno nel mondo dottorale pisano. Nella lista includo anche a Francesco Mancuso con chi abbiamo condiviso lunghe discussioni sull'attualità geopolitica, strategica e militare e con chi abbiamo costruito una pregiata amicizia. Ugualmente, non potrei non ringraziare ai miei colleghi Irene, Matteo e Volodia con chi abbiamo condiviso diversi passaggi, avventure e sventure del nostro percorso.

Al professore Gori di Firenze ringrazio i suoi preziosi consigli su come fare l'approccio dell'ambito strategico e aggiungerei un altro ringraziamento a Marta Pagnini nella quale ho trovato una gran amicizia e una persona di una gran curiosità accademica a chi auguro un brillante futuro academico.

Outside Pisa, I would start thanking Professor Nicolai Petro for his valuable contribution and support in the final part of this work and for its subsequent publication, besides the fact that he took the time to come from Rhode Island to Pisa to participate in my dissertation and he represents a first-rate example of academic excellence. I also thank Professor Martin Riegl from Charles University in Prague for his valuable comments to this research in its final steps.

In Ukraine the list is vast. I would start with Professor Perepilitza, who dedicated me his time on many occasions to discuss my research and the ongoing political situation in the country. Besides, indirectly, the Spanish language teachers in the KIMO, Marina and Alyona, allowed me to know more about the student perception during the political crisis of 2013-14. Also, I would like to thank the library personnel, both in this institution and in the Mohyla Academy for their disposition. Likewise, in the Mohyla Academy I had the opportunity to meet professor Andreas Umland and Florian Kuchler. The former gave me valuable advices and contacts and the latter advised me on the approach of the complex study of Pridnestrovia.

В Киеве я хотел бы поблагодарить также Ольгу К и Анастасию Б, которые показали мне многочисленные уголки Киева и за то, что они привели меня на мои первые митинги на Майдане, кроме того, чтобы связать меня с разными активистами и, прежде всего, за их дружбу.

Кроме того, я хотел бы поблагодарить Ирину С. за то, что она показала мне другую сторону местной украинской повседневной жизни и фантастическое гостеприимство, которое ее семья проявила в Ковеле. От Катя Я, Яна Б и Ани Б, Я глубоко ценю, как они делились своим опытом об их вынужденном выезде из Донбасса. Они принадлежат к группе тысяч людей, вынужденных покинуть свой город войной, которая радикально изменила их жизнь. Для них и всех беженцев из Донбасса я также посвящаю эту книгу.

В Российской Федерации я хотел бы поблагодарить профессора Анна Барсукова из Института Канта в Калининграде, который внес свой вклад в организацию отличной летней школы об отношениях между ЕС и Россией в тот момент, когда эти отношения проходили через сложный момент, а затем она предоставила чтобы дать мне ценные комментарии к книге. Я также хотел бы поблагодарить Марию Свиткович не только за советы и контакты, но за ее дружбу.

In Moldova I would like to thank professor Victor Chirila for the numerous books and material provided which were very useful during the chapter about this country.

В Приднестровье я хотел бы поблагодарить Ирину Бурис, которая дала мне многочисленные контакты и оказала большую помощь во время моего первого визита в эту страну. Точно так же я благодарю Наталью М за ее ценную поддержку в Тираспольском университете и за несколько советов и практическую помощь во многих отношениях. Кроме того, я хотел бы поблагодарить академический вклад и время, проведенное профессором Бабилунга и профессором Бомешко, который также предоставил мне материалы и с которыми у меня были очень интересные беседы о Молдавской Республике Приднестровья.

In Deutschland möchte ich mich bei den Mitarbeitern des ibidem-Verlags bedanken, die an dieser Veröffentlichung beteiligt waren, hauptsächlich bei Valerie Lange und Florian Bölter für ihre Geduld und ihre Hilfe während des gesamten Prozesses.

Le menzioni non sarebbero complete se non ringraziassi eternamente alla Dottoressa Sara Iacobelli per ricordami l'importanza di stare in contatto con la nostra parte emotiva e mostrarmi una piccola parte del complesso mondo che rappresenta il nostro inconscio.

E per ultimo, un ringraziamento a tutti quelli coinquilini che mi hanno sopportato durante la mia ricerca, soprattutto ma non solo ad Andreea, Raffaella, Abdellah, e per il gran sostegno di José in momenti complessi.

Y ahora si para concluir, agradecería a mis padres por haber contribuido cada uno a su manera también a este esfuerzo.

Prologue

The terms state-building and nation-building are often confused. The former should, technically, be used to refer to the promotion of a state's capacity to govern effectively, whereas the latter should refer to the processes necessary to achieve a viable nation. Although it is customary to speak of countries as "nation-states," these terms do not always coincide. One important difference is that, while the latter can gain strength from short term external reinforcement (at least this is the lesson that many in the West took from the Marshall Plan), the former seems to be the result of historical, cultural, and religious patterns that proceed at a glacial pace.

And while almost everyone agrees that the long term objective for states should be to build viable societies and governments—to become, in the words of Alberto Alesina, "state capable nations"[1]— there is sharp disagreement about how this is accomplished. For some, the primary obstacle to overcome is the hesitancy of new regimes to abandon the past; for others, the greaer danger lies in a new regime's often fanatical rejection of that past. It often boils down to a debate over which is better, revolution or evolution.

Nowhere is this debate more fractious than in the countries that emerged from the former Soviet Union. The young scholar Rolando Dromundo now wades boldly into the fray with this book about the struggles of building and strengthening new states in the midst of geopolitical struggle.

Born and raised in Mexico City, he attended UNAM university, one of the largest and most prestigious in Latin America. While at UNAM he studied journalism and languages, but the Kosovo war proved to be a turning point in his life. He was struck both by the multiplicity of unresolved social and ethnic conflicts that permeated the region, and by the overbearing impact that influential neighbors can have in a domestic conflict. This is something that Mexicans can easily relate to.

---

[1] Alberto Alesina and Bryony Reich, "Nation Building", *NBER Working Paper* No. 18839 (Issued in February 2013, Revised in April 2015). http://www.nber.org/papers/w18839

After a brief stint in government, Dromundo first pursued a career as a sports journalist. He never forgot his interest in politics, however, and seized opportunities to conduct investigations into the Mexican political campaigns, the coup d'état in Mali, the Drug War in Mexico and human trafficking from Central America to the United States.

In the early 2010s he found himself in Europe, and decide to pursue further studies in international relations at the University of Bologna in Italy. It was as a student there that he first began travelling to and studying both Ukraine, and its neighbor Moldova. After completing his Master's Degree, he decided to continue on to a doctorate at the nearby University of Pisa, focusing on the problems of state-building in the post-Soviet area.

His doctoral dissertation, on which I was honored to serve as an external reviewer, serves as the basis for this book. It explores the difficulties that post-Soviet states exhibit during the early stages of state-building, focusing particular attention on what many observers choose to overlook—that deep cultural, historical and even religious ties had been established between many of the national communities of the Russian Empire and Soviet Union, and that despite the efforts of new national elites to pretend otherwise, these persist more than a quarter century after the collapse of the U.S.S.R. The tension between the desires of the local population to preserve this heritage, and the desires of new political elites to eradicate it, he concludes, has become the major impediment to successful nation-building in some of these countries.

Moldova and Ukraine are prime examples of this. In Ukraine, the mutually exclusive nationalist rhetoric that dominates political discourse in that country has led to a "cleft country," fulfilling a conflict scenario foreseen by the late Samuel P. Huntington two decades ago.[2] The cultural fracture of the country led those exasperated with the slow pace of domestic change to foist a radical and decisive change upon the Ukrainian people. They argued that only by essentially relinquishing Ukrainian sovereignty to Western financial and

---

[2] Ibid.

security institutions, could the success of a Western-oriented "civilizational choice" be guaranteed, and the survival of Ukraine statehood assured.

As Dromundo point out, they anticipated Russia's opposition to this geostrategic shift. Some even anticipated a struggle over Crimea and Donbass, regions that have consistently sought to preserve their Russophile culture within Ukraine. But they failed to consider the extent to which regional political and economic elites would mobilize resistance to the shift of political and economic influence from Eastern Ukrainian clans to western Ukrainian clans. The consequence of this failure are the loss of Crimea, and the civil conflict in Eastern Ukraine that is now entering its fifth year.

Another, unanticipated consequence of this haste to accomplish a radical break with the past was the failure to properly appreciate how low priority Ukraine is for the West. While sanctions have been imposed on Russia for its role in the crisis, they have had no perceptible impact on Russian policies in Ukraine. Most galling of all, Russia continues to do better economically under sanctions than Ukraine does as the recipient of Western assistance.[3] As the "Revolution of Dignity" has become mired down in domestic scandals and political back-stabbing, the best and the brightest flee from Ukraine in the millions, to make their fortunes and their futures elsewhere.

Among the many insights Dromundo provides, an important one is that the persistent failure of each new Maidan, which were truly popular social protests both in 2004 and 2014, is in no small measure due to oligarchical elites within Ukraine undermining civic society's efforts to become a truly independent political voice. That is as true today for Poroshenko, as it was for his predecessors.

Shifting attention to Moldova, where he also conducted extensive interviews and field research, Dromundo sees a similarly weak polity, albeit with a more complicated way out.

The key issue in Moldova, as he sees it, is the inheritance of Transnistria, which he refers to by the local name—Pridnestrovie. In contrast to most other analysts, Dromundo underscores the relative political stability of Pridnestrovie compared with Moldova and

---

[3] Ben Aris, "A tale of two countries: Russia vs Ukraine in 2017," *BNE Intellinews*, January 9, 2017. http://www.intellinews.com/a-tale-of-two-countries-russia-vs-ukraine-in-2017-113302/

even Ukraine. This political stability, he feels, is the product of an anachronistic, Soviet-style multiethnic polity that derives broad local support from eschewing the radical transformations that reformers in Moldova and Ukraine say are necessary. Indeed, in both rebel Donbass and Transnistria, local officials eagerly point to what is happening in their respective metropoles as cautionary examples.

The overall lesson that Dromundo's comparative study provides is well worth repeating. Paradoxically, denying the Soviet past and the deep and symbiotic relationship that has developed with Russia, often undercuts the state-building process. Attempt to create stability through external realignment, in total disregard of the domestic cultural context, generally wind up undermining national unity rather than strengthening it.

In conclusion, I'd like to note that Dromundo's skills as a journalist have given him not only a keen eye for local details, but also a cultural sensitivity that many political scientists lack. Traveling throughout Ukraine, he notices many similarities to life in Russia, but also a key difference—the sense of frustration at belonging to a weak polity. This reminds him of his native Mexico, where many people also suffer from a similar sense of hopelessness, rationalized as "whatever happens in the territory is supposed to be that way." At the same time, however, he says he never encountered the sense superiority and arrogance, stemming from exaggerated patriotism, that is often found in countries like Russia, China, or the United States.

This work does not lead the reader to definitive conclusions. Rather, it provides valuable insights into the complexity of the tasks that face countries in political transition, and how they are influenced by the perpetual geopolitical struggles going on around them. For this reason alone, it is a study well worth reading.

Nicolai N. Petro
Silvia-Chandley Professor of Peace Studies and Nonviolence
University of Rhode Island (USA)

Introduction

The fall of the Soviet Union brought the last massive change to the world's political geography. It meant not only the arrival of 15 new countries to the international scene; it brought a completely new set of political, social, economic, cultural, ethnic and linguistic repercussions both regionally and globally. For some, it meant the fall of many paradigms, while for others it gave the opportunity to study from different perspectives the complexity of a new political reality. All these events happened under a new organization of global capitalism guided by the precepts of globalization, while the region that used to be part of the Union of Soviet Socialist Republics became part of the global geopolitical stake.

The new countries had the assignment of building a state that in many cases had never existed before. In some cases, it was an attempt to build a sort of 'ethnonational state' in a multi-ethnic and multilingual environment. All of them were formed in the middle of an economic crisis and were forced in different ways to dismantle the Soviet system of social guarantees.

So, why did I choose Ukraine and Moldova? There are many reasons that pushed me to select these two polities as the object of my research. First, both have the intricacy of a multi-ethnic and multilingual population and a Soviet heritage as a link. Second, they are both at the European border of the former Soviet Union and, also, these two polities have been subsumed into different empires, headed by stronger nations that until the fall of the Soviet Union had never been allowed to have a polity of their own. Besides, the current political geography puts them in the middle of different geopolitical projects. Therefore, the population in these two territories had to affront the consequences of the assertive impulse of these geopolitical proposes, headed by the United States, Russia and to a different degree by Germany and the EU.

Besides, to make it even more intricate, the attitudes towards independence from the Soviet Union were completely diverse among the local population depending on the region they came from. There was a complete difference in stance between ethnonational political groups and the group of Russian-speaking people with Soviet identity.

In that sense, to write about state sovereignty after all the political transformations that globalization brought is a complex issue. First, because nation states have undergone dramatic changes and second because the role of *Capital*[4] has evolved and extended into wider spheres. Capital for this reason is understood not only as an economic system, but also as a social system in which social relations acquire the form of the capitalist exchange, which is not like any other exchange.[5]

The evolution of capitalism brought a new set of political changes that permeated all the domains of the Soviet and post-Soviet reality. Additionally, a notable difference in the post-Soviet space was that instead of having nation states influenced or modified by the logic of, in such cases, the new polities had to create a new state under the new political and economic order of globalization. In the studied polities, attempts to institute any kind of sovereignty were threatened when the newly arrived republics were experiencing hyperinflation, economic collapse and with no national currency. Moreover, all this happened while they had to build institutions like a national army, a ministry of foreign affairs and to establish new links with the outside world—without still acknowledging the complex geopolitical restructuration that occurred worldwide and in which the United States intended to have a hegemonic role.

In this context, the goal of this research is to attempt to answer the following question:

Is it possible for Ukraine, Moldova and Pridnestrovia to build a sovereign state in the current global context while in the middle of a geopolitical struggle? To this end, it will be fundamental to understand how the relation between Russia and the West has influenced the political developments and the state-building processes in these polities after the fall of the Soviet Union.

---

[4] In this sense, I retake Marx's understanding of Capital as a set of social relations of domination. Marx, Karl, *El Capital*, Vol. 1, Mexico, D.F., Fondo de Cultura Economica, 1995.

[5] In that sense, Avalos Tenorio sustains that human beings are moulded inside the logic of Capital, either directly or indirectly. Avalos Tenorio, Gerardo and Hirsch, Joachim, *La política del capital*, México, UAM-X, 2007, page 59.

The methodology followed for this research starts with an analysis from a geopolitical perspective of the state of the relation between Russia and the West (including the United States, the EU and its members). For the theoretical part, it considers Schmitt's notions of sovereignty and it presents some of the main geopolitical schools of thought in the United States and Russia to understand each of the dominant geopolitical trends in the area.

In subsequent sections, the research examines the historical and political developments that have taken place in the area mostly from the fall of the Soviet Union until the first quarter of 2016. The local study of Ukraine, Moldova and Pridnestrovia also includes the use of local data, documents, field-research,[6] and diverse local and foreign journals as well as interviews with local scholars together with a wide range of journals and publications of diverse origins.

*****

This work contains four chapters. The first one describes the process of redesigning a Russian state after the Soviet fall. It portrays first the political, economic and social events that meant the crumble of the Soviet empire and how it reflected in many senses in the new Russian polity. The period from 1992 to 2000 had a deep impact on Russian society; meanwhile, Moscow stopped being a geopolitical actor in the global scene. At the end, if there was no real state in practical terms, it was impossible to enforce a national interest in the new global context. The process of rebuilding a Russian State was no simple affair. The decade after the Soviet fall saw not only numerous disputes between the parliament and Yeltsin but also the rise of the oligarchs while the newly established Russian army also intended to frame its own agenda. Russia had lost its primacy in determining foreign policy, while Moscow could not allow itself to act unilaterally in many areas of the world as before.

---

[6] Besides, during my field and documentary research in Kiev, I found myself in the Ukrainian capital during the events that occurred in the last quarter of 2013 around *Maidan* square. Afterwards, I also had the opportunity to visit the war zone in Donetsk on January 2015, therefore, adding numerous local experiences and findings to this work. To that extent, Ukraine, Moldova and Pridnestrovia were visited more than once, and numerous materials of different kinds were found during those journeys. .

Besides, since 2000, after assuming the presidency, Vladimir Putin acknowledged first the lack of real political power that Yeltsin's administration had, and the increased role the new oligarchs had acquired in political spheres. Putin intended from the beginning to retake control of most of the strategic assets that were in the hands of the oligarchs while also pursued an intricate struggle to recover state control over all the territories of the Russian Federation including the military operations in Chechnya together with a new organization of the Russian army.

Overall, Putin's first term also benefited from an increase in global oil and gas prices together with the designing of what would become the new Russian 'National Champions', the way to refer to the new public state enterprises related to energy that allowed for the first time in many years the Russian economy to grow notably. After all these events, it then became possible to redefine a Russian foreign policy that had been invisible in the former decade. Nevertheless, a more assertive presence in the international scene brought consequently a collision against opposing geopolitical projects. To that end, the events following the 2008 war in Georgia would signal a renewed Russian foreign policy. Russian authorities used the Kosovo precedent, set by the United States, to allow Moscow to also act unilaterally to recognize Abkhazia and South Ossetia as independent countries, bringing them in the orbit of close Russian protection and transforming them into de facto Russian protectorates.

The reconstitution of a renewed Russian foreign policy saw on the one side renewed armed forces but also a parallel foreign policy handled by Gazprom through the production of gas supplies towards countries that showed a considerable dependence on Russian provisions. Besides, this new international stance included later the attempt to establish a new geopolitical design in several areas of the former Soviet space that were being tempted to join other political organizations led by rival actors, either by China in Central Asia or the United States and the EU in Europe.

In this regard, the constitution of the Eurasian Union at Moscow's initiative has already integrated five former Soviet Republics, with Tajikistan being the probable sixth and Uzbekistan remaining as a sort of 'maybe' member. On the contrary, in Europe, the intention to draw Moldova and Ukraine closer to this project had to deal with the opposing geopolitical interests of the United States and some EU members. To that extent, the promoters of a future NATO enlargement and the EU Eastern Partnership have noted the strategic importance Ukraine and Moldova enjoy, especially the former because of its size.

The role of the so-called colour revolutions, with clear US involvement, forced Moscow to seek alternative ways to try to increase its control in the Near Abroad. Therefore, being part of that struggle, Ukraine, Moldova and, in a different way, Pridnestrovia would become the theatre in which part of this confrontation occurs. All this while inside these polities, there was also a struggle proper of state building in which different and opposing attempts were made to build a polity in which its citizens could feel identified.

The second chapter starts with an historical-political background to understand the geopolitical role Ukraine's territory has enjoyed for years. Kiev, which functioned as the capital of the Kievan Rus', would be of significance to both Russians and Ukrainians in the future. Later, Mongols occupied almost all the region and, centuries later, the territory had to deal with being subsumed by the Lithuanians and then the Polish-Lithuanian Commonwealth. Subsequently, a complex relation with the Tsarist Russia started to develop since the uprising against the poles organized by Khmelnitsky in the 1648 and the subsequent Treaty of Pereyaslav that would signal the incorporation of the territory from the left bank of the Dnieper into the Tsarist Russia. Besides, it is noteworthy to underline the opposing historical processes in the region that was part of the Russian Empire and in the ones that used to belong to the Austro-Hungarian Empire. The influence both had in each region would also have a deep social, cultural and political impact on future events.

Later on, the Soviet regime made the first attempt to gather state support to build a Ukrainian identity, even though it also had to deal with the contradictions proper of the Soviet regime while the Ukrainian territory had to suffer more than any other territory in Europe the vicissitudes of World War II, also known in the Soviet sphere as the 'Great Patriotic War'.

The first years after the Soviet fall show the ambivalence of both Kravchuk and Kuchma towards the complex process of state building. The former, used seldomly the support of nationalist groups from Western Ukraine to gain support but without endangering the control of the former Soviet political class that continued to rule after 1992. On the contrary, Kuchma, although he had close links with the Russian-speaking southeast Ukrainians, had an ambivalent foreign policy, recognizing that on the one hand he needed Western support, but on the other, he could not be anti-Russian. Therefore, Ukraine under Kuchma's regime gave military support to the US operations in Iraq while sustaining close economic links with Moscow and stopped any attempt by Ukraine to join NATO. In addition, during his term, Ukraine adopted a constitution, being the last country in the Soviet world to adopt one, which shows precisely the complexities of how the state-building process was evolving.

A section of this chapter also considers the emergence and the evolution of the oligarchs, the new group of businessmen who were capable of amassing huge fortunes in a matter of few years and who, later on, also started to pursue political power. The rise of the oligarchs, who were mostly from Eastern Ukraine, was not exempt from the struggles proper of groups linked with organized crime that are in the quest for more power, except that in this case, it would happen through interactions with foreign actors interested in taking advantage of local political events in Ukraine.

Later on, the so-called 'Orange Revolution' would signal the arrival of a president with a strong pro-Western stance, Victor Yushchenko. Even though, he had still to negotiate many issues with the oligarchs. Consequently his regime was seen as weak and incapable of achieving any of his campaign promises and became to a certain extent a hostage of the oligarchs while attempting to approach the country into NATO orbit.

In 2010, the arrival of Victor Yanukovych to the presidency marked the strengthening of oligarchs belonging to the so-called 'Donbass clan' while he intended to adopt a 'neutral' stance on foreign policy and to settle the 'language issue' with the regional language law. It appeared that once the NATO issue was not on the agenda, and that Kiev had officially assumed a non-aligned status, it would be possible to establish closer links with the West through economic agreements with the EU. For the oligarchs, it was significant to obtain the Association Agreement with the EU as it would allow them to expand their activities to different territories once they stopped being just raw-material producers but had expanded their influence through banking and investment-related services while owning luxury-settlements in EU member countries.

Even though the strong efforts by Moscow to 'convince' Kiev to join the Eurasian Union, instead of the EU's Association Agreement, clashed with the EU's lack of a proper political handling of the issue, it allowed the Kremlin to reconsider the initiative and forced President Yanukovych to retreat from his decision to sign the agreement with the EU on autumn 2013. The following reactions and the repression against protesters in Kiev would trigger the deepest political crisis in the short history of the new Ukrainian polity. It would not only show the complete failure of the state-building process of the previous years, but also the degree of foreign involvement at many levels in the local political events. These events would force the premature departure of Victor Yanukovych and pushed for a new kind of reaction by Moscow that brought the incorporation of Crimea into the Russian Federation while the new Ukrainian authorities had no possibility to react. Meanwhile, the eastern part of the country had to face a civil war, after the notably unprepared Ukrainian army suffered considerable desertions on the Russian side. Besides, the remaining part of the Ukrainian polity was on the verge of a power struggle in which the new Ukrainian authorities had to depend considerably on local warlords to confront the rebels in the Donbass that counted with unofficial Russian support. Altogether, the country was submerged in a deep economic crisis and had to depend fully on Western economic support that in exchange required complete political submission to the IMF and US economic agenda in the region, which included naming an until then US citizen as the new Ukrainian Minister of Finance. Meanwhile, without knowing the outcome in the separatist regions of Donetsk and Lugansk, and if they could go back under Kiev's control, the first and second round of the Minsk agreements showed that the whole ordeal is not something that will be decided by Ukrainians, but in the global geopolitical agenda among Russia, the United States and the EU.

In the third chapter, the evolution of Moldova and Pridnestrovia are treated separately. The reason for a separate analysis of both polities lies in the fact that they function independently. In addition, both territories had for many years different historical and political evolutions and only from 1812 to 1918, they were part of the Tsarist Russia and from 1940 to the Soviet fall they were both part of the Moldovan Soviet Socialist Republic.[7]

The Republic of Moldova had to address similar problems as in Ukraine, but it also emerged from civil war with the idea of a future incorporation into Romania as a possibility. The local political elite, aware that an incorporation into Romania would probably mean a diminution of their political role, backed up the idea of a Union with Romania, while nationalist groups were left aside from the government as happened in Ukraine. Besides, the changing foreign policy of the Republic of Moldova has reflected a pragmatic stance by local political parties, but has avoided an anti-Russian position that would diminish the possibility of a solution to the Pridnestrovian issue in Moldova's favour, that is, with Pridnestrovia remaining under the authority of Chisinau. In addition, the Moldovan Government has also showed the same signs of endemic corruption at all levels but with the local elites in a weaker position than Ukrainian oligarchs, for instance. Moreover, the fact that the country does not enjoy the same strategic importance as Ukraine and has a smaller population has reduced the interest of some foreign actors in this polity.

Meanwhile, Moscow is aware of the animosity of local minorities in Gagauzia and Taraclia to a hypothetical incorporation into Romania and often reminds through diplomatic means 'Russian concern' for Russian-speaking minorities in Moldova. In the same way, Russian authorities understand perfectly the advantage gained by the tacit support to the Moldovan Republic of Pridnestrovia. In that sense, Moldova had to deal since 1992 with the fact that it does not control its own alleged borders while considerable sectors of the population did not identify themselves with the idea of a new Moldovan polity, complicating even more any process of state building.

---

[7] An exception to this period would be the Romanian occupation of Bessarabia after operation Barbarossa in 1941 that brought the appearance of the Transnistrian protectorate.

Instead, the analysis about Pridnestrovia shows that after more than two decades of the Soviet fall, it is only one of the three studied polities in this research that by the time of these lines being written will control fully its own alleged borders. Russian support has been of considerable importance together with the presence of a reduced number of Russian peace troopers, but it does not diminish the fact that political authorities in the Pridnestrovian Moldovan Republic have enjoyed notably more stability than those of its two neighbours. Pridnestrovia, at least in its constitution, has three official languages and acknowledges its multi-ethnicity in a way that its neighbours have not been able to do. The war against Moldovan authorities and the opposition against a possible 'Romanization' have also allowed the development of an opposed political identity even while enjoying the same Soviet past as in Moldova. Besides, the PMR has benefited from Russian support to develop a non-recognized 'independent' polity. The non-recognition has also allowed some benefits because it denies any international obligations while conceding strategic decisions in foreign affairs to the Kremlin's agenda.

In that sense, the stalling of the negotiations in the 5+2 format to settle a future status of Pridnestrovia have signalled the impossibility of the involved foreign actors to find a solution that fits them with regard to this subject. Meanwhile, the status quo benefits Moscow and jeopardizes any further approach of the Moldovan Republic to join the EU or NATO.

Finally, the last chapter intends to signal some conclusions on the ongoing relation between the Western powers and Russia and its effects on the failed processes to achieve a successful state-building process in Ukraine and Moldova. The extension of the sanctions by the United States and the EU against Russia at least until 2016 and the ongoing situation in Syria do not point to a possible outcome regarding Ukraine's state-building process. Instead, they show that whatever happens, it seems to be decided on the global agenda while the Ukrainian population is not considered.

In that sense, after 24 years of the Soviet fall, it is evident the impossibility to achieve political unity to allow the edification of a solid Ukrainian polity, at least in the whole territory that used to belong to the Ukrainian SSR. Ukraine had the best chances of the three studied polities to achieve it but, as shown, lost many opportunities. The biggest failure of the *Maidan* was precisely that it was not capable of producing a political force independent of the oligarchs and of the traditional political parties that function around them. Instead, the heirs of the same political class are still in power, only this time with an increased dependency on the United States and its allies.

To conclude, this study does not pretend to draw definite conclusions about the ongoing political situation in the three mentioned polities but intends to give an insight into the complex political processes that have evolved and the influence of the external political and geopolitical struggle around them. Initially, it envisioned, very ambitiously, to understand, analyse and seek for the possibility of a genuine state-building process in a territory that is immersed in this geopolitical struggle.

In this regard, the word 'democracy' is seldom used, first, to avoid confusion with the classical liberal use of the expression that refers only to electoral democracies but also because, in fact, democratic expressions have been almost non-existent in the local political life. Many of the numerous people that participated in the rallies in *Maidan* between 2013 and 2014 represented the desire of the local population to be more actively involved and to show their disapproval against the pillage they have suffered by the local political class for years. Unfortunately, this enthusiasm was not enough to transform itself into a counterbalancing political force. At the end, it disappeared as spontaneously as it arrived. Now that Ukraine is fully aligned with the West, the question remains if a future *Maidan* could achieve the same impact, results or foreign recognition as happened before.

This work does not endeavour to be a comparison of the three polities, as each one has different historical backgrounds even though the regions share a common Soviet past and similar problematics. Even though it is important to consider that the area shares a multi-ethnic population with a mostly Christian orthodox background, and lies in a border of encountered geopolitical projects. In this sense, this research attempts to underline the geostrategic value of the area, and to contribute to the academic discussions surrounding the current local political trends mostly from a geopolitical angle.

1 Some theoretical considerations

The theoretical framework for this research is rather complex. It attempted to include different perspectives to analyse the political trends in the given region. Initially, it considers how globalization was imposed on states and former Soviet Republics. This factor, consequently, brought a loss of sovereignty at the same moment that former Soviet Republics were struggling to assert their own.

Meanwhile, under the new globalized order, a new geostrategic and geopolitical conflict between Russia and the West arose. This struggle between sovereign[8] actors included the emergence of different nationalities, entities and identities in the former Soviet Union that became in a certain way hostages of the same struggle. These new local political actors have pretended in some cases to become also assertive participants, but they have in many cases proved themselves powerless to be so by themselves.

Therefore, the aim to relate globalization, geostrategic conflict and local nationalisms required different analytical perceptions, making the task at certain points complex and even baffling. In that regard, in the subsequent sections I intend to showcase first the political impact of globalization, then an evolution of geopolitics and the geopolitical thinking, and finally the possible relation or the role played by local identities in the region in the political events.

2 Geopolitics of Capital or Geopolitics of states under the logic of Capital?

As part of the welfare state model, Capital is comprised of three different political configurations: the liberal democracies, the fascist regimes and the Soviet Union with its satellites. In the first two, Capital had its expression through private companies of a national base, while in the third, there was no possibility for the Western companies to participate. With regard to this, as Avalos Tenorio

---

[8] Sovereign as explained in the following lines in Schmitt's terms.

wrote, a 'despotic political administrative bureaucracy' at all levels of society substituted the 'despotic control' that capital develops in production.[9] In that sense, Avalos adds:

> No está de más recordar, entonces, que esa configuración social y política no era socialismo sino un gran Estado de bienestar, con sustentos, en términos de relaciones de poder, similares a los que el capital implica. Y aquí también se puede interpretar que aun el Estado soviético formó parte de esa estrategia de contención de la revolución socialista. Es esa la razón profunda del título de la célebre obra de León Trotsky: La revolución traicionada.[10]

After the crisis of the welfare state, dramatic changes occurred in the sphere of capital with several effects on the political order that included a loss of national sovereignty while 'democracy' transformed from a type of government to a set of equitable procedures for selecting representatives to legitimate the power of capital.[11]

This new order included an ideological disguise to legitimize the privatization of public spaces where more 'market' meant the private distribution of public goods like energetics, water or air space for the transmission of electromagnetic waves. Altogether, the state became one of the great organizers of the privatizations during globalization.[12] In that sense, the Washington Consensus[13] in 1989, promoted around the world to follow the recipes by IMF and the World Bank, demanded a 'structural adjustment' and a variety of measures that made undeveloped countries more vulnerable to the pressures of US-led capital.[14]

As Ellen Meiksins Wood says, globalization did not become a truly integrated economy as the so-called 'transnational' corporations generally have a base, together with dominant shareholders and boards, in single nation states and depend on them in many

---

[9] Avalos Tenorio, Op. Cit., page 115.
[10] Idem.
[11] Ibidem, page 28.
[12] Ibidem, page 26.
[13] Those were a set of 10 policy instruments suggested by Washington to face the reforms. The first experiment was in Chile during the military dictatorship of Pinochet. For more about the content of these policy instruments, see Williamson, Jon, 'What washing means by policy reform,' in *Latin American Adjustment: How Much Has Happened?*, edited by Williamson, Jon, Washington, D.C., Peterson Institute for International Economics, April 1990.
[14] Wood, Ellen Meiksins, *Empire of Capital*, London, Verso, 2007, page 133.

Introduction 27

fundamental ways. Meanwhile, wages and conditions of labour remain widely diverse around the world.[15] She adds:

> The global movements of capital require not only free transborder access to labour, resources and markets but also protection from the opposite movements, as well as a kind of economic and social fragmentation that enhances profitability by differentiating the costs and conditions of production.[16]

Meanwhile 'politics', at least with its visible façade, was reduced to the subordination of state authority to the great global companies and the exclusion of citizens from the most important decisions. The recent Greek case as part of the Euro crisis could be just a tiny example. Even after the Greek population voted against the austerity measures imposed by the EU, the European Central Bank and the FMI, the government headed by the until then leftist party SYRIZA, and Alexis Tsipras, had no choice but to surrender to the harsh measures that included privatizing public property, decreasing pensions and reducing social spending. There was simply no political way out while the supposed economic measures became a matter of power politics between Berlin and Athens. In that sense, the so-called democracy substituted the welfare state as the source of legitimation of governments while it increased the possibility of repressive actions by the elected governments against the ones who disagreed with the implicit exclusion in the dismantling of the welfare state.[17] At the end, this global economy would be part of a new geopolitical order as Wood points out:

> The very essence of globalization is a global economy administered by a global system of multiple states and local sovereignties, structured in a complex relation of domination and subordination.[18]

As part of this new political order of the capital in the last two decades, the United States continues to play the leading role. Contrary to what appeared immediately after the Soviet fall, two new actors became challengers to the US hegemonic dominance: China and, to a lesser degree, Russia. Both, even if still far from challenging US

---

[15] Idem, pages 135–136.
[16] Idem, page 136.
[17] Avalos Tenorio, Op. Cit., page 119.
[18] Wood, Op. Cit., page 141.

supremacy, are at least capable of unbalancing US geopolitical proposals in different regions of the world. There is another actor, which has the characteristics and the potential to become a fourth global geopolitical force, namely the European Union; but internal divisions and its own weaknesses have obstructed its progress.

All the mentioned leading geopolitical actors agree on the new way in which capital expresses itself and none of them is trying to modify it. The fact that all recognize the WTO rules and the IMF and promote their own 'free trade' areas shows to what extent they agree on the way capitalism should order itself politically. The only difference would be in who should lead it or how it should be led. Besides, times have changed and the label rival is not used anymore while the constant reference 'partner' is more suitable to express the relation between the big three players despite their constant geopolitical differences.

So how do all these ideas fit into the research? Precisely the political transformations part of globalization imposed on many existing states brought not only the dismantling of the welfare state but also a loss of sovereignty. Meanwhile, the former Soviet Republics were still battling to obtain some sovereignty.

These new 'pretending to be states' had to build a polity while the global conditions pushed them to cede to authority in many areas, including economic measures which provoked the population to suffer a social and economic crisis without precedents since 1992. Economic measures, as seen, responded also to a political agenda and only increased the social impacts of the crisis. While the population in other existing national sovereign states had only 'to adapt' to these political and economic transformations but still with an already existent own polity, Ukraine, Moldova and Pridnestrovia had first to build one.

Therefore, it became essential for this research to underline the political transformations brought by globalization in nation states in the last decades, and how they contributed to shape a new political order. In that sense, I would try to design a link between different geopolitical premises. Nevertheless, it would leave the question open whether the geopolitics mentioned are also the geopolitics of Capital or the geopolitics of states in the logic of Capital.[19]

3 About geopolitics and Carl Schmitt

Initially, it is important to consider a suitable definition of geopolitics, as this word is frequently misinterpreted in the colloquial language. Born at the end of the nineteenth century, the notion arises as the geographical contribution to the political doctrines from a period in which the idea of state-powers developed while Germany arose as a world power.[20]

Geopolitics evolves from a principle in which international relations are dominated by an intrinsic conflict related to the idea of politics and sovereignty. It could be said, reusing the Schmittian view, that the 'other' (referring to any state) is a potential enemy. Therefore, there are two basic premises that need to be considered with regard to geopolitics. First, that it belongs to the realm of states, but also that there are different geopolitics, as each state, being an independent political entity, will have its own geopolitical view. It belongs to a specific historical moment and to the political conditions that allowed it. In that sense, the consideration precedes the political action. Geopolitics pretends to become the 'geography of the Prince',[21] the Machiavellian prince in whom sovereignty falls, and who uses geography within political rationality to pursue what is best for the state.

The objective of geopolitics as a scientific discipline would be precisely to individuate and analyse the consequence of those representations that recall the concept of the Schmittian 'sense of

---

[19] The discussion about the existence of an own geopolitics of capital or the geopolitics of states under the influence of Capital would be the subject of another complex and deep argument that would intend to define in different ways the role of states in the new global order. Different interpretations are found among authors like Ellen M. Woods, Joachim Hirsch, Avalos Tenorio, John Holloway or Antonio Negri that in different ways analyse deeply how the states evolve or are subsumed into the logic of capital, but they do not arrive to the point of establishing a proper GEO-politics of capital, underlining the 'geo' prefix with all what it means. .
[20] Jean, Carlo, *Geopolitica del mondo contemporaneo*, Bari, Editori Laterza, 2012, page 2.
[21] Concept mentioned by Marta Pagnini and quoted in Jean, Idem, page 5.

space'.[22] To extend the definition, Carlo Jean adds that political geography expresses events that already occurred, while geopolitics relates to the politics of the future. It would be like a metaphysics of the dominion of space that reinterprets history and anticipates previsions for the future.[23]

There are two common conceptions related to geopolitics. The first is that a state defines its own politics in relation to its geography. The second instead considers that politics itself pushes to define its own geography. Personally, I would lean more to the second one, as geopolitics refers to a social activity and therefore is the consequence of two or more wills that interact in a struggle proper for 'the political' (reusing Schmitt), applied to a chosen territory.

Altogether, during the last two centuries, rather different geopolitical schools have appeared, representing diverse geopolitical notions. The following list enumerates only some of the founders of the discipline that foresaw the geostrategic importance of the Russian territory and surroundings.

The first use of the term 'geopolitics' goes back to the Swedish academic Rudolf Kjellén. He was the first to mention that the territory of the state should coincide with the nation that lives in it while noticing the importance of stable relations between Germany and Russia.[24]

Another academic, Friedrich Ratzel, included concepts like 'mobile border', 'sense of space' or the famous German notion of 'Lebensraum' implemented by the Nazi regime decades later. The German biologist and geographer rejected the geographical determinism and sustained the importance of the state's will to expand itself.[25]

It is also worth mentioning Sir Halford John Mackinder, who became famous for his theory of the Heartland which he referred to

---

[22] Jean, Carlo, *Geopolitica*, Editori Laterza, Bari, 1996, page 14.
[23] Idem, page 13.
[24] The Scandinavian author mentioned the importance of a sort of balance between Great Powers and divided the world in three macro regions: one under the United States, the second under a German-Scandinavian control that would include good relations with Russia and the third dominated by Japan.
[25] Jean, Carlo, *Geopolitica del mondo contemporaneo*, Bari, Editori Laterza, 2012, page 6.

as the 'Geographical Pivot of the earth', a territorial mass that included part of the current Russia with a piece of Eastern Ukraine and understood Russia's position as one that could eventually gain control of the whole world. He based his geopolitical ideas on his famous premise:

> Who rules East Europe commands the Heartland:
> Who rules the Heartland commands the World-Island:
> Who rules the World-Island commands the World.[26]

Later, Karl Haushofer also pushed for the primate of the land as Mackinder. The German general also understood the impact that an alliance between Germany and Russia could have on the global scene. His conception was similar to Bismarck's ideas and those same principles would be later in line with the content of the Molotov-Ribbentrop pact in 1939. At the end, this notion of a strong German-Russian alliance would later influence German foreign policy and the geostrategic line followed by Gerhard Schroeder and Vladimir Putin in the first decade of the twenty-first century.[27]

Nevertheless, there are other significant contributions with rather different postulates around the geopolitical thinking. For instance, Yves Lacoste, founder of the Journal *Hérodote*, suggested the creation of a mapping of each nation's geopolitical representations to show, as Jean said, its ratzelian 'sense of space'.[28] In fact, that proposal could help understand current geopolitical struggles like the ones regarding the post-Soviet space. In that sense, his contribution towards this research would be precisely to underline the knowledge of the geopolitical trends around Ukraine and Moldova. For Lacoste, considering the geographical pretensions of each state allows to better understand the ongoing geopolitical struggles and to take the analysis not just from a single state's will but to the domain of what is possible, in which a single state goal interacts with others. In that sense, he wrote:

---

26 Mackinder, H.J., *Democratic Ideas and Reality*, New York, NDU Press, 1942, page xviii.
27 Jean, Idem, page 24.
28 Idem, page 11.

La géopolitique ce n'est pas seulement des considérations d'envergure planétaire sur la stratégie des superpuissances, c'est aussi le raisonnement qui peuvent aider à résister à cette hégémonie.[29]

Altogether, Lacoste's contribution signalled a renaissance of the idea of geopolitics. It is important to remember that after World War II, the use of the concept became seriously questioned. On one side, in the Western Hemisphere, because it could be related with the Nazi expansion and its pretensions, and on the other, in the Soviet sphere of influence, because it was considered a 'bourgeois discipline'.[30] Nevertheless, states continued to engage in politics in relation to their own geography. In fact, the Cold War, before being an ideological ordeal, was above all a geopolitical conflict. How many examples is it possible to find where a geopolitical reason preceded an ideological position? Nixon's policy towards China in the 1970s, the war between the Socialist Republic of Vietnam and Democratic Kampuchea or the Soviet Union concurrence with the United States to provide military supplies to Iraq during the war against Iran show how the named ideological warfare was after all a geopolitical ordeal while the most basic concepts of capitalism prevailed.

The list of contributors to the geopolitical thinking is wide and all are not included in this research.[31] Instead, for the same purpose I point directly to more contemporary authors that reflect the vision of current proposals for a new world order related with each of the dominant geopolitical projects.

The first consideration is about US hegemonic views with its different shades. Zbigniew Brzezinski and Henry Kissinger retain the need for the United States to keep its hegemonic role to guarantee global stability. Both not only are well-known names in the academic world but also have played significant roles in designing US foreign policies during crucial moments of the twentieth century. In

---

[29] Lacoste, Yves, 'D'autres geopolitiques,' Herodote, 2e trimester, 1982.
[30] Idem, page 12.
[31] A wider list should mention contributions like the foundation of the *Critical Geopolitics* by Ó Tuathail, or the work by John Agnew or Klaus Dodds who are also relevant scholars in the field. Tuathail, Ó, *Critical Geopolitics: The Politics of Writing Global Space*, London, Routledge, 1996; Agnew, John, *Geopolitics: Re-visioning World Politics*, New York, Routledge, 2nd edn., 2003; Dodds, Klaus, *Geopolitics: A Very Short Introduction*, Oxford, OUP, 2007.

that sense, their pragmatic approaches suggest possible US policies for Ukraine and Russia. Regarding Brzezinski, it is interesting to note how his perception changed between 1997, when his book *The Grand Chessboard* was published, and when his last book, *Strategic Vision: America on the Crisis of Global Power*, was published.[32] During the nineties, it seemed as if the US hegemony could not be challenged in any way while the role of China was diminished. But by 2012, the former US National Security Advisor recognized the increasing presence of China, which even if still far away, from his point of view, to represent a serious threat, needed to be handled with caution, and considered it to be the only real danger to US hegemony. He thus suggested that the 'Core of Global Stability' should include not only all of Europe with its NATO members but also Russia, obstructing an alliance with China, guaranteeing US hegemony and limiting China's options to counterbalance US influence.[33]

Brzezinski also noticed the strategic role of Ukraine. He already foresaw in 2012 the geostrategic importance Ukraine had for Russia and warned about a possible explosive situation,[34] even though he thought Russia should join before an alliance with the West including NATO. That pragmatic proposal gave priority to the relations with Moscow rather than with Kiev. Still, it is worth mentioning that even if he understood the importance of establishing an alliance with Russia, he proved himself wrong with regard to two issues: First, he thought that the West could handle Russia and, second, he did not foresee that the alliance between Moscow and Beijing would get stronger and be in China's favour.

Kissinger also suggested that the United States should maintain its hegemony but in alliance with regional actors in a sort of hub-and-spoke system with the United States at the centre but with regionalized peripheries that did not annul the advantages of a unipolar US-controlled system. This way, Washington would share the security maintenance responsibilities in each region, creating a sort of balance of power without losing control.[35]

---

32 Brzezinski, Zbigniew, *Strategic Vision: America and the Crisis of Global Power*, New York, Basic Books, 2012.
33 Idem, page 156.
34 Idem, page 101.
35 Jean, Op. Cit., page 305.

Besides, it is interesting how the former Secretary of State views US relation with Russia. He also thinks this relation should be a priority while suggesting that it would be a mistake to pretend to push Ukraine into joining NATO, considering the strategic importance it has for Moscow, and the risks the hypothetical Ukrainian entry would bring. In an article published just before the Crimean referendum, he suggested to confront Moscow directly on this subject to obtain an agreement considering the ethno-political divisions present in the territory. He wrote:

> A wise U.S. policy toward Ukraine would seek a way for the two parts of the country to cooperate with each other. We should seek reconciliation, not the domination of a faction.[36]

Later, he criticized the way the Ukrainian crisis was handled by the West:

> Russia and the West, and least of all the various factions in Ukraine, have not acted on this principle. Each has made the situation worse. Russia would not be able to impose a military solution without isolating itself at a time when many of its borders are already precarious. For the West, the demonization of Vladimir Putin is not a policy; it is an alibi for the absence of one.[37]

Brzezinski and Kissinger are not the only US scholars with a realist approach, but their position contrasts with those of many neoconservatives that far from a credible realist position had also notable influence in determining US foreign policies. The ideas of scholars like Robert Kagan sustained by former officials like Paul Wolfowitz and Condoleezza Rice clash with the realist approach of the authors mentioned earlier. This contrast in the way of applying policy by the 'neocons', as they are commonly known, proved itself wrong constantly, with examples like the failure of US interventions in Iraq,

---

[36] Kissinger, Henry A., 'Henry Kissinger: To Settle the Ukrainian Crisis, Start at the End,' March 5, 2014. https://www.washingtonpost.com/opinions/henry-kissinger-to-settle-the-ukraine-crisis-start-at-the-end/2014/03/05/46dad868-a496-11e3-8466-d34c451760b9_story.html

[37] Idem.

Libya or the role of Victoria Nuland[38] in Ukraine. We end this discussion by quoting Kissinger: 'The test of policy is how it ends, not how it begins.'[39]

On the other hand, it is important to consider the Russian geopolitical thinking. For example, a renowned Russian academic, who was noticed for his role as foreign minister and, later, the prime minister of the Russian Federation, Sergei Primakov, had the tough task to attempt rebuilding a Russian foreign policy when there was de facto none after the Soviet fall, as explained in subsequent sections. He noticed the impossibility of the Russian Federation to have the same geopolitical goals as the Soviet Union and, therefore, pushed, as an official and as an academic, the idea of a multipolar order. Multipolarity should include Russia, China and India as a strong counterbalance to US hegemony, but also in which Europe and Latin America could have stronger roles as regional blocks. He tried to point out the fact that key geopolitical issues in the world cannot be solved unilaterally by the United States and without Moscow's cooperation.[40] In that sense, he justified the Russian reaction in Georgia in August 2008 as logical while pointing out the importance of future cooperation between the United States and Russia precisely as part of the multipolar order he proposed. Primakov's ideas played a primordial role during Putin presidency: a pragmatic approach that did not pretend to break fully with the United States, considering US supremacy in many spheres.

Primakov's ideas proper of a simple realist approach are not the only ones present in Moscow. Others such as the ones from the highly controversial Alexander Dugin exist. Similar to the US neocons, Dugin seems to push too far for an idealistic view, in this case defending the restoration of the Russian Empire to include all the Russian-speaking areas of the world. He draws a parallel as if Eurasia and Russia were more or less the same thing while justifying

---

[38] Victoria Nuland is the Assistant Secretary of State for European and Eurasian Affairs that belongs to the US State Department. She is the wife of the neoconservative academic Robert Kagan. Her role in the Ukrainian crisis will be mentioned in the second chapter. Note of the author.
[39] Idem.
[40] Primakov, Evgeniy, *Мир без России?*, Moscow, Российская газета, 2010, page 251.

his Eurasianist views in a mix of Russianness and Slavophile values.[41] He reconsiders the importance of Mackinder and the Heartland while portraying Russia as a leading subject of world history.[42] Even though Dugin's ideas, besides its inaccuracy, have been used by the Kremlin mostly for propagandistic purposes, opposed nationalist groups in Ukraine or other former Soviet territories showcase Dugin as an ideologue of the Kremlin. Instead, Putin's stance is guided more by a mere realist and pragmatic approach and he would not pretend as a matter of principle to break absolutely with the West, as Dugin would like.

The other geopolitical view considered is the sometimes baffling but also strategic one of the European Union and its members. The case of the EU is rather interesting. It is the biggest economy in the world. It comprises of an army with more than 500 nuclear warheads and enough quality armed forces to pose a considerable threat to any army around the world. Even if technologically behind Russia and the United States in some fields, the size of its arsenal and air force would make it difficult for its possible rivals to instigate a military action as the costs and risks would be always higher than the benefits. Altogether, the EU has the economic and political potential to become the fourth world power and in that context, it has developed its own geopolitical agenda even though in many cases under US protection; and, precisely as long as it remains under this shield, it will not have the possibility to play a more assertive role. In that sense, European geopolitical scholars' ideas would coincide with what Simms mentioned:

> The fundamental issue has always been whether Europe would be united—or dominated...[43]

Italian general Carlo Jean explains it the following way:

> Durante il periodo del dominio europeo sul mondo, dal 1500 al 1900, l'Europa conobbe una lunga epoca di sanguinose guerre interne, attraverso le quali gli Stati europei consolidarono la loro identità nazionale, che rimane tuttora l'ele-

---

[41] Clowes, Edith W., *Russia on the Edge*, Ithaca, Cornell University Press, 2011, page 44.
[42] Idem, page 50.
[43] Simms, B., *Europe: The Struggle for Supremacy, From 1453 to the Present*, New York, Basic Books, 2013, page 530.

mento essenziale della loro coesione sociale e politica. È proprio questa caratteristica che ostacola l'integrazione politica e militare dell'Europa, impedendole di essere una grande potenza globale in grado di competere con gli Stati-continente che oggi dominano l'ordine mondiale della politica e dell'economia, quali Cina, Brasile e India, otre agli Stati Uniti e alla Russia.[44]

Precisely these words explain why the EU has not been able to adopt structures and mechanisms to become a globally efficient actor.[45]

These antagonizing geopolitical views show the global scenario that includes what I define as 'the three and a half full sovereign actors'. It would include the three mentioned actors United States, China[46] and Russia while the 'half' would be Germany within a 'germanized' European Union[47] that has the possibility to play a stronger role even if sometimes it seems it (Germany) does not intend to enforce its whole potential to do so. Each of these entities has different geopolitical views, of which the views of United States, the EU and Russia will be the ones of interest for this research precisely because they are the ones that have influenced the events in Ukraine, Moldova and Pridnestrovia.

After these initial considerations, it is important to analyse the possibilities in the studied polities, to achieve any degree of sovereignty during the state-building processes and to that end, Carl Schmitt's contribution is significant. 'The Concept of the Political'[48] is one of his texts in which it is possible to understand his idea of sovereignty and his notion of 'friend' and 'enemy'. The German philosopher considered that a state recognizes itself as one, as long as it has the capacity to discern between friends and enemies and to decide with whom to establish alliances or to break them. His basic

---

[44] Jean, Op. Cit., page 192.
[45] Idem, page 196.
[46] China's geopolitical view is not included in this research, as the events in Ukraine, Moldova and Pridnestrovia do not affect them directly. Chinese leaders are fully aware of the dispute around the area and reacted accordingly. Part of this strategy would be the strengthening of the Sino-Russian relations in the last years, especially in the energetic sphere. Note of the author.
[47] When I refer to a 'germanized' EU, I do not intend to bring back the idea of a German-controlled Europe, but one in which Berlin simply takes the political leadership in the EU with all the system of checks and balances existent, while Germany serves also as the economic engine without losing a European perspective above a national one.
[48] For this purpose, I used the French edition: Schmitt, Carl, *La Notion de Politique*, Paris, Calmann-Levy, 1972.

premise of 'the political' rests in the capacity of establishing a difference between 'we' and the 'others' meaning that when humans regroup between friends and enemies, it means there is political activity.[49]

The same logic applies to the state as the supreme political entity. In that sense, a sovereign state has the capacity to determine the friend-enemy distinction in relation to a 'raison d'état', whatever it is. Therefore, a weak polity in which an inner struggle does not allow the state to decide when to go to war, or who the enemies are, for Schmitt means that it has lost political unity.

> Si, au sein d'un peuple, le potentiel politique d'une classe ou de quelque autre groupe se borne a empêcher toute guerre a l'extérieur, sans qu'il y ait dans ces groupes la capacité ou la volonté de prendre en main le pouvoir de l'Etat, d'opérer de leur propre initiative la discrimination de l'ami et de l'ennemi et de faire la guerre si nécessaire, l'unité politique est détruite.[50]

The Ukrainian and Moldovan cases show how opposed local political elites struggling for power did not allow the achievement of political unity and, eventually, the determination of a genuine state interest. Besides, it will be shown in the following pages how foreign interests involved have been capable of influencing or even determining the actions of the local elites. With regard to those kinds of struggles Schmitt would add:

> Si elles sont assez puissant pour empêcher une guerre voulue par ceux qui gouvernent l'Etat mais contraire a leurs intérêts ou a leurs principes, sans cependant de l'être assez pour déterminer a leur tour, de leur propre initiative, une guerre conforme a leur choix, ce la signifie la fin de toute unité politique constituée.[51]

The lack of a political unity and the incapacity to decide who the enemies are would mean the polity ceased to exist as politically free and became subordinate to another political system.[52] In that sense, the events in the former Soviet Republics showcase on the one side

---

[49] In that sense, an individual has no political enemies. Conflicts and wars are caused not only by purely religious, economic or juridical motives but by political ones. Therefore, the political becomes the criteria to understand diverse dimensions of the human conduct. To deepen your understanding of the subject, see Avalos Tenorio, Gerardo, *El Monarca, El ciudadano y el excluido*, México, D.F. UAM-X, CSH, 2006, pages 224–225.
[50] Schmitt, Op. Cit., page 79.
[51] Idem, page 81.
[52] Idem, page 93.

a quest to build a state but without the achievement of political unity, therefore allowing the possibility of becoming a hostage of the hypothetical enemies of an emerging state.[53]

The impossibility to maintain political unity, therefore, would bring the disappearance of that political community. Schmitt argues: 'Qu'un peuple n'ait plus la force ou la volonté de se maintenir dans la sphère du politique, ce n'est pas la fin du politique dans le monde. C'est seulement la fin d'un peuple faible.'[54]

Schmitt also considers that sovereignty allows declaring the state of exception and suspending the current legal order in its totality, going then from legality to legitimacy.[55] The last idea could be crucial when analysing the attempts to build a foreign policy of the European Union. Precisely, the impossibility to decree a state of exception reduces the quickness and the political impact of the EU leaving the initiative to its members, or forcing them just to adjust to what the United States decided to do. In that sense, the failure to act by the EU during the Ukrainian crisis would be an example.

The *Nomos of the Earth*[56] could be considered also as a geopolitical treatise. It explains conflicts to obtain territorial gains and its further division as something belonging specifically to sovereign states. Here, the German author relates wars during a certain period in which the state became the holder of a new spatial order on the earth with a Eurocentric and interstate character, after the confessional wars had been overcome. From 1648 until 1914, the European family of sovereign states were treated as *justi hostes*, a fair enemy, in which these sovereign states divided among themselves

---

[53] In that sense, Schmitt wrote: 'Si une partie de ce peuple déclare ne plus se connaitre d'ennemi, elle se range en tout état de cause du côté des ennemis et leur prête son appui sans faire disparaitre pour autant la discrimination ami-ennemi.' Idem, page 95.
[54] Idem, page 97.
[55] The discussion about the state of exception is very complex. It is not the purpose of this work to deepen it, but it is important to consider just how fundamental in Schmitt's political thinking it is to go beyond legality to legitimacy. Declaring the state of exception means the capacity by the sovereign to decide and re-establish the constitutional order, by whatever means possible, and in that sense to go beyond the law. Therefore, the capacity to decide those circumstances becomes a forging element of his concept of sovereignty. For a deeper understanding of this concept, I suggest: Avalos Tenorio, Op. Cit., pages 230–232.
[56] Schmitt, Carl, *Il nomos della terra*, Milano, Adelphi Edizioni S.P.A., 1991.

the European territory and the rest of the world became free land to be occupied by the European states.[57] The same geopolitical order allowed a juridical delimitation of war in which sovereign states could go to war and distinguished the state from traitors and criminals. The end of a war between sovereign states would usually include a peace treaty and an amnesty.

That Eurocentric global order stayed in force until 1914. Afterwards, World War I started with those precepts, but the primacy acquired by the United States changed completely the idea of war. The Treaty of Versailles, the peace agreements afterwards and the institution of the League of Nations considered for the first time states as actors that could carry on an illegal war or an 'unjust' war.

> El adversario no se llama ya enemigo, pero por eso mismo es presentado como violador y perturbador de la paz, hors-la loi y hors-l'humanité, y una guerra efectuada para el mantenimiento y la ampliación de posiciones económicas de poder debe ser transformada, con el recurso de la propaganda, en la 'cruzada' y en la 'última guerra de la humanidad'.[58]

That new perception allowed the United States to export its hegemonic vision of the world. They influenced the new borders established in Europe while making sure that the Doctrine Monroe was recognized by the European nations.[59] In that same sense, Schmitt explains the importance of recognition to other states and how since the end of World War I, the recognition of the 'legality' of a determined country was in function of the needs of a new global order headed by the United States.

> Conformemente vennero riconosciuti solo quei governi che erano legali nel senso di una costituzione democratica. Che cosa democratico e legale significassero in concreto veniva in pratica definito, interpretato e sanzionato ovviamente dallo stesso governo che esercitava il riconoscimento, vale a dire nel nostro caso dal governo degli Stati Uniti. Evidentemente tale dottrina e tale prassi del riconoscimento di nuovi governi avevano un carattere interventistico.[60]

These concepts allow understanding of how the idea of war has changed—from one that considered war as between sovereign states to another in which a new global order promoted by the United

---

[57] Op. Cit., page 165.
[58] Schmitt, Carl quoted in Avalos Tenorio, Op. Cit., page 245.
[59] Schmitt, Carl, *Il nomos della terra*, Op. Cit., page 325.
[60] Idem, pages 404–405.

States legalizes or even moralizes the use of war. In fact, the new order which appeared after the fall of the Soviet Union only recognized one global order as legitimate. So where would Russia fit? Moscow under Putin precisely had the pretension to be taken again into account as a world power, or as Slavoj Zizek mentioned, they were considered one power as long as they would not act like one:

> Back in the 1990's a silent pact regulated the relationship between the great western powers and Russia. Western states treated Russia as a great power on the condition that Russia didn't act as one. But what if the person to whom the offer-to-be-rejected is made actually accepts it? What if Russia starts to act as a great power? A situation like this is properly catastrophic, threatening the entire existing fabric of relations-as happened five years ago in Georgia. Tired of only being treated as a superpower, Russia actually acted as one.[61]

In that sense, the Russian reaction in Georgia in 2008, in Ukraine in 2013–2014 or even in Syria recently is also part of a struggle for that recognition as a great power. Schmitt would add:

> Il riconoscimento di una grande potenza da parte di un'altra grande potenza rappresenta la forma più alta del riconoscimento giuridico-internazionale.[62]

Meanwhile, Ukraine and Moldova, in fact, have not enjoyed the opportunity to evolve as sovereign countries but instead were allowed to exist by the world powers in exchange for not challenging the global order. In the Ukrainian case, as explained in the following chapters, it is fundamental to understand the great importance given by the United States and Russia to forbid Ukraine, to keep its nuclear arsenal as a precondition to be accepted in the new order. This action could be interpreted like a hidden message to the emerging Ukrainian Republic that implied: 'You can exist as long as you don't pretend to be one of us', denoting that the property of a nuclear arsenal, which gives expectancy of a completely different treatment in the global scenario, must remain a privilege of a reduced number of countries. Therefore, losing the nuclear weapons meant also to lose the capacity to eventually discern from a stronger position between 'friends' and 'enemies'.

---

[61] Zizek, Slavoj, 'Who can control the post-superpower capitalist order?,' *The Guardian*, May 6, 2014, accessed on February 22, 2016. http://www.theguardian.com/commentisfree/2014/may/06/superpower-capitalist-world-order-ukraine
[62] Schmitt, Op. Cit., 234.

Altogether, a new geopolitical order between sovereign states appeared after the Soviet fall, but in this case it was guided solely by the United States. Meanwhile, Russia and China later attempted to obtain recognition at the same level. Schmitt wrote:

> Si vede qui in modo più chiaro che mai l'obbligo generale che conferisce forza giuridica ad un ordinamento interstatale di potenze sovrane, non dipende di ogni singolo membro, ma dall'appartenenza ad uno spazio e ad un territorio comuni la cui suddivisione costituisce il 'nomos' complessivo dell'ordinamento.[63]

Therefore, from a Schmittian interpretation, it is possible to affirm that the recent resurgence from Russia and China brought a renewed will to participate in the design of a new 'nomos of the earth'. To that extent, what the German author considered 'die grosse Politik' was precisely the one that occurred at a global level.[64]

Overall, as will be shown, diverse current geopolitical projects intersect with the attempts to achieve a successful state-building process in Ukraine, Moldova and Pridnestrovia and diminish for them the possibilities to reach some sort of sovereignty after their arrival to the international scene.

4 About strategy and geostrategy

Each geopolitical vision needs also a strategy to pursue its aim. In that sense, it became necessary to consider[65] some notions of the strategic thinking when applied to political action and its possible application by the involved political actors in the area. Among the spheres of action, there will always be the military one. As Clausewitz wrote, war is a simple continuation of politics by other means.[66] One of the contributions by the Prussian general was precisely to individuate military actions as part of a political agenda. That means there is nothing autonomous from the political ordeal.[67] Pol-

---

[63] Idem, page 236.
[64] Avalos Tenorio, Gerardo and Hirsch, Joachim, *La política del capital*, México, UAM-X, 2007, page 59.
[65] The inclusion of some classics of strategic thinking was done after an interview with Professor Gori from the Università di Firenze. Note of the author.
[66] Von Clausewitz, Carl, *Della Guerra*, Torino, Giulio Enaude Editore s.p.a., 2002, page 38.
[67] *Ein Teil des politischen Verkehrs*, as referred in Idem, page 230.

itics would have always the preponderant role meanwhile war remains simply englobed as part of politics.[68] He shows the difference between strategy and tactics, then depicts how the political aim is the one that determines the military goals and the means to achieve it.

Moreover, the relation between war and politics remains after the armed conflict. For instance, it has to be considered how a decisive military defeat is a major precondition for breaking the enemy's will to resist, but is not enough precondition for lasting peace. It becomes more important to win the heart of the enemy so that his population is no longer hostile. Heuser, reusing the ideas from Clausewitz, agrees that a victory must be built on military success, but has to contain a very large mixture of politics with a peace settlement that should not prelude another war.[69] These lessons could be perfectly applicable to the search of any solution in the Donbass or in any other areas of the post-Soviet space where military conflicts have occurred.

Once the political nature of war is clear, the words 'strategy' and 'tactic' become opportune—'strategy' as a way to obtain a goal and 'tactics' as the doctrine of the use of the armed forces during combat. In that sense, for Clausewitz, for instance, strategy is the doctrine of using combats for the purpose of the war. At the end, the political sense of the military action also requires understanding the strategic sphere.

The notable *Traité de Strategie*[70] written by Coutau-Bégarie gives some insight not only into the terminology of the word 'strategy'[71] but also into the different ways in which it is applied. He differentiates, for instance, between a major strategy and a minor

---

68   Idem, pages 229–238.
69   Heuser, Beatrice, 'Clausewitz ideas of strategy and victory,' in *Clausewitz in the Twenty-First Century*, edited by Strachen, Hew and Herbrer-Rothe, Andras, Oxford, OUP, 2007, pages 161–162.
70   Coutau-Bégarie, Hervé, *Traité de Stratégie*, Paris, Economica, 2003.
71   The word comes from the Greek *Stratos Agein*, the army that pushes forward and its association creates the word *stratogos* to refer to the general. There is the word *strategikos*, for the adjective and the plural noun becomes *strategika* to refer to the functions and qualities of the general. Therefore, strategy would be the art to conduct an army or more generally the art of commandment. Idem, page 57.

strategy; the first one is used in politics and military, while the second would refer to the strategy in a secondary operations theatre that is mostly in the military sphere. The notion of strategy goes beyond violence to include intimidation and constraints while it coordinates and determines how to command the action. Coutau-Bégarie defined it as: '...l'art de coordonner l'ensemble des forces de la nation pour assurer a celle – ci la place et le rôle définis par le projet politique du gouvernement'.[72] All this while politics keeps its primacy as an active counterbalance to any possible excesses of the military Chiefs of Staff.

In that sense, Coutau-Bégarie relates also the term 'geostrategy' and its obvious relation with geopolitics. He considers that while geopolitics suggest what to acquire, geostrategy determines if it is possible to achieve and would show the necessary means required.[73] Military geography is a fundamentally static concept, while geostrategy is essentially dynamic. In that sense, the importance of a certain zone is less determined with regard to the function of its own characteristics compared to its place in the global strategic system.[74] Coutau-Bégarie explains precisely the close relation between geopolitical and geostrategic thinking.

> Le raisonnement géostratégique n'est, souvent, qu'une rationalisation des représentations géopolitiques qui empruntent moins à une réalité spatiale qu'a des images, a des stéréotypes. Il propose une logique qui se veut objective et qui, surtout, est médiatiquement transmissible.[75]

Moreover, similar to geopolitics, he questions if geostrategy is only reserved to the great powers with a wide range of means operating at a continental or global scale.[76] Finally, he shows geostrategy to be quite related with nuclear strategy, as this, he mentions, brought the apparition of the dissuasion[77] strategy.

---

[72] Idem, page 447.
[73] Idem, page 721.
[74] Idem, page 731.
[75] Idem, page 737.
[76] Idem.
[77] He defines dissuasion as the prevention of an action by the fear of the consequences. That is a state of mind resulting from the existence of a credible menace of unacceptable reaction. Idem, page 457.

'La géostratégie, finalement est sœur de la stratégie nucléaire. Le nucléaire porte l'apparition de la stratégie de dissuasion.'[78] Thus, portraying again the importance of possessing a nuclear arsenal that allows a completely different treatment in the global scenario.

Later, it becomes necessary to consider one of the more brilliant contributions to the notion of 'strategy', the one by Basil Henry Liddell Hart. His analysis of the 'indirect approach' allows a completely different perspective of the analysis not only of military but of political and geopolitical thinking.

> Indeed, it might even be said, in a deeper and wider sense than Clausewitz implied, that the defensive is the stronger form of strategy as well as the more economical. For the second compound, although superficially and logistically an offensive move, has for its underlying motive to draw the opponent into an 'unbalanced' advance. The most effective indirect approach is one that lures or startles the opponent into a false move—so that, as in ju-jitsu, his own effort is turned into the lever of his overthrow.[79]

He underlines two maxims for an offensive strategy:

1) In face of the overwhelming evidence of history, no general is justified in launching his troops to a direct attack upon an enemy firmly in position.
2) Instead of seeking to upset the enemy's equilibrium by one's attack, it must be upset before a real attack is, or can be successfully launched.[80]

He readapts Lenin's ideas to show his case:

> The soundest strategy in any campaign is to postpone battle and the soundest tactics to postpone attack, until the moral dislocation of the enemy renders the delivery of a decisive blow practicable.[81]

He also emphasizes the search for a weak spot in any military action instead of a direct confrontation. That way, success in any strategy can be achieved. To that extent, he defines strategy as: 'The art of distributing and applying military means to fulfil the ends of policy.'[82] Besides, and consequently, with his theory of the indirect approach, strategy's purpose is to diminish the possibility of resistance, and it meets this purpose with the elements of movement and surprise. Movement lies in the physical sphere and surprise in

---

78   Idem, page 743.
79   Liddell, Hart, *Strategy*, New York, Meridian, 1991, page 146.
80   Idem, page 147.
81   Idem, page 147.
82   Idem, page 321.

the psychological sphere. Tactics lies in and fills the province of fighting. Strategy not only stops on the frontier but also has for its purpose the reduction of fighting to the slenderest possible proportions. Accordingly, he suggests that a perfect strategy would be, then, the one that produces a decision without any serious fighting.[83] For instance, the Russian operation allowed the Russian Federation to take control of the Crimean Peninsula without a single shot and before any possible reaction by the United States, by the EU or by the then disorganized Ukrainian army.

Liddell Hart suggests, then, that the strategist's true aim is not so much to seek battle as to seek a strategic situation so advantageous that if it does not itself produce the decision, its continuation by a battle would definitely achieve this.[84] Nevertheless, plans should consider the risks in any cases and, therefore, ponder the importance of anticipating the enemy's capacity of frustrating any strategy.

'Any plan must take account of the enemy's power to frustrate it; the best chance of overcoming such obstruction is to have a plan that can be easily varied to fit the circumstances met; to keep such adaptability, while still keeping the initiative, the best way is to operate along a line which offers alternative objectives.'[85] Exactly this lack of vision by the EU can be seen in the way the Ukrainian crisis was handled, or better to say mishandled, while EU bureaucracy tended to remain without immediate response to Russian actions.

Finally, another notable aspect of Liddell Hart's contribution is how he recovers the Aristotelian view of temperance as a fundamental virtue in politics. 'The combatant who can keep a cool head has an advantage over the man who not. The statesman who gives that instinct its head loses his own; he is not fit to take charge of the fate of a nation.'[86] In that sense, the Ukrainian case could be an example of a lack of a statesman. Or why did the Ukrainian authorities and warlords sent armed militias to combat in the Donbass without clear military goals and without any possibility to succeed? Was

---

[83] Idem, page 324.
[84] Idem, page 325.
[85] Idem, page 330.
[86] Idem, page 357.

there a cool head taking the military decisions or there was just nationalist passion that did not consider the real circumstances?

To conclude this brief list of theorists of strategy, it is important to mention Edward Luttwak. His contribution is significant for how, among other things, he analysed the elements of surprise and paradoxes during a military struggle. Surprise, he says, is only one advantage among many that creates a brief suspension of the predicament of strategy.[87] Meanwhile, it is part of the elements that contribute to the paradoxes proper of any strategic advantage. It suggests precisely that by each strategic benefit, the condition for a disadvantage is being created. It is as if any offense creates a weak point. Any initiative even if it achieves its goal opens the possibility for a reaction from the opposing actor. Luttwak wrote: 'In strategy's dynamic paradox, a defense as much as an offensive can be too successful. It can evolve into a wider failure, whether in defending outposts, in protecting fleets that technical advances are making from servant to master.'[88]

Therefore, in the analysed territories, it is possible to notice how different political strategies by the United States, the EU or Russia allowed a new kind of reprisal to appear. Hence, when the EU and the United States did not respect the agreements regarding Yanukovych's exit, the Russian reaction was to act on Crimea. Consequently, the EU and the United States decided to apply sanctions against Russia, Moscow responded by applying economic reprisals that hurt the EU even more. The same can be said about the sanctions and countersanctions by the Ukrainian Government and Moscow.

Globally, the Kremlin perceived the actions in Ukraine as part of a strategy by Washington, and the response was then to open a military front in Syria to unbalance the West and sustain Assad. Still, that action had as a consequence the bombing by members of self-proclaimed Islamic State against the Metrojet flight 9268 that carried mostly Russian tourists. The same way, French military operations in Syria had the consequence of the tragic Paris events on November 2015. Meanwhile, the intentional downing of a Russian Air

---

[87] Luttwatk, Edward N., *Strategy, The Logic of War and Peace*, Cambridge, The Belknap Press of Harvard University Press, 2001, page 4.
[88] Idem, page 49.

48   State-Building in the Middle of a Geopolitical Struggle

Force by a Turkish plane brought a new set of reprisals against Ankara plus the detachment of the most modern anti-aircraft system in the world, the S-400, by Russia and so on.

Ultimately, each move, even the clever ones, has consequences. That is the key for understanding the paradox and logic in any strategic analysis and the key to allow a minimum comprehension of the fluctuating situation of the geopolitical struggle between Russia, the United States and other global actors. Luttwak notes, 'Grand Strategy'[89] requires coordinated action in diplomacy, propaganda and secret operations and in the entire economic sphere.[90]

5   Identities in post-Soviet societies

The complex political and economic external context became even more intricate as Ukraine and Moldova were forced in a matter of months to become independent entities while they had to define another composing element of the state-building process, which is to build an identity of their own, and which became quite complex in a multi-ethnic and multilinguistic society that shares the heritage of the Soviet period. Therefore, it is also worth acknowledging the evolution of the local *ethos* and how it interacted with the state-building attempts in Ukraine, Moldova and Pridnestrovia even if, as will be shown, foreign guidance has been crucial in the development of local political events.

In that sense, the fall of the Soviet Union brought, among other issues, a new conflict of identity among many of its citizens. On the one side, many republics besides building a state had also to create a local identity, sometimes depending on baffling symbols and a blurry Soviet past that produced diverse effects among the local population. To make it even more complex, the Russian-speaking population that lived outside the Russian Federation had also to confront being treated as a sort of 'foreigner' in their own land. These new polities envisaged new identities for a population formed in a Soviet past. Meanwhile, a new sense of confusion arrived for the Russian-speaking populations, which did not know if they

---

[89]   In this sense, the idea of 'Grand Strategy' by Luttwak could be compatible with Bismark's idea of '*Die Grosse Politik.*' Note of the author.
[90]   Luttwak, Idem, page 262.

should call themselves Soviets, Russians or belonging to the home republic.

The high social mobility of the Soviet society was also a heritage.[91] Several examples are present in the ex-Soviet world, where it is very difficult in many cases to distinguish what is Soviet, what is Russian and what belongs to the local republic. People were used to being born in one city, studying in another and getting a job somewhere in Central Asia, the Caucasus or in the Baltic Republics. This was even more common for people in the Soviet Armed Forces, which occupied a considerable sector of the population and were used to migrating quite often. At the end, for many former Soviet citizens, identity was determined more by the land and territory than from the ethnic group to which they claimed to belong. In that sense, David Laitin[92] describes in a profound sociological analysis the different attitudes that appeared in some of the Russian-speaking populations in the Near Abroad and the difficulties they were confronted with when trying to incorporate themselves into these new societies. Some of them in a few countries suffered hard conditions of exclusion and discrimination like in the Baltic countries, while in others, they fit in smoothly.

Altogether, it is worth analysing the identities in the studied polities with the sometimes amalgamating or dividing symbols among them. To that extent, to determine the development of an identity in Russian, Ukrainian, Moldovan, Pridnestrovian, post-Soviet, Gagauzian, Taraclian or any other state would be the subject of a thorough scrutiny even though it is important to evidence some characteristics.

To begin, understanding the Russian-Ukrainian relation, with regard to identity, is very complex. A historian like Graziosi considered it as fundamental to explain the Soviet collapse:

---

[91] As an example, I remember once, when flying to Ukraine, I met an ethnic German born in Turkmenistan, where he had finished his studies. Then, he moved to Kazakhstan, then Russia and finally stablished himself in Lutsk, where he got married with an Ukrainian-speaking woman and even if he understood Ukrainian language perfectly, he always spoke Russian, so he was used to having bilingual dialogues.

[92] Laitin, David D., *Identity in Formation*, Ithaca, Cornell University Press, 1998.

> La questione russa e quella ucraina sarebbero insomma al cuore del collasso, confermando che l'Urss – come sapeva anche Stalin – non era mai riuscita a risolvere la prima né a sistemare in maniera soddisfacente la seconda.[93]

At the end, the evolution of both ethnic groups through history, as commented in the first chapter, allows to understand how in most of today's Ukrainian territory, the emergence of a Ukrainian identity separate from the Russian identity was difficult.

The two most prominent Ukrainian writers, Nicolai Gogol and Taras Shevchenko, also had different perspectives on how they confronted the issue. For instance, Gogol acknowledged the following:

> I myself do not know whether my soul is Ukrainian (khokhlatskaia) or Russian (russkaia). I know only that on no account would I give priority to the Little Russian (malorossiianinu) before the Russian (russkim), or to the Russian before the Little Russian. Both natures are too richly endowed by God, and, as if by design, each of them separately contains within itself what the other lacks—a sure sign that they complement one another.[94]

Instead, as opposed to Gogol, Taras Shevchenko, who is considered one of the founders of Ukrainian literature, is also one of the symbols of Ukrainian nationalism. One difference being that while Gogol wrote in Russian, Shevchenko did so in Ukrainian.[95] Still, his ideas were shaped during the Soviet period, making Shevchenko an 'internationalist' who was against tsarism. These two diverse writers who are at the same time representative of Ukrainian literature are just one example of the complexity of characterizing a Ukrainian identity. Certainly, it would be absurd, as some Russian nationalists would like to express, if Ukrainian identity does not exist. On the contrary, it is its perception, due to its complexity, that makes it difficult to define only one 'Ukrainian identity'; instead, it would be

---

[93] Graziosi, Andrea, *L'Unione Sovietica 1914–1991*, Bologna, Il Mulino, page 652.
[94] Letter from Gogol to his long-time friend Alexandra Smirnova, also born in Ukraine, December 24, 1844, in N.V. Gogol, Sobranie sochinenii, Vol. 10 – collected letters (Moscow: Russkaia kniga, 1994), page 276 as quoted in Wilson, Andrew, *The Ukrainians: Unexpected Nation*, New Haven, Yale University Press, 2002, pages 88–89.
[95] Even though it is worth to mention that the same Shevchenko used mostly Russian and Shurzhik for his mail and diary as noted by Oles Buzina. More details can be consulted in Buzina Oles. 'Истории от Олеся Бузины: Тарас Шевченко—эталон двуязычия,' October 10, 2010. Consulted on August 22, 2016. http://www.buzina.org/povtorenie/2204-taras-shevchenko-etalon-bil engvizma.html

Introduction 51

more proper to consider it a cross-breed of different elements, as a sort of 'mestizo'[96] culture in which the product is a mix of Russian, Ukrainian and Soviet elements.

In that sense, it is imperative to understand the different historical events in today's Ukrainian territory to appreciate the different regional characteristics present. Orest Subtelny, for instance, mentions that national identity should be considered in terms of a three-part rather than a two-part scheme. That is from Western Ukraine, Central Ukraine and the southeast Ukraine.[97]

For instance, West Ukraine includes the territories incorporated into the Ukrainian SSR only after 1945. This region had a completely different historical development and never interacted with the Soviet Union or the Tsarist Russia as the rest of today's Ukraine did. The conditions in which the Habsburg Empire was organized allowed the renaissance of a strong nationalist identity within the Austro-Hungarian Empire. Later, once this region became part of the Soviet Union, locals had to recognize that their perception of what Ukrainian meant was completely different to the one existing in the rest of the territory. Western Ukrainians developed a high degree of national consciousness, but still they represent only 20% of all Ukrainians.

The second area of identity is the one related to southeast Ukraine. On the one side, it is notably Russian-speaking, it includes the most important industrial areas in the country and for centuries it has interacted with ethnic Russians. The southeast is an ethnically heterogeneous region where inhabitants identify themselves with

---

[96] The term 'mestizo' comes as consequence of the Spanish conquests in America and its subsequent colonization. It brought the appearance of a mestizo identity product of the mix of the Spanish and the Indian population. The brutality in which this process took place brought in some cases the refusal by one sector of the mestizo population to acknowledge itself as mestizo while attempting to redefine itself as Indian or even pretending to be perceived as white. Even though, it is clear in a cultural, social and anthropological perspective that the new societies were a crossbreed of both. In the use of this term regarding this research, it is obvious that the conditions related to the Ukrainian case are rather different to the ones occurred in Latin America but the word is retaken precisely to show the case of a new '*ethos*' consequence of a mix of cultures. Note of the author.

[97] Subtelny, Orest, 'The ambiguities of national identity: The case of Ukraine,' in *Ukraine: The Search for a National Identity*, edited by Wolchik, Sharon L., and Zviglyanich, Volodymyr, Lanham, Rowman & Littlefield, 2000, page 5.

the imperial policies or the Soviet policies. It has a multi-ethnic composition with the Russian language as a lingua franca. Finally, Central Ukraine serves as a mediator or buffer zone between both regions. In this sense, Subtelny added that this area holds the country together.

> In this scheme, the west and the southeast Ukraine represent the two extremes of the national-consciousness spectrum, while the central Ukraine occupies an intermediate position.[98]

Besides, there is the local elites who adapted themselves in other ways.

> Over the centuries, their elites have repeatedly assimilated into those of Poland, Russia, and the Soviet Union. Rarely did they identify primarily with their land of birth. It was this 'invisibility' of Ukrainians in spheres of high culture, politics, and economics that led many to question the very existence of a Ukrainian nation.[99]

Altogether, under the Austro-Hungarian and Tsarist Empires, opposed identities developed, namely the so-called *Rusyns*[100] and *Malorossistvo*.[101] Under Tsarist rule, both Ukrainians and Russians were orthodox and there was no confrontation with the peasantry as in Poland. The identity Tsarist officials wanted Ukrainians to adopt was broader, looser and flexible than the exclusionist, ethno culturally based Polish-type identity. Ukrainians were to become *rossiany*[102] but not necessarily *russky*[103]. In that sense, they could retain a *maloros* identity and a *rossianin*. It was more flexible.[104]

---

[98] Idem, page 4.
[99] Idem, page 2.
[100] This is the common term to refer to the Ukrainians, who lived under Austrian rule. Most of them came from the region of Trans-Carpathia. The ones that lived in territories that eventually became part of the Ukrainian SSR 'evolved' or assimilated into the idea of being Ukrainians while some groups remaining in Slovakia or ex-Yugoslavia. Taras Kuzio considers them a branch of the Ukrainian nation. Kuzio Taras, 'The Rusyn question in Ukraine: Sorting out fact from fiction,' Canadian Review of Studies in Nationalism, XXXII, 2005, http://www.taraskuzio.net/Nation%20and%20State%20Building_files/national-rusyns.pdf
[101] This word refers to the residents of Ukraine under the Tsarist Empire.
[102] The term refers to citizens of the Russian empire.
[103] The term refers to ethnic Russians.
[104] Idem, page 3.

Later, Soviet policy made them choose between two ideas: the Soviet one which is still being built and the Ukrainian, which still had not the opportunity to establish itself.[105] Besides, in the Soviet period, Russians and Ukrainians became closer as they identified themselves in conflict with other nationalities present, like the ones from the Caucasus, Central Asia or the Balts. There was no tension among them but only an awareness of the distinctions when both sides communicated in Russian. Altogether, this complex ethnolinguistic tissue showed few tensions for two decades but, as will be explained, remained fragile and exposed to the geopolitical vicissitudes surrounding these societies.

Moreover, with regard to the development of the different identities in the Ukrainian territory, another factor that is worth analysing is the role of the Russian-speaking populations in what became known as the 'Near Abroad'. As mentioned, after the Soviet fall, the Russian-speaking populations found themselves in a complex situation, and in the cases of Ukraine and Moldova they became a minority among the dominant ethnic group in the republic, and in a certain sense started to develop a different identity.

For this purpose, it is important to keep in mind the effects of *Korenitzatsia*, the name for the affirmative action policies implemented in the Soviet regime, which showed different effects with regard to integrating the local elites. The Ukrainian case showed a higher level of integration and brought a high percentage of bilingual citizens together. There was also a notable asymmetry with regard to language learning. In some cases, ethnic Russians would learn the language of the titular republic easier, as happened in Ukraine; while, in other cases like in Kazakhstan this seldom happened. Instead, as Laitin noted, for the Ukrainians and Kazakhs there were more incentives to learn Russian. Meanwhile, there were not the same incentives for the Baltic population. On the contrary, there was incentive for the Russians or for the 'Russianized Balts' to come back as rulers.[106]

The Language Law 1989 produced numerous effects among the Russian-speaking population also. Besides, it provided, as Laitin

---

[105] Idem, page 4.
[106] Laitin, Op. Cit., page 82.

noted, a sense of loss, insult and uncertainty that pervaded the everyday life of the Russian-speaking populations in the newly independent post-Soviet Republics. That included also the appearance of new interrogations:

> Should they learn the titular languages should they apply for citizenship in their new countries, how were they were to go about constructing a new social and political identity?[107]

In that sense, there were different approaches in Ukraine and Moldova also on how to handle the issue, and these became one of the mitigating factors in the civil war that brought the appearance of Pridnestrovia. In Ukraine, for instance, Kuchma pushed for assimilation and a multi-ethnic state-building process, at least at the level of speech. Instead, strong opposition came from Western nationalistic groups that also enjoyed notable diasporic support.[108] Therefore, Kuchma did not go as far as making Russian the second state language.

It is worth noting how language switching is something very common in Ukraine, mostly in Central Ukraine. Bilingual conversations are quite common, either in the parliament or on TV. Cabinet meetings are frequently in Russian, even with the current government. Besides, in Kiev, street life is conducted in Russian, including most of the commerce; but, the cultural life tends to be in Ukrainian as it is often organized by the local *intelligentsia*. Besides, with university life something peculiar happens as students have to receive the lectures in Ukrainian but once out of the classroom they speak mostly in Russian among themselves. Only the Mohyla Academy, which is linked to a different kind of university, includes notably more Ukrainian-speaking pupils, while in the public schools students speak mostly Russian. It is also common to notice university professors, who by law have to speak in Ukrainian, switch during the middle of a lecture or just greet in Ukrainian and go back to Russian.

Even though the most common 'language' to be heard around Central Ukraine would be Surzhyk, most people in Central Ukraine

---

[107] Idem, page 86.
[108] Idem, pages 99–102.

Introduction 55

commonly use a mixed dialect between Ukrainian and Russian.[109] Many people claiming to speak Ukrainian in fact are speaking Surzhik while just as many would say 'Chisto Ukrainski' is mostly heard only in West Ukraine. Meanwhile, bilingual conversations are quite common depending on the region. For instance, in Kiev, if a group of three to five people gather with only one of them being Russian-speaking, the conversation usually would take place in Russian. Instead, if the same conversation takes place in West Ukraine, more probably it would be in Ukrainian. There is also a latent preference for pop culture and diverse mass culture in Russian. At the end, what happens is that both, Russian- and Ukrainian-speaking populations have an almost perfect comprehension of both languages. Therefore, why is the language issue sometimes concerning? Simply because there have been different attitudes from the local governments in Ukraine or in Moldova towards the Russian-speaking population and also different attitudes from the Russian-speaking population towards the titular's nationality. In some cases, they adapted, in others they migrated or they attempted to defend their linguistic rights with limited success, like in the Baltics. Altogether, it was not only a black-and-white issue as Laitin observed:

> It would be a grave error to think about identity politics in the post-Soviet republics as a bipolar conflict between titular and Russians. When categories or identity change, the old labels are no longer relevant.[110]

Even if in many cases, the Russian-speaking population was quite integrated, in other cases a huge variety of names were used by the dominant ethnic group to refer to them.[111] That pushed them, in

---

[109] A study from the Kiev International Institute of Sociology showed in 2003 that from 11 to 18% of the population were found to communicate in Surzhyk. Khmelko, B.E., 'ЛІНГВО-ЕТНІЧНА СТРУКТУРА УКРАЇНИ: РЕГІОНАЛЬНІ ОСОБЛИВОСТІ ТА ТЕНДЕНЦІЇ ЗМІН ЗА РОКИ НЕЗАЛЕЖНОСТІ,' Kiev International Institute of Sociology, 2003.

[110] Idem, page 198.

[111] Laitin numbers a wide list of names to refer to the Russian-speaking population in other republics. From Russian-speaking, Russians, foreigners, occupants, Slavs, colonists, Cossacks, residents, Soviets or migrants were some of the adjectives used with either a positive, negative or neutral stance towards them. Idem, pages 265–268.

some cases like the Moldovan one or in the Baltics to mould a different identity and Laitin even suggested creating a path towards a nationality of the Russian-speaking population.

In this sense, the term Russian-speaking identity could be more prevalent than other terms like Slav or Soviet.[112] 'Russian-speakingness' became a distinction or an identity marker. Many of them had received rights for the land on which they constructed dachas. Soviet citizens became attached to the land and got a sense of rootedness. One good example in the opposite sense can be seen in the movie recently nominated for an Academy Award in 2015 for the Best Foreign Language Film, *Tangerines,*[113] which illustrates how in Soviet societies, even if people belong to a definite ethnic group, it was also the feeling of attachment to the land that gave an identity.[114]

Besides, in many cases, the Russian-speaking population in the Near Abroad also shared Soviet symbols, songs, holidays, the memory of the great Fatherland War and jokes, part of the internationalist society that was tried to build.[115] It was a sort of new conglomerate identity, the one that arose:

> ...the construction of a conglomerate identity is clearly an alternative strategy to that of assimilation ....[116]

Moreover, the Russian-speaking population who were not always ethnic Russians became a geopolitical tool for Moscow. Since the 1990s, it was even referred to as a Russian diaspora:

> So it has turned out that twenty-five million Russians all of a sudden live outside Russia. This is the biggest diaspora in the world. The leaderships of Ukraine and Kazakhstan are both extremely shortsighted. They have taken upon themselves a task that culturally cannot be worked out. For example, in Kazakhstan they will have to turn those Russians into Kazakhs.[117]

---

[112] Idem, pages 295–299.
[113] The movie gives an interesting insight of the Georgian-Abkhazian in 1992. It showed a group of ethnic Estonians residing in Abkhazia during the war. They decided not to leave their lands and relocate in Estonia. Instead besides the armed struggle, they preferred to wait to harvest their tangerines. Note of the author.
[114] Idem, pages 296–297.
[115] Idem, page 297.
[116] Idem, page 298.
[117] Remnick, David, in Laitin, Idem, page 318.

The use of the term diaspora could be controversial because, as seen in the Ukrainian case, the Russian-speaking population had been for centuries. Something similar could be said about the Moldovan case, in which Chisinau since the period of Tsarist occupation became a partially Russified urban centre compared to the Romanian-speaking countryside.

The fact is that there was a tendency for multi-ethnic regions or cities to use Russian as lingua franca, and until now they felt more attachment to Moscow even though the majority were from a non-Slav ethnic group. That explains why in many cases pro-Russian activists are not always Russian. One example could be the Gagauz, an ethnic group of Turkish origin that since the fall of the Soviet Union pretended to obtain more autonomy and until now have received open support from Moscow, when the local authorities express their desire to follow Moscow-attached policies instead of the Western-oriented policies that the government adopts.

In this sense, Russia tries to present itself as the defender of the multilinguistic and multi-ethnic Russian-speaking population that is a product of the Soviet past. Besides, it shows the lack of capacity by the governments in Moldova and Ukraine to integrate minorities in a polity in which its inhabitants can feel identified.

For example, ethnic Ukrainians have been divided on the question of a civic or culturalist national programme to address state building. The radical nationalists in the West, until the 2014 events, were not able to undermine the electoral weight of the civic nationalist in the East. Until now, radical nationalists have pretended to humiliate Ukrainians who do not use Ukrainian in public.[118] Instead, Russian-speaking areas have also defended their rights and acted collectively.[119] Laitin goes even further to suggest that they could emerge as a new national form.

> It is most likely in the Baltics, but also possible in Ukraine, that a Russian speaking population will have the memories, the interest, and the possibility of emerg-

---

[118] I remember, for instance, in Kiev, I was with a professor from Western Ukraine in a restaurant. He denied to pay the bill until the waiter would speak to him in Ukrainian. In fact, the waiter who was Bulgarian and had attended a Russian-speaking school did not know Ukrainian at all and only one of the present personnel at that time could speak Ukrainian freely.
[119] Idem, page 361.

ing as a new national form. But in all four republics, the social formation of 'Russian-speakingness', an identity group forged from the double cataclysm will continue to play an important political role as titular leaders in the post-Soviet republics seek to fashion, within their republican boundaries nation-states.[120]

In this sense, it will be interesting to follow up on the current events in the Donbass while they manage to develop separate local identities, among the locals and the rest of Ukraine. Since 2014, the war has exacerbated nationalist passions. In that sense, the oligarchs, while looking also for political survival, promoted a new patriotic wind through their own Media and received considerable acceptance in many Ukrainian regions only with a strong opposition in the Russian-speaking Donbass.

Laitin sustained more than a decade ago that the linguistic issues had produced until then only few cases of violent reaction.[121] At the end, as will be explained, this is never based only on linguistic or ethnic reasons but on political reasons also. Therefore, tensions appeared in Latvia and Estonia with no deep effect, while, it should be noted, there was a war in Moldova that among other things used the linguistic argument as one of many arguments to push for the creation of Pridnestrovia.

Altogether, the Moldovan and Pridnestrovian cases are rather different to the Ukrainian case. First, Moldova has an elite group related to a Soviet past that tries for political survival to appear different from Romania. Hence, it becomes even more complicated to find unique elements that are not either Romanian, Soviet or Russian and that would be solely 'Moldovan'. Moldova emerged in the international scene in the middle of a civil war and, until now, it is one of the poorest countries in Europe. Therefore, this fact reduces even more the appeal among other ethnic groups to feel identified with the Moldovan polity.

---

[120] Idem, page 363.
[121] Laitin suggested that violent reactions are product of a low possibility of acceptance in the population of their movement. He compares the Catalan, the Basque cases, even though the context I would say are rather different as other geopolitical actors do not influence Catalans, and Basques, and they are not part of polities that pretend to build a new state only in the recent years.

Introduction 59

It would be naïve to suggest an Estonian approach towards minorities applied for Moldova, as Montanari did,[122] precisely considering the numerous socio-economic differences they had after the Soviet collapse. Estonia has well-developed Scandinavian economies as neighbours while Moldova has an undeveloped Romania, along with the Pridnestrovian issue.

Finally, with regard to the development of the Pridnestrovian identity, discussed carefully in the third chapter, it is worth considering the words from Professor Mikulas Fabry: 'Denials of state recognition have had a far stronger affirmative impact on national identity than recognition.'[123] In that sense, the lack of recognition together with the war against the Moldovan Armed Forces, chosen elements from the Soviet past and the presence of different ethnic groups have allowed the formation of a sort of 'Pridnestrovian identity', which serves the political goal of the local authorities and reinforces an antagonistic idea against Moldova. Therefore, this case would be not only a Laitin's conceived identity around the Russian-speaking populations in the Near Abroad[124] but would include more reinforcing elements.

Finally, to understand the pretension to build local identities today in Ukraine, Moldova and Pridnestrovia it is also important to consider Eric Hobsbawn's analysis of the role played by the invention of traditions in the nation-building process.

> Inventing traditions ... is essentially a process of formalization and ritualization, characterized by reference to the past, if only by imposing repetition.[125]

The formation of a just or legitimate new political elite requires the creation of a completely new set of values to reinforce the idea of a

---

[122] Montanari, Arianna, 'Un caso di nazionalismo normativo: l'Estonia,' in *La fine del Sistema Sovietico e i Paesi Baltici, Il caso dell'Estonia*, edited by Pirzio Ammassari, Gloria and Montanari, Arianna, Milan, Francoangeli, 2003, pages 61–63.
[123] Fabry, Mikulas, 'Unrecognized States and National Identity,' Geopolitical Conference, Prague, November 13, 2015.
[124] Laitin, Op. Cit.
[125] Hobsbawn, Eric, 'Inventing traditions' in Ed. Hobsbawm, Eric and Ranger, Terence, *The Invention of Tradition*, Cambridge, Cambridge University Press, 1983, page 4.

certain political community. Therefore, even if invention of traditions has occurred often throughout history, it appears more often in certain conditions:

> ... we should expect it to occur more frequently when a rapid transformation of society weakens or destroys the social patterns for which 'old' traditions had been designed, producing new ones to which they were not applicable, or when such old traditions and their institutional carriers and promulgators no longer prove sufficiently adaptable and flexible, or are otherwise eliminated: in short, when there are sufficiently large and rapid changes on the demand or the supply side.[126]

Hobsbawm catalogues three types of invented traditions:

a) Those establishing or symbolizing social cohesion or the membership of groups
b) Those establishing or legitimizing institutions, status or relations of authority
c) Those whose main purpose was socialization, the inculcation of beliefs, value systems and conventions of behaviour[127]

The second and third, as he underlined, are devised, flags, anthems or emblems for example. Imagine how, after the Soviet fall, 15 new anthems had to be created, together with a new list of holidays or to be readapted from the old ones, even though sometimes they do not have the same roots as others. For example, the first Russian anthem never got the same acceptance as the former Soviet one, something that Vladimir Putin noticed; so when he arrived to power one of his first actions was to go back to the old one with slight modifications.[128]

Altogether, the study of invented traditions cannot be separated from the wider study of the history of society. Invented traditions, as far as possible, use history as a legitimator of action and a cement for group cohesion.[129] Therefore, they become highly relevant to the

---

[126] Idem, pages 4–5.
[127] Idem, page 9.
[128] Another example could be the Russian Holiday known as Unity Day on November 4 that tried to replace the celebrations of the October Revolution on November 7.
[129] Idem, page 12.

historical innovation of a nation and associate themself with phenomena like nationalism, the nation state, national symbols, histories, etc.[130]

> Modern nations and all their impedimenta generally claim to be the opposite of novel, namely rooted in the remotest antiquity, and the opposite of constructed, namely human communities so 'natural' as to require no definition other than self-assertion.[131]

In that sense, Hobsbawm's ideas are pertinent to this research. The situation becomes even more complex in a multi-ethnic and multinational territory like Ukraine or Moldova where the selection of a selected tradition is also a political choice. Therefore, holidays like May 9, or other Soviet festivities, even if they have a great acceptance among the local population, still cause controversies.

Altogether, when the Ukrainian Government stipulated, since 2015, that the end of the World War II would be celebrated on May 8 (as if that would make Ukraine more Westernized) instead of May 9, it also provoked a local outrage from another sector of the population, increasing the political and cultural fracture with the local population in Eastern Ukraine, especially in the Donbass. The same way, the current government intends to abolish or modify old holidays while creating new ones precisely to give certain legitimacy to the new regime that could make it seem different from the former one.

Overall, the formation of local identities has also played a role in the state-building process while interacting with the geopolitical projects that surround the studied polities. Therefore, after laying out these introductory ideas, it is possible to proceed to the analysis of the geopolitical implications of the struggle between Russia and the West.

---

[130] Idem, page 13.
[131] Idem, page 14.

1 Geopolitical Issues Between Russia and the West

When Vladimir Putin declared on 26 April 2005: '.... the collapse of the Soviet Union was the greatest geopolitical catastrophe of the century',[132] Western media throughout the world suddenly started to moan that the Russian president was disapproving the fall of the Soviet regime.[133] The Polish Foreign Minister at that time, Adam Rotfeld, even complained of what he thought was an apology of the USSR.[134] In fact, if we listen to the complete speech, there was no single word defending the Soviet regime, but otherwise he wanted to underline the event simply and purely as what it was, that is a geopolitical (not only political) tragedy.[135]

This means there was a geopolitical confrontation and a winner. It depicts the fact that the Soviet collapse and the separation of the 15 SSRs into new entities meant that huge areas of the world were not under Moscow's control and could become part of other geopolitical projects. In that sense, he was right; no other country had lost so much territory and influence in such a short period.[136] In this case, not only did the country lose territory but the state also crumbled.

The fall of the USSR represented the end of a politically and economically organized system together with the arrival of 15 new pol-

---

[132] 'Putin: "Collapse of the Soviet Union was a major geopolitical disaster of the century",' published January 12, 2014. http://www.youtube.com/watch?v=nTvswwU5Eco

[133] Eckel, Mike, "Putin calls Soviet collapse a 'Geopolitical Catastrophe,'" Associated Press, 26-IV-2005. http://www.utsandiego.com/uniontrib/2005 0426/news_1n26russia.html

[134] Idem.

[135] The idea of a geopolitical tragedy should be understood as it was mentioned in the foregoing pages as the fact that each sovereign state has its own geopolitics. It does not give any moral judgement of what they mean or they intended to but only to the fact that one of those geopolitical projects succumbed against other.

[136] Even though it could be argued that the Great Britain or the French Republic suffered huge losses during the decolonization still they retained a huge influence and economic dominance on many of their ex colonies, a lot less, comparable to what happened to the Soviet sphere of influence.

ities. This fact meant not only several changes in the political geography but in the interests of all the global actors involved. The Cold War disappeared, together with the bipolar world that had a central part in the international relations after World War II. Russia lost the privileged position it had enjoyed for decades that allowed the USSR to influence or decide whatever happened in different political and social processes that occurred throughout the world. The sustainance of the Cuban regime after the revolution, the aid sent to Nicaragua during the first Sandinista Government, the Soviet implication in Vietnam and similar kinds of support given to Third World countries conditioned to be an ally became something of the past. From being a creditor nation, Russia became a country with a huge debt and dependent in a huge way on the aid given by foreign banks and the international financial system.

The Warsaw Pact, the pact that allowed the Soviet Union an alliance with nations that formed a counterweight against NATO, also disappeared. This treaty allowed the Soviet Army to intervene in Hungary in 1956 against the uprising led by the local population or to send tanks to oppose the reforms carried out by Alexander Dubcek in Czechoslovakia in 1968. Even if it was an alliance, in which other nations participated, at the end it was always to protect Soviet interests and with a preponderance of Soviet troops. The same way NATO's role has been to protect the United States' interests, for instance like in Iraq's war, where the troops that participated included more than 90% of US forces. The fall of the Soviet Union allowed the United States to establish itself as the only global power and without a counterbalance. This way, the United States advanced in geographical areas which they could not have entered before without any geopolitical opposition. Besides, to make the Russian perspective even more intricate, Warsaw Pact members started gradually to adhere to NATO. At the end, even if some Russian leaders wanted to react against NATO enlargements or intervene in the ex-Yugoslavia, they had to face the fact that there were 15 new entities in a territory, where there used to be one.

The will to influence world political events had secondary importance because the main issue was to build a state, and, in many of the former Soviet Republics, to try to mould nation states that had never existed before. This problem was of a greater importance than having a foreign policy that could have a decisive role in the world politics.

Meanwhile, almost every region in the globe had the tendency to apply what later became the Washington Consensus of 1989 with a series of reforms that encouraged the disappearance of the welfare state and changed the state's role in the economy. Undeveloped countries suffered this impact even more, complicated by their peripheral position in the world economy.

At the end, as Wallerstein said, the USSR was englobed in the same logic of a World System.[137] Even the Soviet Union, with all its state economic planning, was also part of the world economy in an equal global context. In that sense, as Joachim Hirsch points out, the breakdown of the Soviet state must be seen as part of the crisis of Global Fordism.[138] That crisis brought a new set of political and economic transformations that led to the globalization being considered as a political strategy aimed at restructuring capitalism in its political, economic and social dimensions.[139]

---

[137] Wallerstein, Immanuel, *Geopolitics and Geoculture*, Cambridge, Cambridge University Press, 1991.
[138] Hirsch considers that Global Fordism was based on a particular societal model lead by the United States. It enforced Taylorist mass production and mass consumption with the development of the welfare state and Keynesian intervention aimed at economic growth and full employment. Hirsch, Joachim, 'Globalization of capital, nation states and democracy,' *Studies in Political Economy*, Vol. 54, University of Toronto, 1997, pages 40–42.
[139] Idem.

"Soviet Union Administrative Divisions, 1989," accessed on July 18, 2017.
Source: Wikimedia Commons, licensed under CC BY-SA 3.0
(https://creativecommons.org/licenses/by-sa/3.0/)

Altogether, it is not possible to explain how the failure of the economic system and the social demographic problems brought the separation of the 15 republics without considering the role of the 'national' factor in local politics. In that sense, the general economic decline and the detrimental opinion of the ruling class brought a loss of legitimacy to the government. Political reforms carried out by Gorbachev together with the complex multi-ethnic balance that persisted in the Soviet Union allowed the emergence of nationalist movements in several republics or regions. Overall, the economic crisis pushed the revival of ethnic movements throughout the Union. The Soviet federal structure was based on territorial ethnic entities, and individually, each Soviet citizen officially recognized the ethnic group to which they belonged. Therefore, there were 15 republics of the Union with a different constellation of diverse inferior ethnic entities. The status of a republic was higher, but there were other entities like autonomous republic, autonomous province or national district. This sort of federalism intended to create a cohabitation between different nationalities in a multi-ethnic state.[140] It was never implied that these borders would become part of independent republics and that the coexistent complex divisions would be threatened because of the partition of the Soviet state. The preferential treatment of ethnic groups in their own territory and the protection of their educational and professional interest of the middle class and the local political elites were part of this political order.[141]

Moreover, Gorbachev's reforms changed the role of the coercive apparatus. The government thus had to face the non-programmed consequences of more freedom of speech and information access that allowed ethnic discontent to emerge. The reforms applied by Gorbachev had a boomerang effect not foreseen by the United States. He visibly wanted to gradually transform Soviet economy, as desired by the West, while keeping the integrity of the Soviet state, excluding maybe the Baltic countries. This plan generated many resistances among hardliners in the Communist Party of the Soviet Union and in the Red Army. Besides, the increasing power of the representatives of the republics, legitimized by their elections, threatened the authority of the Kremlin and created a power struggle between Gorbachev and Boris Yeltsin.[142] The new Union Treaty previously drafted and intended to be signed on 20 August 1991, attempted to handle this struggle. The agreement intended to give wide economic autonomy to the republics and conserve a strong union responsible for defence, foreign policy and monetary policy mostly.

History was different. The failed coup attempt of August 1991 urged the representatives of the republics to secede from the Union, leaving Gorbachev without real power after the images of Yeltsin as

---

[140] The affirmative action introduced at different levels and stages will be analysed deeply in the Ukrainian case. Martin, Terry, *The Affirmative Action Empire, Nations and Nationalism in the Soviet Union: 1923–1939*, Ithaca, Cornell University Press, 2001.

[141] Zaslavsky, Victor, *Dopo L'Unione Sovietica, La perestroika e il problema delle nazionalità*, Bologna, Il Mulino, 1991.

[142] Boris Yeltsin was from May 29, 1990, the chairman of the Presidium of the Supreme Soviet of the Russian Soviet Federative Socialist Republic and from July 10, 1991, was the president of the Russian SFSR, mandate that transformed itself later in the one of the Russian Federation.

on top of a tank were publicized worldwide.[143] These events pushed consequently for the quick dissolution of the Communist Party of the Soviet Union on August 29. Finally, on 8 December 1991, the representatives of the Russian, Ukrainian and Belarussian Soviet Socialist Republics signed the Belovezh Accords that undid the USSR after the impossibility to establish a new Union Treaty even if, as Schrad wrote, 'vodka politics' was not out of place.[144]

Besides Yeltsin's drunkenness, which raised doubts about the legitimacy of the agreement, the whole outcome should be analysed thoroughly even if sources confirm that the original document is missing.[145] The constitution of the Commonwealth of Independent States (CIS) that followed left most of the problems to be solved by the to-be ex-Soviet Republics. The population found itself with a new citizenship[146] and with the heritage of a high social and ethnic mobility that had permeated the Soviet society. The multi-ethnicity issue was handled by the republics in different ways,[147] and without

---

[143] Even though it is seldom mentioned that the day before the coup on August 18, Yeltsin was in Almaty, concluding a weekend trip to shore up relations with the Kazakh republic and Nursultan Nazarbayev. Yeltsin was completely drunk and Nazarbayev remembered how he tried to ride a horse and kept drinking during the day. 'We had to push him up the aircraft steps to get him on his plan,' recalled Nazarbayev. Schard, Mark Lawrence, *Vodka Politics, Alcohol Autocracy, and the Secret History of the Russian State*, Oxford, Oxford University Press, 2014, page 289.

[144] In an event supposed to be Yeltsin's final political triumph, he got so drunk that he fell out of his chair just as the doors were opened for the ceremony. According to one witness: 'Everyone began to come into the room and found this spectacular scene of Shushkevich and Kravchuk dragging this enormous body to the couch. The Russian delegation took it all very calmly. They took him to the next room to let him sleep. Yeltsin's chair stayed empty. Finally, When Kravchuk finished his short speech to everyone about what had been decided, he said, "There is one problem that we have to decide right away because the very existence of the commonwealth depends on it: don't pour him too much" Everyone nodded. They understood Kravchuk perfectly.' Schrad, Op. Cit., page 292.

[145] Parfitt, Tom, 'Document proclaiming death of Soviet Union missing,' February 7, 2013. http://www.telegraph.co.uk/news/worldnews/europe/russia/98546 19/Document-proclaiming-death-of-Soviet-Union-missing.html

[146] Or even without citizenship as happened to many ethnic Russians in Latvia and Estonia. Note of the author.

[147] Ethnic Russians, in many cases, had never lived in the Russian Federation and the same could be mentioned of several ethnic groups. People were used to be Soviets and to have a high mobility within the USSR. The fact that in many cases the local elites pretended to build a state in an ethnonational basis on a multi-ethnic territory was cause of many disputes. At the end, the defence of

considering the Red Army which held considerable political power and controlled the entire nuclear arsenal. In fact, its resistance to change would be noticed afterwards. Altogether, the hurry to dissolve the Union created a long list of geopolitical consequences, which can be seen until now. This way, on 21 December 1991, the leaders of the republics of what became the CIS assembled and signed the Alma Ata Declaration,[148] with Yeltsin drunk again and only occasionally raising his head to mutter a slurred 'What you say is right' before passing out. Yeltsin again had to be carried from the room.[149]

> This is terrible! Who's ruling Russia? growled a scornful Armenian president Levon Ter-Petrossian to one of Yeltsin's aides. How are you Russians going to live? We don't envy you.[150]

Therefore, independent Russia was born.

1.1 The first post-Soviet years: A stateless Russia

After the failed coup d'état in August 1991, the central government of the Soviet Union entered into a crisis. The real power remained in Yeltsin's hands who was the president of the Russian Federation since July. Meanwhile, the ministries of the Russian Federation did not know how to proceed. Suddenly, the governments of the SSRs had become the sole legitimate authority and assumed control of instances that belong to the Soviet Government, even if in many cases they were unprepared for this. There was a complete lack of direction to build national policies capable of facing the complex situation present since 1992.

The urge to build a state was urgent but no steps seemed to be taken in that direction. It is worth considering that when we say state-building process, we do not refer to the institutions only, but

---

ethnic Russians and Russian-speaking population in the Near Abroad became afterwards a strong element for the Russian Federation to be used in the designing of a foreign policy.
[148] 'АЛМА-АТИНСКАЯ ДЕКЛАРАЦИЯ,' December 21, 1991, Archive Egor Gaidar, http://gaidar-arc.ru/file/bulletin-1/DEFAULT/org.stretto.plugins.bulletin.core.Article/file/2880
[149] Schrad, Idem.
[150] Idem.

to the whole social process that legitimates or enforces the creation of a new polity in which a community organizes itself politically and legally. In that sense, what happened in the Russian Federation after 1992 was exactly the opposite.

The chaos occurred during Yeltsin's government, displayed something that looked like an ungovernable territory. The emerging institutions from the Russian Federation were not ready to handle what happened; besides, the fight for power between different actors, the economic crisis and the social degradation worsened throughout the whole territory after the fall of the USSR. Local mafias soon raised to power; meanwhile the old *nomenklatura* and every actor with a little bit of power tried to take advantage of the situation to get some benefit for themself.

During the last years of the Soviet Union, Yeltsin's struggle against Gorbachev took him to invite the republics, regions and other political entities to 'take as much sovereignty as you can swallow'[151] to debilitate the Soviet regime and, especially, Gorbachev's authority. This proved to be costly, especially because some regions in the Russian Federation were not willing to recognize Moscow as an authority. Chechenia was an example, maybe not the only one but the bloodiest.[152] The continuous losses of the Russian Army in the First Chechen War (1994–1996) evidenced not only the degrading condition of the armed forces but also showed the absence of a state policy to try to build or enforce a new and lasting political order.

Referring to the first years after the Bolshevik Revolution, Wallerstein said: 'Holding the state together was a monumental task, especially since Russia was an empire and not a nation-state.'[153] The

---

[151] Idem.
[152] There was an urgent need to define the roles and powers of federal subjects and on March 31, 1992, a treaty was signed bilaterally with 86 of 88 federal subjects. Some obtained regional autonomy or tax privileges. The only ones that did not sign the subject were Chechnya and Tatarstan. The latter signed a different agreement on 1994, leaving the Caucasic Republic as the only one that was incorporated by force after the Second Chechen War. Note of the author.
[153] Wallerstein, Immanuel, *Geopolitics and Geoculture*, Cambridge, Cambridge University Press, 1991, page 89.

same could be said about the period in which Russia could be considered a failed state or simply that there was a lack of state at all.[154]

Crisis and economic reform

The political authorities of whatever kind of polity existed in Russia in January 1992 had to face the humongous task of improving the local economy. Production activities were falling, inflation rising and there were no clear delimitations of the roles of the political authorities in each region or autonomous republics. The Red Army had already been forced to recognize the new political order and the population was deprived suddenly of what remained of the welfare and social protection that had prevailed for years.

Even though the Soviet economy was always immersed in global economy,[155] at least there was some sort of an idea of national development and state planning. Gorbachev wanted to keep a degree of sovereignty over strategic assets to allow economic transformations in a controlled manner. Even in the last year of existence of the Soviet Union, the economic figures were already alarming. In the first semester of 1991 the Gross National Product diminished 10% and inflation passed from 19% in 1990 to more than 100%.[156]

On 2 January 1992, there entered into force a new decree for price liberalization. The reality of January and February 1992 confirmed the worse scenarios of the ones that opposed the reforms. Boris Yeltsin and his then finance minister Yegor Gaidar had mentioned that inflation would not cross 300% during the first trimester, and that inflation would have decreased to 10–12% by April and at the end of the year, it would be under two figures, together with a reduction in production of no more than 10–12%. The reality was completely different. During the first trimester, prices increased from 800 to 900% for most of goods and services; meanwhile salaries only doubled. Production fell by more than 20%.[157] On September 6, the next evaluation was published:

---

[154] The idea of failed state or stateless polities was discussed on the introductory pages.
[155] Wallerstein, Op. Cit. Idem.
[156] Graziosi, Andrea, *L'Unione Sovietica 1914–1991*, Bologna, Il Mulino, 2011, page 634.
[157] Medvedev, Roj, *La Russia post-sovietica, Un viaggio nell'era Eltsin*, Torino, Giulio Enaudi Editori, 2000.

> Al momento si può dire soltanto una cosa: il tentativo di applicare una terapia d'urto in Russia secondo il modello polacco e in base ai consigli del Fondo monetario internazionale e di un gruppo di esperti occidentali è risultato doloroso.[158]

In 1993, production continued to fall, causing high social and political tensions. The GDP fell by 12.5% and the national income by 14%. Industrial production was reduced by 25% and agricultural production by 5.5%. In 1990, the Soviet rouble reached a parity value with the US dollar, while at the end of 1992, one dollar was worth 450 roubles and in the last days of 1993, its value was 1,250. The results of 1994 were even worse, compared to the previous year. Public spending for the maintenance of state and administrative entities was double the size of the GDP. Production was only 85% that of 1993. Agricultural production fell again, this time almost 10%. The results of the five-year period meant an economic collapse not seen since the Bolshevik Revolution and the civil war that followed (1917–1921). In 1995, the GDP was only 40% of that in 1990, the industrial production was 42% and agricultural production 65%. Capital investment had shrunk to 28% from 1990. These numbers were even challenged by some experts who claimed that the situation was even worse.[159]

The reforms did not have any planning. They tried to impose changes without considering the conditions present in the Russian territory. Roy Medvedev remarked:

> A una monopolizzazione irrazionale, poteva subentrare una razionale concorrenza, e metodi economici di regolamentazione potevano integrare o sostituire parzialmente i metodi puramente amministrativi ecc. Occorreva un lento e prudente processo di riforma, basato su studi scientifici, discussioni e sperimentazioni. Solo in questo modo si poteva dare all'economia sovietica la flessibilità e il dinamismo caratteristici del mercato senza privarla dei vantaggi della centralizzazione e della pianificazione.[160]

Instead, they tried to apply the economic theories that dominated in the Western World as if they would magically lead Russia to development. Economists like Jaremenko considered that Western macroeconomic theories were not applicable to Russia mostly be-

---

[158] Bogomolov, Oleg, 'Resta la speranza,' Moskovskoe Novosti, 1992, quoted in Medvedev, Idem.
[159] Medvedev, Op. Cit.
[160] Idem.

cause of the great disparity between the aeronautic and spatial industry and the military production system on one side with the most modern technology available and a civil industry with a mass resource to manual labour on the other. The Soviet Union had dedicated many resources in the attempt to maintain military parity with a rival that was economically stronger and, at the end, that proved itself disastrous.[161]

The reformers had little account of the industrial infrastructure of Russia and the enormous potential of its qualified employees. Military supremacy could have been used to transform the civil industry; instead, the government reduced the order of goods produced by the military industry. That way, Yeltsin's regime gave a strong blow not only to the military complex but also to all the civil economy that could have modernized, thanks to the resources and the qualified personnel from the most advanced area of the Soviet economy.

In other areas, social policy mostly disappeared during the decade. When Ella Pamfilova, minister of social protection, sent a letter of demission to Boris Yeltsin, she declared that the social policy was a complete fiasco. In the Soviet Supreme of the USSR, she had directed one commission about the privileges of public officials and knew well how high officials used to live but commented that compared to the current abuses of power, the former abuses were like a children's game.[162] Other areas like science and higher education were completely disrupted even quicker than industry and agriculture. Tens of thousands of scientists and researchers from each branch of science had to leave the country. Significant research centres of basic or applied research were closed.

Local economist Galina Rakckaja explained the reforms as follows:

> Il presidente e il suo governo sono stati bravissimi nell'attuare con rapidità e competenza il programma del Fondo Monetario Internazionale, che prevedeva la distruzione, in larga misura, dell'economia russa, la trasformazione della Russia in un Paese di tipo coloniale, con un tenore di vita molto più basso di prima per la maggior parte della popolazione, con una disoccupazione massiccia, e con un'industria incapace di competere sul mercato mondiale; la trasformazione

---

[161] Idem.
[162] Idem.

della Russia in una fonte esclusivamente di manodopera e di materie prime a buon mercato per il primo mondo.[163]

It was not fortuitous that during those years the same economic policies were promoted in different regions of the world, be it Latin America or in Africa. In that regard, Western financial circles were blamed for the influence. At the end, the new dynamics of the world economy were just part of the way in which Capital was being reorganized in a new global system.

The political transformations throughout the world in this period as part of the global crisis brought what Joachim Hirsch considered 'Der Nationale Wettbewerbstaat.'[164] This 'National Competition State', as conceptualized by Hirsch, became a new system of political and social relations together with new ways of production around the world. The reforms accomplished in Russia, with their own particularities, were part of this phenomenon. Besides, the logic in which the new global system functioned included in this case many local particularities. For instance, the way privatizations occurred was catastrophic. State budget did benefit. All profit went to agencies that functioned as intermediaries of bonds and single businessmen.[165]

In that sense, Medvedev compared how companies were managed in Soviet times and by those of the new 'democratic nomenklatura'. The old one formed with administrators in a certain way diligently and consciously tried to promote the constant expansion of state property, because their own well-being depended on the proper functioning of the productive apparatus that they controlled.[166]

In the case of the military industry, a big coup was attempted against a fundamental part of what used to be the Soviet development. Military investment in this area had been always important and should have remained the same way in future reforms with a

---

[163] Rakickaya, Galina, Nezavisimaya Gazeta, 5 gennaio 1996.
[164] For a biggest comprehension of how state policies around the world were adapted in favour of the needs of Capital around the globe, it is worth to check Hirsch, Joachim, *Globalización, Capital y Estado*, México, UAM Xochimilco, 1996.
[165] Medvedev, Op. Cit.
[166] Idem.

transformation that could adapt this industry and canalize it to develop other areas. Instead, what happened was the opposite.[167]

Corruption was rampant in all privatizations and, at the end of 1995, 80% of what used to be state companies were in private hands.[168] In 1995, tenders were organized for Russian oil and gas companies. The buyers paid tens or hundreds of millions of USD but the companies were worth hundreds of billions. Yukos, for instance, was worth more than $2 billion but 78% of the stake was sold for 350 million USD. Public officials justified themselves mentioning nobody in Russia had the money to pay the real value, but this was obviously an excuse. There were even several cases when production efficiency became worse after privatization. In others, instead, foreign companies used Russian local firms as agents or as nominees to buy Russian companies, take benefit of the technology and then make the recently bought company go bankrupt to prevent it from becoming a dangerous competitor.

According to information provided by the Duma's Commission for goods and privatizations, at the end of 1993 near 50 big Russian industrial, metallurgic, mechanic, oil, gas and chemistry firms with a market value of 200 billion USD were sold only for 7.2 billion and ended up in the hands of foreign investors that bought them through local nominees.[169] Medvedev remarks that it is unknown how much of that money got to the state treasury and how much remained in foreign accounts of intermediates and operators.[170]

---

[167] American corporations Boeing and Sikorsky used local firms to buy at low cost one-third of the share of helicopter producer M.L. Mil. The goal of the acquisition was to obtain access to high technology and to the projects from the establishment and at the same time eliminate a dangerous competitor in aviation technology from the world market.

[168] There are some absurd cases: The controlling stakes to control the northwest navigation line that consisted of more than 100 vessels (worth more than 450 million USD) and other land properties of more than 400 million USD were ceded for only 6 million, the value of a single ship. The Hercules establishment, a notable factory in Moscow's outskirts that produced cereals for breakfast, was acquired for 20,000 USD. There were also many cases in which the buyer was not even solvable. For instance, with the Vnukovo airline, the buyer with actives of 1 million USD got a firm with an annual income of 400 million. Delovoj, Vtornik, Delovoy '*Mir*,' February 3, 1996, quoted in Medvedev, Op. Cit.

[169] Rossiskaya, Gazeta, January 24, 1995.

[170] Medvedev, Op. Cit.

Even cynical confirmations of the events can be found, as the one from current oligarch, Mikhail Prokhorov,[171] who recognized that privatizations were not fair and that current oligarchs just profit from the situation; meanwhile he defended his role and said the entire fault lies with the government.[172]

The level of pillage found here could be even compared to the one occurred in territories that were Spanish or Portuguese colonies between the fifteenth and seventeenth centuries. Boris Fedorov, former state finance minister, indeed names it the biggest robbery of the century and maybe in history.[173] In this sense, the Russians were deprived of their own heritage without being aware of it. By 1996, 70% of the market consumer goods had passed to foreign companies while Russia became a provider of raw materials.

The people who benefited the most from the reforms were state company managers, commercial brokers and public officials from different ministries while a new class enriched itself at a speed that could have been impossible in any other region of the world. Corruption was found at all levels of the government.

The same level of corruption was found among people like Anatoly Chubais who was in charge of the privatizations and also the Yeltsin entourage as Garrad and Newell wrote: 'Members of the Yeltsin family including his two daughters and their husbands were accused of gross financial violations of amounting billions of dollars. During the scandal, Yeltsin's financial manager was accused for the alleged misappropriation of 30 million USD in the form of bribes from foreign contractors.'[174]

---

[171] Mikhail Prokhorov became in 1995 owner of Norilsk Nickel, the world's leading producer of nickel and palladium, and then separated his assets in this company in 2007 but still owed a fortune worth $10.92 billion as showed in his profile on the *Forbes* List on April 2014, http://www.forbes.com/profile/mikhail-prokhorov/

[172] Presidential candidate debate between Vladimir Zhirinovsky and Mikhail Prokhorov. The quote can be watched at 1:04:00 in 'Поединок: Жириновский VS Прохоров,' published on February 5, 2012. https://www.youtube.com/watch?v=6B0LR7mn7-k

[173] Izvestiya, March 21, 1995.

[174] Garrad, John and Newell, James L., *Scandals in Past and Contemporary Politics*, Manchester, Manchester University Press, 2006, page 186.

Another problem was foreign debt. At the beginning of 1991, Soviet debt was near 71 billion USD. By the beginning of 1992, the Russian Federation's debt was $69 billion. In 1993, it reached $82 billion, in 1994 it went up to $120 billion, by 1995, it was $130 billion and in 1996 it reached 150 billion USD.

The economic decline in Russia brought also a lowering of living standards for most of the population and a drastic reduction of every kind of welfare or social protection with terrible consequences. Life expectancy dropped in Russia more than in the rest of the Soviet Union, especially because of the increase in alcohol consumption. The Russian population arrived to consume of 20 litres per capita that represented the highest in the world.[175] This mark was a lot higher than during Soviet times. The fall in life expectancy became similar to countries in the middle of civil wars, like Angola, Sudan or Somalia.[176] In addition, just to give an example of the demographic impact, Soviets lost 14,000 troops in Afghanistan; meanwhile Russia lost more than 400,000 victims to alcohol every year since the collapse of the Soviet Union.[177] Schrad added, 'Vodka facilitated the wholesale demodernization of Russian economy and society while unleashing a demographic catastrophe unlike anything before seen in the peacetime history of the world.'[178] Besides, the hyperinflation present in Russia allowed the use of Vodka as a currency to become common during the 1990s.[179]

The average life expectancy for men was 65 at the height of the anti-alcohol campaign in 1987 but plummeted to 62 in 1992. Two years later, it dipped to below 58, indicative of a demographic catastrophe without parallel in peacetime human history, so dramatic was Russia's fall. The average life expectancy was 57.6 in 1994.[180]

With regard to nutrition also, numbers were catastrophic. The average caloric consumption was 2,100 calories, which is below the

---

[175] Zafesova, Anna, *e da Mosca è tutto, storie Della Russia che cambia e che non cambia*, UTET, Torino, 2005.
[176] Medvedev, Op. Cit.
[177] Schrad, Op. Cit., page 14.
[178] Idem, page 13.
[179] The concept 'бутылка за услугу', which means a bottle for a service, was widely shared in many Russian regions especially if we considered the hyperinflation, how long it took sometimes to receive wages or the fact that local vodka was produced easily in many houses. Idem, page 313.
[180] Idem, page 321.

level recommended by the World Health Organization. Between 1980 and 1985, it was 3,400 calories compared to 3,732 in the United States. In 1997 a survey showed that 15% of the population lived better than before the Perestroika, 68% worse or a lot worse and 14% felt no difference.

Reforms were not part of a global strategy; they were brought about on advice from international financial institutions. It is common to listen to the concept 'shock therapy' [181] with regard to all the changes implemented. The inflationary spiral created for some the opportunity to enrich themselves very quickly. Several foreigners and Russians made profit. The acquisition of almost any goods at Russian inner price and the immediate selling at world prices brought huge profits. This occurred in many areas, like the energy sector. Just to mention some examples, one apartment in downtown Moscow could be bought for 2 or 3 thousand dollars, the same ones that today cost around 1 million USD.

Between 1992 and 1993, Russia was ruined and impoverished and exported capitals to the West for more than 30 billion USD. These 'new Russians'[182] were afraid of investing their own money in the local economy or in local accounts. Therefore, the prosperity of Russian entrepreneurs happened in a scenario of general decline in production, increase of poverty levels, inflation and the almost general ruin of the country.

This new elite had specific origins. The Sociology Institute of the Russian Academy of Sciences indicated that at the end of 1995, 75% of Yeltsin's administration and his entourage were members of the old Soviet elite with an eminent position at the Communist Party of the Soviet Union. From the *nomenklatura* came 82% of the regional elites and 74% of the whole government. Regarding the business

---

[181] Idem.
[182] The term 'new Russian' (Novyi Russkie) refers to those that enriched themselves at great pace after the fall of the Soviet Union. This new social class that could travel throughout the world, which allowed Russia to become the biggest consumer of Mercedes Benz cars during the 1990s, became the new dominant class. Vladimir Kortunov considers that this people were mostly ex members of the old *Nomenklatura* that found themselves at the right spot during the privatizations or were also members of criminal organizations that learned how to operate sagaciously in conditions of social and political legal instability and that could operate safer under a commercial brand. Kortunov Vladimir, Nezavisimaya Gazeta, December 5, 1996.

elite, 61% came from the same source, mostly from the Komsomol and the Soviet economic administration.[183] Other sources consider that between the new rich business elite there were even 85% of ex members of the CPSU.[184]

The events here were similar to what occurred in many Central and Eastern European countries that belong to the Soviet sphere. Even though, in this case, the political elite from the Communist Party did not just stay only in power with a new brand but they became oligarchs and owners of huge economic assets not available in smaller East European countries.

Therefore, in a territory with new oligarchs that became the most powerful elite, a weak president, regional disputes, economic crisis, unpaid wages for months and obviously corruption at all levels, little could be expected of the justice system. 'Contract killings of businessmen, politicians, journalists shattering public trust on a regular basis. Yet, more often than not, no one was arrested or sentenced.'[185] On one occasion the murderer of the TV Star Vladimir Listyev was named in the media. The detective handling the case and the prosecutor general said they knew who the murderer was but allegedly Yeltsin forbade the arrest.[186] In this context of general decline and complete chaos, Yeltsin battled to stay in power. He even ordered the bombing of the Russian Parliament,[187] in a kind of embarrassment for Western governments that defended him as a democrat a couple of years before and had to keep silence as the legislature was set on fire following Yeltsin's orders.[188]

In this sense, it seemed impossible that Yeltsin could win a re-election, for a second mandate. His continuous gaffes while drunk plus the complete lack of direction of government policies made it difficult to improve his public image. It was precisely at this point

---

[183] Medvedev, Op. Cit., page 208.
[184] 'Argumenty I Fakty,' 1996, n. 4, page 6.
[185] Garrard, John and Newell, James L., *Scandals in Contemporary Politics*, Manchester, Manchester University Press, 2006, page 186.
[186] Idem.
[187] That parliament had been elected on March 4, 1990, as the Congress of People's Deputies of the Russian SFSR. After the events in October 1993, it was dissolved.
[188] It should be mentioned that this decision was taken while Yeltsin was drunk and was easily 'convinced' by his minister of defence, Pavel Grachev. Schrad, Op. Cit., page 297.

that he had to turn to the oligarchs for support to his campaign. The new Russian billionaires that had amassed fortunes in the last five years were also owners of huge media holdings that proved decisive in campaigning during the presidential election in 1996, when it seemed that the Communist Party with Gennady Zuganov could win. The campaign included national TV channels like ORT, RTR and NTV. This last one was a property of the oligarch Vladimir Gusinsky who sent the head of his channel, Igor Malashenko, to lead Yeltsin's media relations.[189] Meanwhile, during that time, the government owned two of the three most important channels and provided funding for most independent newspapers, so that their support could be assured. This way, Yeltsin's domination of media presence became one of the decisive factors.

There are clear indicators of the partiality with which media actively campaigned for Yeltsin. The European Institute for Media found that 'Yeltsin earned 53% of all media coverage of the campaign, while Zyuganov claimed only 18%. Second, EIM evaluated the bias of the stories. For each positive story, EIM gave a candidate 1 point; for each negative story, it registered a -1. In the campaign for the first round of the presidential elections (June 16), Yeltsin scored +492; Zyuganov scored -313. In the final round of the election (July 3), Yeltsin scored +247; Zyuganov scored -240.'[190]

Even though it was not only a matter of media coverage, financing was rather unequal. The campaign limit was 2.9 million USD but private estimate costs of Yeltsin's campaign were hundreds of millions.[191] In addition, the Central Bank provided an additional billion USD to keep campaign promises before the election.

With regard to the vote counting, although in many regions the count was properly done, the fact that in Chechnya, severely bombed by the Russian army, Yeltsin received more than 70% of the votes was amazing.[192]

---

[189] Allison, Graham T., and Matthew, Lantz. 'Assessing Russia's democratic presidential election.' http://belfercenter.ksg.harvard.edu/publication/2362/assessing_russias_democratic_presidential_election.html
[190] Idem.
[191] Idem.
[192] Idem.

The United States also played a role, while the IMF gave a 10 billion USD loan and NATO's expansion to the East was not mentioned during those months.

Altogether, when the campaign started in January, Yeltsin's approval rating was 6%. In June, he won 35% of the votes and in July, to the Western governments' relief, Yeltsin managed to 'win' or to impose himself with 54% of the votes, in what any independent electoral observer considered as a fraud but was recognized in the West as a free election.[193] Even the OSCE's mission chief was pressured not to make public all the irregularities that had been documented during the voting.[194]

Consequently, from day one of his second term, Yeltsin was like a lame duck president. He was politically indebted to the oligarchs as the Russian economy lurched from one crisis to another, culminating in the government's default and economic collapse amidst the 1998 financial crisis.

The financial crisis in 1998, together with the Chechenia War, took the Russian Government to their lowest point of popularity. It was just in 1998 when it seemed that Russia could start to improve again that a new devaluation and the fall of the Russian stock market that same year took Yeltsin's popularity to a historical low. When Yeltsin left office, his approval rating was around 3% in polls with a margin of error of +− 4%.[195]

The absence of a foreign policy

The chaos of Yeltsin's era influenced the building of a foreign policy or, let us say more precisely, the absence of one, because at the end, if there was no Russian state, it is impossible to consider the existence of a real Russian foreign policy.

It was difficult to transform the foreign policy interests of the Soviet era into the ones of a Russian polity. There was an emerging conflict between an empire that had disappeared and the desire to have one, as Alessandro Vitale said:

---

[193] Zaitchik, Alex and Ames, Mark, 'How the West helped invent Russia's election fraud: OCSE's whistle-blower exposes 1996 whitewash,' December 9, 2011. http://exiledonline.com/how-the-west-helped-invent-russias-election-fraud-osce-whistleblower-exposes-1996-whitewash/
[194] Idem.
[195] Schrad, Op. Cit., page 306.

> La sospensione fra un'identità imperiale perduta e una statuale-nazionale difficile da acquisire, provoca imponenti tensioni disgreganti per lo Stato territoriale, sottoposto in molti suoi punti anche a forze d'attrazione esterne e crea difficoltà di controllo politico.[196]

During Yeltsin's term, the relations with the United States had a central role but in a completely different way as during Soviet times. This time, relations were meant more to keep peace so the United States could guarantee foreign aid mostly from financial institutions like the IMF or the World Bank. The continuous support from Bill Clinton during moments of crisis, or the way Yeltsin's international bloopers[197] were ignored, showed how important it was also for the Western governments and especially for the United States to have an ally that allowed the economic policies promoted by the United States to be followed. Some epic comments from Clinton, 'Yeltsin drunk is better than most of the alternatives sober' or 'I want this guy to win so bad it hurts', showed how fundamental it was for the US foreign policy to keep him in power even with all the difficulties it included.

Something similar happened in Europe, when Boris, drunk again, made the fool of himself trying to direct an orchestra in Berlin and pushed everybody away as they were trying to approach him.[198] In addition, another scandal occurred during an official visit to Ireland, in which he could not get out of the plane because of the drunk state in which he was.

The numerous episodes of Yeltsin's drunkenness, for this analysis, go way beyond the meaning of a funny episode, giving journalists a theme to sell more news. Let us imagine, first, an average Russian citizen that grew up in the Soviet System and was proud that his country was always at the top in any field, be it sports, culture or international politics. He grew with the idea that the USSR was a world super power in which Soviet authorities could really allow themselves to threaten the United States of America. Instead, now, all that remained was an alcoholic president that went to the United States, made the fool of himself while begging for money while the

---

[196] Vitale, Alessandro e Romeo Giuseppe, *La Russia post imperiale, la tentazione di potenza*, 2013, Italia, Rubbettino, 2009, page 3.
[197] Schrad, Op. Cit., page 301.
[198] 'Best of Drunk Boris Yeltsin,' published April 7, 2014. http://www.youtube.com/watch?v=v9YnDirqwT4

country was subsumed in chaos, criminals became rich and scientists had to migrate or drive a taxi to survive.

This lack of presence in international politics, not to say the decreased role in other fields like sports where the Soviet teams used also to head medal tables at the Olympics, had a very negative impact on the public opinion.

The Russian Government might have liked to enjoy the same influence in the foreign sphere as before; instead, every time Yeltsin showed himself as drunk to the public, he showed more weakness and what was even worse was that he was never able to defend a Russian position strongly enough. The fiasco of the Russian participation in conflict resolutions, first in Bosnia and then in Kosovo, showed the impossibility to lead a sovereign foreign policy as in Soviet times.

Russian position was never taken seriously during that period, but how could they influence or participate actively in conflict resolution in the Balkans while they had an ongoing war in Chechnya. The Russian Federation could just watch as Eastern European countries became NATO members and was in no position to oppose them.

One of the first matters that influenced the creation of a Russian foreign policy was to define, to put it in Allen C. Lynch terms,[199] the questions: What is Russian? What is foreign? And what is policy?

1. The first question intends to redefine the political content of Russianness in the wake of the disintegration of the imperial state that, in Soviet as in Tsarist times, undergirded Russian power at home and abroad.
2. The second refers to understand what is foreign when, amidst the debris of that lost empire, about one-sixth of the 'Russian nation' resides outside the borders of the Russian state.
3. Finally, what is policy when the state lacks the resources, institutions and coherence to perform many of the minimal functions of governance, including the levying of collectable taxes, control

---

[199] Lynch, Allen C, 'The realism of Russia's foreign policy,' *Europe-Asia Studies*, Vol. 53, No. 1 (January, 2001), pages 7–31, published by Taylor & Francis, Ltd, http://www.jstor.org/stable/826237. Accessed on October 17, 2014, 11:48.

of the armed forces, suppression of internal rebellion, macroeconomic regulation of the economy and satisfaction of external financial obligations?[200]

The three mentioned points were never clear during Yeltsin's presidency, mostly owing to inner power struggles between different actors and the incapacity to consolidate a solid state. The first concept is tricky, starting with the translation. In that sense, first it would be necessary to underline the difference between the Russian words 'русский' (*russkii*) and 'россиский' (*rossiski*). The former refers to the ethnic Russians and the latter to the citizens of the Russian Federation. Both concepts are usually translated in Western languages as Russian but they mean completely different ideas. Therefore, when the idea of Russianness is used, it is not always precise to which of the two references is made. That lack of choice is not without a political intention, considering all the ethnic Russians and Russian speakers that find themselves in many ex-Soviet countries, mostly but not only in Ukraine, Kazakhstan, Moldova, Latvia and Estonia. In that same sense, the idea of 'foreign' does not always apply to the Near Abroad, as for many Russians at least in the social imaginary they belong to the same polity. Finally, the third point, regarding the definition of a policy becomes more complex when the foundational bases of a Russian state are not present.

This way, we found completely different issues the Russian foreign policy should be considering, what Yeltsin and his entourage wanted, what the Russian Army intended (the biggest heir of the Soviet army) and what the Russian parliament (mostly dominated by members of the Communist Party) pretended. Those three actors portrayed different ideas of the three terms mentioned above. This chaos created a huge complication when anything that wanted to look like a foreign policy was to be framed. The weakness itself of the Yeltsin's government allowed even more other actors to take the initiative when, in their opinion, the 'Russian' National interest should be otherwise. In the example of the Russian Army it is clear in the way it handled specific conflicts in the Near Abroad[201] or in

---

[200] Idem.
[201] The case of Pridnestrovia will be explained in the following pages.

the Balkans without taking into account what the government wanted.

There were three ministers of foreign affairs during the Yeltsin's presidency. The first one was Andrey Kozyrev, who was widely criticized by different sectors of the opposition in Russia. During his term, the Russian position in the war in Bosnia was almost never taken into account; meanwhile Yeltsin and Kozyrev were always subordinates like Lynch said '... to the need to maintain at least the appearance, if not the substance, of partnership with the West.'[202] At first, Russia participated in a contact group that included the United States, France, Germany and Great Britain where the Russian voice was heard with regard to some subtle matters but once Russia was no longer needed as an interlocutor, the NATO members acted by themselves. The rejection of Croatia's president Franjo Tudjman of an invitation to participate in Moscow in a conference with Russia and Serbia on 10 August 1995, shows how the Russian position was insignificant in the international scene.[203] In fact, the start of NATO's bombing on August 30 saw Russia effectively marginalized as a military and diplomatic factor.

Altogether, the urgency of a stronger foreign policy surely influenced the choice of Yevgeny Primakov[204] as minister of foreign affairs in 1996 in which his continuous attempt to build a foreign policy is notable. He tried to re-establish Russia, China and India as a triangle that could have some weight in the most important issues in Asia; but the general economic and social decline stopped almost any possibility of improvement for the Russian position in foreign affairs. He even tried to stop or to slow NATO's advance while cooperating within the NATO-Russia Council, even though the effects

---

[202] Lynch, Op. Cit., page 15.
[203] Idem, page 17.
[204] Yevgeny Primakov was minister of foreign affairs from 1996 to 1998 and then prime minister from September 1998 to May 1999. He was a high trusted academic with a reputation as someone that wanted to recover a privileged position for Russia in the international scene and pushing for multilateralism in the international relations to oppose the hegemonic vision of the United States. After being removed by Yeltsin, he became presidential candidate against Putin but at the middle of the campaign, he resigned and then became a close advisor in foreign politics for the Kremlin once Putin had won the election.

were minimum. Besides, he tried to maintain a cohesive and disciplined diplomatic relation at all levels and isolate it from the vicissitudes of the Russian daily political scene. He had a vast experience as foreign correspondent, academic and member of the Academy of Sciences after being also the director of the Institute of Eastern Studies, which gave him a huge background[205] to understand the global context and the possibilities to act.

Primakov had almost in vain tried to have a realistic approach regarding Russian interests. He was worried about the lost Russian influence in the CIS. Even though, during his term as Foreign Affairs Minister, the key bilateral agreement between Russia and Ukraine was signed in May 1997[206] where borders were mutually recognized. Primakov's primary intention was to assure that Ukraine would not become part of NATO.[207]

The attempts were not enough as, in fact, the Russian Federation was not in a position of power to control the global situation. The next example was during the war in Kosovo, when Primakov[208] was flying to Washington with a solution proposal, and the United States decided to start bombing Serbia.

This war was a tragedy for the Russia and foiled Russia's attempt to build a foreign policy. Russian public opinion was overwhelmingly in favour of a Russian participation to defend Serbia. Besides, it was the first time in history when NATO acted without mandate from the United Nations but also operated beyond their own mission of defending NATO member states. This happened after the Atlantic organization had just enlarged to include the Czech Republic, Hungary and Poland. In that sense, Lynch added 'NATO's war thus underscored in undeniable ways the weakness of Russian power and the extent to which Russia's influence depends upon fissures in its external political environment.'[209]

After the Russian position was ignored, they only managed to be included in the military mission in Serbian territory.[210] Still, there

---

[205] Medvedev, Op. Cit., page 377.
[206] This subject will be treated thoroughly in the next chapter.
[207] Lynch, Op. Cit., page 23.
[208] At this date, Primakov had already become prime minister of the Russian Federation and the minister of foreign affairs was Sergei Ivanov.
[209] Lynch, Op. Cit., page 19.
[210] Idem.

are some facts notable about the participation of the Russian Armed Forces in Kosovo. The episode in which around 200 parachutists entered Prishtina's airport before NATO troops arrived surprised the Western governments and looked like a momentary embarrassment for NATO. This move was made by Russian officials without an order from the minister of defence or the president.[211] This action caught NATO's troops by complete surprise, as it was not foreseen in the previous agreements in which Russians were not taken seriously.[212] The Russian military operation also caught off guard Sergei Ivanov who had mentioned that the Russian troops would leave afterwards.[213]

The following promotion of Viktor Zavarzin[214] to colonel-general after the mission showed that Yeltsin had no other choice but to support the decision taken by his officials or face public embarrassment. Even though this symbolic gesture counted little or nothing in the global solution while the Russian position remained marginalized.

After Primakov was dismissed[215] on May 1999, the relations between Yeltsin and the parliament worsened. A survey conducted during those days showed that 2% of the population trusted Yeltsin while 70% trusted Primakov.[216] Primakov was replaced by Sergey Stepashin, and he stayed in this role for almost three months. Subsequently, there were two tendencies among the Russian elite. The oligarchs wanted a successor for Yeltsin and, on the other side, some of the old apparatchiks had the intention to retake control and

---

[211] Chiesa, Giuletto, 'I congiurati dell'Operazione Kosovo, La Stampa (Torino),' June 13, 1999, page 3. http://www.archiviolastampa.it/component/option,com_lastampa/task,search/mod,avanzata/action,viewer/Itemid,3/page,1/articleid,0494_01_1999_0160_0001_13626651/anews,true/
[212] Idem.
[213] Idem.
[214] He was in charge of the mission that took Pristina's airport. Idem.
[215] One of the official reasons about Primakov's demission was that Yeltsin was not satisfied with the economic results but Roy Medvedev sustains that during his government numerous investigations started by federal prosecutors about corruption touched the oligarchs and different public officials. Names like Boris Berezovsky and others appeared in the press together with their links to Swiss accounts. All this could have been enough to Yeltsin's entourage that was highly influenced by the oligarchs to push for Primakov's exit. Medvedev, Idem, page 377.
[216] Medvedev, Op. Cit.

bring the Russian Federation to a situation of stability. Obviously, foreign policy was a hostage of this situation, as Lynch would agree: 'It is therefore an open question how much longer the relative coherence of the external policy of a very fragile state can be maintained.'[217]

Regardless of how the state is named during this period, as fragile state, failed state or a lack of state or the Russian polity, the fact is that internal political factors, rather than the very narrow external margin of Russian manoeuvres, decided the main contours of Russian foreign policy.[218] For almost a decade, Russia had battled between trying to define and defend whatever was considered national interest and Yeltsin's need to create solid links with the West, mostly because the loans granted by the International Financial Institutions in many cases represented a direct benefit for Yeltsin's family and his associates. The overall situation showed a deteriorating situation in Russia including an insignificant foreign policy.

At this moment, for the average Russian citizen, the need of order to supress the visible chaos was urgent and, precisely in this context, an almost completely unknown, Vladimir Putin arrived at the scene.

1.2 Rebuilding a Russian state

When Boris Yeltsin replaced Sergei Stepashin as prime minister on 10 August 1999, few knew who the new arrival was. Vladimir Putin had been in charge of the Federal Security Service of the Russian Federation, known as FSB,[219] since 25 July 1998, where he managed also to become secretary of the Security Council of the Russian Federation. After being member of Primakov's and Stepashin's Government, the decision announced by Yeltsin that he was going to be his successor came as a surprise to many in the ruling political class. After a long career at the KGV, where he served in east Germany and was present during the fall of the Berlin Wall, he came back to Russia where he served first in the St. Petersburg administration

---

[217] Lynch, Idem, page 26.
[218] Idem.
[219] FSB stands for Федера́льная слу́жба безопа́сности Росси́йской Федера́ции (Federal'naya sluzhba bezopasnosti Rossiyskoy Federatsii).

before moving to Moscow and performed different roles in the presidential administration before obtaining the position at the FSB.[220]

For the Russian political class, the current political situation was not tolerable anymore and there was an urgent need to find a substitute for Yeltsin. The president's entourage and the oligarchs around him were not ready to cede their position of power so easily. They needed to be reassured that they would be untouched. It is obvious that what happened in Putin's career as chief of the FSB, where he surely worked with many ex-KGV colleagues, assured him the possibility to convince or even make an arrangement with Yeltsin so he would receive support to become prime minister and become the next president. A deal would have to include prosecutorial immunity for Yeltsin and his family, similar to how Gerald Ford did when he became president and gave a full and unconditional presidential pardon to Richard Nixon.[221]

At that point, several opposition parties including the Communist Party and other actors like Primakov were already thinking of a coalition that could allow them to win the presidency. At the end, this was not possible; Putin, as prime minister, launched the Second Chechen War together with a strong media support that assured him more visibility. Therefore, he had no problems first to have a decent result in the parliamentary elections of 1999 with his recent constituted party *Unity* where he obtained 23.32% of the votes.[222] This score, even though only represented a fraction of the congress, allowed him to make alliances with independent members of the parliament in the State Duma and with the Communist Party to assure him stability.

Following this, Yeltsin surprised the world by presenting his resignation on 31 December 1999, with Vladimir Putin becoming acting president until the elections to be held on 26 March 2000, where he won his rival Gennady Zyuganov relatively easily with 53.4% of the votes, while Gennady Zyuganov from the Communist Party got 29.5%.[223] It is worth noting that the first decree he signed

---

[220] Medvedev, Op. Cit., pages 402–403.
[221] '*Proclamation 4311*,' September 8, 1974, http://en.wikisource.org/wiki/Proclamation_4311
[222] Nohlen, D. and Stöver, P., *Elections in Europe: A Data Handbook*, Baden-Baden, Germany, Nomos, 2010, page 1642.
[223] Idem.

as acting president was precisely the one titled 'On Guarantees of former president of the Russian Federation and members of his family'.[224] This decree assured Yeltsin the legal basis that he would not be prosecuted.

Putin had secured the presidency for himself. Now, he had the task of ruling after a decade of chaos and trying to reconstitute a solid Russian polity or more precisely to build a new Russian State.

As mentioned, state building entails many difficulties. Throughout history, many modern nation states have passed through a war or series of wars or different kinds of struggles to assure the establishment of a new spectrum of social relations that could help conceive a state. For the matter of this research, state will not be understood either as an apparatus or, as many jurists would consider it, only as population, territory and government. Without going into a deep discussion on political philosophy, it is important to conceive of a state as a social relation and, for instance, the way in which a society organizes itself politically and legally. In this sense, this polity includes citizens that recognize themselves in it and recognize an authority. Besides, a sovereign state, to put it in Carl Schmitt's terms, should be capable of deciding with sovereignty who are the enemies of the state.[225] 'Si une partie de ce peuple déclare ne plus se connaitre d'ennemi, elle se range en tout état de cause du Coté des ennemis et leur prête son appui sans faire disparaitre pour autant la discrimination ami-ennemi.'[226]

None of these elements were present during Yeltsin's presidency during which each actor had a different agenda and impunity, criminality, looting and foreign involvement prevailed. Yeltsin's presidency was seen as one of a corrupt and weak government controlled by the oligarchs and in no position to oppose the Western countries' advances by any means. The power struggle was also present between federal government, the local governors and the Duma. Meanwhile, oligarchs controlled media and the Russian Army had

---

[224] 'О ГАРАНТИЯХ ПРЕЗИДЕНТУ РОССИЙСКОЙ ФЕДЕРАЦИИ, ПРЕКРАТИВШЕМУ ИСПОЛНЕНИЕ СВОИХ ПОЛНОМОЧИЙ, И ЧЛЕНАМ ЕГО СЕМЬИ,' Rossiskaya Gazeta, December 31, 1999, http://www.rg.ru/oficial/doc/ykazi/1763.htm

[225] Schmitt, Carl, la notion de politique, Paris, France, Calmann-Lèvy, 1972, page 86.

[226] Idem, page 95.

its own agenda regarding conflicts in the Near Abroad. The Armed Forces had already exchanged its support in exchange for not having its number of effectives cut drastically.

After Putin assured Yeltsin that no prosecution would follow, members of the Yeltsin family were removed from positions of power and even some investigations started against Tatyana Yeltsina[227] to sideline the family entourage. The first step had been taken; but before increasing his power and after selecting loyal cadres to his cabinet, he had to deal with another thorny issue if he wanted to move in the same direction of reinstating a sole political authority in Russia and that fact was dealing with the increasing authority and power of the oligarchs.

The oligarchs were this figure of newly rich Russians that had amassed fortunes in less than a decade, thanks to their links with political power, many of them with the help of former prime ministers. They had the opportunity to benefit themselves during the privatizations. Several of them were members of the Komsomol[228] in Soviet times, where they managed to establish under the Perestroika rule small businesses like centres for Scientific and Technical Creativity of the Youth. These almost tax-free enterprises allowed them to obtain an economic liquidity due to which they started participating in the privatizations.

Previous sections showed how some of the tenders had allowed these ex-Komsomol members to amass fortunes in only some years. The oligarchs were not happy only with owning villas, planes, yachts and women but had also bought power. They were present heavily in Yeltsin's campaign in 1996 and when it was decided that Vladimir Putin would be the successor. Even though, this moment, as Andrew Muller published in the Guardian, was when 'the oligarchs out-clevered themselves'.[229] Putin, remarks Muller, saw two things: 'That they were potentially more powerful than him and that they

---

[227] 'Survival of the fittest,' May 16, 1999, TIME http://content.time.com/time/magazine/article/0,9171,24834-2,00.html
[228] Komsomol (Комсомо́л) is the abbreviation for the All-Union Leninist Young Communist League (Всесоюзный Ленинский Коммунисти́ческий сою́з молодёжи) but usually known only as Коммунистический союз молодёжи from where the initials are taken.
[229] Muller, Andrew, *The Guardian*, December 3, 2005 http://www.theguardian.com/media/2005/dec/03/tvandradio.russia

were about as popular as with your average Russian as a man idly burning bundles of £50s outside an orphanage.'[230] In that sense, according to the same source, a poll from 2004 assured that only 18% of the population opposed wholesale renationalization of the country's resources.

Even though, the first thing Putin tried to pursue was a deal with the oligarchs. The first approach included names like Boris Berezovsky, Mikhail Khodorkovsky, Vladimir Gusinsky, Roman Abramovich and Moscow's mayor Yuri Luzhkov. The famous 'shashlik agreement' between the president and the oligarchs on May 2000 just after his accession and a later meeting at the Kremlin in July that same year endeavoured to establish boundaries on the principle of mutual non-interference. The government would not interfere in their businesses and they would not participate in politics.[231] Gusinsky and Berezovsky were the first to violate the rules and they exposed themselves suddenly to the consequences. Both had huge media empires that were lost after they continued to attack the president. Gusinsky was arrested and, later, left the country. His channel, NTV, was even taken over by armed forces.[232] The rest of his shares were sold to Gazprom.[233] Many of the staff that worked in the media conglomerate tried to find refuge in Berevozky's TV channel, but he also began to encounter demands for the repayment of debts and to feel the political pressure until he had to cede control of the First National Channel where he was a shareholder. He surrendered his parliamentary seat in July 2000 and went to live in the United Kingdom where he obtained political asylum in 2003.

Still, there was Khodorkovsky, the owner of Yukos and who at that moment had reached the 15th position at the Forbes list of wealthiest men in the world with a fortune of $16 billion. He did not openly finance opposition but his philanthropic foundation had allowed him to stay public and to keep links with different political contacts that could allow him to become a potential presidential

---

[230] Idem.
[231] Kryshtanovskaya, Olga and White, Stephen, 'The sovietization of Russian politics,' *Post-Soviet Affairs*, Vol. 25, No. 4 (2009), page 287.
[232] Idem, page 288.
[233] Idem.

candidate in 2004. His case is rather peculiar because once the Kremlin started to pressure him, he preferred rather to defy Putin.

For instance, Yukos, on 28 May 2003, signed a 20-year oil-delivery contract with China as if Khodorkovsky and Yukos were sovereign powers. 'Here they were, making foreign policy with China, something Putin regarded as the state's and his, not an oligarch's, prerogative.'[234]

Besides, he tried to sell a portion of Yukos' share to either Chevron or Exxon Mobil and even a protocol of understanding was signed three weeks before his arrest. It is not a surprise, in that sense, he received a sentence of nine years for fraud and tax evasion after a highly controverted trial[235] meanwhile his company was renationalized.[236] Khodorvkovsky had gone too far.

Other oligarchs faced the same fate. Vladimir Bryntsalov, owner of a pharmaceutical holding, was forced to take residence in Monaco and Yevgeny Chichvarkin was forced to sell his telephone company at $400 million and moved to the UK[237] where he still actively campaigns against the Russian Government. Instead, others like Roman Abramovich preferred to deal with the issue and accepted the conditions offered by the government and continued to do well under Putin's presidency and even invited other oligarchs to concede as shown in the BBC documentary 'Russian Godfathers'.[238] For instance, he sold his 72% share of Sibneft to Gazprom for $13 billion.[239]

After putting the oligarchs into order, Putin then proceeded with his long-time goal of building new 'national champions'. This idea of new renationalized state companies should be the base from

---

[234] Goldman, Marshall I., *Petrostate: Putin, Power and the New Russia*, Oxford, Oxford University Press, 2008, pages 111–112.
[235] Kryshtanovskaya, Idem, page 289.
[236] Schrad, Op. Cit., page 343.
[237] Kryshtanovskaya, Op. Cit., page 289.
[238] 'Russian Godfathers,' published August 20, 2012, http://www.youtube.com/watch?v=w_LE77YFnGk
[239] Goldman, Op. Cit., page123.

which Russian economy could retake growth. He had written a dissertation[240] in 1996–1997 in which he pushed for the idea of companies that would promote state interest above profit maximization. That meant to subsidize prices locally and for exports to use these companies as a foreign policy tool.[241]

To achieve this success, there was an urgent need to retake state control in the oil and gas industry after the dubious privatizations carried out during Yeltsin's period. When Chernomyrdin was prime minister, Gazprom evaded taxes on large scale, causing a huge deficit to the state finances. In 1995 and 1996, despite having generated earnings of almost $2 billion, Gazprom paid only $3.5 million in dividends to the state. Even stranger, the state at the time held 38.4% of the company's stock.[242] Gazprom shares were stripped away and divided between people near to Chernomyrdin; meanwhile, ITERA,[243] a company highly controversial during those years in many ex-Soviet countries, became owner of many of Gazprom's assets.

Gazprom was then, during Putin's first presidency, one of the first companies over which state retook control. In his initial fight against the oligarchs, Chernomyrdin, who was chairman of Gazprom, was fired and replaced by Rem Vyakhirev (CEO) and by Dmitry Medvedev and Alexei Miller, both of who knew Putin from St. Petersburg. The idea was to stop asset-stripping and to regain lost possessions. ITERA was then almost forced to declare bankruptcy or sell the stolen assets back to Gazprom.[244] 'As an indicator

---

[240] His dissertation had 16 pages copied almost intact from a similar study from Pittsburgh University as it was discovered by Clifford Gady and Igor Dachenko as it was mentioned in Goldman, Op. Cit., pages 98–99.
[241] Idem.
[242] Goldman, Marshall I., *Petrostate: Putin, Power and the New Russia*, Oxford, Oxford University Press, 2008, page 140.
[243] ITERA is a company that used to have its headquarters in Jacksonville, Florida, with its main business in Russia. They used to sell gas from Central Asia to third countries, mostly Ukraine but also to Moldova, Georgia and the Baltic countries through Russian pipelines. Igor Makarov was the CEO for many years. During Yeltsin's term, they were known for acquiring underpriced Gazprom assets and getting huge profit from them. They have lost or sold many of the shares they had in the gas and oil industry but still have a considerable presence in the energy sector. The headquarters is now in Cyprus. Idem, page 146.
[244] Idem.

of Putin's success in reclaiming the state's ownership of the country's oil output, when he took over as president in 2000, the state's share of total crude oil production was 16 percent; by late 2007, it had increased to about 50 percent.'[245] Even though it is noteworthy how Chernomydin and Vyahirev, who were related to several corrupt deals through ITERA, did not suffer the same fate as the non-loyal oligarchs. Maybe, as Goldman considers, both were two corrupt long-time members of the public administration but they were not considered enemies of the state.[246]

The establishment of these new *national champions* was noticeable. The idea, just as described before, was to have strong state companies that could be competitive in the West and even have a strong corporate presence worldwide. The fact that Gazprom or Rosneft became sponsors in considerable sport activities, including UEFA's champions League, shows the level of expansion they obtained several years after being recovered by the state.

Aggressive tactics were used to retake the companies that had been adjudicated as belonging to the oligarchs. These methods included the use of tax authorities to find unpaid taxes and fill them with unpayable fines or forcing the owner to sell by different means. In many cases, oligarchs understood the message, in others, like in the already mentioned Khodorkovsky's case, they resisted and at the end, they lost everything or almost everything.[247] Even vodka production suffered a similar fate as other strategic assets.[248]

At the end, as Mark Schrad wrote: 'Say what you will of the tactics, by the end of Putin's second term as president in 2008, he had not only leveraged many Yeltsin-era cronies from power, but he had

---

[245] Idem, page 99.
[246] Chernomyrdin was later named ambassador in Ukraine meanwhile Vyahirev received in 2001 the order 'for merits for the Fatherland' by president Putin. Goldman, Idem, page 105.
[247] The main renationalizations carried out during Putin's first two presidencies are available at Idem, page 134.
[248] On August 4, 2000, armed men under the authority of the Federal Tax Police Service took control of the Krystall Distiller, the largest and most famous vodka manufacturer in Russia. By then, the company was controlled at a 51% by Moscow's city government, headed by Yury Luzhkov. He was another of Putin's rivals and had a stronghold in the Russian capital where he ruled for 18 years. Putin afterwards created Rosspirtprom to consolidate state control over vodka factories in which the federal government retained a majority interest and took control over the vodka market. Schrad, Op. Cit., page 341.

also recentralized many important sectors of the Russian economy, including vodka.'[249]

After Putin retook control over strategic assets, still, the issue of assuring total territorial control remained pending. The second Chechnya war was convincingly won by the Russian Army, although at a high cost to the local civilian population that suffered 25,000 casualties.[250] A new constitution was 'approved' in which Chechens recognized themselves as part of the Russian Federation; meanwhile a considerable sector of the Russian public opinion sustained the war.

Besides, through the years, Putin made it clear to the governors that only those who were loyal would remain in power and especially after the Beslan school hostage crisis in September 2004, he created the legal framework in which regional governors would be proposed by the president and only ratified by local legislatures.[251] Only autonomous republics stayed with the possibility of electing directly their own executive as part of the complex federal structure of the Russian Federation.[252]

Reusing political control also included founding a new political party as happened with United Russia. After the parliamentary elections in which the party obtained just 23.32% of the votes and 73 seats in December 1999, by 2003, it won a comfortable victory with 37.6% of the votes and 223 of the 450 seats at the Duma. Afterwards, the 17 legislators of the People's Party together with many independent parties joined this party, giving Putin a comfortable majority at the Duma. United Russia, a party that became then the party of the regime won by a landslide in the next parliamentary elections in 2007 and 2011, allowing the president to have no real opposition at the parliament.

This process arrived with a new economic stability that, even if it did not correct the social inequalities that recently emerged, allowed the economy to grow, thanks to the increase in the oil prices, and gave rise to a period of stability after a turbulent decade. For

---

[249] Idem, page 343.
[250] 'Russian federation: What justice for Chechnya's disappeared?,' AI Index, EUR, 46/015/2007, Amnesty International, May 2007.
[251] Kryshtanovskaya, Op. Cit., page 286.
[252] 'The constitution of the Russian federation,' Chapter 3, The Federal Structure. http://www.constitution.ru/en/10003000-04.htm

the Russian people, the image of Putin that did not drink persecuted the oligarchs and imposed order was quite preferable to Yeltsin's chaotic rule. Order was more important to the common Russian than the idea of democracy, respect for human rights or freedom. That is why, while the West admired Gorbachev for his humanism, the Russians saw him as weak and incapable of exercising authority. The average citizen of the Russian Federation preferred a president that defended publicly Russia's interest and was not afraid to oppose foreign powers when they went against something considered a Russian public interest. A survey in 2011 showed that only 32% of the Russian citizens preferred democracy to a strong leader.[253]

Altogether, in his first years of government, Vladimir Putin managed to consolidate a new Russian state that could then focus on elaborating sovereign foreign policy and politics or, to be more precise, redesigning what would become the new Russian geopolitics.

1.2.1 Renaissance of a foreign policy

When Putin rose to power, it was urgent to reinstate order to the government and stop the precipitous decline of Russian position in international affairs.[254] This decline had to deal with different issues. First, to define the real possibilities to act for the Russian Federation, after a decade in which its position deteriorated. It is obvious that many areas that were of strategic interest to the Soviet Union could not receive the same attention as Russia. It was essential to set realistic goals to enforce a Russian position.

Besides, it is worth reminding that the idea of an empire remained present in the Russian collective imaginary. In that sense, any foreign goal would pretend somehow to recover the lost Soviet space; meanwhile, in the new borders it was confined to the idea of Russianness.[255] Therefore, the new foreign policy would include the idea of a sort of 'must be' Russian area of influence. Precisely since

---

[253] 'Confidence in democracy and capitalism wanes in former Soviet Union,' December 5, 2011. http://www.pewglobal.org/2011/12/05/confidence-in-democracy-and-capitalism-wanes-in-former-soviet-union/

[254] Lo, Bobo, *Vladimir Putin and the Evolution of Russian Foreign Policy*, The Royal Institute of International Affairs, Russia and Eurasia Programme, Oxford, Blackwell Publishers, UK, 2003.

[255] The idea of Russianness is always vague and imprecise in most speeches. It could refer to the citizens of the Russian Federation, to ethnic Russians, to the Russian-speaking population or even to ex-Soviet citizens. Note of the author.

the nineties, the notion of the Near Abroad[256] (*ближнее зарубежье, blizhneye zarubezhye*) came to be understood as:

> Un limbo ritenuto ancora di pertinenza ex imperiale russa, sospeso fra dimensione 'interna' ed 'esterna' in cui non valgono le rigide delimitazioni tipiche degli Stati nazionali di origine occidentale.[257]

Therefore, to retain strategic influence over the Near Abroad became one of the first goals of a renovated Russian foreign policy—first, through the CIS and then within other supranational organizations like the Customs Union and the Euro Asiatic Union.

It is important to keep in mind that for any Russian polity throughout history, the syndrome of encirclement has been a constant driving force of the Russian foreign policy. The fact that Russians or Soviets were always concerned by a possible external menace by other powers, namely Germans, Japanese or the United States, just to name some cases in the twentieth century, caused the Russian diplomacy and also the armed forces to be deeply alarmed by any new configuration around their borders. In that sense, the Near Abroad became a zone of concern, even more so after East European Countries that were in the Soviet sphere of influence started to adhere to NATO. That fact awakened the elite in power in Moscow to reinstate a stronger foreign policy to be carried out by the державники' (proponents of the imperial power) and the 'силовики'[258] (proponents of the force).[259]

In that sense, Russia granted itself the right to intervene in the affairs related to the ethnic Russians and Russian-speaking population abroad. Besides, after the disappointing outcome of the NATO intervention in Kosovo, there was an urgent need to re-establish new priorities. It was also the first time in history that the Atlantic organization acted without the approval of the Security Council of

---

[256] The Near Abroad refers to the countries that emerged after the fall of the Soviet Union, conceived as a zone of geopolitical interest for the Russian Federation.
[257] Vitale, Op. Cit., page 3.
[258] Силовик (Silovik), which can be translated as person of force, is used to describe all the people related to the security apparatus in organs as the FSB, FVR, the military of the Federal Drug Control.
[259] Vitale, Op. Cit., page 3.

the United Nations.²⁶⁰ These events made it possible that unilateral actions by the United States against Russian interests could be carried out.

The Military Doctrine of 2000 pushed more for a multipolar order in which Russia recognized its strategic role in the Euro Asiatic area and in global processes, thanks to its economic, military and scientific potential.²⁶¹ In former documents, a distinction appeared between sources of external military danger and immediate military threats. This distinction disappeared in the publicized draft form in October 1999, and then was approved in late April 2000.²⁶² The document mentioned continuous attempts to weaken Russia's position in international affairs to resolve thorny issues in different regions. It also presented terrorism as a big threat and very critic of NATO's actions without the approval of the Security Council.²⁶³ In that sense, the new military doctrine tried to determine a starting point to deal on the one side with issues like terrorism that had affected Russia in recent years while also trying to demark the role of Russia in Eurasia.

The 11 September 2001, attacks against the United States would have a deep impact on the international relations. First of all, because nobody was willing to oppose the United States' 'right' to respond to a clear and direct attack on their territory but also because the menace of terrorism looked like the motive that could gather or reorganize a multinational force headed by the United States without being opposed.

The Russian position was very clear. They gave complete support to the US mission in Afghanistan and they even agreed that CIS countries could host military bases of the Multinational Coalition that followed against Afghanistan. At this point, Russia tried to keep in a good tone the relation with the United States, noting that there were common goals and worries at the international scale.

---

260 The first major NATO operation had been in 1995 in the Balkans over Bosnia and Hercegovina, even though at that time, the Russian Government did not oppose the approval of the Security Council of the UN. Note of the author.
261 Vitale, Op. Cit., page 34.
262 'Военная доктрина Российской Федерации,' February 5, 2010. http://kreml in.ru/supplement/461
263 Vitale, Op. Cit., page 114.

Moscow understood terrorism as a common enemy and they wanted to adjudicate themselves the same right to respond if similar menaces would happen on Russian soil. With that in mind, Putin intended to improve the relations with NATO which had been deteriorated after the events in Kosovo.

As the Kremlin became more assertive in foreign politics, Washington also reacted. The first decision that implied a serious disagreement between the two governments was when the United States decided to retire from the Anti-Ballistic Treaty in June 2002. This act not only represented the first time that the United States denounced an international military treaty but it also gave a serious blow to Putin's aspirations of introducing Russia as a solid partner with the Western world. In fact, more than once Russia made note of a possible Russian aspiration to become a NATO member that would have to be negotiated in preferential terms and almost without any conditions. The idea of a possible NATO membership was consequent for Russia, as there was no more a cold war; to sustain the existence of NATO seemed from that perspective illogical. Putin proposed at that time, in one of the first news conferences he gave after he became president, that the current Atlantic organization should be replaced by another that included all of Europe and Russia.[264] At that point, he mentioned that NATO's expansion was creating different levels of security that did not correspond with present realities.[265] NATO members and above all the United States did not echo the Russian proposal but allowed the message of a deeper cooperation to continue. Therefore, the NATO-Russia Council emerged.

In that sense, the NATO-Russia Council was established on 28 May 2002, after the NATO summit in Rome.[266] The idea was to work as partners in the fight against terrorism, in the non-proliferation of weapons of mass destruction and in different areas in the

---

[264] 'Putin wants NATO to let Russia join,' July 18, 2001. http://www.deseretnews.com/article/853851/Putin-wants-NATO-to-let-Russia-join.html?pg=all
[265] Idem.
[266] Nato-Russia Council Statement, May 28, 2002. http://archives.nato.int/nato-russia-council-statement-28-may-2002-rome-italy;isad

military sphere.[267] The speech of NATO members and Russia mentioned common ambitions and mutual challenges and it remained the same way for the next few years, even though gradually serious differences appeared, as the United States continued to handle their foreign security policy in the area independently from the possibility of having any agreements in the Council. This, in fact, turned the organism from the Russian perspective into 'a body where scholastic discussions were held' as Russian envoy to NATO, Dmitry Rogozin, declared once.[268]

Following the United States' withdrawal from the Anti-Ballistic Treaty, Russia withdrew from the START II Treaty[269] the next day. The following negotiations for new treaties in the area like SORT that same year or the new START in the future were influenced by the fact that the Anti-Ballistic Treaty was not valid and that the United States had the intention of building an anti-ballistic system placed in NATO member countries, specifically in Poland and the Czech Republic.

All these facts together forced the Russian side to look for different strategies to have a more assertive presence in the international scene. The war in Iraq and the insistence to develop the anti-missile system in Eastern Europe were perceived directly as an act of aggression against the Russian Federation.

1.2.1.1 Gazprom and the new Russian energy politics (and policy)

One of the most important elements the Kremlin used to reinforce its foreign policy was energetics. By reusing state control over gas and oil companies, Russia strengthened its position in foreign affairs. Having the biggest gas-proven reserves in the world,[270] which represented 28% of the world's reserves,[271] and the 8th position in

---

267 Idem.
268 'Russia does not rule out future NATO membership,' April 1, 2009. http://euobserver.com/defence/27890
269 The treaty had been signed by Boris Yeltsin on January 3, 1993, but ratified only on April 14, 2000.
270 'Natural gas proved reserves,' The World Factbook, accessed on February 22, 2015. https://www.cia.gov/library/publications/the-world-factbook/rankorder/2253rank.html
271 Goldman, Op. Cit., page 139.

oil[272] allowed them also to develop foreign policies directly or indirectly linked with the use of energy as a bargaining tool to push for geopolitical goals.

Russia, Iran and Qatar account for more than half of the world reserves while other countries account for not more than 3%. Therefore, Russia is in a strong bargaining position. By 2006, Gazprom had become world's third largest corporation after Exxon Mobil and General Electric.[273]

> More generally, by revising strategic expectations Putin has set achievable targets. Russia has very real levels of influence on Eastern Europe (as energy supplier) and the former Soviet Union (across the board), but the key to their effectiveness is not to overstrain them. Ultimately, then, it is not that he has thrown out the idea of spheres of influence, but that he has reworked (or modernized) it taking into account Russia's capabilities and the changed regional and global environment in which it operates.[274]

Assuring state control did not mean that foreign companies were not allowed in joint projects in Russia or abroad with Gazprom, *Rosneft* or other companies. Instead, Western oil and gas corporations joined specific regional projects like *Sakhalin* or the Shtokman reserves.[275] The cases in which they were allowed depended on the one side on the technological support that could be offered by those companies, but it also became a geopolitical choice depending on the alliances that could be more convenient for the Kremlin. In that sense, sometimes an alliance with the French Total was chosen for some projects even if Shell or Exxon offered more technological support, but the choice was not technical but political.

In that sense, the political capabilities of Gazprom became huge. Not only did Russia increase the share of the natural gas provided to European countries but also many of them became completely dependent on Russian gas.

Besides, for many years, Russia had granted gas subsidies to many former USSR countries. At a certain point, that was not profitable and the fact of bargaining for a new price with each country

---

[272] 'World proven oil reserves by country,' OPEC, December 31, 2013. http://ww w.opec.org/library/Annual%20Statistical%20Bulletin/interactive/current/Fi leZ/XL/T31.HTM
[273] Goldman, Op. Cit., page 142.
[274] Lo Bobo, Op. Cit., page 83.
[275] Goldman, Idem, pages 129–131.

became the subject of tough political negotiations that represented for many countries the act of choosing between political loyalty to Russia and the West. Russia's position as provider became a powerful tool to pursue foreign policy goals. In that sense, Alexei Miller, Gazprom's CEO, had enormous power with Gazprom playing the role of a second ministry of foreign affairs. In more than one occasion, tense gas negotiations with deep regional impact were carried out only by Gazprom's staff and were portrayed as 'business only' deals. The Ukrainian gas crisis, described in the next chapter, was one of many examples of this new kind of energetic foreign policy.[276] Therefore, even close allies like Alexander Lukashenko in Belarus were obliged to renegotiate gas deals that were more favourable to Russia and with little margin for bargaining. In that sense, Gazprom extended participation in gas and oil companies and buying assets not only in the CIS countries but also in many EU countries. The growth included the creation of many subsidiaries in several industrial sectors like finance, media and aviation.

These huge global gas corporates or 'National Champions' as had been conceived by Putin years before allowed the government to have different kinds of foreign policy. The official one was carried by the minister of foreign affairs, first Igor Ivanov and since 2004 by Sergei Lavrov and the 'business one' in the hands of Alexei Miller. This possibility also allowed many obscure negotiations to take place between Gazprom and selected oligarchs related to the local governments that referred to the gas deals. The case of Dimitry Firtash in Ukraine would be one of many examples. Firtash helped to leave ITERA out of the business deal to bring gas from Turkmenistan to Ukraine, therefore increasing Gazprom's role in the transit while allowing Firtash to obtain great profit in the Ukrainian market through Eural Trans Gas[277] from 2002 to 2005. This company was half property of Gazprom and half of Firtash who owned it

---

[276] In fact, it is possible to find throughout the world many countries with huge oil or gas reserves that use them as a tool to get benefits in other areas. Venezuela's example under Hugo Chavez that created Petrocaribe to push for further Latin American integration through subsidized oil to other neighbours or Qatar's Government that also uses gas financed companies to sponsor selected Western companies are only some examples of how big energetic state conglomerates can become a powerful foreign policy tool. Note of author.
[277] Goldman, Op. Cit., page 147.

through Austrian frontrunners like Raiffeissein Investment AG.[278] That company disappeared later in favour of RosUkrEnergo (RUE), which would play a considerable role in the Ukrainian gas crises in 2006 and 2009.

Altogether, Gazprom did not mind dealing with different oligarchs or any government that could facilitate pursuing Kremlin's political goals. The Russian company could finance loyal regimes or punish disloyal ones by simply demanding expired payments as any business partner would do. Besides, Gazprom extended its coverage through EU member states, creating in many cases a huge dependency on Gazprom as gas provider.

According to the European Commission,[279] the share of Russian natural gas in the EU member states in 2007 was the following:

Estonia 100%
Finland 100%
Latvia 100%
Lithuania 100%
Slovakia 98%
Bulgaria 92%
Czech Republic 77.6%
Greece 76%
Hungary 60%
Slovenia 52%
Austria 49%
Poland 48.15%
Croatia 37%
Germany 36%

---

[278] It is notable that since 2003 the FBI and the US Department of Justice had been investigating Firtash's companies in relation to their links with the Ukrainian and Russian mafia and mostly in relation with Sergei Mogilevich, now in the FBI's most wanted list. It was only recently on March 2014 that Firtash was arrested in Austria and left free after paying a bail of €125 million, the largest in Austria's history. The why and when of the arrest could probably be understood only in relation with Firtash's role in the Ukrainian political turmoil those days. Idem.

[279] ASSESSMENT REPORT OF DIRECTIVE 2004/67/EC ON SECURITY OF GAS SUPPLY, Commission Staff Working Document, Brussels, SEC, (2009) 978 final, 16/7/2009. http://eur-lex.europa.eu/LexUriServ/LexUriServ.do?uri=SEC:2009:0978:FIN:EN:PDF, pages 64–76.

Italy 27%
Romania 27%
France 14%
Belgium 5%

Besides, Ukraine was strategic to the gas deliveries to Europe as seen in the map. In fact, more than 70% of the Russian gas exports to the EU arrived by 2006 via this country and made it imperative for Germany, the biggest consumer in EU, to develop new alternatives with Russia. In that sense, the *Nord Stream* gas pipe, mostly negotiated during Gerhard Schröder's term as German Chancellor, allowed the possibility to deliver gas directly to Germany, while avoiding Ukraine and also the Baltic countries that could frequently take an anti-Russian position. The first line of this pipeline, the longest sub-sea pipeline in the world, was inaugurated in November 2011 and the second line in October 2012. It is not by chance, then, that after Schröder stepped down as chancellor he became almost immediately chairman of the board of Nord Stream AG, the consortium that operates the pipeline.

The same plan was intended in the south where Russia projected the South Stream pipeline. Even though this pipe has found notable political difficulties, it began its construction on the Russian side in 2012 and in the Black Sea, and even though Bulgaria and Serbia, two of the participants in the project, were openly committed together with Italy, strong resistances by the United States pushed the European Union to suspend the project due to the conflict in Ukraine in 2014. First, there was a non-binding resolution[280] by the European Parliament on 17 April 2014, and then Bulgaria temporarily stopped the works due to an EU's infringement procedure.[281]

The development of the project managed also to force out the concurrent Nabucco.[282] Meanwhile the future of the project is unclear but a big pressure is expected, mostly by Austria and Italy that

---

[280] 'MEPs oppose south stream, seek sanctions against Russian energy firms,' April 17, 2014. http://www.novinite.com/articles/159923/MEPs+Oppose+South+Stream,+Seek+Sanctions+against+Russian+Energy+Firms
[281] 'Austria pleads for south stream pipeline,' June 24, 2014. http://www.euractiv.com/sections/energy/austria-pleads-south-stream-pipeline-303010
[282] Nabucco was a project financed by the United States and the European Union that pretended to build a pipeline from the Shah Deniz gas field in Azerbaijan

would like to secure also the Russian gas furniture without regarding the outcome of the conflict in Ukraine. Russia officially suspended the construction of the underwater pipes in December 2014 due to the decision by Bulgaria to discontinue their part of the construction.[283]

Major Russian pipelines, accessed on July 18, 2017.
Source: Wikimedia Commons, licensed under CC BY-SA 3.0
(https://creativecommons.org/licenses/by-sa/3.0/)

---

through Georgia and Turkey to the EU via Bulgaria and Romania. The project was considered over when on June 2013 the Azerbaijan gas field chose another pipeline. 'EU-backed Nabucco project 'over' after rival pipeline wins Azeri gas bid,' June 27, 2013, http://www.euractiv.com/energy/eu-favoured-nabucco-project-hist-news-528919

[283] 'Россия останавливает строительство Южного потока,' December 2, 2014. http://korrespondent.net/business/economics/3450548-rossyia-ostanavlyvaet-stroytelstvo-yuzhnoho-potoka

The European Union does not have an independent energy policy and still leaves a lot of margin to the member states but has the tools to pressure some members as happened with Bulgaria. This creates confusion on the when and how of political decisions on these matters and how the pressure from the United States operates.

South Stream pipeline as projected.
Source: Wikimedia Commons, licensed under CC BY-SA 3.0
(https://creativecommons.org/licenses/by-sa/3.0/)

Moreover, Gazprom's control of the pipeline network that once belonged to the USSR became one of Russia's strategic assets. Instead, Central Asian countries could export to Europe only through Russian pipelines.[284] In Turkmenistan, for example, a country that has the fourth biggest gas reserves in the world, the government preferred also to negotiate the use of Russian pipelines to ensure that Russia did not interfere in their inner affairs.[285]

Kremlin's use of energy has also been widely perceived in different areas of the world. Gazprom and Rosneft have active investments in distant countries like Venezuela and Bolivia. The gas giant

---

[284] Goldman, Op. Cit., page 149.
[285] Turkmenistan's close political system and gas abundance have allowed them to build a regime with tough control on any civilian liberties and in practice does not allow real political opposition thus remaining a sort of single-party system—by law during the presidency of Saparmurat Niyazov and in practice with the actual one Gurbanguly Berdimuhamedow.

has also acquired subsidiaries that deliver gas to Armenia, Austria, Belarus, Bulgaria, Czech Republic, Estonia, Finland, France, Germany, Greece, Hungary, Italy, Kazakhstan, Kyrgyzstan, Latvia, Lithuania, Moldova, Netherlands, Poland, Romania, Serbia, Slovakia, Slovenia and Switzerland, among others. In many cases, Gazprom controls totally or partially the local distribution and also has several investment funds throughout the world and in places usually considered tax heavens like Cyprus, Switzerland and many British territories.

The expansion of the Kremlin's energy policies has also allowed focusing on two other areas of the world considered of great strategic importance. The first of them is China and the other is the Arctic Ocean. Regarding China, although the Asiatic giant has experienced through the years a changing attitude towards Moscow, the fact of enjoying a big economic growth in the last decade has also enlarged their energy needs. In that sense, Moscow seems as an ideal partner for China with whom most of the energy needs can be met while complementing their needs with other Central Asian countries like Turkmenistan. This way, Moscow with increasing gas exports to China would like to reduce the interdependence with Europe. The next map shows some of the pipelines built and planned to deliver Russian gas to China.

It is worth mentioning that the last deals reached with China in May 2014 included building new pipelines for 4,000 kilometres and stock structures for liquefying gas for which Russia will receive a loan of $50 billion from China.[286] The deal also included the first talks about a pipeline from Siberia to China. Altogether, the transaction between Gazprom and the China National Petroleum Corporation (CNPC) is worth $400 billion, which includes annual supplies for 30 years starting in 2018.[287] It is obvious that the partnership that Russia would like with China is as equals, but the way their Asian neighbour is expanding its geopolitical role, Russia would

---

[286] Mini, Fabio, 'La strana coppia Russia-Cina, figlia delle manipolazioni e degli errori di Obama', Limes, Rivista italiana di Geopolitica, Agosto 2014, Pagina 49–63.
[287] Idem.

also be at a risk of becoming just a kind of a junior partner as Carlo Jean considers.288

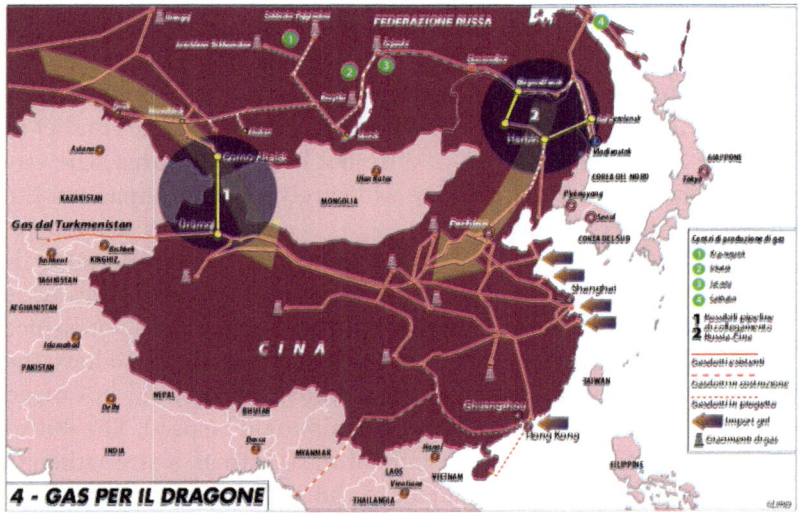

"Gas per il dragone," LIMES.
Source: Limes online http://temi.repubblica.it/UserFiles/limes/Image/altro3/RU-CINA_ga s%20per%20il%20dragone_big.jpg. Reprint with kind permission.

The exploration in the Arctic instead has been one of the most aggressive projects in which Russia has been expanding the role of its 'national champions', to borrow Goldman's definition. The volume of energy reserves, either gas and oil in that area, is still in some areas unexplored but the amount found and the strategic role they play will have a deep strategic impact in determining Russian foreign policy. The fact that Russia considers itself owner of the Artic or at least most of it, as shown in August 2007 when a team of Russian scientists descended more than two miles and planted Russia's flag,289 symbolizes the geostrategic importance of the area.290 In fact, 10% of the world's petroleum resources are estimated to be in

---

288 Jean, Carlo, *Geopolitica del mondo contemporaneo*, Roma-Bari, Editori Laterza, 2012.
289 'Russia's claim under Polar irks Americans,' February 19, 2008. http://www.nytimes.com/2008/02/19/world/europe/19arctic.html?adxnnl=1&adxnnlx=1311810481-IXSrMDBjzhfGopGmYcf6tw&_r=0
290 De Bonis, Mauro, *Le mani sul Polo*, Limes, Rivista italiana di Geopolitica, March 2010.

the Arctic. This way, Russia plans to develop the area as its top strategic resource by 2020[291] disregarding possible environmental damage.[292]

Besides, it is noteworthy how in this region of the world, Gazprom and Rosneft invited foreign companies to participate in different investment projects disregarding the current rivalries with the West. This way, Exxon and Chevron were before the conflict in Ukraine considered partners at different levels in the area. The way the events take place in Ukraine will surely have an impact on the different projects in the Artic.

To conclude, the energy policy of the Russian Federation is strictly related to its foreign policy. State-owned companies have become an instrument to reposition Russia's role in the globe since Putin's arrival to power. In that sense, the impossibility to have the same geopolitical influence, as during Soviet times, did not mean that new ways of enforcing the own goals could be used. The Putin-Medvedev tandem in the government meant, then, a strengthened foreign policy but still dependent of the vicissitudes proper of the oil prices. Therefore, there is still one weak spot: The high dependence on energy income for the Russian Federation could become a weakness, as seen with the fall of oil prices orchestrated by the United States[293] at the end of 2014 as a response to the Ukrainian crisis.

This weakness has been clear to the Kremlin for many years. In that sense, it was considered in other ways to sustain a respectful geopolitical impact where needed and this included a restructuration not only of the Russian Armed Forces and how they could be

---

[291] 'Russia to boost Artic research,' 23-IX-2009. http://blogs.nature.com/news/2010/09/russia_to_boost_arctic_researc.html

[292] 'Russia to charge greenpeace activists with piracy over oil rig protest,' *The Guardian*, September 24, 2013. http://www.theguardian.com/environment/2013/sep/24/russia-greenpeace-piracy-oil-rig-protest

[293] Larry Elliot sustained that the United States together with Saudi Arabia agreed on a fall of the oil prices. First, the United States had notably increased their domestic production; secondly, the Saudis did not accept to reduce production in the OPEP to keep former prices, even if this brought a negative effect for them. Nevertheless, these actions had a deep impact on Russia and Iran among others, countries that are not aligned geopolitically with the United States. Elliot, Larry, 'Stakes are high as US plays the oil card against Iran and Russia,' *The Guardian*, November 9, 2014. http://www.theguardian.com/business/economics-blog/2014/nov/09/us-iran-russia-oil-prices-shale

used and act upon actions considered a threat to Russian interests. The Georgian War in 2008 would be one of many examples of use of the military force outside Russian borders.

1.2.1.2 From the Commonwealth of Independent States to the Eurasian Union

The energy policies together with a renewed Russian Army also included a vigorous military industry that gave some elements to rebuild an assertive foreign policy at least in the Near Abroad and to a lesser degree in the rest of the world. A renewed Russian geopolitics would therefore intend to have a strong Eurasian presence. In that sense, after the Soviet collapse, it became obvious that new ways of organizing and enhancing neighbour countries to keep themselves in the same geopolitical orbit were necessary. Therefore, Russian foreign policy pursued the objective of integrating the Near Abroad in a new political project that could fit into the political and economic order proper of the post-Soviet era.[294]

The CIS was the consequence of the political rush to negotiate the disappearance of the Soviet Union. It occurred in extremely complex conditions and was initially negotiated by the leaders of only 3[295] of the 15 republics. The new supranational organization intended to keep influence and coordinating powers on trade, finance, law making and security and to promote cooperation on cross-border crime. This loose association of independent countries was exactly the opposite of the proposal Gorbachev had tried to implement before. The Union Treaty pretended to transform the Soviet Union into a new kind of federation in which each Soviet Republic would retain great economic and cultural autonomy, among others; meanwhile foreign monetary policy and defence would remain part of the polity that used to be the USSR but now with the initials standing for Union of Soviet Sovereign Republics. In fact, the question of whether the failure of the Soviet economic system should also mean the separation of the republics remains open.

---

[294] In this sense, I refer to the political order proper of the globalization, understood as the political answer to the crisis of the welfare state as referred to by Joachim Hirsch. Avalos Tenorio, Gerardo and Hirsch, Joachim, *La política del Capital*, México, D.F., UAM Xochimilco, 2007.

[295] Even only two (Kravchuk and Shuskevich) if considered that Yeltsin was completely drunk during the negotiations as documented by Schard, Op. Cit.

Instead, Boris Yeltsin saw that the only way he could obtain absolute power in Russia was avoiding the existence of any authority above him. US Political Analyst Brzezinski agreed with this idea:

> The disintegration of the Soviet Union in December 1991 was not, therefore, the consequence of an irresistible wave of non-Russian political self-assertion. The old Soviet Union had outlived its day, but the precipitating impetus for its disintegration came from the political conflicts in Moscow, from the struggle between Boris Yeltsin and Mikhail Gorbachev within a demoralized and fractionated Communist Party of the Soviet Union (CPSU)—reinforced by pressures from outside the center for a genuine redistribution of power (especially economic power) between Moscow and the formally 'sovereign' capitals in Kyiv, Tbilisi, or Tashkent. The combination of these forces led, to the astonishment of all those who had assumed that the national problem in the Soviet Union no longer existed, to the rapid dissolution of the Soviet Union and its replacement by a quickly improvised new entity called the Commonwealth of Independent States.[296]

In that sense, the CIS pretended from its origins to be just like a coordinating forum to resolve all the problems related to the dissolution of the USSR. There were always strong resistances that the new organization could become a Russian-oriented supranational order from which Russia could restore control over the ancient republics. The reality was more complex. Some countries because of the economical or geographical conditions had easier ways of resolving their own issues and developing in an autonomous way, but the social tissue was well deeply interconnected at different levels and in many cases, it was impossible to impose just a border. Besides, in the logic of the Soviet economic planning, some regions were only supposed to produce certain products and receive the rest from other areas, like cotton production in Uzbekistan or wine in Georgia to mention some examples. In fact, if we notice how much time it took the Central Asian countries to declare independence it was because they had noticed the economic difficulties that would follow without Moscow's support. 'Nonetheless, the independence that came in late 1991 came largely because the center of Soviet power had collapsed so rapidly.'[297] In fact, as Brzezinski mentions, independence was not the consequence of a national liberation

---

[296] Brzezinski, Zbigniew, *Russia and the Commonwealth of Independent States: Documents, Data and Analysis*, Armonk, ME Sharp Inc., 1997, page 6.
[297] Idem.

struggle or a political contest.[298] That allowed the same local elites from the Communist Party of the Soviet Union to stay in power without any resistance until now.

After the Soviet collapse, every country handled the crisis in a different way. For the Baltic countries, it was easier, first because they were smaller and second because they received strong sums of foreign investment mostly from Scandinavian countries and Finland. They exchanged any degree of sovereignty they could have for Western support and the possibility to incorporate themselves in Western Institutions and thus the European Union and NATO. Some others like Azerbaijan or Turkmenistan could count on huge energy resources from oil and gas to develop commerce and sustain without rivalries the same elite in power throughout years. Others like Armenia, Kyrgyzstan or Tajikistan were in poor conditions to develop and were with almost no energy reserves. Others like Georgia and Moldova had even complicated inner conflicts that could not be resolved without Russia. Altogether, this allowed the CIS to become a necessary institution on the one side but on the other there was never the political will to give it more power or any kind of a supranational authority. Therefore, while the idea of the CIS was to regroup at least 12 of the former Soviet Republics,[299] it was never possible. All 12 members ratified the protocol at different moments between December 1991 and April 1994, with Moldova being the last country to do so. But Turkmenistan and Ukraine never ratified the charter. Besides, after the Russian-Georgian War of August 2008, Georgia withdrew from the CIS, leaving it officially with nine countries as members and two as associates.[300]

---

[298] Idem.
[299] The three Baltic Republics were never part of the project to become CIS members.
[300] Recently in Moldova and Ukraine, there have been legislative initiatives to withdraw from CIS. For the Moldovan initiative, see: 'Proiectul legii cu privire la denunțarea Acordului de constituire a Comunității Statelor Independente nr.40-XII din 08.04.1994,' March 25, 2014. http://www.parlament.md/Proc esulLegislativ/Proiectedeactelegislative/tabid/61/LegislativId/2230/languag e/ro-RO/Default.aspx The Ukrainian initiative can be found in 'Проект Постанови про питання участі України в Співдружності Незалежних Держав,' November 27, 2014. http://w1.c1.rada.gov.ua/pls/zweb2/webpro c4_1?pf3511=52424

Therefore, the results achieved by the CIS in different areas were very poor, both in promoting the social and economic development and even in the human rights agenda[301] where Central Asian countries have very low records. Besides, even though the CIS Charter establishes a council of ministers of defence to coordinate military cooperation, it has proved useless in resolving the different regional conflicts.

At the end, Russia has always held the position of power and, in many cases, the countries that find themselves in a weak economic position have preferred a negotiated solution with Russia that allows the local elites to prevail in power in exchange for aligning the country geopolitically with Moscow. This process took years and in that sense, the failure to develop the CIS shows on the one side the lack of an assertive Russian foreign policy during the 1990s together with the lack of interest by the other members to try to regroup in other supranational organizations.

CIS's limits together with local and foreign interests urged for the creation of different organizations to regroup former Soviet Republics—most of them with Russia as a leading member but others precisely with the intention of counterbalancing Moscow, like GUAM[302] or the Organization of Central Asian Cooperation.[303]

The logic of how Capital[304] organizes itself also has influenced how supranational organizations have transformed themselves

---

[301] There have been several cases of rights abuses and repression against political opposition visible in Central Asian Republics. 'Central Asia: Widespread Rights Abuse, Repression,' January 31, 2013. http://www.hrw.org/news/2013/01/31/central-asia-widespread-rights-abuse-repression

[302] GUAM, founded in 1999, represents the initials of its members, Georgia, Ukraine, Azerbaijan and Moldova, and counted for some years with the membership of Uzbekistan. The organization, opposed by Moscow, also served as a trampoline of US interests in the region. In the following chapters, Ukraine's and Moldova's role in it will be discussed. Note of the author.

[303] This organization has changed its name and members often since its origins. Kazakhstan, Uzbekistan, Turkmenistan, Kirgizstan and Tajikistan founded it. Then Russia became a member in 2004 and at last, the organization merged into the Eurasian Economic Community.

[304] Again, retaking Hirsch, when I refer to how Capital organizes itself, I refer to the way in which the global process of accumulation and the social relations around the globe have transformed in the recent decades. This includes all changes that forced nation states to be actively involved in adjusting national economy to global capital requirements meanwhile diminishing their local

around its needs. In 1994, there was an agreement to create a free trade area between CIS members, but it never became a reality. Years later, eight members signed the CISFTA, the Free Trade Agreement of the CIS members excluding Azerbaijan and Uzbekistan but including Ukraine,[305] on 18 October 2011.

The intention to have a free trade area among CIS members evolved in the Eurasian Economic Community with the participation of many CIS members. The EAEC, founded in the year 2000 with a treaty signed in Astana on October 10, included the membership of Belarus, Kazakhstan, Kyrgyzstan, Russia and Tajikistan. Later, it was decided in 2005 that Uzbekistan would join while Armenia, Moldova and Ukraine were observers.[306],[307] There are a couple of facts worth mentioning. First, the EAEC was only the first step of a project of deeper integration that would become later the Eurasian Economic Union. Second, the fact that Armenia, Ukraine and Moldova were only observers at this point shows that these countries were valuing until what point a further integration with CIS members was convenient to the ruling elites in these countries; meanwhile there was an already present temptation of extending economic links with the West, in this case with the EU. Therefore, for GUAM members there was no deep interest in joining the EAEC.

Contrary to the ambiguous position of GUAM members, the participants in the Custom Union of Belarus, Russia and Kazakhstan agreed first on the creation of a united customs tariff and created a schedule for a unified customs territory. The agreement also included the formation of a Single Economic Space from 1 January 2012. Finally, on 29 May 2014, the presidents of those three countries agreed to establish the Eurasian Economic Union from 1 January 2015. Consequently, an agreement to terminate the EAEC was signed in Minsk on 10 October 2014, as the new Eurasian Economic

---

capabilities to oppose it. Hirsch Joachim, Globalización Capital y Estado, Hirsch Joachim, UAM Xochimilco, 1996.

[305] 'CIS leaders sign free trade deal,' November 18, 2011. http://sputniknews.com/russia/20111018/167833875.html

[306] 'ЕВРАЗИЙСКОЕ ЭКОНОМИЧЕСКОЕ СООБЩЕСТВО,'. HTTP://EVRAZES.COM/EN/ABOUT/

[307] Official documents related with the foundation of the EAEC. http://www.evrazes.com/about/history

Union englobed the functions previously handled by EAEC. Besides, the idea of the Eurasian Union expanded to include Armenia, once this country finally decided to stop bargaining between the West and Russia and noticed that it was preferable, considering their geopolitical context, to have a strong alliance with Moscow rather than a cloudy prospective of integration into the EU. Moreover, energy dependency towards Russia and the unresolved conflict in the Nagorno-Karabakh where Russian troops are peace guarantors forced the Armenian Government to prefer an alliance with Moscow that includes entering the Eurasian Union. In addition, the weak Armenian position towards Azerbaijan, both militarily and economically, forced the authorities in Erevan to choose Moscow as an ally that also appears as the protector of the orthodox faith in a region surrounded by Muslim neighbours. In that sense, Armenian elites were in no position to bargain for Western support, and neither the EU nor the United States were willing to offer it. In this case, for the West it is preferable to have an energy alliance with Azerbaijan rather than support Armenia. Altogether, the EAEC started functioning on 1 January 2015, with five members that also includes Kyrgyzstan, which signed the treaty on 23 December 2014.[308] The Union probably will include Tajikistan as a member in the near future and a slight perspective that Uzbekistan[309] could join even if Uzbek officials have expressed contradictory statements regarding a possible membership.

Therefore, the Eurasian Economic Union appears as a new geopolitical and economic bloc concurrent with other similar ones and portraying a geopolitical goal of the Russian foreign policy to achieve a privileged position in Eurasia.[310] Even if Kazakhstan's president, Nursultan Nazarbayev, often declares that the Union is

---

[308] 'Putin: Kyrgyzstan signs deal to join Eurasian Economic Union,' December 23, 2014. http://sputniknews.com/business/20141223/1016151391.html
[309] 'Post-Soviet integration process to benefit Moscow-Tashkent relations,' December 10, 2014. http://itar-tass.com/en/economy/766223
[310] 'A brief primer on Vladimir Putin's Eurasian dream,' February 18, 2014. http://www.theguardian.com/world/shortcuts/2014/feb/18/brief-primer-vladimir-putin-eurasian-union-trade

Geopolitical Issues Between Russia and the West 117

purely economic, and that his country will preserve full sovereignty,[311] it is clear though that the EEU antagonizes with other geopolitical projects in the globe, either with China in Asia or with the EU in the West.

The EAEC has a political governance in a certain way similar to the European Union. The following scheme explains how the decisions are taken among the Eurasian Economic Union. The Commission has two authorities, the Board and the Council, the former, composed of equal number of members of the adherent states with the final number still to be determined once the entrance of Armenia and Kyrgyzstan is taken into account. Also as part of the Commission, the Council is composed of the vice prime ministers of all members and has to meet every three months.

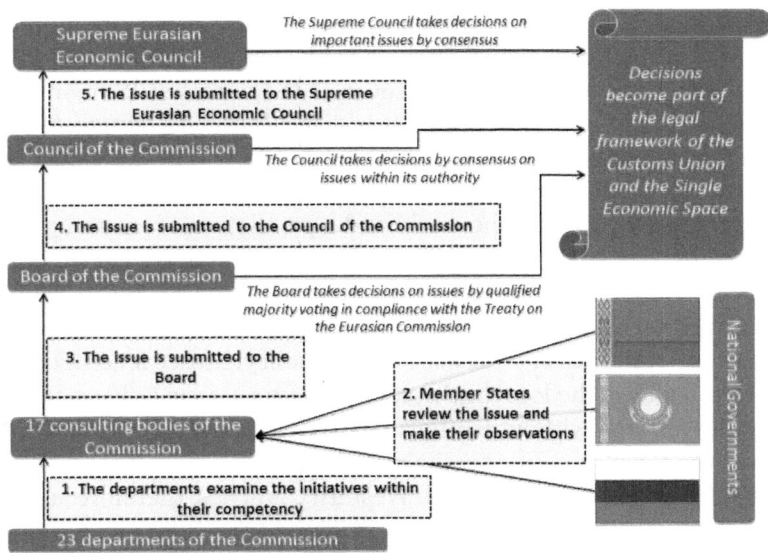

"Decision making processes of the Eurasian Customs Union and Single Economic Space."
Source: Wikimedia Commons, licensed under CC BY-SA 3.0
(https://creativecommons.org/licenses/by-sa/3.0/)

---

[311] 'Customs Union, Eurasian Union no threat to Kazakhstan's sovereignty council,' August 27, 2014. http://itar-tass.com/en/world/746905

The possibility to create a parliament[312] has been mentioned and exhorted by Vladimir Putin but is still considered premature by some members. Besides, the Union has a court that has two judges from each member approved by the Supreme Eurasian Council for a nine-year term.[313]

Finally, there is also the Eurasian Development Bank that comprises currently of six members, the five members of the Eurasian Union plus Tajikistan. The bank had in 2014 a capital of US$ 7 billion,[314] which is relatively small compared with others like the Inter-American Development Bank or the African Development Bank but still manages to finance considerable projects mostly for transport infrastructure and power generation and electricity.

Altogether, the Eurasian Economic Union has seen growth at a respectable pace and achieved partially some of its goals. The idea of a common currency has been mentioned and it has still more to grow. The prospective entrance of Tajikistan and maybe even Uzbekistan could allow it to have seven of the once 12 CIS members. Still, there are also limitations. It is difficult that Turkmenistan or Azerbaijan would join the EEU in the near future. Turkmenistan because with a stable income, as a consequence of having the fourth biggest gas reserves in the world and a population of around 5 million people, does not consider it necessary to join another economic bloc. Turkmen constitution makes a strong emphasis on their own neutrality. This neutrality can be understood as a compromise of not developing an anti-Russian foreign policy. Moscow accepts this fact and allows the local authorities to have a strong hold on power at all levels and without caring about any criticism that could come from the West. Instead, Azerbaijan also has big oil reserves and has established good relations with Western countries, therefore, assuring them an affordable partner that can be a provider and a transit country for gas and oil, mostly when relations with Russia do not

---

[312] 'Creation of Eurasian Parliament deemed possible,' November 20, 2013. http://itar-tass.com/en/russia/708233
[313] 'Treaty on the Eurasian Economic Union,' May 29, 2014. https://translate.google.com/translate?hl=en&sl=ru&tl=en&u=http%3A%2F%2Fwww.alta.ru%2Fshow_orders.php%3Faction%3Dview%26filename%3D14bn0044&sandbox=1
[314] 'Facts and figures,' Eurasian Development bank. http://www.eabr.org/e/about/figures-facts/

flow smoothly.[315] These facts transform this small Caucasian country in 'geopolitically critical' as Brzezinski said.[316] In this sense, if Turkmenistan[317] and Azerbaijan do not tolerate political opposition, any freedom of expression or do not care about human rights, it won't be a concern for the West, as much as they do not integrate closer with Russia. This scenario leaves the possibility of further enlargement of the Eurasian Economic Union to other CIS members as complicated.

Besides, the speed with which the constitution of the Eurasian Union was established in Central Asia was very different to the level of conflicts that confronted this project in the West. Obviously, the idea pretended to include Moldova, Georgia and Ukraine, but the geopolitical conflict between the West and Russia as to who will englobe these countries in their area of influence has at least for the time being stopped any possibility for them to be considered as possible candidates to join the Eurasian Union. Even though, the Kremlin still has different ways to pressure Moldova, as for instance, with the influence they exercise in Pridnestrovia and Gagauzia[318] and in Ukraine while the current crisis is not over. In the Georgian case, even if the government as mentioned has tried to improve relations with Russia it cannot go as far as to relinquish the Association Agreement signed with the EU. Therefore, still the only bargain possibility for Russia for a deeper integration would be a change in the status of South Ossetia and Abkhazia, something that seems not plausible for now. Besides, local elites in Ukraine and Moldova, and especially local oligarchs, have more to win with the EU than any benefit the Eurasian Union could offer them.

---

[315] Doroshko, M.C., *Геополітичні інтереси та зовнішня політика держав пострадянського простору*, Kiev, Nika Centre, 2011, page 128.
[316] Brzezinski, Zbigniew, *The Grand Chessboard: American Strategy and its Geostrategic Imperatives*, New York, Basic Books, 1997, page 38
[317] Reporters without borders consider Turkmenistan the third most censured country in the world. 'Most censored countries,' May 2, 2006. http://cpj.org /reports/2006/05/10-most-censored-countries.php
[318] On February 2014, a consultation was held in Gagauzia to decide whether they wanted to join the Customs Union. Even if it received an overwhelming majority of the local population, the results were not recognized either by the Moldovan Government or by the West. 'Таможенный союзник Гагаузия хочет к России, Белоруссии и Казахстану' February 3, 2014, accessed on February 20, 2014. http://www.kommersant.md/node/25241

The Union and its expansion has become the biggest geopolitical project for the Kremlin. The subsequent chapters will discuss carefully the Ukrainian and Moldovan cases, but it is important to anticipate that the Kremlin's wishes clashed with antagonist projects that precisely pretend to diminish Moscow's assertiveness in the area by including Georgia, Moldova and Ukraine in other geopolitical areas. Therefore, the confrontation between Russia and the West involved other actors and different strategies to reach their own goals, which included using ethnic differences and divisions remaining after the Soviet fall.

Besides, it is worth mentioning a theme of considerable importance for Moscow, the idea of a common security and defence. As antecedent, the Soviet Army always saw with distrust the reforms carried out by Gorbachev and then the disappearance of the Soviet Union. In fact, the last political actor to recognize the Soviet fall was precisely the Soviet Army, which only on the last days of December 1991 recognized Boris Yeltsin as the authority in Russia.

The process of transforming the Soviet Army into 15 different national armies was complex. The military strategy used to cover all of Soviet territory and was devised within the logic of the Cold War. Therefore, it was not possible just to divide the military equipment into 15 proportional components. The agreement after the Soviet fall was that Russia would keep the greatest amount of strategic assets including all the nuclear weapons. Consequently, the Russian Army became mostly an adaptation of the Soviet Army only with a reduced territory; meanwhile the other 14 republics had to scratch wherever possible to obtain some equipment that was never of the same quality as the one available to the Russian Federation.

Besides, the rush in which the Soviet collapse occurred left conflicts erupting in different regions like Tajikistan, Armenia, Moldova or Georgia. It created civil wars that brought ceasefires sustained only by the presence of Russian troops. These struggles brought the 'de facto' independence of South Ossetia, Abkhazia or Pridnestrovia[319] while territories like Adjara obtained considerable

---

[319] Pridnestrovia's case and its relationship with Moldova will be explained in the Chapter 4.

autonomy.[320] Russia, to different degrees, sustained tacitly the breakaway republics as a bargaining tool towards Georgia[321] or Moldova, while Moscow kept the upper hand, either with regard to economic or energetic pressure or guaranteeing security.

Meanwhile, the same structure, personnel and chiefs of staff from the Soviet Army but acting on behalf of the Russian Federation remained present in different arenas, while the presence of Russian troops in Armenia, Moldova, Georgia, Tajikistan and Crimea allowed to conceive, if not legally at least symbolically, that all these territories belong to the same area of defence, maybe in a similar way as the US North Command, the one responsible of the security of most of the United States' territory, englobes Mexico and Canada in the same Unified Combatant Command[322] and proceeds to organize its strategic defence accordingly.[323]

Therefore, on 15 May 1992, six ex-Soviet states signed the Collective Security Treaty Organization: Russia, Armenia, Kyrgyzstan, Tajikistan, Uzbekistan and Kazakhstan. The next year Georgia, Azerbaijan and Belarus joined and currently, after some withdrawals, it has five members from the Eurasian Union plus Tajikistan.[324]

The treaty can be considered as an intergovernmental military alliance and constrains the members to join other military alliances; meanwhile aggression against one of them would be considered an act of aggression against all. Besides, there is also a Collective Rapid

---

[320] Adjara had a considerable degree of autonomy under the rule of Aslan Abashidze until the Georgian Government decided to retake control of the region in 2004. Eke, Steven, 'Profile: Aslan Asabidze,' May 4, 2004. http://news.bbc.co.uk/2/hi/europe/3683629.stm

[321] In the Georgian case, the outcome of the ethnic and political division among the territory got even more complicated after the Georgian War in 2008. Note of the author.

[322] 'Unified combatant commands,' accessed on February 22, 2016. http://upload.wikimedia.org/wikipedia/commons/e/e6/Unified_Combatant_Commands_map.png

[323] Jacoby, J.R. and Charles, H., 'Statement of General Charles H. Jacoby, JR. United States Army Commander, United States Army Commander, United States Northern Command and North American Aerospace Defense Command before the Senate Armed Services Committee,' March 13, 2014. http://www.northcom.mil/Portals/28/Documents/2014%20NC%20SASC%20Posture%20Statement.pdf

[324] 'Организация договора о коллективной безопасности,' accessed on February 22, 2016. http://www.odkb-csto.org/

Reaction Force that has organized military exercises on different occasions.[325],[326] Another interesting point is that the organization forbids since 2011 the establishment of new foreign military bases in the member states.[327] This last action would limit future NATO operations like the ones carried out against Afghanistan that comprised of air bases in Kyrgyzstan and Uzbekistan during the conflict. In fact, the last foreign base, Manas Air Base, was finally closed on 3 June 2014.[328]

Therefore, a common security policy follows a similar trial like the Eurasian Economic Union. It includes the same members with the addition of Tajikistan and changing attitudes from Uzbekistan that retired from the Treaty[329] in 2012. Still, the same problem persists, with NATO trying to englobe Moldova, Georgia and Ukraine. Meanwhile Turkmenistan prefers to stay neutral and Azerbaijan does not want to participate in a military agreement that includes Armenia with the conflict in Nagorno-Karabakh unresolved. Besides, the Azerbaijani Government has developed different levels of cooperation with the United States and NATO, discussing even the possibility of military bases[330]; all this while Russia has continued to be the main weapon provider for this Caucasian country.

There is still one fact worth mentioning regarding both geopolitical projects, the Eurasian Economic Union and the Collective Se-

---

[325] 'Учение КСОР ОДКБ 'Взаимодействие-2014' началось в Казахстане,' August 8, 2014, accessed on February 22, 2016. http://www.odkb-csto.or g/news/detail.php?ELEMENT_ID=3600&SECTION_ID=91

[326] 'Московский комсомолец': 'Хочешь мира, готовься... Страны ОДКБ провели успешные маневры в Кыргызстане,' August 7, 2014. http://ww w.odkb-csto.org/news/detail.php?ELEMENT_ID=3594&SECTION_ID=92

[327] 'CSTO tightens foreign bases norms,' December 20, 2011. http://ww w.thehindu.com/todays-paper/tp-international/article2736607.ece

[328] This airbase handled 5.3 million personnel in 12 years of operations in the Afghan conflict. Kucera Joshua, 'U.S. formally closes its Kyrgyzstan Air Base,' June 3, 2014, accessed on February 23, 2016. http://www.eurasianet.org/n ode/68430

[329] It is worth mentioning that Serbia and Afghanistan have an observer role in the treaty and Iran has been mentioned as a possible candidate. 'Афганистан и Сербия стали наблюдателями при ПА ОДКБ,' accessed on November 5, 2014. http://www.odkbcsto.org/news/detail.php?ELEMENT_ID=1779&SEC TION_ID=92&sphrase_id=8903

[330] Doroshko, M.S., Геополітичні інтереси та зовнішня політика держав пострадянського простору, Kiev, Nika Centre, 2011, page 136.

curity Treaty Organization. Its members have not shown deep interest in creating strong supranational authorities. There is on the one side the fear to lose sovereignty, while Moscow would like to keep control over both organisms and that is exactly what other members do not want. In fact, only a complex supranational authority with a proper system of checks and balances would allow members a deeper integration, with a single defence policy and a single customs union not decided unilaterally by Moscow; and that would present itself as more attractive to other members. Either way, Moscow would keep the upper hand, but symbolically it would have allowed a supranational authority in which all participants could feel included at the same level. Besides, Russian influence could remain similar to the German one in the EU but without the capacity to decide unilaterally. Therefore, a deeper integration could mean a stronger geopolitical impact towards other regional actors, in particular against China, the EU and the United States.

Of all the European CIS members, Ukraine has been, since the Soviet collapse, the most important to keep in the same geopolitical project. The causes will be explained in depth in the following chapter. The same causes were well known by Western powers which also developed their own strategies to try to englobe or at least approach Ukraine.

To conclude, the future of the Russian geopolitical project has a block at the West, where two other projects, sometimes overlapping among them, clash with Moscow's ambitions. This means that Moldova, Georgia and, especially, Ukraine as the main goal, cannot be englobed by now in the geopolitics depicted by Moscow. The new assertive Russian foreign policy must deal either way with these two Western geopolitical configurations. Therefore, it is worth analysing first the most antagonistic of those projects, that is NATO, its enlargement and its repercussions in the Near Abroad.

1.3 United States' strategic interests in Eurasia after the Cold War

After the crumble of the Soviet Union, it appeared as if the global order and hegemony guided by the United States could not have any rivalry of real consideration. The Cold War was over; therefore, it seemed that the United States could impose their geopolitical will with ease. It is interesting in this sense to reconsider Brzezinski's words from his famous book *The Grand Chessboard*, wrote precisely in 1997, just some years after the Soviet fall.

> For the first time ever, a non-Eurasian power has emerged not only as the key arbiter of Eurasian power relations but also as the world's paramount power. The defeat and collapse of the Soviet Union was the final step in the rapid ascendance of a Western Hemisphere power, the United States, as the sole and, indeed, the first truly global power.[331]

In this sense, he reconsidered Mackinder's idea of the importance of controlling Eurasia and noted that a non-Eurasian power had become hegemonic but recognizing that this area of the world was the chessboard in which global supremacy continued to be played.[332] Besides, the United States had been able at the end of the 1990s to build a system of alliances that guaranteed them the control of Eurasia and ensured the impossibility of any other regional power to try to defy them.

> ...the American global system emphasizes the technique of co-optation (as in the case of defeated rivals—Germany, Japan, and lately even Russia) to a much greater extent than the earlier imperial systems did. It likewise relies heavily on the indirect exercise of influence on dependent foreign elites, while drawing much benefit from the appeal of its democratic principles and institutions. All of the foregoing are reinforced by the massive but intangible impact of the American domination of global communications, popular entertainment, and mass culture and by the potentially very tangible clout of America's technological edge and global military reach.[333]

Besides, considering the strong influence the United States had at the world's financial institutions at the end of the 1990s, US hegemony was guaranteed, to put it in Brzezinski's terms.

> ...one must consider as part of the American system the global web of specialized organizations, especially the 'international' financial institutions. The International Monetary Fund (IMF) and the World Bank can be said to represent 'global' interests, and their constituency may be construed as the world. In reality, however, they are heavily American dominated and their origins are traceable to American initiative, particularly the Bretton Woods Conference of 1944.[334]

---

[331] Brzezinski, Zbigniew, *The Grand Chessboard: American Strategy and Its Geostrategic Imperatives*, New York, Basic Books, 1997, page 7.
[332] Idem, page 29.
[333] Idem, page 23.
[334] Idem, pages 26–27.

US hegemony exercised a strong cultural influence which was visible in many tangible circumstances. The ex-US National Security advisor added: 'Cultural domination has been an underappreciated facet of American global power. Whatever one may think of its aesthetic values, America's mass culture exercises a magnetic appeal, especially on the world's youth. Its attraction may be derived from the hedonistic quality of the lifestyle it projects, but its global appeal is undeniable. American television programs and films account for about three-fourths of the global market.'[335]

The strategy suggested for the United States by Brzezinski in 1997 showed some changes from the one he suggested in 2012 in his book *Strategic Vision, America and the Crisis of Global Power*.[336] In 15 years, it is notable that the United States had to deal with two unexpected facts. First, the incredible growth of China at all levels and, second, the reconstitution of the Russian state that did not align itself with the West as Brzezinski had suggested in his previous book. Still, there was a common idea, the importance of having a hegemonic position in Eurasia.

Therefore, precisely this idea of building a strong position in Eurasia from which the United States could sustain its hegemonic position played a preponderant role in its foreign policies. Its role in the Balkan Wars and later during NATO's enlargement were some of the successes achieved by the United States during the 1990s. After that, there were some backlashes. The failed interventions in Afghanistan or in Iraq, even though they obtained relatively easy military victories, were not capable of sustaining a political order that could secure stability in those regions for US interests. The fact that more than 13 years after the intervention in Afghanistan[337] US military presence is still needed shows the lack of capability to build a new stable political order and displays the impossibility to control a complex region.[338]

---

[335] Idem, page 23.
[336] Brzezinski, Zbigniew, *America and the Crisis of Global Power*, New York, Basic Books, 2012.
[337] It is worth to note that for the Soviets it took 10 years to understand that they could not control Afghanistan as intended. Note of the author.
[338] NATO formally ended operations on December 28, 2014, but a considerable number of armed forces mostly from the United States will remain for assistance and training plus others for counterterrorist activities and logistical assistance. Rasmussen Sun Engel, 'NATO ends combat operations in

The same problem is visible in the current unstable situations in Iraq, and Libya, where the United States pushed to ouster rulers that were not aligned geopolitically with them, but managed through a tyrannical regime to impose a sort of secular political order that avoided religious extremists. These regimes could only on a case-by-case basis negotiate with the West, but that did not seem to align with US interests.

The failures in Iraq and in Libya, after the 2011 intervention that ousted Mohamad Gadhafi in which the territory is still in a continuous civil war, made it necessary to form a pact with other regional powers if steps needed to be taken against uncomfortable regimes like in Syria and mostly in Iran. This allowed a renewed Russian presence that negotiated with the West the disruptive use of chemical weapons[339] by the Syrian regime with the agreement that there would not be any Western intervention against Assad.[340]

Therefore, the continued assertiveness of Russian foreign policy also made it a priority for the United States to counterbalance its influence. Strategy against Russia would also have to take into account relations with China[341] and to understand one of the weaknesses of the Russian Federation, which is the gross dependence from oil and gas incomes to the local economy.

Therefore, different strategies by the United States became visible since Vladimir Putin arrived to power to try to influence the Near Abroad and to change the geopolitical orientation of some of

---

Afghanistan,' December 28, 2014. http://www.theguardian.com/world/20 14/dec/28/nato-ends-afghanistan-combat-operations-after-13-years
[339] Gordon, Michael R., 'U.S. and Russia reach deal to destroy Syria's chemical arms,' September 14, 2013. http://www.nytimes.com/2013/09/15/world/ middleeast/syria-talks.html?pagewanted=all&_r=1&
[340] The negotiated agreement for the destruction of the Syrian chemical weapons became a diplomatic victory for Russia. By one side, they eliminated the possibility of a US intervention in Syria. In practice, the agreement also assured that Assad could stay in power and he could continue to massacre local resistance only this time without chemical weapons. Note of the author.
[341] Brzezinski in 2012 considered that it was preferable to englobe Russia in the same geopolitical area with Europe and the United States to counterbalance China. He proposed that it was preferable to englobe a sort of pro-Western Russia with NATO and that the inclusion of Ukraine would be part of the deal. Brzezinski, Op. Cit.

these countries. Altogether, the geostrategic importance of one territory became crucial to counterbalance the relation with the Russian Federation, of course, that meant Ukraine.

1.3.1 NATO's enlargement towards Eastern Europe

It is not a secret to describe NATO as a geopolitical masterpiece by the United States after World War II. The logic of the Cold War and the impossibility of the Western European countries to contain by themselves a possible Soviet threat made it imperative to build a military alliance that could assure them security. Meanwhile, the United States guaranteed a continuous military presence that portrayed at that time as indispensable in a confrontation with the Soviet bloc.

After the Cold War, NATO passed through several changes. It had to change its goals and to find a justification to exist once the Warsaw Pact and the Soviet Union, the enemies they were supposed to confront, did not exist anymore. It had to justify also a gradual enlargement from the 12 members it originally had to the 28 it now includes.

After the reunification of Germany in 1990, NATO had its first expansion towards territory that once was under Soviet influence. At that time, Soviets received assurances by their US counterpart that no further NATO enlargements would follow to the East. Years later, Gorbachev was quoted saying 'The Americans promised that NATO wouldn't move beyond the boundaries of Germany after the Cold War but now half of central and Eastern Europe are members, so what happened to their promises? It shows they cannot be trusted.'[342]

---

[342] Gorbachev, Mikhail, quoted in Blomfield, Adrian and Smith, Mike, 'Gorbachev: US could start a new cold war,' May 6, 2008. http://www.telegraph.co.uk/news/worldnews/europe/russia/1933223/Gorbachev-US-could-start-new-Cold-War.html

128   State-Building in the Middle of a Geopolitical Struggle

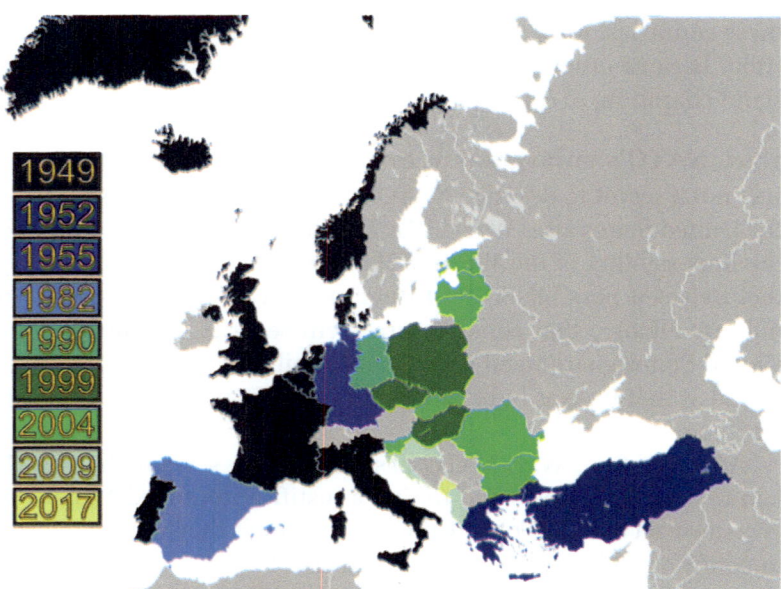

"Enlargement of NATO," accessed on July 18, 2017.
Source: Wikimedia Commons, licensed under CC BY-SA 3.0
(https://creativecommons.org/licenses/by-sa/3.0/)

Beyond the question if the United States could be trusted, Gorbachev did not understand that before being matter of trust it was simple politics, to put it in Frank Underwood's terms.343 It was naïve of Gorbachev to think that the United States would not pursue a further NATO enlargement once the opportunity arose.

After the definitive Soviet crumble, and without Russian opposition, NATO easily englobed three new members from the Visegrad Group344 in 1999: Poland, Hungary and the Czech Republic. Moscow perceived the act as an encirclement; but at that point, they had

---

343   At this point, I retake a quote of Frank Underwood, a character of the famous TV series *House of Cards*, which at a certain point asks Jackie Sharp, the Democratic majority whip, to organize an impeachment against the US president that belongs to their same party. In that scene, the majority whip says: 'What you are asking me is just shy of treason' to which he answers: 'Just shy, which is politics.' 'House of Cards,' Season 2 Episode 12. Written by Beau Willimon, directed by James Foley. Netflix, 2014.

344   This was an alliance between Poland, Hungary, and Czechoslovakia 1991 and once it divided with the Czech Republic and Slovakia. Its primary goal was to promote further European integration. Once the four members became part of both NATO and the EU, the group lost its preponderance.

no way to oppose it. Neither could they resist the subsequent NATO enlargement in 2004 that included seven other members. By 2009, the enlargement included Croatia and Albania, and Montenegro in 2017. Moreover, if we see the earlier figure, it becomes clear how the United States increased its presence in Europe while for Moscow, the expansion signalled an approach of the Atlantic Alliance against its borders.

It is also worth noting how there was no real serious European opposition to NATO's enlargement. European security was conceived as something that went together with US foreign policy. Therefore, for the United States, Europe became the geopolitical entrance to a stronger presence in Eurasia.

> At this stage of American-European relations, with the allied European nations still highly dependent on U.S. security protection, any expansion in the scope of Europe becomes automatically an expansion in the scope of direct U.S. influence as well. Conversely, without close transatlantic ties, America's primacy in Eurasia promptly fades away. U.S. control over the Atlantic Ocean and the ability to project influence and power deeper into Eurasia would be severely circumscribed.[345]

To that extent, the Balkan Wars were an example of the impossibility of the Europeans to solve among themselves a crisis they helped to create.[346] 'The crisis in Bosnia offered painful proof of Europe's continued absence, if proof were still needed. The brutal fact is that Western Europe, and increasingly also Central Europe, remains largely an American protectorate, with its allied states reminiscent of ancient vassals and tributaries.'[347]

NATO's enlargement also benefited from a weak Russia. Nevertheless, the notable enlargement still needed one member to control the 'Critical core of Europe's Security'. Hence, the geostrategic importance of the Ukrainian territory and the Black Sea is once again visible, as seen in the next figure.

---

[345] Brzezinski, Idem, *The grand chessboard: American strategy and its geostrategic imperatives*, New York, Basic Books, 1997, page 47.
[346] Even though acknowledging the high level of ethnic tensions present in former Yugoslavia, it is clear that once Germany and other European governments started to recognize the independence of former Yugoslavian Republics without a clear proposal to resolve the ethnic issues present, they opened the door to the establishment of ethnic republics in multi-ethnic territories, therefore allowing the possibility of many atrocities. Note of the author.
[347] Brzezinski, Idem, page 47.

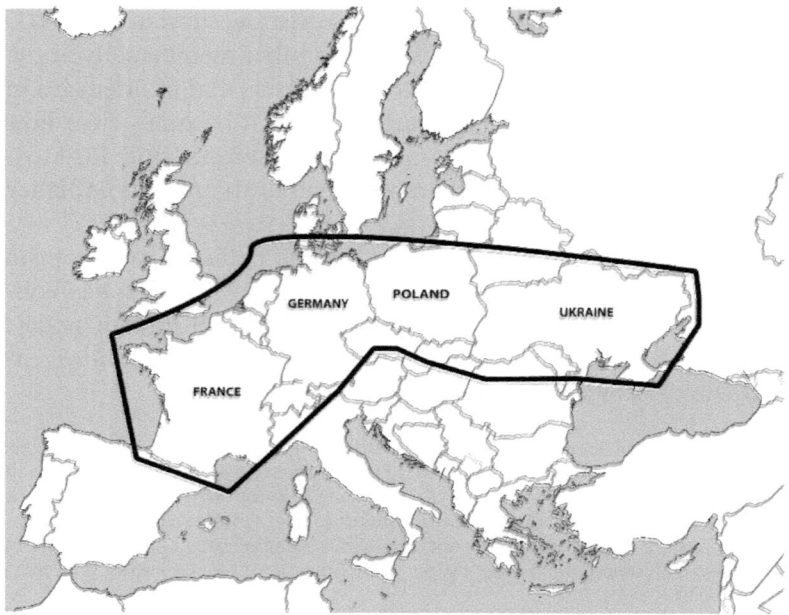

The critical core of Europe's security.
Source: Modified map based on Wikimedia Commons Map of administrative divisions of Europe. Licensed under CC BY-SA 3.0
(https://creativecommons.org/licenses/by-sa/3.0/deed.en)

Ukraine, a new and important space on the Eurasian chessboard, is a geopolitical pivot because its very existence as an independent country helps to transform Russia. Without Ukraine, Russia ceases to be a Eurasian empire. Russia without Ukraine can still strive for imperial status, but it would then become a predominantly Asian imperial state, more likely to be drawn into debilitating conflicts with aroused Central Asians, who would then be resentful of the loss of their recent independence and would be supported by their fellow Islamic states to the south.[348]

Therefore, it was clear that for the United States, Ukrainian territory had a geopolitical importance that collided with Russian interests. Meanwhile, Moscow would argue that they relate to Ukraine by deep historic, cultural, linguistic, social and economic links. The fact is that Ukraine became, since the fall of the Soviet Union, again the object of a clear geopolitical confrontation. How the United States would try to pull Ukraine into its orbit would be part of a US

---

[348] Brzezinski, Op. Cit., pages 37–38.

foreign policy priority in Europe that would use different strategies. Now it is worth analysing one of those approaches.

1.3.2 The 'colour revolutions'

The term 'colour revolution' became widely used by media to refer to a series of political movements in countries located in Eastern Europe or that used to belong to the USSR. The following pages show the role of foreign involvement in these actions, and in the next chapter, when inner politics of Ukraine will be analysed, it will also be shown how the proper inner factors with foreign support allowed them to succeed in the Ukrainian case.

Camille Gangloff's detailed research[349] showed how the political conditions in Serbia, Kyrgyzstan, Ukraine and Georgia were ideal to allow foreign intervention to succeed in financing political movements capable of ousting the local regime. The last three cases were ex-Soviet countries, where members from the old Soviet *nomenklatura* had stayed in power. These regimes, even though considered authoritarian from a Western liberal perspective, allowed the possibility to protest to a limited extent. The conditions were rather different as in other former Soviet republics as Belarus or Turkmenistan, where the attempt to promote this kind of movements would have been in vain.[350]

In fact, among most CIS members or ex members there is a low degree of tolerance to political opposition. In Russia and Armenia, there is a visible opposition present in the parliament while one single party has continued to rule for the last decade. Still, not allowed opposition could suffer consequences like blogger Alexander Navalny[351] to mention one example. In Uzbekistan, instead, no real op-

---

[349] Gangloff, Camile, *L'import-export de la démocratie: Serbie, Géorgie, Ukraine, Kirghizistan*, Paris, L'Harmattan, 2008.
[350] Aleksandar Maric sustained that once in an interview, former president of Turkmenistan, Saparmurat Niyazov, responded on how he would react if a Turkmen organization invited Serbian students as in other countries to promote democracy to which he answered that he would shoot them all in the airport. Maric, A., 'Les faiseurs de revolutions,' *Politique International*, No. 106, hiver, 2004–2005. Quoted in Gangloff, Idem, page 212.
[351] Vasilyeva, Nataliya, 'Conviction of Putin's foe sets off protest in Moscow,' December 30, 2014. http://news.yahoo.com/putin-foe-arrives-court-hear-verdict-061609972.html

position to President Karimov exists with all the political parties endorsing his policies.[352] Similar cases can be seen in Azerbaijan[353] and Turkmenistan, where the government is able to quickly supress or control any visible guise of political activity not supported by the regime or where any push to develop independent journalism is not possible.

The Georgian, Ukrainian and Kirgiz cases had several internal differences, even though the common element was a weak state, perceived by the population as corrupt and authoritarian. It is worth noting that governments in these three countries were tolerated by Moscow, as long as they were willing to maintain good relations with Russia and do not seek an alliance with the West, which in the Georgian and Ukrainian cases meant considering a possible entrance to NATO.

These facts motivated the United States to promote by different means a change in the regimes. The argument of promoting democracy, an 'open society' and defending human rights has always been one of the favourite tools of the United States to intervene in other areas of the world. In this sense, we can find examples in all parts of the globe, from Latin America to the Middle East, in which the excuse of promoting what the United States considers as democracy becomes the starting point for their involvement. The Freedom Support Act[354] of 1992 illustrates how US foreign policy considered the importance to finance a 'democratic' development in Eastern Europe. Therefore, it was not through military power, political or

---

[352] 'В Узбекистане прошли парле выборы без оппозиции,' December 21, 2014. http://korrespondent.net/world/3458976-v-uzbekystane-proshly-parlamen tskye-vybory-bez-oppozytsyy

[353] The case of journalist Khadija Ismailova in Azerbaijan is a clear example. She became famous as an investigative journalist and the way she has portrayed state-level corruption involving current president Aliyev and his family members. She has been threatened, blackmailed and imprisoned on charges of inciting suicide, in a case widely criticized by human rights activists. She is still one of the few independent voices in the local media. 'The Khadija project,' accessed on February 23, 2016. http://occrp.org/free-khadija-ismayilova/

[354] Freedom Support Act, Enrolled Bill as passed through the Senate and the House of Representatives, S.2532 1992, accessed on November 5, 2014. http://thomas.loc.gov/cgi-bin/query/F?c102:1:./temp/~c102yFQjHe:e926

economic influence but with soft power that the United States tried to influence political events in this area of the world.[355]

> Cependant, cette politique de promotion de la démocratie doit se combiner avec les autres intérêts en jeu, comme les intérêts géostratégiques, énergétiques, etc. Ainsi dans certains cas, la promotion de la démocratie sert ces intérêts géostratégiques. Les exemples géorgien et ukrainien en sont une bonne illustration.[356]

Therefore, the United States developed a complex network to allow them to subsidize political activism around the world. Sometimes directly funded by the US Government and others through different ONGs or organizations whose policies are in line with their foreign policy. The most important of them is the Federal Agency USAID, but there is also the National Endowment for Democracy that appears as a non-profit organization but is financed mostly by the US Government. It also has two dependencies, the IRI and NDI, each of them directed by the Republican and the Democratic parties. Furthermore, there is Freedom House, an ONG with links to the CIA or the Eurasia Foundation that also receives funds from the US Government.[357]

Adding also the Open Society Foundation subsidized by billionaire George Soros, which coincidently finances projects concordant with US foreign policy, there is a well-elaborated structure of different institutions capable of training, organizing, advising and financing political activism around the world.

The context of these colour revolutions was also in the middle of discredited regimes that wanted to remain in power throughout electoral frauds but did not have the political means to impose themselves after stealing the elections as it has happened in other regions of the globe in cases I define as geopolitically tolerated frauds.[358] Therefore, here, it was easy for foreign actors to organize

---

355   Orlando, Cristiano, *La partita eurasiatica, Geopolitica della Sicurezza tra occidente e Russia*, Roma, Archivio Disarmo, 2009, page 62.
356   Gangloff, Op. Cit., page 48.
357   Idem, page 31.
358   The Russian presidential election in 1996 and the Mexican 2006 presidential election are two of many cases of 'successful' frauds in which the regime in power managed to stay in the government besides the numerous proofs that they rigged the election. In these two cases, there was a clear interest by the United States for the same regime to continue in power, therefore diminishing severely the worldwide effect of the public opinion that could be against the frauds. Note of the author.

and canalize the discontent present against the regime. In that context, Gangloff said:

> Les révolutions colorées sont donc aussi un concept marketing séduisant et motivant, participant à la réussite même du mouvement, et attirant d'avantage l'attention de la communauté et de l'opinion publique internationales.[359]

The starting point of these movements involved a complex organization that involved ONGs and student organizations with appealing slogans while their leaders were trained and advised by different foreign organizations with US support. The first case was Otpor, the Serbian organization that committed itself to overthrow Slobodan Milosevic by non-violent means. It is interesting how the organization grew while it received the proper funding and how it disappeared quickly after its goal was achieved. The NY Time portrayed months later how US financial support was key to the success of the movement. 'Otpor was no ramshackle students' group; it was a well-oiled movement backed by several million dollars from the United States.'[360] The United States was not the only country involved in these activities but was the one that more actively supported political opposition before and during the elections first in Serbia and then in Georgia, Ukraine and Kyrgyzstan once the model of action proved successful.

The influence and the transcendent role of US involvement is visible in the documentary 'Bringing down a dictator'.[361] The film narrated by Martin Sheen depicts how the political opposition against Slobodan Milosevic in Serbia was organized and managed to stop a possible runoff between Milosevic and Vojislav Kostunica and therefore assure Kostunica's win in the first round after a new count of votes. It shows the originality and the way they managed to gather public support together with proper coordination and funding as mentioned to bring about a movement.

Later, many leaders of this movement participated directly or indirectly in the 'Rose Revolution' in Georgia and in the electoral campaign in 2004 in Ukraine. In fact, it is not difficult to understand

---

[359] Gangloff, Op. Cit., page 123.
[360] Cohen, Roger, 'Who really bought down Milosevic?,' November 26, 2000. http://www.nytimes.com/library/magazine/home/20001126mag-serbia.html
[361] 'Bringing down a dictator,' https://www.youtube.com/watch?v=UBvzsDUh8eY

that colour revolutions for Moscow represented a way of destabilizing regimes to establish others that would be favourable to the United States.[362]

It is important to mention that the most important element in the game was not a deep democratic change in the regime that meant a more open and a democratic society, instead a simple change in the geopolitical orientation that the new government would take. This new geopolitical orientation would include the opening of strategic assets to Western companies in energy-related issues and above all an increased presence of NATO in the area. In that sense, 'promotion of democracy' was part of the rhetoric, but it did not mind if members of the old political elite that pretended to change their geopolitical orientation towards a pro-US position would stay in power like in the Ukrainian case.

> Ce sont en faits de révoltes civiques, menées par une grande partie de la population en réaction à ces fraudes électorales manifestes, et non des révolutions au sens strict qui ont eu lieu, mais on comprends aisément toute l'importance de la qualification de 'révolution'.[363]

Portraying them in the media as revolutions conveyed exactly the idea that a dramatic change was brought about in which a Western US-oriented political order was the only 'acceptable' possibility, a new order in which these countries would free themselves from 'evil tyrannies' or rulers that were completely dominated by Moscow. But, it was not mentioned that in reality new elites, formed and backed by the United States, were acceding to rule the country like Saakashvili in Georgia or Victor Yushchenko in Ukraine. Later, their foreign policy would prove to be a lot more in favour of the United States, the way the supposedly former pro-Russian governments were favouring Moscow.

Hence, the clue to understanding these movements is the foreign and mostly US interests to build a political opposition capable of installing a government aligned with US policies. This feature shows these countries as an object of a political dispute between a more assertive Russia and the United States. Therefore, during the

---

362 Cordsman, Anthony H., 'Russia and the color revolution,' Center for Strategic and International Studies, May 28, 2014. http://csis.org/publication/russia-and-color-revolution
363 Gangloff, Op. Cit., page 123.

colour revolutions, there was a common strategy present. 'L'élaboration progressive d'une stratégie d'action standardisée exportable et exportée est une caractéristique majeure de ces révolutions, dont les similitudes ont souvent marqué les esprits.'[364]

It is important to comment on the specific inner conditions that allowed the movements to prosper. Foreign ONGs were the undoubted stimulants of these Colour revolutions but even if there were necessary, they were not enough to overthrow the regime by themselves.[365] Mostly, local discontent was present at a very unpopular regime which could not use the same repressive measures against the population as in other ex-Soviet countries. Some countries like Belarus still have a certain amount of local support while others like Uzbekistan use more authoritarian methods that simply would make it impossible for this kind of colour revolution to succeed. The case of the Andijan massacre is a clear example.[366] In this Central Asian republic, pacific protests and political rallies were not enough to overthrow the regime as in Georgia or Serbia. Therefore, the colour revolutions operated in a sort of failed state where the government did not have full authority, power or legitimacy to sustain itself. These countries also had societies in which the appeal of the West tempted the local middle classes, mostly in the Serbian and Ukrainian cases, an appeal that allowed to propagate the idea of some sort of liberal values (understood as such) in different ways.

Therefore, there was discontent among society, while the United States, could be said, gave the political direction to this dissatisfaction. Political discontent often takes so many forms and expressions;[367] but in this case, the foreign involvement rather guided the dissatisfaction with a geopolitical direction.

---

[364] Idem, page 193.
[365] Idem, pages 218–219.
[366] This massacre occurred when the Uzbek Government fired into a crowd of protestors on May 13, 2005, killing between 187 and 1,500 people, as there are different testimonies from the event. 'Preliminary findings on the events in Andijan, Uzbekistan 13 May 2005,' June 20, 2005, accessed on February 23, 2016. http://www.osce.org/odihr/15653?download=true
[367] It is notable mostly in the Western world, how political displeasure increases the appeal of the so-called anti-systemic parties. UKIP in the UK, the Front National in France, Movimento Cinque Stelle in Italy or different sort of populist parties that in their proper way refer a displeasure against the political and economic order. Note of the author.

The initial success of these 'revolutions' obliged the Russian counterpart to take measures; but many of the regimes that felt they could suffer the same fate took precautions. Consequently, the Russian Federation increased regulations over the activity of NGOs or Lukashenko in Belarus augmented pressure over any hint of opposing activity in his country.

The so-called colour revolutions were perceived by Moscow as part of a strategy to constrain their influence in its areas of geopolitical interest. In the mentioned cases, Yugoslavia was out of reach and, at that time, Moscow did not have a real possibility to influence the events. Instead, the events in the Near Abroad, starting with Georgia in 2003, alarmed the Russian Federation more and created the perception that new ways of aggression were being used, as a new kind of warfare as mentioned by the Russian Defense Minister Sergei Shoigu and by Foreign Minister Sergei Lavrov.[368]

To conclude, there are two points worth remarking about these events. First, the scarce capacity of these countries to determine sovereignly its own decisions. It is clear that either way the political course of action would go, it was in favour of a different geopolitical project, and therefore, it had almost no possibilities of favouring independent policies that could consider local interests. The Georgian, Ukrainian and Kirgiz cases showed how the population of these territories had only the option of incorporating themselves into another sphere of influence without really deciding sovereignly which option would be better.

The second point is that with these events, the United States had changed notably the plan of action against Russia. It was clear at this moment that it was not an option to have Russia as a geopolitical ally. The idea of advancing political projects against Russia instead of trying to englobe the Russian Federation in the same course of action, as during the nineties, marked a change in the US foreign policy. This was also a consequence of Moscow's assertive foreign policy since Vladimir Putin's arrival.

---

[368] Gorenburg, Dmitry, 'Countering color revolutions, Russia's new security strategy and its implications for U.S. policy,' PONARS Eurasia Policy Memo No. 342, September 15, 2014, CAN, Harvard University. http://russia mil.wordpress.com/2014/09/15/countering-color-revolutions-russias-new-s ecurity-strategy-and-its-implications-for-u-s-policy/

Alessandro Vitale considered that it was a change between the idealist and the realist perspective as to how to handle relations with Russia.

> In quest'ottica, in una prospettiva di allargamento della NATO a Ucraina e Georgia vi sono due ipotesi possibili di cui una sola potrà essere la più percorribile. Una idealista, che sottende la difesa ad ogni costo di un'enclave occidentale nel Caucaso con l'ingresso di Tbilisi nella NATO, e una realista per la quale gli Stati Uniti hanno troppo bisogno di una Russia partner piuttosto che avversaria. In caso contrario, un confronto con Mosca porrebbe l'Occidente di fronte a difficoltà economiche e militari nel mantenere posizioni dominanti in Medio Oriente come in Asia Centrale.[369]

There is still one more element to consider. The EU played an active role in the process but with a different model from that of the United States.[370] The EU members had pledged themselves to the US involvement in the Russian Near Abroad. Still, they had to determine where the European interest and that of its members could coincide with the US foreign policy. That question still needs an answer.

1.4 The EU and Eastern Europe

After explaining Moscow's and Washington's pretensions for Ukraine, it is important to also consider the EU perspective; but to do so it is important to write a few words about its members, and the EU as a whole, and how their capabilities to contend as a geopolitical actor have evolved.

The end of World War II signalled the end of the European era in world politics.[371] At this point, and throughout the Cold War, although Eurasia was still the focus of geopolitical interest, the United States and the Soviet Union, and not Western European countries, were the main actors in the international scene. 'Germany's defeat was sealed largely by the two extra-European victors, the United States and the Soviet Union, which became the successors to Europe's unfulfilled quest for global supremacy.'[372]

---

[369] Vitale, Op. Cit., page 94.
[370] Gangloff, Op. Cit., page 221.
[371] Brezinski, Op. Cit., page 10.
[372] Idem, page 10.

Meanwhile, since the first after-war years, the Western European nations were obliged to immerse themselves in different geopolitical projects, European integration and NATO membership. Therefore, Western European nations were obliged to comply with the US project to build NATO[373] while the task of achievement of further integration had to proceed only at the economic level. But, this bold move, mostly by the French Government in the after-war years, was also a unique political move. In addition, this political action assured to eliminate the reasons for future conflicts between members as the Schuman declaration established.

> This merging of our interests in coal and steel production and our joint action will make it plain that any war between France and Germany becomes not only unthinkable but materially impossible.[374]

Not only was the groundwork for a new political entity laid, but there also emerged the possibility of a new geopolitical player that could evolve further.

> By pooling basic industrial production and setting up a new High Authority whose decisions will be binding on France, Germany and other member countries, these proposals will bring to reality the first solid groundwork for a European Federation vital to the preservation of world peace.[375]

Therefore, European integration could proceed in a certain direction while accepting that in many matters Western European foreign policy was in the middle of the Cold War and could not develop itself independently of the US foreign policy.

During the subsequent years, further European integration was at a crossroads, where EU members had been subsumed and that restrained the development of any further integration. First, it has not been defined properly until what point European unification is a process or a cause, and second, more integration usually requires ceding sovereignty to a supranational organ, something that does not like the largest members, usually United Kingdom and France.

---

[373] It is worth to remember that there was an effort to build the European Defence Community, proposed by French Minister Rene Pleven in 1950. A treaty was signed on May 27, 1952, but it was never ratified. Judt, Tony *Postwar: A History of Europe since 1945*, New York, Penguin Press, 2005.

[374] 'Schuman declaration,' May 9, 1950. http://www.schuman.info/9May1950.htm

[375] Idem. Underlined in the original.

Besides, the continuous growth of the EU through the years urged it to frame its own foreign policy. The development of this foreign policy did not always match the goals of the national foreign policies. This contradiction has sometimes been resolved, as seen in the fact that over the last decades, the EU managed to transform itself from being the European Coal and Steel Community to what it is right now. The Single European Act[376] that came into effect in 1987 served as a forerunner of what in the Treaty of Maastricht would be the arrival of the Common Foreign and Security Policy.[377]

But, the struggle was not an easy one. De Gaulle had already mentioned that the United Kingdom could become the Trojan horse that takes over the United States if they would enter the European Economic Community in 1963.[378] Thenceforth, each enlargement made it already more complex to find common solutions and the possibility to make advances towards the establishment of a common foreign policy.

The key word has been always sovereignty. No single state wants to lose sovereignty without a cause. The reason that made Western European countries lay the foundation of the EU was precisely to avoid another conflict of the dimensions that had just ended. Later, there could have been political reasons but they did not carry enough weight to convince all the members that together they would be a stronger geopolitical actor. Therefore, France and subsequently the Great Britain, when they joined the Union, were not willing to accept easily to trade sovereignty with a supranational authority. Only afterwards, French government up to a certain stopped being so reluctant in that sense but that did not change in the British side. Hence, the clue to a commitment to advance in the European integration has been always when there is a French-German thrive in that direction.

---

[376] 'Single European Act, 1986,' accessed on February 23, 2016. http://en.wikisource.org/wiki/Single_European_Act
[377] 'Treaty on European Union/ Title V: Provisions on a common foreign and security policy,' http://en.wikisource.org/wiki/Treaty_on_European_Union/Title_V:_Provisions_on_a_Common_Foreign_and_Security_Policy
[378] 'Biographie: La Consolidation du regime,' http://www.charles-de-gaulle.org/pages/l-homme/accueil/biographie/1962-1968-la-consolidation-du-regime.php?id_article=375

Only Germany conceived that it is only through a deeper integration they could manage to improve the weak position they had in the international scene in the after-war years.

> Federal Germany was, until the unification of 1990, a semi-sovereign state, dependent on its allies for protection against the Soviet threat and inhibited by the history of the Second World War from defining or explicitly pursuing its own national interests. The WEU, and later EPC, both served to contain a revived and rearmed Germany within multilateral frameworks devised by their neighbours.[379]

Hence, most of the German post-war leaders have understood that only through a commitment to a further European integration can an assertive German foreign policy be achieved.

> Germany sees in its fervent commitment to Europe a historical cleansing, a restoration of its moral and political credentials. By redeeming itself through Europe, Germany is restoring its own greatness while gaining a mission that would not automatically mobilize European resentments and fears against Germany. If Germans seek the German national interest, that runs the risk of alienating other Europeans; if Germans promote Europe's common interest, that garners European support and respect.[380]

Thus, those moments when German and French governments have agreed that their own foreign policies would benefit with more Europe, then the proper changes for a deeper European integration have been achieved.

In that sense, the text edited by Christopher Hill in 1996 showed precisely the complexity that was present already two decades ago when trying to unify or at least coordinate foreign policies, which more than a foreign policy through the years has been more a sort of coordinated mechanisms for framing the policy of the member states.

> It will therefore be that much harder to build a collective foreign policy by coordinating national policies, if they are increasingly domestically oriented and developed by politicians who are forced to have a keen idea of the short-term electoral implications of any stance which they might choose to adopt.[381]

---

[379] Hill, Christopher and Wallace, William, 'Introduction,' in *The Actors in Europe's Foreign Policy*, edited by Christopher Hill, London, Routledge, 1996, page 11.
[380] Brzezinski, Op. Cit., page 10.
[381] Allen, David, Conclusions in Hill, Op. Cit., page 300.

Hence, this balance of national interests not always has allowed one to observe that only further integration would have a deeper geopolitical impact. Consequently, the development of a European foreign policy has always struggled to gain acceptance among member states and tried not to compete with the inclusion of most of its members in NATO's structures.

The Common Foreign and Security Policy appeared in Maastricht and was improved in the subsequent treaties. Besides, the existence of a Common Security and Defence Policy as part of the same policy gave the opportunity to develop structures that could pursue European interests and not only the ones from the United States.

Even though, the first missions only achieved to establish a certain presence in areas like the Balkans.[382] Even if in these cases, it was only to continue missions were NATO had been the leading actor and in situations that were also part of US policy. Therefore, the possibility of establishing an assertive and independent European foreign policy was far from true. Besides, it has not been free of scandals[383] like the one in Kosovo in 2014.

Altogether, different scholars like Alessandro Vitale have noted the importance to build a stronger foreign policy:

> Appare, però, necessario affiancare a questa crescita tecnica una crescita politica che porti ad una maggiore coesione all'interno dell'EU. E fondamentale inseguire l'obiettivo di una autentica affinità nella politica estera dei diversi paesi membri, senza la quale Bruxelles è condannata a rimanere un attore con poca autorevolezza e affidabilità diplomatiche.[384]

The position of High Representative of Common Foreign and Security Policy that appeared in 1999 and expanded after the Treaty of Lisbon was also an important achievement. Still, together with the formal existence of the job it did not have the capacity to implement

---

[382] In 2003, the EU substituted the police force from the United Nations located in Bosnia with the mission EUPM. In addition, EUFOR Althea substituted from 2004 NATO mission SFOR and from 2003, the Common Security and Defence Policy substituted NATO in Macedonia with a mission named EU Concordia. Orlando, Idem, page 22.

[383] One of the European Union's flagship foreign missions was accused of severe failings and cover-ups in several corruption allegations in Kosovo. 'EU accused over Kosovo mission failings,' November 6, 2014. http://www.theguardian.com/world/2014/nov/06/eu-accused-over-kosovo-mission-failings

[384] Vitale, Op. Cit., page 23.

a strong foreign policy. Nevertheless, it is worth mentioning that after the Treaty entered into force in 2009, it counted also with the External Action Service, which allows the EU to have its own diplomatic corps and serves as a kind of foreign ministry. It can be said, then, that the EU has built the tools to frame its own foreign policy but still lacks the power to use these tools.

Besides, its first[385] High Representative Catherine Ashton was much criticized often for not having enough diplomatic experience and secondly for not having the political maturity to assert EU's position.[386] Therefore, in many cases, the EU was restrained from having its own foreign policy. Thus, it could just follow the agreements pursued by some member states.

This contradiction between the need of most of the member states to have a solid and unified foreign policy on the one side and the lack of political will to implement it by others has not allowed the EU to present itself in a strong position. In Palestine, Middle East, the Arab Spring, Africa and Eastern Europe there are several examples where the attempts by the EU to have its own foreign policy have mostly reflected the policies of the member states, which does not mean that the interest of one or some member states would have to coincide with the EU interest. Therefore, other actors mostly the United States and also Russia and China prefer to negotiate directly with France, the United Kingdom and Germany, leaving the other members in a weak position.

Simms, for instance, even goes further and compares the current perception of the EU to other episodes in the history of Europe.

> Will Europeans persist in regarding the EU as a modern-day Holy Roman Empire, which enables them to coexist more easily than ever before but is incapable of effective collective action, or will they conclude that all these problems can only be mastered by establishing a new constitutional settlement on the lines pioneered by the Anglo-Americans in the eighteenth century: a mighty union

---

[385] Some would consider Catherine Ashton was in fact the second as Javier Solana had a similar appointment before but not with the same attributions, as it was expanded in the Treaty of Lisbon. Note of the author.

[386] I could also remember the words of one member of the Euro parliament part of the Progressive Alliance of Socialists and Democrats, as he told me one day during a conversation about the problems to build an EU foreign policy. He referred that in the best case, at important meetings, the only thing that Catherine Ashton could do was open the entry door, trying to evidence that she had no power at all. Note of the author.

based on a common debt, strong central institutions responsible to a directly elected parliament and a common defence against common enemies?[387]

Altogether, the prevailing situation leads us to examine the relations with Russia together with the stance the EU and its members have assumed towards Eastern Europe. Recent enlargements in 2004, 2007 and 2013 made the situation more complex and show that there is still an absence of a solid EU foreign policy. In fact, in this scenario, the Ukrainian crisis discussed in the following chapter is a very clear example.

1.4.1 EU policy towards Eastern Europe: The 2004, 2007 and 2013 enlargements

After the Soviet collapse, there was a clear willingness by the EU, mostly Germany, to approach the countries that used to be under Soviet influence,[388] and to englobe them in the Western European structures.[389] The same way, these countries wanted assurances against a possible Russian reawakening. Amidst all the political and economic transformations taking place in the world during those years, NATO for them guaranteed military protection, the United States still being looked upon as a saviour.

> La Nato rappresenta per questi paesi un appiglio più solido. In essa vengono visti gli Stati Uniti, la cui eroica immagine di antagonisti del nemico sovietico non si è sbiadita nell'immaginario collettivo e nell'opinione pubblica.[390]

Besides, the EU through the investments of its member countries offered them the only possibility to include them in the new political and economic world order in which they could not count on Soviet support. There was simply no option for them. Small countries like

---

[387] Simms, B., *Europe: The Struggle for Supremacy, from 1453 to the Present*, New York, Basic Books, 2013, page 531.
[388] In this case, I refer to the Central and European countries that entered the EU in the 2004 and 2007 enlargements and used to be in the Soviet sphere of influence: Bulgaria, Czech Republic, Estonia, Hungary, Latvia, Lithuania, Poland, Romania and Slovakia. Meanwhile, Slovenia and Croatia that joined the EU in 2004 and 2013 were part of Yugoslavia but had to affront similar inner transformations while Cyprus and Malta could be considered different cases. Note of the author.
[389] Orlando, Op. Cit., page 24.
[390] Idem, page 26.

the Baltic States could not do otherwise but accept most of the conditions for admission both to NATO and to the EU without bargaining. They changed from being a Soviet geopolitical area to a West-led geopolitical project or projects, if we count both, NATO and the EU.

In any case, for the EU members, it was also a bold political and geopolitical move. I have already mentioned how in the moments where the French-German relation presents an assertive push towards a stronger Europe, it has usually achieved positive results. In that sense, when Chirac and Schroeder, both with the perspective of a strong EU, saw the chance to extend its borders, as it had never been done before, they did not miss the opportunity.

Therefore, in Lars S. Skalnes words: 'Besides the emphasis on using EC policy to promote economic and political reforms and by extension stability in Eastern Europe, geopolitical considerations explain why the EC decided to commit itself to enlargement at Copenhagen in 1993 and why accession talks were expanded in 1999 to include countries previously excluded.'[391]

Still, the notions of enlargement differed a lot in the United Kingdom compared to the ones of France or Germany. In that sense, the Germans have also understood that an enlargement does not have to mean itself a weakening of the EU and to turn institutions looser. On the contrary, the British have always expected that the larger the EU, the more difficult it will be to agree on a deeper integration and then remain just like a big free trade area.

> The British seem to believe (most vociferously during Mrs Thatcher's premiership) that any enlargement is attractive because it will lead to a weakening of the Union's supranational elements and federal ambitions... The French have always shared the British view of the relationship between widening and deepening but have tended to come to the opposite conclusion about the attractiveness of further enlargement to Eastern and Central Europe. This, however, brings the French into conflict with Germany for the Germans have never accepted the notion that wider means weaker and have instead tended to perceive the question of enlargement towards the East as both essential and as a welcome stimulus towards deepening the present Union.[392]

---

[391] Skalnes, Lars S., 'Geopolitics and the eastern enlargement of the European Union,' in *The Politics of European Union Enlargement, Theoretical Approaches*, edited by Schimmelfennig, Frank and Sedelmeier, Ulrich, New York, Routledge, 2005, page 230.
[392] Allen, David, Conclusions in Hill, Op. Cit., pages 292–293.

146   State-Building in the Middle of a Geopolitical Struggle

The largest enlargement in 2004 included ten new members[393] and left Bulgaria and Romania for later in 2007, both with a weaker economy and with lower life standards. The ambitious plan allowed to carry out on 1 May 2004, the largest expansion of the EU in terms of territory, population and number of countries, but not in terms of gross domestic product, which shows the real differences between the new and the old members. Until now, it is possible to perceive the real inner differences at the economic level.[394]

It is clear that the EU members were conscious of the differences when they took the decision. They even allowed many exemptions or failings in transparency, respect for minorities and human rights[395] and all those issues in which the EU always tries to promote itself as an example.

Altogether, it was not clear, if the newcomers could insert themselves in the EU without becoming a liability; meanwhile in France and other member states the myth of the Polish plumber[396] emerged. At the end, the enlargement was nothing more than a real European geopolitical decision; but that again went together with a NATO enlargement to most of those countries in the list. Therefore, again, it was in line with a US geopolitical interest.

---

[393]   Czech Republic, Cyprus, Estonia, Hungary, Latvia, Lithuania, Malta, Poland, Slovakia and Slovenia.

[394]   Just as example, countries like Netherlands, Belgium, Germany, France or Luxembourg have minimum wages above €1,400 Euros a month; meanwhile in the Baltic countries or in Slovakia, it goes something above €300 and not to mention Bulgaria and Romania where it is even lower.

[395]   As an example, it is worth mentioning the case of ethnic Russians in Latvia and Estonia. Even if they represented a considerable percentage of the local populations, they were deprived of citizenship after the Soviet fall; therefore, people that had lived in those territories for generations were not allowed to vote or to have any political right. Besides, in many cases, the access to basic education in Russian language became limited together with the public use of the language on the streets or for advertising. 'Citizenship rows divide Latvia,' March 25, 2005, accessed on February 23. 2016. http://news.bbc.co.uk/2/hi/europe/4371345.stm

[396]   The myth of the Polish plumber was first used by the now famous French satirical magazine *Charlie Hebdo* as a symbol of cheap labour coming from Eastern Europe. Then it became widely used by extreme right groups to promote the fear that huge waves of migrants would arrive with the 2004 enlargement of the EU. '"Polish plumber" beckons French,' June 21, 2005, accessed on February 23, 2016. http://news.bbc.co.uk/2/hi/europe/4115164.stm

It is possible that from the French-German perspective there was the belief that the enlargement would also transform itself in a stronger Europe once the Constitution was ratified. Unfortunately, for the EU cause, Chirac failed his political calculations when he preferred to call for referendum on the Treaty establishing a Constitution for the EU and turned it into a big political defeat that brought as a consequence the diminished Treaty of Lisbon.

There is one notable fact to underline about the enlargements. Most of the new members saw their European conviction mixed with their Atlantic military integration to NATO, in fact NATO membership seemed to weight more than the EU one.

> I paesi dell'Est tendenzialmente sono più atlantisti che europeisti e sono molto più inclini a seguire la politica estera di Washington piuttosto che quella dei principali paesi europei. Dimostrazione lampante ne è l'appoggio incondizionato di molti dei loro governi alle coalizioni di willing volute da G.W. Bush e la partecipazione ai combattimenti in prima linea delle forze armate polacche, estoni e lituane al fianco delle truppe anglo-americane sia in Iraq sia in Afghanistan. Questo genera la differenza, per dirla con le parole sprezzanti dell'ex segretario alla Difesa USA, Donald Rumsfield, tra la vecchia e la nuova Europa.[397]

Therefore, it became clear once the enlargement became a reality that the United States could not only find support from the United Kingdom but also from Poland and the Baltic States that were completely loyal to the US foreign policy, especially regarding Russia. Therefore, subjects like a EU foreign policy and mostly a EU Defence Policy outside NATO became more improbable. Altogether, the timeframe in which the Treaty of Lisbon became operational reduced seriously the possibilities of a consensus in the EU from the enlargement in 2004 until 2009. For example, the US intention to build a missile shield based in Poland and the Czech Republic counted on automatic support from the Eastern members and did not really consider the opinion of the French and German partners on the subject. Although it is true Cristiano Orlando mentions in his book that the Eastern European countries should show more consistency in their Europeanism,[398] it is also true that the EU has not tried to enforce it. Although in Lithuania or Latvia, European Union

---

[397] Orlando, Op. Cit., page 26.
[398] Idem, page 26.

spending and investments account for a gross portion of the GDP[399] compared to that of other members, that fact has not transformed itself in a stronger bond with the EU more than the one with the United States. Besides, the reinforced cooperation between the large Western European countries in political and economic spheres has created in the new arrivals, in some cases, the perception of being excluded from the main decisions and of being treated as belonging to Europe's periphery. Even the reduced reaction from the EU in cases where Russia has acted[400] against the Baltic countries made it easy for them to give more weight to the alliance with the United States in acts that could be perceived as a serious geopolitical flaw for the European Union in its goal of gaining consistency.

Therefore, the EU indeed achieved a great geopolitical status with the recent enlargements until 2013 and became a Union with 28 members; still, it has left behind many problems that have transformed it, as journalists love to refer, into a Europe at two speeds. Hence, an EU was formed in which not all states are members of the Schengen Area, the Eurozone, the Common Security and Defence Policy or the Charter of Fundamental Rights, the fact being that there is a wide list of opt-outs with the risk of leading to what the French consider 'Europe a la carte'.

> Un Europa a più velocità, senza un'identità geopolitica forte, rischia di non trovare una strada percorribile per attribuirsi un ruolo fondamentale, ed è di questo che è da sempre convinto.[401]

---

[399] In Lithuania, the spending and contributions from the EU represent 5.82% and in Estonia 5.65%; meanwhile, in countries like Finland or the Netherlands, it is only 0.73% and 0.36%, respectively. 'European Union spending and contributions 2010,' January 26, 2012. http://www.theguardian.com/news/datablog/2012/jan/26/eu-budget-european-union-spending#data

[400] Just to mention some examples in the recent decade: In the spring of 2007, Russia diminished 30% the flux of refined products to Estonia as an answer to the destruction of a monument to the Red Fleet in the Tallinn. In other cases, there was an interruption of the oil flux to a refinery in Lithuania in 2007 and the Hacker Attacks against the Estonian Government that same year. Quotes 21 and 22 in Vitale, Op. Cit., page 25.

[401] Op. Cit., page 50.

This complexity, seen at different levels, makes it extremely difficult to operate a foreign policy that is truly a European policy and not one of certain member states only.[402]

Even though the EU went further to frame policies towards Moscow's area of influence, this time the goal was penetrating little by little in its orbit countries, which not only were ex-Soviet Republics but were already part of the Community of Independent States and overlapped directly with Moscow's intention of getting them to join the Eurasian Union. That is how the EU Eastern Partnership originated.

1.4.2 EU Eastern Partnership

The Eastern Partnership is an initiative promoted mostly by Poland and Sweden in the European Union to strengthen its relationship with Armenia, Azerbaijan, Belarus, Georgia, Moldova and Ukraine. It was inaugurated in Prague on 7 May 2009.[403] From the formal point of view, the idea was to create a mechanism to discuss themes like visa agreements, free trade deals and strategic partnership agreements without discussing concretely their accession to the EU.

The interpretation of each member state and each country participating with the EU was rather different. Therefore, while for Germany and France the partnership should not become a chamber previous to an EU membership, for Poland it was the opposite, it meant to open the possibility of an entrance to the EU and NATO altogether.[404] For Belarus, it was just a forum, seeing that they have no intention of further engaging in deeper agreements with the EU

---

[402] Once during a conference in which I participated with Euro parliamentarian Antonio Panzieri, he was explaining how in practice, the EU's foreign policy was mostly influenced by specific member interests. That is, France mostly decided for North Africa and the Maghreb, the British in their ex colonies, Spain in Latin America or Poland and the Baltic countries in what regarded as Eastern Europe but that unfortunately many times it was not in line to what could be the EU's political interest. 'La politica estera europea, tra mediterraneo, primavere arabe e crisi ucraina,' Panzieri Antonio e Dromundo Rolando, Conference organized by the Partito Democratico at Iseo, Lombardy, Italy, March 20, 2014. https://www.youtube.com/watch?v=EeBgkT8dJuE

[403] 'EU pact challenges Russian influence in the East,' May 7, 2009. http://www.theguardian.com/world/2009/may/07/russia-eu-europe-partnership-deal

[404] 'Uomini Verdi, Uomini Neri, Ominicchi e Quaquaraquà,' Editoriale, Limes, Rivista italiana di Geopolitica, December 2014, page 18.

and neither its members would like to make a similar arrangement with Lukashenko's regime. Armenia preferred to join the Eurasian Union whereas in Azerbaijan, even though it is a key geopolitical ally of the West, Aliev's regime was not interested in going with a further integration with the West not even with regard to establishing the political reforms that would be required.

Hence, this leaves Ukraine, Georgia and Moldova, the countries that through this mechanism started to build the association agreements with the EU. The details of the association agreements will be discussed with particularities regarding Ukraine and Moldova in each chapter but if a simplistic description could be anticipated, they are a kind of free trade agreement with the EU in which these three countries would adapt to EU legislation in different areas and at different levels.

Geopolitically, the EU intended to establish a buffer zone between itself and Russia. In fact, one of the notable facts is that the EU pretended to play geopolitics without being still a real geopolitical actor. In this sense, the words published in a Limes editorial in December 2014 are illustrative:

> Poiché l'Unione Europea non è un soggetto geopolitico, quando a negoziare è la Commissione e/o il servizio europeo per l'Azione esterna entra in campo la burocrazia. Il caso ucraino conferma che ogni organizzazione burocratica, tanto più se internazionale, quando chiamata a far politica agisce come se fosse diretta dall'intelligence avversaria. Risultato: un dossier eminentemente geopolitico è stato trattato da Bruxelles come fosse solo economico, anzi contabile.[405]

Therefore, the Eastern Partnership, even if it appeared as a good idea in principle, did not have the requisite political tools to function. In addition, here appears one of the great difficulties proper of this partnership. There was not a uniform awareness of what the EU expected and it was just taking a top-down approach in which the EU would tell these three countries what to do. Besides, the goals being different from the member states, and the lack of a geopolitical EU approach transformed the Eastern Partnership into a kind of agreement that would approach Ukraine, Moldova and Georgia but did not want to compromise itself for another enlargement about which most of its members were not very enthusiastic.

---

[405] Limes, Op. Cit.

From the geopolitical point of view, the EU was advancing straight against Moscow's interests. It pretended to show a soft approach without the NATO factor present, but still, it was advancing into Moscow's geopolitical area, which certainly could allow any one with a little bit of political rationality, to expect a possible reaction by the Russian Federation. Thus, this was a case, in which some EU member states that also strongly support US foreign policy defined a EU policy and endangered it of having a solid and unified approach on a very delicate subject.

Hence, it should be asked what can the Eastern Partnership achieve, and besides the association agreements with Georgia, Moldova and partially with Ukraine until now, it should be mentioned that one of the most significant 'achievements', if it is possible to use that word, would be then the current Ukrainian crisis.

1.4.3 Can the European Union build a common and sovereign policy towards Russia?

It seems like if the EU did not handle the Eastern Partnership from a European perspective but to advance the interest of some member states, the other members would propose policies conflicting with their specific area of interest. However, the bigger question would be, how to build a truly sovereign relation between EU and Russia. What would be the EU's interest in that relation, and how it can differentiate itself from the interests of single members or from the ones of the United States?

Apparently, it could seem almost impossible to find similar terms on how to handle the relation with Russia. The United Kingdom supports the United States without doubt mostly; the Baltic countries seem sometimes to even expect a war against Russia while Poland actively supports all sanctions against Russia even though they will have an effect against them also. On the contrary, Germany and Italy, for instance, have strong economic links at different spheres with Russia that they would like to keep and develop even more. Therefore, which should be the rationale used to decide what is more important? What weighs more?

The fact is that the relation prior to the Ukrainian crisis and, mostly for sure afterwards, is a one of mutual dependence. Both actors, the EU and Russia, need each other. Even if they do not agree on several political and geopolitical matters, the fact remains that in the last two decades, mostly in the last decade, both partners have benefit from each other in different ways.

Russia is the third trading partner of the EU and the EU is the first for Russia. EU exports to Russia are mostly machinery and transport equipment, chemicals, medicines and agricultural products. EU imports from Russia are dominated by raw materials, mostly oil and gas. Besides, it is estimated that 75% of foreign direct investment in Russia comes from the EU.[406]

Besides all these aspects, it is worth noting the energy dependence, already mentioned. The EU presents a notable dependency towards Russia but mostly it worsens by the fact that there is no common energy policy from the EU. These two factors are weak points from the energy perspective of the EU and need to be taken into account if there is an intention to define a European interest in its relation with Russia.

Alessandro Vitale has already mentioned about the need to diversify energy supplies for the EU but the situation is complicated. There are still weak topics that need to be addressed:

First, the EU needs to present itself unitarily at least as a consumer and therefore to present itself as a great energy consumer as India or China. Second, bilateral contracts from the companies weaken every possible common policy at medium term and difficult to the possibility to have some uniformity in the costs and supply for the EU consumers.[407]

> Quindi, il successo dell'-UE sarebbe trovare una sintesi nelle prospettive di consumo e di gestione delle relazioni commerciali tra le imprese. Uno spazio di consumo omogeneo permetterebbe di migliorare le relazioni commerciali con i paesi produttori, soprattutto la Russia.[408]

The fact is that Western Europe receives 70% of Moscow's energy resources and depends from those supplies in almost 40% for its own energy consumption.[409] Therefore, a little bit of political vision, and mostly the will to think from a European perspective and not

---

[406] 'Countries and regions: Russia,' Last updated October 27, 2015, accessed on February 23, 2016. http://ec.europa.eu/trade/policy/countries-and-regions/countries/russia/
[407] Vitale, Op. Cit., page 168.
[408] Idem.
[409] Op. Cit., page 169.

from a national one, would allow to foresee that it would be fundamental to have a single energy policy. An energy policy coordinated by the EU could also prevent and resolve any possible shortage consequence of supplying issues regarding transit countries, in this case, mostly Ukraine. Instead, when countries like Lithuania or Estonia are dependent to a large extent on Russian gas and oil and still want to apply further sanctions against Russia, it seems like they are not thinking even of their own national interests but on behalf of other geopolitical actors.

In this case, for Russia there is also a real interest to become an affordable partner and the projects to develop further gas pipes like South Stream tend precisely also to avoid third parties that could block the relation. In that sense, the suspension of that project seems like a failure of the EU to determine its own interest prior to that of the United States. With regard to South Stream, for the United States its suspension can be considered a victory after Russia had managed to block the Nabucco pipeline some years before. For European countries, instead, it meant the loss of direct gas supply that could be independent of the vicissitudes in Ukraine that have not been few since the arrival of Victor Yushchenko to the presidency in 2005 until now. Even if members like Austria,[410] Italy, Hungary and Slovenia were going to receive a direct benefit from the pipeline, the pressure from the United States on the Bulgarian government was enough to convince a key participant to suspend the building of a segment of the South Stream project. Therefore, without Bulgaria, the rest of the pipeline lost any sense.

The relation of mutual dependence with Russia is not visible only in the energy sphere. Russian oligarchs have made large investments in banks in Cyprus, Luxembourg and the United Kingdom to mention a few, besides notable investments in real estate in the United Kingdom. It is true that not all the members have the same degree of economic relations with Russia and obviously Portugal does not have the same interest as Estonia for instance; but a common ground can be found. From a realistic point of view, there is no gain by imposing sanctions against Russia. Sanctions will be thor-

---

[410] 'Austria pleads for South Stream pipeline,' Op. Cit.

oughly discussed later, but the question here is what is more important for the EU, the relation with Ukraine or Russia? Ukraine as a buffer zone with Russia or Russia as a stable affordable energy partner? A possible EU enlargement to Ukraine or Ukraine as a place for mutual EU's and Russia's investments where Ukraine remains neutral?

Therefore, for the United States it seems the goal[411] is to separate Ukraine from Russia's area of influence, for Europe should it be the same? Again, the United States can and has the means to maintain a long political standing against Russia but could the EU do it alone? The answer is no, which makes it again dependent on the US protection through NATO, therefore losing the capacity to have an independent position on Ukraine and Russia.

Hence, the Ukrainian crisis and the relation with Russia puts the EU at the same crossroads already mentioned, the one in which there is an absence of a real foreign policy and only the policy of the member states and mostly that of the United States prevail.

Thus, to redefine the idea of a European interest it is necessary to have more political will and vision from the different levels of authorities. That means a continuous growth from the EU at different levels should translate also in more cohesion and above all, more supranational authority.

> Appare, però, necessario affiancare a questa crescita tecnica una crescita politica che porti ad una maggiore coesione all'interno dell'EU. E fondamentale inseguire l'obiettivo di una autentica affinità nella politica estera dei diversi paesi membri, senza la quale Bruxelles è condannata a rimanere un attore con poca autorevolezza e affidabilità diplomatiche.[412]

Altogether, to act independently could allow building a different approach with Russia in which both actors could benefit. The EU has the tools, still needs to become precisely a geopolitical actor and to

---

[411] Even if former Secretary of State Henry Kissinger considers the current US approach regarding Ukraine a mistake, it would be more important to think about the long-term relation of Russia to the West. 'Henry A. Kissinger Looks back on the Cold War,' November 4, 2014, accessed February 23, 2016. http://www.cfr.org/united-states/henry-kissinger-looks-back-cold-war/p33741

[412] Vitale, Op. Cit., page 23.

develop EU geopolitics. The EU is in fact a bigger economy[413] than the United States. In the military sphere, the EU has 450 active nuclear warheads[414] and would have the potential to have an army that could serve as a deterrent against any possible Russian invasion. The tools exist. What it lacks is only the political will. Therefore, the key element to define a sovereign relation with Russia goes hand in hand with separating the European interest from the US interest without severely affecting the kind of privileged relation it enjoys with the United States.

Germany sporadically has acknowledged this fact. The German companies in different areas also consider more important the commercial relation with Russia than adopting an anti-Russian stand just for Ukraine. The last proposal from Angela Merkel to Vladimir Putin to end the Ukrainian crisis with a vast free trade zone area from Lisbon to Vladivostok is similar.[415] Still, as Merkel mentioned, an agreement between the EU and the Eurasian Union still leaves unresolved the question of where to fit Ukraine, Georgia and Moldova.

A 'Germanized' Europe, then, reconsidering Carlo Jean's words, still seems better than the 'No Europe' option. That could be the only way in which EU can find a common ground to build a different kind of relation and in which the United States does not despise the EU's position as happened several times in the present Ukrainian crisis.[416]

Altogether, the complexity of the European position has been notoriously seen in the complexity of the events in Ukraine and Moldova. Both cases are analysed thoroughly in the following pages.

---

[413] As of 2013, the seize of the European Union's GDP was larger than the one from the United States. '*GDP at Market Prices*,' World Bank, accessed on November 23, 2014. http://data.worldbank.org/indicator/NY.GDP.MKTP.CD/countries/EU?display=graph

[414] That is counting the once in possession of the United Kingdom and France. 'Status of world nuclear forces,' accessed on February 23, 2016. http://fas.org/issues/nuclear-weapons/status-world-nuclear-forces/

[415] 'Меркель—Путину: Мир в Украине—в обмен на ЗСТ с Евросоюзом,' January 23, 2015. http://korrespondent.net/ukraine/politics/3470382-merkel-putynu-myr-v-ukrayne-v-obmen-na-zst-s-evrosouizom

[416] The famous 'Fuck the EU' from Victoria Nuland is just one example. '*Ukraine: des enregistrements clandestins embarrassent les Etats-Unis.*' http://www.lemonde.fr/international/article/2014/02/07/ukraine-quand-une-diplomate-americaine-s-emporte-contre-l-ue_4361896_3210.html

1.5 Conclusions

This chapter intended to show the current state of the relation between Russia, the United States and the European Union and how the three actors have handled their relations with Ukraine and Moldova. This interaction together with the geopolitical consequences brought by the fall of the Soviet regime are central to understanding the attempts by ex-Soviet countries to build an independent state.

It was essential to consider the renaissance of a Russian state after the chaotic decade that meant the end of Yeltsin's presidency—a decade in which the dismantling of the Soviet regime allowed other geopolitical actors to advance their own projects without resistance; a decade in which crisis, inflation, looting and pillage at unseen levels allowed a new class of oligarchs to emerge in Russia; a decade where Russia had no relevant presence at the international scene and the armed forces decreased their capacity as shown in the First Chechen War.

The rise of Vladimir Putin to the presidency brought the reappearance of the Russian Federation as a state with an assertive and sovereign policy that from a realistic perspective tried to become a respected actor in the international scene. The recovery of energy companies back to state control allowed the Russian Federation to subsidize economic growth and to build again a more assertive position in the international scene together with a renewed role of their armed forces. A new Russian polity reconstituted a new foreign policy while Russian geopolitics remerged.

The renewed Russian geopolitical project had as a priority to regain influence in the Near Abroad, firstly, to stop the advance of other geopolitical actors in this area, either China in Central Asia or the United States and the EU with its members in the West.

This policy is visible in the Eurasian Economic Union, a supranational organization, that together with the Collective Security Treaty Organization, reinstates an area of the world under Russian influence and opposes with more firmness rival projects. The idea of the Eurasian Union advanced notably in Central Asia but still did not manage to include Ukraine, Moldova and Georgia in the West, which were under pressure to subsume themselves into other geopolitical projects, both NATO and a rapprochement with the EU.

Meanwhile, the United States also changed the way in which they handled relations with Russia, trying at first to integrate slowly or at least approach the Russian Federation to convince them to join Western institutions with the NATO-Russia Council for instance. Afterwards, continuous NATO enlargements and the developing of a vigorous strategy to include Georgia, Ukraine and Moldova into NATO's structures marked the change of approach in relations with Russia.

The colour revolutions represented for Moscow a sort of Western-oriented movement financed by the United States to impose regimes aligned geopolitically with the West. Therefore, after the success of these movements in Serbia, Georgia and Ukraine and partially in Kirgizstan, Russia decided to have a firmer response against moves that conflicted with their own interests.

This converted Russian response was present in the Georgian War in 2008 in which the renewed Russian Armed Forces displayed an effective and quick reaction to an attack against their forces stationed in South Ossetia. This became a starting point in which Moscow was willing to show that they would act outside of their borders if they felt their strategic interests were under threat. The recognition afterwards of South Ossetia and Abkhazia was part of the geopolitical effect.[417] In that sense, as Alessandro Vitale wrote: 'La dichiarazione di indipendenza di Pristina dalla Serbia si è trasformata in un boomerang geopolitico con la vicenda georgiana.'[418]

Altogether, the message was clear.[419] Russia did not want an extended enlargement of NATO in the Caucasus. The Russian Federation with its renewed armed forces became an actor to consider for

---

[417] Currently, both republics are only recognized by Russia, Venezuela, Nicaragua and Nauru plus the breakaway republics of Pridnestrovia and Nagorno-Karabakh. Note of the author.
[418] Vitale, Op. Cit., page 94.
[419] Vladimir Putin warned the United States and many Western countries when they decided to recognize Kosovo as an independent country that a precedent was being established that could follow with dangerous consequences in different breakaway regions. The precedent meant that borders recognized by the United Nations could be modified by geopolitical interests. The Kosovo argument was exactly the same that allowed him then to recognize two new 'states' that included the presence of Russian troops, the Russian rouble as currency and a considerable percentage of the population that happen to be also citizens of the Russian Federation. Note of the author.

negotiating the outcome of any secessionist conflict in similar scenarios like Pridnestrovia, Nagorno-Karabakh or in Tajikistan. The outcome in Georgia was a clear message to the United States showing that Moscow was not in the same position as it was one decade before.

> ... la guerre avait pour cibles réelles les Etats Unis et la communauté des pays occidentaux. C'est à eux qu'un double message était adressé par le biais de ce conflit que nul ne pouvait ignorer, tant son effet sur les relations internationales- une guerre au cœur de l'Europe, conduite par un grand pays – était important, et considérable l'entorse aux règles qui avaient présidé aux relations internationales depuis la fin de la guerre froide. C'est le souci d'être entendu et compris des véritables destinataires de ce message qui explique l'ampleur de l'action russe.
> ...le geste russe signalait l'existence d'une limite à ne pas franchir : la Russie indiquait par la que les empiètements constants sur ce qu'elle tenait pour sa zone d'influence n'étaient plus acceptables par elle. L'avertissement valait aussi pour le projet d'extension de l'OTAN à l'Ukraine, et les Ukrainiens ne s'y sont pas trompés.[420]

It showed that any advance against their own geopolitical interests would be met with similar answers. But, it seems the West did not learn the lesson before the 2013–2014 Ukrainian crisis.

In the meantime, the European Union and its members created the Eastern Partnership to not only promote a kind of a buffer zone between Russia and the EU but also to use a soft approach to pull the countries from this area into NATO's and the EU's orbit. The lack of a deep definition of the goals of this partnership between EU members has given rise to the different results achieved until now.

Altogether, the main intention of this chapter was to show how different geopolitical projects coincide in Ukraine, Moldova and Pridnestrovia and how each external actor has had different goals regarding these territories. To make it even more complex, these projects portray a geostrategic game that uses inner ethnic, cultural, political, social, religious and economic differences present. Besides, this happens in an attempt to build an independent state, something that, for instance, had never existed in Moldova[421] and Pridnestrovia and practically never in the Ukrainian case besides

---

[420] Carrère d'Encausse Héléne, *La Russie entre deux mondes*, Paris, Fayard, 2010, pages 301–302.
[421] In this case, I refer to the region of Bessarabia and not all the territory of the ancient Moldavia.

the short-lived Ukrainian People's Republic[422] after the Russian Revolution.

Therefore, in the following chapters, it will be analysed how internal political forces were influenced by the external factors mentioned and until what point the local populations proved successful in creating or advancing an independent polity that could become one day a sovereign state.

---

[422] Even though the Ukrainian People's Republic exists as a reference, it would be arguable if it could be considered as an independent state. The country was in the middle of a Civil War and continuously invaded by all sorts of foreign armies during that period. The second chapter shows more details about these events. Note of the author.

2 Ukraine

To understand the role of the Ukrainian territory in the geopolitical chessboard should be the starting point of any analysis of the different attempts to build a state in this area. A pivot, keystone, cleft country, cushion state, borderland or so many definitions used by scholars portray the geostrategic importance of this territory in many different means. Being the second largest country in Europe, with more than 50 million people, and an estimated 5% of total world mineral resources, adds more complexity to a territory that also has become strategic to deliver oil and gas to many European countries today. Ukrainian territory suffered more than any other impacts of World War II, and after the Soviet fall it recovered its geostrategic importance while becoming the reason for different actors in the international scene to bring Ukraine under their orbit. Therefore, it is worth mentioning some notable features that have influenced the political processes and the society that inhabit this territory.

Ukraine means 'borderland'[423] and to have at least a slight understanding of the people that live in this land, it is imperative to traverse the long interaction between so many different civilizations across this territory. The land that we actually know as Ukraine has been a border between so many civilizations, ethnic groups, languages, religions, armies, nomads and others included between Europe and Asia or between the Slavic world and the Arabic world, between Greeks and the Caucasus or so many other civilizations that have added to the complexity of this territory. Therefore, it has been always the object of geopolitical interest of different foreign powers through centuries.

Besides, different historiographical viewpoints also have rather different perceptions on the historical developments of the current Ukrainian land. Therefore, Polish, Russian or Soviet historiography have usually different standpoints and, in most cases, conceive this

---

[423] It comes from the word 'ukraina' (оукраина), which was used to refer to the borderlands of the Rus'. Subtelny, Orest, *Ukraine a History*, Canada, University of Toronto, 2000, page 3.

territory as part of different polities but not as one with its own *ethos* from which it could build a state.[424]

Moreover, two of the most important academic contributions of Ukrainian history focus on different perspectives. One of them, Paul Magocsi, focuses more on the events that happen on the Ukrainian territory, and the other by Orest Subtelny focuses more on the endeavours of the Ukrainian people. This minor difference, in a multi-ethnic territory could mean a lot for the historical narrative. Nevertheless, neither diminishes the quality of other historiographical research that serves to give some notions about the happenings in this land.

Ukraine also has one peculiarity. People in the Ukrainian territory have never had a state or polity of their own, where its society organizes itself politically and legally around a common 'ethos'.

In that sense, historian Orest Subtelny says: 'In most national histories the acquisition and development of the nation-state is a paramount feature, but in the Ukrainian case the opposite is true. The frustration of the Ukrainians' attempts to attain self-government is one of the key aspects of their historical experience. Therefore, the Ukrainian past is largely the history of a nation that has had to survive and evolve without the framework of a full-fledged national state.'[425]

Therefore, as a reference, the following pages show some of the most important events that marked the history of this territory underlying the key political and geopolitical cleavages and their impact always immersed in the relations with neighbouring polities until the Soviet period. Therefore, after the Soviet collapse, it becomes easier to understand the vicissitudes of the last two decades and the failed attempts to build a Ukrainian state.

---

[424] Magocsi, Paul Robert, *A History of Ukraine*, Toronto, University of Toronto Press incorporated, 1996, page 12.
[425] Subtelny, Op. Cit., Preface to the first edition, page xiii.

2.1 Historical background

"Principalities of the Kievan Rus," accessed on February 28, 2016.
Source: Wikimedia Commons, licensed under CC BY-SA 3.0
(https://creativecommons.org/licenses/by-sa/3.0/)

The Kievan Rus'[426] was the first polity established within the territory with Oleg as the first recognized ruler from the year 882. The growth and development of Kiev included already the participation of several ethnic groups and the interaction between Slavic and Scandinavian groups.[427] The first key political and geopolitical decision was to opt for the Christian religion. When Prince Vladimir had to choose between the Muslim and Christian world, he chose the latter after requesting the hand of the Byzantine Emperor's sister in 988. Ukrainian nationalists try hardly to affirm that the Kievan Rus' was the ethnic and cultural precedent of the Ukrainian tradition while Russians descended from Finno-Ugric groups.[428] Instead, Russians would like to demonstrate that they are the heritage of the Kievan Rus'. In fact, there was no Ukrainian, Belorussian or Russian state back then, just diverse ethnic groups with the Kievan Rus' as predecessor. The territory was a multi-ethnic agglomeration with common religious background. In addition, some authors sustain that they spoke the same language,[429] a dispute that also highlights the differences between Russian and Ukrainian historiography.[430]

---

[426] The origin of the word Rus' is also the origin of different historiographic disputes. There is one version that sustains that it comes from the Finnish word 'ruotsi' or 'rodr' in Swedish that means *rower*. Another sustains that it comes from the river Rus or Rusna in Central Ukraine. The latter version tries to prove that locals were able to organize itself without foreign support. Historian Subtelny sustains that the only certain thing is that it was first applied to the Scandinavian Varangians, then to the territory of the Poliany in Central Ukraine and last to refer to the political entity Kievan Rus' (Киевская Русь). Subtelny, Op. Cit., page 23.

[427] Pritsak, O., *The Origin of Rus'*, Cambridge, Harvard Ukrainian Research Institute, 1981, pages 8–33.

[428] Lieven, Anatoly, *Ukraine & Russia, a Fraternal Rivalry*, Washington, DC, United States Institute for Peace, 1999.

[429] Lunt, Horace, 'The language of the Rus' in the eleventh century; Some observations about facts and theories,' *Harvard Ukrainian Studies*, Vol. 12–13 (1988–1989), pages 276–313, referred in Wilson, Andrew, '*The Ukrainians Unexpected Nation*,' New Haven, Yale University Press, 2002, page 7.

[430] The Kievan Rus' was the dominant language until the adoption of Christianity, language that is a little bit closer to the Ukrainian language. Either way, this language became the language of the peasantry given that the elites adopted the Church Slavonic as their language. The Russian language instead emerges from Kievan Rus' mixing itself with other languages as the Church Slavonic and the influence of other Finno-Ugric local tribes. Therefore, the three east Slavic languages started to develop in the XIII and XIV centuries after the Kievan Rus' had fallen. Ibidem.

The Mongol invasion of 1237 and the fall of Kiev in 1240 brought the disappearance of this precursor of Russia and Ukraine. Subsequently, the Russian Empire expanded with cultural, linguistic and religious liaisons with the Kievan Rus'; meanwhile there emerged a notable division with the regions of Galicia and Volhynia. The latter suffered less from the Mongol invasions, which allowed them to preserve more their own identities. Rutheny became a peripheral area of low interest for the Golden Horde and became a sort of semi-independent vassalage that paid a tribute, thus becoming a political base of the Ukrainian people. Subtelny remarks: 'The two principalities absorbed much of the Kievan heritage and at the same time prevented the absorption of Ukrainian lands by Poland. By so doing, they preserved for Ukrainians, or Rusyns as they were called, a sense of cultural and political distinctiveness at a crucial points of their history.'[431] This distinction was not only ethnic but also a political and geopolitical.

After the Mongol invasions, the people of the former Kievan Rus' never had again their own polity and were always part of different political entities. Lithuanian expansion arrived in the fourteenth century without a fierce resistance from the population as it was preferred to that of the Golden Horde. Lithuania had a scarce population and even invited some local Ukrainian nobility to access the government and, as they had not adopted Christianity, they allowed Ukrainians to keep their faith. Meanwhile, the Poles had invaded Galicia and Volhynia in the same century. The Polish population was catholic and had established that religion in Galicia with an eparchy in Lvov that also became the biggest landowner in the region while trying to stop the advance of the orthodox faith. This fact added another layer of religious and political division between this territory and the rest of the current Ukrainian territory.

---

[431] Subtelny, Op. Cit., pages 64–65.

166 State-Building in the Middle of a Geopolitical Struggle

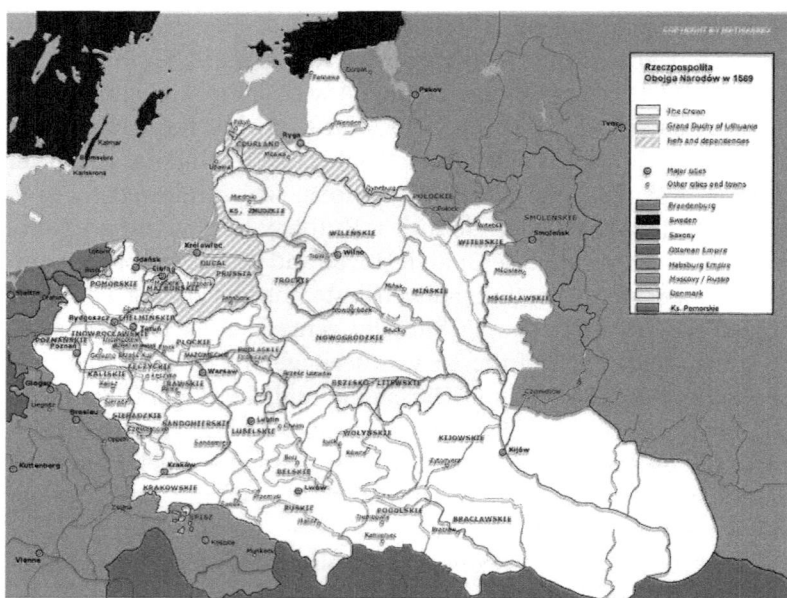

"The Polish-Lithuanian Commonwealth in 1569."
Source: Wikimedia Commons, licensed under CC BY-SA 3.0
(https://creativecommons.org/licenses/by-sa/3.0/)

The Union of Krewo[432] in 1385 wanted to prevent the Teutonic and Russian expansion and allowed a great preponderance of the Catholic Church while diminishing the agreements among Ukrainian nobility and the Lithuanians. The Union deepened in different stages until 1585 when the Union of Lublin created a single state between Poland and Lithuania.

Besides, Polish domination withheld local population under extremely harsh conditions. The system was based on established rights in which the limits between the polish nobility (*szlachta*) and other social classes were unsurmountable and most of the land, mostly at the right bank of the Dnieper, was under the control of just a few Polish families. Therefore, this started a great rivalry between the Ukrainian peasantry and Polish nobles.

Meanwhile, Moscow's outstanding territorial growth from the fifteenth century led to the emergence of the idea of the 'Third

---

[432] This treaty sealed the Union of Poland and Lithuania under a single crown. A translation from the original treaty can be found at http://polishkingdom.co.uk/unionkreva.html, accessed on January 4, 2015.

Rome', after Rome and Constantinople, and Moscow had as 'destiny' to become the sacred and universal empire; meanwhile Ivan III called himself 'gosudar' of all the Russians and assumed that all the territories that used to belong to the Kievan Rus' should belong to Moscow. Therefore, even under Polish domination, the current Ukrainian territory was already in Moscow's geopolitical expectations even though Poland at that time was the largest state in Europe.

In the territories dominated by Poland, the nobles were catholic and spoke Polish but the peasantry kept the orthodox faith and spoke Ukrainian or Ruthenian, considered the language of the lower classes.[433] The attempt by the Polish rule to co-opt the orthodox Ukrainian nobility with the Union of Brest[434] failed and revealed the arrival of the local society divided into three religious groups: The Polish nobility was Catholic; some of the Ukrainian nobility became Greek Catholic or Uniate while the largest number of the peasantry kept their faith to the Orthodox Church. This split added another element of division to the population of this territory but started to allow the development of a Ukrainian identity around the orthodox faith against the antagonistic Catholic Pole. To this element, it is possible to add another that became crucial in the development of the Ukrainian identity, Cossacks.

The Cossacks

The Cossacks were people established mostly near the eastern borders of the Polish kingdom and being far away from the centre, they obtained tacitly a certain autonomy. Even if they recognized Polish

---

[433] Ruthenian or rusyn (русин, *rusin*, in lingua) is a Slavic language of the Eastern Group together with Russian, Belorussia and Ukrainian that shows a straight similarity with Ukrainian language. There is a controversy between linguists if it should be considered a language of its own or a dialect of Ukrainian. Magocsi, Paul Robert, 'The Rusyn language question revisited,' in *Of the Making of Nationalities There is No End*, edited by Magocsi, Paul Robert, Vol. I., New York, Columbia University Press/East European Monographs, 1999, pages 86–111, http://www.rusyn.org/images/4.%20Rusyn%20Language%20Question%20Revisted.pdf

[434] The Union of Brest in 1595 established that the Ruthenian Church of Rus' would break relations with Constantinople while recognizing the authority of the Vatican. It allowed them to retain their liturgy and traditions proper of the Orthodox Church while recognizing the Pope as the only authority. It is commonly known as Greek Catholic Church. Subtelny, Op. cit., pages 99–102.

authority and were a functional unit of the kingdom, as they would help against attacks carried on by Tartars, the Cossacks were independent people that defended themselves and had military knowledge. Families grew far from the Polish *Szlachta* and took care of the border, therefore having a non-official approval of the kingdom. Cossacks did not belong exclusively to one ethnic group even though the majority were in today's Ukrainian territory.

Many of them founded the 'Zaporozhian Sich', a sort of military fortress for those who escaped from feudal lords or the Tartars. Cossacks had the same rights and a council known as 'Rady'[435] would take the decisions. The head called 'Hetman' meanwhile ensured that there prevailed a sort of ethos of fraternity and equality even if certain economic differences were present.

At the end, even though there were different kinds of Cossacks, the ones from the Zaporozhian Sich, the ones paid by Poles, and the ones in the borders, Cossacks became an element of national consciousness.[436] Cossackdom and Orthodox faith became gluing symbols against Polish domination, mostly in the left bank of the Dniester. In that sense, the novel *Taras Bulba*[437] by Nicolas Gogol gives a colourful and vivid picture of how Cossacks organized and related against the Tartars, Poles or Russians.

Altogether, when Hetman Bohdan Khmelnitsky commanded an uprising against the Poles in 1648, his success was also due to the fact that locals were clearly exhausted with the Poles and the Jew population that administered the land.[438] At this point, after liberating the lands of the left bank of the Dnieper, the Cossacks again took a key geopolitical decision. To prevent any Polish reprisal, they

---

[435] From this word comes the term 'Rada' to define the current Ukrainian parliament. Subtelny, Idem, page 110.
[436] Subtelny wrote that as Vikings for the Scandinavians. Subtelny, Op. Cit., page 122.
[437] Gogol, Nicolai, '*Taras Bulba e gli altri racconti di Mirgorod*,' Milano, Garzanti, Grandi libri, 2012.
[438] At the time of the rebellion, in 1648, Jews, who rented the properties for 2–3 year contracts, administered more than half of the land. This took them to look to obtain the greatest profit possible at the expense of the local peasantry in that period. Therefore, once the rebellion proved itself successful, the local population took vengeance mostly against the Jew populations. Paul Magocsi calculates that about 50% of the Jew population that was around 60,000 was reduced in more than 50% because the war. Magocsi, Paul Robert, '*Ukraine: A History*' Toronto, Toronto University, 1993.

needed protection by a foreign power. The Cossacks opted for the Russians. The 1654 Treaty of Pereyaslav, of which no copies remained, became a forging point in the relations between Ukraine and Russia. In this agreement, Cossacks accepted Czar's authority. Historians Venedikt Miakotin and Mykhailo Hrushevsky agree that the agreement was kind of a vassalage in which the Czar would protect the Ukrainians and not interfere in their inner affairs and in exchange, they would pay tribute and military assistance when needed.[439] Throughout the years, this agreement became also a Russian justification to possess these lands.

Besides, Czar's perception about the agreement was rather different. The idea of autonomy even if apparently accepted in first instance diluted in the following century and completely disappeared once Catherine II was in power in the eighteenth century. Meanwhile, Ukrainian identity forged around the idea of Cossack 'freedom' antagonized with the czarist autocracy; meanwhile ethnic and religious similarities with the Russians prevailed.[440]

From this moment, 'the fate of Ukraine became inextricably linked with that of Russia'[441]. Afterwards, Ukraine's strategic role was present in different wars Russia had against Sweden and the Ottoman Empire. Meanwhile, the Cossacks had to pay the price that a group of them headed by Ivan Mazepa had decided to combat with the Swedish, in what meant another diminution of Cossack autonomy and the further disappearance of the Zaporizhian Sich. Finally, the Hetman's authority was abolished during the eighteenth century, ending officially Cossack's local authority while the term *Malorosy*[442] became common usage to refer to the local population. Besides, the oppressive measures that were part of the 'slovo i delo' included the prohibition to express any criticism against the regime

---

[439] Subtelny, Op. Cit., page 135.
[440] Wilson, Andrew, *The Ukrainians: Unexpected Nation*, New Haven, Yale University Press, 2002, page 70.
[441] Subtelny, Ibidem, page 135.
[442] In Russia-dominated Ukraine, the perceived idea was that Ukrainians were merely a variant of Russians. The term 'malorosy' comes from the Малороссия (Malorossiya) that means little Russia and was used to refer to most of the current Ukrainian territory. Subtelny, Orest, Introduction, the Ambiguities of National Identity: The case of Ukraine in Wolchik Sharon, L., Ukraine: The Search for a National Identity, Rowman & Littlefield, 2000.

and these were not exclusively against the Ukrainian population, applied to all the subjects of the Russian Empire.443

The Russian Empire

The incredible growth of the Russian Empire cannot be compared to any other one in the world. In 1462, Muscovy had 24,000 square kilometres and in 1914, it counted with 13,800,000 square kilometres, the sixth of the world, after having grown at a level of 80 kilometres per day. Ukraine served as a platform for invasions against the Khanate of Crimea and Ukrainians participated in the fight against Tartars. Besides, it is worth to acknowledge that present-day Ukraine suffered by then most of the Tatar raids.444

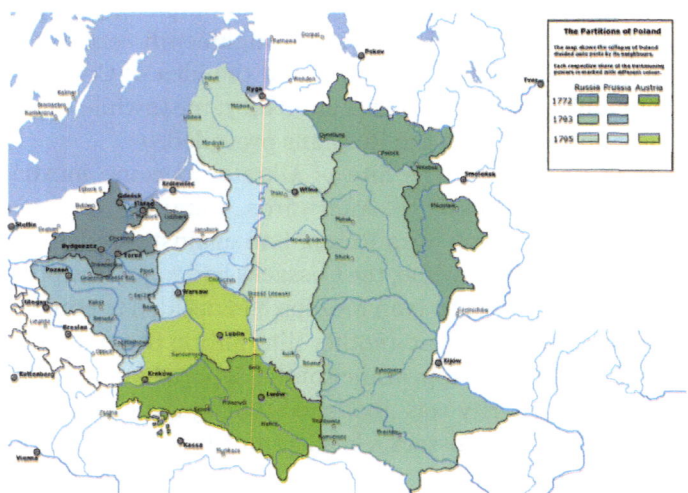

"Partitions of Poland," accessed on February 4, 2015.
Source: Wikimedia Commons, licensed under CC BY-SA 3.0
(https://creativecommons.org/licenses/by-sa/3.0/)

The partition of the Polish-Lithuanian Commonwealth occurred in three phases. This division assured that Russia would remain with

---

443   *The Great Soviet Encyclopedia*, 3rd edition. S.v. 'Slovo i Delo Gosudarevo,' accessed on February 4, 2015. http://encyclopedia2.thefreedictionary.com/Slovo+i+Delo+Gosudarevo
444   Kolodziejczyk, Dariusz, 'The Crimean Khanate and Poland-Lithuania, International diplomacy on the European periphery (15th–18th century).' A study of peace treaties followed by annotated documents, Boston, Brill, 2011.

62% of the territory and 45% of the population; the Austro-Hungarian Empire would take 18% of the land and 32% of the population and Prussia 20% and 23%, respectively.[445]

At this point, more than 80% of territory currently known as Ukrainian was already under Czarist Russia; meanwhile, the other 20%, the regions of Galicia and Bukovina, were under Austro-Hungarian domination. Hence the same way as the Ukrainian population under Czarist authority received the name Little Russians or Malorosy, the ones under the Austro-Hungarian crown were known as Ruthenes or Rusyns.

The partition of the Polish Confederation meant that after approximately a century and a half, the two banks of the Dnieper became part of the same Russian political system. Nevertheless, the impact that this period of separation meant is noticeable, for instance, on how on the left bank more people speak today Russian than in the right bank.

Altogether, the Ukrainian territory continued to function as a strategic background for Russian expansion, while Ukrainian peasantry like all the subjects of the Czar were under a severe domination with new reforms to the land property that forbade peasants from moving freely from one settlement to another. The same Ukraine peasantry that had battled for freedom against the Poles after 130 years were serfs again. At this point, Cossacks were 40% of the population, peasants 53.7%, city habitants 4%, nobility 1.6% and priests 0.7%.

Meanwhile, a new process of Russification occurred. Anyone who intended to include itself in this society and to arrive to a considerable position as official or in the government. Besides, any enthusiasm for separatist movements disappeared; meanwhile the old Cossack elite, the *starshyna*, stayed loyal to the tsar. They saw themselves as a tribe of the same Russians. The Napoleonic invasion was one of the cases in which Cossacks fought loyally to defend the tsar. New universities and schools appeared in Russian language to substitute the Polish ones while Romanovs ruled through a multi-ethnic bureaucracy in which Ukrainians could arrive to the

---

[445] Subtelny, *Ukraine a History*, Op. Cit., page 177.

top. Political loyalty was more important than ethnic origin. The imperial elite was a caste but the rest included names not only Russians but from Ukrainian, Baltic, German, Georgian or Tartar origin.[446] By the mid-nineteenth century, remained only Russified nobility from one side and poor Ukrainian peasants at the other, what allowed to use the denomination of 'Ukrainian' to refer to someone from the countryside with a residual folklore tradition.[447]

Ukrainians under the Austro-Hungarian Empire
One of the most notable differences present between this empire and the Tsarist Russia was that in the Austro-Hungarian case, no nationality was a majority. There were 11 nationalities with other minor ethnic groups and with one-seventh of the European population. Besides the ethnic diversity, there was no centralized government as in Russia.

Most of the Ukrainians were in Galicia and others in Bukovina and Transcarpathia. Galicia had Polish as a majority in the West and the Ukrainians in the East while being an extremely poor region. The peasantry were still serfs and there were few optimal spaces for agriculture. In fact, being one of the poorest regions of the empire, the region was quite poor and represented 12–15% of the empire's population, a considerable fraction in a territory with so many ethnic groups. In this case, they were confronted with the Polish influence and with continuous attempts to Polonize the territory, which were later reduced with the Constitutional reforms that occurred.

---

[446] Wilson, Op. Cit., page 77.
[447] Ibidem, page 78.

"Ethno-linguistic map of Austria-Hungary, 1910," accessed on February 4, 2015.
Source: Wikimedia Commons, licensed under CC BY-SA 3.0
(https://creativecommons.org/licenses/by-sa/3.0/)

During this period, a notion of independence developed among Western Ukrainians. The reason that made Galicia become an avant-garde of Ukrainian nationalism was a consequence of how the Austro-Hungarian Empire was organized. The 1848 reforms allowed the development of a sense of identity while they started to call themselves Ukrainians instead of Rusyns. For these Ukrainians, the idea of nationality included the fact of having education, local government, alimentation and social legislation while at the same time opposing the Polish. Therefore, the relation with the Habsburg Empire was one of mutual benefits that accrued on each side from 1772 to 1918 as portrayed by Paul Magosci.[448]

The Ukrainians started to mould their own 'ethos' and recognize themselves as a different group in the empire. The political conditions were rather different. The events in the West had no influence on the East where there was no plan to conceive a nationalist movement. There was not the desire or the possibility to look for changes

---

[448] Magosci, Paul, *The Roots of Ukrainian Nationalism, Galicia as Ukraine's Piedmont*, Toronto, University of Toronto Press, 2002, page 82.

or to create a national movement. There was no link between intellectuals and peasants and, therefore, there was no national consciousness as in the West. In Kiev, at the beginning of the twentieth century, there were no books printed in Ukrainian, whereas in Lvov, there were newspapers, schools, cooperatives and they had a parliamentary representation. Therefore, the fact that later, the views of the local population towards Russians or to the idea of building a state were extremely diverse should not be amazing. In Galicia, the ambitions were to go even further, beyond autonomy and look for independence.

Cossacks' role had a deep impact in developing the local identity; thus, the biggest reason that would cause the local Ukrainians to go against the Russian Empire was not ethnic or religious but political. Therefore, this created a dichotomy that on the one side attracted some and on the other differed from Ukrainian society within the Russian rule or as Anatoly Lieven would name it, the development of a fraternal rivalry[449].

The differences in the political organization between the Czarist Empire and the Austro-Hungarian meant also completely different approaches from the different social classes towards the idea of building a Ukrainian nation and state.

2.2 The Soviet years

World War I and the Russian Revolution

World War I brought the collapse of different empires: the Austro-Hungarian, the Ottoman and in a different way the Russian. The geopolitical repercussions were enormous and allowed the possibility for new nation states to emerge on the international scene.[450]

In Russia, the resentment against the Tsar had increased notably due to the war. Sending unprepared soldiers and suffering high losses in extremely unfavourable conditions created a bigger resent-

---

[449] Lieven, Op. Cit.
[450] That includes the return of Poland to the international scene plus Czechoslovakia and Yugoslavia while Finland, Estonia, Latvia, Lithuania declared independence from Russia and received further recognition. Becket, Ian, *The Great War*, Great Britain, Pearson Longman, 2007, pages 552–553.

ment towards the ruling family. Besides, many soldiers fought almost without munitions or proper guns while there was a visible corruption in the bureaucratic elite. To that extent, Trotsky's account is a good source that portrays the harsh conditions in which the armed forces sent to the front.[451]

It was not a surprise, then, that while Nicholas II was at the front, big strikes organized by the workers in Petrograd grew and many troops loyal to the Tsar instead of repressing the protesters adhered to their cause. After some days, Nicholas II abdicated power and a new provisional government was established on February 1917, headed by Kerensky.[452]

At this point, another attempt to create a Ukrainian polity was made, to a great measure as consequence of the complex political and geopolitical context that surrounded the Ukrainian territory. After the February Revolution, a Congress of the Workers and the Central Rada (*Центральна Рада*) was established, reusing the name of the Council that gathered the Cossacks. There was a great variety of ideologies present, from moderates, liberals, social democrats and the socialist revolutionary Ukrainian party. They tried to establish an autonomous government and to act as an independent country against the foreign menace but the conflict against the Bolsheviks was long and became even more complex because of the existence of White troops that wanted to retake power for a monarchic Russia again. Therefore, in the Rada, there were those who wanted to build a nation state while still many sectors of the Ukrainian society were highly Russified and without an interest in the development of a Ukrainian national consciousness. Later, many of the members allied themselves with the Bolsheviks and after less than a year it collapsed.[453]

The period from 1917 to 1919 was very anarchic. Six different armies occupied Ukraine: Bolsheviks, the Whites, the Ukrainian nationalists' troops, Poles, the Austro-German troops and the anarchists. Kiev changed hands five times within a year. The Rada tried

---

[451] Trotsky, Leon, *The History of the Russian Revolution*, Chicago, Haymarket Books, 2008, pages 15–18.
[452] Becket, Op. Cit., page 523.
[453] Subtelny, Op. Cit., page 353.

to establish a government but after the failure, the Bolsheviks established another Ukrainian Government. Afterwards appeared a new conservative government guided by Pavlo Skoropadsky with support from the Germans and Austrians. After their defeat in the war, consequently, the government crumbled. Andrew Wilson wrote:

> The Ukrainian movement was also unable to build a broader political base in the towns, where they were a small minority, compared to Russian monarchist, Russian radical and even Jewish and polish forces... Kharkiv and Donbas were controlled either by the Bolsheviks or by the local workers' militias. Kiev was invaded by the Bolsheviks three times, with considerable assistance from workers inside the city. In the absence of any outside forces, this was too narrow a base on which to build the new Ukrainian nation.[454]

After two years of war, the new Bolshevik Government negotiated peace with the Polish Government accepting to lose Volynia. Galicia would remain under Polish control and the rest passed to the Ukrainian Soviet Socialist Republic. The peace between the Soviet Government and the Poles did not mean an end to fighting in the region. Western Ukrainians did not want to be part of a Polish state again. They tried to establish the West Ukrainian National Republic (Zakhidno Ukrainska Narodna Respublyka – ZUNR) and managed to create an army that brought a long uprising in which Poles had to send numerous forces to control the Ukrainian rebellion. At the end, besides the effort, Ukrainians were not capable of winning against a stronger army and by 16 July 1919, the conflict was over.[455]

Hence, it was again a matter of geopolitics that a West Ukrainian Republic was not included in the logic of Woodrow Wilson's famous 14 points, which allowed the creation of a Polish state and the Baltic states.[456] Western Ukrainians did not obtain reconnaissance as other nationalities did in the after-war period to have their own

---

[454] Wilson, *'Ukrainians Unexpected Nation,'* Op. Cit., page 124.
[455] Subtelny, Op. Cit., pages 367–370.
[456] Even if idealists in international relations love to consider the Fourteen Points, from January 8, 1918, as a starting point to define the self-determination of the people, actually, those points were strictly based in geopolitics. In fact, the result achieved was to create a buffer zone between the recently formed Soviet Union and Germany; meanwhile the disappearance of the Austro-Hungarian Empire meant that allied countries like France and the United Kingdom stayed as the strong states in Europe. There is no idealism in that only simple and pure geopolitics. Note of the author.

states. Polish pressure saw Ukrainians as a possible Bolshevik ally and the fact that Poles had populated the region made it difficult for Ukrainians to find recognition by the Western powers. Even though, at the beginning of the century, Ukrainians from Galicia had already developed a strong sense of local nationalism that defined their identity against Poles, they did not want to link it with the rest of Ukraine.

The difference between both territories was huge, the ones in the Soviet Union were in many senses deeply integrated with the Russians and, above all, without a clear will to create a national identity even less an independent state. Many Ukrainians were deeply immersed in Russian culture, and it seemed difficult for them to see the difference or to conceive an existence separated from Russia. Instead, in the West, even if smaller and poorer, there was a stronger sense of belonging to an ethnic group and nationality. In the West, external factors did not allow the success of the movement that pretended to even create a nation state at least in the region of Galicia. Instead, at the East, the social transformation seemed more important to most of the population and from there to transform the socio-economic conditions of the region. The failure of the Ukrainian Republic in the West brought the development of a strong ethnonationalist Ukrainian identity that was strongly anti-Polish and also anti-Russian. Therefore, when these territories united again in 1945, it was in conditions completely different from the ones in 1919.

2.2.1 Ukraine within the USSR

The Soviet years in Ukraine or in the rest of the Soviet Union are commonly referred as one single era, instead of acknowledging the great differences present in the politic, economic and social sense. Each one of them had specific characteristics and the first two, the period under Lenin and later under Stalin, left profound impacts in Ukraine, in completely different ways. Therefore, it is worth underlining how the idea of nation building was present and conceived by Lenin and then by Stalin. Besides, even if at this point, most of the current Ukrainian territory was under undisputed Soviet control, it was not exempt from geopolitics.

The first thing to notice is how the Soviet authorities handled the nationality issue. Terry Martin in *The Affirmative Action Empire*[457] demonstrates how there was a positive attempt to build a multi-ethnic and multinational state after the Bolshevik Revolution and the Civil War. It was a very complex environment and it was not easy in a territory where ethnic Russians had been in the position of power. Therefore, changes that would be accepted otherwise would certainly bring resistances. Hence, it is worth remembering what Lenin said to his fellow Bolshevik companion Georgy Pyatakov: 'Scratch any Communist and you find a Great Russia Chauvinist.'[458]

The process was complex and the idea was to deeply transform the society and make all the ethnic groups feel part of the same ethos with a very careful approach. Lenin had already raised the question in 1913 when he wrote the *Theses on the National Question*.[459] Once the Bolsheviks were in power, Terry Martin mentions three different premises that were on deliberation:

1. The Marxist premise: Considered that the above-class appeal of nationalism could be disarmed by granting the forms of nationhood.[460]
2. The Modernization premise: The formation of nations came to be seen as both an unavoidable and positive stage in the modernization of the Soviet Union.[461]
3. The colonial premise: Mostly pretended to simply repress any nationalist expression and Lenin once denounced Dzherzhinski, Stalin and Ordzhonikidze as Great Russian Chauvinists for defending this position.[462]

The idea was that 'National identity would be depoliticized through an ostentatious show of respect for the national identities of no Russians.'[463] The Bolsheviks attempted to fuse the nationalist demand for national territory, culture, languages and elites with the socialist

---

[457] Martin, Terry, *The Affirmative Action Empire, Nation and Nationalisms in the Soviet Union, 1923–1939*, Ithaca, Cornell University Press, US, 2001.
[458] Quoted in Martin, Op. Cit., page 3.
[459] 'Theses on the national question,' accessed on February 6, 2015. https://www.marxists.org/archive/lenin/works/1913/jun/30.htm#fwV19E085
[460] Martin, Op. Cit., page 5.
[461] Ibidem, page 6.
[462] Ibidem, page 7.
[463] Ibidem, page 13.

Ukraine 179

demands for an economically and politically unitary state. This demanded for positive action (Положительная деятельность) or affirmative action to defend non-Russian culture against an unjust fate.[464] In that sense, Martin calls them Bolsheviks internationalist nationalists or Affirmative Action nationalists, because the idea was that the Soviet Union would sustain both national minorities and majorities.

The USSR was the first country in world history to establish Affirmative Action programmes, for national minorities and no country have yet approached the vast scale of the Soviet Affirmative Action.[465] Precisely this premise allowed the USSR to structure itself not only as a multi-ethnic state but also a state provided with multi-ethnic institutions.

Korenizatsiia (коренизация)[466] was the starting point to develop the early concepts of nationhood and state building in early Soviet years. The idea was that the central state should not be identified as Russian even though, as Martin underlines, ironically, this fact preserved the national structure of the old empire, just with another name.[467]

The concept of *Korenizatsiia* was related also, even if not as a primary motivation, to what Martin defined the Piedmont Principle. It refers to the Soviet attempt to exploit cross-border ethnic ties to project political influence onto neighbouring states. For example, Ukraine was used as a Piedmont[468] to contrast the negation of Ukrainian culture in Poland in 1924.[469]

Altogether, the 1920s was a decade in which Ukrainian culture and language received their largest impulse in history. During this

---

[464] Ibidem, page 16.
[465] Idem, page 18. Besides, different kinds of Affirmative Action programmes can be found in the twentieth century in countries like Yugoslavia, Brazil or the United States in different ways. Note of the author.
[466] This word means nativization or in a literal sense 'putting down the roots' to underline precisely the promotion of the roots of the different nations present in the Soviet Union. Note of the author.
[467] Martin, Op. Cit., page 20.
[468] Ibidem, page 9.
[469] This policy is not far from the current use of the Russian ethnic minorities by the Russian Federation in ex-Soviet countries to project its geopolitical interests. Note of the author.

period, several Ukrainian schools opened and strived for a completely new educational system. It included Ukrainian not as a second language but also as a national language. The Soviet Government during these years allowed the appearance of a culturally and educational trend which was diverse and independent. Besides, the people that knew how to read rose from 24 to 57% in that decade.

The creation of national Soviets, districts and all different kinds of political entities at all levels was bound to promote the development of different nationalities, so they would all be at a certain point majority or minority in the same area. In fact, the Affirmative Action Empire strategy, as Martin underlines, called for the strengthening of national identity and even measures of de-Russification.[470] This policy received support until a certain point in the Ukrainian SSR, but met many resistances in the Central Asian republics, where it proved quite more difficult to create new native local cadres that shared the Soviet policies.[471] In fact, the emergence of national Soviets in Ukraine was used as a model for the whole Soviet Union.[472] Ukraine had, in fact, 21.3% of the population of the USSR in 1926.

Overall, the 1920s became the first attempt in Ukrainian history to develop from a state policy a Ukrainian identity, in this case as part of the USSR. The success was considerable at many levels even with the Ukrainian authorities, where a notable Ukrainization was visible not without notable resistance from the urban sectors in Eastern Ukraine.[473] The only spaces where Ukrainization did not succeed was at the factories and in the federal public services. Even though, as Martin noted, in Ukraine, *Korenizatsiia* had a great support but also more contradicting local resistances.[474]

---

[470] Martin, Ibidem, page 32.
[471] Martin, Ibidem, Chapter 2.
[472] The process of korenizatsiia was quite different in the Eastern Republics. In cases where some kind of ethnic tension was present between Russians and no Russians like in Kazakhstan or Kirgizia, it became more difficult to apply. In others like Armenia or Georgia, it was accepted smoothly as there was already an educated local elite that could easily transform itself into a Soviet local elite. Martin, Idem, page 77.
[473] Martin, Idem, page 26.
[474] Those resistances came precisely from Russified urban centres and from some cadres of the same communist party. Martin, Idem, page 79.

Altogether, again, the linguistic differences that had prevailed for years in Ukraine were present in this process. As an example, at the Ukrainian Government level, 10–15% of the paperwork was in Ukrainian while in the village almost 100% was in Ukrainian. Also, while in the Kiev or Vinnitsa regions most work in the public administration was in Ukrainian, in the Donbass the level of Ukrainization was above zero.[475] Still, the efforts made and the results promoted by party members like Mykola Skrypnik[476] were quite considerable. All this while Lenin's New Economic Policy (NEP) remained in action.

This linguistic thrive had great impact in defining an Ukrainian identity within the USSR, then, the future happenings were not exempt from the inner political changes in the Soviet Union. Stalin's consolidation in power, after Trotsky's expulsion from the Communist Party in 1927 and Bukharin's in 1929, allowed gradually a change from the former NEP to point for two deep changes in Soviet policies, for industrialization and collectivization.

The years between 1933 and 1938, known as the Great Retreat, had a huge impact on the Soviet population including the Ukrainian territory. To understand the complexity of these policies, it is important to put them in the general political context that prevailed. Usually in Soviet times, as in many other regimes, there coexisted two kinds of policies: hard policies and soft policies and sometimes there were contradictions between them.

Korenizatsiia was part of a soft policy, while the hard-line policies, among other goals, intended to repress nationalist deviations especially in matters that could be a risk for the Soviet National Security. Therefore, while linguistic Ukrainization and *Korenizatsiia* were of considerable political interest, they did not receive the same attention given to other hard policies required. Linguistic Ukrainization in general was a great success, mostly from 1923 to 1932.

Stalin's hold on power increased even more after the Great Purges since 1934. For example, Lazar Kaganovich, someone who could be considered close and loyal to him, had a double role in

---

[475] Ibidem, page 84.
[476] Mykola Skrypnik was a Bolshevik and leader of the cultural Ukrainization. He was appointed head of the Ukrainian Commissariat for Education in 1927 and stayed there until 1933 when he was removed as part of the Stalinist purges.

Ukrainization and in terror campaigns. Therefore, as general secretary of the Ukrainian Communist Party of the Ukrainian SSR, he was promoting both policies.

One consequence of *Korenizatsiia*, even if not planned, was the deepening of a bilingual atmosphere with a pronounced cultural and economic split. Russian would be the dominant language in the economic, industrial and hard-line political spheres while Ukrainian would predominate in the cultural, rural and soft-line political spheres.[477]

> There were signs that a territorial Ukrainian identity was emerging, but this was bilingual and open to adoption by ethnic Russians. It is true that for this new equilibrium to emerge fully, the dominance of Ukrainian in the press, education, and government paperwork would have had to be loosened. However, this would have occurred without the massive 1933 terror. The terror was a response to the political and not the social consequences of Ukrainization.[478]

Besides, the considered foreign menaces against the Soviet Union gave rise to a deep concern by the Soviet foreign policy to acknowledge the risk certain ethnic groups could represent. Therefore, foreign policy requirement would use the label of 'dangerous' ethnic groups in the case of possible foreign threats. Poles, Germans, Finns, Estonians, Latvians, Koreans, Chinese, Kurds and Iranians were in the list. Belonging to these ethnic groups was considered dangerous only when located near a border region but not when located deep inland.[479]

This marked a big shift in the national policy. Even though, it is important to underline that these modifications were always part of a political approach rather than an ethnic ordeal.[480] Moreover, it is worth underlining the differences between the Great Retreat and

---

[477] Martin, Op. Cit., page 123.
[478] Martin, ibidem.
[479] This means that the actions carried out against specific ethnic groups or nationalities was with a political base and not ethnical. In fact, many cases in which these groups were established in the inner regions of the Soviet Union, they would be allowed to normally function respecting their rights for promoting their own local languages and culture and with the possibility to be promoted to a position of authority. Ibidem, page 311.
[480] This argument does intend to justify ethically in any means the massive deportations to which different nationalities within the USSR were subject as part of this power struggle. Note of the author.

the Great Terror. The first one was a fundamental shift in social and cultural policy. The second was a matter of power politics.

Stalinist terror had a deep impact on Soviet society and was not something specifically addressed to the Ukrainian people. Stalin, a Georgian, not Russian, carried out centralizing policies without considering local differences in each region. The goal was to control all aspects of political life and therefore make all possible opposition disappear. NKVD[481] sources claim that as a consequence of the purges, during 1937–1938 around 800,000 people were executed or became victims of the Gulags,[482] including 35,000 sub officials, officials, generals and marshals of the 80,000 that had the Red Army. Other estimates put the figure in the range from 900,000 to 1.2 million. To this extent, Ellman explains the origin of the different estimates including Rosefield's (1.075 million), Wheatcroft and Davies (1.15 million) and the controversial Conquest estimate, which suggested the number of victims to range from 2 to 3 million based on unofficial sources that before Glasnost were the only ones available.[483] Overall, the most accurate estimate for academic purposes remains around 1 million.[484]

Besides those alarming numbers, there was a deep social impact that among other issues brought the disappearance of a considerable part from the local *intelligentsia* and meant the arrival of a new kind of peasants and proletarians that would take their place and create a new kind of *intelligentsia* but this time a more Soviet one.

The Stalinist regime touched all levels of society and it imposed harsh measures in Ukraine and in other nearby territories with the effects of the Great Famine or Holodomor (*Голодомор*) of 1932 and 1933. It was not the first famine under the Soviet period. In fact, there was another between 1921 and 1923; but in that case, a public campaign with the government and the Orthodox Church helped the population to avoid further damage.

Instead, the 1930s had seen the introduction of the collectivization of agriculture. Ukraine was one of the territories more affected,

---

[481] It was the predecessor of the KGB and the initials meant Народный Комиссариат Внутренних Дел.
[482] Ellman, Michael, 'Soviet repression statistics: Some comments,' *Europe-Asia Studies*, Vol. 54, No. 7 (2002), page 1154.
[483] Ibidem, pages 1154–1158.
[484] Ibidem, page 1162.

precisely because of a long tradition of local farms while most of the Russian territories were common property. This is again a political difference in the Ukrainian society rather than ethnic.

The new Soviet policies that replaced the NEP damaged deeply the agricultural production, even though Ukraine was the most productive area, for instance, at the beginning of the twentieth century, and more than 50% of the flour produced in the imperial Russia came from this territory. The effects of the new policies were devastating. Besides the reduction in production, Soviet authorities asked for an even higher increase in the harvest in 1931 making it an unreachable goal. The famine affected mostly the rural population. The impact was disastrous. In a few months, Ukrainian land, known to be very fertile, was the scene of a terrible famine. There is no precise number about the victims but accounts vary from 1 to 10 million depending on the source and on the political intentions. The most accurate account based on demographic statistics comes from R.W. Davies and S.G. Wheatcroft who give a balanced figure of around 5.5–6.5 million in all of Soviet Union with almost 3 million in Ukraine.[485] Others like Robert Conquest increase the toll to 5 million[486] in Ukraine but without the same statistical robustness. Soviet sources mention the regime's attempt to limit the effect of the famine authorizing a total of 320,000 tons of grain, but ocular witnesses have detailed the repression caused by the forced collectivization together with the recollection of all available nourishment during the campaign and the millions of victims caused by it.

Until now, nationalist groups denounce the word 'genocide', but even though it was brutal and intentional, it was an ideological war and not a national one. Other Soviet regions like the lower Volga, Kazakhstan or Kuban also suffered.[487] Besides, many Ukrainian officers participated in the requisitions. There were Ukrainian officials in the NVKD and there were Russian peasants among the victims. Therefore, it was a political but not an ethnic ordeal. It was a mere decision again of power politics. It was the will of the Soviet

---

[485] Davies, R.W. and Wheatcroft, S.G., *The Years of Hunger: Soviet Agriculture, 1931–33*, New York, McMillan, 2004, page 415.
[486] Conquest, Robert, *The Harvest of Sorrow. Soviet Collectivization and the Terror-Famine*, New York, Oxford University Press, 1986, page 306.
[487] Wilson, Op. Cit., page 145.

elite and mostly by Stalin to impose a policy against the peasants, ergo, of one class against another. Curiously, most of the authors that promote the use of the term 'genocide' come precisely from the region of Galicia, which in fact did not even suffer.[488] As Wilson wrote:

> Nationality was of minimal importance to this campaign. The famine was not an intentional act of genocide specifically targeting the Ukrainian nation.[489]

Besides, there is until now a clear political use of the statistics around the famine. For instance, Wheatcroft even accused once former Canadian prime minister Steven Harper of exaggerating by three the total toll number.[490] Historian Timothy Snyder also criticized President Yushchenko for increasing the estimate by three, creating an erroneous perspective of what happened.[491] Instead, nationalist scholars like Roman Szporluk and Bohdan Kravchenko recognize that specific regions from Russia suffered the same way as Ukraine during this period. Altogether, the term 'genocide' would be a mistake.[492] The famine was, then, a cruel Stalinist crime and a deliberated massacre but not an ethnic crime.

Russians did not consider Ukrainians as foreigners from another ethnic group; for them, they were also Russians or very close and belong to the same confederation. Therefore, if it had been an ethnic question, it would be like if Hitler instead of exterminating the Jews would have done the same with the Bavarians or the Saxons. It would make no sense.[493] Therefore, 'the national interpretation

---

[488] Ibidem.
[489] Ibidem, page 305.
[490] 'Harper accused of exaggerating Ukrainian genocide death toll,' Kiev Ukraine News Blog, October 30, 2010, accessed on February 10, 2015. http://news.kievukraine.info/2010/10/harper-accused-of-exaggerating.html
[491] Snyder, Timothy, 'Holocaust: The ignored reality,' Eurozine, June 26, 2005, accessed on February 28, 2016. http://www.eurozine.com/articles/2009-06-25-snyder-en.html
[492] Genocide would be the case of an ethnic group that exterminates another like the Turkish against Armenians in 1915, the Hutu against the Tutsi in Rwanda or the Holocaust itself. In the Great Famine, it was done with a political and ideological finality but not ethnic. Note of the author.
[493] Lieven, Anatol, *Ukraine & Russia, A Fraternal Rivalry*, Washington, DC, United States Institute for Peace, 1999.

then was not a cause of the grain requisition crisis and famine. Rather, it emerged as a consequence of it'.[494]

The famine meant also a diminution of the reduced Ukrainian intelligentsia that existed and the arrival of a new one that included Ukrainians who benefited from the purges and became the new promoted or Выдвиженцы (vydvizhentsy).[495]

Beyond this tragedy, only some years later the arrival of World War II would leave an even deeper impact that would hide partially the impact of the famine. Again, Ukraine was the field of geopolitical interests between two powers, and it was deeply affected. If we consider that the Soviet Union lost 20 million people during the war, it is worth mentioning that at least 6 million were Ukrainian. The 'Great Patriotic War'[496] affected Ukraine more than any other European territory. Many important battles were over Ukrainian territory and the Nazi occupation from 1941 to 1944 represented for the locals a new type of domination until then that had a huge amount of victims.

The German Army arrived with the Barbarossa operation in June 1941. In the West, locals initially received them as liberators but after some time, they proved themselves wrong. After three years of occupation, 70% of the Jews were exterminated. During the occupation, there were two factions under which the population organized either for conviction or survival. In general, most partisan groups organized by the secret soviet police had a lot of success in Central and Eastern Ukraine.

Instead, in the West, nationalist elements related to diverse political parties worked with the German troops against the Soviets. In fact, even an SS division was created almost entirely with Ukrainian population. In the West, the OUN, Organization of Nationalist Ucrainians (Організація Українських Націоналістів, *Orhanizatsiya Ukrayins'kykh Natsionalistiv*) which had appeared during

---

[494] Martin, Op. Cit., page 303.
[495] In this class, the first two Ukrainian presidents Kravchuk and Kuchma belong to this new class, the same as former Prime Minister Lazarenko. Wilson, Op. Cit., page 146.
[496] The denomination 'Great Patriotic War' (*Великая Отечественная Война*) was given by Stalin to call to defend the 'great mother land'. This campaign gave a great result and until today, it is common that most of the post-Soviet population independently of their political position refer to World War II this way with exceptions mostly in the Baltic countries. Note of the author.

the 1920s remerged. This organization pretended to create an independent Ukrainian state but, generally, it failed to attract the population from Central and Eastern Ukraine. In their congress from 1941, they even promised to eliminate Jews from Ukraine, as they were considered loyal to Bolsheviks and Russians while their units promised to give the Ukraine state a rebirth with cooperation with the National Socialist Germany. The 'Nachtigall' Battalion fought together with the Germans and was the first unit with foreigners to become part of the SS, in this case with elements that belong to the ONU. In Galicia, there was another SS division with the name of SS Galicia.

Another partisan group, instead, organized against the Soviets was the Ukrainian Insurgent Army, known as UPA,[497] from their initials in Ukrainian, which included members from Galicia and Volhynia and were like the armed forces from the ONU. In fact, once Soviets had retaken control of the Ukrainian territory they had to fight against UPA members for some years after the war.

UPA received in the after-war period aid from the CIA and the British MI6 even if not in sufficient amounts to continue resistance against the Soviets. This movement, allied sometimes with the Nazis, came also to West Ukraine and portrayed the differences in political perception depending on the region.

Altogether, the level of devastation on the Ukrainian territory was huge. For every village destroyed in France or in Czechoslovakia, there were 250 destroyed in Ukraine. One-sixth of the population perished and 2.3 million went to labour camps in Germany. Around 16,000 industrial factories were destroyed together with 28,000 collective farms.[498]

Besides, more than 2 million Ukrainians fought in the Red Army against only 90,000 in the Ukrainian Insurgent Army (UPA). Soviet propaganda had been very specific in each region, and in the Ukrainian cases, it went with slogans like 'Slavic people to the battle' that pretended to push for a Pan-Slavic Union.

---

[497] President Victor Yushenko proposed that ex-UPA warriors should be taken into account as war heroes, proposition that was met with a big refusal from a great part of the population.
[498] Subtelny, Op. Cit., page 480.

Therefore, the massacres of the Great Patriotic War masked the horrors of the Great Purge and forced collectivization. This way the Ukrainians sided in most cases with Soviets except in Galicia. The war created the myth of liberating armies that fought the Nazis. The events brought a completely different historical narrative about the war for the population of central and Eastern Ukraine than to the one from Galicia and other Western territories. This division can also be seen in the current political class, while still many people today have relatives that fought with the Red Army against the Nazis and consider them heroes.[499]

Altogether, there is a notable fact that appeared after the war. The world conflict allowed for the first time, since the Union with the Czarist Empire, the unification of all the current Ukrainian territories, this time as part of the Ukrainian SSR. After the war, there was a need to amalgamate the territories, rebuild all the destroyed industrial and production activities and to include the new portion of territory that became part of it, including Galicia.

Therefore, industrial modernization signalled an economic recovery while the Greek Catholic Church became outlaw,[500] to eliminate any possible traces of the Polish occupation. Besides, and maybe without wanting, the after-war arrangements between Stalin and Western Powers included that Polish population would be deported within the new Poland borders. Therefore, the Polish presence in Ukrainian territories ended for the first time in more than five centuries, allowing locals then for the first time an autonomous development of the Ukrainian identity without Poles.

The arrival of Khrushchev in the period known as 'The Thaw' and his report to the 20th Congress of the Communist Party of the

---

[499] A very different situation occurred in Latvia and Estonia, where locals do not perceive Soviet as liberators but as occupants. In fact, the parliamentary decisions to remove after-war monuments dedicated to Soviet soldiers brought a vivid reaction by the numerous ethnic Russian population. Le Temps, June 7, 2006. There are even people in Latvia that still honour each year the Latvian Legion that fought with the Waffen-SS. 'Why does Latvia still honour the Waffen-SS?' March 16, 2012, accessed on February 28, 2016. http://www.newstatesman.com/blogs/the-staggers/2012/03/latvia-riga-waffen-european

[500] What happened in fact was that some priests were convinced by the Soviets to organize a group that would denounce the Union of Brest and break with Rome and then reunite with the Russian Orthodox Church. Subtelny, Op. Cit., page 488.

Soviet Union[501] marked the start of the de-Stalinization. Ukraine's role grew in different USSR organs with the Ukrainian culture and language gaining more recognition. That allowed one to consideor, as one scholar mentioned, the notion of 'Second among equals'[502] in relation with the other republics. This notion of junior partner allowed many Ukrainians to rise to the highest levels of the party and the government.

Altogether, to encourage this relation in 1954, and to celebrate the 300 years of the Pereyaslav Treaty, Crimea was a 'gift' from the Russian SSR to the Ukrainian SSR to celebrate the 'everlasting union' between Russians and Ukrainians. Once again, inner borders changed to respond to the internal dynamics of Soviet politics without considering ethnic or linguistic boundaries.

The 1950s and the 1960s were years with a great economic growth around the world. In this case, the after-war decades brought a notable increase in the workers' income that just in Ukraine increased by 230% between 1951 and 1958. Consumption also increased and for those that had lived during the famines and the war, the difference was notable together with the improvement of services at all levels. Altogether, Ukrainian role was considerable: It accounted for 40% of the iron, 34% of the carbon and 23% of the agricultural products of the Soviet Union.

Besides, as Subtelny said: 'Certainly there was less reason to complain about the Soviet System in the Khrushchev years than during the Stalin era.'[503] There were no mass arrests, purges and terror tactics and that for the Soviet population meant a lot.

Therefore, when Nikita Khrushchev lost the leadership of the Communist Party in 1964 as part of the power struggle in the USSR

---

[501] Khrushchev's report from February1956 known also as the 'Secret Speech' was the starting point of the condemnation of the Stalinism. He surprised many of the presents at the Great Hall of the Kremlin when he condemned Stalin and his crimes and begun a new era that ended with the precedent terror. That meant 'the all-encompassing fear and the paralysis of creativity that characterized the Stalin period eased considerably.' Ibidem, page 500.
[502] Referred by Subtelny Orest, Ibidem, page 499.
[503] Subtelny, Ibidem, page 506.

at least, the biggest contribution, in his own words, was that the terror was over. 'The fear is gone, and we can talk as equals. That's my contribution. I won't put up a fight.'[504]

The sixties and the seventies also saw the increased role of the Soviet Union in the international scene and at all levels. For the average Soviet citizen, this was a period in which the continuous achievements of the regime in sports, culture, politics or science were a reason to be proud. Ukrainians accepted the Soviet regime as their legitimate government and identified themselves with it. Stalinism or the Great Patriotic War remained in the collective imaginary and brought a sort of passive acceptance. Soviet Ukrainians usually took pride from the USSR prestige and the improvement of the social system, access to social education and the high mobility. Altogether, the high level of state propaganda increased this acceptance.

There was a high social mobility among the USSR from one republic to another. Ethnic Russians were half of the Soviet population; it occurred that in many cases the number of Russians that arrived increased. Most of them arrived in Donetsk, Dnepropetrovsk, Kharkov and Zaporozhe, while ethnic Russians constituted 21% of the population that lived in the Ukrainian territory with 30% of mixed marriages in the cities. Ethnic mix was something common, even more so between Russians and Ukrainians.

East Ukraine became even more Russified and more industrialized and the linguistic division, which was already present, increased. This division reinforced the stereotype within the USSR, associating the Ukrainian language and culture with the countryside while the city dwellers and the ones from the economic, politic and scientific elite associated modernity with Russian. Ukrainian was something related with collective farms, local habits, etc., similar as it was during the czarist era. Meanwhile, the political profile of Ukraine outside the Soviet Union was very low.

Besides, a new approach in the nationality policies had been evolving to arrive at the commonly known Дружба народов (Druzhba narodob), which can be translated as Friendship of the Peoples. Therefore, after a first phase, in the twenties that pretended to

---

[504] Khrushchev's words quoted in Taubman, William, *Khrushchev: The Man and His Era*, New York, W.W. Norton & Co., 2003.

build national elites, the second phase strived more to understand nationalism as part of the Soviet nation. At the end, the idea of the friendship of the peoples was an imaginary Soviet community as Terry Martin said:

> The Soviet turn toward primordial nationality, then, was not intentional. It was the result of unforeseen consequences of the original Soviet nationalities policy combined with the affinity of primordial ethnicity with broader Soviet social processes such as the statist cult of the popular.[505]

Brezhnev's regime also meant a gradual deterioration of the standards obtained in the former decades and by the end of the seventies it resulted in widespread economic and social stagnation in Soviet society.[506] The deteriorating conditions were notable in every Soviet Republic. Meanwhile, the Soviet constitution from 1977 preserved the existence of the national republics and the national identities while Russian became 'the language of friendship and cooperation of the peoples of the Soviet Union'.

There was also another interesting aspect, increased urbanization; for instance, in 1959 there were 25 cities in Ukraine with more than 100,000 inhabitants and by 1979 there were 46. This increased the already mentioned bilingual dimension of the Ukrainian SSR but also created 'a highly educated, bilingual nationally conscious, and largely urban population whose very existence ensured the survival of Ukrainians and their evolution into a distinct and viable nationality'.[507]

These were some of the most notable changes until the eighties when the hand of Mikhail Gorbachev brought a new air of reforms to the Soviet state and, without intending, led to its disappearance in the subsequent years. The following events brought the unexpected and sudden independence of Ukraine.

2.2.2 Different attitudes towards independence

Glasnost and Perestroika brought a new opportunity for nationalities to express themselves. As it happens in many parts of the world, when an economic and social stagnation is present added with many signs of social discomfort, nationality becomes a usual refuge

---

[505] Martin, Op. Cit., page 451.
[506] Magocsi, Op. Cit., page 659.
[507] Idem, page 665.

from which to create a political base. In this sense, the Soviet Union in general and the Ukrainian SSR were no exceptions.

In the Ukrainian scenario, different political actors appeared. Among them, there was Ukrainian Writers' Union that reunited writers that pushed for a wider use and teaching of the Ukrainian language. In addition, several political forces appeared and represented a breakthrough in the monolithic political activity common in the Soviet regime. Among them, there was the emergence of Rukh, which stands for Народний Рух України (Narodnii Ruh Ukraini), that called for the rebirth and comprehensive development of the Ukrainian nation.[508] In 1989, Rukh did not call for independence, but rather for the transformation of the Soviet Union into a union of sovereign states, similar to Gorbachev's proposal months later. Later, it tried to copy the model that nationalist parties adopted in the Baltics, but it only managed to build a notable political base in Western Ukraine. Another opposition group, maybe the more effervescent anti-Soviet, was the Ukrainian Helsinki Union, dominated by former political prisoners. These two focused mainly on the national question. Another one was from the Democratic Platform within the local Communist Party that was a Rukh crossover and another was from the independent trade unions after the miners' strikes in the Donbas in 1989.[509]

Among these opposition groups, sometimes there were few elements in common. The miners' movement in the Donbas, even though it became strong, was extremely local and was part a reminder that the people from this area considered themselves part of a different identity.[510]

Besides, there was also the return of the Greek Catholic Church, which received permission to register its parishes in 1989, ending with the prohibition from force since the late forties.[511] The same happened with the Autocephalous Orthodox Church, which increased the division present among the Orthodox Patriarchies.

Moreover, an important element that had played a big role and still does today is the diaspora, a Ukrainian diaspora, mostly located

---

[508] Magocsi, Op. Cit., page 670.
[509] Wilson, Op. Cit., 157.
[510] Idem.
[511] Magocsi, Op. Cit., page 671.

in Canada and the United States but with presence in Brazil, Argentina, Western Europe and Russia, one of the best organized politically.

Altogether, the end of the eighties brought a rebirth of the political life together with the weakening of the Soviet state. The first elections that allowed political opposition in the Soviet Ukraine showed from the beginning the deep differences that have been portrayed in the earlier pages. Rukh would have expected to have the same results that nationalist groups obtained in the Baltic states. Instead, they got a big share of 108 seats out of 450, still far away from a majority. The Communist Party got 239 seats; even though the number was higher, some defections began almost immediately after the elections. Besides, the democratic platform got 28 deputies and there were many independents.[512]

> The elections confirmed that Ukraine was still a highly regionalised country. The population remained divided by ethnic, linguistic and religious differences and by the variety of historical experiences of the regions in which they lived.[513]

Therefore, the trajectory for independence was completely different from the one in other ex-Soviet republics. It is true that there was a dissatisfaction with the Soviet regime but on the other side this did not transform itself into a will to build an independent state. To this extent, Wilson added:

> The word revolution hardly fits at all. Events had been enormously accelerated between 1989 and 1991, but then choices made in haste can quickly be set in stone. There was only a limited transcendence of the historical divisions between the Ukraine represented by Rukh and a deeply disoriented Soviet Ukraine. As such there was little momentum to carry forward after 1991, and no all-powerful independent movement like the Vietcong, capable of shaping the new state in its image. The old guard were still in charge, a little dazed perhaps, but still perfectly capable of looking after their own interest.[514]

The same *nomenklatura* was always in power, the political divisions present could not allow the achievement of independence without including the local ruling class. It is interesting to note the changing moods of the Ukrainian electorate in the two referenda held in the last year of existence of the Soviet Union. First, on March 17 with a

---

[512] Wilson, ibidem, page 160.
[513] Ibidem, page 161.
[514] Ibidem, page 171.

83% turnout, people voted yes to the question: 'Do you consider necessary the preservation of the Union of Soviet Socialist Republics as a renewed federation of equal sovereign republics in which the rights and freedom of an individual of any nationality will be fully guaranteed?'.[515] The votes in favour were 71.48%, therefore, supporting Gorbachev's proposal for a new Union Treaty. This meant a complete support to the Union even though in different conditions. Even though, it is worth mentioning that in the referendum Kravchuk[516] added a second question mentioning a union of Sovereign states which also got the vote yes in 80.2% of the cases. In fact, few people understood the difference. The second question wanted to create a marge of manoeuvre for eventually a treaty with more attributions to the republics or even independence, even though the word was not mentioned at the beginning. Besides, in Galicia, that included the Lvov, Ivano Frankovsk and Ternopol regions, there was also another referendum about complete independence that was received obviously with a huge support from the locals in the region. Therefore, it seemed as if the independence push was only regional and would not succeed to create a national movement like in the Baltics or in Georgia.

Meanwhile, going back a little bit to a geopolitical topic, the United States acknowledging the turmoil happening in the USSR had advised against secessionist movements within the Union. They preferred to deal with a single and weak Soviet state than 15 unpredictable new political entities that potentially could count on nuclear armament, as until that point, there had not been discussions on that matter yet. After the famous speech given by George Bush, on 1 August 1991, in Kiev, Ukrainian nationalists and Rukh members later criticized the fact that he openly summoned Ukrainians to stay within the Union.

---

[515] Nohlen, D., Grotz, F. and Hartmann, C. *Elections in Asia: A Data Handbook*, Vol. I, 2001, page 492.
[516] Since July 18, 1990, Leonid Kravchuk had become chairman of the parliament in substitution of Volodymir Ivashko. Note of the author.

Americans will not support those who seek independence in order to replace a far-off tyranny with a local despotism. They will not aid those who promote a suicidal nationalism based upon ethnic hatred.[517]

Liberals considered it a treason, but the United States still had not outlined a policy in which Ukraine would play a separate role from the Soviet Union, even though, once the Soviet crumbled, all that changed suddenly. Therefore, those words, and the speech written by Condoleezza Rice, were extremely calculated and gave preference to the good relation present with Gorbachev at that moment. The failed coup in August orchestrated against Gorbachev accelerated the local response in many Soviet Republics. Leonid Kravchuk had at the beginning a completely ambivalent attitude towards the coup, neither of condemnation nor support.[518]

After the denunciations against the Communist Party of the Soviet Union everywhere, Rukh proposed a vote for independence in the parliament and gathered support from some deputies of the Communist Party; therefore, this created the momentum to call for a vote on 24th August and a call for a referendum that occurred on December when the moods had changed drastically. The same people that had approved a new treaty of the Union massively this time voted for independence with a 90% support and nobody campaigning against it.

As in many other Soviet republics, this was a move of political survival. To change so nothing changes, pure 'gattopardismo'[519] in Giuseppe Tomasi's terms. Therefore, Kravchuk took the opportunity presented by Rukh and the nationalists to acquire more power. The referendum in fact served to have presidential elections the same day in which Kravchuk won with almost 62% of the votes and, far away in second place, Rukh's candidate Viacheslav Chornovil with 23.3%.

---

[517] Kranish, Michael, 'Bush says Ukraine should accept loose union with USSR,' *The Boston Globe*, August 2, 1991, accessed on February 28, 2016. http://highbeam.com/doc/1P2-7671451.html
[518] Wilson, Op. Cit., page 166.
[519] I retake the name of the novel from Giuseppe Tomasi, *The Leopard*, in which he acknowledges how the local ruling class in Sicily adapts to stay in power after all the political changes during Italian unification. The term 'gatopardismo' comes from the ones that think it is necessary that something changes so as to everything remains the same. Note of the author.

During the arrangements between Kravchuk, Yeltsin and Shushkevich, mentioned in the first chapter, Yeltsin only needed to get rid of Gorbachev's authority and was willing to make any concessions in that regard. Besides, being drunk for most of the meeting, the outcome could come only in beneficial terms for Kravchuk and Shushkevich, meaning in practice a full break with the Kremlin.

Therefore, as other Soviet republics, Ukraine had found itself independent without really looking for it, as Andrew Wilson named it on his book *The Ukrainians, Unexpected Nation*. Now, they had to confront a more difficult task and that was to build a state in the middle of an economic chaos.

2.3 Kravchuk: Trying to build a state in the middle of chaos

As in Russia, there was the need to build a new polity in Ukraine, added that the political and economic conditions were even more complex. Ukrainian politics had not existed on its own for centuries and the patterns appeared after the Soviet collapse became also a representation of the ethnolinguistic divisions present in the territory. Besides, to build a nation state in that political context with the same elite in charge became a challenge. At least, as some authors consider, the fact that the same group remained in charge avoided a violent transition and ethnic conflicts as in other Soviet republics. There was no ethnonationalist model in the Ukrainian case. Here, it was the same ruling elite, which adapted to the circumstances, and used sporadically an alliance with Rukh to rule. Therefore, there was no political transition.

Nonetheless, without transition appeared neither the fight nor the struggle proper of state building. Ukraine had found its independence without even looking for it and in hands of the same cadres that used belong only some months before to the Communist Party of the Soviet Union. It was all a matter of pragmatic politics for the political survival of the elite. There was a need to establish a new system of social relations that could be pointing to become a new state. It was urgent a new kind of social pact to make all the people that were living in the former Ukrainian Soviet Socialist Republic to feel themselves part of the new polity and recognize themselves in it.

State-building process is always complicated and it has been very difficult in different regions of the world. The same way after the Italian unification there was one famous phrase 'Abbiamo Fatto l'Italia, ora bisogna fare gli italiani',[520] in the Ukrainian case, there was a need to create the idea of statehood and nationhood or even multinational statehood.

As the following quote notes a state cannot be created by decree: 'States are not created or destroyed, or frontiers are drawn or obliterated by arguments or majority votes; nations are freed, united or broken by blood and iron.'[521] Therefore, if the political steps were not taken to assure and promote the building of a new polity, the new political entity would be very weak.

Ukraine was in a complex situation in which most of the population was under a kind of shock in which practically somebody decided for them a sudden and dramatic political change. The same way as in ex-Yugoslavia, locals could not become easily used to the idea from one day to another that instead of Yugoslavian citizens they belong to a different political entity. Here it was a case with a territory where the 73% of the population was ethnic Ukrainian, more than 21% Russian and notably Hungarian, Romanian and Tatar minorities present, among others. Many of them were used to being Soviets, and the Ukrainian language was not a unifying factor as happened with the local language in other ex-Soviet republics.

Kravchuk noticed this aspect and in fact, only two of the first four Ukrainian prime ministers were ethnic Ukrainians and only one Ukrainian speaker. He noticed that without support from the Donbas elite, he could run the risk of a kind of a Pridnestrovian scenario

---

[520] It is not clear who said the original quote, as there are sources that attribute it to Massimo d'Azeglio, others to Cavour or to Ferdinando Martini. I do not pretend to look for the original source but I pick up the political message that after the Italian unification there was the need to build the idea of nationhood and a state. Accessed on February 15, 2015. '1861. L'Italia unita fanalino di coda rispetto all'Europa,' March 10, 2011, accessed on February 28, 2016. http://www.corriere.it/unita-italia-150/11_marzo_10/de-cesare-italia-unita-fanalino-coda_13e7441c-4b22-11e0-9e9a-b429a0ac9415.shtml, 'Massimo d'Azeglio,' accessed on February 28, 2016. http://it.wikiquote.org/wiki/Massimo_d%27Azeglio

[521] Garnett, Sherman W., 'The integrationist temptation,' *The Washington Quarterly*, Vol. 18, No. 2 (Spring 1995), pages 40, quoted in Kuzio, Taras, Ukraine Back from the Brink, European Security Study No. 2, Institute for European Defence and Strategic Studies, MCP Litho Ltd., 1995, page 8.

in southeast Ukraine. It seems, by the way, the current government that took office since 2014 did not learn that lesson even though the current conditions as we shall see are rather different.

The need to consider the regions to avoid separatism became also important. Crimea had already declared independence in 1992 and the process of the reincorporation back into the Ukrainian polity was part of a hard negotiation with the locals but mostly with Russia.

'Kravchuk therefore obtained the support of local elites in key areas such as the Donbas and the Crimea by giving them a share of the financial benefits of independences as well as agreeing to continue without major changes to the pre-independence chain of command and distribution of power.'[522] This way, Kravchuk played both sides, by giving the minimum necessary to the nationalist in Rukh while also looking for alliances with the Donbas.

Religion also became a factor, the creation of the Ukrainian Orthodox Church, or to be more precise, the appearance of their own patriarch became a reason of conflict because many parishes also continued to be loyal to the patriarch in Moscow. Besides, the role of the autocephalous Orthodox Church that for a moment seemed could be united with the Kiev patriarchate brought the existence of three different Orthodox Churches in the territory, plus the already present Greek Catholic Church in the West.[523] Therefore, during the next decade, the devotees of the Orthodox faith found themselves divided, with 69.5% belonging to the Orthodox Ukrainian Church that followed the Moscow Patriarchate, 22% that followed the Orthodox Ukrainian Church with Patriarchate in Kiev, 7.7% that followed the autocephaly church with a patriarchate in the United States and 0.8% belonging to others.[524]

The government had to deal with the urge to build new institutions like a ministry of defence, the Ukrainian Central Bank and also a tax collection entity and system that were non-existent. In that

---

[522] Kuzio, Taras, '*Ukraine Back from the Brink*,' European Security Study No. 2, Institute for European Defence and Strategic Studies, MCP Litho Ltd., 1995, page 9.
[523] Boyko, Natalia, 'Eglises orthodoxies et identité nationale en Ukraine postsoviétique,' in *L'Ukraine dans la Nouvelle Europe*, edited by Lepesan, Gilles, Paris, Espaces Milieux, CNRS Editions 2005, pages 84–92.
[524] Ibidem, page 87.

sense, the account by the first Ukrainian Minister of Defence, Kostiantyn Morozov, is revealing.[525] He explains how from having nothing, not even office or personnel, he had to start building a defence policy while the Red Army was not willing to cede any material resources to the new Ukrainian Army. Among the tasks, establishing a new army was required to define the future status of all the nuclear weapons stationed in Ukrainian territory or the future of the Black Sea Fleet.[526] Both issues were part of a complex negotiation and were settled already during Kuchma's presidency, while the country was at this point also in the middle of an economic stagnation that required more attention.

The case of the division of the Black Sea Fleet took more than five years to find a solution. It shows the complexity of the situation, in which on the one side, commanders chose allegiance either to Russia or Ukraine almost randomly but allowed the local officers to present themselves in a position of force. At this point, when the armed forces do not recognize any authority and become themselves another force it only shows a lack of state authority on both sides.

Kravchuk with Leonid Kuchma, as prime minister, made the necessary reforms to transform Ukraine into a centralized government. They started nominating presidential representations for all the regions. Therefore, until now, the regions in Ukraine even though they had their local parliaments had a governor nominated by an authority in Kiev that had been either the president or the prime minister depending on the period.

Besides, there was a need to create a new central bank and a currency. For some years, some kind of coupons, named *Karbovanets*,

---

[525] Morozov, Kostiantin, *Above and Beyond, From Soviet General to Ukrainian State Builder*, Harvard, Harvard Ukrainian Research Institute Publications, 2001.
[526] The process of creating a Ukrainian Navy and more specifically the division of the Strategic Black Sea Fleet was more complex. Initially both governments agreed on an interim treaty establishing a Russo-Ukrainian fleet under bilateral command. This proved complex to handle as commanders also chose each to swear allegiance to the country of their preference. Besides, many officers became a separate power claiming that the fleet could not be separated. Therefore, the situation remained unsettled during Kravchuk's presidency. Zaborsky, Victor, 'Crimea and the black sea fleet in Russian-Ukrainian relations,' discussion paper 95-11, Center for Science and International Affairs, September 1995.

were in circulation to replace the Soviet rouble but they were subject to the hyperinflation present. Afterwards, the Hryvnia entered into circulation until 1996.

Inflation was very high and by 1993, it reached 5,371% (other sources calculating 10,200%). Only Serbia's inflation was higher in those transition years.[527] By 1996, the GDP was half that of 1991, and by 1998, it was only 41%. Only after the first half of 2000, real growth reappeared. Whole sectors of productions disappeared and investment declined or stopped.

Economic reform did not start as quick as in Russia and there were high levels of corruption and black activity. Wage arrears of several months were the norm at all levels and, for example, they represented 6.3% of the GDP in 1998.[528] Besides, the arrival of new 'Biznezmeni', as were called the new dealers that were regularly murdering one another, made Ukraine one of the most corrupt countries in the world. Wilson said:

> Powerful economic interest groups operated beyond the control of the state, or themselves controlled the state, and were robbing the country blind—left largely untouched by the 'Grand Bargain' negotiated during independence and Leonid Kravchuk's stability of cadres' policy.[529]

A huge humanitarian crisis appeared altogether. Population declined from 52.2 million in 1992 to 49.3 in 2000. Meanwhile, average life span decreased from 66.1 to 63.5 for men in March 1995. Average daily calorie intake declined by 23% and the industrial output has dropped by half since 1990.[530]

There was an urgent need to build a sort of Ukrainian economy, but that was simply impossible. In addition, how can a national economy be created in the middle of globalization and with neo-liberal policies? This time, it was not 1917. Ukraine was no longer a self-sufficient rural economy relatively immune to trade disruption, and dismantling the highly integrated Soviet industrial economy would have to be a slow and careful process. People had as a sole option to look for survival as part of an informal economy. Besides,

---

[527] Wilson, Op. Cit., page 254.
[528] Idem, page 255.
[529] Idem, page 256.
[530] Kuzio, Op. Cit., page 24.

with all the black market, money outside the banking system was 25% in 1995 and 49% in 1998.

Instead, domestic policies only served to empower Ukraine's elites to take benefit of their position. The new business groups did not produce merchandises but became private circles for the appropriation of public goods. Therefore, a weak state (to avoid saying non-existent) proved an easy prey for more powerful interests.

Besides, Ukraine made a late start on economic reforms compared to what happened in Russia, so capital concentration was three years behind in that sense. The most powerful economic interests were still semi-dependent on the state and on its still wide range of administrative powers in 1998. It created big corporate interests around public figures that laid the bases for the development of a different kind of oligarchs than the ones present in Russia already during Kuchma's administration. In this sense, it is interesting to note how Wilson considers the Ukrainian type of oligarch that emerged during that decade as much closer to the Indonesian type rather than Russian or Latin American oligarchs.[531]

Besides, local politics were far from the left-right system common in Europe. The electoral system allowed single constituency seats in which elected members bargained their position to the best dealer. This practice is common even now. In a territory where people did not have the habit of participating in elections, the scene became more complex.

In those years, for instance, the national communists and Rukh made a sort of alliance to rule the country since 1992; therefore, Rukh was not in the opposition anymore and had some ministries while Kravchuk kept the most important positions for his group. Kravchuk used a nationalist speech when needed and limited it when required. He did not compromise with a position and proved himself very pragmatic. That way he managed to divide Rukh.[532]

---

[531] Wilson, Op. Cit., page 265. To that extent, Wilson may refer as how in the Latin American or Russian cases, the oligarchs emerged as outsiders that just benefit from political contacts, bribing the political elites. Instead, in the Ukrainian or Indonesian cases, the same political elite sponsored the emergence of the oligarchs, while they became a political force of its own with its own political parties. The Latin American cases would be very heterogeneous to classify it in just one kind. Note of the author.
[532] Wilson, ibidem, pages 174–175.

Something comparable to left political forces managed to organize itself as a strong opposition in the first years. A Socialist Party appeared guided by Oleksandr Moroz, while the Communist Party was headed by Petro Symonenko. The Socialist Party took example from the European social democracy while the Communist Party included new faces that remained after the events of 1991. They were both cadres with second-grade positions, but once the leaders left the party, they took those places.

These parties benefited themselves from being at the opposition during a great economic crisis. The communists were very different from the Russians. They pretended to establish good relations with Russia and to go back as much as possible to the structure that existed during the Soviet Union including all the social guarantees. They were the first majority in the parliament after the 1994 and the 1999 parliamentary elections and that fact allowed them to become a huge pressure for the government that had to consider them in many issues, even though the representation of the parties had a clear attachment also to regional preferences. Altogether, the instability proper of the first years brought a continuous dispute between the parliament and the president, but they did not arrive at a breaking point as in Russia.

The socialists tried to distance themselves from the Soviet errors and tried to present themselves with a different façade. The Communist Party, the Socialist and the Rukh were the only ones that functioned in the parliament as a party while there were a big number of 'independents' that would change from parliamentary block depending on the case. The 1994 parliamentary elections established several blocks that forced Kravchuk to negotiate with each of them separately.

Meanwhile, Leonid Kuchma emerged as a political actor, first as a prime minister but with his own agenda. He was only in charge from 1992 to 1993 and left the post in the middle of a huge economic crisis while his call to make economic reforms was the starting point to distance himself from Kravchuk and start campaigning for the presidency.

The parliamentary election of 1994 required that in each of the districts participation would be above 50%; that way, many precincts did not achieve the required minimum and went to further elections. The Communist Party was the first political force with 86 deputies but out of a total of 450. The other groups that managed to constitute themselves as fractions did not cross 20 members in congress. There were 168 independents and 112 vacant constituencies.[533] Political blocks appeared but they changed frequently during the duration of the legislature.[534]

That same year, in 1994, presidential elections took place and they have many particularities. First, Kravchuk sought re-election against the former prime minister Leonid Kuchma. The former made an alliance again with the nationalists while the latter did a campaign urging for economic reforms. It became also a presidential election, in which the ethnolinguistic borders were also present on how people voted. Therefore, the western part of the country voted for Kravchuk and the southeast for Kuchma. In the first round, Kravchuk obtained 38.4%, Kuchma 31.8% and Oleksandr Moroz 13.3% of the votes.

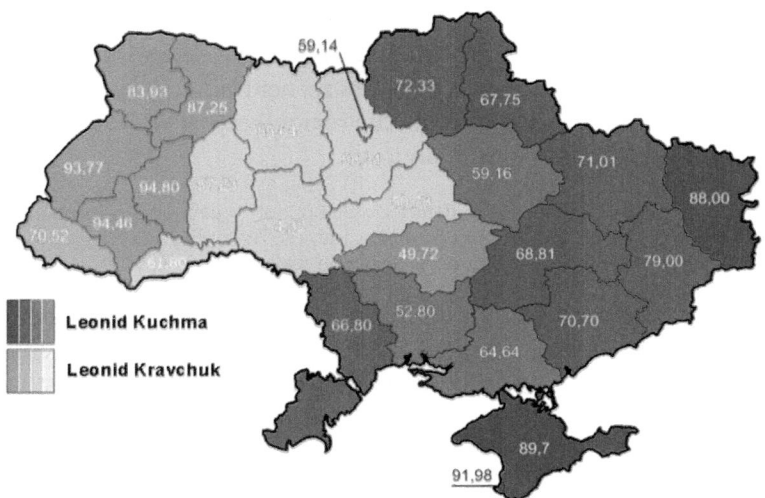

"Ukraine presidential elections: 1994 second round," accessed on February 28, 2016.
Source: Wikimedia Commons, licensed under CC BY-SA 3.0
(https://creativecommons.org/licenses/by-sa/3.0/)

---

[533] Wilson, ibidem, page 183.
[534] 'Політичні партії України у взаємодії зі структурами влади,' accessed on February 16, 2015. http://analitik.org.ua/ukr/publications/joint/3dd12dea/3dd13f15/

After Moroz decided to support Kuchma together with the Communist and the Socialist Parties in the second round, he won with 52.3% of the votes against 45.2% from Kravchuk.[535] This made Kuchma become the second president of Ukraine. It was also the first time in the CIS, in which a president coming from the Soviet regime lost an election and stepped aside peacefully.

Next to the events in Russia one year before, when Yeltsin ordered to bomb the parliament, this seemed like a good sign that a transition was possible without bloodshed. Even though, if we analyse carefully, the fact is simply that the elements of power had been slipping out from Kravchuk's hands while Kuchma became stronger, both were at the end of the same regime of the Soviet Union.

Foreign policy

In foreign politics, Kravchuk's presidency focused on a policy of neutrality. Meanwhile, the Western world noticed again the importance that Ukraine would have to contain Russia; while for the Russian part, the risk that Ukraine would take side with the West became a cause of concern.[536] Therefore, neutrality, at least in those years, proved itself handy while the region kept its strategic role in the global scene as Wolczuk noticed:

> The emergence of an independent Ukraine not only redefined the geography of the region it also introduced new stakes into the reckoning and fundamentally challenged the hitherto long-established regional security norms.[537]

On 19 January 1993, a group from the socialist deputies together with the managers of the most important industries pressed Kravchuk to sign a new CIS treaty that he considered as a restoration of the Soviet Union. Even though Ukraine never became a full member of the CIS it tried to balance its position with the West, from which they received big sources of financial aid while also

---

[535] 'Вибори-99: Кучма і КПУ – знову разом!,' May 15, 1999, accessed on February 28, 2016. https://web.archive.org/web/20140923002907/http://www.day.kiev.ua/uk/article/podrobici/vibori-99-kuchma-i-kpu-znovu-razom
[536] Subtelny, Op. Cit., page 598.
[537] Wolczuk, Roman, *Ukraine's Foreign and Security Policy*, 1991–2000, New York, Routledge Curzon, 2003, page 4.

keeping a stable relation with Russia, considering the possible risks present.

One of the worries for Russia, the United States and Western countries was that Belarus, Kazakhstan and Ukraine should not emerge as nuclear powers. President Kravchuk felt justified in using nuclear weapons as a bargaining chip to obtain greater Western attention, security assurances and financial compensation. He started the negotiations that were later finished during Kuchma's presidency, the negotiation regarding the Black Sea Fleet. All those issues were part of a complex relation with Russia in which Ukraine pretended to keep above all territorial integrity. He refused to participate in a common currency or armed forces within CIS and promoted the Guidelines for Ukraine's foreign policy, which was approved by the parliament on 2 July 1993.[538] This document advocated the creation of an all-embracing national system of universal and all-European security and the participation in it as a basic component of its security.

Hence, it is noteworthy how englobing different European countries became a foreign policy choice without becoming anti-Russian and without recurring to NATO or the United States. It was a wise political and geopolitical decision, a pan-European choice that pretended to maintain Ukraine's sovereignty. It is true that Russia was not in a strong position by then, but also it was neither a foreign policy that could be perceived as a menace for Moscow, as the concept pan-European left open the option for anyone. It was also the only starting point available to the future administration to negotiate for the status of the nuclear arsenal, the Black Sea Fleet and also the status of Crimea which still at the end of Kravchuk's administration pretended to become independent or part of the Russian Federation.

At the end, with a little bit of more than two years and a half, Kravchuk's presidency represented an attempt to build a new Ukrainian polity. He pushed to break with Moscow after the failed coup against Gorbachev and managed to defend CIS more as a light institution without real powers, which allowed members of the

---

[538] 'Periods of the foreign policy of Ukraine,' Pak-Ukraine Trade and Culture Information Centre, accessed on February 28, 2016. http://pakukrainec entre.com/fpou.htm

USSR to become independent countries. His decision together with Yeltsin's incapacity (or his alcoholism) to propose any other solution to overcome the authority of the Soviet Union allowed Kravchuk to become with a great support the first president of Ukraine.

Afterwards, a complex power struggle, lack of institutions, economic stagnation and social deterioration made it impossible to push for the establishment of a new polity that could defend its sovereignty at the international scene. Besides, Kravchuk left the bases to constitute a new elite, which until now was the de facto real power that managed to control most of the strategic assets in the country. Within this elite, I refer to the new appeared oligarchs.

2.4 Kuchma: The emergence of the oligarchs

Liberal scholars tend to perceive the change from Kravchuk to Kuchma as a successful transition from one government to another. A simple case in which the opposition candidate won and the ruling and defeated candidate accepted his defeat and ceded his post. Reality would be rather different. Leonid Kuchma and Kravchuk were members of the same Soviet bureaucracy. The former was a member of the Communist Party of the Soviet Union also and through his ranks made a political career. At the end of the 1980s he was already a fierce critic of the party. Besides, he was chief manager of the Yuzmash factory, an industrial complex in Dnipropetrovsk, in charge of manufacturing space rockets, satellites and agricultural equipment among other equipment. There, he managed to build a network with the industrial area in Eastern Ukraine and had a solid base that allowed him to become member of the Rada, first in 1990 and again in 1994.

After the Soviet collapse, he became the prime minister and increased his power, thanks to his links precisely with the Donbas, it was this rebirth of the region politically that allowed him to run for president with great initial support. Kuchma was as pragmatic as Kravchuk and both belonged to the same regime. The difference was that Eastern Ukraine regained importance in relation with the reforms that were to take place, and this allowed the elite in power to prefer Kuchma rather than Kravchuk. Until this point, no transition had happened in Ukraine, it was always the same political class that was ruling, but this time with Kuchma pretending to accelerate economic transformation.

Economic transformations meant to privatize a great variety of public assets in different sectors. It meant the government would decide the which and how and for how much each privatization would be, allowing Kuchma not only to select the beneficiaries but to benefit himself from them. Several personalities acquired great wealth during this period. After the resignation of Vitaliy Masol as prime minister and then of Yevgen Marchuk, Pavlo Lazarenko held the post from May 1996 to June 1997 and became one of many names that allowed building great fortunes around privatizations.

For example, Ukrainian companies did not give annual reports by then or information to the press about their situation. United Energy Systems turnover was 1.5 million USD before its main sponsor, Pavlo Lazarenko, became prime minister in 1996. In 1996–1997 turnover was as high as 3 billion. UES paid 11,000 in taxes while Lazarenko accumulated 72 million in Swiss bank accounts.

Watching closely, all the oligarchs who appeared during Kuchma's presidency had links with the regime that allowed them to amass fortunes in a very short term. Victor Pinchuk, for instance, got married to Kuchma's daughter who became owner of the telephone company Kievstar. Pinchuk until now is the second richest man in Ukraine. By that time, the so-called group of five became notorious: Oleksandr Volkov, Hryhorii Surkis,[539] Ihor Bakai,[540] Viktor Pinchuk and Vadym Rabinovych.[541]

Other oligarchs would follow afterwards and built their fortunes during Kuchma's term. Rinat Akhmetov,[542] Dimitry Firtash, Ihor

---

[539] Hryhorii Surkis was the president of the Ukrainian Football Federation until 2012 and is one of UEFA's five vice-presidents. His brother Ihor is chairman of the football club Dynamo Kiev. In 2008, he and his brother were considered owners of a fortune of $926 million. 'Суркис Григорий Михайлович,' April 14, 2015, accessed on February 28, 2016. http://file.liga.net/person/284-grigorii-syrkis.html

[540] Ihor Bakai was head of the State Accommodation Department and played a considerable role in the privatizations. After the fall of the Kuchma regime, he escaped to Russia and has not come back.

[541] Wilson, Op. Cit., page 265.

[542] Rhinat Ahmetov became the richest man in Ukraine through his properties in the carbon industry and arose to become the most influential personality during the next decade according to the journal *Korrespondent* above then president Yushchenko, Prime Minister Yanukovych and the head of the

Kolomoyskyi, Serhiy Tyhipko and current president Petro Poroshenko are part of that list. Most of the oligarchs made their fortunes in the energy sector and metals as well as machine-building and food industries. The degree of profitability depended on the preferential treatment they would receive from the government. Besides, public energy companies like Interhaz and Naftohaz had links with Kuchma from his days as head of the giant missile factory.

Heiko Pleines explains very accurately four developmental phases during the arrival of the Ukrainian oligarchs:

1. From the end of the 1980s until the mid-1990s, the oligarchs acquired their start-up capital and their first company shares.
2. Spanned to the second half of the 1990s, some of the oligarchs' holding companies disappeared when their political connections lost power (like Timoshenko); others managed to expand.
3. The end of the 1990s saw the stabilization of the surviving holding companies and the incipient economic upturn led to the rise of several new names.
4. Around 2002, the oligarchs developed strategic preferences and invested in vertical integration and modernization. A number of holdings became increasingly integrated in the global economy. As a result, the holdings of the oligarchs formed one of the most productive parts of the Ukrainian economy. They started to enter the EU market not only as exporters but also as investors. As a result, their economic interests were diversified away from Russia and they started to promote closer economic cooperation with the European Union.[543]

Phase number 4 will be mentioned later, but until now, it was a struggle in which the ones with better political connections made fortunes very quickly.

For instance, 'In the sphere of trade activity, metals could, for example, be purchased on the Ukrainian market at subsidised prices and then sold abroad at world market prices. The profit margin was as high as 900%.'[544]

---

parliament, Oleksander Moroz. 'TOP 100,' Korrespondent, Kiev, Number 32(221). August 17, 2006.

[543] Pleines, Heiko, 'The political role of the oligarchs,' in *Ukraine on Its Way to Europe, Interim Results of the Orange Revolution*, edited by Besters-Dilger, Juliane, Peter Lang, New York, Frankfurt am Main 2009, page 104.

[544] Ibidem.

Ukraine 209

In the banking sector, the National Bank would give credits to different banks below the interest rate; then, these banks would lend the money to customers at the usual interest rate and would keep all the interest for themselves.[545]

In the energy sector, two factors allowed the individuals close to the government to amass huge fortunes, even though Ukraine did not produce a lot of energy, besides a considerable amount of the local gas for its own consumption. One was the strategic role Ukraine played in the transit for all the gas that arrived at Europe from Russia and Central Asia and second, the local distribution allowed the possibility to accumulate huge fortunes. Oil, for instance, went directly to private distribution monopolies, which received the concessions from the government. Gas instead was distributed by regional monopolies while a national gas company was kept so production would be under the Ministry of Energy. One clear example in that sense was the enrichment of Iulia Timoshenko. She created with her husband and Oleksander Gravetsas the Ukrainian Petrol Company with the help of Pavlo Lazarenko and in 1995 reorganized it as United Energy Systems of Ukraine. At that moment, Lazarenko had become deputy prime minister for energy and negotiated gas supplies with Russia and Turkmenistan. They bought gas from Gazprom and then redistributed it through Ukraine in a scheme in which the bills were highly inflated by different oligarchs. By 1996, it was the biggest trading gas company in Ukraine and invested in other sectors like banks, metallurgy and machine building and even an airline besides investing in pipelines abroad in Turkey and Bolivia. The company's turnover in 1996 was $10 billion with profits of $4 billion.[546] When Lazarenko became prime minister, numerous accusations against him and mostly differences with Kuchma forced him to resign. By then, Iulia Timoshenko had already become a member of the parliament and enjoyed immunity.[547] Both Lazarenko and Timoshenko were under numerous accusations of corruption, monopolizing gas trade and even in Lazarenko's cases of

---

[545]   Ibidem.
[546]   Rutland, Peter, *The Challenge of Integration, Annual Survey of Eastern Europe and the Former Soviet Union*, New York, East West Institute, 1998, page 172.
[547]   Ibidem, pages 173–174.

misusing $2.7 million to restore his dacha. After the accusations, both Lazarenko and Timoshenko used their own media to defend themselves. The difference was that the latter preferred to negotiate with Kuchma and the accusations remained in the air while Lazarenko fled and the Rada voted to waive his immunity.[548] According to the United Nations, he looted more than $200 million from the government of Ukraine before he was sentenced in the United States for fraud.[549] The sudden fall of Lazarenko and the accommodation of Timoshenko in the opposition reflected also that Kuchma did not want to let any other possible political rivalry to rise against him.

Meanwhile, the economic situation only became worse while Kuchma prepared for the 1999 presidential election. By then, foreign reserves hit a low point in 1999 and foreign debt increased from zero to 38% of the GDP by 1998. A fund of social protection controlled by Oleksander Volkov had more than a billion and a half US dollars to spend for Kuchma's campaign. Besides, the Russian oligarch, Boris Berezovsky,[550] contributed $150 million to protect his investments in Ukraine.[551] At the end, Berezovsky's participation became a constant and later he was accused of contributing also to Viktor Yushchenko's campaign.[552]

Altogether, many similitudes could be found between the events in Ukraine and Russia during the 1990s, in either the political or economic sphere. At the end, Kuchma was not so different to Yeltsin in his relation to the new oligarchs, how he treated the opposition and in the use of media or the way of conducting politics. As Wilson

---

[548] Even Transparency International considered him one of the 10 most corrupt leaders of the last decades. 'World's ten most corrupt leaders,' accessed on February 29, 2016. http://www.infoplease.com/ipa/A0921295.html

[549] Kravets, David, 'Former Ukrainian PM sentenced for fraud,' The Associated Press, August 25, 2006, accessed on February 16, 2015. http://www.washingtonpost.com/wp-dyn/content/article/2006/08/25/AR2006082500897.html

[550] At that point, he was still a key figure with close links to the Kremlin while Yeltsin was still in power. Finally, after Putin arrived to the presidency and the oligarchs started to be pressured, he escaped to the United Kingdom.

[551] Dubrova Irina, Kharismatiki y Ortodoksy, Novoe vremia, July 26, 1999. Quoted in Wilson, Idem, page 202.

[552] 'Пан Березовский вершит историю Украины,' September 15, 2005, accessed on February 29, 2016. http://lenta.ru/articles/2005/09/15/money/

said: 'The common soviet heritage has led to similar patterns in the exercise of powers emerging in both states.'[553]

There was a great mistrust within the population towards political parties. In 1999, there were 71 parties in Ukraine but with only 350,000–400,000 people affiliated to any party. The amount was equal to less than 2% of the voting population. A survey in 1995 showed that only 31.2% believed in the existence of a multiparty system and only 8.8% would like to give power to any of the ones present. That showed a great mistrust in the political system and in the Kuchma Government.

The 1999 election results were until now the only ones that were not under an ethnolinguistic base as the others. This proves again the volatile mood of the Ukrainian electorate. These elections had also a greater amount of irregularities than before including how Kuchma's allies picked up lots of funding to be paid off afterwards by the government.

Once starting his second period, Kuchma nominated Viktor Yushchenko as prime minister and Iulia Timoshenko as vice prime minister. Yushchenko tried to apply neo-liberal reforms without having a strong relation with the different clans and that way he became more valuable to the West. Some authors consider that Kuchma only wanted to use the prestige he obtained while head of the Ukrainian Central Bank to obtain a better negotiation with the IMF. Instead, Timoshenko used her position to accumulate resources to build herself an image as an opposition figure. In that sense, Kuchma's political platform was kind of a 'catch all' that took elements from the left, the liberals or as Wilson considered, it was a period in which the government worked by default.[554]

There was a struggle between clans for power. The lack of clarity but mostly the scarce possibility for the West to influence inner events made them important to sustain Yushchenko once he became the prime minister. In any case, it allowed the appearance of a new opposite bloc with Yushchenko, Timoshenko, the Socialist Party and eventually turned them and the communists against Kuchma. Altogether, maybe without knowing it, Kuchma created

---

[553] Wilson, Op. Cit., page 199.
[554] Wilson, Idem, page 206.

the conditions for what would become the polemic 2004 presidential election. This kind of 'an opposition bloc' was present in the 2002 parliamentary election.

The parliamentary election of 2002 had brought the arrival of 'Our Ukraine' as a new political force headed by Victor Yushchenko. His party obtained 111 seats[555] in the elections but did not manage to obtain enough support to force a majority in his favour. Therefore, the recently created party of regions and allies managed to barely obtain enough votes in the parliament (236 out of 450) to promote Victor Yanukovych as prime minister since November 2002. Meanwhile, the Communist Party remained as the second party in number of votes and received more than 20% of the ballots.

Altogether, during 2003, internal politics had regrouped by one side most of the oligarchs around the Party of the Regions and its allies meanwhile at the opposite side, Victor Yushchenko with clear Western support and the Ukrainian diaspora in alliance with oligarchs that had been excluded from Kuchma's exclusive circle. This included names like Iulia Timoshenko or Poroshenko that had also been part of the political establishment and had lost for different reasons their positions of power. Therefore, it became more convenient for them either economically for keeping their own assets or politically to adopt Western-oriented political views.

---

[555] Even if as usually happens in Ukrainian politics, the number of members of the parliamentary fraction changed and by 2005 it had diminished to less than 50.

Ukraine 213

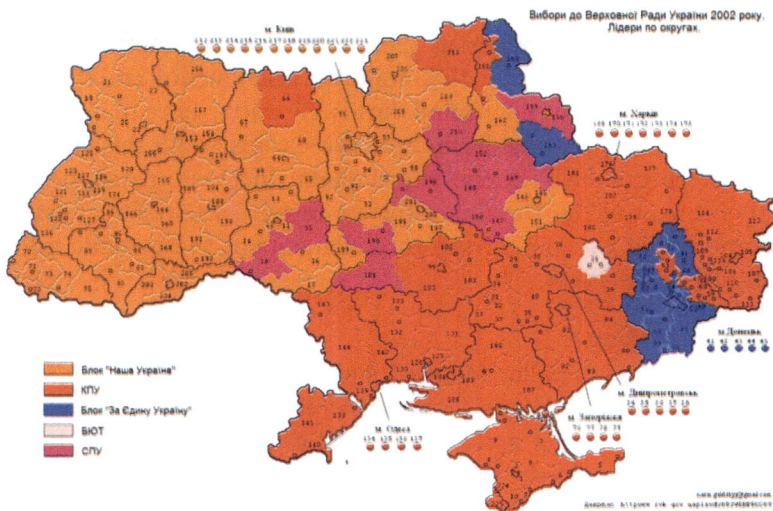

Map downloaded from Ukrainian parliamentary election, 2002. "Ukrainian parliamentary election 2002," accessed on February 29, 2016.
Source: Wikimedia Commons, licensed under CC BY-SA 3.0
(https://creativecommons.org/licenses/by-sa/3.0/)[556]

Meanwhile, the position of the Communist Party and the Socialist Party diminished their presence and they were forced at best to seek alliance with each of the different sides of the conflict but with fewer possibilities of obtaining power.

Besides, the regime still was capable of buying the loyalty of different members of the congress during that period to ensure a favourable majority, in fact, after the 2002 parliamentary election until $500,000 could be offered for a defection.[557]

By then, the political role of the oligarchs had increased even more. First, they had acquired mass media to influence the public opinion, and, second, they built an informal network with the political elite and then they themselves took public office.[558] Mostly, by

---

[556] The former figure shows how Our Ukraine in Orange became the leading political force in the West while the Communist Party was the leading party in almost all the eastern regions except Donetsk while the Socialist Party was the leading force in Poltava. "Elections of people's deputies of Ukraine," accessed on February 29, 2016. http://www.cvk.gov.ua/pls/vd2002/webproc0e

[557] Wilson, Andrew, *Ukraine's Orange Revolution*, London, Yale University Press, 2005, page 65.

[558] Pleines, Op. Cit., page 108.

this time, the oligarchs were organized into three clans, the Donbas Clan with Rinat Akhmetov as the most important representative, the Dnipropetrovsk clan with Kolomoiski and Pinchuk and then the Kiev clan with Medvedchuk and Surkis. By 2003, more than 50% of the economic elite came from these three clans.[559] All this extreme empowering of the oligarchs contributed to increase greatly the disappointment of the Ukrainian society towards the political establishment and was one of the core elements of the polemic 2004 presidential election.

Foreign policy

Kuchma's foreign policy followed a similar line as Kravchuk's but with some notable changes. He was inclined towards neutrality and a multivector foreign policy that could assure a peaceful relation with Russia and slowly deepen relations with Western powers. The period in which Kuchma arose to power still presented a weak Russian Government that had not managed to establish a sustainable foreign policy while the country was in the middle of a political and economic crisis; therefore, Ukraine was able to seek different ties with the West at the same time.

In that context, the first topic concluded under his government was related to the nuclear arsenal. Therefore, Ukraine abandoned its nuclear stock and in exchange, it received assurances from Russia, the United Kingdom and the United States. Those assurances appeared in the form of a memorandum[560] signed on 19 December 1994, which specified that the three nuclear powers would respect independence and sovereignty of Ukraine and the existing borders. Assistances were offered through the United Nations and seemed like the guarantees were established to recognize territorial integrity. Taras Kuzio considers that even though those were not guarantees legally binding because they are in the form of a memorandum,[561] these 'security assurances' supported Ukraine's territorial

---

[559] Ibidem.
[560] 'Memorandum on security assurances in connection with Ukraine's accession to the treaty on the NPT,' December 19, 1994, published February 6, 2014, accessed February 29, 2016. https://www.msz.gov.pl/en/p/wiedenobwe_at_s_en/news/memorandum_on_security_assurances_in_connection_with_ukraine_s_accession_to_the_treaty_on_the_npt
[561] Kuzio, Op. Cit., page 30.

integrity and independence, at a moment in which Russia was also in a chaotic situation and would have found itself difficult to act in a more assertive way.

During his inauguration speech, Kuchma referred to Ukraine as one of the leaders of the Euro-Asian integration, even though he continued to follow a two-faced foreign policy, mostly because of the economic benefit that he could gain from the West. For instance, by 1996, Ukraine was the third largest recipient of US aid after Israel and Egypt, and replaced Russia as the largest one in the CIS.[562] This shows how the United States understood the geostrategic importance of the country, and consequently, attempted to pull Ukraine by different means into the Western orbit. During Kuchma's visit to Washington in 1996, he met also with the heads of the IMF and the World Bank and announced that the IMF had agreed to begin negotiations for a new three-year loan of $3 to $4 billion.[563] Besides, he managed to obtain another credit of $2.3 billion from Western countries as financial aid for the costs of closing down the Chornobyl nuclear plant.

Another thorny issue was regarding the Black Sea Fleet. In 1997, Kuchma managed to agree on the partition of the Fleet with Russia, establishing two independent national fleets and dividing armaments and bases. The agreement included to lease most of the bases until 2017. It also arranged for Russia to take 81.7% of the Black Sea Fleet and Ukraine the remaining 18.3%. Meanwhile, it gave Russia the right to maintain 25,000 troops, 24 artillery systems, 132 armoured vehicles and 22 military planes on the Crimean Peninsula.[564]

Afterwards, during his government, Kuchma also signed the Partnership and Cooperation Agreement with the European Union with a modest framework that entered into effect in 1998 with a duration of 10 years. In 1997, the first Ukraine-EU Summit took place

---

[562] Nahaylo, Bodan, *The Ukrainian Resurgence*, Toronto, C. Hurst & Co. Publishers, 1999, page 501.
[563] Ibidem, page 502.
[564] Ukrainian version of the Partition Treaty on the Status and Conditions of the Black Sea Fleet signed on May 28, 1997. 'Угода між Україною і Російською Федерацією про статус та умови перебування Чорноморського флоту Російської Федерації на території України,' May 28, 1997, accessed on February 29, 2016. http://zakon4.rada.gov.ua/laws/show/643_076

in Kiev. The second summit of that kind took place in 1998, and it was mentioned for the first time that Ukraine would like to acquire associated membership of the EU.[565] The subsequent summits in 1999 and 2000 brought no big changes in relation with the EU. Even though the fact of becoming an associate member of the EU had been mentioned, no specific steps were taken in that direction, and there were only promises of increasing cooperation.

During his second period in office, he showed a weak foreign policy and during that time the EU-Ukraine Summits obtained few results, making the then EU Commissioner for Enlargement Gunter Verheugen to say that 'a European perspective for Ukraine does not necessarily mean membership within 10 to 20 years.'[566] In fact, the enlargement of the 2004 and 2007 were so complex to the EU to swallow that to think of the possibility of another one with a country with more than 50 million people depicted it clearly needed further discussions among members.

After re-election in 1999, Leonid Kuchma had also to confront a scandal that troubled his stay on power and therefore meant a reposition in relation with Russia. The 'Cassette scandal'[567], also known as the *Gongadze affair,* caused Kuchma's popularity to drop below 9%. The ongoing protests made him also change his foreign policy preferences. The scandal brought about huge demonstrations against Kuchma and a general mood that he should leave office. Western countries reduced their support to Kuchma and therefore the then new Russian president Vladimir Putin offered backing.

From this point, Kuchma gave preference to relations with Russia even without losing the ties with the EU and the United States.

---

[565] 'EU-Ukraine summits: 16 years of wheel-spinning,' February 28, 2013, accessed on February 29, 2016. http://ukrainianweek.com/Politics/73494

[566] Gressova, Maria, 'Ukraine-possible new member state of the EU with post-transition economy—and the EU' in Collection of Papers from the 1st PhD Students' International Conference 'my PhD,' Friedrich Ebert Stiftung, Slovakia, 2007, page 115.

[567] The Cassette scandal was an event that happened after the disappearance of the journalist Georgiy Gongadze. His body was found beheaded and weeks later tapes were presented by Oleksandr Moroz, part of the opposition on 28th November 2000 in which it was heard how Kuchma was ordering to kidnap Gongadze.

He supported the invasion in Iraq by US forces and even contributed with Ukrainian troops to the mission,[568] which ensured that the *Gongadze affair* would not be a problem at least in relation with the United States.

Regarding relations with other CIS countries, in 1997 GUAM appeared as a consultative forum between Georgia, Ukraine, Azerbaijan and Moldova. During Kuchma's period, it tried to be just an alternative forum to deal with different subjects including energy, transport, trade and security among others. The fact is that the new organization had a clear geopolitical goal and therefore received a clear support from the West. Its origins go back to a meeting between Kuchma and President Aliyev of Azerbaijan in October 1996. There, they discussed the potential role of Ukraine in the transportation of Caspian oil. Afterwards Ukraine, Azerbaijan and Georgia signed an agreement to create a transport corridor between Europe and Asia during the same days that Xavier Solana, and then NATO General Secretary undertook a tour of the Caucasian region.[569]

Altogether, the organization became a source of worry for Moscow, after the idea that Turkey may join, which would mark the entrance of a NATO member in alliance with countries of the Near Abroad, and with most of the Black Sea at their disposal. Uzbekistan announced their plans to join GUAM in 1999, afterwards many CIS members refused to sign the CIS Collective Security Treaty; therefore, it seemed by then, Moscow had not been capable of stopping the pace of integration of this forum that also opposed some of the functions that were part of the CIS. Besides, an agreement had even been made to initiate negotiations for the creation of a free trade area and even pretended to encourage Romania to join, which by then was more interested in joining the EU. Altogether, during this period, GUAM (or GUUAM)[570] facilitated Ukraine in its goal of avoiding further integration within the CIS.[571]

---

[568] 'Operation iraqi freedom,' accessed on February 15, 2015. http://c21.m axwell.af.mil/iraq.htm#willing
[569] Wolczuk, Roman, *Ukraine's Foreign and Security Policy*, 1991–2000, New York, Routledge Curzon, 2003, page 148.
[570] The extra U in the initials refers to Uzbekistan that abandoned the organization in 2002. Note of the author.
[571] Wolczuk, Op. Cit., page 155.

GUAM's organizational structure[572] established since its first summit a council of heads of state, a council of ministers of foreign affairs and seven working groups together with an economic forum related to the Secretariat in Kiev together with a parliamentary assembly and a working group related to cooperation between GUAM and the USA.[573]

One of the geopolitical goals of the organization was clearly to regroup former Soviet countries without Russia but with US support. Even though the changing political situation in member countries did not allow it to succeed to achieve any degree of deeper integration, even if it proved to be convenient to handle issues as the situation in Pridnestrovia, Nagorno Karabagh or other conflicts related to the post-Soviet space. In 2002, Uzbekistan announced that the country was leaving the organism and by the last years of Kuchma's government, GUAM had lost the original impulse it had enjoyed, maybe also because a reinvigorated Russian foreign policy in the region had appeared.

The last two years of Kuchma in power showed him to be more dependent on the one side on Russian support for political survival and on the other the Western governments, waiting for the presidential election in which an alliance formed with Victor Yushchenko.

For instance, the EU-Ukraine summits of 2003 and 2004 brought few changes to strengthen the relation between both EU and Ukraine. During the seventh summit in 2003, Ukraine only obtained the status of neighbourhood country within the European Neighbourhood Policy and through the eight summit in 2004; Kuchma did not manage to obtain a cooperation plan while the EU showed that was willing to cooperate only within this policy. The then president of the European Commission Romano Prodi even commented that 'This policy is not linked with membership—this issue is as yet not in the agenda.'[574]

---

[572] 'GUAM organizational structure,' accessed on February 29, 2016. http://guam-organization.org/en/node/269
[573] 'GUAM-USA framework programme,' accessed on February 29, 2016. http://guam-organization.org/en/node/291
[574] 'EU-Ukraine summits: 16 years of wheel-spinning,' February 28, 2013. http://ukrainianweek.com/Politics/73494

Meanwhile, Kuchma had to depend even more on the support from the oligarchs mostly regrouped in the Party of Regions. By that time, Rinat Akmetov established himself as the main figure[575] among the oligarchs related to the Donbas and Eastern Ukraine. Consequently, it became a need for them also to find a candidate that could represent them and replace Kuchma who could not run for re-election and had since the Gongadze affair kept his popularity very low.

Therefore, the oligarchs representing the Donbas economic elite chose Victor Yanukovych[576] as their candidate, the same person that had been functioning as prime minister and that would assure Kuchma a peaceful transition and guarantee for his entourage.

At this point, the local political struggle for presidential succession was not exempt at all from the geopolitical struggle present to have influence over Ukraine. Vladimir Putin's position was well established in the Russian presidency and he was pushing for a more assertive Russian foreign policy in the Near Abroad. Meanwhile, the United States and the EU members had found in Victor Yushchenko a candidate that could allow them to pull Ukraine to the Western orbit of influence. It is curious, though, to note how in both cases, both Russia and the United States supported candidates that came from the same political establishment that had been ruling Ukraine. The only difference was in the kind of links they had built in the last years.

In that sense, the last two years of Kuchma's term saw not only the lack of a strong foreign policy but instead Ukraine being again a prey to foreign policies from Russia, the United States, the EU and some of its members. Therefore, inner politics became a hostage of

---

[575] Even if Rinat Akhmetov was the most visible of the oligarchs, thanks to the ownership of the Football Club Shaktor Donetsk, others like Dimitry Firtash, Ihor Kolomoyskyi or Serhiy Tyhipko had also great leverage and all of them controlled a considerable group of congressmen besides owing TV channels and media that could be used for political pressure in their benefit. Note of the author.

[576] Victor Yanukovych had served as Vice-Head and then Head of the Oblast Administration of Donetsk—a position in which he cultivated close relationship with Rinat Akmetov which allowed him to become prime minister with only 234 votes on November 2002. 'Политическая карма Виктора Я,' June 10, 2005, accessed on February 29, 2016. http://www.from-ua.com/articles/7569-politicheskaya-karma-viktora-ya.html

this struggle that used also the ethnolinguistic divisions present in the territory.

Altogether, Kuchma thought that he could overcome the risk of losing the election by controlling the Central Electoral Commission and managing to guarantee the result he wanted for Victor Yanukovych. Therefore, the 2004 presidential election became strategic as much for the United States as for Russia that wanted to have an influence on Ukraine. Several issues worried the involved actors. The Russians needed urgently to renegotiate a deal to use Sevastopol as a base for the Black Sea Fleet. Besides, any Ukrainian approach to NATO would be a serious threat for their national security. The outcome of the new assertive Russian foreign policy made it also imperative for Western countries to have more influence in Ukraine and to improve ties with NATO. Besides, the just enlarged EU with 25 members on 2004 included Poland that pushed also for a more assertive presence of the EU in the presidential election. Altogether, there was a notable change in the EU-Ukraine relations after the enlargement.

All those elements became evident in the events that in the West were portrayed as the 'Orange Revolution'.

2.5 Yushchenko: The myth of a revolution

The 2004 presidential election in Ukraine and the events that followed were the first of many clashes between the West and Russia after the fall of the Soviet Union to determine the sort of future Ukrainian territory should have. In any case, it was not the Ukrainian people to decide even though they got involved. It would be simplistic and erroneous to explain the events of 2004, just as a fight for democracy against an authoritarian regime. It is true that a considerable sector of the Ukrainian society was tired after more than a decade of crisis and economic failure in the country. The decline of the living standard and the former Soviet welfare while watching how an elite became richer while depriving the country of their resources was part of the natural outrage against Kuchma's regime. All this while, corruption was visible at all levels of the government. But, this inner discomfort was not exempt from the geopolitical struggle already present. Therefore, the interested actors precisely took advantage of this scenario and of the ethnolinguistic divisions present in the territory. In fact, social discomfort in a failed state can become an easy prey for foreign interests to canalize a determined political project like in the Ukrainian case as occurred in the other colour revolutions.

Altogether, the magnitude of the events made it difficult for any candidate to compete in the presidential election independently from the geopolitical struggle present. That fact reflects until this point the failure to build the minimal foundation for an independent and sovereign Ukrainian polity. Therefore, local elites in different ways also searched for foreign support to obtain an electoral victory at all costs.

It is noteworthy that each candidate represented mostly one ethnolinguistic side of the population in the Ukrainian territory while they also represented two geopolitical projects with two slight different economic models. Viktor Yushchenko as head of the Ukrainian Central Bank and as a prime minister was a fervent defendant of neo-liberal policies and pretended to apply them in Ukraine as he had tried while being prime minister. Meanwhile, Yanukovych, as the representative of a clan, the Donbass clan, sustained the idea of building a sort of 'Ukrainian national capitalism'.[577] That meant to protect the investments of national investors, in this case the oligarchs, so foreign investment would not make profits in favour of transnational companies that were mostly of US and Western European origin.

Therefore, the election between Yushchenko and Yanukovych represented a struggle first on how capitalism should be organized in Ukraine, second about the geopolitical orientation of the Ukrainian polity and third, it used the ethnolinguistic and religious divisions present to campaign for either one or the other candidate in the ballots.

Altogether, even though Yushchenko had a great support in Western Ukraine, the inner alliance with Iulia Timoshenko together with the support of another dissident oligarch, Petro Poroshenko,

---

[577] It is worth to note that even if Yanukovych did not push openly for neo-liberal policies in his speech, his idea of a national capitalism was strictly related to the well-being of the oligarchs and their interests. That meant to allow them not to pay taxes, to block any concurrence in their areas of interests and when needed, to promote 'free trade'. Note of the author.

brought to the campaign considerable electorate from Central Ukraine, which is less influenced by an ethnolinguistic vote. This area together with a great sector of the local *intelligentsia* reflected an anti-Kuchma or even anti-establishment tendency more than a tendency to actually support Yushchenko that campaigned with a liberal platform.

There were 26 registered candidates for the presidential election but since the beginning, it was clear it was going to be a fight only between the two strongest contenders: the still prime ministers Yanukovych and Yushchenko. Besides, there was the candidate Oleksandr Moroz, who had been a notable figure in the opposition and Petro Simonenko from the Communist Party. There were some minor candidates like Natalia Vitrenko, who were only there to play the game for Yanukovych and tried to divide the opposition. But, their role was minimal at the end.

Kuchma had envisioned promoting a constitutional reform to run for a third term but it was not possible. At the end, he had to accept the will of the oligarchs and Yanukovych's candidacy while another oligarch, Tihipko, became chief of campaign.[578] Therefore, with a not very charismatic candidate they started the campaign while Russian political advisers helped to design the promotion. It is worth mentioning that those same campaign advisers were tempted by Poroshenko to join Yushchenko's campaign as Wilson described.[579]

On the other side, Yushchenko received a clear support not only from the diaspora but also from the United States and other Western governments that supported his campaign by different means. Therefore, the election became more like a clash between Russia and the West in which each side invested in their own candidate. US support arrived through different means—first, by the National Endowment for Democracy and the International Republic Institute, the National Democratic Institute and USAID. There were several programmes to finance ONGs during the campaign, and a programme to help build 'independent' media in the CIS also supported the opposition.

---

[578] Wilson, Op. Cit., page 84.
[579] Idem, page 88.

Ukraine 223

In fact, it is interesting to note the allocution before the US Senate of John E. Herbst when he was going to be confirmed as the next ambassador in Ukraine after having served in the same role in Uzbekistan. There, he stood for the need to help Ukraine to democratize and join the euro-atlantic community and he would do whatever possible to assure that; the presidential elections in 2004 would occur in good conditions precluding a strong US involvement in the process.[580] The comment about the fact by Camille Gangloff seems quite precise.

> Cela pouvait paraitre paradoxal, puisqu'il était alors encore en poste en Ouzbékistan, ou les standards internationaux en matière d'élections étaient loin d'être respectés, preuve une fois encore que des intérêts autres que la démocratisation peuvent entre en jeu.[581]

Besides, there was the support from the Ukrainian diaspora in the United States. The funding was clearly visible but it would be difficult to calculate the amount in terms of economic support because there were numerous private donors that contributed. Moreover, Yushchenko's wife was from the diaspora herself and a former employee of the US State Department and during the Reagan presidency, she was the administrations' ethnic affairs liaison in 1988. This raised numerous suspicions on the Russian side and gave more elements to Yanukovych's campaign to portray Yushchenko as a strong pro-US candidate.

Both candidates played their game dirty just with different means. Yushchenko pulled a small group of oligarchs that had been excluded from the other clans. This group included the already mentioned Petro Poroshenko that owned the Channel 5 and a huge chocolate and candy industry that earned him the nickname the Chocolate King. Besides, there was Evgenii Chervonenko who used to smuggle caviar[582] and then became a businessman close to the Kuchma regime where he was an adviser to President Kuchma and afterwards became Yushchenko's chief of security during the campaign. Another name was David Zhvania, of Georgian origin, who

---

[580] Gangloff, Idem, page 97.
[581] Ibidem.
[582] Ibidem, page 63.

with common acquaintances with Boris Berezovsky owned the energy company Brinkford based in Cyprus, but was later accused by Yushchenko of collaborating for his poisoning in September 2004.

Altogether, Yushchenko also gave roles to several players of the Kuchma circle. Meanwhile, in media the campaign was portrayed as a battle between the West and the East. For the Russophones in the East, NATO's menace, extreme Ukrainization and Yushchenko's links to the West were shown during the campaign for Yanukovych. Instead, Yushchenko's side campaigned more against Kuchma's corrupt regime and the need to establish reforms and push for more 'democracy', an easier electoral argument to sell, mostly for the changing electorate of Central Ukraine.

PORA, an ONG that copied the model of OTPOR in Serbia had also a considerable role. Its members were trained with foreign counselling, and the organization disappeared as quickly as it had emerged some months after the election. Even though PORA's members always denied receiving US support, there were indicative signals of the strong US link. Altogether, USAID assistance to Ukraine was $70,490,000 in 2002, $23,950,000 in 2003 and $30,880,000 in 2004.[583] Meanwhile, NED provided more than $240,000 for projects to mobilize Ukrainian youth to vote and only $100,000 in 2004 alone.[584] Besides, George Soros foundation also gave notable support to different NGOs and years later Boris Berezovsky was found to have donated $21 million to the opposition in Ukraine.[585]

On the opposite side, Kuchma dedicated also a big amount of public resources to help Yanukovych. Besides, most of the oligarchs belonging to different clans cooperated. Mostly the Donbass Clan with Akhmetov but also the ones from Dnipropetrovsk helped to finance the campaign. At the end, all of them had deputies in their side and were expecting a huge stake as a payback if Yanukovych

---

[583] 'US assistance to Eurasia,' fiscal years 2000–2004, SEED Act implementation report 2002–2004, quoted in Gangloff, ibidem, page 47.
[584] Ibidem, page 160.
[585] One year later, after he felt he had not received in return what he expected, he decided to make public the support given during the election. 'Berezovsky's funded revolution,' November 12, 2005, The Independent. http://www.independent.co.uk/news/world/europe/berezovsky-funded-revolution-514948.html

would become president. In addition, there was considerable Russian support that arrived through different channels after Russian oligarchs that sympathized with Yushchenko had been encouraged by the Kremlin not to sustain him. Moreover, Russian TV that was seen by most Ukrainians campaigned actively for Yanukovych and even the Russian magazine *Profil* claimed that Vladislav Surkov who was then Kremlin's chief of staff authorized personally $50 million.[586]

Altogether, it would be difficult to account which side contributed more money, whether the United States and allies or Russia but at the end, the undeniable fact is that there was an election with huge foreign spending to influence the outcome. That is purely geopolitics and not democracy at all. Meanwhile, Ukrainian voters were trapped in the logic of a failed state with marked ethnolinguistic divisions and did not manage to build different political options independent of the geopolitical struggle while there was also a considerable dissatisfaction against Kuchma's regime and the deteriorating living conditions in the last decade. Something similar would happen in 2014.

Afterwards, during the campaign, there was also the famous poisoning episode, in which Yushchenko ingested dioxin during a September 2004 meeting with SBU officers that caused him to be hospitalized for several weeks and left him with visible scars on his face. This event increased Yushchenko's popularity after he survived and it became evident that somehow Kuchma was behind the act. As it became known later, the scheme was organized by Medvedchuk, Deputy Prime Minister Andri Kluiev and one of the Russian political technologist Glev Pavloski.[587]

Another element during the campaign was the Orthodox Church. It heavily campaigned for Yanukovych. As mentioned, the Orthodox Church in Ukraine is divided between those who follow the Kiev's patriarch and Moscow's patriarch. The latter campaigned heavily in favour of Yanukovich. Yushchenko was also orthodox but from the Kiev patriarchate.

---

[586] Barinova, Maria, 'Проект Россия,' November 22, 2004, accessed on February 17, 2015. http://www.profile.ru/archive/item/45597
[587] Ibidem, page 100.

Besides, Kuchma foreseeing that it would be difficult to obtain the results he wanted set the bases to arrange for election. During the first round, the turnout was increased so as to help increase the numbers of the candidate from the Donetsk clan. Altogether, different actors contributed to the effort, so Kuchma and the oligarchs could have the desired score.

> The key powers at election time were the local governors, who since 1994 had been directly appointed by the president (Kuchma), and the Territorial Election Committees (TECs), nearly all of which were controlled by the authorities via the 'technical candidate' method.[588]

Even though during the election they had to make up their own figures, as Wilson shows, 'Administrative resources failed to deliver a fake vote in line with their fake polls.'[589] Instead, the small candidates like Vitrenko, Kinah and Jakovenko that were supposed to take votes from Yushchenko 'were not allowed' to get votes in the Donbass and other areas of East Ukraine. Altogether, after the first round, a slight lead stayed for Yushchenko; meanwhile Oleksandr Moroz came third and the leader from the Communist Party, Petro Symonenko, performed poorer than before and came fourth. Overall, the first round of results were as follows:

The candidate to the post of President of Ukraine	Percent of votes cast for each candidate	The number of voters cast for each candidate
Viktor A. Yushchenko	39.90	11,188,675
Viktor F. Yanukovych	39.26	11,008,731
Oleksandr O. Moroz	5.82	1,632,098
Petro M. Symonenko	4.97	1,396,135
Natalia M. Vitrenko	1.53	429,794
Anatoliy K. Kinakh	0.93	262,530
Oleksandr M. Yakovenko	0.78	219,191
Oleksandr O. Omelchenko	0.48	136,830
Leonid M. Chernovetsky	0.46	129,066

"Elections 31.10.2004," accessed on April 23, 2015.
Source: http://www.cvk.gov.ua/pls/vp2004/wp0011e

---

[588] Wilson, Op. Cit., page 117.
[589] Ibidem, page 112.

Also, there were 1.98% voters who chose the option 'against all', an interesting particularity present only in some countries that until then was still present in Ukraine.

For the second round on November 21, it became obvious that Kuchma would not take any risks and since the beginning of the count, Yanukovych was always on top with a safe margin until the results were published with the option 'against all' with 2.31% of the votes. Moroz had supported Yushchenko in the second round.

The candidate to the post of President of Ukraine	Percent of votes cast for each candidate	The number of voters cast for each candidate
Viktor F. Yanukovych	49.46	15,093,691
Viktor A. Yushchenko	46.61	14,222,289

"Elections 21.11.2004," accessed on April 23, 2015.
Source: http://www.cvk.gov.ua/pls/vp2004/wp0011e

There were numerous evidences of the electoral fraud orchestrated to make Yanukovych the winner. Wilson, in his book *Ukraine's Orange Revolution*, and many other historians, journalists and political scientists have explained in detail how Kuchma managed to modify the results, increase the turnout, allow voters to vote several times in different cities and even cancel votes for Yushchenko or transfer votes from other candidates to Yanukovych.

There is no doubt there was an electoral fraud, the fact that interests this research is the reaction or more precisely the geopolitical reaction that followed, underlining both the response by the United States and EU members and of course the Russian one.

First, on the Russian side, Putin congratulated Yanukovych, in what later became a terrible embarrassment. It was followed by a telephone call by Alexander Lukashenko to Yanukovych and support or recognition from the presidents of Kazakhstan, Uzbekistan and Kyrgyzstan was seen.[590] Meanwhile, all EU members summoned their ambassadors to show their discontent while in the United States, George Bush, who curiously had become president in a controversial presidential election in 2000, refused to acknowledge the results.

---

[590] 'Georgia in the foreign press,' November 27, 2004, accessed on February 29, 2016. http://www.kvali.com/kvali/index.asp?obiektivi=show&n=195

Ukraine was not the only country in the world where rigged elections happened in the last two decades. Many countries in Africa, Latin America, Asia or Europe can be found to have electoral processes far from any liberal democratic standards even though they hardly provoke the same reaction by Western governments. Paul Biya has been re-elected as president of Cameroon unopposed for decades and no Western government has complained. The same can be said of Abdelaziz Bouteflika in Algeria, who has won the last four presidential elections, one of them with even more than 90% of the votes. Even clear electoral frauds like the one in Mexico in the 2006 presidential election[591] seemed to be ignored or simply did not receive the same level of attention. Instead, the Ukrainian case received unusual attention, highlighting Yushchenko as the candidate of the 'democratic forces' and Yanukovych as 'pro-Russian'.

How each of them was democratic or pro-Russian in reality will be discussed in the subsequent pages but the most important fact is that suddenly the world attention focused on the huge protests that occurred in the *Maidan*.[592] The opposition headed by Yushchenko and Timoshenko had been also counting on the protests to improve their international support. 'The mass protests watched around the

---

[591] In a case very similar to the Ukrainian one, a colossal operation of electoral fraud was carried out to take Felipe Calderon to the presidency and avoid the victory of Andres Manuel Lopez Obrador in Mexico. The authorities refused a recount besides the numerous evidences of unlawful acting by the electoral officials. A huge political turmoil together with protests that gathered even 1 million people followed but the reaction was completely different by the Western governments to the one that occurred in Ukraine. The huge difference was that here the affected candidate was a social democrat that pretended to have a sovereign policy towards the United States and not a follower of the neo-liberal policies the United States wanted for Mexico. In the Latin American scenario, especially when there were so many leftist governments in place at that time, that was not in line with US foreign policy interests. My comments published on the issue mentioned on the article by Rodriguez Araujo Octavio, '*México y el ejemplo de Ucrania*' La Jornada, July 27, 2006, accessed on February 29, 2016. http://www.jornada.unam.mx/2006/07/27/index.php?section=politica&article=032a1pol

[592] *Maidan* is the Ukrainian word for 'square', so the Independence Square, which in Ukrainian language is known as Maidan Nezhalezhnosti, became the centre of the protests also because of its strategic position in the city near all the most important government buildings where the presidency and the parliament are located. Note of the author.

world after the Ukrainian election were obviously pre-planned, but then so was the fraud that led to them.'[593]

Even if the opposition commanded by Yushchenko and Timoshenko had been planning on the protests before the election, there was still the question on how much the population could mobilize itself during winter and how effective it could be. After a first meeting with around 25,000–30,000 people on the night of the elections, on Monday November 22, more than 100,000 people gathered after a poll had suggested that Yushchenko had won and people armed with leaflets crowded around the *Maidan*. The reaction therefore was mixed, with thousands of people rallying against the fraud on the one side and an international reaction encouraging it even more on the other. Wilson explained:

> One thing the organisers of the Maidan got spectacularly right was their understanding of the power of TV images to form public opinion in the West, and, to an extent, at home. The Yushchenko team hired a satellite station so that any TV company in the world could easily obtain pictures of the peaceful but determined crowds. This ensured that the Maidan would always be the main story, the implied epicentre of the events.[594]

The level of the protests increased the next three days; meanwhile the government and the electoral authorities had announced Yanukovych as the winner. A crackdown was considered but never too seriously; even though officials like the chief of the presidential administration Medvedchuk or the same Yanukovych wanted a stronger approach at the end, Kuchma never allowed it. They did not have the internal unity for that kind of operation and the government was in a very weak position.

In the EU, there were also new factors that affected the international reaction like the recent enlargement with 10 new EU members that included Poland and the Baltic countries. Polish president Aleksander Kwasniewski took the leading role first to avoid a violent crackdown against the demonstrators but also to look for an exit from the political crisis that followed. There were, as Wilson showed, many polish economic interests at stake together with the

---

[593] Wilson, Op. Cit., page 122.
[594] Ibidem, page 131.

oligarchs and therefore they were ready to compromise for a solution.[595]

At the end, Kwasniewski managed also to gather support from different EU members. It included some like German chancellor Gerhard Schroder, who normally had a more negotiating stance[596] towards Russia, the Czech president Vaclav Klaus, the Austrian president Wolfgang Schussel and the Dutch premier Jan Peter Balkenende (while the Netherlands held the EU presidency) together with Javier Solana that was the EU's common foreign policy High Representative.

After a long meeting, Kuchma pushed for the idea of a package, a compromise on the election in return for constitutional reform and his own personal guarantees. The interesting thing to notice is how the meetings happened and how the EU together with US support had an effective participation to push for a solution favourable to their interests. Russia was outmanoeuvred. Putin had few options to offer instead and he stayed without the possibility of counterbalancing the proposal. He had suggested during a telephone conversation with Kuchma that he could decree a state of emergency and handle power to Yanukovych but the Ukrainian president did not accept.[597]

Afterwards, the parliament met on November 27 and voted for a resolution that considered that the elections took place with violations of the law by 255 deputies. Some oligarchs excluded themselves from the Donetsk clan and sided with the opposition. Meanwhile, the negotiations with Kwasniewski and the opposition continued until the acceptance of Kuchma's proposal. On Friday, December 3, the Supreme Court ordered to repeat the second round of the election considering the numerous violations mostly with the formation and checking of voters list and the intrusion of government officials in the process.[598] All this while Kuchma and Putin had

---

595 Idem, page 139.
596 The first chapter mentioned how a close alliance between Schroder and Putin took to the construction of the Northstream gas pipe and the former becoming the head director of the project at the end of his term as chancellor in Germany. Note of the author.
597 Wilson, Op. Cit., page 136.
598 Idem, page 147.

Ukraine   231

met at Vnukovo airport on December 2 but it seems little could be done at that point for the Russian side.

Altogether, the compromise was simple. Kuchma got immunity and economic guarantees which included that his interests would not be touched. Besides, a constitutional reform was done that diminished the power of the president and transformed the government into a kind of semi-presidential republic similar to France or Poland. The regime could remain untouched at the end. Finally, as Wilson notes,[599] an estimated 300 out of 450 Rada deputies were dollar millionaires and therefore they transformed the Rada into a kind of organ to allow them political survival and breaking line with Medvedchuk and Kluiev, figures more tied to Kuchma. The Rada became a 'safe haven for the old elite, which would, it was hoped, feel less like a retirement home and more like a business club.'[600]

The political reform included the fact of lowering the barrier to enter the parliament to 3% and to elect it wholly on national party lists. Meanwhile, deputies would not be allowed to simultaneously serve in the government or hold other positions. The Rada would have clearer powers over the National Bank, members of the CEC and state executive agencies. It would appoint half of the Constitutional Court, and the president the other half. Moreover, the president would propose the ministers of defence and foreign affairs. The reform was going to be applied since 2005 or 2006 and it envisioned some kind of struggle between the president and the parliament because of the new powers that the prime minister would have.

Altogether, the third round occurred on December 26 while the turnout diminished by around 4% and the expected results were as follows:

---

[599]   Idem, page 149.
[600]   Idem, page 149.

The candidate to the post of President of Ukraine	Percent of votes cast for each candidate	The number of voters cast for each candidate
Viktor A. Yushchenko	51.99	15,115,712
Viktor F. Yanukovych	44.20	12,848,528

"Elections 26.12.2004," accessed on April 26, 2015.
Source: http://www.cvk.gov.ua/pls/vp2004/wp0011e

Therefore, after what the West portrayed as a huge victory of the 'Orange Revolution' against Russian interests, Viktor Yushchenko became the third president of Ukraine and assumed office on 23January 2005. Besides, Putin had to affront the shame of having congratulated Yanukovych as the winner and then retract with the facts. From the outside, it seemed as a considerable victory for the United States and the EU. Inside, there were still obstacles Russia could use to keep Ukraine in its orbit. Ukrainian oligarchs kept huge power and controlled the parliament, which nominated Timoshenko as a prime minister. Still, Polish president Kwasniewski is supposed to have used the following phrase: 'For every great power Russia without Ukraine is better than Russia with Ukraine', [601] a phrase that reflects the geopolitical importance for the West of controlling the Ukrainian territory as part of a struggle against Russia. During the next years, events would show that what seemed a complete Western victory over Ukraine became a fallacy.

Consequently, to consider the events occurred in November and December 2004 as a revolution would be inaccurate. A revolution brings a change in the regime. Instead, what we witnessed was simply a change in the government while the essence of the regime remained untouched. In this case, only the geopolitical orientation was different, but still it would be worth acknowledging the level of the mass protests that arose against the regime after the fraud, which due to a lack of an own political project, at the end the social and political explosion became also hostage of geopolitics.

---

[601] Wilson, Op. Cit., page 193.

Yushchenko's presidency

Yushchenko's term presented since the beginning huge divisions with his ally, Iulia Timoshenko. They had signed an agreement before the elections on how the government would be divided, considering the electoral results each one had in the 2002 parliamentary election. Timoshenko was declared as Ukraine's prime minister on 4 February 2005, with 373 out of 450 votes. Only the Communist Party voted against her. The agreement also included that 55% of government posts would go to Our Ukraine, 23% to the Timoshenko bloc and the 22% reserved to any other formation needed to secure a majority. Poroshenko also tried to get a shot at the premiership but his links with Mykola Azarov[602] and the fact that he had invited him to the *Maidan* worsened his position. In fact, there are testimonies that Kuchma had talked with Poroshenko and offered him the premiership at the height of the protests. On January 4 Timoshenko declared that people who have business should not pretend to obtain a place in the new government in a comment directed at Poroshenko. Once in the government, it was common to hear that they were spying on one another.[603] Poroshenko was named as head of the National Security and Defence Council the same day Timoshenko was nominated and four of his close allies were named governors in regions near his hometown Vinnitsa.

Since the beginning, the relation among members of the government was complicated. The assigning of cabinet positions[604] included oligarchs and people related with the old regime. Many conflicts of interest arose. For instance, Yevhen Chervonenko, who ran a transport business, became the minister of transportation. Corruption scandals arose afterwards, first with Justice Minister Roman Zvarych who was accused of self-interest and then of faking his title studies from Columbia University. Timoshenko's close ally,

---

[602] Mykola Azarov became the acting prime minister after Yanukovych's resignation and stayed in charge from January 5 to January 24, 2005.
[603] Wilson, Op. Cit., page 160.
[604] Appointments of regional governors and cabinet by President Yushchenko compiled by the Action Ukraine Report Monitoring Service on February 4, 2005, accessed on February 29, 2016. http://www.europarl.europa.eu/meetdocs/2004_2009/documents/fd/ua_20050223_04_/ua_20050223_04_en.pdf

Oleksandr Turchynov, became head of the SBU, which is the Security Service of Ukraine. Conflicts between Timoshenko and Poroshenko continued and when some allegations of corruption appeared[605] against Poroshenko, Aleksandr Tretyakov, director of the presidential cabinet, and Nikolai Martynenko who was the head of the 'Our Ukraine' parliamentary group, the government was dismissed. By then, Poroshenko had already given his resignation as Head of the Security Defence Council.[606] The 'orange love' between Yushchenko and Timoshenko lasted only little bit more than six months.

Altogether, it seemed obvious that meanwhile Yushchenko had a clear support from the Western governments; still he did not count on the inner backing to do the reforms he claimed to and had to depend a lot on the alliance with Timoshenko who meanwhile had her own agenda. Timoshenko was looking already at the 2006 parliamentary elections to improve the share of the votes she had obtained in 2002.

The destitution of Timoshenko forced Yushchenko for new ways to establish a majority. He named Yuri Yekhanurov as a prime minister but he stayed short of obtaining the necessary 226 votes from the Rada. Therefore, he was forced to make a deal with Victor Yanukovych who by then at the opposition controlled enough deputies to give the majority to a government headed by Yekhanurov. The funny thing if not tragic is that in the deal Yushchenko obliged himself to draft a bill to give amnesty to all of those that participated in the election fraud in 2004[607] and, besides, after that, not a single senior official from the Kuchma regime was prosecuted for corruption. These measures proved unpopular in Ukraine but the fundamental question would be why would he concede so much to the side that used to be his rival? Maybe the goals he was pursuing in foreign policy were considered more important than some corruption charges or, let us say, maybe the foreign policy of the United

---

[605] Gangloff, Op. Cit., page 124.
[606] 'Ukraine leader sacks government,' *BBC News*, September 8, 2005, accessed on February 29, 2016. http://news.bbc.co.uk/2/hi/europe/4225566.stm
[607] Gallina, Nicole, 'Ukraine knocking at the door? The Ukraine-EU relationship after the Orange Revolution,' in *Ukraine on its Path Meandering Path between East and West*, edited by Lushnycky, Andrej N. and Riabchuk, Michola, Bern, Peter Lang AG, 2009.

States could sacrifice incarcerating corrupt officials in exchange for trying to pull Ukraine into NATO's orbit. Altogether, Yekhanurov's government lost a vote of no confidence on January 10 after the first of many gas crises but stayed in power until the next parliamentary election.

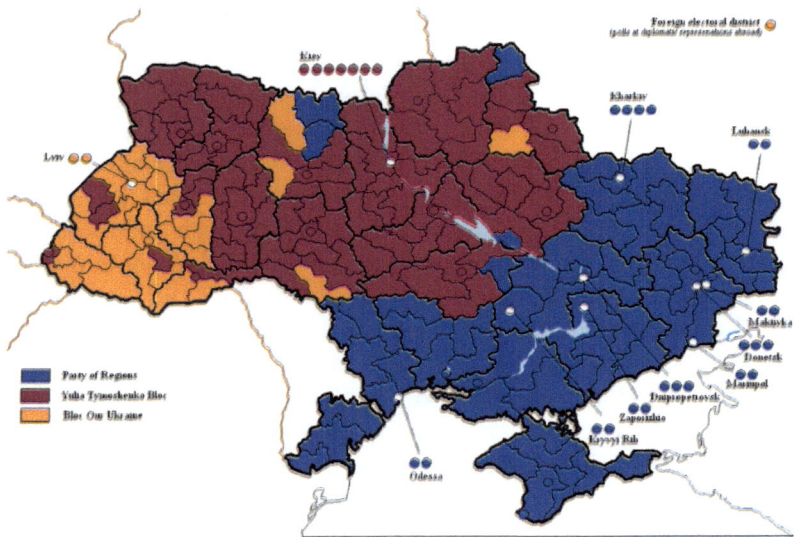

"Wahlkreise Ukraine, 2006 eng", accessed on February 29, 2016.
Source: Wikimedia Commons, licensed under CC BY-SA 3.0
(https://creativecommons.org/licenses/by-sa/3.0/)

Therefore, the 2006 parliamentary elections that took place on March 26, which for the president should have represented the confirmation of his political project, saw a repetition or even a deepening of the regional and ethnolinguistic vote already present in the 2004 election. Besides, it saw also a notable increase of the Iulia Timoshenko Bloc with respect to the role of Yushchenko's party Our Ukraine. Therefore, after having dismissed Timoshenko from the government and agreeing with Yanukovych, Yushchenko's list was relegated as the third political force with only 13.95% of the votes. Meanwhile, Victor Yanukovych, who was extremely discredited after 2004, this time heading the list of the Party of Regions, obtained 186 seats and 32.14% of the votes, finishing first, and Timoshenko came second with 129 seats and a 22.29% share of the polls.[608] The next graphic shows the leading party in each electoral district, clearly showing that while the Party of Regions confirmed itself as the leading force in the southeast, Iulia Timoshenko did so in Central Ukraine and Kiev, while Yushchenko had only kept his support in Western Ukraine and abroad with the diaspora.

The political division was rather the same as in 2004, but some slight differences occurred this time. It is true that Yushchenko and Timoshenko together would have a greater number of seats than Yanukovych, as they had in 2004, but it would be accurate to say that then they counted on the Socialist Party of Oleksander Moroz to build a majority. In this election, he obtained 33 seats, and 5.69% of the votes but opted to negotiate with Yanukovych and the Communist Party of Ukraine of Petro Symonenko, which obtained 21 seats and 3.66% of the votes.

The negotiations to form a new government were tough. Timoshenko thought she deserved to become the prime minister again, but she did not consider the fact that the Socialist Party decided to change sides, a common move in the Ukrainian parliamentary reality. At the end, after months of impasse, Victor Yushchenko had to confront the fact that he had no options. He nominated Victor Yanukovych as prime minister, the same person that had participated in an electoral fraud against him in 2004, the same person that certainly was directly or indirectly involved in poisoning him and the same person that represented the regime Yushchenko had campaigned against. Therefore, for many people that had participated in the protests in Kiev in 2004, this was seen as a step back; instead, for Yanukovych it was a victory and also for Russia which after the first gas crisis now had an ally with whom they could deal in other terms.

The following year saw a complex struggle between the president and the parliament and brought, as a consequence, a lack of govern-

---

[608] Official results can be consulted in: 'ВИБОРИ НАРОДНИХ ДЕПУТАТІВ УКРАЇНИ 26 березня 2006 року П Р О Т О К О Л ЦЕНТРАЛЬНОЇ ВИБОРЧОЇ КОМІСІЇ ПРО РЕЗУЛЬТАТИ ВИБОРІВ НАРОДНИХ ДЕПУТАТІВ УКРАЇНИ,' accessed on February 29, 2016. http://www.cvk.gov.ua/info/protokol_cvk_2006.pdf

ability, especially considering the foreign factors which are explained in the following pages. Therefore, Yanukovych carried out his own agenda that in practice was the agenda of the oligarchs while Yushchenko tried to push his liberal agenda and Timoshenko became a fierce oppositioner.

'Our Ukraine' had originally nominated some members of the cabinet but they were gradually dismissed or resigned. Again, after less than a year, another political crisis arose when the president claimed to dissolve the parliament and the government and what remained of the coalition majority[609] opposed in a long standoff that lasted from April to June 2007. After consultation with the constitutional court and a negotiation with the parliament, finally the call was made to have new parliamentary elections on 30 September 2007. Therefore, after more than two years in power, Yushchenko had been struggling internally to pursue his reforms while the idea of a political paralysis was visible for the general Ukrainian electorate.

The results were again rather similar with the same ethnolinguistic divisions already present but presented again two slight differences. On the one side, the Socialist Party of Oleksander Moroz did not obtain the 3% necessary to enter the parliament and a 'new' arrival, the Lytvyn Bloc,[610] entered the parliament.

The election outcome was as follows:

---

[609] After the 2006 parliamentary elections, the majority that included the Party of Regions, the Communist Party of Ukraine and the Socialist Party added also five votes more from Our Ukraine and six from the Timoshenko Block to total 249 deputies. It increased to 260 at a certain point and before the elections, it had been reduced to 238 with the votes from Our Ukraine and Timoshenko having left. 'Коаліція офіційно всохлася до 238 депутатів,' April 6, 2007, accessed on February 29, 2016. http://www.unian.ua/politics/40758-koalitsiya-ofitsiyno-vsohlyasya-do-238-deputativ.html

[610] The Lytvyn Bloc was a new created party headed by Volodymir Lytvin that used to be the chair of the parliament during Kuchma's presidency. Note of the author.

Party	Votes	%	Swing %	Seats	2006
Party of Regions	8,013,895	34.37	+ 2.23	175	−11
Yulia Tymoshenko Bloc	7,162,193	30.71	+8.43	156	+27
Our Ukraine	3,301,282	14.15	+0.21	72	−9
Communist Party of Ukraine	1,257,291	5.39	+1.73	27	+6
Lytvyn Bloc	924,538	3.96	+1.53	20	+20
Against all	637,185	2.73			

Parliamentary election 2007. I mention only the parties that entered to the parliament and the option against all. "Протокол Центральної виборчої комісії," September 30, 2007, accessed on February 28, 2016.
Source: http://www.cvk.gov.ua/info/protokol_cvk_2007.pdf

Therefore, as perceived, Iulia Timoshenko was the big electoral winner and had the possibility to establish a majority only with Our Ukraine. The second Timoshenko Government then was appointed on 18 December 2007. The short majority of 228 votes reduced itself to 226 votes only, the date of the voting giving it just the minimum necessary for the government to be approved. After one year, a reshuffle of the cabinet included a coalition with the Lytvyn Bloc to cover some possible defections in the ruling coalition.

Afterwards, during 2009, Poroshenko also came back to the government as minister of foreign affairs and was reappointed by the president to the National Security and Defence Council. Therefore, the same inner struggle continued while for the government it became difficult to have a coordinated inner and foreign policy; and besides they had to deal with a new gas crisis with Russia.

Altogether, the strong support by the United States, the EU, most of its members and the Ukrainian diaspora was not enough to give Yushchenko an inner governability. At the end, he was very fragile inside and his government was perceived as weak, incapable of taking decisions and Russian media portrayed him as very US-oriented.

Besides, choices like redefining World War II history while attempting to establish the UPA fighters as national heroes became very unpopular. It is important to remember that OUN-UPA combatants, even though popular only in West Ukraine and the diaspora, had ties with the SS during World War II. Besides, the number of Ukrainians that fought as UPA fighters was around 90,000 compared to the more than 2 million that fought for the Red Army. Therefore, when he proposed a bill in which UPA fighters would be considered war veterans,[611] he decreased even more his popularity in Central and Eastern Ukraine where still like in many Soviet countries the remembrance of the Great Patriotic War has still strong significance in the local identity.

It is also worth noting that the oligarchs, mostly the Donbas Clan, continued to have a prominent role in the political life. The Dnipropetrovsk clan and the Kiev clan had lost their political contacts, instead Akhmetov and his entourage with Victor Yanukovych included still kept a lot of power. It is interesting to note that while in 2004 there were no Ukrainians in the Forbes list, by 2006 there were seven with fortunes exceeding US$1 billion. In that same year, 29 entrepreneurs had amassed fortunes worth at least US$ 200 million.[612]

Their presence in politics was in most cases continuous. Some like Viktor Pinchuk publicly retired from active political life but most of them continued. In 2006, there were 12 oligarchs in the parliament, 8 of them in the orange fraction and the number decreased to 8 after 2007 of which 5 were orange. The decrease did not mean they were less active. What happened is that besides the bought loyalties already mentioned, they commonly included their loyal ones in the lists and as they were not in the first places, they were never questioned. For instance, Rinat Akhmetov had his former driver become a deputy, while Firtash did the same with his chief of security. Therefore, only a few oligarchs, for instance, could control a huge number of members of the parliament while they could retire to attend their businesses.

---

[611] 'Yushchenko pushes for official recognition of OUN-UPA combatants,' January 10, 2008, accessed on February 23, 2015. http://zik.com.ua/en/n ews/2008/01/11/121551
[612] Pleines, Op. Cit., page 105.

Altogether, by 2008, Taras Kuzio mentioned the scandalous figure that the 50 richest oligarchs represented 85% of the country's GDP compared to 35% in Russia.[613]

For example, a survey was published in 2008 by WorldPublicOpinion.org. In different countries it asked the question: 'Whose benefit is country run for?' Frequently, the most common answer was the option: 'A few big interests', but in the Ukrainian case, it was the highest amount (84%) of the answers that voted for this choice, compared, for instance, with 59% in Russia or France.[614]

Therefore, the role of the oligarchs did not diminish in Yushchenko's term, it only changed. Kiev's and Dnipropetrovsk's clans lost force and the Donbas clan increased power. Some personalities rose to power more like Dmitri Firtash who after the so-called 'Orange Revolution' seized a monopoly position in Ukrainian natural gas imports and was accepted by both Yanukovych and Yushchenko and both supported the formation of his related business connections.[615]

To conclude, Yushchenko took no concrete steps to build a solid polity in Ukraine and was hostage of the struggle between oligarchic clans in the territory. All this while he tried to take also sides in the already changing geopolitical struggle between Russia and the West. Therefore, it would become important to notice the significant changes present in the foreign relations of Ukraine once Yushchenko assumed the presidency.

---

[613] Kuzio, Taras, 'Oligarchs wield power in Ukrainian politics,' *Eurasia Daily Monitor*, Vol. 5, No. 125 (July 1, 2008), accessed on February 25, 2015. http://www.jamestown.org/single/?no_cache=1&tx_ttnews%5Btt_news%5D=33765#.VRl1Q_msWZw

[614] 'World publics say governments should be more responsive to the will of the people,' May 12, 2008, accessed on February 29, 2016. http://www.worldpublicopinion.org/pipa/articles/governance_bt/482.php?lb=btgov&pnt=482&nid=&id=

[615] Pleines, Heiko, 'From competitive authoritarianism to defective democracy: Political regimes in Ukraine before and after the Orange Revolution,' in *Presidents, Oligarchs and Bureaucrats, Forms of Rule in the Post-Soviet Space*, edited by Stewart, Susan, Klein, Margarete, Schmitz, Andrea and Schroder, Hans-Henning, Presidents, oligarchs and Bureaucrats, Farnham, Ashgate, 2012, page 132.

Foreign policy

The modifications in the Ukrainian Constitution diminished by a considerable degree the authority of the president, even though he retained the possibility to nominate the minister of foreign affairs and the minister of defence. From the beginning of his term,[616] Yushchenko made it clear he wanted Ukraine to become a NATO member and to build closer ties with the West. This goal included pushing for more integration with the EU with close US support. He thought that maybe if he did not endanger the oligarchs' interests, he could pursue his foreign policy goals that coincidently were also US foreign policy goals for Ukraine. Altogether, when he gave priority to these objectives instead of pursuing the corruption allegations under Kuchma and the electoral fraud, it cost him a lot more of the remaining popularity he had among the people that had protested in the events of late December 2004.

Meanwhile, Yushchenko rejected the former multivector policy openly.[617] The approach towards NATO, even if it was publicly sustained by the United States and many EU members, especially the Baltic countries and Poland, brought many inner resistances mostly but not only in the Russian-speaking Ukraine. During his period, NATO kept being extremely unpopular among the Ukrainian society, which was perceived as a US-headed military alliance that in a post-Soviet society represented the enemy against whom they had grown.

The Ukrainian Army and NATO troops carried out some military exercises in Crimea and produced numerous protests by the local population. There was a Ukraine–NATO Partnership for peace exercise scheduled to take place starting 17 July 2006. One month before, Crimean parliament even without official jurisdiction had declared Crimea a NATO-free territory. When 200 US Marines arrived, it provoked hundreds of locals to protest against their presence in Feodosia. Meanwhile, Russia warned against the risks Ukraine would face if they joined NATO. At the end, the military

---

[616] Even if his first foreign visit was to Russia to try to improve the links after the election, in a visit that by the way did not count with the participation of Iulia Timoshenko against whom was a pending order of arrest in Russia for corruption.
[617] Wilson, Op. Cit., page 190.

exercises had to be cancelled due to the local opposition that had the military trapped in their barracks[618] while the arrival of provisions was blocked. From a geopolitical analysis, this military exercise was obviously a provocation against the Russian counterpart that had precisely the Black Sea Fleet in Crimea, motive enough for Russia to oppose the exercises by different means. Besides, the protests in Crimea showed how the population was quite reticent about an approach to the Atlantic organism and did not understand what the benefits could be besides troubling the relation with Russia. At the end, again, the fact is that Ukraine was trapped in a geopolitical struggle between Russian interests and US ones the later pursuing a clear goal of pulling Ukraine near its orbit while Russia was getting help from local sympathizers in Ukraine to pressure on its behalf.

From a realistic approach, the multivector policy had helped balance and keep in a neutral position Ukraine so it would not fluctuate between different stronger geopolitical projects. Once governments pushed from either side of the balance, it risked producing fractures in the already fragile multi-ethnic social tissue in this territory. During my master's thesis in 2007,[619] it was advised precisely to try too hard to pull Ukraine into NATO orbit could make the country break itself and lose its territorial integrity. The events in the following years proved that I was not wrong.

The relation with the EU
Meanwhile, the relations with the EU saw a notorious change since Yushchenko took charge. The ninth summit held in December 2005 allowed Ukraine to obtain some preferences by the EU like starting preliminary consultations to replace the Agreement on Partnership and Cooperation and the fact of obtaining the status of 'market economy'.[620]

---

[618] 'Russia tells Ukraine to stay out of NATO,' June 8, 2006, *The Guardian*, accessed on February 24, 2015. http://www.theguardian.com/world/2006/jun/08/russia.nickpatonwalsh
[619] Dromundo, Rolando, 'Ucraina: Un conflitto geopolitico fra la Russia e Occidente,' Thesis to obtain the Master's Degree in International Relations, EU-Latin America at the Bologna University, Italy, 2007.
[620] The nomination 'market economy', in fact, acquires a clear political value in this case. The EU gives it to countries aligned precisely with neo-liberal policies and as a territory that could enter into the EU's own geopolitical space. Note of the author.

After the change of government from Timoshenko to Yanukovych in 2006, there was some confusion among the EU as to where Ukraine was heading, but after Timoshenko got back to the government, the summit in 2008 finally included a compromise to look for an Association Agreement. Pleines added in that sense: 'The offer made to Ukraine by the EU in summer 2008, comprising a free trade agreement but no membership perspective, may therefore satisfy most of the Ukrainian oligarchs.'[621]

But, at the end, the last EU-Ukraine summit under Yuschenko's term in 2009 could not hide the disappointment in the EU by the fact that he had not been capable of carrying on with the reforms that the EU pretended. In that sense, the European Commission president, Jose Manuel Barroso, declared: 'I will be honest with you, Mr. President. It very often seems to us that the promise of reforms is fulfilled in part only, commitments to reforms are fulfilled only in part, and words are not always accompanied by deeds',[622]

In fact, the proposed reforms meant above all to give EU companies the possibility to invest in Ukraine with more concurrence and in conditions that are more profitable. This would have affected directly the role of the oligarchs in favour of foreign investors and challenged their monopoles. Hence, the approach to the EU became more rhetorical because there was no political context to jeopardize the control of the oligarchs over the economy at that time. Therefore, it is possible to witness here another confrontation, about who should profit in Ukraine, the oligarchs or the transnational corporations residing in the EU with clear support from their governments, another clash in which the Ukrainian people were not being consulted.[623]

Another notorious point worth mentioning with a huge visual impact around the world was the bid to organize the UEFA EURO 2012. The idea of a joint bid with Poland had obviously a clear geopolitical goal. First, why a joint bid with Poland and not another

---

[621] Pleines, Heiko, 'The political role of the Oligarchs,' in *Ukraine on Its Way to Europe, Interim Results of the Orange Revolution*, edited by Besters-Dilger, Juliane, Peter Lang, Frankfurt am Main, 2009, page 117.
[622] EU-Ukraine Summits: 16 Years of Wheel-Spinning, February 28, 2013. http://ukrainianweek.com/Politics/73494
[623] From a Marxist point of view, it would be like asking the Ukrainian citizens who they did prefer as exploiter. Note of the author.

neighbour? In 2006, it would have been quite easier to coordinate with other neighbours like Belarus or Russia for example. The choice of Poland, besides the fact that still could bring some resentment among Ukrainians for the domination the suffered under the Poles, had as a goal to organize the competition with a country well integrated in the EU and NATO structures in an event that would certainly need to coordinate issues like security, among others. That had a clear geopolitical goal and showed the kind of direction the government wanted to give to Ukraine.[624] Certainly, when the bid was asked, Yuschenko thought that maybe by 2012 he would be in his second term as president. He could never have guessed that by then Victor Yanukovych would be the president.

Relations with Russia and the gas crises
The relations with Russia became complex even though the first visit Yushchenko did as president was precisely to Moscow. The aim was to keep appearances of a good will to keep stable diplomatic relations, considering Russia was Ukraine's most important economic partner. For the Kremlin, there were mainly three geopolitical goals of extreme importance regarding Ukraine. First, to assure that Ukraine would not join NATO, second, to extend the lease of the naval base in Crimea for the Black Sea Fleet that was due to expire on 2017, and third to assure that Ukraine would be a trustable territory for gas transfers to the West while trying to create a gas transit consortium among other possibilities. To pursue these goals, Russia had to diminish US presence and coordinate with single EU members to weaken a solid EU position. Besides, there were many strong points from which the Russian Government could exert pressure on Ukraine against Yushchenko's foreign policy wishes.

First, there was the Ukrainian gas dependence with Russia, second the role of the Orthodox Church from the Moscow Patriarchate, the defence of the Russian language in Ukraine and the Russian ethnic minority and besides there were many economic interests present in Ukraine. There was a notorious Russian presence in non-

---

[624] Dromundo, Rolando, 'La Geopolítica de la Eurocopa Polonia-Ucrania 2012,' *El Internacionalista*, April 19, 2012, accessed on February 25, 2015. http://elinternacionalista.com/2012/04/19/la-geopolitica-de-la-eurocopa-polonia-ucrania-2012/

Ukraine 245

ferrous metallurgy, petrochemical, telecommunications and machine building, and Russian companies controlled four of Ukraine's largest oil refineries while the Ukrainian ones processed raw material shipped from Russia.[625] Meanwhile, by 2000 already, 82% of Gazprom's European exports had transit via Ukraine.[626] This amount diminished in the following years but it was still 68% in 2009.

In addition, there was the issue of the subsidized gas that Ukraine received. It is important to remember that after the fall of the Soviet Union, Russia had been selling to most former Soviet Republics gas under the market price. By 2005, Russia charged Ukraine $50 for 1,000 cubic metres while they paid Ukraine a transit fee of $1.09 for that amount per 100 kilometres but by barter. Since his arrival, Yushchenko intended to move away from barter in gas trade and ask for cash in the transaction. Altogether, this allowed Gazprom a perfect opportunity to ask to modify the prices, and he announced on March 2005 the intention to increase the price from $50 to $160 per 1,000 cubic metres.

Altogether, by mid-2005, besides the troubling relation Yushchenko had with Timoshenko, he had to assume that there were not only disputed transit contracts with Russia but also a similar situation regarding supply arrangements, gas debt and an absence of a transit network consortium.[627]

It is important to consider that Ukraine is the largest CIS gas market with annual consumption reaching 70–75 billion cubic metres and its annual domestic production of around 20 billion cubic metres only covers residential sector consumption while the rest came mostly from Russian and Central Asian (mostly Turkmen) imports.[628] From 1998 to 2002, Gazprom did not supply Ukraine any other gas than supplied for transit. The rest was purchased by Ukrainian gas traders (different oligarchs) from Turkmen Neftegaz and ITERA. From 2003, Naftogaz became the single buyer of Turkmen gas at the Ukraine-Russia border from ETG, which became the

---

625 Perepelytsia, G.M. Ed., *Foreign Policy of Ukraine*, Annual Strategic Review 2008, Kyiv, Stylos Publishing House, 2009, page 166.
626 Yafimava, Katja, *The Transit Dimension of EU Energy Security*, Oxford, Oxford University Press, 2011, page 140.
627 Ibidem, page 150.
628 Ibidem, page 151.

shipper in substitution of ITERA. ETG did not last long and in July 2004 Gazprom and Naftogaz agreed that a new company RosUkrEnergo (RUE) would operate. The company was a 50/50 joint venture by Gazprombank and Austrian Raiffeisenbank registered in Switzerland. Raiffeisenbank acted on behalf of undisclosed beneficiaries that appeared to be Dmytro Firtash and Ivan Fursin, owning 45% and 5% each. It is notable in this case, how on the one side the Russian part gave Gazprom its share in the gas trade, instead the Ukrainian side did not give it to Naftogaz but created a complex scheme registered in Switzerland and related to one of the newly arrived oligarchs, Firtash.

Altogether, when Ukraine refused to pay the new prices, they tried to look for other sources. There was an attempt to establish a deal to buy Turkmen gas even though, it was not possible at the end because Turkmenistan already had agreements with Gazprom that compromised most of its production. Gazprom threatened to cut gas supplies from 1 January 2006, while sending only transit gas to the EU market. Gazprom's demand was to create a joint venture for distribution and a price increase.

There were tough negotiations during December in which, at the beginning, EU members and the European Commission stayed out of the discussion. For the EU, it was complicated to sustain publicly neo-liberal policies and complain about gas subsidies, and on the other hand criticize the measure by Russia, even though it obviously had a political goal. Vladimir Putin offered a $3.6 billion loan to Ukraine to pay for the increase but Yushchenko rejected it. Therefore, on January 1, Gazprom started to reduce the pressure on the pipeline system and gradually the Ukrainian counterpart started to withhold some of the gas destined to Europe even though it was denied at the beginning. The diminution affected countries in a different way. For instance, Slovakia suffered a decrease of 33%, Poland 14%, France 25–30%, Hungary 40% and Italy 24% to mention some. In the Balkans, Macedonia and Bosnia and Herzegovina saw a 100% reduction of the gas supplies in that period.[629]

---

[629] 'Ukraine "stealing Europe's gas",' January 2, 2006, accessed on February 25, 2015. http://news.bbc.co.uk/2/hi/europe/4574630.stm

On January 4, an agreement was made. It resulted in Naftogaz losing its role as a wholesale importer, and excluding it from supplying the industrial sector. The deal was signed between Gazprom, Naftogaz and RUE that now played a leading role. Therefore, RUE would be the only seller of gas to Ukraine and a new joint venture between RUE and Naftogaz was set up for local distribution, UkrGazEnergo (UGE). This complicated scheme became unprofitable for Gazprom in the following years, but mostly it was for RUE and the subsidiary that would sell in Ukraine; therefore, the leading benefactor in this case was Firtash again. It is interesting to notice how Firtash continued under Yushchenko to benefit the same way as under Kuchma and now (indirectly) by participating in trilateral agreements with Russia and Ukraine.

The first gas crisis ended also with a deal in which around one-third of gas arriving to Ukraine would be Gazprom's (through RUE) at $230 per 1,000 cubic metres and the rest would be from Turkmenistan, and all combined, Ukraine would be paying $95 per 1,000 cubic metres during 2006. Besides, the fact that eventually Naftogaz retained during the crisis some of the gas destined to the EU was overlooked.

This episode was locally a small victory for the Kremlin even though Gazprom did not manage to enter the internal and transit market in Ukraine as wanted but the most important effect was in the relations with the EU. First, European media magnified the diminution of the supply even though consumers were never affected, sounding the alarms in Brussels.[630] For the EU members, it was a clear signal that they could not afford to push Ukraine so much without suffering a boomerang effect. If the United States pretended that Ukraine broke ties with Moscow, they could handle it, but the EU could not afford the same struggle over Ukraine with the gas dependency already described.

The timing of the deal is also completely related with the Nord Stream pipeline. Since the end of 2005, Nord Stream gathered notable support from Germany. Ten days before the 2005 German parliamentary election, an agreement was signed to build the pipe-

---

[630] Yafimava, Op. Cit., page 166.

line and some days after stepping back as chancellor, Schröder assumed power as head of the shareholders committee. The new pipeline, for Germany, meant a full and direct supply from Russia by sea, avoiding the involvement of any possible third parties. The move, agreed before the gas crisis, was also a strong blow to the Baltic countries and Poland, which exposed them in their bilateral relation with Moscow. Therefore, this gave room for Moscow to divide EU members due to a lack of a unified EU energy policy, but above all because members had assumed a different position with regard to what would be more important to assure a stable energy supply or to have Ukraine as an ally.

During the following years, Gazprom noticed that intermediaries were not an advantage in any sense mostly because debt started to accumulate once the prise rose again in 2007. On 2 October 2007, Gazprom threatened to cut supplies because of an unpaid debt of $1.3 billion, but the dispute was settled in the following days. Even though the concept of the debt was very confusing, there were not only four different companies participating in the gas transactions (Gazprom, Naftogaz, RUE and UGE) but also the regional distributers in the Ukrainian oblasts which apparently were controlled by Firtash.[631] Altogether, for Gazprom there was a clear 'Ukrainian debt' even if it was not transparent who owned whom and how much once dividing the debit between Naftogaz, UGE, the oblast distributors or UGE.

In addition, Iulia Timoshenko once back as prime minister pushed to establish a direct relation between Naftogaz and Gazprom, mostly because Firtash was a political rival close to the Party of Regions, so even if weakening RUE would mean to strengthen Gazprom she saw it as a lesser evil.[632]

Afterwards, Yushchenko and Putin reached an agreement on 12 February 2008, creating two new joint ventures for the gas delivery, but this time as joint ventures of Gazprom and Naftogaz, respectively.

---

[631] Even though Yafimava does not document any concrete evidence, she shows there were several hints that portrayed most of the oblgazy and even a claim in 2009 that he controlled two-thirds of them. Yafimava, Op. Cit., page 170.
[632] Ibidem, page 173.

In the meantime, the inner struggle between Yushchenko and Timoshenko had an effect in the gas disputes. Timoshenko as a prime minister had spoken clearly against joint ventures and therefore did not support the new agreement. Meanwhile, the debts continued to accumulate with Gazprom, which gave a reason to the Russian side to cut again partially the supply on 3 March 2008, by 25% and an additional 25% the next day. Gas supplies were restored on March 5 after Alexei Miller agreed with Naftogaz CEO, Oleh Dubyna, on the debt, but afterwards, the cabinet refused to execute the gas agreements signed by the president. Altogether, the debt continued to grow.

New terms were agreed on more than once, first between Timoshenko and Putin in October 2008, and then between Naftogaz and Gazprom. These terms included smooth conditions for the price increase to the Ukrainian side, but condition to the full payment of the debts. The problem was that this included very short terms to pay the total amount required and it needed the acceptance of RUE to transform Naftogaz's debt to RUE into debt to Gazprom. The last two reasons led to the failure of the agreements. First, because RUE and Gazprom differed on the amount of the debt and also because the new deal was a great blow to RUE and particularly to Firtash and, as his approval would be needed, this became an obstacle. It is obvious at this point that Firtash would move all his pieces to end the deal. At a certain point, Gazprom issued an ultimatum that any new deal would have to include the previous payment of the existing debt.[633] At the end, Naftogaz paid on December 30 without the existing penalties while Dubina as CEO of Naftogaz and Timoshenko agreed on a new contract but were ordered not to sign it by Yushchenko, only six hours before the contract expired. Therefore, as promised, Gazprom cut supplies to Ukraine on 1 January 2009, starting what Yafimava considers 'the most dramatic supply and transit crisis in the history of the European (and global) gas trade'.[634]

---

[633] The last days of 2008 passed by without Naftogaz paying which Yafimava speculates could be because of two reasons: to use the delay as a bargaining tool for a new contract or that part of the Ukrainian elite had an interest in preserving the existing arrangements that benefited Firtash directly. Ibidem, page 181.
[634] Ibidem, page 183.

At the beginning, Western governments thought that the crisis would evolve as in 2006, with no real harm to the EU supply. The difference was that, this time, Moscow was not willing to accept the Ukrainian authorities to be taking gas destined to EU buyers for their own use. On January 5, Gazprom stated that 65.3 mmcm of gas were 'stolen' by Ukraine to which the Ukrainian authorities responded saying that in the absence of a contract they were entitled to take the gas they thought necessary for transit. This time they admitted openly to taking gas.

What followed was a diversification of the Russian supply to the EU, which increased the cuts and created direct damage to the countries supplied exclusively through Ukraine. 'The fact that for 13 days no gas from Russia flowed to Europe via Ukraine was an unprecedented event in the Russia-Europe gas relationship.'[635]

Ukraine meanwhile used its reserves and reversed the system to feed the industries in the eastern part of the country.[636] Even the phone conversations of German Chancellor, Angela Merkel with the Russian and Ukrainian Governments did not help to find a quick solution to a problem that deeply affected the supply, above all of the countries that had mostly only one supplier, in this case, Gazprom.

Many countries remained without the sufficient level of gas storage to face the interruption in the supply, precisely in the harshest month of winter. Instead, it seems that Naftogaz had already been planning the Ukrainian reaction for a long time considering the speed to reverse the system that had never been stopped since it was built in Soviet times as Yafimava suggests.[637]

Altogether, 12 EU members were affected to different degrees together with the Balkan countries and Moldova.[638]

After long negotiations, it was agreed that a gas-monitoring mission[639] would be established and Russian offers to restart partially

---

[635] Ibidem, page 184.
[636] Ibidem, pages 186–187.
[637] Ibidem.
[638] To consult the degree in which each country was affected, see: Gas Coordination Group, 'Member state general situation according to significance of impact,' Memo 09/3, Brussels, January 9, 2009, accessed on February 26, 2015. http://europa.eu/rapid/press-release_MEMO-09-3_en.htm
[639] Yafimava, Ibidem, page 187.

the pumping of transit gas were rejected by the Ukrainian side which wanted a whole restitution of the supply. On January 11, the monitoring agreement was signed but at the end, there was nothing to monitor because there were not flows at all. Besides, observers were not allowed to monitor Ukrainian storages despite the fact that the Ukrainian Government had committed to it.

The final solution came only after a bilateral agreement between Putin and Timoshenko signed on 18 January 2009, and a supply and transit contract signed between Gazprom and Naftogaz the following day. The agreement included a discount of 20% for 2009 in exchange for keeping the same transit price of 2008 during that year. In addition, they agreed that since 2010 all prices and tariffs would follow to market standards. Gas flows to Ukraine and to Europe did not restart until January 20 and returned to normal for all European customers on 22 January 2009.

There are many interesting facts to note from this agreement, the first, which will be mentioned afterwards, was that the deal signed by Timoshenko in his role of prime minister cost her future accusations for abuse of power and took her to prison. The second fact is that the contract signed in January 2009 was a lot worse to the Ukrainians than the one offered by Gazprom on 30 December 2008. Therefore, the inner struggle in Ukraine had only damaged the country. It neither improved its position against Russia or with the EU. Nothing was obtained while Yushchenko's reputation with the EU was damaged and, at the end, it seemed as if the Ukrainians were sabotaging themselves, a clear indication again of a failed state.

The Ukrainian Government did nothing to allow, as stipulated, the transit gas to arrive to the West, thinking perhaps that EU governments would tolerate some fluctuations with the supply as part of their support to Ukraine. The EU had to confront the fact that they were not in a position to handle the issue as a single entity, facilitating the Russian position and at the end, Russia had indirectly made them pay the price for their support to Yushchenko in the 2004 events. However, Moscow was also in a complicated position because on the one side, they did not want to lose trust from the European buyers but they wanted to remind Ukrainian authorities that the further they went against Moscow, the effects would be bigger.

At the end, it is worth remarking how Russia used the same tools and speech that were part of the IMF, World Bank, the United States or the EU when trying to act on weaker countries regarding the need to reduce subsidies, pay debts and privatize monopolies to allow foreign investment. It showed, just to another side of the world economy, how at the end, commercial deals are not only economic, but above all political.

During an interview, Alexander Medvedev, maybe the second most important individual in Gazprom, declared:

> Tra il 2006 e il 2008, l'Ucraina ha ricevuto l'equivalente di oltre 30 miliardi di dollari in sovvenzione legate al commercio del gas a prezzi scontati. Questa cifra corrisponde a 50 volte gli aiuti dell'UE all'Ucraina dopo la rivoluzione arancione.[640]

The fact that Putin always tried to show the gas crisis as a commercial issue that should be solved between Naftogaz and Gazprom confirmed the political logic of how capital works.[641] Above all, it was always politics and geopolitics. Therefore, the gas dispute was part of the same struggle, while at the end, the price had a political cost to the Ukrainian authorities and to the Ukrainian population that would lose subsidies and would have to pay for the gas increase in the already complex economic situation they have to live every day.

Ukraine and GUAM

Once Yushchenko had portrayed his intentions with regard to foreign policy towards Russia and the West, he also tried to revive GUAM, an organization that tried since its origins to organize some CIS countries without (or against) Russia. Once Uzbekistan confirmed they were leaving the organism in 2002, the summit in

---

[640] Interview with Aleksander Medvedev, deputy chairman of the Board of Executive Directors of Gazprom, published in Limes, Rivista italiana di Geopolitica, 3/2009, page 60.
[641] In the introductory chapter, it was explained precisely the political logic in which Capital has restructured itself in the last decades.

2004, before Yushchenko was president, counted only on the participation of two of their presidents when they met in Yalta. The 2005 summit in Chisinau, instead, received a strong impulse with the presence of the Lithuania's and Romania's presidents, the secretary general of the OSCE and a special representative from the State Department of the United States. All this while, Russia was not invited. At that time, Yushchenko declared 'Our organization is emerging as a powerful force, participating in resolving problems in the Caspian-Black Sea region... [GUAM] member states share a common approach against terrorism and separatism.'[642] It is not a coincidence that proposals were made to resolve the issues of the frozen conflicts in Pridnestrovia, Nagorno Karabagh, Abkhazia and South Ossetia.[643] This integration without Moscow became a source of concern for the Kremlin when this renewed GUAM considered even creating a peacekeeping force of their own[644] that concretized in 2007 in a 500-personnel battalion to combat any possible separatists in their countries.[645]

In this context, the close relation Yushchenko had with Georgia's president, Saakashvili, due to their close relation with the United States increased after the Russo-Georgian War in 2008. In this case, Yushchenko again took sides notoriously with his Georgian counterpart including the shipping of military aid.[646] Ukraine supplied also air-raid complexes, which defended Georgia from Russian air force bombing during Russian-Georgian conflict.

---

[642] 'GUAM leaders Hail Chisinau summit,' April 22, 2005, accessed on February 26, 2015. http://www.civil.ge/eng/article.php?id=9677
[643] Kapitonenko, Mykola, 'Resolving post-Soviet "frozen conflicts": Is regional integration helpful?,' *Caucasian Review of International Affairs*, Vol. 3, No. 1 (2009), accessed on February 26, 2015. http://www.cria-online.org/6_4.html
[644] 'Ukraine suggests setting up GUAM peacekeeping unit,' May 31, 2006, accessed on February 26, 2016. http://today.az/news/politics/26721.html
[645] 'Russia suspicious of GUAM motives,' June 20, 2007, accessed on February 22, 2015. http://www.isn.ethz.ch/Digital-Library/Articles/Detail/?lang=en&id=53439
[646] There were many discussions about the alleged illegality of the arms supply to Georgia, and even a parliament commission in the Rada found that the arms were sold at artificially low prices in detriment of Ukraine's military capabilities. The commission chairman sustained that some $100 million from the sales did not go to the state coffers and that a fire was provoked at an Ukrainian ammunition depot to cover the smuggling. Considering the extreme polarization of the parliamentary forces, it is difficult to know how accurate

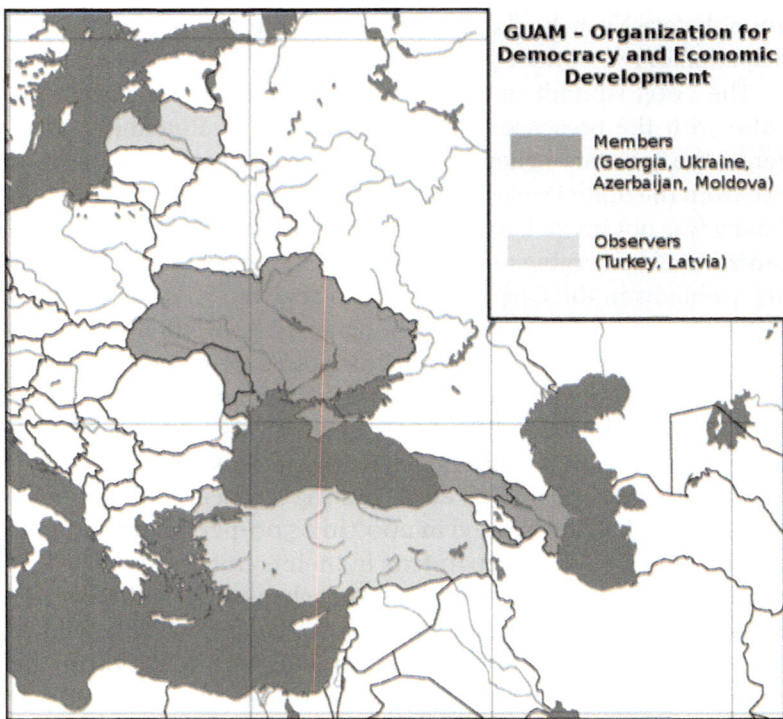

Location of GUAM member states (orange) and observers (green) in Eastern Europe and the Caucasus. "GUAM organization for democracy and economic development," accessed on February 27, 2015.
Source: Wikimedia Commons, licensed under CC BY-SA 3.0
(https://creativecommons.org/licenses/by-sa/3.0/)

Besides, there were declarations by Yushchenko, threatening to increase the price for the rent of the Sevastopol Base to the Black Sea Fleet. He also issued a decree[647] about regulating the Black Sea Fleet in which they should give notice of their itineraries. These actions

---

the accusations were, either by the parliament or by the government, but the undeniable fact is that arms were provided to Georgia (legally or not), signalling a clear anti-Russian stance by Yushchenko. Korduban, Pavel, 'Were Ukrainian arms supplies to Georgia Illegal?,' *Eurasia Daily Monitor*, Vol. 5, No. 22 (November 19, 2008), accessed on February 27, 2015. http://www.jamestown.org/single/?no_cache=1&tx_ttnews%5Btt_news%5D=34145#.VVCoZCHtmko

[647] Yushchenko, Victor, 'Georgia and the stakes for Ukraine,' *The Washing Post*, August 12, 2008, accessed on February 28, 2015. http://www.washingtonpost.com/wp-dyn/content/article/2008/08/24/AR2008082401856.html

were more rhetorical than real as they had no possibility of being enforced.

Altogether, the inner struggle with Timoshenko again was present. Timoshenko did not take the same anti-Russian stance and her declarations were more moderate than Yushchenko's, maybe to portray herself as a more restrained alternative towards the 2010 presidential election. This pragmatic approach caused her to be accused of being pro-Russian by the president. Meanwhile, she accused Yushchenko of fanning national flames to improve his severely decreased popularity.[648] Ex-president Kravchuk also suggested that Yushchenko did not need to include threats to the Black Sea Fleet. Even deputy fraction leader from 'Our Ukraine' (the faction that supported the president), Taras Stetskiv, considered that the ideological stance of the president was more an act of immaturity instead of an act of principle, based on a lack of a realistic analysis and 'anti-Russianism'. He considered that Ukrainian national interests did not need tension with Russia.[649]

Precisely from a pragmatic perspective, after one gas crisis and the possibility of a second one already present in 2008, the strong Western orientation of Yushchenko did not need to still add another confrontation against Russia that was always in a stronger position than Ukraine. Playing this role served perfectly to strengthen the US position, but was not in line with an Ukrainian interest. The same as Kuchma before had acted around Russian needs when looking to survive politically, this time Yushchenko functioned around US needs while showing the general lack of acknowledgement of an Ukrainian interest at all.

At the end, when foreign powers determine so easily the actions of a polity, it would be worth reconsidering Carl Schmitt's words:

> Si le peuple accepte qu'un étranger lui dicte le choix de son ennemi e lui dise contre qui il a le droit ou non de se battre, il cesse d'être un peuple politiquement libre et il est incorporé du subordonné a un autre système politique.[650]

---

[648] By then, Yushchenko's support was around 5%. Kuzio, Taras, 'Strident, ambiguous and duplicitous, Ukraine and the 2008 Russia-Georgia war,' accessed on March 1, 2015. http://www.taraskuzio.net/International%20Relations_files/Kuzio_Georgia_Demok.pdf, page 364.
[649] Idem, page 365.
[650] Schmitt, Carl, *La notion de politique*, Paris, Calmann-Levy, 1972, page 93.

Altogether, Yushchenko contributed to fracture in many senses even more the complex social tissue in Ukraine while his popularity decreased to unseen levels for an acting president. He carried most of the political weight of the gas crisis, a failed approach to NATO, a slight approach to the EU with few concrete goals accomplished and with the oligarchs untouched, he still thought that he could repeat in 2010 the success he had in the presidential elections in 2010.

Meanwhile, the oligarchs, especially the Donbas clan, had increased their political leverage. They decided it was time to choose one of their own to run the country. This set the base for a predictable 2010 presidential election, in what would mark the return (as if they had really gone) of the oligarchs.

2010 presidential election

The 2010 presidential election had many known names in the Ukrainian political scene but only two with real chances to achieve victory: Victor Yanukovych and Iulia Timoshenko. Both had been critics of Yushchenko but also had participated with him in running the government as prime ministers. Besides, they had mutually managed to obtain Russia's support '... following V. Putin's sad experience during the Orange Revolution, the Kremlin will no longer bet on one and single candidate. V. Putin will count simultaneously on two candidates, Y. Timoshenko and V. Yanukovych, inspired by their pro-Russian orientation'.[651]

Altogether, the following candidates competed for the presidency: Victor Yushchenko seeking re-election, the oligarch Sergei Tihipko, Arseniy Yatsenyuk, Petro Symonenko from the Communist Party of Ukraine, Oleksandr Moroz from the Socialist Party, the pragmatic Volodymyr Lytvyn, the extreme right candidate Oleh Tyahnybok and the former minister of defence under Yuschenko, Anatoliy Hrytsenko.

On the other side, Yushchenko's popularity was so low that he obtained one of the lowest scores in the history of electoral process around the world for an acting president.[652] There was a decrease in

---

[651] Perepelytsia, *Foreign Policy of Ukraine, Annual Strategic Review 2008*, Op. Cit., page 247.
[652] Another similar example occurred when Lech Wałęsa got only 1.4% of the votes in the 2000 Polish presidential election even though in this case it was 5 years after he had finished his presidential term. Note of the author.

the total turnout compared to the 2004 presidential election and, at the end, the first round results confirmed Yanukovych in the first place and Timoshenko in the second. Tihipko came as a surprise in the third place which assured him a strong position to negotiate with the future government even though he did not endorse any of the candidates for the second round. Yushchenko finished in a disappointing fifth place with 5.45% of the votes. Symonenko and Lytvyn were far from being serious candidates while Yatsenyuk also with almost 7% of votes was fourth.

The first five places were from people from the same political establishment and all had worked under Yushchenko in different circumstances. Tihipko had headed the National Bank of Ukraine and had Yatsenyuk as his deputy when Yushchenko was prime minister, while as mentioned Timoshenko and Yanukovych had been in charge of the government during Yushchenko's presidency. Besides, all had some sort of relations with the oligarchs. Firtash sustained at different points, Yushchenko, Yatsenyuk and Yanukovych mostly because he did not want Timoshenko to get to the presidency after she had damaged his business in RosUkrEnergo.[653]

The only considerable difference was regarding foreign policy. Yushchenko proposed more of the same pro-Western orientation while Timoshenko had a more realistic approach. She had proved herself capable of negotiating with Putin on specific items. Yanukovych instead was portrayed in the West as a pro-Russian candidate even though he responded more to the oligarchs, who did not want to cut at all their ties with the West. Even if the oligarchs could eventually concede to strategic Russian interests on specific issues, including the lease contract for the Naval Base in Sevastopol, which was due to expire in 2017, and became therefore an issue part of the campaign.

Altogether, the results in the first round for the most known candidates on 17 January 2010, were as follows:

---

[653] Wilson, Andrew, 'Yatseniuk loses fresh-face label, popularity after his financial backers exposed,' *Kyiv Post*, October 22, 2009, accessed on March 2, 2015. http://www.kyivpost.com/opinion/op-ed/yatseniuk-loses-fresh-face-label-popularity-after--51159.html

Candidates	Nominating Party	Votes	%
Victor Yanukovych	Party of Regions	8,686,642	35.32
Iulia Timoshenko	All-Ukrainian Union 'Fatherland'	6,159,810	25.05
Serhiy Tihipko	Self-nominated	3,211,198	13.05
Arseniy Yatsenyuk	Self-nominated	1,711,737	6.96
Victor Yushchenko	Self-nominated	1,341,534	5.45
Petro Symonenko	Communist Party of Ukraine	872,877	3.54
Volodymyr Lytvyn	People's Party	578,883	2.35
Oleh Tyahnybok	All-Ukrainian Union 'Freedom'	352,282	1.43
Anatoliy Hrytsenko	Self-nominated	296,412	1.20
Against all		542,819	2.20

"Протокол Центральної виборчої комісії про результати голосування у день виборів Президента України," published January 25, 2010, accessed on March 4, 2015.
Source: http://www.cvk.gov.ua/info/protokol_cvk_17012010.pdf

The second round of the election[654] took place on 7 February 2010. Victor Yanukovych obtained 48.95% of the votes and Timoshenko 45.47%. Besides, 4.36% voted for the option 'against all' the same option received more than 8% of votes in the Kiev area. The vote had again present similar ethnolinguistic lines with the southeast supporting Yanukovych and the West supporting Timoshenko even though the latter had some inroads in the southeast and Yanukovych did the same in Timoshenko's Central Ukraine.

The most interesting fact about the second round was the apparent support of Yushchenko to Yanukovych.[655] There was a supposed agreement between both parties, in which after the election Yushchenko would become prime minister under Yanukovych. The deal included some cabinet positions like the Ministry of Foreign Affairs

---

[654] 'Протокол Центральної виборчої комісії про результати повторного голосування з виборів Президента України,' published on February 14, 2010, accessed on March 4, 2015. http://www.cvk.gov.ua/info/protokol_cvk_07022010.pdf
[655] 'Yushchenko to back Yanukovych in runoffs,' November 10, 2009, accessed on February 29, 2016. http://zik.com.ua/en/news/2009/11/10/204057

for Yatsenyuk and other ones for people related to Yushchenko.[656] Both parties denied the existence of the agreement leaked by Yaroslav Kozachok, the deputy head of the presidential secretariat's department. Even though, some actions by Yushchenko, first to pressure TV channels not to discuss publicly the issue and then, an investigation ordered by the president to the prosecutor general about how the document was leaked[657] would increase the suspicions, about the actual existence of the deal.

Altogether, it was difficult that the parliament would have approved Yushchenko's candidacy as prime minister, but in case it was true, it would show until what point the power struggle between Timoshenko and Yushchenko grew. Besides the fact that the supposed deal included points like diminishing NATO aspirations, and a middle ground about the intention of making Russian become second state language in Ukraine, it would mean that with a pro-Western stand, as Yushchenko had assumed, his initial foreign policy goals were far from reachable.

The election was recognized by the European Union, the United States and most EU members congratulated Yanukovych. Only Iulia Timoshenko did not accept the results. She initially challenged the score but withdrew her appeal on February 20 and declared that she would not challenge the results any more.[658]

At the end, the United States and the European Union had to swallow the idea that the beaten candidate in 2004, the one depicted in the West as the 'corrupt and undemocratic pro-Russian' successor of Kuchma's regime, was now to become the president of Ukraine. Yushchenko, even with strong US support, had failed to carry out the reforms desired by the West. He pushed too far. It is true that he was uncomfortable with Russian foreign policy interests, in cases like the Georgian War, but the result for Ukraine was

---

[656] 'President's office ex-official blows Yushchenko-Yanukovych secret deal,' January 8, 2010, accessed on March 5, 2015. http://zik.com.ua/en/news/2010/01/08/211289
[657] Kuzio, Taras, 'Yushchenko and Yanukovych forge an electoral alliance,' January 5, 2010, *Eurasia Daily Monitor*, Vol. 7, No. 2, accessed on February 29, 2016. http://www.jamestown.org/single/?tx_ttnews%5Btt_news%5D=35871&no_cache=1#.VVTDnvntmko
[658] 'Yulia Timoshenko will not challenge the results in Supreme Court,' February 20, 2010, accessed on March 5, 2015. http://www.tymoshenko.ua/en/article/vu8az6s6

catastrophic. He proved to be divisive among an already divided population and put US foreign policy interests before a more pragmatic approach that could allow him to keep an eye on a supposed national interest. Besides, the oligarchs remained untouched and as the element that still had the strong grip on power. He never even tried to confront the inherent issues regarding corruption in public affairs even though as everything proves he was quite well informed and he kept being, as Andrew Wilson defined him a 'banker among thieves'. Altogether, the West had lost this battle with Russia.

2.6 Yanukovych: The Donbas clan stakes their hold on power

Victor Yanukovych was sworn into office as the fourth president of Ukraine on 25 February 2010. His political development had been quite different from Kuchma's or Kravchuk's. Native from Makiyivka, a mining village in Donetsk, he was sent to prison for teenagers with a three-year conviction after his activities in a local gang but was granted an amnesty in 1967. He also had another conviction for inflicting harm during an armed robbery two years later.[659] With this history, it would have been tough to develop a political carrier but with the patronage of the local hero cosmonaut Georgy Beregovoy, he managed to enter the party and during the 1980s started to head a series of local factories in the area.

Meanwhile, after the Soviet collapse, the local Donbas industry was extremely dependent on Kiev's subsidies. It became tougher to obtain them from Kiev rather than from Moscow. Therefore, the local industry organized strikes and started to threaten with separatism issues, helped with the fact that the population in the Donbas had always developed a strong local identity. This forced Kiev to turn its attention to the Donbass and kept the subsidies flowing.

Afterwards, local industry directors started to be challenged by local mafias that started to establish 'legitimate' businesses. The most dominant one was headed by Akhat Bragin, who started to expand to different activities, like banking or football by buying the team Shakhtar Donetsk. Bragin managed to wipe out all the rival groups including their leaders. The Industrial Union of the Donbas

---

[659] Wilson, Op. Cit., page 10.

(IUD) was established in 1995 to serve as a lobby for the new clan. When it started to clash with the interests Pavlo Lazarenko, who was from the rival region of Dnepropetrovsk, a series of murders followed against members of the Donetsk group. Bragin was killed by a bomb in Shaktar's stadium in October 1995 while his business partner, Yevhen Shcherban, was also assassinated and many related to the circle too. This allowed a younger generation from the clan to appear. One of these new arrivals was Rinat Akhmetov. Rumours related him with Bragin's assassination while he used mafia methods to push aside the 'red directors' of the IUD.[660]

He developed highly lucrative schemes. First with coal and the subsidies the local industry received and then with a scam using regional financial groups to acquire shares in energy-generating and distribution companies to provide another cheap input for the local industry he owned or controlled. To promote the idea of a free economic zone for the Donbas was also part of his proposals.

In this context, Yanukovych's links with Akhmetov allowed him to become vice-head of Donetsk Oblast Administration in August 1996 and governor in May 1997. Always in relation with Akhmetov, he purged Lazarenko supporters from the local administration and helped Rinat take over local rackets. Later, Kuchma promised the clan to give it autonomy in its own affairs if they supported him in the 1998 presidential election.

Meanwhile, with administrative resources, he managed to build a party to combat the influence of the Communist Party of Ukraine in the local elections. The results gained by the party locally helped him gather enough support from Kuchma to take him to Kiev and eventually be nominated as prime minister in 2002. All that time, Yanukovych's links with Akhmetov were clear who managed to develop a complex business empire. It included four parts: System Capital Management group (SCM), which controlled iron and steel production; the ARS joint stock company which coordinated mining and supplies; a company that supplied local pits with mining equipment; and Concern Enerho, another regional energy supplier. Afterwards, he formed relations with other groups belonging to the

---

[660] Ibidem.

food industry. Altogether, he had few businesses in Russia compared with other groups from Kharkov or other areas. The most important issue concerned export to China.[661] All this while, he was Ukraine's richest man.

Therefore, even if Western media portrayed Yanukovych as the pro-Russian candidate, it would be very simplistic to conceive him as just that. He was the candidate of the oligarchs and more precisely of the Donbas clan and Akhmetov's. Still, it is clear that to be elected to the presidency, he had to make a pact with the different groups from different areas. The ordeal would include like Firtash, Tihipko and other names. His career had grown, thanks to the impulse given by the oligarchs, and in the measure he responded to them. Kravchuk and Kuchma were party pragmatic apparatchiks from another generation. Instead, Yanukovych grew with Akhmetov and with his protection.

At the beginning, he was a supposed public servant that benefited by serving the oligarchs, but once in power, he tried to become an oligarch himself. The development of a big fortune by his son would confirm his position during the following years. Therefore, once he started to obtain political and economic weight close to others like Akhmetov and Firtash, they did not always take it with good eyes. Nobody likes new arrivals that only bring more rivalries in the elite. These divisions became apparent in the 2013–2014 political crisis.

2.6.1 Pro Russians or pro oligarchs?

The first issue Yanukovych had to confront, as a president, was the nomination of a prime minister. Once it was clear Iulia Timoshenko could not remain in charge, he suggested three possibilities,[662] which illustrated that he did not have an apparent intention of breaking completely with the Western-oriented economic policies. The candidates were Sergei Yatsenyuk, Sergei Tihipko and Mykola Azarov. The first was, as noticed, a strong supporter of neo-liberal

---

[661] Ibidem, page 12.
[662] 'Yanukovych has yet to secure ruling majority in parliament,' February 25, 2010, accessed on February 29, 2016. https://www.kyivpost.com/content/ukraine/yanukovych-has-yet-to-secure-ruling-majority-in-pa-60468.html?flavour=mobile

policies and had been in the Ukrainian National Bank under Tihipko, an oligarch, who had a strong presence in the presidential election and could become a balancing force against other oligarchs. The third one, Azarov, headed the state tax administration (1996–2002) and was not per se a political force, but he had strong links with the Donbas. Of course, all of them had links with different oligarchs.

As mentioned, Yanukovych did not win with a majority in the parliament, but after the election, enough members from 'Our Ukraine', changed sides to assure him the possibility to nominate Azarov who became prime minister with 242 votes. Still, it remained a country politically divided on ethnic lines and deeply affected by the world economic crisis in 2008–2009. The GDP had fallen 15% only during 2009. At the end, the ones more affected by the inner power struggle were the Ukrainian people, who had again to pay the price with a decline in the social and living standards.

The new cabinet considered personalities related to the oligarchs, and Tihipko became deputy prime minister in charge of economic issues; later, in December, he became vice prime minister and minister of social policy. Yuriy Boyko, that used to head Naftogaz, became the strategic minister of fuel and energy.[663] Boyko and Serhiy Lyovochkin, who became the head of the presidential administration, were people related to Firtash; and in this way they wanted to secure a strong position in the government.

One notable feature during Yanukovych's first year in office was that the Constitutional Court of Ukraine decided that the political reforms carried out in 2004, which changed Ukraine into a kind of semi-presidential republic, were not constitutional, therefore returning to the old constitution and giving more powers to the president again. The decision became highly controversial, as it is not common for a court to consider the unconstitutionality of an issue six years after it occurred. Altogether, it allowed Yanukovych to concentrate more power.

---

[663] 'Le nouveau président ukrainien forme une coalition pour sortir le pays de la crise,' March 12, 2010, accessed on March 1, 2015. http://www.lemonde.fr/europe/article/2010/03/12/le-nouveau-president-ukrainien-forme-une-coalition-pour-sortir-le-pays-de-la-crise_1318204_3214.html

Meanwhile, the fact that Timoshenko did not recognize his victory allowed her to become a strong opposition figure. Therefore, another of the first political steps by Yanukovych was to go after Timoshenko. The judicial and political process that followed were not exempt from the geopolitical struggle present around Ukraine. It is true that numerous judicial procedures were opened against Timoshenko before Yanukovych took office, and it is true, that in some sense they had some sort of a judicial base. But, in this case, it was decided with political precision to prosecute him for one of the numerous cases of abuse of power present in the country but against his strongest political rival. In fact, Yanukovych did the same thing Timoshenko would have done if she had won the election, to hit the other at his or her weak spot. Simple political strategy.[664]

Accused of having signed a gas deal with Gazprom was considered unfair to Ukraine in 2009, Timoshenko became therefore the subject of a judicial process started under Yushchenko. At the end, she was condemned to seven years in jail and ordered to pay the state $188 million. The case received huge media attention throughout the world and it is worth also mentioning that Yushchenko testified against Timoshenko and considered it a 'normal judicial process'.[665] This shows again until what point the 'orange love' between the two persons that led to the so-called 'Orange Revolution' had disappeared and transformed into a huge political rivalry.

There were other cases opened against her, involving the use of funds regarding the selling of quotas under the Kyoto Protocol and with the inappropriate buying of ambulances, even though only the first charge was enough to get her to jail. Since her incarceration, Timoshenko portrayed herself as a victim of a 'Stalinist purge' and showed herself as being prey to Yanukovych retaliations against the opposition. Her position was widely publicized in the West, where

---

[664] As a similar example, when Nicolas Sarkozy took office, he opened procedures against Jacques Chirac and some years later, Francois Hollande did the same against Sarkozy. Even if the judicial systems are not comparable, it is quite common around the world to find the opening of judicial procedures against a political rival like in a logic of check and balances, even though to determine how fair is each one of the procedures would be a completely different ordeal. Note of the author.

[665] 'Ultimate betrayal: Ukraine retreats to a Dark past,' October 18, 2011, accessed on February 25, 2015. http://www.spiegel.de/international/europe/ultimate-betrayal-ukraine-retreats-to-a-dark-past-a-792458-2.html

she complained about the unfair judicial process she had went through. Altogether, she became more pro-Western than during her presidential campaign and her liberation would become one of the demands from the United States, the EU and its members made to the Yanukovych Government during the following years.

Another considerable development during his term was the law regarding regional languages. Yanukovych had for many years pushed for Russian to become the second state language, something quite logical in a country where more than 40% speak Russian as a mother tongue. Everybody who has lived in Ukraine can easily notice the bilingual atmosphere present around the territory, where bilingual conversations even in TV, the parliament or elsewhere are the norm. There was a strong resistance from Western Ukrainians due to the fear of a supposed Russification, while it was an old demand from the Russian-speaking regions of South-Eastern Ukraine. Finally, the law was approved and signed with controversies that included a fistfight in the Rada (something common in the last decade).

At the end, to raise the status of Russian as a regional official language was an important step that could allow the state-building process to go to another level, not only around one language or ethnic group but around a new common *ethos* based more on a political idea of a Ukrainian citizenship rather than on an ethnic idea. Instead, the language issue has always been used by nationalist groups in the West or by Russia to push for their policies of interest and has been one of the main dividing issues in Ukrainian society which has clearly a multilingual basis.

The new law expanded the role of all the languages from any minority that represents 10% or more of the population of a determined area into a regional language.[666] That way, not only Russian but also in some cases Romanian and Hungarian became regional languages.[667]

---

[666] 'Yanukovych signs language bill into law,' August 8, 2012, accessed on February 29, 2016. http://www.kyivpost.com/content/ukraine/yanukovych-signs-language-bill-into-law-311230.html

[667] Six regional councils declared Russian a regional language and Crimea drove similar provisions. Meanwhile, Romanian and Hungarian became also regional languages in some villages. There was even one more that declared Moldovan to be the regional language in the village of Tarasivtsi in the

During the first two years of his presidency, there was also a general disenchantment with the political system. Not only Yushchenko's presidency had failed to make any concrete changes to the Ukrainian living standard, it had severely deteriorated. Besides, the general perception was that either side of the political spectrum represented just the same habits of a cronyism proper of the ruling political class. Yushchenko had established before 'to combat corruption' as a national priority, the fact is that it was only a matter of speech and the same happened during Yanukovych first three years. At the end, there was no notable difference during his term with regard to the lack of will to tackle the evident issues of cronyism and chronic corruption at all levels of the public administration.

Differences started to arise between the oligarchs for diverse reasons; the ones that had already amassed fortunes, like Akhmetov, Firtash and Tihipko, were looking to become legitimate. If we remember, how Pleiko Heines[668] mentioned the different phases of development of the oligarchs, by now, they owned already big holdings, well integrated with the global economy. Therefore, they were also investors in the EU and were not reduced to exporters of raw materials. Their interests were always more related to the EU market. Consequently, to do business worldwide they needed to be seen as trustable partners. To this end, remembering the famous novel by Mario Puzo, *The Godfather,* which afterwards became an Academy Award winner for best picture in 1972, the most important goal of 'the Family' was to become legitimate, that is to stop being a criminal organization and to manage a 'socially accepted' family business. At the end, this goal was not different from that of the Ukrainian oligarchs. Even with their criminal past, the way their holdings had grown made it imperative to look for some sort of legitimation.

Meanwhile, since Yanukovych arrived in the presidency he did not want to play just the role of Akhmetov's puppet, but endeavoured to become an oligarch too; but it was obvious that he was back

---

Chernovtsy region but as we shall see the difference between Romanian and Moldovan is political not linguistic. 'Romanian becomes regional language in Bila Tserkva in Zakarpattia region,' September 24, 2012, accessed on February 29, 2016. http://www.kyivpost.com/content/ukraine/romanian-becomes-region al-language-in-bila-tserkva-in-zakarpattia-region-313373.html

[668] As mentioned in Section 2.4 'Kuchma: The emergence of the oligarchs'.

in the race of amassing a fortune like his former protector. Moreover, there are two figures interesting about the notable preference for the Donbas. First, the fact that more than 46% of the budget subventions for social and economic development were allocated to the Donbas (Donetsk and Lugansk). Second, for instance, in January 2014, two months after the political crisis had started, Yanukovych's son, Oleksandr, was allegedly winning more than 50% of the public tenders while Akhmetov's businesses obtained only 31%.[669] Yanukovych seemed not worry so much about the appearances and the social legitimation the other oligarchs were looking for. After his fall in 2014, the way his abandoned estate showed the extremely sumptuous conditions in which he lived confirmed the reasons for the lack of trust among most of the Ukrainian electorate towards the ruling class.

The lack of legitimacy in the dealings he carried out in the first two years of government contributed also to another electoral reform before the 2012 parliamentary election. After two years, there was a general disenchantment towards the biggest political parties. For instance, it is interesting to know that the Ukrainian electoral law had until then an option in which the voters could vote 'against all' candidates. A poll before the election indicated that more than 17% of the voters would have voted against all, if the option had remained for the election.[670] Imagine what public embarrassment would be if among the leading parties in the election the option 'against all' emerged as the winner? Therefore, it is no surprise that a new electoral law removed that option and reduced by half the candidates elected by proportionality while the others could be elected in single constituencies. The new legislation was approved by a comfortable majority, which included support obviously by both, the Party of the Regions and Timoshenko's Party (Batkivshchyna).[671]

---

[669] 'Ukraine crisis: Oligarchs are Yanukovych's weakest link,' February 20, 2014, accessed on February 20, 2014. http://www.bbc.com/news/world-europe-26277970

[670] 'R&B poll: 17% of Ukrainians would vote 'against everybody' during elections,' November 11, 2012, accessed on November 11, 2012. http://en.interfax.com.ua/news/general/128943.html

[671] 'Parliament passes law on parliamentary elections,' November 17, 2011, accessed on February 29, 2016. http://www.kyivpost.com/content/politics/parliament-passes-law-on-parliamentary-elections-117151.html

In this context, it is not a surprise that 'new' political forces arrive when the present ones are quite discredited. Therefore, a new party appeared, UDAR. It was headed by the boxer and world heavyweight champion Vitali Klitschko. His popularity as a sportsman and as someone outside the ruling political class allowed him to figure quite well in the polls before the election, especially because his party avoided touching thorny issues like the language and ethnic issues. Still, it is important to notice that his electoral list contained several names related to oligarchs Dmytro Firtash and Ihor Kolomoysky.[672] Therefore, the three main parties heading the parliamentary election had again some kind of link with the oligarchs. Besides, it is interesting to notice here the pragmatic step taken by Petro Poroshenko. He had entered the government as minister of economy in March 2012, but quit to become a candidate in a single constituency from Vinnitsa.

Overall, the result from the parliamentary elections left the three main parties related to different extents to the oligarchs as the main political forces, while two parties not related to them managed to obtain considerable regional success: the Communist Party of Ukraine and the extreme right party Svoboda. Both had only local acceptance in the southeast and in the West, respectively. The Communist Party campaigned only in Russian while Svoboda also in Ukrainian; so, even they were critical of the role of the oligarchs, the strong ethnolinguistic remarks each one had in their programmes made it difficult for them to obtain more preferences nationwide. Altogether, the results were as follows:

Parties	%	Swing %	Seats (proportional representation)	Seats (single constituencies)	Seats (total)
Party of Regions	30.00	▼ 4.37	72	113	185
All-Ukrainian Union 'Fatherland'	25.55	▼ 5.16	62	39	101

---

[672] 'After the parliamentary elections in Ukraine: A tough victory for the party of regions,' November 7, 2012, accessed on November 7, 2012. http://www.osw.waw.pl/en/publikacje/analyses/2012-11-07/after-parliamentary-elections-ukraine-a-tough-victory-party-regions

UDAR (Ukrainian Democratic Alliance for Reform)	13.97	N/A	34	6	40
Communist Party of Ukraine	13.18	▲ 7.79	32	—	32
All-Ukrainian Union 'Svoboda'	10.45	▲ 9.69	25	12	37

Official results of the 2012 parliamentary elections published on: "ПРОТОКОЛ ЦЕНТРАЛЬНОЇ ВИБОРЧОЇ КОМІСІЇ ПРО РЕЗУЛЬТАТИ ВИБОРІВ НАРОДНИХ ДЕПУТАТІВ УКРАЇНИ У ЗАГАЛЬНОДЕРЖАВНОМУ БАГАТОМАНДАТНОМУ ВИБОРЧОМУ ОКРУЗІ," November 10, 2012, accessed on March 5, 2015.
Source: http://www.cvk.gov.ua/info/zbvo_2012.pdf

The Party of Regions managed to conserve a similar amount of seats as in the last election with 185 while the great defeat was to Timoshenko's party that lost more than 50 to obtain only 101. UDAR and the Communist Party were close to 13% both, but thanks to the new electoral law, instead of obtaining around 60 seats, they only got 40 and 32, respectively, while Svoboda had 37 seats. It is worth noting also that independents and minor parties obtained 50 seats in single constituencies and 5 of those had to repeat the election due to irregularities. The independents as usual proved themselves 'available' to assuring the Party of Regions the majority. Therefore, it seemed that Azarov would have again a slight majority to repeat as prime minister. It is in this political inner context that Ukraine was headed to the 2013–2014 political crisis.

Foreign policy

Once knowing the inner developments that occurred in the first three years of Yanukovych's term, it is fundamental to analyse the external context and its evolution until the events of 2013–2014.

The arrival of Yanukovych marked a deep change in the Western-oriented foreign policy intended by Yushchenko. As mentioned, it would be a mistake to portray Yanukovych mainly as pro-Russian. The oligarchs needed both, the West and Russia. In that sense, the EU market was more tempting for the oligarchs as it could be more profitable, even though a deeper relation with the EU would have to be subject to the EU concurrence laws and that would damage their monopolies. They understood perfectly how Russia could still supply cheap gas for their energy local monopolies and how they still represented a considerable market for their products. Russia's possibility to dissuade any rapprochement with the West made it imperative to look for a different foreign policy that without being pro-Russian would not be interpreted as anti-Russian. Yanukovych proposed a bill to exclude Ukraine from any military bloc. The non-bloc status obtained 226 votes at the parliament on 3 June 2010. This status mostly pointed against any enrolment in NATO but did not exclude further cooperation with the EU, even though, still there was a great degree of Russian insistence so Ukraine would participate in the Customs Union with Russia, Belarus and Kazakhstan, which later became the Eurasian Economic Union.

Altogether, the arrival of Yanukovych meant also for Russia a great victory after the events of 2004. As described earlier, one of the biggest worries of the Russian foreign policy was the Ukrainian approach to join NATO during Yushchenko's term together with the fact that the contract to lease the Sevastopol base was due to expire in 2017. There was an urge to find a solution to guarantee first the permanence of the base, at least in a medium term and to stop NATO advances against CIS members. The solution obtained by Russia was the Kharkov agreement.

The January 2009 gas supply contract stipulated that Naftogaz would have to pay the full European gas price beginning from 2010. As explained, the conditions to get the 2009 gas crisis to an end were worse than the once offered by Russia before it started. Therefore, it was in Ukraine's interest, but more precisely in the interest of the oligarchs related to energy distribution to reduce the price. The government intended to decrease the price to $250 with the excuse they claimed to balance its budget with IMF requirements while it would represent losses to Gazprom of 3bn. Russia was not willing to concede a discount on gas that would also mean an economic loss without obtaining political concession. Therefore, the priority for the Russian foreign policy was to assure precisely the presence in Crimea. The negotiation between Azarov, Boyko and Vladimir Putin, who by then was prime minister, allowed the final agreement to be signed on 21 April 2010, in Kharkov between Victor

Yanukovych and Medvedev. The agreement, ratified during the following week, stipulated that Ukraine would receive a 30% drop in the price of natural gas from Russia in exchange for receiving permission to lease the naval base in Sevastopol for 25 years with an additional 5-year renewal option.[673] The agreement stated that the money saved by Ukraine, as a result of the price reduction, would constitute an obligation of the Ukrainian state in case the lease was not respected. Besides, the only instrument that would allow Ukraine to claim a price discount would be precisely the agreement on the lease.[674] It was offered a consortium for a gas transportation consortium but as Ukraine only offered management but not ownership, the issue was finally not part of the deal[675] while it is true that Russia's interest in the gas network had also decreased. The idea of having a consortium might have avoided the unauthorized offtakes and the 2006 and 2009 gas crises but by now, Moscow was more interested in the development of Nord and South Streams. The first of those was already under construction in that year. Still, the offer to merge Naftogaz and Gazprom was made by Putin and the discussion on some kind of joint venture with the perspective of a merger stayed on the Russian agenda for a while until a declaration by Deputy Prime Minister Tihipko finally rejected the idea.[676]

Altogether, Russia had obtained already the non-bloc status by Ukraine, stopped NATO's enlargement and assured a military presence in Ukraine for three decades. In that sense, some of the Russian foreign policy goals had been obtained. There remained the idea of pulling Ukraine into the Customs Union, something that seemed complicated considering that Yanukovych also seemed to pursue further cooperation with the EU to establish the Association Agreement.

---

[673] 'Договор Януковича и Медведева о базировании флота до 2042 года. Текст документа,' Украинская правда, April 22, 2010, accessed on February 29, 2016. http://www.pravda.com.ua/rus/articles/2010/04/22/4956018/
[674] Yafimava, op. cit., page 197.
[675] The gas network in Ukraine has always been state owned and it has been a controversial subject in Ukraine, as the constitution forbids privatization of the network. Therefore, the strategic importance it has for the oligarchs allows it to be considered like 'family silver' like Yafimava states and its potential sale would be seen as the sale of statehood. Ibidem, page 198.
[676] Ibidem, page 206.

In that sense, Ukraine's decision to become an 'observer' in the Customs Union of Belarus, Kazakhstan and Russia could be interpreted as a symbolic gesture that intended to show that they pretended to sustain economic links with Moscow but on the other hand, they intended also to pursue further cooperation with the EU. Russia actively insisted that Ukraine join the Customs Union but did not succeed. At the end, Ukraine was trapped between two geopolitical projects and received pressure from both actors, the EU and Russia. Besides, the ambivalent position of the Ukrainian Government that tried to keep a good relation with the International Monetary Fund at the end generated a common mistrust among the EU, the IMF and Russia.

Specifically, the relations with the United States also got colder after the arrival of Yanukovych. Moreover, there was a clear repercussion due to the state of the relations between the United States and Russia and the famous 'reset' that claimed to rebuild the relation after the arrival of Barack Obama to the presidency in 2009. Therefore, thorny issues like the missile shield in the Czech Republic and Poland stayed temporarily out of the agenda.

> The reset of US-Russia relations induced a certain re-grouping of the US Role in Eastern Europe. For the sake of securing Russian support in tackling Iran and Afghanistan problems, achieving progress in non-proliferation of weapons of mass destruction and stabilizing situation in the Middle East the US lessened their strategic interest in Ukraine.[677]

The United States, at least publicly, seemed to accept the renunciation of NATO membership perspective by Ukraine.[678] Common declarations by Hillary Clinton as US Secretary of State and by President Victor Yanukovych showed their willingness to accept either the middle ground that the term 'non-allied state' portrayed, together with acceptance by the United States of the victory of Victor

---

[677] Perepelytsia, G.M., Ukraine's relations with the USA and Canada in *Foreign Policy of Ukraine Annual Strategic Review 2009/10*, Kiev, Stylos Publishing House, 2011, page 270.

[678] In Kiev, I remember how once a professor that used to have contact with the US embassy confided to me how he noticed a clear diminution in the embassy's activities in comparison to what happened during Yushchenko's term in office.

Yanukovych in the 2010 presidential elections, considering them 'free, fair, transparent'.[679]

At the end, the United States commonly recognized elections or regimes independent of their democratic credentials, but in relation to their geopolitical need in determined areas of the world. Therefore, it is not a surprise that even if the victory by Yanukovych had meant a defeat for them, still they wanted to keep the door open for possible negotiations. Possibly a soft-policy approach was needed to keep Ukraine near the Western orbit and that approach could certainly be given by the European Union.

In that sense, the relation between the EU and Ukraine during Yanukovych's term in office was plagued with contradictions. The 14th summit between the EU and Ukraine took place in November 2010 and was the first attended by Victor Yanukovych as president. Since then, an action plan to introduce free-visa[680] travel was introduced. Herman Van Rompuy, who by then was the president of the European Council, noticed the 'progress' Ukraine had made in relation with the EU but underlined that still Ukraine needed to fulfil some conditions related to the visa policy. The most significant issue of that summit became the joint commitment on establishing a joint free trade zone.[681]

The next year, relations stiffed. The EU-Ukraine summit in 2011 was affected by the incarceration of Iulia Timoshenko. Her widely publicized trial had shown her in the West as a victim of an oppressive regime while many EU members openly pushed for her liberation. Therefore, the geopolitical goal of pursuing the Association Agreement contradicted itself with the push from the United States and some EU members to put on top of the agenda the Timoshenko

---

[679] As quoted in Perepelytsia, Op. Cit., page 273.
[680] Until now, the visa-free regime has been openly the most pursued goal by the Ukrainian authorities regarding the EU. To them, it means to legitimize themselves with the EU while allowing the middle classes to travel freely and to stay legally or not to work in easier conditions than until now. Even though the subject continues to be freezed by the EU because of the notable complications it would include, especially after the events of 2014–2015, a visa-free regime to the EU would risk of bringing a much higher increase in migration from Ukraine, mostly considering the deteriorating economic conditions. Note of the author.
[681] 'EU-Ukraine summits : 16 years of wheel-spinning,' February 28, 2013, http://ukrainianweek.com/Politics/73494

issue. By December 2011, the EU left the 'technical issues' of the agreement solved but left the rest (the Timoshenko case) in the hands of Ukraine's government.[682]

Therefore, the relation during 2012 continued to be influenced by the different positions regarding Timoshenko. Even though by that time there was a general opposition among the EU towards the Ukrainian Government asking for her liberation, there were different views regarding what should be done with the Association Agreement.

The UEFA EURO 2012 complicated even more the issue. An event originally proposed by Yushchenko, to be organized together with Poland with the already explained geopolitical effect, became instead an activity in which Poland had to coordinate with Ukraine, besides the obvious political and geopolitical differences present. Some leaders were asking for a boycott of the event.[683] The highly publicized hunger strike[684] by Timoshenko increased her popularity in the West while the government did not show any intention to change its position in that subject.[685] At the end, even with the absence of several EU leaders in the competition, the Euro Cup evolved as expected while allocated huge public spending beneficial to the oligarchs in different sectors related to the competition venues.

Altogether, for the 16th summit on 25 February 2013, there was a common statement in which Ukraine was 'determined to comply' with the prerequisites to sign the Association Agreement, including what they defined 'a deep and comprehensive free-trade area'.[686] By

---

[682] Ibidem.
[683] Stroophants, Jean Paul, ' L'UE divisée sur un éventuel boycott de l'Euro 2012 en Ukraine,' *Le Monde*, May 14, 2012, accessed on May 14, 2012. http://www.lemonde.fr/europe/article/2012/05/14/l-union-europeenne-divisee-sur-un-eventuel-boycott-de-l-euro-2012-en-ukraine_1701148_3214.html
[684] 'Ukraine : l'opposant Timoshenko cessera sa grève de la faim mercredi,' *Le Monde*, May 8, 2012, accessed on May 8, 2012. http://www.lemonde.fr/europe/article/2012/05/08/affaire-timochenko-l-ukraine-boycottee-annule-un-sommet-international_1697787_3214.html
[685] 'L'Ukraine met en garde Berlin contre un "boycott politique" de l'Euro 2012,' April 30, 2012, accessed on April 30, 2012. http://www.lemonde.fr/sport/article/2012/04/30/l-ukraine-met-en-garde-berlin-contre-un-boycott-politique-de-l-euro-2012_1693037_3242.html
[686] 'EU-Ukraine summits : 16 years of wheel-spinning,' February 28, 2013, http://ukrainianweek.com/Politics/73494

then, it had been clear that the Ukrainian Government was playing a double card by showing the intention to continue negotiations on the Association Agreement while also having talks about the Customs Union with Moscow. In that sense, the EU made it clear that it was not possible to join both spaces.

On March 12, an action plan on priority measures for European Integration for Ukraine, issued by the National Security and Defense Council of Ukraine, following the decree by the Cabinet of Ministers of Ukraine of the second Azarov Government entered into force by decree of the president.[687] The idea was to show the EU that a commitment was made. Meanwhile, on May 2013, there were also meetings in Astana regarding the Customs Union.

By then, the EU members started to urge to sign the Association Agreement in November. The idea was to use the Eastern Partnership summit to sign it. Instead, Russia increased the pressure to convince Ukrainian authorities about the advantages that it would give them to join the Customs Union. Meanwhile, the Ukrainian authorities continued to flirt with some aspects of the Customs Union[688] while still intending to sign the Association Agreement and trying to find a middle ground.

It is also important to notice the complete lack of a proper approach by the EU to handle the issue. The handling of foreign affairs by the EU authorities headed by Barroso and Catherine Ashton was unsuitable. They handled the affair as a technical issue when it was something that needed to have a clearly political and geopolitical approach. The goal was to bring Ukraine a step near to the EU and it could be achieved with the signature of the agreement. A realist approach would have understood the real potentialities of the EU to act and the Russian ones to react. It was not a deal only about 'free trade'; it was an agreement to take the Ukrainian territory out of the Russian orbit, at least in some spheres.

---

[687] 'УКАЗ ПРЕЗИДЕНТА УКРАИНЫ № 127/2013,' March 12, 2013, accessed on February 27, 2015. http://www.president.gov.ua/ru/documents/15520.html

[688] 'Больше трех не собираются,' Газета 'Коммерсантъ Украина,' №172 (1875), November 24, 2013, accessed on November 24, 2013. http://www.kommersant.ru/doc/2326962

When many EU members continued to pressure for the liberation of Timoshenko[689] or at least to allow her to receive medical treatment abroad (which in practice meant her liberation), they complicated more the decision by the Ukrainian Government. They were asking the president to sign an agreement with the EU and to free his biggest political rival, besides the big enmity that divided both actors (Yanukovych and Timoshenko) as former Polish president Aleksander Kwasniewski suggested.[690] Besides, the EU did not have the capacity to enforce this demand.

By then, it was obvious that Russia had also many aces on the table to pressure the Ukrainian authorities. All this should have been foreseen. Anyone with a slight historic understanding of Russia knows what Ukraine means to Moscow, therefore, any political advisor could easily predict a reaction by the Kremlin.

Since September, the Russian Government had been warning about the economic risks the agreement would bring and suggested that Ukraine would suffer a financial catastrophe and a collapse of the state. At the end, it became true.[691] That same month, Armenia announced that they had opted to join the Customs Union instead of signing the Association Agreement. That left only Georgia, Moldova and a dubious Ukraine as possibilities for the November summit to sign the deal.

The real negotiation had to be between the EU and Russia. It never happened. At a certain point, the Baltic states, Sweden and Poland were willing to sign the Association Agreement as negotiated without further preconditions; instead Germany continued to push for the liberation of Timoshenko.

On November 20, the Ukrainian Government signalled that there was no intention to liberate Timoshenko while the general

---

[689] In this sense, I do not judge if it was fair or unfair, but in many cases the EU has closed its eyes in front of notable human rights violations in other areas of the world in relation to its geopolitical interest. Here, it could have done the same if the political goal was to sign the agreement. Note of the author.

[690] 'Квасьневский рассказал о ненависти Януковича к Тимошенко,' November 19, 2013, accessed on November 19, 2013. https://news.mail.ru/inworld/ukraine/politics/15706634/

[691] 'Ukraine's EU trade deal will be catastrophic, says Russia,' *The Guardian*, September 22, 2013, accessed on September 22, 2013. http://www.theguardian.com/world/2013/sep/22/ukraine-european-union-trade-russia

prosecutor linked her with accounts in Switzerland worth $500 million.[692] Not surprisingly, this last information did not receive much attention in Western media.

Attention instead went to the Rada where deputies dropped the legislation that would have allowed Timoshenko to be released. All this, only some days after, three semi-secret meetings between Vladimir Putin and Victor Yanukovych signalled the final defeat for the EU. On November 21, Ukraine officially refused to sign the Association Agreement.[693] Moscow had won another battle and opened the door for what would be the events that would deeply affect the political life of Ukraine for the subsequent years. It started, then, another scenario of the battle for Ukraine between Russia and the West.

2.6.2 The Ukrainian crisis, 2013–2014

The refusal to sign the Association Agreement was enough to organize most of the parliamentary opposition against the government. Three of the four opposition parties complained that the rejection to sign the Agreement was detrimental to the Ukrainian position while the Communist Party that had opposed the deal preferred to keep a low profile. UDAR, headed by Klitschko, Fatherland by Yatsenyuk and Svoboda even with notable inner differences among them, especially the last one, decided to seize the opportunity to convene a protest for the next Sunday after the announcement. It was the first time the opposition tried to invite a massive rally in many years. The protests organized in recent months for the liberation of Iulia Timoshenko had not enjoyed the support of a considerable part of the population that saw 'the blonde with pigtails' as usually portrayed in the West as just another oligarch from the corrupt political class in Ukraine. Instead, this time, it was expected that the refusal to sign the agreement could give rise to bigger protests against the government, even though it was not at all perceived directly which would be the immediate benefits the agreement

---

[692] 'Юлия Тимошенко нажила врагов в Швейцарии,' November 20, 2013, accessed on November 20, 2013. http://www.kommersant.ua/doc/2347889

[693] 'L'Ukraine renonce à s'associer avec l'UE, Ioulia Timochenko reste en prison,' *Le Monde*, November 21, 2013, accessed on November 21, 2013. http://www.lemonde.fr/europe/article/2013/11/21/ioulia-timochenko-reste-en-ukraine_3518120_3214.html

would bring to the population. In fact, the expectation among the middle class went from the desire to more transparency, diminish corruption, but mostly to have access to the Schengen Zone without visa and maybe even get a work permit easily for the EU. Little was known about what exactly the Association Agreement meant, something a little bit more than a free trade deal with the intention to adapt in certain aspects to the EU legislation. By then, only 45% of the Ukrainian population supported the signature of the Association Agreement.[694]

The first notable rally on November 24 gathered maybe almost 50,000 participants that even though they were not enough to challenge the government were a notable advance. Meanwhile the president declared already until what point Russian pressure[695] and the risk of an economic blockade were factors to decide the refusal to sign the Agreement. Besides, in the EU, there was a reaction of disappointment by the European Commission,[696] but not a clear unified voice by the EU to try to look for a deal with Moscow to unblock the Agreement. Only German chancellor Angela Merkel mentioned the possibility of discussing the issue[697] with Putin; meanwhile, the EU commission continued to deal with a clearly geopolitical portfolio only as a technical issue.

At that point, Ukrainian authorities suggested the possibility of receiving a compensation package to the EU authorities to avoid the economic effect that Russia could impose, but nothing was obtained.[698] It was obvious that an Ukrainian Government and the oligarchs would suffer from Russian economic sanctions and, therefore, if there was any intention of convincing them to change sides,

---

[694] 'Ukraine faces critical East-West Tug of war over association agreement,' *The Guardian*, November 20, 2013, accessed on November 20, 2013. http://www.theguardian.com/world/2013/nov/20/ukraine-eu-association-agreement-europe-russia

[695] 'Russia "blackmailed Ukraine to ditch EU pact"' *The Guardian*, November 22, 2013, accessed on November 22, 2013. http://www.theguardian.com/world/2013/nov/22/russia-ukraine-eu-pact-lithuania

[696] 'Statement by EU high representative Catherine Ashton on Ukraine,' Brussels, November 21, 2013, 131121/04. www.eeas.europa.eu

[697] 'Меркель намерена поговорить с Путиным об Украине и Восточном партнерстве,' November 23, 2013, accessed on November 23, 2013. http://www.kommersant.ua/news/2351686

[698] 'Евросоюз не расслышал предложения Украины,' November 26, 2013, accessed on November 26, 2013. http://www.kommersant.ua/doc/2352676

there was a need to put something more on the table than just the Association Agreement. A declaration by Angela Merkel some days later, made the point exactly in that sense when she referred about never to let Ukraine choose between Russia and the EU.[699] In fact, at this initial point, the only oligarch that positioned himself against the government and sustained the opposition rallies was Petro Poroshenko, whose businesses, mostly related with the chocolate and candy industry, would benefit more with an open EU market.

Until then, the Ukrainian Government with tacit Russian support seemed able to handle the rallies that had emerged. The Eastern Partnership summit in Vilnius on November 28 and 29 developed with obvious tension the consequence of the Ukrainian refusal to continue its alignment with the EU. Meanwhile, the Georgian and Moldovan signing did not receive the same attention due maybe to the size of the countries but also because of an obvious smaller geostrategic importance.

In the meantime, in Kiev, the events in the following hours after the summit would change the wave that had allowed Russia to obtain a symbolic victory by stopping the signature of the Association Agreement. On Saturday, November 30, after the political failure in Vilnius, the police violently dispersed a group of students still present in the *Maidan*. The action would not be out of controversy and would have a deep political effect. At that point, early in the morning, before the first rays of sun would appear in a slight cold autumn night, there were only some hundreds of protestors, mostly students from the last day. Most of them were planning to leave in the following hours and it was clear by then, the protests had not achieved the desired political goal.

It was common in Kiev during December that a big Christmas tree was built in the *Maidan* before the holidays and, therefore, the metallic structure had already been positioned partially. Therefore, with the excuse of liberating the area to continue the works, local

---

[699] 'Меркель: Нельзя ставить Украину перед выбором между Россией и ЕС,' December 18, 2014, accessed on December 18, 2014. http://korresponde nt.net/world/worldabus/3278376-merkel-nelzia-stavyt-ukraynu-pered-vybo rom-mezhdu-rossyei-y-es

police forces violently vacated the area, leaving numerous injured in between before the eyes of media.[700]

During the whole day, the actions and the effects were continuously repeated in the opposition media that included among others the 5th Channel, property of Petro Poroshenko. The outcome had a huge political effect. The image of the injured protestors created a huge outrage against the political repression that occurred and immediately pushed for a huge rally the following day that this time became a lot bigger than the ones before. Therefore, the fear of an authoritarian reprisal by the government became a sort of catalyst that allowed the emergence of a huge movement of discomfort against the government.

Before analysing the inner and external political effects that would change completely the flow of the political events, it is important to ask the question of the why and how all this happened. The first question that arises is why to send police forces to vacate the square and use violence when the students were already leaving? Who gave the order? For what reason? It is difficult to find any apparent political goal with this action, especially considering the divided political scene in Ukraine and the deteriorated reputation of the government. The police forces even if they were under the direct authority from the Kiev administration received instructions from someone in a higher position. At this point two hypotheses can be made:

1. The action counted on presidential support and pretended to give a lesson to the protestors.
2. The reprisal did not count on presidential support and pretended to erode the president's authority in the already fragile Ukrainian political scene.

During that same day after these events in the *Maidan*, there were two notable developments; first, the president and the prime minister condemned the actions against the protesters and did not recognize giving the order, second, early in the morning that same day,

---

[700] 'Ukraine: Les partisans de l'UE dispersés,' *Le Monde*, November 30, 2013, accessed on November 30, 2013. http://www.lemonde.fr/europe/article/2013/11/30/ukraine-la-police-disperse-les-partisans-de-l-europe_3523130_3214.html

Serhiy Lyovochkin resigned[701] as head of the Presidential Administration of Ukraine. This man was very close to Dmitry Firtash, by then the second most powerful oligarch in the country, who had been displeased during Yanukovych's administration because the president had favoured notably more his own son's businesses together with Akhmetov's instead of his. The conflicts of interests among the oligarchs were not always easy to handle, especially with Akhmetov continuously improving his position in relation with the others. Therefore, a weakened Yanukovych could be an easy prey for blackmail by Firtash, who could exchange political support for more benefits. Local scholars also sustained this theory, which was published some days after the events on a local newspaper.[702]

The same Yanukovych, more than a year after the events, sustained that the events which took place that day had been extremely prejudicial to him and it would have been senseless for him to order the violent dispersal of the protestors.[703] Therefore, an action ordered by Yanukovych would have been extreme political clumsiness, which cannot be excluded; but if it was instead planned by Lyovochkin, it would show the great fragility present in the Ukrainian Government and, how at the end, the public was held by the oligarchs in what would be another case of a failed state. Nevertheless, this action, motivated or not by Firtash, changed completely the political scene and put in jeopardy the stability of the regime.

Besides, this action brought a great new impulse to the turmoil. The new wave of protests showed hundreds of thousands of people gathered to express their discomfort at the government. That same Sunday saw a mix of spontaneous masses that appeared in the *Maidan* while other big groups arrived; but these were organized by the

---

[701] More suspicion generates the fact that it took several days to the president to react and finally refute Lyovochkin's resignation. 'Виктор Янукович не отпустил Сергея Левочкина в отставку,' Kommersant Ukraine online, December 2, 2013, accessed on December 2, 2013. http://www.kommersant.ua/doc/2358759

[702] 'Куда идет страна, 5 главных вопросов и ответов по поводу текущих событий в Украине,' Вести, December 2, 2013, pages 4–5.

[703] 'Янукович заявил, что не собирался разгонять Майдан,' December 24, 2014, accessed on December 24, 2014. http://korrespondent.net/ukraine/politics/3460021-yanukovych-zaiavyl-chto-ne-sobyralsia-razghoniat-maidan

main parties with participants mostly from West Ukraine. The almost unprecedented mass congregated that day did not have a single political position but just wanted to show a clear disapproval of the repression that just occurred. What the refusal to sign the Association Agreement could not do, was achieved instead by the fear of political repression, and the condemnation of an authoritarian act.

During that afternoon, the three main opposition parties already controlled the platform from where speeches were made and where the instructions to the crowd were communicated. Therefore, once they controlled the high ground, all the discourses and the action were directed by the three main parties even though at the beginning many participants were completely alien to the main political forces, in fact, in many cases they were against them. This is not a minor issue, because even if the participation was huge, it is quite notorious that most of the people went out on a spontaneous participation but with a lack of a clear political goal. That meant that from then on, all the political actions were decided by the parties from the establishment that many people participating were willing to oppose.

That same Sunday on 30th, there were some groups trying to promote violent actions against the authorities. Masked participants using a tractor were shown worldwide as they were confronting the police near the government building. Some warning shots and a fire occurred that did not bring any serious consequences. There were two notorious facts. First, many of the violent groups that day were later related to the 'Pravyi Sektor',[704] an extreme right organization with a full organized way of acting that did not care how the rest of the political leadership in the *Maidan* decided. Second, there was among the hundreds of thousands of participants only enthusiasm as a common element, and while some let themselves to be carried away by the emotions of the violent actions

---

[704] The Pravyi Sektor was an organization derived from *Tryzub*, an extreme right paramilitary organization that had as its leader Dmytro Yarosh and then mixed with street-fighting soccer fans and other far right groups to create the Pravyi Sektor. They became notorious for their actions against authorities between November 2013 and February 2014 in the *Maidan* and afterwards in different Ukrainian regions. Shekhovstov, Anton and Umland, Andreas, 'Ukraine's radical right,' *Journal of Democracy*, Vol. 25, No. 3 (July 2014), accessed on February 27, 2015. http://muse.jhu.edu/journals/journal_of_democracy/v025/25.3.shekhovtsov.html

pushed by radical groups, a majority opted to push for a pacifist protest.

The huge crowd that participated during the first day, and more in the following weekends, counted also on foreign support. Different foreign participants, mostly from Georgia on the first day and related to Saakashvili's party, contributed to the protest.[705] By December 3, the still German Minister of Foreign Affairs, Guido Westerwelle, visited the *Maidan*. This visit also meant a clear support to the protestors at the square.[706] It was also common to find ambassadors from the Baltic countries and the governments from Poland and Lithuania actively campaigning for the demonstrators. Even the High Representative of the European Union for Foreign Affairs, Catherine Ashton, assisted in the demonstration in the *Maidan*.[707] This entire active foreign role on either side of the game is nothing but a symbol of a failed state in many senses. What would happen if any foreign minister or ambassador would participate in a rally against a government in any other sovereign state? Could anyone imagine a US ambassador rallying in support of the Tibet in China, or an Argentinian diplomat organizing an event in the United Kingdom for the restitution of the Malvinas Islands? Or what about Cuban diplomats organizing a rally in the United States against the embargo? At the end, this lack of response by the government and a greater lack of capacity to react to these foreign interventions are all symptoms that the Ukrainian polity was crumbling.

The degree of foreign involvement either in the protests or in support of the government in the first weeks of the crisis allowed again a clear geopolitical struggle; meanwhile each side interacted

---

[705] 'В киевском Евромайдане принимают участие грузинские оппозиционеры,' December 3, 2013, accessed on December 3, 2013. http://korrespondent.net/world/3273941-v-kyevskom-evromaidane-prynymauit-uchastye-hruzynskye-oppozytsyonery

[706] 'Министр иностранных дел Германии Гидо Вестервелле посетил митингующих на Евромайдане в центре Киева,' December 3, 2013, accessed on December 3, 2013. http://korrespondent.net/ukraine/politics/3274431-hlava-myd-hermanyy-posetyl-evromaidan-v-kyeve

[707] 'Эштон перед встречей с Януковичем побывала на Майдане,' December 10, 2013, accessed on December 10, 2013. http://korrespondent.net/ukraine/politics/3276159-eshton-pered-vstrechei-s-yanukovychem-pobyvala-na-maidane

with local actors to improve its position. The images of Victoria Nuland,[708] the Assistant Secretary of State for European and Eurasian Affairs within the US Department of State, giving cookies to the people in the *Maidan* or of US Senator John McCain talking to the masses would be greatly used by Russian media to underline US involvement.

Foreign media showed mostly what happened in the *Maidan*, but the political actions were decided always between the leaders of the three main parties, Klitschko, Yatsenyuk and Oleh Tyahnybok from *Svoboda*, the extreme right party. It was sometimes different to settle inside this sort of 'collective leadership' which also had close contact with Western governments. The United States mostly preferred Yatsenyuk to head a future Ukrainian Government while Klitschko had more contact with Germany.[709] Besides, the role of the Ukrainian diaspora[710] that resides mostly in the United States and Canada was also visible.[711]

During the second week of December, the government initiated dialogue that was not received with interest by the opposition. There was not a clear political will, on either side to advance, maybe because they both felt they had strong foreign support, either from Russia or from the West. Therefore, this first effort for a dialogue did not produce any concrete results.[712] By that time, there was also a growing fear that the government could try to retake by force the *Maidan* and the public buildings already in control by opposition

---

[708] As mentioned in the introductory pages, besides, Victoria Nuland is married to Robert Kagan, one of the leading neoconservative scholars in the United States.

[709] 'Round two: EU grooming Klitschko to lead Ukraine,' December 10, 2013, accessed on February 39, 2016. http://www.spiegel.de/international/euro pe/eu-grooms-boxer-vitali-klitschko-to-lead-ukraine-opposition-a-938079.h tml

[710] It is worth mentioning that in most cases, the Ukrainian diaspora is not composed of Ukrainian citizens entitled to vote but of Canadian and US citizens of ethnic Ukrainian origin that have lived in those countries for many generations already.

[711] 'Украинская диаспора в 20 городах мира присоединяется к Маршу миллиона,' December 8, 2013, accessed on December 8, 2013. http://k orrespondent.net/ukraine/politics/3275314-ukraynskaia-dyaspora-v-20-hor odakh-myra-prysoedyniaetsia-k-marshu-myllyona

[712] 'Что и говорить,' Газета 'Коммерсантъ Украина,' №207 (1910), December 12, 2013, accessed on December 12, 2013. http://www.kommersant.ua /doc/2365723

forces, even if the government assured more than once that there was no intention for a violent eviction.[713]

After days passed, the protestors took control of some nearby government building and the organization evolved. For example, the Kiev City Administration building was occupied by people related to *Svoboda*. Besides, the number of spontaneous participants diminished during weekdays and increased on Saturdays and Sundays, while each political party brought people from different regions of Ukraine. These demonstrators, usually paid, where provided with shelter, food, and a daily cash allowance depending on the conditions. You could usually tell, mostly after several weeks of protests, who was a spontaneous and who was a paid militant. It is impossible to know the exact number of how paid and spontaneous protestors; but it is undeniable that for many of them present, it became a way of earning a living. For some participants, it assured them an income of even 700 Hryvnia a day that by that time meant something around €50, more than half of a monthly salary for many Ukrainians, at the end of 2013.

It is worth noticing also the great political differences among those present in the Maidan. There were groups organized by the three main opposition parties, UDAR, Fatherland and Svoboda, which to different degrees included paid militants from different Ukrainian regions, mostly from the West. Besides, they were foreign groups, students from the Taras Shevchenko University or from the Mohyla Academy that had a completely separated organization, and there were also participants related to Poroshenko, who openly accepted to finance the movement. There was also the already mentioned Pravyi Sektor, and different political organizations that tried to make themselves visible. At a certain point, it was possible to find a tent with fliers challenging the role of the oligarchs while the next would be sustaining Iulia Timoshenko and portraying her as a martyr of freedom. Besides all these differences present, the three main parties managed to hold the leadership and exclude any other movement willing to interfere in the decisions the movement was

---

[713] 'Разгона Майдана не будет—Захарченко,' December 11, 2013, accessed on December 11, 2013. http://korrespondent.net/ukraine/politics/3276258-razghona-maidana-ne-budet-zakharchenko

taking. At the end, there were the two main parties, with the extreme right trying to pull a little bit to its side, the ones that guided the movement. Those same parties were also in touch with the Western Government and in different ways received their support.

Besides the unproductive first dialogue between the opposition and the government, there was another important turning point. On December 13, the next day after Rinat Akhmetov had a meeting[714] with Victoria Nuland, the richest man in Ukraine declared publicly that he sustained the protests in the *Maidan* and called both sides of the conflict to find an agreement.[715] The threat by the United States to the strongest oligarch in the country who also controlled more than 50 deputies in the Rada was a turning point. He would be the first of many oligarchs that above all thought of defending their own interests. Besides, many of the oligarchs as mentioned before had disliked the way in which Yanukovych had handled the crisis and how he had been concentrating a lot of power and pretended to change from being their puppet into another oligarch.

The United States played therefore on different fronts, threatening the oligarchs and financing the opposition; and those facts did not go unopposed by Russia. By those days, the Russian Minister of Foreign Affairs had offered to have discussions with EU members to find a common solution. Meanwhile, the next days, the Russian Government presented a proposal to solve the crisis, while giving an assurance to the economic elite that they could also receive a benefit with the refusal to sign the Association Agreement. On December 17, after Victor Yanukovych had visited Moscow, the Kremlin announced an aid plan for Ukraine of around $15 billion. It included a new price for gas of $268 for 1,000 cubic metres instead of the $400 they were paying by then.[716] Instead, the EU was not able

---

[714] 'США требуют от Ахметова и Клюева поднять партийный бунт против Януковича. Иначе—санкции,' December 13, 2013, accessed on December 13, 2013. http://censor.net.ua/news/263364/ssha_trebuyut_ot_ahmetova_i _klyueva_podnyat_partiyinyyi_bunt_protiv_yanukovicha_inache_sanktsii

[715] 'Ахметов поддержал Евромайдан и призвал стороны конфликта сесть за стол переговоров,' December 13, 2013, accessed on December 13, 2013. http://korrespondent.net/business/economics/3276964-akhmetov-podde rzhal-evromaidan-y-pryzval-storony-konflykta-sest-za-stol-perehovorov

[716] 'На каких условиях Россия профинансировала Украину,' Forbes Ukraine, December 17, 2013, accessed on December 17, 2013. http://forb es.ua/business/1362429-na-kakih-usloviyah-rossiya-profinansirovala-ukrai

to offer a counterproposal and the intricate mechanisms proper of the European organism to take decisions, made it very difficult to answer in the same terms. At that point, it seemed that the economic offer could be enough to keep on Moscow's side the Ukrainian elite, while there was still a need for a political inner solution to end the crisis. The West did not have a counterproposal even if they had been grasping more deputies to their side to decide on a new government. Besides, Moscow continued to push for an offer that could include three side negotiations to protect Russian's interest with a possible Association Agreement with the EU.[717] Meanwhile, the Ukrainian Government insisted that they were willing to sign the Association Agreement and remain as observers in the Customs Union with Russia, Belarus and Kazakhstan but the legal terms under which both roles would remain were not clear.[718]

At this point, it is worth mentioning the fragility of the Azarov Government. He had presented his resignation and Yanukovych nominated him again on December 9 and received the necessary votes on December 13. He got the support of 252 members out of a 450-member chamber, still a more than enough amount. However, it was not clear how long it could last, considering the changing position of the oligarchs and the dubious sustain by the Communist Party and the 'independent' members of the parliament. It is worth also noticing how the Communist Party of Ukraine lost all political cleavage during the events. After the outstanding results obtained in the 2012 parliamentary elections, where they got more than 13% of the votes, this time they did not manage to position themselves separately from the government. The CPU criticized the oligarchs but at the other side saw the protests as US-oriented and therefore did not take sides with them, since they were in favour of the Cus-

---

nu?utm_source=korrespondent.net&utm_medium=picstrip&utm_campaign=KorrMain

[717] 'Никто же ни фига не читает! Читать умеете?' Путин о Соглашении Украины с ЕС, December 18, 2013, accessed on December 18, 2013. http://korrespondent.net/business/economics/3278646-nykto-zhe-ny-fyhane-chytaet-chytat-umeete-putyn-o-sohlashenyy-ukrayny-s-es

[718] 'НГ: В Украине может полыхнуть с новой силой,' December 20, 2013, accessed on December 20, 2013. http://korrespondent.net/world/worldabus/3278895-nh-v-ukrayne-mozhet-polykhnut-s-novoi-syloi

toms Union. This lack of a visible position made them lose a considerable political role and become a void force while the opposition tried to convince their deputies to change sides frequently.

By December 22, there was a kind of political impasse. Another demonstration gathered more than 100,000 people that day, while the oppositions asked for the demission of the Minister of Internal Affairs Vitaliy Zakharchenko and created the Maidan's People Union[719] to make the role of a political organ that took the decisions related to the movement. In practice, it consisted of the leaders of the main opposition parties plus Petro Poroshenko and other personalities related with the Yushchenko Government or with Iulia Timoshenko. There was the symbolic inclusion of some 'independents' like Ruslana[720] and the president of the Mohyla Academy, Serhiy Kvit[721] to take the role of a sort of a student representation.[722] Even though, it was mostly the same political class, which at that time sided with the opposition.

The speculation about a violent crackdown on the protesters continued but with no clear evidences. Even though, crimes against people involved in the *Maidan* under suspicious conditions raised the question how much the government was really preparing a violent repression or just wanted to calm down the animosity. The Ukrainian journalist Tetiana Chornovol was a victim of assault on December 25, while before the member of the anticorruption group Road and Control was shot. The case of the Chornovol was widely

---

[719] 'Участники Народного вече приняли резолюцию и выбрали сопредседателей гражданского объединения Майдан,' December 22, 2013, accessed on December 22, 2013. http://korrespondent.net/ukraine/politics/3279454-uchastnyky-narodnoho-veche-prynialy-rezoluitsyui-y-vybraly-sopredsedatelei-hrazhdanskoho-obedynenyia-maidan

[720] Ruslana was a famous singer that won the Eurovision Contest in 2004 and since the beginning of the protests she sided with the opposition. Her public inclusion as an 'independent' wanted to show that the three main parties were willing to include additional people in the leadership. Her political contributions were scarce besides often appearances to sing for the public in the *Maidan*.

[721] Besides being the president of the Mohyla Academy, Kvit is member of the extreme right organization 'Tryzub' that became the basis of the formation of the Pravyi Sektor. He is also considered to be the friend of Dmytro Yarosh.

[722] From my personnel experience in university movements, the fact that the rector of a university would assume the representation of the students in a political movement would be a motive of a huge outrage among them; instead, in this case, it seems they did not mind at all. Note of the author.

portrayed in the West and even after recovering she blamed the government, some testimonies linked two of the recognized perpetrators with the Klitschko brothers.[723]

By the end of the year, the Azarov Government introduced criminal liability to the seizure of public buildings but still with no way of really enforcing that law without a forceful stance against the protestors. Meanwhile, another law giving amnesty to the participants in the protests was approved.[724] Altogether, the year ended while again several thousands gathered in the *Maidan* to celebrate New Year with the end of the crisis not visible in the near future. Besides, numerous well-known foreigners for their role supporting the rallies at different levels were forbidden to enter Ukraine. Among them, was the Georgian ex-president Saakashvili and the US scholar Taras Kuzio.[725]

By then, the support against or in favour of the *Maidan* also had a notable division among ethnic lines, the same way the voting was usually influenced in Ukraine, while more than 80% of West Ukraine were in favour and more than 80% of Eastern Ukraine instead were against.[726] More divisions were evidenced in a rally to remember Stepan Bandera, the nationalist leader of the OUN, the far right organization allied with Nazi Germany during World War II. This rally counted with the support of more than 15,000 participants but a sector of the leadership including Klitschko excluded themselves from the event besides numerous participants related to

---

[723] 'Police implicate, link Klitschko brothers, other opposition members to Chornovol beating suspects,' December 27, 2013, accessed on December 27, 2013. http://www.kyivpost.com/content/ukraine/police-implicate-link-klits chko-brothers-other-opposition-members-to-chornovol-beating-suspects-33 4343.html

[724] 'Янукович подписал закон об амнистии арестованных активистов Евромайдана,' December 23, 2013, accessed on December 23, 2013. http://www.kommersant.ua/news/2375677

[725] 'Саакашвили запрещен въезд в Украину по требованию нардепа Царева—Ъ,' December 24, 2013, accessed on December 24, 2013. http://ko rrespondent.net/ukraine/politics/3279907-saakashvyly-zapreschen-vezd-v-ukraynu-po-trebovanyui-nardepa-tsareva

[726] 'На Евромайдане происходит внутренний конфликт—социолог,' December 23, 2013, http://korrespondent.net/ukraine/politics/3279399-na-evromaidane-proyskhodyt-vnutrennyi-konflykt-sotsyoloh,

the *Maidan*.⁷²⁷ At the end, the desire to portray Bandera as a national hero has always been a political goal of the extreme right and people from Galicia and some regions in West Ukraine, while the rest of the country saw them as a group allied with the enemy that invaded Soviet Ukraine.

Other motives divided the participants in the *Maidan*. During those days, massive anonymous SMS arrived to many Kiev residents complaining of the 'dirty Galicians' that spoiled the city in a clear intention to create animadversion against the thousands of Western Ukrainians residing in the *Maidan*.⁷²⁸ Meanwhile, local media had openly antagonizing positions, so while oligarchs close to the government sustained the presidency, media related to Poroshenko sustained the opposition.

The first two weeks of January saw a decrease in the number of the participants in the *Maidan*. Protests numbered between 10,000 and 50,000 and after local courts banned the protests in Kiev, it made believe the ones present that there would be an attempt by public force to take them out.

Here again, after a long standoff between the government and the opposition, the president perpetrated again a disastrous political mistake. On January 16, the government proposed new legislation directed to punish the participants in the riots. It pretended also to create the background for a more repressive ending to the crisis, once the participation had diminished. This proved to be a catastrophic error. It is true that by January a sector of Ukrainian society was tired of the protests while to a lesser degree, spontaneous participants were present and political parties depended more on paid militants. But, Yanukovych did not seem to take into account the fact that the protests were precisely triggered after the repression in November. Therefore, adopting again repressive measures, even with a passive approach typical of many Soviet societies, did not change the fact that there was still a general anger against the government. Besides, extreme right groups still had

---

727 'Кличко откресстился от Бандеры и его "героизма",' January 2, 2014, accessed on January 2, 2014. http://news.mail.ru/politics/16349438/
728 'Киевляне стали чаще жаловаться на Евромайдан—КГГА,' January 6, 2014, accessed on January 6, 2014. http://korrespondent.net/kyiv/3282855-kyevliane-staly-chasche-zhalovatsia-na-evromaidan-khha

been very active and had proved themselves the best organized of the groups participating in the movement.

The new laws included provisions like mandatory licensing for internet providers and provisions for legal governmental internet censorship. Punishment included up to 15 days of jail sentence for unauthorized installation of tents and sound equipment. Defamation by social media or press to carried a penalty of up to one year in prison. Besides, non-governmental associations that received foreign funds needed to register as 'foreign agents' and it extended and applied amnesty for prosecution to those who applied crimes against prosecutors.[729] To make it even more controversial, the new laws were approved without following the common parliamentary procedure with electronic vote; instead, they used hand vote to barely get the needed majority.

The new laws received a rejection by most of the Western governments accusing Yanukovych of denying the possibility of a peaceful solution while the Ukrainian Minister of Foreign Affairs, Leonid Kozhara, defended them with the argument that similar laws existed in other Western countries.[730]

The reaction was obvious. It not only pushed again a sector of the demonstrators to return to the *Maidan*, but it also motivated extreme right groups to get a stronger attitude against the authorities. This included also the well-coordinated Pravyi Sektor and other similar groups that started to organize themselves with Molotov bombs and other improvised arms in the *Maidan*. This created a complicated position both for the opposition leaders and for the Western governments sustaining them.[731] For the West, it was an

---

[729] 'Депутаты приняли закон о блокировке сайтов, продаже SIM-карт по паспорту и наказании за «экстремизм» в соцсетях,' January 16, 2014, accessed on January 16, 2014. http://ain.ua/2014/01/16/508940?utm_source=ain&utm_medium=fb&utm_campaign=social

[730] 'FM Kozhara tells US, EU ambassadors Rada's laws meet democratic standards,' January 17, 2014, accessed on January 17, 2014. http://www.ukri nform.ua/eng/news/fm_kozhara_tells_us_eu_ambassadors_radas_laws_meet_democratic_standards_316142

[731] 'A Kiev, l'opposition dépassée par la colère des manifestants,' January 20, 2014, accessed on January 20, 2014. http://www.lemonde.fr/europe/article/2014/01/20/a-kiev-l-opposition-en-passe-d-etre-depassee-par-la-colere-des-manifestants_4350966_3214.html

awkward situation to support Yatsenyuk and Klitschko while several groups occupied different governmental buildings and promoted violent actions. They were supposed to sustain a struggle for 'democracy' while they complained about the new legislation but they had to ignore the fact that also at their side there were people promoting violence. At the end, the geopolitical goal was more important; therefore, this subtle difference had to be ignored by the West.

On January 20, the president asked Andrey Kuliev, the Secretary of the Council of National Security, to form a working group to find a solution to the crisis. By then, both sides accused the other of promoting the violence. The United States threatened to impose sanctions against government officials while the minister of interior declared on January 21 that there had been 119 injured police officers, 35 journalists and more than 120 demonstrators.[732] At this point it was obvious that neither the new legislation had allowed the government to improve its position to solve the conflict nor they were in the position to implement the new laws without increasing the level of confrontation with the already numerous violent groups present in the *Maidan*.

The number of injured increased on both sides. By January 23, they were already more than 400 on both sides[733] while the United States imposed sanctions[734] against some Ukrainian officials. By then, it was clear that the opposition leaders had lost control of a considerable sector of the protestors and they were in no position to negotiate any kind of truce in the clashes against the police forces.[735] It was also a complicated situation for the government and

---

[732] 'Глазами Беркута, МВД обнародовало свое видео, снятое на Грушевского,' January 21, 2014, accessed on January 21, 2014, http://korrespondent.net/ukraine/events/3287130-hlazamy-berkuta-mvd-obnarodovalo-svoe-vydeo-sniatoe-na-hrushevskoho

[733] 'В беспорядках в Киеве пострадали уже 254 правоохранителя—МВД,' January 23, 2014, accessed on January 23, 2014, http://korrespondent.net/ukraine/3296288-v-besporiadkakh-v-kyeve-postradaly-uzhe-254-pravookhranytelia-mvd

[734] 'США вводят санкции против ряда граждан,' Украины, January 22, 2014, accessed January 22, 2014, http://korrespondent.net/ukraine/politics/3287579-ssha-vvodiat-sanktsyy-protyv-riada-hrazhdan-ukrayny

[735] 'Оппозиция уже не в состоянии контролировать радикалов— Захарченко,' January 25, 2014, accessed on January 25, 2014. http://korresp

for Yanukovych, who did not have the means to solve the crisis. On January 25, during the negotiations with the opposition leaders, he offered the post of prime minister to Yatsenyuk and to Klitschko the vice premier in charge of human rights affairs.[736] He thought that with the two main opposition parties in the government, it was possible to find a solution to the crisis.

By then, there were numerous signs of a dismantling Ukrainian polity. Not only the government had lost is legitimacy, the institutional opposition neither had the capacity to offer a real solution. The regional groups had been starting to push for different answers ignoring what happened in Kiev. For example, Crimea's parliament had called the presidency to bring order to the country and bring back the constitutional order.[737] Different groups in Sevastopol started to call for the creation[738] of a new country with the name of 'Malorossiya', while in Donetsk, there were patrols organized by veterans[739] and self-denominated Cossacks to avoid the presence of extreme right groups in the area and defend public buildings. Besides, the Communist Party of Ukraine definitely withdrew his support to the government.[740] To complicate things even more, Prime Minister Azarov presented his resignation[741] on January 28, only

---

[736] ondent.net/ukraine/politics/3297085-oppozytsyia-uzhe-ne-v-sostoianyy-kontrolyrovat-radykalov-zakharchenko
'Предложение Януковича занять пост премьера повергло Яценюка в шок – СМИ,' January 25, 2014, accessed on January 25, 2014. http://korrespondent.net/ukraine/politics/3297200-predlozhenye-yanukovycha-zaniat-post-premera-poverhlo-yatsenuika-v-shok-smy

[737] 'Парламент Крыма призывает Януковича жестко навести порядок в стране,' January 20, 2014, accessed on January 20, 2014. http://korrespondent.net/ukraine/politics/3286979-parlament-kryma-pryzyvaet-yanukovycha-zhestko-navesty-poriadok-v-strane

[738] 'В Севастополе заявили о возможности создания государства Малороссия,' January 26, 2014, accessed on January 26, 2014. http://korrespondent.net/ukraine/politics/3297354-v-sevastopole-zaiavyly-o-vozmozhnosty-sozdanyia-hosudarstva-malorossyia

[739] 'Донецк патрулируют отряды казаков и ветеранов-афганцев,' January 26, 2014, accessed on January 26, 2014. http://korrespondent.net/ukraine/politics/3297360-donetsk-patrulyruuit-otriady-kazakov-y-veteranov-afhantsev

[740] 'Симоненко больше не поддерживает Януковича,' January 26, 2014, accessed on January 26, 2014. http://delo.ua/ukraine/simonenko-bolshe-ne-podderzhivaet-janukovicha-225502/?supdated_new=1390867181

[741] 'En Ukraine, le premier ministre a démissionné,' January 28, 2014, accessed on January 28, 2014. http://www.lemonde.fr/europe/article/2014/01/28/en-ukraine-le-premier-ministre-a-demissionne_4355497_3214.html

that this time, there was no clear perspective if it was possible for the Party of Regions to give confidence by itself to another government.

The situation was so complex that the session of the parliament that received the resignation of the prime minister also decided to abrogate nine of the 10 repressive laws just approved some days before because of their enormous unpopularity.[742] This was not even close to bringing a solution. Yatsenyuk did not reject the proposal to enter the government but neither accepted it. It was obvious there was an interest, but without the full support of other political forces, it was complicated. Besides, the visible divisions between Klitschko and Yatsenyuk would have deepened if they would share the government. At the end, it was more comfortable for the opposition to ask for more guarantees for the exit of Yanukovych.

It was obvious by then, that the solution would come from the outside, in the sense of a political agreement between Russia and the EU or its members or the United States. Russia had been pushing for an agreement with the EU without the United States. During the EU-Russia summit on January 2014, in which obviously the most important subject became the Ukrainian crisis, Putin proposed to create a free trade zone between the EU and the Eurasian Union.[743] It was an open political proposal to seek a global solution that even if it left in the air many subjects like the role of Ukraine it allowed advancing to a geopolitical solution accepted for both of the actors. The scholar Oleg Bondarenko also agreed in that sense. He also thought that only a mediation of both the EU and Russia would help to unlock the political impasse present. He considered that any one-sided attempt to solve the conflict would bring heavy consequences with the risk of breaking the country apart.[744]

---

[742] Ibidem.
[743] 'Путин предложил создать зону свободной торговли с Евросоюзом,' January 28, 2014, accessed on January 28, 2014. http://news.liga.net/n ews/politics/969816-putin_predlozhil_sozdat_zonu_svobodnoy_torgovli_s _evrosoyuzom.htm
[744] 'Без вмешательства ЕС и России решить конфликт в Украине уже не получится – политолог,' January 28, 2014, accessed on January 28, 2014. http://korrespondent.net/ukraine/politics/3297944-bez-vmeshatelstva-es-y-rossyy-reshyt-konflykt-v-ukrayne-uzhe-ne-poluchytsia-polytoloh

The next week, the audio recording of a conversation[745] between Victoria Nuland and US ambassador in Ukraine, Geoffrey Pyatt, would become an excellent example of how the United States and the Russia were acting; meanwhile, the EU had not been able to push for a proposal of its own. The recording, which appeared on YouTube the first week of February, referred to a conversation between them in which they discussed the convenience of having Yatsenyuk enter the government and why Klitschko should stay out of it besides Yanukovych invitation. The audio, probably filtered by Russian Security Services, evidences which were the priorities for each side of the conflict and how both of them understood their actions as part of a geopolitical struggle. First, because by making it public, the Russians were conscious of the effect it would carry and second because it shows how the United States had an enormous influence above Yatsenyuk and why they preferred him to guide the government instead of the not so trustworthy Klitschko. The audio and the famous 'Fuck the EU' from Victoria Nuland also reflected how the United States despised the EU position and did not care at all what they thought about handling the situation. Besides, the way in which they expressed themselves about each of the actors in the Maidan reflected, as *Le Monde* noted, the arrogance with which they pretend to install governments around the world with ease.[746]

That same day, a senior adviser to President Putin, Sergei Glazyev, accused the United States of supplying opposition groups with $20 million a week, to obtain arms among other things.[747] True or not, the level of US involvement became also a source of concern for Russia, which therefore would not allow a change of regime so easily. At that point, the EU could be the balancing factor. A second

---

[745] 'Марионетки майдана— puppets of the Maidan,' Published January 6, 2014, https://www.youtube.com/watch?v=YBWP48O_5Mo

[746] 'Les cinq leçons du "fuck the EU!" d'une diplomate américaine,' *Le Monde*, February 9, 2014, accessed on February 9, 2014. http://www.lemonde.fr/europe/article/2014/02/09/les-cinq-lecons-du-fuck-the-eu-d-une-diplomate-americaine_4363017_3214.html

[747] 'Ukraine crisis: Putin adviser accused US of meddling,' February 6, 2014, accessed on February 6, 2014. http://www.bbc.com/news/world-europe-26068994

audio[748] filtered around the same days, showed a conversation between the Deputy Secretary for Political Affairs of the European External Action Service, Helga Schmid, and EU's ambassador in Ukraine, Jan Tombinski. During the recording, Schmid complained that the United States was spreading the rumour that the European position was weak regarding Ukraine because the EU was not sustaining the sanctions the United States was applying. The audio also showed how EU officials acknowledge the complexity they have in the decision-making process and the short conversation portrayed also how they planned to operate.

Those two conversations received great coverage in the West, even if several media tried to point public opinion against 'the evil role' of Russian Security Services. Meanwhile, the EU did not even publicly complain about the famous 'Fuck the EU' by Victoria Nuland in something that showed the weak and diminished position of Catherine Ashton during his period as High Representative of the Union for Foreign Affairs and Security Policy. Instead, the only strong voice from the EU criticizing the way the United States was acting came from Angela Merkel. In fact, after the revelations by Edward Snowden, in which it had been demonstrated that the United States had been spying on German agencies and on Merkel's phone, she had no problem expressing her outrage against the comments made by US officials.[749] It is therefore here possible to remember Carlo Jean's words when he analyses the EU's geopolitical role that even if it is not desirable a Germanized Europe, it is always better than the No-Europe. Therefore, again the only voice that showed a 'sort of' European voice came from Berlin.

Altogether, during the next days, two things were noticeable; first, besides the political crisis present in Ukraine, the country was on the verge of economic collapse. The money Moscow had promised could help but to complete the whole transaction would obviously go hand in hand with a solution favourable to Russian's interests. On the other hand, the West openly had not been capable of

---

[748] 'Как они делят Украину,' Published February 4, 2014, accessed on February 4, 2014. https://www.youtube.com/watch?v=kOjrACdTQE8
[749] 'Ангела Меркель сочла высказывания Нуланд "недостойными",' February 8, 2014, accessed on February 8, 2014. http://korrespondent.net/world/3302950-anhela-merkel-sochla-vyskazyvanyia-nuland-nedostoinymy

counteroffering even if Yatsenyuk had filtered that in case the opposition obtained power the IMF and the EU would give them access to funds totalling $15 billion.[750] The second thing was that the lack of credibility of the traditional opposition parties together with the increasing level of violence in the *Maidan* made it difficult to obtain a solution without the participation of all external forces present in the conflict.

By February 9, new defections in the Party of Regions included at least 30 deputies related to Sergei Tihipko.[751] Those votes, together with the ones of the Communist Party, made it impossible for the government to get a majority. The opposition still did not have a concrete proposal. By February 14, Klitschko refused to participate in the new government,[752] maybe following US advice as shown in Nuland's audio. By that time, Yatsenyuk and Timoshenko still in prison had been speculating on a government of the *Maidan*, obviously headed by them. Two days later Yatsenyuk changed his mind. By that time, the continuous violence and the polarization of one sector of the opposition linked with the far right made it impossible for the moderate sector of the opposition to accept the offer to join the government with support from the *Maidan* or maybe because they were already pointing to the exit of Yanukovych.

Altogether, violence increased during the next days. The government accused[753] the opposition of acting violently; mostly the Pravyi Sektor and the opposition accused the government of the same. By that time, at the second half of February the *Maidan* was far from

---

[750] 'Заявление Яценюка о финансовой помощи ЕС безосновательны – политолог,' February 3, 2014, accessed on February 3, 2014. http://korrespondent.net/ukraine/politics/3300787-zaiavlenye-yatsenuika-o-fynansovoi-pomoschy-es-bezosnovatelny-polytoloh

[751] 'Не менее 30 регионалов готовы пойти против Януковича – Шевченко,' February 9, 2014, accessed on February 9, 2014. http://news.liga.net/news/politics/976974-v_partii_regionov_poyavilas_gruppa_gotovaya_idti_protiv_yanukovicha.htm

[752] 'Кличко исключил участие УДАРа в "правительстве Януковича",' February 14, 2014, accessed on February 14, 2014. http://news.liga.net/news/politics/979991-klichko_isklyuchil_uchastie_udara_v_pravitelstve_yanukovicha.htm

[753] 'Ответственность за поджог Дома профсоюзов лежит на "Правом секторе" – МВД,' February 19, 2014, accessed on February 19, 2014. http://korrespondent.net/ukraine/politics/3307613-otvetstvennost-za-podzhoh-doma-profsouizov-lezhyt-na-pravom-sektore-mvd

being the place it was when the protests started in November. By this date, security guards from different factions were posted in the entrances and checked the unknown arrivals. Tension was visible among the present groups while differences arose among groups with ease. Improvised and enthusiastic groups had notably diminished their participation together with a notable sector of the students. The calls to keep the protests peaceful were ignored at this point by many participants in the *Maidan* while some groups gathered material to improvise Molotov bombs, shields and whatever could be used against the authorities.

The confrontation between different security forces and the protestors incremented around the country, mostly in Kiev. Not only many supporters of the *Maidan* had taken control of public buildings in several regions in West Ukraine, the number of arrests, injured and suspicious beatings increased. On February 18, 20,000 protesters[754] advanced to the parliament to ask for the return of the 2004 Constitution. The police responded by firing rubber ammunition and tear gas while demonstrators responded with crude weapons and explosives. By February 19, more than 240 people were hospitalized in Kiev while the number of killed that day reached 25. Among the injured, there were 79 members of the security forces, 5 journalists and a member of the Rada.[755] The day before also more than a hundred had been hospitalized. Until that point, the minister of interior, Zakharchenko, had denied the use of fire weapons.[756] By the next day, he decided to authorize the use of live ammunition. The general lack of trust on the Ukrainian authorities made it difficult to believe until what point the minister of interior was telling

---

[754] A clearly reduced number considering the amount present at the beginning of the protests in November. Note of the author.

[755] It is worth to notice the high number of security forces injured. This number sends suspicion until what point one section of the opposition activists were already prepared to confront the Ukrainian security forces. '*В столкновениях в Киеве погибли 25 человек – Минздрав*,' February 19, 2014, accessed on February 19, 2014. http://korrespondent.net/ukraine/politics/3307609-v-stolknovenyiakh-v-kyeve-pohybly-25-chelovek-mynzdrav

[756] '*Милиция не использовала огнестрельное оружие во время "освобождения улиц Киева" – МВД*,' February 19, 2014, accessed on February 19, 2014. http://korrespondent.net/ukraine/politics/3307616-mylytsyia-ne-yspolzovala-ohnestrelnoe-oruzhye-vo-vremia-osvobozhdenyia-ulyts-kyeva-mvd

the truth, but the fact is that there were numerous injured on both sides. Another audio[757] released some days after the events showed a conversation between Catherine Ashton and the Estonian Minister of Foreign Affairs, Urmas Paet. In the recordings, Paet related about testimonies in the *Maidan* of the doctors present helping the protesters. They acknowledged that the same snipers were shooting either to the police or to the people on the streets and that they were not part of the governmental forces.

Besides the obvious question of who started the violence,[758] which until certain point becomes rhetorical, what appeared at this point was again the clear dismantling of the Ukrainian polity. There was a discredited president; a lack of government with parliamentary majority, the opposition was not willing to enter the government. This coexisted with repression against protestors but also armed violent groups that challenged the police forces. Overall, there was a lack of any kind of a sustainable political order with the legitimacy to become an authority, therefore, a lack of state.

The image of the bloody injured and several bodies in the *Maidan* together with the firing and the improvised guns by the protestors circulated around the world. It urged for a political solution that obviously required international intervention. The question that arose was, what kind of international intervention or how. It was obvious that any kind of political solution would have to include Moscow to avoid an extension of the bloodbath. Therefore, the pressure increased on Putin to negotiate some kind of exit for Yanukovych.

At that point, seeing the tardiness of the EU, the ministers of foreign affairs of Germany, France and Poland took the lead to urge Yanukovych to leave power. It became a complex negotiation in which a Russian representative was also present. The lack of a direct negotiation between the West and Russia transformed it into a conciliation in which the diplomats from Poland, Germany and France

---

[757] 'Ukraine, Appel intercepté Catherine Ashton/Urmas Paet (26/02/14) VOSTFR,' published March 16, 2014, https://www.youtube.com/watch?v=equgXlRLePs

[758] Until December 2015, there had been no independent investigation about the details of what happened those days in the *Maidan*. Note of the author.

negotiated with Yanukovych and Vladimir Lukin as the Russian envoy, while sporadic calls to Putin were made. Altogether, for the first time since the beginning of the crisis, a geopolitical agreement was reached. This was of fundamental importance because for the first time since the beginning of the hostilities and the refusal to sign the Association Agreement, there was an understanding between the representatives of three EU governments and Russia about how to handle the Ukrainian crisis. The lack of the same representation from the United States in the meeting makes one wonder how much of it was planned or was part of the tension that had arose between the EU and the United States after Nuland's conversation was released. The significant thing is that the agreement negotiated on February 21 allowed for the first time a political solution to the crisis. The three leaders of the opposition were obliged to sustain this political arrangement. Klitschko, Yatsenyuk and Tyahnybok, therefore signed the agreement with Yanukovych. The agreement included establishing a national unity government, a constitutional reform and presidential elections no later than December 2014. It also agreed on conduction investigation into the recent acts of violence monitored by the Council of Europe and included the handing over of illegal weapons to the Ministry of Interior in the next 24 hours.[759]

The agreement meant a capitulation for Yanukovych, but still allowed him to remain in charge to organize the next presidential election. The next day, the Russian Minister of Foreign Affairs, Sergei Lavrov, put pressure on his colleagues from Germany, Poland and France so the opposition would be compelled to sign the agreement but what happened was completely the opposite. The night before, Yanukovych abandoned Kiev and went to Kharkov where he tried to make it look as a regular state visit. Meanwhile the parliament had voted, 386-0, to return to the 2004 Constitution and by a 332-0 majority it decided to remove Zakharchenko as interior minister. That last action created a huge vacuum of power in the secu-

---

[759] A complete version of the Agreement can be consulted on: 'Agreement on the settlement of the crisis in Ukraine-full text,' *The Guardian*, February 21, 2014, accessed on July 26, 2017. http://www.theguardian.com/world/2014/feb/21/agreement-on-the-settlement-of-crisis-in-ukraine-full-text

rity forces. Therefore, the president's residence and most of the government buildings stayed without security. Nobody in charge of the *Berkut*[760] wanted to take the responsibility once Zakharchenko was not in charge any more.

Meanwhile, another sector of the opposition, including the Pravyi Sektor, rejected the Agreement. Many protestors, then, took most of governmental buildings and the president's estate where they exhibited the luxurious style of living Yanukovych had as a president. This event allowed the public opinion to validate empirically the wide level of corruption in the regime.

Afterwards, the parliament also voted the day after to liberate Iulia Timoshenko from jail. At that point, Yanukovych even if officially still in power was in fact powerless trying to secure safety somewhere in East Ukraine. Later, the Rada started a procedure of impeachment against Yanukovych while the parliament declared Turchynov, the newly elected leader of the parliament, as acting president. The Ukrainian Constitution clearly established the procedure for impeachment but it was ignored. Article 111 of the Constitution establishes that the Rada should establish a special investigatory commission to formulate charges against the president, seek evidence to justify the charges and reach a conclusion about the president's guilt so the Rada to consider the outcome. Then, to prove him guilty, at least two-thirds of Rada members must assent.

Besides, prior to a final vote, the procedure requires that the Constitutional Court of Ukraine reviews the case and certifies the procedure and the Supreme Court must certify that the acts of the president are worthy of impeachment. Then, to remove the president from power, at least three-quarters of Rada members must assent. Instead, no investigatory commission was established and the Courts were not involved. Therefore, when the Rada simply passed a bill removing President Yanukovych from office with 328 votes, less than the three-quarters necessary, the Western Governments tacitly recognized the illegal removal of a president whose election

---

[760] The Berkut were the forces of special police under the control of the minister of foreign affairs. They became quite controversial during the conflict because of the sustain they gave to the regime. After the events in the *Maidan*, the Berkut were officially disbanded. Note of the author.

they recognized in 2010.[761] Instead, Moscow described the events as a coup d'état.

Edward Luttwak defines in the following terms a coup d'état. 'A coup consists of the infiltration of a small but critical segment of the state apparatus, which is then used to displace the government from its control of the remainder.'[762] Therefore, considering this definition, the actions occurred in Kiev would perfectly fit.

Even though Coup or not, this action together with the first movements carried out by the new government headed by Turchynov, a close ally of Iulia Timoshenko, forced Russia to react. They had negotiated for an agreement with the EU and the opposition and it was not respected. There was not even consideration to build a national unity government including the Party of Regions, and besides, among the first actions carried by the Rada (as if there were no other priorities), was to abolish the law of language policies. The approval of this parliamentary bill, even if it was not signed by Turchynov afterwards[763], gave Moscow more arguments to sustain that the new government was ethnonational oriented and ignored the rights of the Russian-speaking people in Ukraine, while Russian media underlined the 'fascist' members of the new cabinet.

Vladimir Putin had already warned weeks before, that the precondition for Ukraine to keep its territorial integrity was to avoid discrimination and to respect the rights of the ethnic, linguistic and religious minorities.[764] If we read carefully that comment, it was a

---

[761] 'How William Hague deceived the house of commons on Ukraine,' March 10, 2014, accessed on February 28th, 2016. http://www.huffingtonpost.co.uk/david-morrison/ukraine-willliam-hague_b_4933177.html

[762] In this rather peculiar and pragmatic book, the author intends to show the steps to operate a coup d'etat sustaining that by its nature, it is neutral and it is not by definition left wing or right wing. Luttwak, Edward, *Coup d'Etat, A Practical Handbook-a Brilliant Guide to Taking Over a Nation*, New York, Fawcett Publications, 1968, page 12.

[763] 'Турчинов отказался подписать решение Рады об отмене закона о языках,' March 2, 2014, accessed on February 28, 2016. http://korrespondent.net/ukraine/politics/3314338-turchynov-otkazalsia-podpysat-resheny e-rady-ob-otmene-zakona-o-yazykakh

[764] 'Путин назвал условие сохранения территориальной целостности Украины,' February 10, 2014, accessed on February 10, 2014. http://korrespondent.net/ukraine/politics/3426731-putyn-nazval-uslovye-sokhranenyia-terrytoryalnoi-tselostnosty-ukrayny

clear warning. He was exposing which were the issues he would exploit in case the government in Kiev would not consider the Kremlin's pretentions. Therefore, the new authorities not only ignored a possible Russian reaction, they even provoked it, and considering the fragile and changing political condition, it was rather stupid or intended exactly to seek a Russian reaction as a clear political goal. It is impossible to know, until what point the United States supported this kind of 'coup' and how much they knew about the decisions the Rada was planning, but as it has been shown, there were serious divisions among the main opposition forces. Therefore, while UDAR along with Klitschko were closer to the EU, Yatsenyuk and Timoshenko had closer links with the United States. It is not a surprise, then, that even though a deal existed between the EU, the opposition and Russia it was not respected.

For the Russian side, it was also a complex situation. Since February 7, the 2014 Winter Olympics had started in Sochi, where Russia was trying to present itself as a modern global power properly integrated in the world order. A strong and violent reaction by Moscow while hosting the main winter sports competition in the world would damage the image they were trying to build. Consequently, the Kremlin reacted only after the Olympics concluded on February 23. By February 24, the Ministry of Foreign Affairs affirmed, for instance, that they considered the new authorities in Ukraine to be illegitimate.[765]

Before concluding this chapter, it is worth mentioning the biggest failure of all. The *Maidan* was supposed to be an expression of discontent against the regime. It pretended to show the nuisance of the Ukrainian population against the loot and pillage that had characterized all the precedent regimes. It pretended to express a call for a more democratic government that would consider the majority of the population's opinion. It was not ethnically oriented at the beginning even though it had several extreme right groups among them. It pretended to erode and decrease the power of the oligarchs

---

[765] 'Россия считает новые власти Украины нелегитимными – МИД РФ,' February 24, 2014, accessed on February 24, 2014. http://korrespondent.net/world/russia/3310699-rossyia-schytaet-novye-vlasty-ukrayny-nelehytymnymy-myd-rf

and the way they had ruled the country for years. Thousands of people showed their discontent within Ukraine and many lost their lives. Even if they had not exposed clearly their goals or how to carry them out, it was at least evident what they did not want. Maybe naïvely but very enthusiastically, they expected something more than the deteriorating political, economic and social context in which they had lived for the last two decades. Consequently, even if some authors[766] would like to believe that it was a victory of the 'democratic forces', the reality was quite different. Besides, the lack of a clear and own political project became a weakness profited precisely by the foreign actors involved and by the traditional political class that pretended to keep its influence. Therefore, the consequence was exactly the opposite. The same ruling political class stayed in command with the oligarchs mostly untouched. They did not allow the founding of a political force proper of the *Maidan* independent of the oligarchs but also all the participants present were not able to push for it.

In that sense, when confronted with the question whether to consider the February events as a revolution or a coup d'état, it is possible to say that neither of them would be correct. First, because a revolution includes a change of regime that did not happen. It was only a change of government with the same ruling political class in place and the oligarchs practically untouched, but just with another geopolitical orientation. Neither a coup d'état would be proper, because the way all the events developed and considering the deep involvement of foreign political forces, it is not possible to have a coup d'état when there is no state at all or maybe it was just a coup without the 'd'état' component in it.

Therefore, from a political perspective, it would be more proper to consider the events in February as a revolt that brought a change in the government and afterwards as will be analysed transformed itself into a civil war with still a high degree of international involvement.

Altogether, the fragility of the new Ukrainian Government and the imperative for Russia to defend what they considered Russian geostrategic interests allowed them to look for a response in one of

---

[766] Arjakovsky, Antoien, *De la Guerre a la paix?*, Paris, Parole et silence, 2014.

weakest points of the fragile Ukrainian polity, and they found it in Crimea.

2.7 Crimea

Crimea symbolizes the complexity and the fragility present in the Ukrainian polity after the fall of the Soviet Union. The territory received huge historical and strategic importance during the Tsarist period. Later on, it was the only region in Ukraine after the Soviet fall, where ethnic Russians were a majority. Russians made up 67% of the population and 81% spoke Russian as mother tongue.[767] Hence, the success or failure to build a Ukrainian state would go well naturally with the fact of including the inhabitants of Crimea as part of the country and to make them feel part of it. Therefore, before analysing the political events of March 2014, it is worth mentioning some historical events in the peninsula. In that sense, the research done by Gwendolyn Sasse[768] describes some of the key actions occurred during the twentieth century and its effects in the area. Sasse considers that 'Crimea is a place apart from Ukraine.'[769] An affirmation that seems true but also it is true that many regions in Ukraine had a very specific ethnic, social and religious context, that makes so complex the social tissue found in the different regions of the Ukraine that appeared after the Soviet fall. At the end, the differences present between Crimea, Galicia, Volhynia, the Donbass or Central Ukraine are all notable. Some particularities are necessary to comment in the Crimean case.

The peninsula of Crimea was part of the Crimean Khanate, a vassal territory of the Ottoman Empire. Ironically, then, as the Polish historian Kolodziejczyk comments: 'When the Crimean Khanate was annexed by Russia in 1783, few Western intellectuals would disagree with Catherine II, who praised this move as the triumph of

---

[767] Data from 1991 published in Wilson, Andrew, *The Ukrainians: Unexpected Nation*, Yale University Press, 2002, page 151.
[768] Sasse, Gwendolyn, *The Crimea Question: Identity, Transition, and Conflict*, Cambridge, Ukrainian Research Institute, Harvard University, 2007.
[769] Ibidem, page 4.

civilization.'[770] This was part of the long standoff between the Russian and the Ottoman Empire and therefore the control of Crimea had a strategic place in that rivalry.

Once under Russian control, there was a massive Christianizing programme, which refashioned the region's identity as an Orthodox holy place for Russians and other Orthodox believers[771] even though a considerable number of Tatars remained residing in the peninsula under Czarist Russia. Years after, data showed that Tatars made up 34.1% of the population in Crimea in 1897, 25.9% in 1921, 19.4% in 1939, .3% in 1979, 1.6% in 1989 and 12.1% in 2001. Meanwhile, Russian population increased from 45.3% in 1897 to 51.5% in 1921, 68.4% in 1979 and then 58.5% in 2001. Meanwhile, Ukrainians were 13.7% in 1939, 25.6% in 1970 and 24.4% in 2001. Between 1897 and 1921, no distinction was made between Russian and Ukrainians.[772]

Under the Soviet Union, mass deportations carried out under Stalin had a deep impact in Crimea. Soviet documentation recorded 225,009 deported people from Crimea, among them 183,155 Crimean Tatars, 15,040 Greeks, 12,422 Bulgarians, 9621 Armenians, 1,119 Germans and 3,652 others. Most Crimean Tatars (151,604) were reported to have been relocated to Uzbekistan and 31,551 to the Russian Soviet Federative Socialist Republic.[773] During the war, a number between 8,000 and 20,000 Tartars fought with the Germans, and around 20,000 fought in the Soviet Army. Besides, it is important to consider the effects of the war. Sevastopol, for instance, became one of those examples of Soviet reconstruction used afterwards by Soviet propaganda. In fact, the damage had been so severe that only 3% of the buildings were intact after the war.[774]

Altogether, the history of Crimea had a fundamental event in 1954. An event that could have been of trivial importance during the Soviet period but after the Soviet fall acquired a great significance.

---

[770] Kolodziejczyk, Op. Cit., page XVI.
[771] Kozelsky, Mara, *Christianizing Crimea, Shaping Sacred Space in the Russian Empire and Beyond*, DeKalb, Northern Illinois University Press, 2010, page 13.
[772] Sasse, Op. Cit., Appendix 1, page 275.
[773] Ibidem, page 5, Note 12.
[774] Qualls, Karl D., *From Ruins to Reconstruction, Urban Identity in Soviet Sevastopol After World War II*, Ithaca, Cornell University Press, 2009, page 1.

The transfer of Crimea from the Russian SFSR to the Ukrainian Soviet Socialist Republic became a controversial issue in the relation between Russia and Ukraine after the Soviet fall.

By that time, in 1954, the context that prevailed was the destalinization promoted by Nikita Khrushchev. Magosci considered the transfer had a dual approach: to integrate Ukraine more into the Soviet System, while it would loose (at least formally), Moscow's control as part of the destalinization. Officially, the transfer was part of the events to commemorate the 300 years of the Treaty of Pereyaslav. The event received little attention in the Western and Soviet media while the 300th anniversary celebrations overshadowed the transfer.[775] Altogether, the reasons are not all clear. It could have been an attempt by Khrushchev to obtain support from the Ukrainian Communist Party, at a time where still Malenkov was the Premier and had a strong position. Sasse also speculates that it could represent an attempt by the Soviet leadership to dilute the Ukrainian notion in the Soviet Union.[776] But, considering the period, it does not seem probable by then, as the Ukrainian issue was kind of 'solved' from the Soviet point of view. Still, an interesting fact to acknowledge is the lack of Crimean officials in the 1954 celebrations, something that could evidence that there was a local resistance to the transfer.

Meanwhile, the overwhelmingly Russophone Crimean population remained the hegemonic ethnic group. Therefore, as Sasse wrote: 'Three layers of Soviet identity were promoted simultaneously: the Soviet bond throughout the USSR, the common Slavic roots of Russians, Ukrainians, and Belarusians, and the Russian nation and its achievements.'[777] Instead, after being deported and written out of history,[778] the Crimean Tatars were excluded from the 1954 celebrations and the transfer of Crimea.[779]

---

[775] Sasse, Op. Cit., page 98.
[776] Ibidem, page 100.
[777] Ibidem, page 103.
[778] Tatars would not be allowed as other ethnic groups to re-enter with the laws of 1957 promoted by Khrushchev and it was only during Gorbachev that they were able to return to the peninsula.
[779] Sasse, Op. Cit., page 104.

As Sasse analysed, archival material suffices to challenge the conventional wisdom about the transfer of Crimea to the jurisdiction of the Ukrainian SSR in 1954. Khrushchev played a central role in conceiving the idea and its implementation. The different Soviet organs quickly approved the whole process in January and February 1954, while at that time, even if Nikita still did not have enough power to decide by himself, it seems it was his initiative.[780] Khrushchev always had strong links with Ukraine as he had started his career close to Lazar Kaganovich[781] and had resided in this territory for many years. Even though, he certainly had to defeat some resistances appeared in the Russian elite to be able to cede Crimea. For instance, at the voting from the Presidium, 11 of the 26 members were absent and since decisions usually were made unanimously, absence could reflect disapproval.[782] Besides, evidence suggests that on January 1954, the first secretary of the Crimean Party, Pavel Titov, was summoned to Moscow where he was informed of the decision. His apparent protests forced his replacement by Dmytro Polianskyi.[783]

Moreover, the legality of the procedure is doubtful. Mainly because the Supreme Soviet of the RSFSR was not consulted and the transfer was only approved by the Presidium. The Constitution of the RSFSR then in force considered that any change of the borders needed the approval of the Supreme Soviet of the RSFSR.[784] Therefore, the transfer contravened Soviet law.

At last, Sasse also adds two interesting episodes that show the will of Khrushchev to pursue the idea of the transfer. One of them occurred in October 1953 during a trip to Crimea, when his son in law, Aleksei Adzhubei, noted Khrushchev's impatience with economic conditions in the region and had one spontaneous reaction like the ones he used to. He decided to fly to Kiev and in a dinner with party officials voiced the idea of the border change as part of

---

[780] Ibidem, pages 107–108.
[781] Kaganovich was one of the close associates of Stalin and was famous for his role as long-time full member of the Politburo from 1930 to 1957 and as First Secretary of the Communist Party of Ukraine from 1925 to 1928 and again in 1947. For more details, consult: Rees, E.A. 'Iron Lazar: A Political Biography of Lazar Kaganovich,' London, Anthem Press, 2012.
[782] Sasse, Op. Cit., page 109.
[783] Idem, pages 110–112.
[784] Idem, pages 109–112.

the plan to rebuild and develop Crimea.[785] Another one, that includes the first hint about the transfer, comes from 1944 during the war. Then, Stalin asked Khrushchev to relocate 100,000 Ukrainians to Russia to help with the post-war reconstruction. Referring to this episode, in a dialogue with Lavrentii Pogrebnoi, an apparatchik close to Nikolay Shvernik, the first secretary of the All-Union Central Council of Trade Unions and head of the Presidium of the Supreme Soviet of the RSFSR, Khrushchev allegedly said to him: 'Ukraine is in collapse and everything is pulled out of her. What about giving her Crimea? How they cursed me and what a hard time they gave me after that.' He later added: 'The people I will provide, but Crimea I will have, no matter what.'[786]

The fact is, legal or not, it was an inner administrative reform carried out inside the Soviet Union. Nobody could foresee back then that less than four decades after, the Soviet state would not exist anymore. Besides, the same as many internal border changes during Soviet times, it never considered the local population's opinion. There were political decisions from the elite. Consequently, Crimea became a part of the Ukrainian SSR. The peninsula was Ukrainized in some key aspects. There was also substantial resettlement of Ukrainians from other parts of Ukraine in Crimea and it became part of all the economic linkages of the Ukrainian SSR.

Decades later, there were two cycles of mobilization by the local population—first, the period from 1990 to 1994 and then from 1994 to 1998. During the former, a regional Russian nationalist political mobilization culminated with a push for Crimean separatism. During the latter, the separatist mobilization diminished in intensity until a special constitutional autonomy was granted in 1998.

Crimea entered the post-Soviet period as a stronghold of Soviet perceptions and power structures. The peninsula had an unusual concentration of Soviet structures from military presence and industrial to numerous resort facilities of Soviet ministries, trade unions, and other organizations. As Sasse would portray, there were ideal conditions for making Crimea a bastion of Soviet-minded conservatism. Besides, on 14 November 1989, a decree by the Supreme Soviet of the USSR paved way for the return of Crimean Tatars to

---

[785] Ibidem, page 115.
[786] Ibidem, pages 115–16.

Crimea.[787] Moreover, Kravchuk who was in charge of the Ukrainian SSR by then, allowed on 12 November 1990, an extraordinary session of the Crimean Supreme Soviet which convened to consider Crimea's status. Kravchuk then pushed for a Crimean ASSR.

In this case, the language factor in post-Soviet Crimea was not a useful indicator of political cleavages based on ethnicity as all the Russians, Ukrainians and Tatars spoke mostly Russian.[788] There was a referendum on January 21, and the establishment of the Crimean Autonomous Soviet Socialist made it the last Soviet ASSR, and curiously the first and only one established by a popular vote.[789] In that occasion, the turnout was 81.4%, and 93.3% voted for a Crimean ASSR.

During that same year, a resolution[790] from the Crimean Supreme Soviet pointed out that the transfer in 1954 had not obtained the consent of the people. The drama of the first years after the Soviet fall left the Crimea question as a secondary issue in Ukrainian politics.[791] Meanwhile, the amended Constitution of September 1992 became a prelude to a crisis.

Later, Kiev did not achieve to address the autonomy issue during the initial attempts to draft a constitution, while a more radical and separatist and ethnic Russian mobilization began to appear in the peninsula. Crimean Tatar mobilization also increased their stake in the political process.[792] Besides, both ethnic Russians and Ukrainians in Crimea supported autonomy and secession, a move that highlights the regional rather than ethnic nature of Crimean separatism.[793] At the end, local identity in the post-Soviet space tends to be in many cases more attached to the land rather than the ethnic group as David Laitin showed.[794]

---

[787] Ibidem, page 134.
[788] Ibidem, page 137.
[789] Ibidem, page 138.
[790] 'О Заявлении Президиума Верховного Совета Крымской АССР' Органы власти АРК, Президиум ВР АРК; Постановление, Заявление от 01.10.1991 № 136-1, accessed on March 1st, 2016. http://zakon4.rada.gov.ua/krym/show/rb0136003-91
[791] Ibidem, page 153.
[792] Ibidem, page 154.
[793] Ibidem, page 172.
[794] Laitin, David D., *Identity in Formation*, Ithaca, Cornell University Press, 1998.

One detail is significant. At that point, the desire from the local Crimean population to secede from Ukraine or at least for more autonomy found a political solution in the regional institutions and without violence. This arrangement allowed Crimea to become an autonomous republic as part of Ukraine benefited from the fact that Russia during the nineties was in no position of power, therefore, the Kremlin could not defend its interests in Crimea, as they wanted. Even if different sectors of the Russian Government, including the parliament and the army wanted to act, at the end, the confusion and the lack of Russian action allowed Ukrainian authorities to enforce a constitution with little local resistance and in Kiev's favour.

The Crimean question played a role in Russian politics. The Duma challenged the legitimacy of Ukraine's sovereignty over the peninsula and some members of the government supported the idea. In January 1992, a group of Russian parliamentarians began to discuss the 1954 transfer of Crimea and the status of the Black Sea Fleet. The driving force behind the Russian parliament's moves on the Crimean issue was Vladimir Lukin, a foreign policy adviser to Yeltsin. Lukin pretended to use the Crimea issue to negotiate over the Black Sea Fleet. On 21 May 1992, two weeks after Crimea's Act on State Independence,[795] the Russian parliament nullified the 1954 transfer by an almost unanimous vote. The transfer had violated the Constitution of the RSFSR and Soviet legislative procedures.[796] For instance, the Russian authorities continued to use the same arguments about the legality of the transfer, after the events of 2014.[797] Altogether, the standoff for power between Yeltsin and the Duma reflected also here, and no Russian action followed in that sense at least during the nineties.

Instead, Kravchuk offered incentives to those members of the armed forces which would take oath to Ukraine, such as better pay

---

[795] Originally, the 1992 Crimean Constitution approved on May 5 established self-government. Only on May 19, Crimea accepted to remain as part of Ukraine and annulled their proclamation of self-government. Note of the author.
[796] Sasse, Op. Cit., page 226.
[797] 'Генпрокуратура назвала незаконной передачу Крыма УССР,' June 27, 2015, accessed on June 27, 2015. https://news.mail.ru/inregions/crimea/110/politics/22484922/?frommail=1

and housing, and given the climate, conditions of service, many sailors acted pragmatically in the choice of allegiance to Ukraine.[798] Altogether, by 1998, Crimean autonomy had been constitutionalized in three steps: the incomplete Crimean Constitution passed by the Ukrainian parliament in April 1996, the formation of Ukrainian Constitution of June 1996 and the final revision of the Crimean Constitution ratified by the Ukrainian parliament in December 1998, which anchored the Autonomous Republic of Crimea in the Ukrainian state.[799] It is noteworthy that despite its historical and cultural ties with the Crimean Tatars, Turkey never made any serious attempt to become a mediator or power broker.[800] At the end, what could Ankara expect to claim precisely?

Finally, the solution of what became the Crimean Autonomous Republic was not exempt from geopolitics. A weak Russia, during Yeltsin's term, marginalized the Crimean autonomy issue and concentrated on the negotiations over strategic bilateral agreements with Ukraine, which required acceptance of Ukraine's territorial integrity at that time. Besides, it was a more pragmatic decision to guarantee only the permanence of the Black Sea Fleet in Sevastopol rather than to control the whole peninsula. Meanwhile, in Ukraine, there was the acceptance that Crimea was a constitutional problem that required a compromise. Kiev accepted the principle of autonomy without defining it until they had better conditions to negotiate.

Overall, as in many other post-Soviet territories, 'Crimea illustrates the disjuncture between state boundaries and historically constructed identities in the aftermath of the Soviet Collapse.'[801] It was an example of a contested territory with multiple deeply embedded cultural, historical, and institutional memories. Here, the change of regime and weak statehood and geopolitics provided a source for political mobilization and consequently, as has been the case, when the state is weak, the subnational level gains political importance.

---

[798] Sasse, Op. Cit., page 225.
[799] Ibidem, page 219.
[800] Ibidem, page 248.
[801] Ibidem, page 251.

Crimea was also latecomer in terms of political mobilization after Perestroika compared to what happened in other Soviet territories. A territorial question within the USSR developed into a demand for territorial autonomy within Ukraine and a separatist movement only in 1994. 'Paradoxically, the majority of the Crimean population appeared simultaneously to oppose Crimea's exit from Ukraine, while favouring Crimea's reintegration with Russia.'[802]

It was a territory with a strong Soviet identity where the movement for more autonomy developed at the elite and mass level, even though their options were limited and Crimea finally received fewer rights than Russian autonomies, or Quebec, Scotland or Northern Ireland to mention some examples. Besides, the increase or decrease of the movements for more autonomy in Crimea has been deeply influenced by the geopolitical situation. The peninsula is located in an area where it becomes the middle of a geopolitical triangle between Russia, Ukraine and Turkey [803] but also as mentioned with even more geostrategic importance for NATO, ergo the United States.

After the Crimean issue was solved internally and internationally, the territory for more than a decade seemed integrated in the Ukrainian political activity. Ten regional and national elections plus a regional and a national referendum where held during the period from 1991 to 2002. In the first presidential election, Kravchuk obtained a slim majority in Crimea. Instead, in 1994, Kuchma won. In some occasions, the parliamentary elections were boycotted by the pro-Russian movement, leading to a majority of communist and 'independent' deputies, at the parliament with moderate views regarding Crimea's autonomy. Altogether, by 1995–1996, the balance of power had shifted further away from the political actors that pushed for a separatist position.

As mentioned before, the peninsula again regained notoriety together with the separatist movement on June 2006, when the Crimean assembly followed suit with a resolution declaring the peninsula a NATO-free zone, rejecting in fact the military exercises Yush-

---

[802] Ibidem, page 253.
[803] Ibidem, page 156.

chenko pretended to carry out in the peninsula with the participation of US Marines.[804] The resolution highlighted that the Ukrainian parliament had not authorized the exercise involving foreign troops on Ukrainian territory. It is significant to underline how the protests started again when the status of the relation between Russia and Ukraine changed under Yushchenko's presidency. At the end, the fragile agreement that had helped to build a Ukraine separated from Russia could be easily complicated each time Ukraine was forced to change its geopolitical orientation. Therefore, the Crimean territory was maybe the most sensitive area each time the Ukrainian Government took an approach towards the West, the same way Galicia would reflect the approach of the government in Kiev towards Russia. The existing autonomy in Crimea did not prove itself enough for a foundation to integrate and moderate the regional- and national-level elites. Already in 2006, Crimean elites, both Russian and Tartars, were not satisfied with the autonomy status and the way the relations with Kiev were established.[805] Besides, autonomy status could not resolve the regions' political economic issues,[806] which are similar to those of the rest of the Ukrainian territory.

Overall, three dimensions influenced the situation in Crimea: Kiev and Simferopol, Russia and Ukraine and the Crimean Tatar issue. The Tatar issue had a lesser impact than the others did, even if Sasse considered that the Crimean Tatars could be the key to future regional stability.

To conclude her book, Sasse considered that Crimea was a conflict that did not happen. She proved herself wrong in that sense. The most sensitive point regarding the status of Crimea considering the weakness of the new Ukrainian polity was precisely the impact of the relation with Russia and therefore, after the events in Kiev, in February 2014, there was an immediate effect on the peninsula.

The following days after the ousting of Yanukovych, numerous people in the peninsula started to organize themselves against the

---

[804] Ibidem, page 269.
[805] Kasyanenko, Mikita, 'On the 15th anniversary of the ARC,' ICC News Digest No. 4 (Winter 2006), A Review of the 15th Anniversary of the Founding of the Autonomous Republic of Crimea (ARC), accessed on June 28, 2016. http://www.iccrimea.org/news/newsdigest4.html
[806] Sasse, Op. Cit., page 274.

new government in Kiev and to complain against the abolition of the law on the regional languages.[807] The Crimean Government originally said it would commit itself to the Ukrainian law but on February 25, several hundred people blocked access to the parliament asking for a referendum on Crimea's independence. By February 27, around 60 pro-Russian gunmen seized the Crimean parliament and the Council of Ministers building. That same day a close session decided to remove Prime Minister Anatolii Mohyliov and named Sergey Aksyonov as the new prime minister. That same day, Berkut[808] units from Crimea took control of all the accesses to the peninsula. The next day, men in military uniforms without signs took both airports in Simferopol and Sevastopol.[809]

It is important to underline how the new authorities in Crimea quickly managed to organize a referendum for March 16 and also how the new Ukrainian Government was not capable of reacting in any sense. The Russians had managed to operate a geostrategic marble in response to what they felt was a Western betrayal in Kiev. Besides, the fact is that pro-Russian forces, with considerable local support, were able to take control of Crimea and also to block or take most of the Ukrainian strategic military assets present in the area, from the Ukrainian Army, Air Force and the Ukrainian Navy.[810] Besides, numerous military men from the three forces took side with the forces of the Government of the Autonomous Republic of Crimea. On a notable event without precedent in post-Soviet history, on March 1, Denis Berezovsky, the recently appointed commander of the Ukrainian Navy announced in a televised address

---

[807] The abolition was approved by the parliament but not signed by Turchynov.
[808] Berkut units were dissolved on February 25, 2014, but unofficially remained operational in Crimea. 'Head of Ukrainian Interior Ministry signs order to dissolve "Berkut",' February 26, 2014, accessed on February 26, 2014. http://sputniknews.com/voiceofrussia/news/2014_02_26/Head-of-Ukrainian-Interior-Ministry-signs-order-to-dissolve-Berkut-3065/
[809] Later on, it was known there were Russian Special Troops present in this operation.
[810] The case of the Ukrainian Navy was the most notable as all of the major ships but one, the Frigate 'Hetman Sadaydachniy', were captured by the Russian Black Sea Fleet by March 24, 2014. 'One-ship Ukraine navy defies Russia to the end,' March 26, 2014, accessed on March 26, 2014. http://www.wsj.com/news/articles/SB10001424052702303949704579461513462696086

that he had sworn allegiance to the people of Crimea.[811] By March 5, more than 6,000 members of the armed forces of Ukraine had taken sides with the Crimean authorities.[812] At the end, this is again another symptom of a failed state. It is more than symbolic that when the chief of the Navy takes side with the rivals together with a considerable amount of the armed forces the political unity that should be proper of a state had failed to exist.

Therefore, it was easy for the new Crimean authorities, with implicit Russian support, to push for a referendum. The two questions asked to the inhabitants of Crimea were the following:

1. Do you support the reunification of Crimea with Russia with all the rights of the federal subject of the Russian Federation?
2. Do you support the restoration of the Constitution of the Republic of Crimea in 1992 and the status of Crimea as part of Ukraine?[813]

The results as expected were overwhelmingly in favour of reunifying Crimea with Russia. In the Autonomous Republic, 96.77% voted for the first option and in Sevastopol[814] 95.60% did the same. The legality of the poll was widely contested in many Western countries while only a few openly recognized the results. In the following days, the Russian Federation quickly followed to incorporate from the legal standpoint Crimea and Sevastopol as new subjects of the Russian Federation, thus, assuring to remain with the control of the peninsula and the dominance of the Black Sea Fleet in the area.

---

[811] 'Crimea forms its own fleet as Ukraine navy chief sides with region,' March 2, 2014, accessed on March 2, 2014. http://rt.com/news/navy-chief-ukraine-crimea-485/

[812] 'ARC government: three anti-aircraft missile regiments of Ukraine's armed forces join Crimean side,' March 5, 2014, accessed on March 5, 2014. http://sputniknews.com/voiceofrussia/news/2014_03_05/ARC-Governme nt-three-anti-aircraft-missile-regiment-of-the-Armed-Forces-of-Ukraine-joi n-Crimean-side-8049/

[813] 'При воссоединении с Россией крымчане дискомфорта не почувствуют!,' March 8, 2014, accessed on March 8, 2014. http://www.kryminfo.net/pri-vossoedinenii-s-osiyey-krymchane-diskomforta-ne-pochustvuyut/

[814] Sevastopol was considered administratively separate from the Autonomous Republic of Crimea. The city council had declared since March 6 the city a federal subject of the Russian Federation. Still, the referendum took place but separately. 'Севастополь принял решение о вхождении в состав РФ,' March 6, 2014, accessed on March 6, 2014. http://www.unian.net/politics/8 93910-sevastopol-prinyal-reshenie-o-vhojdenii-v-sostav-rf.html

The Tartar issue did not become a bigger topic. Even if they did not support the referendum, after it happened, they were obliged to negotiate with Moscow. Being around 12% of the local population gives them a voice but still not in a position to challenge the decision. At the end, Tatar elites are not so different from other groups found in the Caucasus or other areas of Russia. The Russian Federation has managed to incorporate peacefully or by force different ethnic minorities without really endangering political control. Besides, the results, even if arguable in their accuracy, certainly show that at least a segment of the Crimean Tartars voted for the incorporation into the Russian Federation.

Meanwhile, the same as following the Georgian War, Moscow argued that they were just following the precedent settled by the United States in Kosovo. Even arguments as Russia having more right to Crimea than the British to the Malvinas Islands appeared among the justifications.[815]

At the end, even if the referendum had a weak legal base[816], either the ousting of Yanukovych from power was, therefore, it was also a political response. It was a matter of simple power politics, where the Kremlin wanted to show that they did not intend to quit on Ukraine so easily. If the EU members and the United States had betrayed the agreement of February 21, then, Russia would act in its own way.

---

[815] 'Russia has more right to Crimea than Britain to Falkands, says Russian MP,' March 23, 2015, accessed on March 1, 2016. http://www.theguardian.com/world/2015/mar/23/russia-has-more-right-to-crimea-than-britain-to-falkands-says-russian-mp

[816] This research does not deepen on the legality of the incorporation of Crimea into the Russian Federation. As a matter of fact, for international law, a referendum in this sense would require the agreement of Ukraine, as happened in Scotland and the United Kingdom, for example, during 2014. In the Crimean case, there are also a cumulous of illegalities surrounding the precedent facts, for instance in Ukraine and the USSR. Therefore, if the referendum could be considered illegal, also the 1954 transfer, the fall of the Soviet Union, the ousting of Yanukovych, and most of the electoral processes in Ukraine. At the end, this research as mentioned underlines the political and geopolitical struggle in the area and the effects in Crimea. Contrary to what some lawyers would think, the legality (or the lack of it) is a consequence of politics and not vice versa.

The de facto annexation or reincorporation (depending of the perspective) of Crimea into the Russian Federation, meant one geopolitical victory for the Kremlin after the events in Kiev of 2014. Nevertheless, this fact, as the classics of strategy[817] describe, opened the door to other fronts, first a reaction by the United States and the EU but also a counteraction by Russia.

2.8 What next?

After the events in Crimea and the preceding actions on February 2014, the new Ukrainian Government was in a very weak position. Turchynov, the acting president, was not recognized by Russia. Yatsenyuk, the US favourite candidate, became prime minister in a cabinet where he predominated over his allies and people related to Timoshenko while conceding also some positions to the extreme right party Svoboda,[818] including the General Prosecutor of Ukraine, who should have been in charge of a serious inquiry of what happened in the *Maidan* during February. Yatsenyuk incorporated also 'independent' personalities like Serhiy Kvit, the rector of the Mohyla Academy as Ministry of Education and Pavlo Sheremeta[819] as minister of economy and trade. There were no members from the UDAR Party or related with Klitschko as the United States had suggested, as noticed during Nuland's audio. Instead, there was one minister related to Poroshenko, Volodymyr

---

[817] In this sense, I retake Luttwak's idea of how measures and countermeasures continuously evolve. Luttwak, Edward N., *Strategy, The Logic of War and Peace*, Cambridge, The Belknap Press of Harvard University Press, 2001.

[818] Svoboda obtained three cabinet positions in the first Yatsenyuk government including the vice prime minister for Humanitarian Policy with Oleksandr Sych, the Ministry of Agrarian Policy and Food with Ihor Shvaika and the Ministry of Ecology and Natural Resources with Andriy Mokhnyk. Besides, they held briefly the Ministry of Defense with Ihor Tenyukh but he resigned after the events in Crimea altogether with the General Prosecutor of Ukraine Oleh Makhnitskyi. Note of the author.

[819] With a reputation of a harsh privatizer and supporter of neo-liberal policies, he acted before as the dean of the Kiev Mohyla Business School. 'Sheremeta explains his resignation as being due to uncoordinated appointment of trade representative,' August 21, 2014, accessed on August 21, 2014. http://en.in terfax.com.ua/news/economic/219334.html

Groysman. Finally, there were only two outsiders from the local political class, which obtained cabinet positions: Oleh Musiy[820] who had been member of the medical service of the Maidan became minister of health and Dmytro Bulatov as minister of youth and sports. Both left the post before the end of the year. Besides, it is worth noticing that mostly people from Western Ukraine composed the cabinet.

Altogether, the actions taken by the new government were completely opposed to any attempt to amalgamate the already fragile social tissue and bring political stability. Ukraine had lost Crimea; meanwhile several groups in Eastern Ukraine were not recognizing the government. By April, it was clear that many regions in East Ukraine were not under government control and that there were separatist groups in different areas, mostly in the Donetsk and Lugansk regions, occupying government buildings. Protesters declared the existence of the Donetsk People's Republic and the Lugansk People's Republic on April 7. Pro-Russian rebels managed also to acquire weapons, mostly from police or army lots in the area, which allowed them to establish protected positions and to become a challenge to the authorities in Kiev. Even in Odessa, groups pretended to organize themselves and call for the creation of an Odessan Republic.[821] In some cases, the Russian support to the opponents became evident[822] but it was also clear that in different degrees there was a local dissatisfaction with the new authorities in

---

[820] Oleh Musiy was one of the few outsiders that managed to enter the government. He pursued a fight against old corrupt schemes in the medical Ukrainian system where bribes account for almost half of the budget in hospitals and where allegedly around 40% of the official budget is stolen. He was suspended from his duty by Yatsenyuk around six months later. Musiy sustained there was never a serious intention to fight against corruption by the government. After his dismissal, the old networks that used to profit with public resources came back to operate. Bullough, Oliver, 'Welcome to the most corrupt nation in Europe,' *The Guardian*, February 4, 2015, accessed on March 1, 2016. http://www.theguardian.com/news/2015/feb/04/welcome-to-the-most-corrupt-nation-in-europe-ukraine#comments

[821] 'Антимайдан» Одессы объявил о создании Одесской республики,' April 14, 2014, accessed on April 14, 2014. http://www.sinoptik.md/ru/news/695?utm_campaign=Informer&utm_medium=referral&utm_source=Kommersant

[822] 'Мэр Славянска подтвердила присутствие российских военных в городе,' April 16, 2014, accessed on April 16, 2014. http://korrespondent.net/ukrain

Kiev. By those days, the United Nations warned for the risk of an ethnolinguistic split in Ukraine.[823] It is obvious, as noticed before, that Russia would support the ethnolinguistic fragmentation to take advantage of its position and it is obvious that they had the tools to destabilize considerable areas of South and Eastern Ukraine and count on considerable local support.

At this point, considering the fragile condition of the Ukrainian Army, the lack of trust of many of the local authorities in East Ukraine and the fragile political situation, the government still decided to retake control with the use of force. During those days, Turchynov declared the beginning of the Anti-Terrorist Operation (ATO), which, as the Minister of Interior Avakov said, pretended to retake by negotiation or by force the buildings and installations controlled by armed rebels. It is funny, though, that if there was a real intention of establishing a political dialogue, the name 'anti-terrorist'[824] was used to design the operation. After some days, the interim

---

e/politics/3350468-mer-slavianska-podtverdyla-prysutstvye-rossyiskykh-voennykh-v-horode

[823] 'Украина под угрозой раскола по языковому признаку – ООН,' April 16, 2014, accessed on April 20, 2014. http://korrespondent.net/ukraine/pol itics/3350493-ukrayna-pod-uhrozoi-raskola-po-yazykovomu-pryznaku-oon

[824] "'Terrorism' may well be the most politicized term in the political vocabulary these days. Used as a label for a certain form of political violence, it reflects, if it 'sticks', negatively on a political opponent, demonizing him and delegitimizing his conduct. In its pejorative dimension, the fate of the term 'terrorist' is comparable to the use and abuse of other terms in political vocabulary terms like 'racist', 'fascist' or 'imperialist'." Schmid, Alex P., 'The definition of terrorism,' in *The Routledge Handbook of Terrorism Research*, edited by Schmid, Alex P., New York, Routledge, 2011, page 40. Therefore, the use of the word depends on the political intention of the rival. For instance, the United States considers Al-Qaeda a terrorist organization but it was not one when they received US support against the Soviets. The same way, the US State Department has a definition and a list of state sponsors of terrorism that changes depending on the geopolitical goals pursued by the United States. Cuba, for instance, was in that list, but was withdrawn recently, as there is an intention to improve the relation with the country. Instead, only some governments recognize Hezbollah as a terrorist organization. The same can be said of the accusations against Israel or the United States and the way they have financed 'terrorist' activities as part of their military activities. These examples display the political nature of the use of the word 'terrorist'. Finally, the word 'terrorist' is commonly used to describe a political rival with whom it is not possible or desirable to reach an agreement. Hence, when the Ukrainian authorities decided to name the rebels in the East as terrorists they were already intending that there was no real intention to negotiate a peaceful ceasefire in East Ukraine.

president, Turchynov had to accept the fact that the Ukrainian forces were not in a position to enforce their authority in Eastern Ukraine.[825] Altogether, the conflict arrived to the brink of a civil war but with the same foreign actors involved, around what remained of the Ukrainian polity, changing roles, now Russia supporting in different ways the opposition while the United States with the EU trying to aid and legitimate as possible the new Ukrainian authorities.

After the tragic events in Odessa,[826] on May 2nd, the regions of Donetsk and Lugansk organized on May 11, at least in the sectors controlled by the separatist forces, a sort of improvised referendum in which the population was asked to comment on the case of Donetsk: 'Do you support the Act of State Self-rule of the Donetsk People's Republic?' Instead, in Lugansk the question was: 'Do you support the declaration of state independence of the Lugansk People's Republic?' In both cases, the answer 'yes' received more than 90% of the votes, while instead the different authorities declared a huge difference on the turnout. The local commissions sustained it was above 74% in both cases while the Ukrainian Ministry of Interior said the participation was only 32% and 24%, respectively.[827] In any case, the Ukrainian Government did not recognize the referendum, consultation or however it was named, while Russia expressed 'respect' for the preferences shown by the people of the Donbass.[828]

Weeks later and in the middle of an emerging civil war, presidential elections were held in Ukraine on May 25, the same day the

---

[825] 'Ukraine forces "helpless" to stop pro-Russia takeover in east,' *The Guardian*, April 30, 2014, accessed on March 1, 2016. http://www.theguardian.com/world/2014/apr/30/ukraine-forces-helpless-stop-pro-russia-takeover-east

[826] After several clashes between pro-Russian and pro-Ukrainian separatist forces, a fire in the Trade Unions House took 46 casualties on the Pro-Russian side. There was never an independent investigation of the events while both sides blamed each other while authorities in Kiev blamed the local authorities. Russia used the event afterwards to underline Kiev's fault on consenting the action of radical nationalists. The mentioned reference takes into account the report by the Russian BBC correspondent in the events. 'Трагедия в Одессе: у каждой из сторон своя версия,' May 5, 2014, accessed on May 5, 2014. http://news.mail.ru/politics/18081380/?frommail=1

[827] 'Турчинов опроверг описанные сепаратистами чудеса явки на "референдум",' May 12, 2014, accessed on May 12, 2014. http://www.pravda.com.ua/rus/news/2014/05/12/7025064/

[828] 'Moscow respects will expressed by population of Donetsk and Luhansk regions of Ukraine,' *TASS*, May 12, 2014, accessed on May 12, 2014. http://tass.ru/en/world/731214

elections to the EU parliament took place while the pro-Russian forces still controlled different areas of the Donetsk and Lugansk regions. Considering how the struggle against Yanukovych had ended, and the fact that Klitschko conceded his support to Petro Poroshenko at the end of March in change of contending for the post of mayor in Kiev, it was obvious that there would be only one candidate with a real possibility to win. Besides, there would be no vote in Crimea and many poll stations would be close in Donetsk and Lugansk. Moreover, the general distrust against what remained of the Party of Regions, made Poroshenko, a supporter of the *Maidan* and, with wide coverage from his TV Channel (5th Channel), the only 'credible' personality known by the electorate. In that sense, even if numerous people still were camping in the *Maidan* considering their original conditions were not fulfilled, Poroshenko easily won the election with 54.70% of the votes. Iulia Timoshenko initially pretended to make a political comeback. She scored very low with 12.8% of the votes, even though she slowed down her campaign in the final days, unofficially conceding ground to Poroshenko. On third, Oleh Lyashko, who used to belong to the Timoshenko bloc, obtained 8.32% of the votes, while Anatoliy Hrytsenko, Yuschenko's former minister of defence, got 5.48%. Serhiy Tihipko, another oligarch that had been a candidate in 2010 and then became part of the Party of Regions, launched his candidacy as 'independent' and received 5.23% of the votes while Mykhailo Dobkin, former governor in Kharkov and contending for what remained of the Party of Regions, got 3.03%.[829]

Altogether, again in the 2014 presidential election, all the mentioned candidates belonged to the same ruling class that had been in power in Ukraine. Therefore, after all the struggles to oust Yanukovych, at the end, it did not imply a renewal of the political establishment as pretended many of the people that contributed to the *Maidan*. Instead, it brought the arrival of another oligarch,[830] but

---

[829] 'ПОЗАЧЕРГОВІ ВИБОРИ ПРЕЗИДЕНТА УКРАЇНИ,' May 25, 2014, accessed on May 25, 2014. http://www.cvk.gov.ua/info/protokol_zvo_28.0 5.2014.pdf

[830] On the week of the election, the fortune of Poroshenko was $1.3 billion and he was ranked the sixth richest Ukrainian. 'Весь бизнес Порошенко. Журналисты составили список активов президента-олигарха,' May 30, 2014, accessed on May 30, 2014. http://korrespondent.net/ukraine/poli

in this case, one that had been for the last decade Western oriented. It was, as *Limes*, the Italian journal of Geopolitics, portrayed, 'Con Poroshenko in Ucraina viene eletto il Gattopardo',[831] the Ukrainian oligarchs remained attached to power, in an election of a sole candidate, when everything was decided before among the oligarchs.

Therefore, almost all the oligarchs pledged alliance to the new government while pretending to conserve the grip of power they had. Akhmetov, for instance, never supported the separatists, but tried to maintain a certain presence in the Donbass by sending humanitarian aid. Others, like Kolomoyskyi, also obtained political positions. He even managed to become governor[832] of the Region of Dnipropetrovsk, while personally financing an armed militia[833] that conducts its own operations in the Donbass. Most of the oligarchs repositioned themselves with the regime while only Dmytro Firtash was held in Austria, accused of corruption.[834]

After Poroshenko[835] took office as the new president, during his inauguration speech, he made special reference to the territorial integrity of Ukraine. There seemed no clear intention to establish any

---

tics/3371259-ves-byznes-poroshenko-zhurnalysty-sostavyly-spysok-aktyvov-prezydenta-olyharkha

[831] 'Con Poroshenko in Ucraina viene eletto il Gattopardo,' May 27, 2014, accessed on May 27, 2014. http://temi.repubblica.it/limes/con-poroshenko-in-ucraina-viene-eletto-il-gattopardo/62419

[832] It is interesting, though, as Ukrainian law forbids persons with double nationality to sustain public office, but Kolomoyskyi then obtained a third one, therefore holding the Ukrainian, Israeli and Cypriot citizenships.

[833] 'Ukraine's secret weapon: Feisty oligarch Ihor Kolomoisky,' June 27, 2014, accessed on March 1, 2016. http://www.wsj.com/articles/ukraines-secret-weapon-feisty-oligarch-ihor-kolomoisky-1403886665

[834] Firtash was arrested in Vienna on March 2014 after an extradition request by the United States on corruption charges. After paying a bail worth of €125 million, the largest in Austrian legal history, a regional court in Vienna rejected the extradition request on the grounds that insufficient prove was provided. It is also important to remind that for years Firtash, that made his fortune mostly under Yushchenko and Yanukovych's terms, had used Austria as a base for his gas deals. Taccani, Matteo, 'Ucraina, La Danza degli oligarchi,' Limes Oggi, May 20, 2014.

[835] It is interesting to note how the United States changed the perception about Poroshenko depending on how he could be useful to the US foreign policy. Back in 2006, the US ambassador in Ukraine described him as a 'disgraced oligarch' and later that year, a cable from Deputy Chief of the US Mission in Kiev, Sheila Gwaltney, mentioned that 'Poroshenko was tainted by credible corruption allegations'. Instead, the opinions changed into positive comments once he became the minister of foreign affairs under Yushchenko in 2009.

kind of dialogue between the parts in conflict. At this point, from the global and local perspective the scenario was quite clear. Globally, as mentioned, the Kremlin did not intend to lose its hold on Ukraine: strategically, historically and politically Ukraine meant a lot for them, and obviously, Moscow had the conditions to prolong the unrest until a better settlement could occur. Instead, among the Western countries, there were different opinions. For instance, for the United States, it could be convenient a long struggle with Russia that even if the Russians could win, it would bring enormous political cost to the Kremlin while the United States would stay as the sole guarantor of stability. Therefore, the different wave of sanctions, which will be explained afterwards, pretended to soften Russia but did not have the possibility of really determining a long-term solution to the conflict. In fact, the only immediate geopolitical effect was to end even more the alliance between Russia and China.[836]

The EU had to choose between pursuing European interests and being loyal to their US ally. The United States could hold a long standoff against Russia, regarding Ukraine. Could the EU allow itself to do it? At the end, the relation with Russia or more precisely, the interdependence with Russia brought more risks and therefore the sanctions applied against Russia had a counter effect for many European countries. Besides, the EU would have to be responsible for most of the economic aid that surely would be needed to help the crawling Ukrainian economy.[837] Western scholars like Anatol Lieven warned on June 2014 how the Western governments should

---

'The not-very-nice things U.S. officials used to say about Ukraine's new president,' May 29, 2014, accessed on May 29, 2014. http://www.washingtonpost.com/blogs/worldviews/wp/2014/05/29/the-not-very-nice-things-u-s-officials-used-to-say-about-ukraines-new-president/

[836] 'It's not Russia that's pushed Ukraine to the brink of war,' April 30, 2014, March 1, 2016. http://www.theguardian.com/commentisfree/2014/apr/30/russia-ukraine-war-kiev-conflict

[837] 'Dancing with the bear: Merkel seeks a hardline on Putin,' March 24, 2014, accessed on March 15, 2015. http://www.spiegel.de/international/germany/merkel-and-europe-search-for-an-adequate-response-to-putin-a-960378.html

avoid helping Kiev to win the conflict by military means. He sustained it was impossible to obtain a military victory considering the current conditions and alarmed of the risk of a prolonged war.[838]

From May to July, the intensity of the military confrontation increased while it was obvious the Ukrainian army did not have the resources to sustain a long war. Besides, it had to rely very often on armed militias or elements of the National Guard, considering the high number of desertions that had been present in the Ukrainian Army. During the whole 2014, the conflict brought numerous casualties and showed the absurdity of pursuing an offensive strategy by military means to defeat an enemy that had on one side support from the local population,[839] and also the obvious logistic and military support from Russia even if the Russian authorities justified the presence of Russian troops as 'volunteers'. Against that force, opposed the lack of awareness of the Ukrainian military forces, together with the increasing power of diverse armed militias that responded to different kinds of warlords, oligarchs or other extreme right movements[840] and even foreign 'volunteer' groups[841] participating. After some months, the gradual intention by the government to incorporate the different militias either to the Ministry of

---

[838] Lieven, Anatol, 'Ukraine-The way out,' June 5, 2014, accessed on March 1, 2016. http://www.nybooks.com/articles/archives/2014/jun/05/ukraine-way-out/

[839] Besides, it is interesting to notice how the bombing of residential areas, even if justified or not as military targets, by the Ukrainian Air Force together with the collateral damage it brought encouraged the local population to oppose even more the authorities in Kiev and to accuse them of genocide against the local population. 'La défiance croissante des habitants de l'Est ukrainien envers l'armée de Kiev,' September 8, 2014, accessed on September 8, 2014. http://www.lemonde.fr/international/article/2014/09/08/la-defiance-croissante-des-habitants-de-l-est-ukrainien-envers-l-armee-de-kiev_4483511_32 10.html

[840] For instance, the Pravyi Sektor conducted its own operations against the rebels while its members managed by themselves to obtain their own guns and even intended to function as a non-authorized police force in different areas of the country. The extreme right organization counted also with the Nazis, Jews and foreigners in the same organization. Evangelista, Joshua, 'Ucraina, la milizia nazionalista con dentro nazi ed ebrei,' December 10, 2014, accessed on March 1, 2016. http://temi.repubblica.it/micromega-online/ucraina-la-milizia-nazionalista-con-dentro-nazi-ed-ebrei/?printpage=undefined

[841] 'Легионеры "Азова": Как иностранцы воюют на Донбассе,' October 9, 2014, accessed on March 1, 2016. http://korrespondent.net/ukraine/politics/3429499-lehyonery-azova-kak-ynostrantsy-vouiuit-na-donbasse,

Interior or to the Ukrainian Armed Forces[842] produced also numerous divisions among the troops and accusations of treason to the ones that resisted or refused to obey the orders. Besides, the high number of Ukrainian casualties, among military and the armed militias was also partially caused by the irresponsibility with which in many cases conscripts were sent to war zones without the adequate preparation and the training to use their own weapons. A witness, for instance, suggested that friendly fire and a poor military kit caused half of the Ukrainian fighters killed.[843]

Altogether, there was not any will by the Ukrainian authorities to look for a political solution convenient for the Ukrainian population. Thus, when an organized polity did not exist, there remained only different groups of interest trying to become hegemonic classes while the civil war continued and the foreign states related either to the West or Russia continued to play their own games. At the end, to quote Schmitt again, when there is no possibility to discern between friends and enemies, the political unity of the polity disappears.

Another event occurred in July 2014, reflecting the complexity of the political situation. In this case, it is the incident of the Malaysian Airlines Flight 17. On July 17, a Boeing 777 travelling from Amsterdam to Kuala Lumpur crashed after being shot down in the area held by the rebels. Western media blamed Russia for the incident (even a British newspaper named its lead as *Putin's missile*) while Putin responded what happened in the Ukrainian territory was the responsibility of the Ukrainian authorities. The tragedy that cost the life of 283 passengers and 15 crewmembers added more tension to the already delicate relation between the parties involved in the conflict. The only thing clear until now is that the plane was shot down by military means. The Ukrainian Government blamed the rebels, while the United States hurried also to claim without show-

---

[842] 'Бойцы батальонов МВД начали переходить в армию,' September 5, 2014, accessed on March 1, 2016. http://korrespondent.net/ukraine/3414884-boitsy-batalonov-mvd-nachaly-perekhodyt-v-armyui
[843] 'Half Ukrainian fighters killed by poor kit and friendly fire,' February 22, 2015, accessed on February 22, 2015. http://www.thesundaytimes.co.uk/sto/news/world_news/Ukraine/article1522268.ece

ing proofs that it was a missile from a BUK system shot by the rebels.[844] Alleged conversation between the separatists were used to blame them for the incident, together with some comments on social sites. Instead, the Russians published satellite pictures which showed around 60 BUK[845] systems property of the Ukrainian army in the area, while only one of them could be with the rebels, even if sources from the Ukrainian Army denied the rebels could have taken the mentioned BUK missile from one of their military bases.[846] Besides, Russian sources assured there was a Su-25 of the Ukrainian Air Force flying nearby. In any case, there is not enough evidence to blame either the rebels or the Ukrainian Armed Forces. The evidence becomes contradictory and cannot fully confirm who did it.

The fact that the BUK missile system tends to be extremely precise when used correctly raises also the question, who would deliberately shoot down a commercial airplane and what was the goal, even though, the lack of sufficient proof until now, makes it impossible to know if the shooting was something planned by the Ukrainian authorities with or without agreement with the United States,[847] or it was a mistake by the pro-Russian rebels.

---

[844] Vernochet, Jean-Michel, 'Ukraine l'escalade,' Chronique ukrainiennes Saison 2, Sigest. Mai/Novembre 2014, page 77.
[845] The BUK missile system is a family of self-propelled surface to air missile systems. It is operated by more than 10 armies in the world including the Russian and Ukrainian Armed Forces. It has an accuracy of 95% and can recognize from a military and civil aircraft. 'SA-17 Grizzly 9A317E BUK-M2 air defense missile system,' accessed on March 1, 2016. http://www.armyrecognition.com/russia_russian_missile_system_vehicle_uk/sa-17_grizzly_buk-m2_9a317e_missile_technical_data_sheet_specifications_description_pictures.html
[846] 'Минобороны Украины: ополченцы не могли захватить украинский "Бук",' October 20, 2014, accessed on October 20, 2014. http://news.mail.ru/politics/19885487/?frommail=1
[847] As an antecedent, on October 4, 2001, the Ukrainian Armed Forces shot down a passenger plane by mistake when a Tu-154 was flying from Tel Aviv to Novosibirsk. Back then, Ukrainian officials acknowledged the mistake. In another incident, the FBI and the CIA had deep knowledge that the former CIA agent Luis Posada Carriles was planning to put a bomb on a Cuban passenger plane, as happened with the Cubana de Aviacion flight 455 on October 6, 1976. Note of the author.

Therefore, it remains for the political analysis to raise the question of who obtained the biggest political advantage from this tragedy: the Kremlin and the pro-Russian rebels or the Western countries and the Ukrainian Government. In practice, the ones who benefited the most from the tragedy were the United States and allies[848] who used the tragedy to push for a stronger stance against Russia while the Ukrainian authorities continued to name the opponents as terrorists. Instead, from the political point of view, it had no sense to shoot down a passenger carrier, considering the huge political cost it would bring.

Among the political instability and the armed conflict, it is also important to consider the enormous number of refugees who suffered consequences of the armed conflict. There are different figures for the number of people displaced, depending on the source but some of them estimate 2 million people until June 2015, most of them coming from the Donbass. Around 800,000 went to Russia but also a considerable number fled to other Ukrainian cities.[849] The numbers are not accurate and only in Kiev it was quite notable the huge number of new arrivals to the city that came from the Donbas, in many cases, people related to the companies owned by the oligarchs that preferred to transfer the companies to Kiev, including in many cases the employees.

The parliamentary elections of October 2014 brought only the confirmation of the same political forces present before. The fact that the same electoral law passed under Yanukovych remained in function allowed a series of old timers to retain their seats as 'independent' candidates, while Poroshenko, after having built his own party named the 'Petro Poroshenko block' managed to become the first political force with 132 deputies. In second place, Yatsenyuk and his party got 82 seats, while a new party, Self Reliance, lead by the incumbent mayor of Lvov, Andriy Sadovyi, obtained 33 seats. The Opposition Bloc that regrouped many from the former Party of

---

[848] In these cases, the Baltic countries and Poland since the beginning of the hostilities were strong supporters of giving military aid to the Ukrainian Government.

[849] 'L'Ukraine, cette guerre que les Européens ne veulent pas voir en face,' June 26, 2015, accessed on June 26, 2015. http://www.letemps.ch/Page/Uuid/456 71aec-1b5e-11e5-9d4e-1dfb5906ea79/LUkraine_cette_guerre_que_les_Euro p%C3%A9ens_ne_veulent_pas_voir_en_face

Regions obtained 32 seats, while the Radical Party from Oleh Lyashko obtained 22 seats and Fatherland with Timoshenko on top got 19 seats. Besides, only 423 out of 450 parliament seats were elected considering the impossibility to hold an election in Crimea and most of the Donbas region. At the end, the results assured Poroshenko and Yatsenyuk the possibility to form a government with little support from the other parties.

The second Yatsenyuk Government was in a certain degree similar to the first with some exceptions. The cabinet members that used to be part of the *Maidan* were left outside the government and in one case that could be unique in modern European history, three foreigners, or at least foreigners until the day they took possession of their cabinet positions became ministries in Ukraine. Natalie Jaresko,[850] a US citizen, became minister of finances, Alexander Kvitashvili, a former minister during Saakashvili's term as Georgia's president, became minister of health and Aivaras Abromavicius from Lithuania became minister of economy and trade. The three of them have in common that they are fervent defenders of neo-liberal policies and of a policy attached to US interests. Besides, it is difficult to imagine, how someone that used to work for the US State Department could defend a hypothetical Ukrainian interest, or what she would do in case both interests are opposed. Besides, it is at least intriguing how these persons, especially Jaresko, decided to take a job in another country in which they would earn only around $200 a month compared to what they earned before. Those were not the only cases. Some months after, more foreigners arrived to the Cabinet. The Georgian Gia Getsadze[851] became vice minister of justice while in one extremely controversial appointment, Saakashvili, the former president of Georgia, became governor of the

---

[850] Jaresko held several positions in the US State Department, including Chief of the Economy Section of the US embassy in Ukraine. She obtained Ukrainian citizenship the same day she took possession of her position. 'В Кабмине будет три министра-иностранца – Луценко,' December 2, 2014, accessed on December 2, 2014. http://news.mail.ru/inworld/ukraina/politics/20329100/?frommail=1

[851] 'Первым заместителем министра юстиции назначили грузина,' January 14, 2015, accessed on January 14, 2015. http://korrespondent.net/ukraine/politics/3466575-pervym-zamestytelem-mynystra-yustytsyy-naznachyly-hruzyna

Odessa region.[852] Besides, this highly controversial and extremely provocative personality, he persecuted in his own country for allegations of abuse of power and organizing the beating of a businessman,[853] he even recognized publicly on his Facebook page that part of his staff is being paid by the United States.[854]

This straight capitulation to the interest of the United States, that seems like part of a complot elucubration, proved itself correct not only with the different nominations to the Ukrainian Government but also by different documents. A letter, addressed by US Senator Richard Durbin, the Senate minority whip, to Prime Minister Yatsenyuk, in which he gives instructions of which ministers should stay in their positions and which ones do not fulfil the requirements from the perspective of US Senate Ukrainian Caucus, confirms the level of US involvement. The tone in which he writes and the lightness with which he addresses the prime minister reflect the ease with which they give instructions to Ukrainian authorities. These facts become a great thrust for Russian propaganda to show the actual Ukrainian Government as a US puppet. The Kremlin once even accused the United States uses Ukraine as a ram[855] while the Russian prime minister Medvedev referred to the relation between the EU and Ukraine as neo-colonialism.[856]

---

[852] 'Михаил Саакашвили стал губернатором Одесской области,' May 30, 2015, accessed on May 30, 2015. Подробнее: http://www.kommersant.ru/doc/2738605

[853] 'В Тбилиси начался суд по делу против Саакашвили,' July 9, 2015, accessed on March 1, 2016. http://korrespondent.net/world/3537567-v-tbylysy-nachalsia-sud-po-delu-protyv-saakashvyly

[854] 'США профинансируют команду Саакашвили,' July 6, 2015, accessed on March 1, 2016. https://news.mail.ru/politics/22574674/?frommail=1

[855] 'Кремль: США используют Украину как таран,' January 29, 2015, accessed on January 29, 2015. http://korrespondent.net/world/russia/3472625-kreml-ssha-yspolzuuit-ukraynu-kak-taran

[856] 'Медведев: Отношение ЕС к Украине похоже на неоколониализм,' December 12, 2014, accessed on January 29, 2015. http://korrespondent.net/ukraine/3455983-medvedev-otnoshenye-es-k-ukrayne-pokhozhe-na-neokolonyalyzm

The letter, dated from June 25, became public on July 5 in different social media pages and was published also by the Ukrainian site Korrespondent. "Яценюк согласовывает министров с США?. В сети появилось письмо премьеру," accessed on July 5, 2015.
Source: http://korrespondent.net/ukraine/3535860-yatsenuik-sohlasovyvaet-myn ystrov-s-ssha-v-sety-poiavylos-pysmo-premeru

Altogether, this total submission to the United States happened amidst a great economic collapse in which the Ukrainian Hryvnia lost more than half of its value in year and a half after the fall of Yanukovych. Economy contracted 6.8% in 2014 and was expected to fall by another 9% in 2015. Amidst the war, the government also reduced drastically social expenses, pensions, budget for education, all while applying a harsh austerity programme designed by the IMF.[857]

At the end, the Ukrainian population became hostage of the geopolitical struggle and had to pay the consequences. The economic collapse, and the unstable situation of the local currency complicated issues even more, for the common Ukrainian who survived in a society where labour rights are easily ignored and where the minimum salary was less than €50 a month in 2015, while the oligarchs continued to enjoy their big share of the Ukrainian GDP. No wonder, how for many average Ukrainian citizens, the EU meant the paradise in which welfare and decent wages and pensions could be obtained.

Another interesting detail of the conflict was the role of the media. In Ukraine, as before, most TV channels and media in the hands of the oligarchs. Most of the channels, especially after the armed conflict begun, transformed their editorial line in a sort of 'patriotic struggle' against the Russian people. Nationalist stories surrounded by flags and dramatic survival accounts became part of the daily TV listings. Even comedy programmes making fun of the Russians and inciting loathing against them became common. Therefore, while Russian media depicted the Ukrainian authorities as controlled by rogues and fascist groups, submitted to the will of the United States, Ukrainian media instead depicted an 'heroic' battle for liberation, where volunteers were fighting for freedom against the 'Russian occupant'. Meanwhile, editorial lines pushed for the need of more military assurances by the 'free world' while showing concern on why they would not commit fully to this struggle for 'freedom' and 'democracy' where obviously of course, the role of the oligarchs was not mentioned. Besides, Russian Channels were prohibited, together with numerous Russian films and TV shows. Sometimes even the Ukrainian channels in Russian languages became 'suspicious' of being part of a foreign fifth column. On New Year's Eve of 2014, the fact that the Channel INTER,[858] invited to its new year

---

[857] 'Кабмин предлагает сократить расходы на образование и науку на 28%,' December 25, 2014, accessed on January 29, 2015. http://news.mail.ru/inworld/ukraina/politics/20578890/
[858] INTER is the leading Russian-speaking channel in Ukraine and is property of Dmytro Firtash.

show some famous Russian singers became a motive for later reprisals by the government. Even members of the government coalition like Oleh Lyashko complained that there was more freedom for the press under Yanukovych than under Poroshenko.[859]

Western media was neither exempt of media geopolitical confrontation, as *The Guardian* pointed out once, as Western media became then anti-Russian.[860] For example, constant comparisons of Putin to Hitler or huge outrage when Western journalists were held by the rebels and ignoring the facts when the Ukrainian forces held them are part of the asymmetry of the media coverage in several Western countries. Besides, in many cases, there was a kind of omission in several Western coverages with regard to the different extreme right groups present in the struggle or the bombing of civilians by the Ukrainian Air Force. At the end, the coverage of the conflict, in Russia, in Ukraine or in the EU portrayed three different realities of how the conflict evolved and was attached in different degrees to the political and geopolitical position of the actors. Therefore, as happens in different armed conflicts, 'independent' journalism is not exempt of assuming a political stance.

---

[859] 'При Януковиче было больше свободы слова, чем при Порошенко – Ляшко,' February 18, 2015, accessed on February 18, 2015. http://korrespondent.net/ukraine/politics/3480836-pry-yanukovyche-bylo-bolshe-svobody-slova-chem-pry-poroshenko-liashko

[860] 'Is western media coverage of the Ukraine crisis anti-Russian?,' August 4, 2014, March 1, 2016. http://www.theguardian.com/world/2014/aug/04/western-media-coverage-ukraine-crisis-russia

"Minsk Protocol" by Goran tek-en, accessed on July 23, 2015.
Source: Wikimedia Commons, licensed under CC BY-SA 4.0
(https://creativecommons.org/licenses/by-sa/4.0/deed.en)

Altogether, the different attempts to solve the conflict have been a failure. The first Minsk Protocol was signed in September 2014 between the representatives of the Donetsk People's Republic, the Lugansk People's Republic, a Russian representative, a representative from the OSCE and Leonid Kuchma representing the Ukrainian authorities. They agreed on a ceasefire and a series of follow-up measures including the delimitation of the area controlled by each side of the conflict and to pull back heavy artillery from the areas shown in the diagram.

After several violations of the agreement, by January 2015, it collapsed, and after another period of hostilities during January and

February in which the Ukrainian Army continued to lose territory, another attempt was made, this time with an increasing participation from Germany and France, to negotiate another agreement. Therefore, Minsk II, again with the Belarus president Lukashenko playing the host, included direct negotiations between Angela Merkel, Francois Hollande, Vladimir Putin and Petro Poroshenko. Altogether, after hours of tough negotiations, they managed to agree on new terms for a ceasefire.[861]

The fragile agreement[862] reflects how the solution of the conflict will still depend on the fluctuations of the relation between Russia, the United States and some EU members. It also shows the impossibility of Ukrainian authorities to solve the issue by themselves while they became hostages of the geopolitical struggle. Besides, it also confirms one transcendent fact. How after more than two decades, the Ukrainian society was not capable of building a solid polity in which its entire population feels included. It shows also the failure of the pretension to build ethnonationalist polities in a multiethnic territory. At the end, the justified desire of the people that live in Ukraine to have their own state did not consider the geopolitical realities. The lack of political vision from many of their leaders or to be more precise the lack of 'state-vision', did not allow to perceive from a realistic perspective which were the imperatives to preserve a Ukrainian polity considering the internal and international context present. Finally, even if the Ukrainians have been victims of geopolitical struggles for centuries, a strong sovereign polity could allow them to defend their interests and play a better role in the world chessboard.

---

[861] 'Minsk agreement on the Ukrainian crisis: Text in full,' February 12, 2015, accessed on July 27, 2015. http://www.telegraph.co.uk/news/worldnews/europe/ukraine/11408266/Minsk-agreement-on-Ukraine-crisis-text-in-full.html

[862] 'Minsk agreement on the Ukraine crisis: Text in full,' February 12, 2015, accessed on July 27, 2015. http://www.telegraph.co.uk/news/worldnews/europe/ukraine/11408266/Minsk-agreement-on-Ukraine-crisis-text-in-full.html

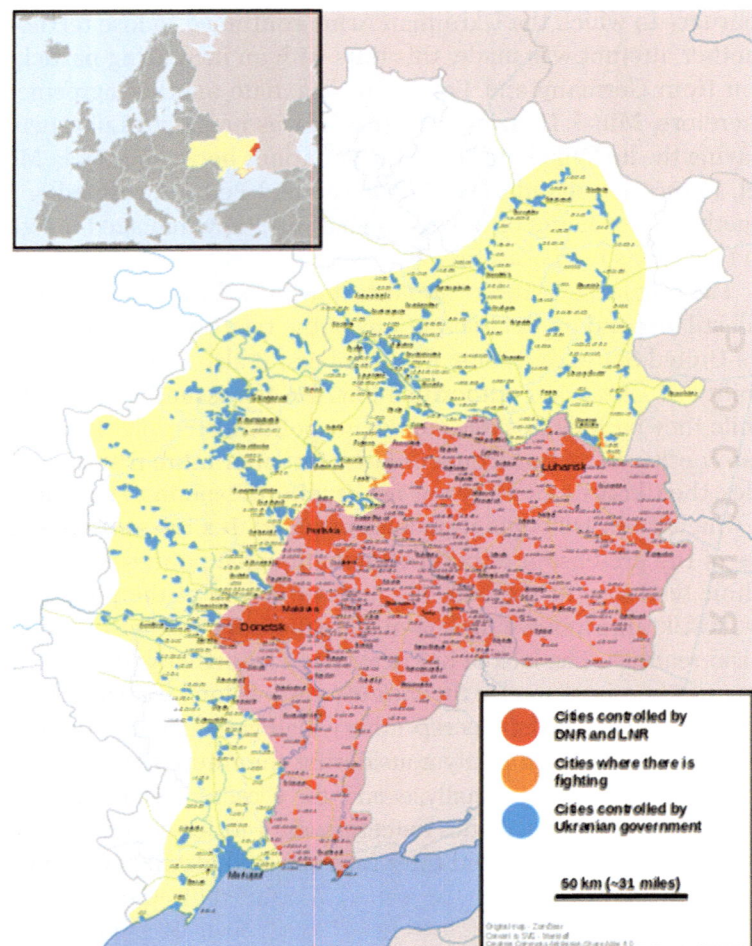

"Map of the war in Donbass, situation on February 2015," accessed on July 30, 2015.
Source: Wikimedia Commons, licensed under CC BY-SA 4.0
(https://creativecommons.org/licenses/by-sa/4.0/deed.en)

In that sense, Ukraine was not the only case in the post-Soviet world that had to confront similar problems but considering size, population and geographical position, it was maybe the most challenging case in which, during the attempt to build a new state, the role of foreign actors was more easily perceived. The cases of Moldova and Pridnestrovia will contribute other elements to the study of the intricate political scenario in the European Near Abroad.

3 Moldova and the Pridnestrovian Moldovan Republic, Historically Justified or Geopolitical Inventions?

3.1 Historical background and the idea of the Great Romania

The question raised in the title of this chapter may sound as a provocation, but it also aims to show the difficulties faced by the inhabitants of these territories during the attempts to build a polity of their own while raising the question until what point they have an ethnohistorical basis, or just mirrors the struggles among surrounding powers. Besides, to separate from the title, Moldova and Pridnestrovia[863] as different entities do not pretend to take sides in a conflict with numerous interpretations, for instance, political, geopolitical, social, cultural and economic. Altogether, there is one undeniable fact. Both function as de facto separate polities, each with its own government, currency, defined borders (even if concurrently), armed forces and even pretending to carry out their own foreign policy.

---

[863] I decided to use the word 'Pridnestrovia' to refer to the polity that names the Pridnestrovian Moldovan Republic. The word 'Transnistria' that came from Romanian can be translated as 'after or through the Dniester', and is not precise considering that the PMR also occupies some small territories at the right bank of the Dniester. Besides, the word 'Pridnestrovia' in Russian should be translated as 'at the Dniester'. The name in Romanian does not reflect an accurate translation. Besides, it has also a political content, as the first time the Romanian Government used the word 'Transnistria' was to refer to the protectorate created during World War II precisely in the lands after the Dniester. The word 'Transnistria' will be only used then, when it refers explicitly to the territories located at the east of the Dniester independently of the PMR. In this sense, it can be added that the Pridnestrovian authorities translate the Russian name Приднестровья directly as Pridnestrovia in English together with the local academic production. Therefore, it is more suitable to recognize the way each polity pretends to be named without considering the different political intentions of different foreign interest regarding this territory. Note of the author.

Moldova also currently denotes two different regions, it can refer to the Romanian region of Moldavia or it could refer to the country that lies between the Prut and the Dniester that includes mostly the ancient Bessarabia which later became part of the USSR. A similar situation to what happens in Macedonia, where Greece refers to Macedonia[864] as a Greek region while geopolitical achievements brought the appearance of a country that pretends to have that same name in the international scene. Therefore, in this research, the word 'Moldavia' will refer to the region that then became part of the Kingdom of Romania and Moldova will refer to the polity created during the Soviet Union that became later the Republic of Moldova.

Overall, Moldova or the idea of a Moldova is sustained by a past, a kingdom and a own history that, in a similar way to Ukraine, was also surrounded by foreign powers that pretended to subsume this territory under their own dominion. It was also a geopolitical enclave that had to deal with stronger neighbours. One of the differences would lie on the linguistic factor, as the Moldovan language is non-existent besides the numerous attempts of recent governments to declare Moldovan the official language[865] instead of Romanian.

The word 'Moldova' comes from a dog named *Molda*, property of Dragos,[866] which gave the name to a river. The principality of Moldavia traces back to 1351 and it is considered part of the medieval precursor of present-day Romania. As it is possible to perceive

---

[864] Officially, the country is named Former Yugoslav Republic of Macedonia (FYROM). This name is not recognized by Greece and it is the main issue that does not allow opening chapters on the candidacy of this country to the European Union. Greece argues with reason that Macedonia is a historical region of Greece and that the current polity named Macedonia should change its name. In fact, when crossing the land border from FYROM to Greece, there is a big sign written in English: 'Welcome to the real Macedonia.' Note of the author.

[865] In practical and linguistic terms, the Moldovan language does not exist and it is a subdialect of Romanian also spoken in northeast Romania. The Declaration of Independence from Moldova stipulates that Romanian is the official language. '*Declaration of independence of the Republic of Moldova,*' August 27, 1991, accessed on March 1, 2016. http://www.presedinte.md/eng/declaration

[866] Dragos was a loyal of Louis 1st of Anjou-Naples, king of Hungary, and gave this territory to Dragos. More about the origin of the word can be found on Ruzé, Alain, *La Moldova entre la Roumanie et la Russie*, Paris, L'Harmattan, 1997.

in the next map, it included territory from the present-day Romania, Ukraine, Moldova excluding the territories after the Dniester, which constitute most of current Pridnestrovia.

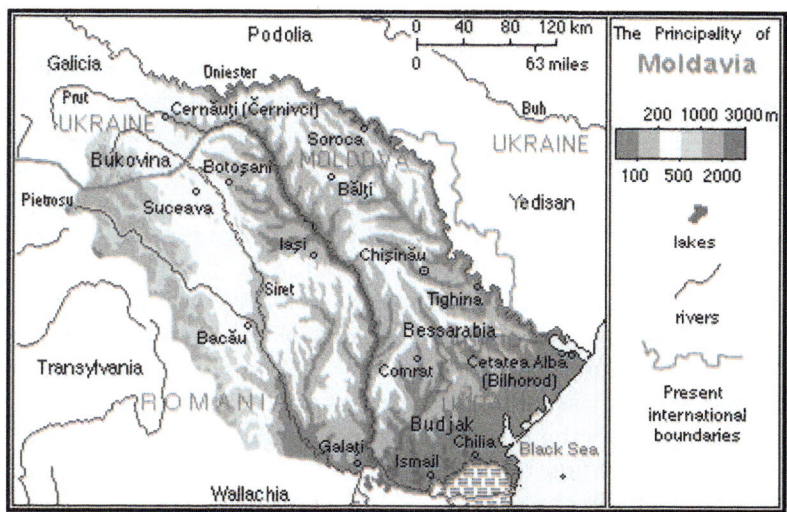

"Moldavia and the modern boundaries," accessed on March 1, 2016.
Source: Wikimedia Commons, licensed under CC BY-SA 3.0
(https://creativecommons.org/licenses/by-sa/3.0/)

During the fourteenth century, the territory served as a wall for the Christian world against possible Golden Horde invasions. The next century, these lands saw a prosperous period under the reign of 'Stefan Cel Mare' (Stephen the Great). He was the Prince of Moldavia for 47 years. He is considered a national hero in both Romanian and Moldovan historiography for defending the territory against invasions from Hungary, Poland and mostly from the Ottoman Empire. He ruled around the same time as Vlad Tepes[867] did in Wallachia, and Stephen managed to inflict famous defeats on the Ottomans, one of the most remembered is the battle of Vaslui. Therefore, the image of Stephen Cel Mare is used as the one of a national hero in both Romania and Moldova.

Gradually, as in Wallachia and Transylvania, they were also affected in their relations with the Ottomans. Therefore, already by

---

[867] Vlad Tepes, better known as Dracula, the son of Vlad Dracul. Note of the author.

the seventeenth century the whole territory of Moldavia was part of the Ottoman Empire, even though Ottomans allow them to keep a certain degree of autonomy if they recognized the suzerainty of the Ottoman authority.

During the eighteenth century, the territory was not exempt from the wars and struggle between the Ottoman Empire and Russia. The Czarist Empire pretended to expand its influence to Moldavia, Transylvania and Wallachia considering those regions were also Christian Orthodox. As part of this struggle, the Treaty of Küçük Kaynarca signed on 21 July 1774, after the Russo-Turkish War of 1768–1774, assured the restitution of Wallachia and Moldavia to the Ottomans but gave Catherine the Great the right to nominate the princes of these territories.[868] Another notable fact was that the territory of Bukovina was separated from Moldavia and became part of the Austro-Hungarian Empire. After yet another war, the Treaty of Jassy in 1792 assured a stronger Russian presence in the area. Those same years the Russians obtained definitely Crimea, and arrived for the first time to Odessa and to the Moldavian border in the Dniester, including present-day Pridnestrovia.[869]

It is visible how Moldova was influenced by the relation between the Ottoman Empire, Russia and later France to gain control of the Black Sea area during the nineteenth century. The Russians agreed with the French regarding the fate of Wallachia and Moldavia, but they did not specified about Bessarabia, an area that had already become of their interest, and was part of Moldavia. Therefore, after yet another Russo-Turkish war, between 1806 and 1812, and the urgence of both parties to negotiate a ceasefire before the French invasion against Russia, the Ottomans ceded Bessarabia, the land located between the Prut and the Dniester, to the Russians, besides the protests of the local Moldavian nobles. Consequently, since 1812, a territory that had been part of the principality of Moldavia since its founding became part of the Czarist Empire. Romanian-speaking populations of Moldavia remained divided. One part was under the still existing principality of Moldavia while the other was

---

[868] Ruzé, Op. Cit., page 57.
[869] Idem, page 58.

incorporated into the dynamic of the Russian autocracy.[870] This division would have also a notable impact for the Ottomans as they lost what they considered a substantial barn.[871]

By 1817, Bessarabia consisted of 86% of Romanians and 8% of Ukrainians and Russians.[872] Initially, Czar Alexander I allowed certain autonomy to the area, something not very common under Czarist rule. But, that self-rule lasted only for a decade and then Bessarabia became totally attached to the Government of New Russia. During the next decades, the number of ethnic Russians increased notably and by 1862, they accounted for 15.7% of the population while the Romanians made up 66.4% and the Bulgarians 5.2%. Russian political control over Bessarabia was not in doubt, but the rivalry against the Ottoman Empire that was present in neighbouring areas had deep repercussions in the area.

For instance, the War of Crimea allowed, for the first time, the existence of Wallachia and Moldavia as quasi-independent polities. One of the causes of the war was the long Russian claim to guarantee better treatment of Orthodox subjects under Turkey. Therefore, the Congress of Paris of 1856 and the consequent treaty signed in March 1856 recognized them as self-governing principalities under the protection of the European powers. The agreement obliged both principalities to have two princes but a loophole in the agreement did not specify that it could not be the same person; therefore, Alexandru Ioan Cuza became the prince of, both Wallachia and Moldavia, what became the united principalities, while Moldavia got back a small portion of Bessarabia from Russia.

The issue of a unified Romanian polity remained completely defined only after yet another Russo-Turkish War in 1877–1878. The Russian intention to recover the territories lost in the last war, plus the intention to expand its influence in the Slavic countries in the Balkans, pushed Russia to restart the military conflict against the crumbling Ottoman Empire. This time, the victory assured Russia to consolidate its position in the Balkans and to obtain a favourable

---

[870] Idem, page 63.
[871] Ruzé also mentions some data about the products that stopped arriving to Turkey after the loss of Bessarabia. Turkey lost 75% of the beef, 72% of the cows and 65% of the grain that arrived from Moldavia. Op. Cit., page 63.
[872] Idem, page 67.

truce in the Treaty of San Stefano on 3 March 1878. Among the features, the agreement included the creation of an autonomous Bulgaria and the recognition of an independent Romania. The treaty was replaced only some months afterwards, by the Congress of Berlin in 1878, which reduced in some degree the size of new autonomous Bulgaria. Besides, the agreement among the big European powers allowed finally, in 1881, the proclamation of the kingdom of Romania. Among the geographic changes, the districts of Cahul, Bolgrad and Ismail went back to Russia, while the new Romania regained the area of Dobruja that originally was assigned to Bulgaria, where the actual port of Constanța is located.[873]

---

[873] Idem, page 92.

"Changes in Turkey in Europe 1856 to 1878," accessed on March 1, 2016.
Source: Wikimedia Commons, Public Domain.

The main fact to acknowledge here is how the Congress of Berlin responded only to geopolitical decisions by the Great Powers. The will and even legitimate desire of some different Slavic nationals or Romanian populations to have its own polity was used and geographically designed around the needs of Russia, Germany, the Austro-Hungarian Empire, the Great Britain and the weakened Ottoman Empire. Therefore, Bulgaria was not allowed to keep the original territory it had gained with Santo Stefano. Romania served perfectly to create a buffer zone between Russia and the Austro-Hungarian Empire while the Balkans were divided, allowing the appearance of Serbian and Montenegrin polities but keeping Bosnia under Austro-Hungarian control. Besides, UK support to the Ottomans against Russia was assured by the acquisition of Cyprus by the British.

Altogether, these complex negotiations carried out in the Congress of Berlin diminished the Russian position obtained in Santo Stefano and became a winning situation for both the British and for Germany guided by Bismarck. Therefore, the creation of the Romanian modern state even if legitimate was solely a geopolitical decision by Germany and Russia, each one with different interests in mind. Overall, the strong role played by Bismarck and how Russia felt betrayed after the Congress were part of the intricate geopolitical causes of World War I in 1914.

Therefore, Romania appeared in the international scene in an extremely weak position. It depended on the recognition of the foreign powers and had to accept Russian occupation of Bessarabia. The new Romanian state recognized already the geostrategic importance of Bessarabia.

A quote found in Basciani's book makes the point:

> Or l'importance géographique de la Bessarabie est incontestable. D'une parte elle commande les bouches de deux fleuves, Dniestr et Pruth, d'intérêt très inégal, et atteint par la le Danube dont elle borde le bras de Chilia sur une assez long distance [...] Toute puissance qui voudra dominer le Detroit et rêvera a l'hégémonie en mer Noire sera intéressée par elle au premier chef.[874]

---

[874] Chantal, Beaucourt, 'L'Union soviétique et la Roumanie,' in *Les frontières européennes de l'URSS*, edited by Jean-Baptiste Duroselle, Paris, Colin, 1975, page 294. Quoted in Basciani, Alberto, *La difficile Unione, La Bessarabia e la Grande Romania 1918–1940*, Roma, Aracne, 2007, page 21.

The new Romanian Government understood the importance of Bessarabia, but they were not in a position to enforce any recovery of the territory. The only option was to negotiate secret deals with Germany.[875] The reason to keep this alliance as a secret was due to the continuous Magyarization in Transylvania, carried on by their central neighbours[876] in a region that had a considerable Romanian population, and those actions caused then displeasure among the ruling Romanian political class.

The complex position of the Kingdom of Romania explains the neutral stand originally taken by Bucharest at the beginning of World War I, even if the development of the conflict obliged them to take part with the allies already by 1916 to pursue the recovery of Transylvania and other regions that had been incorporated to the Austro-Hungarian Empire.

After World War I, the events that took place in subsequent years influenced notably the territory that now constitutes the Republic of Moldova. The deep research by Alberto Basciani[877] shows the complexity of the political events between 1918 and 1940, and the diverse effects afterwards.

Bessarabia, during the nineteenth century had become fully integrated within the Tsarist Empire. Even if a majority of Romanian-speaking population remained in the territory, there was a clear Russification of a segment of the local elites.[878] Besides, most of the Moldovan[879] or Romanian-speaking population lived on the countryside while the urban population became gradually Russified. Chisinau, the regional capital that became famous for being the place where famous Russian poet Aleksander Pushkin lived in exile

---

[875] There was a secret pact agreed with Germany on October 30, 1883, and renewed afterwards. Ruzé, Idem, page 98.
[876] Some numbers about the Magyarization done by the Austro-Hungarian Empire can be found on Ruzé, Idem, page 99.
[877] Basciani, Alberto, *La difficile Unione, La Bessarabia e la Grande Romania 1918–1940*, Roma, Aracne, 2007.
[878] On 1812, there were 145 noble families in Bessarabia, of which 95% were Moldovan. By 1912, there were 468 noble families, of which 30% were Moldovan, 27% Russian and 43% of different ethnic origins. Idem, page 44.
[879] The existence of an ethnic Moldovan is controversial, since at the end, they all belong to the Romanian-speaking population. For the purpose of this research, when the term 'Moldovan' is used, it will refer to the citizens of the Republic of Moldova; when it refers to the Romanian-speaking population, the term 'Romanian' will be generally used.

for three years, was the only place in the area that expanded in a modern sense as an urban centre for the Russian standards of that century. Another characteristic, besides the almost non-existent resistance to the Russification, was the appearance of violence against the Jew population that had grown notably in the cities, mostly in Chisinau.[880]

After the political uprisings in Russia during 1917, the events brought also a renewed political activity to the region. Different groups had tried to organize and recover a Romanian identity among the territory and pursue some sort of local autonomy for Bessarabia. The PNM, the only party that was looking to develop a regional identity obtained only 6 seats in the election for the regional Duma in August 1917. At this point, the divergence between the local Romanian-speaking elites and the countryside became notorious. The PNM campaigned for autonomy or independence; meanwhile the peasants mostly pushed for an agrarian reform, tired of the harsh conditions in which they worked under Czarism. Therefore, the PNM even if not a majoritarian party was well organized and included sectors like the clergy and students. Instead, the peasants, rallied mostly around diverse leftist organizations. The main fact to notice is how the disintegrating Russian Empire created the political conditions in the Governorate of Bessarabia so diverse groups of interest could organize and elect the *Sfatul Tarii*, which became a sort of council that reunited political, cultural and economic organizations present in the territory. The election also had a decisive support from the Moldavian Central Soldiers Committee of all Bessarabia.

Meanwhile, due to the confusion present in Russia during 1917, the Ukrainian National Assembly in Kiev had declared Bessarabia as part of Ukraine, therefore, forcing the local authorities in Bessarabia to ask for protection of the provisional government in Petrograd. Altogether, elections took place in November 1917 and congresses, Soviets and diverse ethnic organizations decided the composition of the future legislative organ.

---

[880] Basciani, Op. Cit., page 48.

The first gathering of this organ took place on 21 November 1917, with 150 representatives plus 10 more areas located after the Dniester, today known as Pridnestrovia. It was decided that the Romanian-speaking community would have 105 delegates, which represented 70% of the total delegates. There were 15 Ukrainians, 14 Jews, 7 Russians, 2 Bulgarians, 2 Gagauzians, 2 Germans and one each for Poles, Armenians and Greek.[881] Originally, the new organ pursued the establishing of a Moldovan Democratic Republic within a Federal Russian state but the changing situation of the international context caused them to proclaim independence from Russia in 1918.

The new legislative organ started to organize an executive power amidst the unstable external political situation. During the last months of 1917, the *Sfatul Tarii* was not in a position to oppose either the Bolshevik Army or the Romanian state. Each one had advanced its interests in recovering the region. Local accounts of the arrival of the troops, mentioned in Basciani's book, comment on how the local population was relieved, not because of a patriotic sentiment to see the Romanians present but because it was expected that after a year of political unrest some order could be established.[882] Besides, Romania was in war against the Central Powers making the circumstances more complex. Russia had capitulated and denied the originally promised support in the conflict against the Central Powers. Consequently, Romania was forced to sign the Treaty of Bucharest in May 1918. This treaty was declared void after the end of World War I but stipulated that Germany would keep control of the Romanian oil fields for 90 years and acknowledged Romania's annexation of Bessarabia into its territory.

At this moment, after external support was guaranteed, and Soviets signed the Brest-Litovsk peace treaty on 3 March 1918, there was no real Soviet menace over Bessarabia. Thus, the Romanian Government conceded at least informally to most of the demands to the *Sfatul Tarii* so they would agree on the accession of Bessarabia into the Kingdom of Romania.

For the peasantry, the Romanian arrival did not generate the same enthusiasm. They had just obtained an agrarian reform that

---

[881] Idem, page 89.
[882] Idem, page 95.

could allow them to become owners of the land they produced. The new Moldovan legislative organ had tried to organize politically the territory and, among the reforms, the peasantry obtained numerous benefits like the right to own land. Therefore, an incorporation into Romania had to guarantee that they would remain with the acquired properties.

The original agreement to annex Bessarabia assured the region some sort of autonomy; meanwhile landowners, recently affected by the reforms, suddenly became unionists aspiring to recover some of the lands they had been forced to give to the peasants. Besides, the numerous ethnic minorities initially worried that an inclusion into Romania would diminish their own rights. Altogether, after long discussions, the *Sfatul Tarii* approved the Union of Bessarabia with Romania obtaining86 votes in favour, 3 against and 36 abstentions, while 25 were not present for the vote[883] on 9 April 1918.[884] The union was approved with the expectancy that numerous issues would be taken into account by the Romania authorities. Some of the expectancies were the following:

1. The Agrarian Reform would be accepted by the Romanian Government.
2. Bessarabia would remain autonomous with its own diet elected.
3. Two Bessarabian representatives would be part of the Romanian Government.
4. A number of representatives of Bessarabia would enter the Romanian parliament.
5. Rights of minorities would be respected.

After the German collapse in World War I, and its consequent capitulation, more negotiations followed regarding Romania and the situation remained unstable until the Treaty of Paris on 1920. In that document, some European Powers recognized the annexation of Bessarabia into Romania. Even though, this document was signed by France, the United Kingdom, Italy and Japan, it was never ratified by Japan and therefore it did not enter into force. Besides, the United States did not sign it, considering that Russia had not

---

[883] Idem, page 101.
[884] The date in the old style calendar was March 27, 1918.

been consulted. That left a very ambiguous legal base to sustain the incorporation of Bessarabia into Romania.

The period between 1918 and 1940, referred by scholars, as the 'Greater Romania' would be used by future Romanian Pan-Nationalists to illustrate the idea of a State that could comprise all Romanian speakers. This concept thoroughly developed by nationalist groups in the interwar period pretended to justify the incorporation of first Transylvania and then Bessarabia[885] and also Bukovina and Dobruja into a Greater Romania. The only detail is that this nationalist idea forgot to notice that some of the territories they pretended to include in this pan-Romanian idea had a notable multi-ethnic population. After World War I, the kingdom of Romania had integrated most of the ancient Moldovan region.

Regarding Bessarabia, as Basciani shows during his research, the Romanian Government mishandled completely the incorporation. Instead of trying to obtain support from the local population, in 22 years, a centralist view struggled to incorporate the local elites and to respect previous pacts. There was, to put it in Basciani's terms, an incomprehension since the beginning between the authorities in Bucharest and the people that lived at the left bank of the Prut river. Altogether, those mistakes would have also a deep effect that would contribute to mould the political events in the region and a future local animosity towards Bucharest.

Besides, Romanian international position was very fragile. Once the Soviet Union had resolved the inner civil war in its territory, they started to look for the means to recover Bessarabia. There was initially a strong diplomatic campaign to recover Bessarabia. That loss was never recognized and the new Soviet authorities understood why Czarist Russian geopolitical claims saw the region as part of an avant-garde for a deeper advance into Romanian territory and in the Balkans.

The Romanian Government found scarce enthusiasm among the local Bessarabian population to incorporate Bessarabia into Romania. The cities were highly Russified, therefore, establishing an even more complex social tissue. Besides, the poverty conditions present

---

[885] Conea, Ion, *L'Unità Geopolitica dello stato romeno*, Bucharest, Amicizia Italo-Romena, 1940.

in most of the territory made it an excellent field for Bolshevik activity, mostly by the Jew and Russian population and also by the poor peasantry.

The shortage of products and poverty already present in most of the Romanian territory worsened here. Besides, the mistrust towards the local population because of their level of Russification brought consequently a severe paralysis in public services and in the local administration. The Romanian Government dissolved the *Sfatul Tarii* and retired the autonomy initially given to the region. Provisional authorities were nominated and the region was divided into nine districts. Initially, both the Russian White armies and the Bolsheviks were present, even though in reduced numbers but enough to cause worry to the government in Bucharest and make them think it was something organized by the ethnic minorities in the region. Therefore, the Romanian government repressed any indications of pro-Russian or pro-Bolshevik affiliation while sustained a very corrupt administration that abused the peasantry.

Besides, the new government did not support the agrarian reform and sided with the former land owners. Peasants obtained only small parcels but without any kind of support to work on them. There was also an attempt to push for the use of the Romanian language in the cities but it was not accepted easily. The local lyceums belong mostly to the minority ethnic groups. Chisinau, for instance, was the second most populated city in Romania but instead as mentioned comprised of numerous minorities, mostly Russian and Jew.

Soviet activity therefore found a good field to organize local groups seeking the reincorporation of the territory into the Soviet Union. During the 20's, there were numerous attempts to organize revolts and resistance by the local population against Romanian authorities. Soviet historiography showed them as part of a struggle to become part of the USSR[886] but the reality was that there were three different groups unsatisfied, for different reasons, with the new Romanian authorities. First, the peasants, without considering their ethnic origin; second, the minorities that inhabited Bessarabia; and third, the Communist organizations. The dissatisfaction of each group was motivated by different motives but sometimes looked

---

[886] Basciani, Op. Cit., page 162.

like if it was coordinated from the outside and Moscow also tried to seek profit from it.

Numerous rebellions organized with Soviet support did not obtain enough force to succeed by themselves.[887] The armed uprisings in 1924 were part of a complete strategy that saw the Soviet intent to pursue the recovery of the area. They obtained the sustain of Communist Party of Romania, that by that time, the same way as in many Communist parties around the world, was completely in line with the directives of the Komintern in Moscow.

Bessarabia during that decade was clearly in the spotlight of the Soviets and they pursued different strategies to recover it. They proposed the Romanian authorities to sustain a referendum to let the inhabitants decide but the idea was rejected by Bucharest. Altogether, the issue stopped both countries from establishing relations during that decade.

Besides, as part of the Soviet strategy, also in 1924, another factor arose that gave rise to great political repercussions, the creation of the Moldovan Autonomous Soviet Socialist Republic as part of the Ukrainian SSR. The decision was approved with uncommon speed and the first congress of the Moldovan Soviet took place on 19 April 1925, in Balta[888] where the capital was established. After some years, it moved to Tiraspol, the city which today is the capital of the Pridnestrovian Moldovan Republic.

The creation of this new autonomous republic fitted perfectly in the already explained Soviet policies that pushed for the claims of different nationalities among the whole USSR. As happened in different regions throughout the country, it pretended to give all the nationalities present a sort of recognition so they could be majorities and minorities at the same time depending on the kind of entity of which they were a part. The difference in this case was that the creation of the Moldovan ASSR[889] was not in Moldova proper, but

---

[887] The rebellions help the Romanian part to demonstrate that there was Russian intervention in the area but still show them that a sector of the Romanian population had helped the Soviets. At the end, even if it clearly was pushed by Moscow, still local population did not feel enough identification with the federal authorities from Bucharest. A detailed account can be read in Basciani's, Idem, pages 206–219.
[888] Idem, page 203.
[889] On the following pages, there are some details of the inner constitution of the Moldovan ASSR.

pretended not only to give recognition to 'ethnic Moldovans' in the Soviet Territory, but also to serve as a bridgehead to continue putting political pressure over Bessarabia[890] in a territory contiguous to the Romanian border.

The answer from Bucharest was to deepen the Romanization of the territory.[891] A General Commissariat for Bessarabia was created. It tried to improve the conditions in which the population lived, but it was not enough. The health and public services were in a terrible condition, while life conditions were worse than in the rest of Romania. At that point, as in the rest of Europe in that period, the economic crisis allowed nationalist extreme right-wing groups to profit and blame everything on the different ethnic minorities; in this case, mostly against Jews because of the privileged position they enjoyed in the commercial activities in the cities.[892]

Altogether, the events developed in an extremely complex way. Foreign diplomats and military advisers noticed the terrible handling of the political situation in Bessarabia by the Romanian authorities. An Italian military attaché noticed how Romanian domination had contributed to accentuate a division among ethnic lines between the locals, while corrupt officials just took profit of the local inhabitants.[893]

Meanwhile, many local elites that had obtained positions in Bucharest preferred to leave the issue of Bessarabia as forgotten. The abandonment of the local population and the increase of the poverty provoked more clashes against the government. Besides, local resentment grew against 'cei de la Bucuresti'[894] as the local peasantry approached the public officials from the capital, who simply showed no interest to solve the local problems, and were only interested in collecting taxes or taking out the resources from the region.

Besides, the arrival of the Nazis to power in Germany increased links with the Romanian extreme right. At that time, the Romanian Government obtained what they thought was a significant success, the establishment of diplomatic relations with the Soviet Union in

---

[890] Basciani, Idem, page 205.
[891] Idem, pages 224–233.
[892] Idem, page 257.
[893] 'ASMAE, Affari Politici, 1919–1930.' Romania. Envelope 1508 report from colonel Baffigi. Quoted in Idem, pages 222–223.
[894] The phrase can be translated as 'those from Bucharest'. Idem, page 318.

1934. Romanian Minister of Foreign Affairs, Nicolae Titulescu, had to confront a notable resistance from different sectors in the government and mostly the Security Services, which did not trust Moscow's intentions.[895] At the end, the establishment of diplomatic relations did not mention Bessarabia or the recognition of the integrity of the Romanian territory. Therefore, the diplomatic relations between both countries did not change Moscow's intentions towards Bessarabia.

Besides, the National Cristian Party (NCP) started to grow notably mostly in Bessarabia and to take a more active role against Jews while sustaining a radical nationalist position. German groups residing in Bessarabia allied with the Nazis pushed for even harsher confrontations against the Jews and sustained the NCP.[896] After the parliamentary elections in 1937, the National Liberal Party that had traditionally won the recent elections in Romania did not obtain enough votes to form a majority and King Carol II chose the NCP, which came only fourth in the election, to form a government. Its leader, Octavian Goga became prime minister and on 21 January 1938, signed a decree, which withdrew citizenship to all the Jews residing in Romania, which in fact where mostly located in Bessarabia.[897] The same government lead by Goga remained in charge for less than two months, because the king preferred to organize a self-coup and design a new ad hoc constitution. Afterwards, the National Renaissance Front founded by the king became the only legal party. Then, a new statute for the minorities appeared in which they became sort of second-class citizens.

Meanwhile, among the political instability and the dictatorship installed by King Carol II, the Soviet activity increased in Bessarabia during 1939. Diverse Communist groups campaigned in different countries[898] for the recovery of Bessarabia while the Soviet presence in the area increased, mostly after the Molotov-Ribbentrop Pact.[899]

---

[895] Basciani, Op. Cit., page 293.
[896] Idem, page 331.
[897] Some of the Jew population tried to resist as they had notorious influence on the commercial activities but it was not enough. Idem, page 334.
[898] There were activities organized in Chicago, San Francisco and New York, for instance, in favour of the oppressed population of Bessarabia. Idem, page 350.
[899] Idem, page 351.

King Carol II established a dictatorship with French and British support while trying to depurate many of the extreme right groups in the territory, mostly the Iron Guard with the expectancy to avoid something similar as in Germany. The geopolitical chessboard was more complex. The Romanian monarch did not know Bessarabia had been part of the Molotov-Ribbentrop[900] deal. The Germans had already agreed that the territory would go back to the Soviets. Besides, the impressive victory by the German army against France and the allies in Western Europe during the campaign in May 1940 left him without expectancy of any support against the Germans.

Therefore, when the Soviets recriminated Romanian authorities for allowing the Polish army to escape into Romania after the Soviet invasion of Poland, it was just part of a long list of recriminations that had as main goal the ultimatum sent by Molotov[901] on June 26, demanding the restitution of Bessarabia, North Bukovina and the territory of Hertza. The Romanian Government was not in a position to resist and thus conceded to the Soviet demands after consulting with the Germans, which showed no sympathy and encouraged them to comply.[902]

General Antonescu who later became Romania's ruler proposed to defend the territory and organize the army but the conditions were very complex. Romania was not in a position like Finland in which it could defend against a Soviet invasion. First, because to defend Bessarabia they would have needed the support of the local population; second, the army was not prepared to go to war and Romania was isolated while still they could expect territorial demands by Hungary and Bulgaria.[903]

---

[900] Article III of the Secret Additional Protocol stated 'With regard to Southeastern Europe attention is called by the Soviet side to its interest in Bessarabia. The German side declares its complete political disinterest in these areas.' The original document in microfilm version can be consulted on: 'Molotov-Ribbentrop Pact,' Moscow, August 24, 1939, accessed on September 1, 2015: https://en.wikisource.org/wiki/Molotov%E2%80%93Ribbentrop_Pact

[901] 'Ультимативная нота советского правительства румынскому правительству,' June 26, 1940, accessed on September 1, 2015. http://r u.convdocs.org/docs/index-23045.html

[902] Basciani, Op. Cit., page 360.

[903] Idem, page 367.

Consequently, the Romanian Government accepted the terms. More than 200,000 people abandoned the three territories and even if there were already established evacuation plans, most of the people left in a clearly unorganized way, together with most of the military garrisons that in some cases abandoned military equipment in hands of the Red Army.[904] Meanwhile in some cases, the remaining minorities applauded the withdrawal.

Altogether, the Soviets recovered Bessarabia; meanwhile the NKVD proceeded also to 'filter' the population of the newly acquired territories to avoid the presence of undesirable 'foreign agents'.[905] Therefore, the phase known as the 'Greater Romania' concluded in a political failure. At the end, even if geopolitics determined the outcome, the continuous gaffes by the Romanian Government in Bessarabia and the impossibility to make the population feel included in a political and national project left a mark. In that sense, Basciani's conclusion in his book are compelling:

> Nella politica internazionale difficilmente le circostanze favorevoli si ripetono due volte; la Romania era stata beneficiata ben oltre i meriti bellici alla fine della Prima guerra mondiale. Allo Scoppio del secondo conflitto mondiale l'incapacità e la mancanza di una moderna visione politica e nazionale della sua classe dirigente condannarono a morte il progetto, prima ancora del revisionismo e dell'opportunismo di Hitler e di Stalin, il progetto della Grande Romania.[906]

Therefore, Bessarabia became part of the USSR related to the same nationality policies that affected Soviet territory and, again, the territory between the Prut and the Dniester would be part of a separate polity composed mostly of Romanian-speaking population. The same multi-ethnic local population that passively accepted to become part of Romania now became one more entity of the USSR.

3.2 The Moldovan Soviet Socialist Republic

The division imposed by geopolitics between the former Bessarabian territory and the rest of Moldavia had as a precedent the creation of the Moldavian ASSR in 1924. It was a case in which as Terry Martin noticed, the Piedmont Principle was the primary motivation

---

[904] Idem, page 365.
[905] Idem, page 366.
[906] Idem, page 367.

to create a national republic in the USSR.[907] Despite its small size, the new territory was given the status of an autonomous republic. The protests of Romanian communists did not impede the establishment of a 'Moldavian' literary language and a separate 'Moldavian' national identity cultivated.[908] The idea was to maximize the political effect of each detail of the republic's formation on the neighbouring Bessarabia.

The new autonomous republic included cities from today's Pridnestrovia, and there were no cities with a clear majority of Romanians.[909] In fact, the clarity of the geopolitical goal was perceived in one Soviet publication as 'the creation of the MASSR, is the beginning of the liberation of Bessarabia. Once the economic and cultural growth of Moldova has begun, aristocrat-led Romania will not be able to maintain its hold on Bessarabia'.[910]

The new entity had by 1936 45.5% Ukrainians and 31.6% 'Moldovans' living in the territory plus almost 10% of Russians[911] while it represented less than 2% of the territory of the Ukrainian SSR. The capital was Chisinau but as the Soviets considered it was 'occupied', then provisionally, first Balta and then Tiraspol functioned as capitals.

This inner border change was completely different from the Crimean case or others very frequent in the Soviet Union mostly during the 1920s and 1930s. In this case, it was to pursue the goal of incorporating Bessarabia. There was a need to 'create' a national identity to justify the possession of Bessarabia as a Soviet Moldova and not as part of Romania and in that sense, the existence of the Moldovan ASSR contributed to its purpose. From 1924 until 1940, the Soviet

---

[907] Martin, Terry, *The Affirmative Action Empire*, Ithaca, Cornell University Press, 2001, page 274.
[908] Idem, page 275.
[909] As Florian Kuchler did, to avoid confusion between ethnicity and citizenship, the term 'Romanian' will be used to denote the dominant ethnic group or national group in Moldova in the Moldovan ASSR or SSR while the term 'Moldovan' will be used to refer to the citizens of that polity. Kuchler, Florian, *The Role of the European Union in Moldova's Transnistria Conflict*, Stuttgart, ibidem, 2006, page 34.
[910] Quoted on King, Charles, *The Moldovans: Romania, Russia, and the Politics of Culture*, Stanford, Hoover Institution Press, Stanford University, 2000, page 54.
[911] King, Idem, page 54.

authorities pushed hardly to develop the idea of a Moldovan identity separated from the Romanian one. That included establishing a separate language, which included using Cyrillic alphabet instead of Latin while also determining a proper Moldavian vocabulary as separate from Romania.[912]

After the Soviet occupation of Bessarabia, North Bukovina and Hertza became a reality in 1940, the Moldavian Soviet Socialist Republic was established and absorbed part of the territory of the Moldovan ASSR. Afterwards, these lands, like Ukraine, had to suffer the vicissitudes of the war.

In Romania, once they had lost territory, King Carol was forced to cede power to general Antonescu and he decided to ally the country with Nazi Germany. Once operation Barbarossa started, Romania participated in the invasion expecting to recover Bessarabia, which they did by July 1941. Here, instead, Romanian authorities committed again a huge mistake. The Romanian political elite legitimated the recovery of Bessarabia; instead, to continue the military operations after the Dniester was highly questioned. Party leaders, even if their role was highly diminished during Antonescu, urged him not to take the war beyond the Dniester.[913] He did not listen and continued the invasion, and as the king wrote: 'By reaching beyond Bessarabia, Romania became a de facto aggressor power, pursuing German aims against the Soviet Union rather than simply reusing the territory stolen by the Soviets.'[914]

Romania established the Governorate of Transnistria to handle the newly occupied territories after the Dniester, with the intention of creating a buffer zone with the Soviets. In fact, there was never a serious intention to incorporate these lands into Romania.[915] Instead, as king accounts, the region witnessed numerous atrocities by Romanian and German troops. For instance, around 123,000 Jews from Bessarabia and Bukovina were transferred to this area before being later deported or killed.[916]

---

[912] Idem, pages 85–86.
[913] Idem, page 94.
[914] Idem.
[915] Idem, page 93.
[916] Idem, page 93.

During the war, Soviets regained back Bukovina and Bessarabia and established finally the same borders for the Moldovan SSR while Bukovina remained part of the Ukrainian SSR. At the end, only a small strip of territory that had never been part of Bessarabia became part of the Moldovan SSR, mostly the same strip that today forms Pridnestrovia. Therefore, this new Soviet Republic emerged with a population of 2.4 million of which around 68.8% were Moldovans[917] and it became the second smallest Soviet Republic, with regard to surface area, only after Armenia with 33,700 square kilometres.

The after-war years presented similar problems as in Ukraine. The territory had deeply suffered the consequences of the war and needed urgent reconstruction. Agricultural production had practically collapsed and a collectivization campaign was established. Moreover, agricultural reforms allowed the arrival of a class of powerful agroindustrial managers out of reach of the central party organs. Meanwhile, a notable industrial development appeared in the cities located on the east of the Dnieper, like Tiraspol, Ribnitza, Dubasari or Bendery, creating also a division between rural Moldavia and what would later become the Republic of Pridnestrovia.

Considering the reduced size and population, the Moldovan SSR acquired great importance in the Soviet agricultural production. It was 0.2% of the Soviet territory and by 1970 it produced 10% of the Union's canned foods, 4.2% of the vegetables, 12.3% of fruits and 8.2% of wines, while agriculture represented 42% of the republic's net material product in 1991.[918] Altogether, there was notable Sovietization. A considerable influx of migrants from different parts of the Union arrived during the 1960s. Besides, Soviets did not encounter a strong national sentiment as in Western Ukraine or in the Baltic countries. Therefore, creating more a multi-ethnic society in which Russian language became also the common denominator was easier. Even though, Moldova was not exempt of the same problems that affronted the Soviet Union, a degrading economy, and the loss of legitimacy of the political elite had an effect here.

Besides, as noticed by the king, the Moldovan SSR functioned as training ground for some future high cadres in the Communist

---

[917] Idem, page 95.
[918] Idem, pages 99–100.

Party. For instance, Leonid Brezhnev was here First Secretary of the Communist Party between 1950 and 1952. Also, Konstantin Chernenko was head of the party's propaganda department from 1948 to 1956 and Khrushchev had also links as party functionary in Ukraine.[919] The multi-ethnic nature present in the territory reflected also in the leadership. Of the 10 First Secretaries of the Communist Party of Moldova, 5 were born in Ukraine, 1 in Russia, 4 in Moldova of which one half in the former Bessarabia and the other in Transnistria.

The Bessarabian question affected the relation between Romania and the Soviet Union and continuously Nicolas Ceausescu campaigned publicly to defend the Romanian position. Besides, another interesting feature of the after-war period was the language issue. The attempts to push for a separate Moldovan language as different from Romanian diminished and in fact as king noted, from 1938 there was a gradual convergence of the grammar, pronunciation and lexicon of 'Moldovan' and Romanian.[920]

Altogether, the Soviet period succeeds in one thing. The Sovietization and the arrival of migrants from different parts of the Union, together with a notable degree of Russification in the cities, contributed to the development of a separate political but not ethnic identity in Moldova. Meanwhile, the linguistic factor did not become the unifying link to merge the population in Bessarabia and Romania. There was a sort of Soviet effect in which the Great Patriotic War, the role of Soviet education, media and the way history was taught in schools counted.[921] Besides the remembrance of the vicissitudes suffered during the period in which the region was part of Romania, these factors contributed to determine a specific identity different from the Romanian one. These factors set or 'stipulated', like king[922] remarked, the idea of a Moldavian nation. Besides, there was also a notable division among the local society—first, a largely rural population with inhabitants from one ethnic group; second, the urban

---

[919] Idem, page 98.
[920] Idem, 108–109.
[921] Danero Iglesias, Julien, *Nationalisme et pouvoir en République de Moldavie*, Bruxelles, Editions de l'Université de Bruxelles, 2014, page 85.
[922] King, Op. Cit., page 108.

centres, which were to some degree Russified and more multi-ethnic and finally the area beyond the Dniester, which had a notable industrial component of workers from different parts of the union. Therefore, this social and demographic tendency would have also decades later a considerable political effect.

Perestroika had also its effects here. On 31 August 1989, the MSSR Supreme Soviet adopted three new laws that declared Moldovan the state language, mandated the transition to the Latin alphabet and set out a programme for the use of Moldovan in the government, education and national economy.[923] Meanwhile, the main opposition group, the Popular Front, pushed during a rally outside to reinstate Romanian as the official language. Besides, the fall of Ceausescu in December 1989 also signalled a thrust for the nationalist sector in Moldova. Between 1990 and 1991, the new Romanian authorities mentioned the idea of an economic confederation and even a reunification of the German model as mentioned by the Romanian Minister of Foreign Affairs Adrian Nastase.[924]

The elections to the Moldovan Supreme Soviet carried out in 1990 allowed the recently formed Popular Front of Moldova to obtain 27% of the seats. Together with some of the 'Democratic' Communists, they managed to form a government. One of their goals pretended to look for the unification with Romania; still there was no unanimity in the political elite. In September, Mircea Snegur became the first president of Moldova. At that point, there was a split among the elite in the Moldovan SSR. The Popular Front had a nationalist agenda and pushed for independence and then unification with Romania. Instead, Snegur, the new president, had no belief to reincorporate Moldova with Romania. Snegur, for instance, in a visit to Romania in February 1991 talked about 'our sister country-Romania', but did not mention the idea of a Union. Besides, the new government of Romania signed also a border recognition treaty that same year with the Soviet Union even though it was never ratified by the Romanian parliament.

This split between two factions complicated a possible union with Romania, even though the Romanian support for a reincorporation was given. It is interesting to notice, though, that the split

---

[923] Idem, page 120.
[924] Quoted on King, Idem, page 150.

was political and not ethnical among Moldovans. Therefore, a sector of the political elite for survival showed no interest for pursuing the union with Romania. Instead, a division among Romanian speakers appeared. Meanwhile, the nationalist pan-Romanian rhetoric of the Popular Front encouraged the different ethnic and linguistic minorities present in the Moldovan SSR to react. The same as after 1918, Romanian authorities had not considered the multiethnic nature of the territory. This time, the agenda of the Popular Front clashed completely with the interests of the ethnic and linguistic minorities. Therefore, the population in the industrial and Russian-speaking zone beyond the Dniester and the Gagauz population organized itself separately towards building their own polity. The fear that the nationalistic rhetoric could achieve its purpose became a powerful unifying element among a sector of the population that did not identify itself with the pan-Romanian idea.

That division deepened when the Soviet authorities decided to organize the referendum on the future of the Soviet Union on 17 March 1991. The poll was conducted in most of the republics except in the Baltic countries, Armenia, most of Georgia and in Moldova where the local authorities decided to boycott it. Even though, it managed to take place in Pridnestrovia and Gagauzia. This event reflects, first as noticed before, the crumbling state of the Soviet Union that could not control what happened in the republics but also the fact that the same authorities in Moldova did not control what happened in their own territory. Therefore, a clear will from the newly established authorities in Gagauzia and Pridnestrovia opposed the pan-Romanian idea of one sector of the Moldovan authorities.

By early August, Snegur announced that they were not willing to sign the new Treaty of the Union and the failed putsch at the end of the month in the Soviet Union, the same as in many Soviet Republics, served as an excuse to declare independence, in this case on 27 August 1991.[925] The language used in the Declaration of Independence became also a reason for controversy. First, it mentioned the dismemberment of the Moldovan principality by Austria and Russia

---

[925] 'Declaration of independence of the Republic of Moldova,' August 27, 1991, http://www.presedinte.md/eng/declaration

and also rejected the political and legal consequences of the Molotov-Ribbentrop Pact. Those points plus the nomination of Romanian language as the official one[926] clearly pointed out that the intention of the new polity would go in the direction of pursuing the union with Romania.[927]

As in the rest of the crumbling USSR, the weak Soviet authorities could not oppose the Moldovan declaration of independence, but the same way, in Chisinau they did not notice that by rejecting the Molotov-Ribbentrop Pact they were also rejecting the deal that incorporated the territory belonging to the former Moldovan ASS. Hence, the same way as in Ukraine, the new local authorities obtained independence but had to deal with the Crimean issue, here in Moldova, a similar scenario happened, just that in this case, geography, politics and geopolitics turned the independence of Moldova in the motive of a war that would divide even more the fragile social tissue present.

Moldova like most of the Soviet republics signed the constitutive act of the CIS on 21 December 1991, and gained official recognition on December 25. This act confirmed the origin of an independent Moldovan polity while the authorities in Gagauzia and the Pridnestrovian Moldavian Republic refused to remain as part of the new Republic of Moldova. Thus, from its origins the new Moldovan polity was already a failed state. Therefore, the Republic of Moldova appeared in the international scene as the weakest of the ex-Soviet republics. Besides, it had to deal with an emerging civil war in which the population at the left bank of the Dniester decided to take side against the authorities in Chisinau, all this while having no army, no national currency, without de facto control of its borders and in the middle of an economic crisis as in the rest of the former Soviet territory.

---

[926] The official language changed several times during the following years. After the Declaration of Independence stated that Romanian was the official language, more than once following governments tried to instate 'Moldovan' as the state language until the Constitutional Court decided finally on the issue in 2013 and declared that the Declaration of Independence had prevalence leaving then Romanian as the state language. 'В Молдове румынский признали государственным языком,' December 5, 2013, accessed on September 2, 2015. http://korrespondent.net/world/3274646-v-moldove-rumynskyi-pryznaly-hosudarstvennym-yazykom
[927] King, Op. Cit., page 151.

3.3 The Republic of Moldova, a failed state from its origins

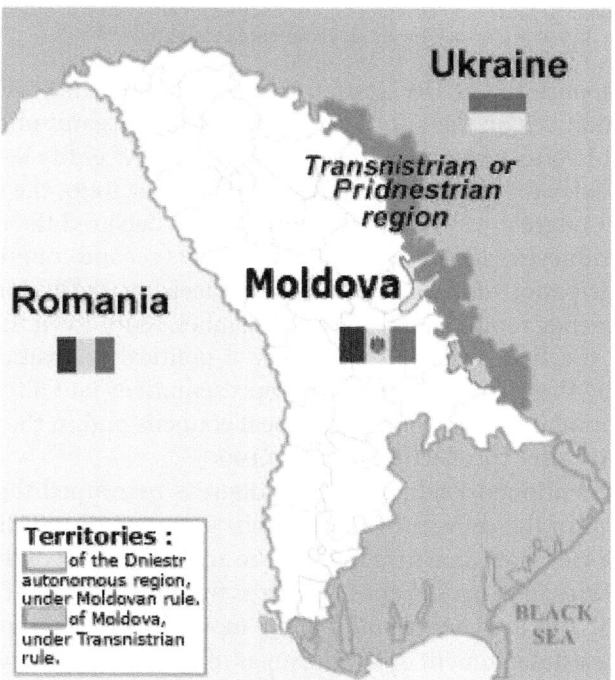

"Map of the Tradnestrian Region," accessed on September 4, 2015.
Source: Wikimedia Commons, licensed under CC BY-SA 3.0
(https://creativecommons.org/licenses/by-sa/3.0/)

3.3.1 The war after the Soviet fall

Already by 1989, the fact that Moldovan authorities determined Moldovan as official language and pursued a policy that could eventually lead to the reunification with Romania was enough motive for other minorities present in the Moldovan SSR to react. Therefore, the Union even if desirable by one sector of the Romanian-speaking population was not politically achievable. In that sense Basciani wrote:

> Al contrario di ciò che avvenne dopo la fine della Prima Guerra mondiale con la caduta della Russia imperiale, nel 1989 la Bessarabia (Repubblica Moldova) e la Romania non hanno trovato però delle classi dirigenti capaci (e desiderose fino

in fondo) di indirizzare verso un credibile progetto unitario quelle istanze unioniste che pure si erano manifestate in tanti settori politici, culturali e dell'opinione pubblica delle due parti. Perso in questa maniera il momento propizio si è permessa l'ingerenza di altre potenze contrarie alla rinascita di uno Stato romeno allargato verso Oriente, segno che quel lungo solco scavato anche tra il 1918 e il 1940 era ormai diventato veramente incolmabile.[928]

As a response to the Declaration from the Moldovan Soviet, local representatives on the left bank of the Dniester organized between 1989 and 1990 a referendum to establish a new entity separated from Moldova.[929] Consequently, on 2 September 1990, the recently created Congress of Pridnestrovian Deputies declared the creation of the Pridnestrovian Socialist Republic, in its second congress with the participation of 636 delegates.[930] The decision was declared void by Gorbachev months later on 22 December 1990. Even though, it marked the first attempt to organize a political opposition, supported by the fact that these local representatives had already obtained numerous positions in the local councils and in the Moldovan Soviet after the elections held on 1990.

The mentioned Pridnestrovian Congress regrouped the representatives of the different local councils and members of the Moldovan Soviet that came mostly from the area at the east of the Dniester. Besides, numerous representatives from the different factories located in this area contributed to the movement that pretended to resist the establishment of Moldovan as official language and a possible reunification with Romania. The movement originally had used strikes in local factories as pressure to oppose the nationalist reforms from Chisinau. It managed to consolidate itself as a political party and obtained most of the city and regional Soviets in the area by 1990.

The different identity built in the industrial areas around Bendery and Tiraspol and mostly at the east of the Dniester allowed a

---

[928] Basciani, Op. Cit., page 368.
[929] Between December 1989 and the first months of 1990, a referendum took place to decide on the creation of a new Pridnestrovian Moldovan Soviet Socialist Republic. The poll first was organized in Rybnitsa, then in Tiraspol and then in other districts located at the east of the Dniester. More details can be found in Bomeshko, B.G. 'Создание, становление и защита приднестровском государственности 1990–1992 гг,' Bendery, Poligrafist, 2010, page 71.
[930] Idem, page 88.

resistance to emerge against the pretension of establishing a Moldova independent from the Soviet Union. At the end, the Soviet elements already mentioned had more weight in a Russian-speaking zone than in the Moldovan or Romanian region.

The first clash occurred on 3 November 1990, when Moldovan police forces pretended in Dubasari to separate Pridnestrovia into two sections. Locals blocked the bridge and Moldovan forces opened fire, causing the first fatalities of the conflict.[931] The political tension remained and it was not until the end of the Soviet Union was imminent that Moldovan authorities attempted once again to regain control of the region beyond the Dniester without success. By then, it was clear that the Moldovan authorities were in no position to exercise control in the area that was to become the Republic of Pridnestrovia. Besides, the armed and failed attempts to retake control allowed the authorities in Pridnestrovian Republic to portray Moldovan authorities as the aggressor and themselves as victims.

Another notorious incident occurred on 29 August 1991. On that day, Igor Smirnov, who had become the leader of the Pridnestrovian Moldovan Republic (PMR), was arrested during a visit to Ukraine together with other members of the delegation who pretended to have a meeting with the Ukrainian leader Leonid Kravchuk.[932] After they were taken to Chisinau, a women's strike committee blocked the Moscow-Chisinau railway line as a response, forcing the Moldovan president Snegur to free them.[933] At the end, the Moldovan Government showed itself incapable to enforce its authority in the Pridnestrovian territory.

The conflict intensity increased by 1992. By then, the Soviet Union officially had ceased to exist. Therefore, allowing each republic to pursue each political goal without Soviet control. In that sense, the situation in the Republic of Moldova was catastrophic as in the rest of the ex-Soviet republics. The Moldovan Government was forced at the same time to organize the creation of the Moldovan

---

[931] A detailed account of the events can be consulted in Bomeshko, Idem, pages 105–107.
[932] Idem, page 166.
[933] Idem, page 167.

Armed Forces, and in the meantime, to attempt to impose legal order in the rebel region of Pridnestrovia.

The fact is that, as mentioned, the former Soviet Forces were the last institution in the Soviet Union to recognize the fall of the USSR. There were numerous military garrisons among the former Soviet territory with considerable military power while from a practical point of view it was not clear under which command they operated. The process of repartition of the military equipment and the establishment of 15 new armies took time while there was an ongoing war in the territory of the former Moldovan SSR. In many cases, weapons were transferred without legal basis. Sometimes they were simply taken by whichever local force had the capacity to seize them. In that sense, Moldova and Pridnestrovia were not different from the rest of the former Soviet territory.[934]

The fact is that at the end of 1991 the police forces of Rybnitsa and Tiraspol swore alliance to the authorities of the PMR. Besides, the Soviet 14th Army that used to belong to the Odessa Military District resided precisely in Tiraspol. At the time of the Soviet fall, it had a considerable amount of military equipment that included artillery equipment, helicopters, armoured personnel carriers and antitank guns together with numerous tanks, mortars and multiple-rocket launchers.

The most serious period of hostilities started in March 1992. By then, the Moldovan authorities had been capable of scratching a decent number of armed forces after having established a minister of defence. After obtaining weapons from Soviet storehouses and together with Romanian support they organized a force of around 25,000–30,000 troops including conscripts, volunteers, police officers and reservists.

On the opposite side, the PMR had around 9,000 troops or officers that armed themselves with the help of the 14th Army. Besides, numerous members of the same 14th Army were from that area, so they openly sympathized with the Pridnestrovian cause and in many cases defected to their side. The official position from the

---

[934] Ozhiganov, Edward, 'The Republic of Moldova: Transdniester and the 14th army,' in *Managing Conflict in the Former Soviet Union: Russian and American Perspectives*, edited by Arbatov, Alexei et al., Cambridge, MIT Press, 1997, page 180.

Moldova and the Pridnestrovian Moldovan Republic 367

14th Army was of neutrality but seeing the unstable political atmosphere in Russia, the ambience in the former Soviet army was for defending the existence of the PMR. Therefore, besides the defections, there was also a passive acceptance of the Republic by the recently renamed Russian troops that just months before were part of the Soviet Army.

The war had on both sides numerous volunteers. Russians and Ukrainians on the Pridnestrovian side, while Romanian volunteers took side with the Moldovan Armed Forces. Therefore, this sort of civil war became also an international conflict and consequently, geopolitical. Besides, there were proofs that Romania continued to provide military aid during the conflict. The 14th Army assured there were four or five railcars which crossed Moldova from Romania each day. Photos and documents of proof were shown in a press conference. An ONG also confirmed the presence of the Romanian troops as documented in Ozhiganov's article.[935]

The war was fought mostly in three different areas. The historiographic research done by B.G. Bomeshko documents many of the details of the struggle between both armed forces, which mostly became a sort of trench war.[936] The three areas were the Dubasari area, Cosnitza and Bendery. Besides, the conflict never was popular in Moldova while the population in Pridnestrovia mostly identified itself with the authorities of the recently formed PMR.

After three months, as it was the logical to foresee, the conflict was decided thanks to Russian intervention, or to be more precise due to the participation of the 14th Army. By those days, there was a deep division between Boris Yeltsin and the vice president Aleksander Rutskoy. For instance, the latter had encouraged the people of Pridnestrovia to obtain their independence and encouraged the 14th Army to take sides with them.[937]

At the end, the Moldovan forces, even if they had improved their coordinated actions against the area, were not capable of securing control of Pridnestrovia. On June 23, Alexander Lebed arrived to

---

[935] Idem, page 178.
[936] Bomeshko, B.G. *Создание, становление и защита приднестровском государственности 1990–1992 гг*, Bendery, Poligrafist, 2010.
[937] The detailed description of the meeting in Tiraspol on April 5, 1992, in which Rutskoy participated, can be found in Bomeshko, Op. Cit., page 287.

take charge of what remained of the 14th Army with the explicit orders to stop the conflict. He relieved general Netkachev who had been in the post since December, and after assessing the situation and stopping the pillage of weapons from the army depots, he went into action ordering the troops to engage directly in the conflict. Lebed, a general who frequently proclaimed a nationalist stance against former Soviet Republics, took sides easily with the Pridnestrovian cause.[938] The fact is that on the eve of July 3, a massive artillery attack by the 14th Army, in fact the most severe of the whole conflict, destroyed the assembling area of the Moldovan forces where they were organizing themselves.[939]

The impact of the military operation and the numerous casualties it caused forced Moldovan president Snegur to fly to Moscow to negotiate with Yeltsin a ceasefire, therefore ending at least formally the military phase of the conflict and signalling the de facto division between the Republic of Moldova and the Pridnestrovian Moldovan Republic. The ceasefire was signed on July 21 between Yeltsin and Snegur and they agreed on a peacekeeping force composed of Moldovan Armed Forces, the PMR units and the Russian Army.[940] In practice, it signalled the division that exists until now and that predestined the development of both the Republic of Moldova and Pridnestrovia as two separate entities. Chisinau did not recognize in any case the PMR as a different entity, but had no way to enforce its position. Therefore, 21 July 1992, signalled the end of the military conflict while the actors involved intended to seek a future political settlement.

Thus, the territory of the PMR became defined with similarities to the historical divisions present before in Moldova, mostly located on the left bank of the Dniester with only the city of Bendery together with some neighbouring towns located on the right bank. Instead, some villages at the east of the Dniester that had never been part of Bessarabia remained under Moldovan control.

---

[938] King, Op. Cit., page 195.
[939] Again a detailed description on the military events can be found in Bomeshko, Op. Cit., page 434.
[940] Bomeshko, Op. Cit., page 467.

For the PMR, it was a political achievement. Even if they did not get official recognition, the war allowed the PMR leadership to acquire more legitimacy. The war, the casualties and the attacks against civilians carried out by the Moldovan forces during the war, allowed the emergence of a sort of new 'national history' about a war for the independence of the 'Pridnestrovian fatherland'. A hero's memorial was erected in Tiraspol together with one of the tanks that took part in the actions.[941] Therefore, the historical narrative of the local troops that fought to 'liberate' the region from 'Moldovan fascists' became part of the schoolbooks and history texts from that day on mix with the memory and symbolism of the Great Patriotic War.[942] Therefore, future generations started to learn that Pridnestrovian fight for independence had included blood from their compatriots. As the years passed, this deepened the already existing political divisions present between the two entities. Besides, by then, the local population after having suffered casualties by the Moldovan Armed Forces did not have any sympathy for the authorities in Chisinau.

On the other hand, the Moldovan Government distrusted the Russian position but needed to bargain with Moscow on several issues. Besides, Romania expected a possible recovery of the former Bessarabia while there was not the same amount of interest by European powers or the United States as appeared in the Ukrainian case. Altogether, there existed a difficult scenario to initiate a state-building process while Chisinau did not control its own assumed border.

3.3.2 The fragile Republic of Moldova

As in the rest of the former Soviet republics, the state-building process had to face an economic crisis. In the Moldovan case, considering the geographical position and the role it had in the USSR, it was more difficult. In 1991, the Moldovan GDP fell by 14%. During the 1990s, Moldova's economy shrunk to around two-fifths of its late Soviet size and only Georgia and Tajikistan had seen a similar

---

[941] King, Op. Cit., page 197.
[942] Idem.

scale of decline.[943] All the economic indicators from that decade were catastrophic and the country only managed to have a growth for the first time in 1997 with 1.6% of the GDP and then in the year 2000 with 2.1%. Besides, Moldova stopped receiving subsidized energy and the population found itself cut from export markets. Therefore, energy prices increased exponentially while the agricultural production got stuck.[944]

Moldova managed to introduce a local currency and privatizations were done quicker than in Ukraine and Russia. There were not so many strategic industries to privatize and many of them were located at the east of the Dniester, outside the control of the Moldovan Government. Altogether, the 1990s was a catastrophic decade for the Moldovan population, which forced many of them to migrate. Around 20–25% of the work force either went to the EU or to Russia in search of better conditions and the remittances sent by them became after some years around the 15–17% of the GDP though some authors believe that the sum could be double considering the illegal transfers.[945] These facts allow understanding why today the Republic of Moldova is one of the poorest countries in Europe. By 2003 already, 38.4% of the population lived with less than 2 USD a day.[946] Besides, the wages are among the lowest in Europe.

After some years of economic and social decline, the expectation of a unification with Romania together with the animosity of the inhabitants of Gagauzia, Pridnestrovia and Taraclia made the Popular Front lose its electoral force in the 1994 parliamentary elections. By that year, the Democratic Agrarian Party of Moldova (PDAM) obtained 56 of the 104 seats in the parliament and was capable of determining the next government in what meant the end of the unifying tendencies of the Popular Front. By then, the new political structure organized around a multi-ethnic formation was led mostly by

---

[943] Hensel, Stuart and Gudim, Anatol, 'Moldov'as economic transition: Slow and contradictory,' in *The EU & Moldova*, edited by Lewis, Ann, London, The Federal Trust, 2004, page 89.
[944] Idem.
[945] Idem, page 90.
[946] Spanu, Vlad, 'Why is Moldova poor and economically volatile?,' In Edited by Lewis, Ann, Idem, page 104.

former collective farm chairmen and mayors that took advantage of the general political decline.[947]

After the election, the new government dropped many of the pro-Romanian decrees. For instance, from 1991 to 1994, the Romanian national anthem was the same as in Moldova. The anthem was replaced by a poem by Alexei Mateevici, 'Limba Noastra'.[948] The strong push for the use of Moldovan (Romanian) language lost its pace and gradually the existence of a bilingual society was accepted. In fact, it was during this period that the status of Gagauzia was resolved and the nationalist tendencies of the pan-Romanians were simply lost as the elite in power preferred to push for economic reforms. Besides, on 6 March 1994, a referendum took place in which the following question was asked to the voters:

> Do you want the Republic of Moldova to develop as an independent and unitary state, in the frontiers recognized in the day where Moldova declared sovereignty, to promote a policy of neutrality and to maintain mutually-benefitting economic relations with all the countries of the world, and to guarantee its citizens equal rights, according to international law?[949]

The poll, which received more than 97% of favourable votes, was a strong blow for unionists while it also sustained the neutrality of Moldova, something that will be commented on in the following pages.

The Democratic Agrarian Party didn't manage to remain in power for a long period. The continuous economic decline affected its popularity while its leader, President Snegur, was not capable of re-electing himself as president in the 1996 presidential election. Snegur for the campaign again took the pro-Romanian stance. Instead, his rival, Petru Lucinschi, a former member of Communist Party of the USSR, former First Secretary of the Communist Party of Moldova and former ambassador in Moscow, took a more moderate position, reassuring minorities and focusing on maintaining links with Russia.[950]

---

[947] King, Op. Cit., page 164.
[948] Danero, Op. Cit., page 96.
[949] Nohlen and Stover, *Elections in Europe: A Data Handbook*, Baden-Baden, Nomos, 2010, page 1330.
[950] Danero, Op. Cit., page 98.

Snegur managed to win the first round with 38.8% of the votes, but lost in the second against Lucinschi, who had also served as speaker of the Moldovan parliament from 1993 to 1997 and presented himself in this election as independent.[951] That was the last direct election to choose the Moldovan president. After that time, the decision was made by the parliament. Besides, it is worth commenting that Moldova's political system gave more power to the prime minister, reducing the margin of manoeuvre of the president. It is curious to notice, though, that Moldova is the only country in the CIS in which the prime minister has considerably more functions and powers than the president.

After Snegur lost the presidential election, the PDAM had a catastrophic result in the next 1998 parliamentary elections, obtaining only 3.63% of the votes and staying out of the parliament. Snegur and Lucinschi both founded new parties to compete in the elections but that poll saw also the resurgence of the Communist Party with the name 'Party of Communists of the Republic of Moldova', which obtained 30.01% of the votes and 40 out of 101 seats in the parliament. The communists benefited from the deteriorating social condition in which by 1998 the 20% richest segment of the population controlled the 50.3% of the wealth, while the 20% poorest only the 3.4%.[952] Altogether, the result of the elections forced the other three parties to ally with themselves to form a government.[953] Lucinschi's party obtained 19.42% of the votes and 26 seats. 'For a Democratic and Prosperous Moldova' had obtained 18.16% votes and 24 seats, while the unionists this time regrouped to form the 'Party of Democratic Forces', which obtained only 8.84% votes and 11 seats.

The score showed how in less than a decade and among the declining economic situation, the desire to reattach Moldova with Romania had faded while parties with a more moderate speech that campaigned for economic reforms and that had a multi-ethnic approach obtained better results. Meanwhile, Lucinschi's party still

---

[951] King, Op. Cit., page 158.
[952] Belostecinic, '*Analiza Barometrului de Opinie Publica 1998, 2000, 2001,*' Chisinau, Institutul de Politici Publice, 2001, page 5.
[953] Horowitz, Shale, *From Ethnic Conflict to Stillborn Reform*, College Station, The Former Soviet Union and Yugoslavia, Texas A & M University Press, 2005.

Moldova and the Pridnestrovian Moldovan Republic 373

remained as the leader in the coalition, even though it had to deal with a strong opposition from the Communist Party.

Later on, Lucinschi's hold on power came to an end. On July 5, he proposed a referendum to change the Republic of Moldova into a presidential republic. The referendum passed with 64.2% of the votes.[954] Even though, the political opposition from the Communist Party managed to reduce again the powers of the president in favour of the government. Altogether, the long effects of the Russian economic crisis together with the degrading image of the rest of the ruling coalition allowed the Communist Party headed by Vladimir Voronin to win the parliamentary elections held on 25 February 2001, obtaining 71 of 101 seats, which meant a clear majority to form the new government. The fact that for this election the threshold had been increased to 6% allowed only 2 more parties to enter the parliament. Therefore, with that comfortable majority, Voronin was also capable of becoming the new president of Moldova as from that occasion the president had to be elected by the parliament with at least 61 out of 101 votes.[955] It was the first time in the post-Soviet history that a Communist Party won the elections in any of the former Soviet Republics, even though the way he handled the country had nothing to do with a supposed Communist guideline. Once in power, he privatized against what he had mentioned during the campaign and had a pragmatic approach focusing on stabilizing the economy, while corruption levels remained the same, with his son, for example, becoming one of the main businesspersons in the country.[956]

At the end, the first 12 years after the disappearance of the Soviet Union saw still the same political elite ruling the country. The first three presidents were part of the Soviet political establishment and had been members of the Communist Party of the Soviet Union. Similar as in Ukraine, the elite used the nationalists sometimes, but still a pragmatic approach by the apparatchiks allowed them to combine a nationalist speech when needed or a multi-ethnic approach in other circumstances. Voronin proved himself capable of

---

[954] Nohlen and Stover, Op. Cit., page 1330.
[955] 'CONSTITUȚIA REPUBLICII MOLDOVA,' accessed on September 5, 2015. http://lex.justice.md/document_rom.php?id=44B9F30E:7AC17731
[956] Danero, Op. Cit., page 103.

staying for a longer period in power. By 2005, his party again won the elections, but this time his party obtained only 56 seats, which forced him to negotiate with the Christian Democratic People's Party (CDP) to obtain the necessary votes to be re-elected to the presidency. On this occasion, again only three parties in total entered the parliament and the Electoral Bloc of Moldova stayed as the main opposition force with 34 seats. Voronin, who by then started to change his geopolitical orientation, obtained the support of the CDP in exchange of the promise of a further approach towards Euro-Atlantic institutions.

The foreign policy of Moldova will be discussed in the following pages but it is worth remarking that the relation with Russia had also a deep effect on the inner politics during these years. Voronin changed his geopolitical orientation once relations with Russia became more tense. In that context, the 2009 parliamentary elections saw again the Communist Party not without controversies[957] to obtain a victory of 60 seats. This was enough to form a government but not enough to vote a new president and in this occasion the other three parties that entered the parliament refused to support its proposal, forcing then a new parliamentary election after two failed attempts to choose a president. Therefore, only three months later, in July, new parliamentary elections took place. This time some defections from the Communist Party did not allow them to have the majority even to form government, obtaining only 48 seats of the 101 seats.[958] The opposition instead managed to put the other four parties together to form a coalition headed by Vlad Filat as new prime minister. Still, the new majority was not able to choose a new president, considering that the Communist Party still had 48 out of

---

[957] Numerous fraud accusations after the April election together with violent clashes against the authorities took place in Chisinau. Originally, the government accused Romania behind the protests but they changed their position afterwards. A recount of votes was ordered by the Constitutional Court and it did not notoriously change the result of the election. 'Moldova recount "confirms result",' April 17, 2009, accessed on March 9, 2015. http://news.bbc.co.uk/2/hi/europe/8004603.stm

[958] 'Courte défaite des communistes en Moldavie,' July 31, 2010, accessed on March 9, 2015. http://www.lemonde.fr/europe/article/2009/07/31/courte-defaite-des-communistes-en-moldavie_1224620_3214.html

Moldova and the Pridnestrovian Moldovan Republic 375

101 votes. Voronin handed his resignation in September 2009 and Mihai Ghimpu became the acting president.⁹⁵⁹

The fragile ruling coalition, still without president, was forced again to go to elections at the end of 2010, before the poll, even though, there was one main issue that divided the ruling coalition. By June 28, the leader of the parliament and acting president, Ghimpu, had scheduled a session to issue a decree instituting 'The Day of Remembrance of the Soviet occupation'. Filat and Lupu, the leaders of the two other coalition parties, rejected the proposal and urged Ghimpu to reconsider the decree. Altogether, this division showed again the different perceptions surrounding the Soviet past and how even if from the Romanian point of view it was clear that the occupation of Bessarabia was a simple annexation still many local Moldovans did not share the same view on this issue. Besides, the intention of the decree allowed a defiant Voronin to sustain that the Soviet Union had liberated Bessarabia from fascism and that the United States had licensed Romania to pursue an irredentist agenda in Moldova.⁹⁶⁰

The parliamentary elections that took place in 2010 gave again the Communist Party the first place although only with 42 seats that meant they were still able of blocking the nomination of a new president. Filat managed to recompose a similar coalition with the other parties and obtain the authorization from Moldova's Supreme Court to remain in charge even though a president was not chosen, therefore, ending the Communist Party's capacity to block the nomination and to force new elections. Besides, new defections in the Communist Party by 2012 allowed finally after three years the parliament to finally choose a president.

The parliamentary election that took place in 2014 showed only some recycling among the same ruling parties. There was a strong

---

959 Two more persons would hold the position of action president, Vlad Filat and Marian Lupu, and it was only until 2012 that the Moldovan parliament managed to choose a president, this time in the person of Nicolae Timofti. Note of the author.

960 Socor, Vladimir, 'Moldovan government chickens out of historical assessment of communism,' *Eurasia Daily Monitor*, Vol. 7, No. 126 (June 30, 2010), accessed on April 5, 2015. http://www.jamestown.org/programs/edm/sin gle/?tx_ttnews%5Btt_news%5D=36552&tx_ttnews%5BbackPid%5D=484& no_cache=1#.VcYl9fntmko

division among the Communist Party that allowed the Party of Socialists, headed by one former member of Voronin's party, to obtain the lead in the elections with 25 seats. Besides, the divisions among the three parties in the ruling coalition forced the Liberal Democratic Party (Filat) together with Democratic Party of Moldova (Lupu) to establish a minority government excluding the liberal party and with the tacit support of Voronin and the communists. Altogether, the results are as in the following table:

Party	Number of votes	%	Seats
Party of Socialists	327,910	20.51	25
Liberal Democratic Party	322,188	20.16	23
Party of Communists	279,372	17.48	21
Democratic Party of Moldova	252,489	15.80	19
Liberal Party	154,507	9.67	13

"Alegerile parlamentare Republicii Moldova din 30 noiembrie 2014," accessed on July 1, 2015.
Source: http://www.cec.md/r/r/

Almost two and a half decades of existence of the Republic of Moldova had shown different political forces in charge. After the first three years, the nationalist pan-Romanian rhetoric stepped back for a more pragmatic and multi-ethnic approach that avoided opposing the Russian or not Romanian-speaking population present in the territory. Under the rule of the Communist Party, there was a sort of *moldovenism* used as a political instrument as defined by Danero Iglesias,[961] first to oppose the pan-Romanians but mostly to allow the elite in power to remain in charge. Afterwards, Moldova would be also greatly influenced by the geopolitical projects surrounding them and therefore the foreign policy would be greatly conditioned by several events as explained in the following pages. The effects of the Russo-Georgian War in 2008 and the Ukrainian crisis are only a couple of examples.

The role of the local oligarchs was not the same as in Ukraine or Russia, only because foreign interests proved to have notably more weight than the local ones. Still there were some local individuals like Vladimir Plahotniuc who managed to have notable influence in

---

[961] Danero, Op. Cit., pages 122–125.

the government.⁹⁶² A rampant level of corruption like in the rest of the former Soviet republics meant that the local finances were severely drained by the people that hold public office. A survey, for instance, acknowledged that in 2012 Moldovans spent around 62 million Euros in bribes with an average of 150–400 EUR for each bribe.⁹⁶³

Besides, another astonishing incident occurred in May 2015 when around 1 billion USD disappeared from three banks that represent one-third of the banks active in the country. The stolen sum is worth 15% of the Moldovan GDP.⁹⁶⁴ At the end, any kind of government that allows that kind of robbery signals a complete lack of any judicial clarity, one of many symptoms of a failed state.

This leaves the population of Moldova to make the daily living in one of the poorest countries in Europe with a devastating social decline. A deteriorated welfare system (if there is one remaining) with a rampant corruption produces also a lack of trust in the political system. A considerable sector of the population remains only with the hope of migrating or to obtain somehow a Romanian passport legally or in the black market with ease, which means an entry to the EU labour market and therefore contribute with remittances from abroad as a considerable sector of citizens of Moldova do. A thorough journalistic research carried out by Adrian Mogos and Vitalie Calugareanu showed how it is possible to acquire genuine documents for false applicants to obtain later a Romanian passport,

---

962 Some oligarchs like Vladimir Plahotniuc have a lot of power. He is the chairman of Victoria Bank, one of the main Moldovan banks, and is among the richest men in Moldova with a fortune of around 300 million USD. He was elected to the parliament in 2010 and again in 2013. He was also vice-speaker of the parliament and just submitted his resignation to his seat on 2015. More information about his fortune can be found on: 'Cum a devenit Vladimir Plahotniuc milionar în euro,' January 27, 2011, accessed on August 10, 2015. http://adevarul.ro/moldova/actualitate/cum-devenit-vladimir-plahotniuc-milionar-euro-1_50ad70757c42d5a663952dc5/index.html

963 'Молдаване за год израсходовали на взятки более 62 млн евро – опрос,' November 3, 2012, accessed on August 5, 2015. http://news.mail.ru/inworld/moldova/society/10823906/?frommail=1

964 'Manifestation contre 1 milliard de dollars " envolé" en Moldavie,' May 4, 2015, accessed on May 4, 2015. http://www.lemonde.fr/europe/article/2015/05/04/manifestation-contre-un-milliard-de-dollars-envole-en-moldavie_4626663_3214.html

and thus a EU citizenship.⁹⁶⁵ At the end, the expectation of a considerable part of the population to migrate, added to the complex multilinguistic social tissue, complicating even more the development of a Moldovan identity and the possibility to build a sort of Moldovan state in which all its inhabitants feel recognized.

Besides, as explained, even if the Romanian-speaking population is a notable majority in the territory, the different minorities, like the Gagauz or the Bulgarians, still have a political impact and have become also tools of the geopolitical struggle in this area of the world. In that sense, before analysing the foreign policy of Moldova during the last decades, it is important to consider the events regarding some of the minorities in the Moldovan territory. It is important to notice how in these cases the political events developed in a different way as in Pridnestrovia, while the local populations accepted to become part of the Republic of Moldova. In this case, I refer to the regions of Gagauzia and Taraclia.

3.3.3 Gagauzia and Taraclia

Gagauzia
The multi-ethnic nature of the Republic of Moldova includes numerous minorities, among them, the Gagauz and Bulgarians. The Romanian-speaking population composes the first majority, while there are Russians and Ukrainians. The Gagauz are the fourth most numerous ethnic group with around 3.5% of the total population and a little more than 153,000 people living in the Republic of Moldova.⁹⁶⁶

The Gagauz is an ethnic group with a language quite similar to Turkish.⁹⁶⁷ There are several theories regarding the origin of the ethnic group, some considering they descend from the Turkic Oghuz.⁹⁶⁸ Other theories link them with Bulgarian groups. The fact

---

[965] 'How to buy an EU citizenship,' September 13, 2012, accessed on March 1, 2016. http://www.balkaninsight.com/en/article/how-to-buy-an-eu-citizenship
[966] Danero, Op. Cit., page 84.
[967] Demirdirek, Hulya, 'In the minority: (Dis) empowerment through territorial conflict,' in *Europe's Last Frontier? Belarus, Moldova and Ukraine Between Russia and the European Union*, edited by Schmidtke, Oliver and Yekelchyk, Serhy, Basingstoke, Palgrave McMillan, 2008, page 127.
[968] King, Op. Cit., page 210.

is that over the years they have established mostly in the region belonging to Bessarabia. During the four centuries of Ottoman domination, they kept their orthodox faith, something that would become a particular characteristic of this group of supposed Turkic origins. Throughout the years they lacked the recognition of other ethnic groups first among Czarist Russia and then during the Soviet regime. The Cyrillic Gagauz alphabet was developed in 1957 and only few schools actually taught in the language. Over the years, considering they were located in one of the poorest regions of the Moldovan SSR, few of them had access to the public administration compared with other minorities of the USSR. Therefore, their relations became largely Russified and by 1989, 73% of the Gagauz considered Russian their second language[969] and not Romanian.

The Gagauz language and culture only received a strong push after 1989 and once the Republic of Moldova came into its existence. Schools, publications and a university were created in Comrat, the capital.[970] After 1989 also, and considering the menace of the return of Romanization, the Gagauz decided to respond and an assembly proclaimed the creation of an autonomous republic with Stephan Topal as their leader.[971] By 1990, the Gagauz had organized their defence units but the degree of confrontation never reached the level of what happened in Pridnestrovia. The same as in Pridnestrovia, the Gagauz welcomed the coup attempt in the Soviet Union in 1991. They thought it could stop local nationalisms that would diminish their position in relation with the Moldovan population. Later on, the Gagauz voted in favour of the new Treaty of the Union in 1991 and then declared itself independent in August of that same year. In December, a referendum held in Gagauzia saw 95% of the voters supporting the independence of Gagauzia with a participation rate of 85%.[972]

It was not until 1994 that the new Moldovan Government without the Popular Front and headed by Snegur managed to obtain a deal with the Gagauz. At the end, as Demirdirek mentioned: 'After

---

[969] King, Idem, page 213.
[970] Idem, page 214.
[971] Idem.
[972] Katchanovski, Ivan, *Cleft Countries, Regional Political Divisions and Cultures in Post-Soviet Ukraine and Moldova*, Stuttgart, ibidem, 2006, page 95.

five years of active political struggle, the Moldovan parliament passed a law on the special legal status of Gagauzia, thus recognizing Gagauz autonomy, on 23 December 1994. This can be seen as one of the most peacefully solved territorial conflicts in the former Soviet Union.'[973]

The current status was negotiated and the Republic of Gagauzia became the Autonomous Territorial Unit of Gagauzia. Besides, the Gagauz autonomy has the right to decide its own status if Moldova reunites with Romania.[974] The new agreement included that the *Gagauz Yeri* (the name in Gagauz of the new entity) would have three official languages: Gagauz, Romanian and Russian.[975] The Moldovan authorities saw it as more advantageous to negotiate with the Gagauz, some autonomy in exchange of them accepting themselves as part of Moldova.

In the Gagauz case, the problem was mostly ethnic and locals did not enjoy the control of considerable industrial resources as in Pridnestrovia. Here, the ethnic elites mostly pretended to have control over local resources and to see a resurgence of the indigenous culture.[976] The fact is that after negotiating, different villages and towns voted to become part of Gagauzia and only those that counted with a majority of Gagauz people voted in favour, meaning that the actual territory of Gagauzia is not contiguous as seen in the following map.

Gagauzia is divided into four enclaves that form three different districts. According to the 2004 census, 82.1% of the population are Gagauz and Bulgarians make up the 5.15%. The rest of the population is composed mostly of Romanians, Russians and Ukrainians.[977]

---

[973] Demirdirek, Op. Cit., page 126.
[974] Idem.
[975] King, Op. Cit., page 219.
[976] King, Op. Cit., page 217.
[977] 'Population census 2004,' Republic of Moldova, accessed on March 1, 2016. http://www.statistica.md/pageview.php?l=en&idc=263&id=2208

"Schematic map of Gagauzia," accessed on March 1, 2016.
Source: Wikimedia Commons, licensed under CC BY-SA 3.0
(https://creativecommons.org/licenses/by-sa/3.0/)

Altogether, the constitution of Gagauzia points to the logic of a multi-ethnic region where the Russian language still plays a significant role in public office and in education while many politically active Gagauz are more fluent in Russian than in Gagauz.[978] Therefore, Gagauzia and Pridnestrovia in some sense are products of the Soviet system. Even if as Demirdirek noticed, the former case was ethnic based but both cases raised against a sort of 'Moldovan' nationalism.[979]

---

[978] Demirdirek, Op. Cit., page 127.
[979] Idem, page 128.

Gagauzia is a poor region that has managed also to obtain numerous supports from Turkey. Ankara has financed numerous development projects including libraries, schools and continuously offers scholarships to Gagauz students, something the Moldovan authorities have accepted to balance Russian influence in the area.[980]

At the end, it is important also that even if the region is poor and does not offer a lot strategically, Moscow may use it to counterbalance any attempt by the Moldovan authorities to pursue a possible union with Romania or simply of block any rapprochement with the West. Therefore, it is not a surprise that while Moldova was negotiating with the EU the Association Agreement, the authorities in Gagauzia organized a referendum in which 98.4% of the voters supported to join the Customs Union with Belarus, Kazakhstan and Russia.[981] The economic weakness of the region allows local elites to become an easy prey of the geopolitical interests around the region while for Russia it is easy to play with the multi-ethnic Russian-speaking card to show themselves as the 'defendants' against a hypothetically Pan-Romanian polity, therefore, making even more complex the context of the fragile Moldovan polity.

---

[980] Op. Cit., Idem, pages 221–222.
[981] 'Таможенный союзник Гагаузия хочет к России, Белоруссии и Казахстану,' February 3, 2014, accessed on February 3, 2014. http://www.ko mmersant.md/node/25241

Taraclia

"Taraclia District," accessed on September 5, 2015.
Source: Wikimedia Commons, licensed under CC BY-SA 3.0
(https://creativecommons.org/licenses/by-sa/3.0/)

Russian, Ukrainian and Gagauz-speaking minorities are not the only ethnic groups present in the Republic of Moldova. Bulgarians account for almost 2% of the local population, more than 65,000, with around 44,000 of them residing in the district of Taraclia. In the Taraclia district, they represent around 65.56% of the population. The Bulgarians living in Moldova mostly speak Russian as a second language instead of Romanian, the same as in the Gagauz.

Bulgarians in Moldova did not organize the same way as the Gagauz but once the final status of Gagauzia was settled they pushed for more autonomy. The Taraclia district obtained the status of a county the same way as other counties in Moldova in 1999.[982] Besides, by 2001 Bulgarian language was taught in 26 schools and, in 2004, the Taraclia State University was founded and co-funded by the Bulgarian Government in the capital of the district which also carries the name Taraclia.[983]

Around half of the population in the district live in the cities while the other half in rural areas. The Bulgarians in Taraclia even if majority in their districts still respond to a multi-ethnic social tissue similar to Gagauzia. As in Gagauzia, both zones traditionally voted for the Communist Party of Moldova also because of the fact that they saw it was closest to Russia. In April 2015, when the Moldovan parliament gave the district of Taraclia the status of national cultural district, there was a strong opposition from the Liberal parties that tend to be more pro-Romanian. The bill only intended some plenary powers on cultural issues while it did not imply autonomy in any other sense.[984] Still, it served to Moscow, like the correspondent from *Le Monde* said to 'advance its pawns in Moldova'.[985]

Altogether, Bulgarians in Moldova and specifically in Taraclia did not achieve the same kind of political organization as the Gagauz but still managed to make themselves politically visible not only for the Moldovan Government but also in neighbouring countries. First to Bulgaria, but also to Russia while the same way as with other minorities, the inhabitants of this region are to a certain degree Russified, and tend to have more sympathy towards Russia and

---

[982] Zaporjoran-Pirgari, Angelina, 'Minority rights in Moldova: Consolidating a multiethnic society,' in *The EU & Moldova, On a Fault Line of Europe*, edited by Lewis, Ann, London, The Federal Trust, 2004, page 67.

[983] Website of the Taraclia State University named Grigori Tsamblak, 'Об Университете, информация о деятельности вуза,' accessed on March 1, 2016. http://tdu-tar.md/ru/about

[984] 'Bill on Taraclia status approved in first reading,' April 6, 2015, accessed on September 5, 2015. http://www.infotag.md/politics-en/201882/

[985] 'La Russie avance ses pions en Moldavie,' *Le Monde*, April 22, 2015, accessed on April 22, 2015. http://www.lemonde.fr/decryptages/article/2015/04/22/la-russie-avance-ses-pions-en-moldavie_4620603_1668393.html

to eventually prefer Moscow's protection in the geopolitical chessboard. Hence, when the Russian ambassador in Chisinau, Farit Mukhametshin, declared in January 2014 that Gagauzia and Taraclia were together with Pridnestrovia, areas of special attention to Russia, he referred not only to the ethnic composition of the territories. He mentioned also the geopolitical orientation these regions could assume in relation with the EU and the West.[986]

Altogether, the Moldovan Government has to consider these factors when trying to design a foreign policy. Authorities in Chisinau do not control their alleged borders, while having a multi-ethnic and multilingual social tissue, an impoverished society, and widespread corruption. Meanwhile Romania still would like to recover Moldova, and Russia would not like that Moldova loses its status of neutrality in favour of joining NATO. Besides, the status of the Pridnestrovian Moldovan Republic and the presence of the Russian peacekeepers complicate even more a scenario while the EU also is trying to take Moldova out of the Russian orbit. Therefore, there exists a very weak polity that remains at the expense of the geopolitical struggle abroad.

3.3.4 The weak and changing foreign policy of Moldova

Since 1992, the Republic of Moldova was immersed in the dilemma of a foreign policy versus West or East. On one side, the Russian troops of the 14th Army became the guarantors of the ceasefire in the Dniester while on the other there were the Romanian claims to recover Bessarabia while there was also the intention to obtain financing from the Western countries for their crumbling economy.

In that sense, it is important to consider in the next pages the evolution of the Moldovan foreign policy regarding different actors. First towards Russia, the CIS and then the Russian pretension to bring Moldova closer to the Eurasian Union. Second the relation with Romania, third the relation with the EU, fourth the relation with the United States and NATO and finally to consider the relation with the Pridnestrovian Republic and the role Moldova had in GUAM.

---

[986] 'Гагаузия и Тараклия вслед за Приднестровьем станут зоной особого внимания России,' January 4, 2014, accessed on January 4, 2014. http://www.kommersant.md/node/24239

The state of the relation will note also four different periods. First, under Snegur from the fall of the Soviet Union to 1994, then the period until 2001 with Lucinschi, third with the arrival of the Communist Party under Voronin, and finally the last years from 2009 until now under the Liberal Democratic Party. In that sense, Moldova's foreign policy was also deeply influenced by the way Russia, the EU or the United States intended to establish the relation with Moldova in relation to how their global interests developed.

The relation with the Russian Federation
When the Republic of Moldova appeared at the international scene, they had to deal with the fact that there were Russian troops in what Chisinau considered Moldovan territory. Therefore, the state of the relation was complicated because Moscow became a guarantor of the ceasefire; meanwhile, after the years they rebuilt a strategic interest in Moldova and Pridnestrovia as part of the Kremlin's geopolitical intentions.

In that sense, the relation between Chisinau and Moscow evolved and changed many times. After 1991, the intension of the Popular Front to adhere Moldova to Romania went completely against Russian interests, even if under Yeltsin's first term, the Russian Foreign policy was not clear at all as explained in the first chapter. That also explains why in that period Moldova did not ratify the CIS agreement signed in December 1991.

After the parliamentary election of 1994, the Popular Front lost its force and the Agrarian Democratic Party took control of the government. This meant a more pragmatic approach, not only in the multi-ethnic construction of the Moldovan polity but also in a more balanced foreign policy that acknowledged a stronger Russian position and above all put aside the aspiration to unify with Romania. It was only then that the CIS Treaty was ratified.[987] In 1995, the foreign policy adopted by the parliament pushed precisely for giving relations with Russia, Ukraine and Belarus a priority.[988]

---

[987] Neukirch, Claus, 'Moldova's eastern dimension,' in *The EU & Moldova, On a Fault Line of Europe*, edited by Lewis, Ann, London, The Federal Trust, page 134.
[988] Idem.

Moldova and the Pridnestrovian Moldovan Republic 387

The dependence with the Russian economy in many senses still kept this relation as a priority until the Russian financial crisis of 1998. At that point, Moldovan leadership tried again to look for other markets while in 1999 a promise was made by Russia to withdraw Russian troops from Moldovan territory, even though this process was later suspended.[989]

The arrival of Vladimir Voronin to power meant during his first years a new attempt to sustain a foreign policy close to Russia. By 2001, Vladimir Putin was already in office and a basic treaty between both countries was signed. Diplomatic relations with the Russian Federation were cordial only until 2003 when on November 2003 Voronin did not sign the Kozak Memorandum[990] to solve the conflict with Pridnestrovia.[991] At the end, even if Voronin wanted initially to sign the agreement, the Western Pressure halted what has been until now the closest moment to solve the conflict in Pridnestrovia.

The refusal by Chisinau to sign the agreement made the relations with Russia more tense. From that point, Voronin started to orientate Moldova's foreign policy towards the EU. One of the turning points in the relation was that on one side Moscow increased support to the regime in Pridnestrovia, while Moldova introduced a new border regime at the Moldovan-Ukrainian border, which for Tiraspol and Moscow meant an economic blockade.[992] The answer by Russia in 2006 was an embargo on the export of Moldovan wines, which had a deep effect on Moldovan economy. Besides, the Kremlin had always the use of gas supply as a foreign policy tool. The gas dependency from Russia allowed Gazprom to impose prices more easily in Moldova after the Russia-Ukraine gas dispute. Quoting Yafimava: 'The Russia-Moldova gas transit relationship is one of high asymmetrical interdependence in Russia's favour. This

---

[989] Vrabie, Radu, 'Relationships of the Republic of Moldova with the Russian federation,' in *The Foreign Policy of The Republic of Moldova* (1998–2008), Chisinau, Friedrich Ebert Stiftung, Cartdidact, page 100.
[990] The Kozak Memorandum was a proposal done by Russia to solve the Pridnestrovian conflict. It is explained in the following pages.
[991] Idem, page 101.
[992] This new border regime in practice meant that Pridnestrovia needed to have Moldovan custom stamps to be able of exporting products produced in Pridnestrovia. Note of the author.

highly favourable initial asymmetry was granted to Russia by Moldova's high dependence on Russian gas imports for which it was not able to pay in full and on time, as well as by its relatively minor transit role, compared to Ukraine and Belarus.'[993] Therefore, leaving Chisinau with a reduced margin to manoeuvre.

Later on, between 2006 and 2009, Voronin tried to improve relations but it did not turn to the state it had before 2003. Besides, Putin lost the trust it had on Voronin and therefore the approach was tougher. Still, by then, after the war on Georgia, Russia had showed another stance against governments that were willing to show a pro-Western position.

After 2009, the new government headed by the Liberal Democratic Party gave a completely new impetus in the relation with the West while still Russia had the Pridnestrovian card to put pressure in different ways. Besides, as with Ukraine, Moldova has a great dependence on Russian energy and, therefore, the country receives all its gas from Russia.[994] The following government headed by the LDP, even though they have been openly pro-Western, have been cautious of diminishing the points of conflict with Moscow. For instance, the NATO issue has not been mentioned and the position of neutrality included in the Moldovan constitution for now forbids any possible membership. In that sense, the most important approach to the West has been through the EU; meanwhile, it is understood that only with Moscow a possible solution could be found for the conflict in Pridnestrovia.

Altogether, Moscow still has the strong hand in the relation, not only the presence of the Russian troops in Pridnestrovia, they have also notorious influence as noted through the Russian-speaking minorities in Gagauzia and Taraclia. Besides, the Russian Orthodox still plays a considerable role. It is important to note that the Metropolis of Moldova is under canonical jurisdiction of the Moscow Patriarchy while the church is one of the most trusted institutions in the country.[995] Another point is Russian media still has a strong influence in Moldova. Here, like in many countries, television represents the main source of information, in this case for 90% of the

---

[993] Yafimava, Idem, page 281.
[994] Idem, page 106.
[995] Idem, page 108.

population, while 50% consider the Russian public television channel 'Первый канал', the most trustworthy.[996] Besides, in another interesting paradox, by 2008, 60% of the Moldovans considered Russia a strategic partner while believing also that Russia should be the partner to help them integrate in the European Union, as remarked by Radu Vrabie.[997]

Moscow was not capable of including Moldova in the Eurasian Union but uses its links with Gagauzia and Taraclia, as explained before, to keep Kremlin's interest in the political agenda. Besides, the continuous interest of opening a consulate in Tiraspol is another issue of the bilateral relation.[998] It is important to remember also that more than 30% of the citizens of Pridnestrovia have a Russian passport; therefore, as long as Moldova considers it as its territory, Moscow would seek how to 'guarantee' consular rights for their citizens.

Altogether, Moldovan foreign policy has lacked consistency. Partially as a consequence of being a weak polity subdued by the turbulent geopolitical struggles around the country. The academic Victor Chila agrees in that sense:

'The danger isn't Russia as such. The real danger is Moldova remaining a weak state controlled by a group of oligarchs, governed by corrupted officials, with an unsustainable economy, flawed democracy and dysfunctional institutions. Such a weak underdeveloped state will be incapable to defend its national interest against ever-growing Russian efforts to re-establish its former sphere of influence in its western backyard.'[999]

Still, it is to be noticed that the authorities in Chisinau did not make the foolish mistake of having an anti-Russian stance or an ethnonationalist position. Moldova is too weak and, if Georgia and Ukraine were not capable for a long period of sustaining an anti-Russian foreign policy, obviously Moldova's position was more

---

[996] Idem, page 107.
[997] Idem.
[998] 'Russia hopes to open consulate in Tiraspol,' September 12, 2012, accessed on September 12, 2012. http://www.allmoldova.com/en/moldova-news/12490 54177.html
[999] 'Moldova weighs up implications of overtures from EU and Russia,' April 30, 2013, accessed on March 2, 2016. http://www.theguardian.com/world/2013 /apr/30/moldova-implications-overtures-eu-russia

complicated. The Moldovan Armed Forces are even outnumbered by the Pridnestrovian forces and to risk a military conflict would not bring any positive solution for the Moldovan side now. Therefore, the approach to the West, after the initial push to become part of Romania, disappeared and a soft-policy approach was mostly used by the West to influence the events in the former Bessarabia.

Moldova and Romania
The Romanian Government was the first to recognize Moldovan independence. If one goes to Chisinau, it is possible to notice that the biggest embassy and the one with more security guards around is precisely the Romanian embassy, which makes you doubt if it is a ministry or any other public office of more importance. That diplomatic representation was also the first established in the Republic of Moldova when inaugurated on 20 January 1992.[1000] In that sense, the interest of Romania was clear. Since the beginning, they wanted to 'recover' the lost territory of Bessarabia. Until now, it is common to find in the Romanian souvenir shops stickers that say: 'Basarabia e România' while on textbooks it is pointed out to show how this territory should be part of Romania. Those minor examples are just to show the geopolitical interest of Romania in what Romanians see as former 'Romanian land'. In that sense, it is understandable that since the war with Pridnestrovia, the Romanian army sent military aid during the war and afterwards they openly suggested any kind of cooperation to help Moldova become incorporated into different international organizations.

The relation between both countries also passed through different periods. First, until 1994 a constructive relation was built, while Romania expected also a further push towards integration. After the arrival of Lucinschi to the presidency, a more pragmatic approach was used from the Moldovan side. Once the Popular Front was out of the government, it became clear that in the near future the Moldovan authorities would not seek to adhere to Romania. Still, a political dialogue continued, but it obtained few results except in the economic sphere where Moldova managed to import electric power

---

[1000] Chirila, Victor, 'Republic of Moldova relations with Romania' in *The Foreign Policy of The Republic of Moldova* (1998–2008), Chisinau, Friedrich Ebert Stiftung, Cartdidact, 2010, page 11.

and Romania was confirmed as Moldova's second economic partner.[1001]

Once Voronin and the Communist Party won the elections, tensions arose between both countries. The initial pro-Russian orientation of Voronin's foreign policy also included antagonizing Romanian's view of Moldova. In October 2001, the Moldovan Minister of Justice Ion Morei accused Romania of expansionism while later president Voronin accused Bucharest of financing protests in Chisinau.[1002] Altogether, after harsh criticism on both sides, by 2003 there was a new attempt of re-launching political dialogue. Only after the failure of the Kozak Memorandum in 2003, again the relations improved.

One of the thorny issues also had been the granting of the Romanian citizenship. In September 2006, the Romanian Government approved an ordinance to amend the law related with the more than 450,000 requests for Romanian citizenship from the Republic of Moldova nationals. Until then, Moldovan citizens enjoyed a visa-free regime with Romania but, seeing the imminent entrance of Romania to the EU in 2007, they lost that right, at least for some years until an agreement was reached with the EU years later.

Another issue that adds tension to the relations between both countries is religion. During the autumn of 2007, the Synod of the Romanian Orthodox Church decided to open three dioceses within the Metropolis of Bessarabia. The decision was met with great displeasure not only by the Moldovan Government but also by the local Metropolis of Moldova in what they saw as an external interference in their affairs. Voronin campaigned to show the act as an aggression of Romania against Moldova while afterwards the Patriarch of Moscow also participated to defend Moldova's position. At the end, after the dispute between both patriarchies, the dioceses were not open while the Romanian Orthodox Church notified the Council of Europe about an alleged case of abuse and intimidation against the community of the Metropolis of Bessarabia.[1003]

[1001] Idem, page 16.
[1002] Serebrian, Oleg, '"Good brothers," Bad neighbours: Romanian/Moldovan relations,' in *The EU & Moldova, On a Fault Line of Europe*, edited by Lewis, Ann, London, The Federal Trust, 2004, page 149.
[1003] Chirila, Idem, pages 36–38.

Once Romania entered the EU, the relations had certain importance, but also they became englobed as part of the whole relation with the European Institutions. That does not change the fact that until now, still Romanian authorities openly support a Union with Moldova even if they acknowledge it would be difficult for now to become a reality.[1004]

Still, Romania plays a considerable role for the West in the attempt to persuade Moldova to move away out of the Russian sphere of influence. For instance, the decision to build a gas pipe between Iasi and Ungheni would allow Romania to export gas to Moldova to cut the Russian dependency in that sector.[1005] Altogether, the Moldovan-Romanian relation is strategic locally for Moldova but globally it is part of the complex process that brought the country to sign the Association Agreement with the EU.

Moldova and the United States
It has been clear that the United States has not shown the same interest in Moldova as in Ukraine, even though it would be a mistake to consider that the United States does not care at all. Moldova has not the same geostrategic meaning, and the presence of the Russian troops in Pridnestrovia is symbolical more than a real military weight, but obstruct the possibility of bringing Moldova into the NATO umbrella. Therefore, until now, Moldova has mostly received technical and financial assistance on specific matters and once the aspiration of joining NATO was not on the because of Moldova's policy of neutrality, the scenarios for cooperation reduced to the economic level.

Cooperation with the United States through NATO happened at different levels without exposing the neutrality policy of Moldova. The Partnership for Peace was signed in 1994 together with other CIS members. Moldova participated in some joint exercises with the United States and economic support was also given to improve the

---

[1004] 'Президент Румынии напомнил, что стремится к объединению страны с Молдовой,' August 13, 2013, accessed on August 13, 2013. http://korrespondent.net/world/1591893-prezident-rumynii-napomnil-chto-stremitsya-k-o bedineniyu-strany-s-moldovoj

[1005] 'Румыния объявила тендер на строительство газопровода Яссы-Унгены,' May 5, 2013, accessed on May 5, 2013. http://news.mail.ru/inworld/moldova/economics/12970816/?frommail=1

Moldovan military. Besides, NATO financed different kinds of humanitarian and scientific projects in the country to make some presence in the territory, something that also is noticed by the permanent office that can be found in Chisinau near the Moldovan State University where a NATO information centre can be found.

Overall, the US presence or more precisely the US interest in Moldova is not so tangible like the one from other countries but still in strategic circumstances, it has been present. For instance, the United States was one of those countries that vehemently opposed the Kozak memorandum, while they also actively participated in the sanctions against 17 Pridnestrovian leaders in 2003.[1006] Altogether, for the United States, the interest in Moldova is related with the global scenario and in that sense, the country retook importance after the Ukrainian crisis in 2013–2014. Still, for the United States it seems difficult that such a fragmented and weak polity could become part of NATO or the EU. Maybe in that sense, a comment from Brzezinski retranslated afterwards by Spanu reads: 'Brzezinski also believed then that the only vehicle by which Moldova might join the EU and NATO was Romania.'[1007] Those same words were repeated years later by the Romanian president, Traian Basescu, who also thought the only way for Moldova to join the EU was as part of Romania.[1008] In that sense, the only immediate vehicle that could be used by the West to approach Moldova was precisely the soft-policy approach of the EU and to try to counterbalance Moscow's influence with organizations like GUAM.

Moldova and GUAM
Moldova, like Ukraine, was a founding member of GUAM together with Georgia and Azerbaijan. As mentioned, it was also backed by the United States, and it pretended to have an influence in settling frozen conflicts within international organizations. Unofficially, it pretended to serve as counterweight against Russia considering also

---

[1006] Vahl, Marius and Emerson, Michael, 'Moldova and the Transnistrian Conflict' in *Europeanization and Conflict Resolution Case Studies* from the European Periphery, Gent, Academia Press, 2004, page 170.
[1007] Spanu, Idem, page 109.
[1008] 'Траян Бэсеску: Молдове нужно присоединиться к Румынии во имя евроинтеграции,' January 6, 2014, accessed on January 6, 2014. http://www.kommersant.md/node/24263

that none of its members signed the CIS Treaty of Collective Security.[1009]

Besides, since its origins, GUAM depended mostly on the coordinated will of the member leaders rather than in institutionalized cooperation, making it extremely ineffective in many cases for the purposes it intended to serve, at least from 1998 to 2005.[1010] After the summit of April 2005, the final declaration among other issues condemned the 'destructive nature of separatism and enhance concerted efforts of the GUAM members states to resolve the separatist conflict in Moldova, Georgia and Azerbaijan'.[1011] By then, economic considerations played a secondary role for the Moldovan authorities as trade was notoriously reduced at least for Moldova in relation with the other members.[1012]

Therefore, the political dimension dominated cooperation among GUAM members since the beginning. As Chirila said: 'Policy makers in Moldova were always aware of Moscow's discontent with the development of a new regional political association with pro Western aspirations on post-Soviet territory that was, furthermore, perceived by Kremlin as a direct threat for the Russian interests in the region.'[1013]

In that sense, as noticed, GUAM had the opportunity to be quite functional for the United States, especially once Russia started to have a more assertive foreign policy under Putin. Coincidentally, since then, Chisinau started since the spring of 2001 also to promote an ambiguous, passive and unpredictable policy with respect to GUAM.

From 2001 to 2008, Moldova opposed the transformation of GUAM into an instrument of political speculations, while the country was willing to take part only in economic projects.[1014] The position was rather ambiguous in general in line with the ambiguity of

---

[1009] Chirila, Victor, 'Cooperation of the Republic of Moldova within GUAM,' in *The Foreign Policy of The Republic of Moldova* (1998–2008), Chisinau, Friedrich Ebert Stiftung, Cartdidact, 2010, page 167.
[1010] Idem, page 169.
[1011] Idem, page 171.
[1012] Idem, page 173.
[1013] Idem, page 174.
[1014] Idem, page 175.

the foreign policy that characterized Voronin's term in office. Therefore, sometimes GUAM was portrayed as a key organ to solve regional issues and sometimes it was ignored by Chisinau. A declaration by Voronin made on 11 March 2008, reflects what could be his final stand in relation with GUAM under his term: 'The presence in any organization should bring tangible benefits. If it does not reap any results there is no interest to be part of such organization. The prospects of GUAM are bleak.'[1015]

At the end, even under the governments led by the Liberal Democratic Party in Moldova, GUAM did not manage to obtain a key political role in the following years. Moldovans preferred to negotiate directly with the EU regarding their issues while by 2015 all GUAM members faced separatism issues, in which the only key actor for the solution is Russia, turning GUAM into a useless political organization, either for seeking integration with the EU or for assuring their territorial integrity. Therefore, for Chisinau, the priority turned to assuring Western support without contravening Moscow. Something apparently complicated seeing the evolving state of the relations between Moscow and the West. In this context, the EU decided to seek to obtain from Chisinau an Association Agreement.

Moldova and the EU

The first legal framework to establish cooperation between both parties was the Partnership and Cooperation Agreement signed on 28 November 1994. It entered into force only until 1998 for a period of 10 years.[1016] The PCA provided an institutional framework to work between the EU and Moldova but achieved few results. Mostly because both actors were not willing to expand their level of cooperation by then. Instead, after the enlargements of 2004 and 2007 that included the incorporation of Romania to the EU, a new impulse in the relation was given not only with Moldova but also with other CIS members as Ukraine and Georgia.

Afterwards, the European Neighbourhood Policy action plan was signed with Moldova on 22 February 2005. It certainly did not

---

[1015] As quoted in Idem, page 178.
[1016] Chirila, Victor, 'Relations of the Republic of Moldova with the European union,' in *The Foreign Policy of The Republic of Moldova* (1998–2008), Chisinau, Friedrich Ebert Stiftung, Cartdidact, 2010, page 61.

assure a prospective entrance to the EU even if for the Moldovan authorities it became the main goal, during Voronin's presidency, after the refusal to sign the Kozak agreement. From March 24, the integration into the EU became legally instituted as a goal and even the Ministry of Foreign Affairs changed its name to Ministry of Foreign Affairs and European Integration. By then, CIS membership was not questioned even if some political parties thought it was not compatible with the geopolitical direction the country intended to take. Subsequently, the EU also took a role as an observer in the '5+2' format to resolve the conflict in Pridnestrovia while Moldova received assistance in the light of the European Security and Defense Policy in the Moldovan-Ukrainian border.[1017]

Years later, at the end of 2008, the basis for the future Eastern Partnership was settled and it became operative in May 2009 as mentioned in Chapter 1. The EP among other things increased financial support to its members from 6 to 20 Euros per capita. The new amount of funds had a substantial impact. First, to push for the loyalty of the Moldovan authorities and second to counterbalance anything Russia could offer. Besides, entry into force of the Eastern Partnership almost coincided with the entrance of the Pro-Western Liberal Democratic Party to the government in Moldova.

As explained before, the goals of the EP intended first, to secure the loyalty of the members to the EU and to try to create a sort of buffer zone between Russia and the EU while not assuring the signatory countries any real prospective candidacy to the EU. Even though, differences remained among EU members regarding where the association would take them. Within time, even former prime minister Vladimir Filat recognized that the EU does not want Moldova to become a member of the EU. In a controversial speech during a rally organized by his own party, he looked more like a resented lover when he addressed the EU with the following words: 'Even if you don't want us, you don't love us, we want you and we love you.'[1018]

[1017] Idem, page 75.
[1018] 'Филат признал, что Европейский союз не хочет интеграции Молдовы,' November 4, 2013, accessed on November 4, 2013. http://point.md/ru/novosti/po litika/filat-priznal-chto-evropejskij-soyuz-ne-hochet-integracii-moldovi

Overall, for the EU it was substantial to have Moldova not only as part of the Eastern Partnership but also to seek as with Ukraine to sign the Association Agreement. The goal again was to obtain a free trade regime while assuring the closest cooperation possible with the EU. Meanwhile, one of the first immediate goals that the Moldovan Government tried to obtain was the visa-free regime. The Association Agreement was negotiated in a contemporary way with Ukraine and other members that had signed the Eastern Partnership. It was expected that all of them would initiate the signing process at the November Summit in Vilnius. At the end, as commented, Ukraine and Armenia refused to do it but the representatives from Moldova signed on 27 June 2014, allowing the agreement to be ratified in the following months by the EU members.

In Moldova, there was no great resistance outside Gagauzia and Taraclia towards the Association Agreement with the EU. There was a kind of tacit acceptance. It is curious that the public opinion showed also more or less the same acceptance for the Eurasian Union and for the EU. For instance, a survey done in November 2014 showed that 51% of the voters would support to join the EU and 36% would vote against it but at the same question whether to join the Eurasian Union, 47% were in favour and 35% against. To make it even more interesting, the same survey asked to whom the Republic of Moldova would be closer? 44% answered to the EU and 43% to Russia.[1019]

In that sense, even if the cabinet changed numerous times since the Liberal Democratic Party assumed the government since 2009, mostly because of corruption scandals, the EU preferred again to disregard those facts, and profit from the pro-EU policies they shared. Altogether, Moldova with a considerable small population did not represent a serious migratory risk as countries with a bigger population like Ukraine; therefore, the EU finally agreed to give consent to visa-free travel for Moldovan citizens. At the end, Moldova has less than 3 million inhabitants excluding Pridnestrovia and only the possession of a biometric passport became the main

---

[1019] 'Imas Sondaj la Nivel national,' Moldova, November 2014, accessed on March 2, 2016. http://ipn.md/infoprim/UserFiles/Image/PDF/Raport_IPN_perspective_alegeri_22.11.2014.pdf

requirement for Moldovans to enter the EU without visa since 28 April 2014.[1020]

The visa-free regime expects to gain the sympathy of the local population towards the EU. It is important to consider that, similar to Ukraine, for the residents of Moldova the importance of the EU reduces to the possibility of free travel within the Schengen area and working in the EU without restraints. Even if the visa-free regime in no way officially means securing working permits, it allows the arrival of undocumented workers, who without proper documents, know the conditions are always better in any EU member than in Moldova.

Altogether, one of the thorny issues has always been about the border with Pridnestrovia. In the Western media, the idea that Pridnestrovia is a no-law zone where smuggling of goods, weapons and even people is common is widespread, but the reality is more complex. Pridnestrovia as will be explained later functions internally with its own Customs system and laws, with the exception that it is not recognized by any country in the world. Therefore, from an international law perspective, no legal authority checks the entrance of goods into Pridnestrovia even if in fact somebody does. Besides, when you travel outside Pridnestrovia in direction to Moldavia, at least until 2013 there were no Moldovan checkpoints to enter Moldova, hence allowing the entrance into Moldovan territory without customs or passport check. At the end, Moldovan authorities always blamed the smuggling on their lack of control of their alleged borders, but meanwhile they were not even controlling in the existing de facto borders as it would mean to recognize it as a real border, therefore, it was better to leave it open. Then, it is curious though how when entering or exiting Moldova from the Western border to Romania any individual is subject to a tough border control, instead when on the return from Pridnestrovia, the control was non-existent. It is like having a bank with the most modern security equipment at the front, while keeping the back door open. At the end, how much of the smuggling of goods, weapons or drugs is fault of the

---

[1020] 'Commissioner Malmström on visa-free travel for the citizens of the Republic of Moldova,' European Commission Statement, April 27, 2014, accessed on March 17, 2015. http://europa.eu/rapid/press-release_STATEMENT-14-137_en.htm?locale=en

Moldovan or Pridnestrovian authorities or both is difficult to know, but it is, true that by refusing to acknowledge an existent border (recognized or not), it made the position of Moldova more fragile. Therefore, since 2013, the Moldovan Government declared the intention to establish border controls in six crossing points with Pridnestrovia to improve this situation.[1021] This measure can be related also as part of the negotiations included for the Association Agreement and to obtain the visa-free regime.

Russia tried within the possibilities they had to stop or slow down Moldovan rapprochement with the EU. A new wine embargo, for instance, having quality problems intended to slow down the process.[1022] The effects again were hard on the Moldovan economy but did not push the Moldovan elite in charge to change geopolitical orientation. Neither the referenda organized in Gagauzia to join the Customs Union had a strong political effect except showing the risks that a pro-Western orientation could carry.

Altogether, even with the ratification of the Association Agreement, it does not seem that Moldova could advance in a deeper association with the EU while still being one of the poorest countries in Europe together with Albania and having the Pridnestrovian issue unsolved. The difference with Ukraine is that the territory is smaller, has a less geostrategic value for the actors involved and the population does not face the degree of ethnic conflict that can be seen in some Ukrainian regions. Moldovans would like to believe also that if Cyprus managed to enter the EU without resolving the division present in the island since 1974, they could also join in a similar way; the difference is that Moldova does not have the same economic value as Cyprus. Moreover, it would not be the same for the EU to negotiate the presence of Turkish troops with Turkey, a

---

[1021] 'Правительство Молдовы подтверждает, что будет осуществлять пограничный контроль на Днестре,' November 22, 2013, accessed on November 22, 2013. http://novostipmr.com/ru/news/13-10-22/pravitelstvo-moldovy-podtverzhdaet-chto-budet-osushchestvlyat

[1022] 'Россия развязала торговую войну с еще одним западным соседом,' September 10, 2013, accessed on September 10, 2013. http://korrespondent.net/business/economics/1601882-rossiya-razvyazala-torgovuyu-vojnu-s-eshche-odnim-zapadnym-sosedom

quasi-eternal candidate to join the Union,[1023] than to do it with the Kremlin, at the end, nuclear nukes also count.

This leaves most of the future status of Moldova again to depend first, on how the country will manage to negotiate for a solution with Pridnestrovia but above all, on how the foreign powers will manage to accept or define that solution. Depending on this circumstance lays the future of the Moldovan polity. Therefore, before analysing the complex state of the relation between Moldova and Pridnestrovia, in which Moldova has to relate to the PMR without officially recognizing the Pridnestrovian polity, it is important to understand also the inner political events in the PM, and how the international lack of recognition affects the relation. At the end, with or without *de jure* international recognition, Tiraspol intends according to its possibilities, to develop also its own foreign policy.

3.4 Pridnestrovia, more sovereign than Moldova?

3.4.1 The inner politics of Pridnestrovia: The 'benefits' of the lack of recognition

Since Soviet times, the authorities that emerged in what today is Pridnestrovia also lacked Soviet recognition. Gorbachev declared void the intention from the improvised Soviet that pronounced the creation of the Pridnestrovian Moldovan Soviet Socialist Republic. Still, the weakness of the crumbling Soviet state made it impossible to stop the integration of most of the communities located at the eastern side of the Dniester. Therefore, Pridnestrovian authorities continued organizing themselves while during 1991, there was not much the Soviet Union nor the Moldovan SSR could oppose. It was only in 1992 after the war that the creation of the PMR was 'settled', mainly as part of the actions carried out by the 14th Army when it decided the course of the war. Even if they were locals fighting for the PMR, it was mostly the decision by Lebed's artillery to open fire

---

[1023] Turkey's application to join the EU was made on April 14, 1987, when it was still the European Economic Community. On December 12, 1999, it was recognized as a candidate. Until now, only one of the negotiating 35 chapters have been closed, while 16 are freeze pending the recognition of the Republic of Cyprus by Turkey. Note of the author.

Moldova and the Pridnestrovian Moldovan Republic   401

against the recently created Moldovan Armed Forces that decided the military struggle. Therefore, as has happened with the origin of many countries in the international scene,[1024] the creation of the PMR was also sustained by a foreign force.[1025] The intervention of the 14th Army allowed the development of a different polity where the local political elite had tried to break links first with the Moldovan SSR and then with what became the Republic of Moldova. The participation from the 14th Army therefore was the fundamental political force that allowed the PMR to emerge. This fact does not pretend to establish the will from the Pridnestrovian elites as illegitimate. There are numerous nations and communities around the world that have tried for centuries to build an independent country and many of these attempts have been stopped by a stronger power that does not allow it. Catalonia, Scotland and Palestine, for instance, are only some cases of communities to whom, even after a long struggle, the dominant world powers are not willing to concede the right to exist as an independent polity simply because they would alter the geopolitical order. Instead, here, the 14th Army made it possible for Pridnestrovia to emerge.[1026]

Similar to the appearance of Romania in the international scene as an independent country was a consequence of the agreements between Bismarck and Russia, or the reappearance of Poland after World War I as part of the Paris Peace Conference and Woodrow Wilson's famous 14 points. In those cases, the new countries de-

---

[1024]   In that case, Uruguay, Panama or Luxembourg are only some examples of countries that appeared in the international scene due to the interest of a foreign power and not precisely because there was an inner struggle that was going to allow it.
[1025]   It would be difficult to sustain that by 1992 the 14th Army represented the interest of the Russian state, because as we have explained the Russian state took almost a decade to refund itself after the Soviet fall. It is possible to say that at least it represented the interest of what was left of the Soviet Armed Forces reintegrated in the armed forces of the Russian Federation. Note of the author.
[1026]   It has been argued in the first chapter how in the first years after the Soviet fall, the Russian foreign policy was not clear and different and even opposed 'policies' were carried out by the government, the parliament and the Russian Army. The intervention in Pridnestrovia could be considered then as part of the immediate strategic interest of the recently conceived Russian Armed Forces that still operated in a Soviet dimension. Note of the author.

pended on a foreign support to become existent. Even if each circumstance would be different, the fact is that these new polities already emerged in a position of weakness because they owed something to a foreign power. That does not deny their right to self-determination; it only underlines the fact that their origin became a reality, thanks to geopolitics.

The same way, geopolitics allowed the appearance of the PMR although with some differences. It is important also to understand that the division that appeared among the Moldovan SSR was not ethnically based but politically based. First, because the ethnical composition of the PMR was not one dominant ethnic group; second, because even the Romanian-speaking population in the PMR allegedly sympathized with the local authorities. In that sense, the newly appeared Pridnestrovia used different elements to create the idea of a 'Pridnestrovian nation' from which to develop a polity even if those elements were based mainly on a political basis, for instance, the war with Moldova. The development of the conflict and the hundreds of casualties that occurred on the Pridnestrovian side gathered the local population around the idea of defending the local population from the menace of a possible 'Romanization'. In that sense, the PMR recognizes the Romanian-speaking populations in its territory as 'Moldovans' but not as Romanians as if they were a different ethnic group. Altogether the PMR managed to use elements like the war against the Republic of Moldova, a strong memory of the glories of the Soviet past while acknowledging a multi-ethnic society although highly Russified in practice but not by law.[1027] The use of some elements in the Pridnestrovian flag and coat of arms also refers to that Soviet past while promoting also the Soviet national holidays such as 9th may to the same level of national importance.

Finally, it is important to consider that the inhabitants at the east of the Dniester were for a longer period part of the Soviet Union. Therefore, they had developed culturally and politically in a different way, while Bessarabia had been incorporated only after the war.

[1027] Pridnestrovia recognizes three official languages: Russian, Ukrainian and Romanian but named as Moldovan.

That explains also how often many of the leaders from the Moldovan SSR came from the eastern part of the Dniester.[1028]

Another element that allowed the Pridnestrovian authorities the possibility of assuring themselves a legal base for its establishment was exactly that the declaration of independence of the Republic of Moldova was mostly based on the denouncement of the Molotov-Ribbentrop Pact. To denounce that treaty meant precisely that most of the territory that today belongs to the PMR should then not be part of the Republic of Moldova, as those territories by then were part of the Moldovan ASSR, meaning as part of the USSR and did not belong to Bessarabia. Therefore, this argument gives a legal basis and the justification to create the PMR or at least not to consider it as part of Moldova.

Afterwards, the inner political developments in the PMR after the Soviet fall were not different from what happened in many Soviet republics, even though there were some interesting differences. Since the end of the hostilities in 1992, and even some months before, Igor Smirnov had been elected the president of the PMR, a position in which he remained unopposed until 2011. He won the elections in 1996, 2001 and 2006 with a clearly comfortable margin. During that time, Western governments complained that the elections were not carried out under what they considered 'democratic standards' but the fact is that the electoral development was not different from what happened in many former Soviet republics. During his long term in office, the legal and political systems now in place in the PMR were organized in a sort of semi-presidential republic. With tacit Russian support, the local authorities managed the economy without opening widely to foreign capitals while not privatizing the entire industrial sector. Besides, in the measure of the possibilities, the Pridnestrovian authorities tried to sustain some of the existing Soviet welfare and that action slightly reduced the deteriorating social decline visible in most former Soviet republics.

The government allowed instead the appearance of local corporations like *Sheriff*, which owns a chain of petrol stations, super-

---

[1028] Even Voronin, who was the president of Moldova for several years, was born in today's Pridnestrovia. Kuchler, Op. Cit., page 49.

markets, the only private TV channel, a publishing house, a construction company, a Mercedes Benz dealer, an advertising agency, a distillery that manufactures the *Kvint* brandies, two bread factories and a local mobile phone network. It also owns the FC Club Sheriff Tiraspol with its notably modern stadium that was worth more than $200 million.[1029] It was long speculated that the company benefited from the fact that Igor Smirnov's son was head of the Customs Service in the PMR[1030] and allowed the firm a reduction on import taxes. The fact is that for a long time, Sheriff was also a considerable support of the regime.

Despite the solid control that Smirnov had over the country over the years, his party was not always capable of securing parliamentary majority in his last years in office. A new arrival party, *Renewal*, headed then by Yevgeny Shevchuk obtained 23 of the 45 seats to secure a majority in the 2005 parliamentary elections. By then, *Sheriff* campaigned actively also for Renewal in what precluded a break between the corporation and Smirnov. That majority increased in the 2010 parliamentary elections when the same party now headed by Anatoliy Kaminski obtained 25 seats. Those results prepared the political terrain for the 2011 presidential election. It was expected that Smirnov would again obtain the victory, instead a highly contended first round saw Shevchuk who was running as 'independent' obtain 38.55% of the votes; Kaminski with open support from the Russian Party United Russia obtained 26.30%, while the still president Smirnov surprisingly got 24.66% and stayed out of the second round.

Western media widely spread the idea that Smirnov had fallen out of grace with Moscow, while Kaminski was the candidate preferred by the Kremlin. The fact is that Shevchuk won easily the second round with 73.88% of the votes becoming then the second person to hold the presidency in the PMR and the result did not seem to bother at all the Kremlin. It is also noteworthy that, democratic

---

[1029] Eberhard, Adam, 'The paradoxes of Moldovan Sports,' Point of View, Centre for Eastern Studies, November 2011, pages 15–16.
[1030] 'The old guard wins in Transdniestria,' September 19, 2006, accessed on March 18, 2014. http://www.kommersant.com/p705753/r_1/The_Old_Guard_Wins_in_Transdniestria/

or not, the victory by Shevchuk allowed a peaceful transition between rival political groups, something not seen quite often in the post-Soviet space.

During more than two decades of existence, the PMR has developed its own legal system.[1031] The republic has also its own currency, the Pridnestrovian ruble attached to the US dollar, while Russian banks operate in place the same way as many Russian firms. Even if the currency is not recognized internationally, thanks to Russian banks, ATMs operate normally in Tiraspol where it is possible to withdraw either Russian rubles or US dollars via the MasterCard, Visa or Maestro circuit. This reflects also an important characteristic of the Pridnestrovian economic life and its dependence with Moscow but also how the lack of recognition can be overcome.

Besides, the Russian Government has subsidized in different degrees the local economy. The gas supply develops into an interesting power play by Moscow to put pressure on Moldova as explained by Yafimava.[1032] In that sense, the Moldovan Transit network consists of four pipelines and all of them transit through Pridnestrovia. The property has also changed hands. Initially it was state Moldova's property but it was sold to Gazprom, which obtained 50% from *Moldovagaz*. The Moldovan Government kept 35.44% of the shares and Pridnestrovia 13.44%, while 1.23% belongs to individual shareholders. In Pridnestrovia, the local distribution is done only by *Tiraspoltransgaz*, a subsidiary of *Moldovagaz*.[1033] In December 2005, the Pridnestrovian parliament approved the decision to withdraw from the *Moldovagaz* JV and *Tiraspoltransgaz* transferred its 13.44% share to Gazprom. The PMR transferred its 13.44% stake to Gazprom under trust management even though, until now, the company's web page announces the PMR as owner also;[1034] meanwhile its stake is held by Gazprom as part of debt settlement, a mechanism

---

[1031] More details can be found on Bomeshko, B.G. 'Законодательная власть в системе приднестровском государственности и её развитие' in *Государственность Приднестровья: история и современность*, Bendery, Poligrafist, 2007.
[1032] Yafimava, Katja, *The Transit Dimension of EU Energy Security*, Oxford, Oxford University Press, 2011.
[1033] Idem, page 264.
[1034] 'Молдовагаз» сегодня,' accessed on August 27, 2015. http://www.moldovagaz.md/menu/ru/about-company/mg-today

that would be more difficult to challenge in court if the Pridnestrovian issue would be solved.

Moreover, Moldova and Pridnestrovia consume the same amount of gas and by 2005 they paid only 70% of their bills. Through the years, gas debt accumulated enormously and while for Moldova, gas debt represents only around 11.4% of its debt, for Pridnestrovia it is 79.1%. Either way, Gazprom continued to 'tolerate' the non-payment by the PMR. That way, core industries-ferrous metallurgy and power sector that represent more than half of the total industrial output and represent 60% of export revenues maintain their competitiveness because of Gazprom's toleration to non-payment. Yafimava adds: 'Essentially Gazprom has supplied gas to the region at half-price, since the level of payment has been only 40–60 percent of the price stipulated by the contract.'[1035]

To make matters more intricate, supply transit contracts are concluded between Gazprom and *Moldovagaz*. Instead, *Tiraspoltransgaz* makes its payments directly to Gazprom but the custom clearance fee is paid by *Moldovagaz*.[1036] Besides, Pridnestrovian consumers have been for years paying domestic prices lower than import costs and the difference is covered by the regional budget. In 2006, the PMR parliament passed a law to pay gas independently from Chisinau to strengthen payment discipline. By 2011 the PMR debt to Gazprom was of 2.8 billion.[1037] The fact is that the government of Pridnestrovia can get away with non-payment, as officially any claims including arbitration would be transferred to Moldova.[1038] At the end, not being an internationally recognized state means that it has no reputation to defend. Thus, as long as the conflict is unsettled, gas transit security to the EU via the Republic of Moldova remains uncertain.[1039]

This way, Russia's aid allows the country to sustain itself economically. Besides, many Pridnestrovian citizens receive also a Russian fund for pensioners while it is possible to obtain credits from Russian banks. Therefore, when Moscow reduced the amount

---

[1035] Yafimava, Op. Cit., Idem, page 271.
[1036] Idem, page 273.
[1037] Idem, page 276.
[1038] Idem, page 282.
[1039] Idem, page 283.

of the aid given to Pridnestrovia during 2014 as consequence of the economic crisis in Russia, the Pridnestrovian economy had to adapt itself as declared President Shevchuk in an interview in 2014.[1040] Even though, Russia is still the first economic partner with a high dependence on Russian imports while Moldova is the second, and the first receiver of Pridnestrovian exports while Ukraine is the third commercial partner.[1041]

Internally it is important to consider the advantages that the lack of recognition carries. Pridnestrovia has its own customs system and controls its own borders, a privilege that, for instance, neither Ukraine nor Moldova can enjoy right now. Besides, the fact that they are not obliged to any international legislation eases the operation of the Pridnestrovian polity. Voices in the EU or in the United States usually refer to Pridnestrovia as a place without law where smuggling and criminal organizations are widespread. The fact is that the smuggling that allegedly exists functions in relation to the Moldovan and Ukrainian authorities. At the end, the three polities have functioning customs systems permeated by corruption but the fact that the one from the PMR is not recognized is what really bothers the EU and the United States because there is no one to account for the legal responsibility.

There are also some notable interesting differences in the daily life between Chisinau and Tiraspol. Tiraspol tries to present itself as a peaceful and harmonic orthodox society. In the Pridnestrovian capital, there are no big malls, or the same nightlife and nightclubs that Chisinau offers. It seems as if Pridnestrovia pretended to give an example where Orthodox morality prevails and no strip-tease clubs or prostitution can be found openly, something quite common in Chisinau for instance. This is not a small ordeal considering the numerous complaints about human trafficking mentioned worldwide regarding Moldova. Besides, the idea of a strong orthodox

---

[1040] 'Президент Приднестровья рассказал за чей счет летает на чартерных рейсах,' April 24, 2015, accessed on April 24, 2015. http://www.kp.md/daily/26371/3252519/

[1041] 'Приднестровье нарастило внешний товарооборот в первом квартале 2014 года,' April 16, 2014, accessed on April 16, 2014. http://www.kommersant.md/node/28572

identity has been reinforced also by the presence of the Moscow Patriarch Kirill in Pridnestrovia. His visits allowed the Kremlin to develop another non-official link with the local society.[1042]

Besides, Russian media plays an important role while giving the locals an idealistic vision of Russia, even considering that many of the Pridnestrovians have never actually been there, while giving also a sort of yearning for the Soviet past. That brings also a strong identification with Russia and explains how many people went into Ukraine voluntary to participate in activities against the current Ukrainian Government. That identification based on an all-orthodox, pro-Russian and anti-US feeling becomes stronger when it happens in a semi-close society. In fact, another interesting detail in Tiraspol is how people are not used to meeting with foreigners, who usually just arrive for one day to the main square, take some pictures of the Soviet monuments and leave while collecting some Pridnestrovian banknotes as souvenirs.

Academically, the Taras Shevchenko Pridnestrovian State University manages to handle 14 faculties and prepare more than 10,000 students while courses are taught in Russian, Ukrainian and Romanian. Besides, it is worth mentioning the considerable amount of publications regarding the Pridnestrovian conflict. There are several indigenous historiographical researches regarding Pridnestrovian history like the ones written by Professor Bomeshko, while also original attempts to justify not just a Pridnestrovian identity but to sustain from a political and geopolitical perspective the separation of Pridnestrovia from Moldova, like the works carried out by Pridnestrovian historian Babilunga.[1043]

At the end, accepted or not, Pridnestrovia has managed to develop a different political identity while still sharing also many Soviet elements with Moldova. Corruption plays also part of daily life and media is used for political and private ends at both sides of the Dniester.[1044] Still, the bond with Russia at the east of the Dniester

---

[1042]   'Патриарх помолился за экономику Приднестровья,' September 9, 2013, accessed on September 17, 2013. http://www.kommersant.md/node/20462
[1043]   Babilunga, N.V., *Повторение пройдённого: феодализм как светлое будущее Республики Молдова*, Tiraspol, Bendery, 2012.
[1044]   Kuchler, Op. Cit., page 50.

allows a deeper understanding of the conflict. The results of the several referenda carried out in the last decades confirm that.

Among the polls that took place in the PMR, it is important to mention the next ones. On 1 December 1991, a referendum was held about formal independence and with a turnout of 78%, 97.7% voted in favour. Another one held in 1995 asked the local population about the permanence in Pridnestrovia of the Russian troops and more than 90% supported their stay. That same year, on 24 December 1995, another poll had taken place, in which the voters approved of the Pridnestrovian constitution with 81.8% of the votes while 90.6% voted in favour of requesting an entry to the CIS. Finally, on 17 September 2006, a second referendum about the Pridnestrovian independence took place. That time with a turnout of 78.6%, 97.2% voted in favour of the question: 'Do you support the course towards the independence of Pridnestrovia and the subsequent free association with the Russian Federation?'[1045] A second question in that same poll asked about renouncing independence and accepting unification with Moldova and 94.9% reject it.[1046]

The referenda were not recognized by any other country in the world. Western governments even complained that they were not held under democratic standards[1047] and it is possible also that most of the population that did not participate was from the Romanian-speaking population in the PMR. Even though, as in the Crimean case, if the polls had been conducted under conditions approved by the West, it is difficult that the results would vary notably. At the end, the refusal of the results has a geopolitical explanation in which the EU and the United States would not like a change in the local geography with the arrival of a new polity, that would not be aligned with them. Pridnestrovia is not Kosovo, therefore it would not be suitable to be managed with ease. Besides, it is undeniable that a

---

[1045] 'Transnistriche Moldawische Republik (Moldawien), 17. September 2006: Unabhängigkeitskurs und Beitritt zu Russland,' accessed on March 18, 2015. http://www.sudd.ch/event.php?lang=en&id=mdo12006

[1046] 'Transnistriche Moldawische Republik (Moldawien), 17. September 2006: Verzicht auf Unabhängigkeit,' accessed on March 18, 2015. http://www.sudd.ch/event.php?lang=en&id=mdo22006

[1047] At the end, the capacity of many Western governments to accept the 'democratic standards' of an election becomes also a political issue and can be accepted or overseen depending on the geopolitical interest in different regions of the world. Note of the author.

majoritarian sector of the population feels a greater attraction and identity with Russia and therefore it points out that many of the events in the PMR will be related with what happens in 'Родина-мать', that is the way still locals can refer to 'Mother Homeland Russia'.

Nevertheless, before analysing Pridnestrovian foreign policy, it is worth mentioning some non-official ways in which the PMR uses to get some sort of recognition. For instance, the Football Club Sheriff Tiraspol becomes also a very interesting case. Sport is the only domain in which Pridnestrovia recognizes itself as part of the Republic of Moldova. The fact that UEFA does not recognize Pridnestrovia forces the clubs located in the region to play in the Moldovan League, and therefore, FC Sheriff Tiraspol and other clubs from Pridnestrovia recognize the Moldovan Football Federation in a unique case. It has been an embarrassment also for Moldovan authorities when they have tried to assist a match in Tiraspol and they are not allowed to enter the stadium.[1048] It has been a useful projection also, as the Sheriff Tiraspol receives considerable funding for the Sheriff Corporation and has enough financing to be frequently the Moldovan Champion, therefore acceding to participate in the preliminary rounds of the UEFA Champions League, which allows also some media presence for the region. Besides, tickets to the Sheriff's games, for instance, have the Pridnestrovian logo while eventually soccer fans in the area recognize it almost as a sort of 'national' representation that plays against Moldovan rivals.[1049]

3.4.2 The foreign policy of Pridnestrovia

Since its foundation, the PMR has tried to obtain international recognition. There is a ministry of foreign affairs that intends to function as similar ministries in other countries. Besides, the PMR obtained recognition from Abkhazia and South Ossetia. Their respective embassies are located in downtown Tiraspol with the pending flags visible. The PMR also is recognized by the Nagorno-Karabakh. That goes for the official relations. Moreover, the PMR

[1048] Eberhard, Adam, 'The paradoxes of Moldovan Sports,' Point of View, Centre for Eastern Studies, November 2011.
[1049] The Moldovan National Division, which is the top tier of Moldovan Football, counts in the 2015–2016 with 10 clubs. It includes two from Pridnestrovia and one from Gagauzia. Note of the author.

has managed to obtain certain success considering the geopolitical context. It has to be recognized at least unofficially by the Republic of Moldova. Besides, the relation with Russia has great importance while Ukraine has shown a changing policy towards Pridnestrovia more on the basis of the foreign interests rather than on what would be in the best interest of Ukraine. Altogether, the fact that the PMR can sit in the negotiating table with representatives from the EU and the United States already gives a sort of non-official recognition that gives them leverage.

In that sense, the foreign policy concept approved by the Pridnestrovian Supreme Council in 2005 considers the priority of establishing cooperation with Russia, Ukraine, Moldova and the three mentioned unrecognized countries that recognize the PMR as the most important relations.[1050]

As shown, the relation with Russia becomes the main support of the regime. On one side, the presence of the Russian troops guarantees the existence of the PMR, although it seems unlikely that Moldova would try to do something similar to what the Georgian Government did while trying to recover South Ossetia with a military operation in 2008. The state of the Moldovan Armed Forces could not allow itself an operation in that sense, while it is foreseen what the Russian answer would be. Just recently, Dmitry Rogozin, deputy prime minister and special presidential representative for Pridnestrovia, declared that Russia is not planning to take the peacekeepers out of Pridnestrovia.[1051] Therefore, the main relation in the Pridnestrovian foreign policy is with Russia, to obtain aid, sustain and recognition. In fact, any visit from members either of the Russian Duma or by the same Rogozin is widely publicized precisely to show the extent of the Russian interest in the region. Even Vladimir Putin declared that Pridnestrovia inhabitants should be allowed to decide their own destiny in a comment that could be perceived as a

---

[1050] 'The foreign policy concept of the Pridnestrovian Moldovan Republic,' November 20, 2012, accessed on November 22, 2012. http://mfa-pmr.org/en/yGL

[1051] 'Рогозин: Россия не выведет миротворцев из Приднестровья,' May 18, 2013, accessed on May 18, 2013. http://news.mail.ru/inworld/moldova/politics/13139361/?frommail=1

tacit backing of the current to the regime.[1052] Besides, recognizing the priority of the relations with the Russian Federation, the PMR acknowledges openly, the geopolitical role of the region as pointed out in the mentioned document.[1053]

> Pridnestrovia considers geopolitical presence of the Russian Federation in the area of the Moldovan-Pridnestrovian conflict as a principal facilitation in maintaining region-wide stability and security. Enduring responsible mission of Russia as a guarantor and mediator in the Moldovan-Pridnestrovian settlement and as a leading force in the tripartite peacekeeping operation is its undeniable contribution to international peace and arrangement of conditions for an equitable final settlement of the Moldovan-Pridnestrovian relations.[1054]

The relation with Moldova, instead, is related with the economic sphere, considering Moldova is the most important economic partner for Tiraspol excluding the gas supplies by Russia. Therefore, each time Moldova decides to establish changes in the import-export rules, Pridnestrovia usually answers with a strong diplomatic campaign denouncing an economic blockade.[1055]

It is not a surprise, then, how the official Pridnestrovian foreign policy recognizes as the major priorities Eurasian integration and the negotiation process.[1056] The first one because it would guarantee a closer integration with Russia and the second because it would allow to establish a definite status recognized by international law. Therefore, it is essential to describe how the negotiation process has evolved and, of course, how it has been influenced by the geopolitical context.

The negotiation process
The process to solve the current situation between the Republic of Moldova and the Pridnestrovian Moldovan Republic has not been

---

[1052] 'Владимир Путин: "Люди в Приднестровье должны сами решать свою судьбу",' Published April 17, 2014, accessed on March 2, 2016. https://www.youtube.com/watch?v=oo6hVmxkcWA
[1053] In this sense, it is notable, because currently few countries allow themselves to mention openly the idea of geopolitical areas as if it were more reproachable. Note of the author.
[1054] 'The foreign policy concept of the Pridnestrovian Moldovan Republic,' November 20, 2012, accessed on November 22, 2012. http://mfa-pmr.org/en/yGL
[1055] 'Тирасполь подчеркнул сырьезность ситуации,' January 31, 2014, accessed on February 2, 2014. http://www.kommersant.md/node/25186
[1056] 'The foreign policy concept of the Pridnestrovian Moldovan Republic,' Op. Cit.

exempted from influence by the international context. In that sense, it has evolved, considering not only the state of the relations between the two direct affected polities of Moldova and Pridnestrovia but also because of the role other actors have played, mostly in Russia, the EU and the United States but also Ukraine when it has decided to play in US favour. Altogether, the process has contained different phases.

The first phase was from 1992 just after the war. The agreement signed on 21 July 1992, between the Republic of Moldova and the Russian Federation would be the only settlement in which the PMR would not be represented as an official signatory.[1057] Afterwards, the PMR assured itself to be recognized as one of the parts in the conflict, therefore assuring a presence in the negotiating table since 1993 when it started to participate in direct talks with the Moldovan authorities.

An initial treaty was proposed by the Pridnestrovian legislature that included two single independent states but with a single membership in the CIS. This proposal was obviously rejected by the Moldovan side while Tiraspol refused also a Moldovan proposal that gave the PMR a special status within the Republic of Moldova.[1058]

The year 1993 also saw the CSCE Mission established in Chisinau with the mandate to assist the two parties in the negotiations. The first proposal included the fact that Pridnestrovia should have the right to 'external self-determination' in case Moldova decided to merge with Romania. It also suggested a possible Moldovan decentralization and to divide eventually the country into 8 or 10 regions.[1059]

The second phase of negotiations could be considered from 1994. By then, Yeltsin pushed to restart negotiations and another

---

[1057] 'СОГЛАШЕНИЕ О ПРИНЦИПИПАХ МИРНОГО УРЕГУЛИРОВАНИЯ ВООРУЖЁННОГО КОНФЛИКТА В ПРИДНЕСТРОВСКОМ РЕГИОНЕ РЕСПУБЛИКИ МОЛДОВА' in *ПЕРЕГОВОРНЫЙ ПРОЦЕСС МЕЖДУ МОЛДАВСКОЙ РЕСПУБЛИКОЙ И РЕСПУБЛИКОЙ МОЛДОВА В ДОКУМЕНТАХ*, Ministry of Foreign Affairs of the Pridnestrovian Moldovan Republic, Poligrafist, 2011, pages 15–17.
[1058] Vahl, Marius and Emerson, Michael, *Moldova and the Transnistrian Conflict in Europeanization and Conflict Resolution*, Case studies from the European Periphery, Gent, Academia Press, 2004, page 163.
[1059] Idem, page 164.

agreement was signed with the OSCE.[1060] Both representatives agreed to start negotiations on the legal and constitutional status of Pridnestrovia and about Russian troop withdrawal and a border agreement. Besides, in 1995, Ukraine became the third official mediator in the conflict.[1061] Afterwards, in January 1996, there was the intention to give Pridnestrovia a special status while Russia and Ukraine in a Joint declaration with Moldova recognized the territorial integrity of Moldova.[1062] The proposal was rejected by the authorities of the PMR later.

Months later, another proposal headed by the Russian Foreign Minister Evgeniy Primakov considered the formation of a 'common state' to unblock the negotiation. This allowed a Memorandum of Understanding between Moldova and Pridnestrovia signed on 8 May 1997, in Moscow.[1063] The document allowed Pridnestrovia to participate in the foreign relations of the Republic of Moldova when it touched up on its interest. The memorandum reaffirmed the presence of Russia, Ukraine and the OSCE as mediators and determined that the presence of the peacekeeping should continue.[1064]

This allowed a third phase of negotiations that, even if it became unsuccessful, allowed agreements at different levels. The agreement called for the reconstruction of two bridges crossing the Dniester and a joint group to combat illegal trafficking of drugs and arms besides programmes related to economic and environmental policy.[1065] This process lead to a new draft agreement and later to a Joint Statement on issues of normalizing the relations between the

---

[1060] The CSCE became the OSCE in 1994.
[1061] The letter in which the leaders of Moldova and Pridnestrovia together with the representatives of the OSCE and Russia asked President Kuchma to participate in the process can be consulted in 'ПЕРЕГОВОРНЫЙ ПРОЦЕСС МЕЖДУ МОЛДАВСКОЙ РЕСПУБЛИКОЙ И РЕСПУБЛИКОЙ МОЛДОВА В ДОКУМЕНТАХ,' Ministry of Foreign Affairs of the Pridnestrovian Moldovan Republic, Poligrafist, 2011, page 31.
[1062] Vahl, Marius and Emerson, Michael, Idem, page 164.
[1063] 'МЕМОРАНДУМ об основах нормализации отношений между Республики Молдова и Приднестровье' in *ПЕРЕГОВОРНЫЙ ПРОЦЕСС МЕЖДУ МОЛДАВСКОЙ РЕСПУБЛИКОЙ И РЕСПУБЛИКОЙ МОЛДОВА В ДОКУМЕНТАХ*, Ministry of Foreign Affairs of the Pridnestrovian Moldovan Republic, Poligrafist, 2011, pages 38–39.
[1064] Vahl and Emerson, Idem, page 165.
[1065] Vahl and Emerson, Idem, page 166.

two polities. After several protocols[1066] signed on 13 July 1999, three days later the Joint Statement included five 'common spaces' which referred to common borders, and common economic, legal, defence and social domains.[1067] Differences appeared instead in the fact that the PMR insisted on keeping a separate military force and its own policies for the weapons and ammunitions, while Moldova wanted a single military force. By July 2000, Putin proposed a state commission to be led by Primakov while Ukraine established a similar one. The Russian proposal became known as the Primakov project but was not accepted either in Tiraspol or in Chisinau. This document proposed a broadened Pridnestrovian participation in the foreign policy and no defence common space was considered.[1068] With regard to other issues, later on Russia committed itself to the withdrawal of Russian troops and equipment from Moldova, which were due to be retired by the end of 2001 and the remaining personnel until late 2002.

The fourth phase of the negotiating process started with the arrival of the Communist Party of Moldova to the government. As mentioned, he had campaigned for a further union with Russia and Belarus. Initially, Voronin showed intentions to settle the conflict but after some months, he saw no consideration for the Pridnestrovian position and a new territorial law reintroduced the structures of the Soviet period dividing Moldova into 31 districts and 2 autonomous regions (Gagauzia and Pridnestrovia).[1069] Together with this action, the mentioned introduction of new customs stamps by Moldova reduced drastically Pridnestrovian exchange with Ukraine in attempt to force the PMR authorities to new negotiations. This was done together with restrictions to travel abroad for more than 70

[1066] The content of the protocols can be consulted in 'ПЕРЕГОВОРНЫЙ ПРОЦЕСС МЕЖДУ МОЛДАВСКОЙ РЕСПУБЛИКОЙ И РЕСПУБЛИКОЙ МОЛДОВА В ДОКУМЕНТАХ,' Ministry of Foreign Affairs of the Pridnestrovian Moldovan Republic, Poligrafist, 2011, pages 88–101.

[1067] 'СОВМЕСТНОЕ ЗАЯВЛЕНИЕ участниковКиевкой встречи по вопросам нормализации отношений между Республикой Молдова и Приднстровьем' in 'ПЕРЕГОВОРНЫЙ ПРОЦЕСС МЕЖДУ МОЛДАВСКОЙ РЕСПУБЛИКОЙ И РЕСПУБЛИКОЙ МОЛДОВА В ДОКУМЕНТАХ,' Ministry of Foreign Affairs of the Pridnestrovian Moldovan Republic, Poligrafist, 2011, pages 102–103.

[1068] Vahl and Emerson, Idem, page 167.

[1069] Idem, page 168.

members of the Pridnestrovian leadership, in a move that was more symbolical, considering many of them had Russian or Ukrainian passports and not Moldovan ones.

The fifth phase saw the conflict arrive near a possible solution as close as it has ever envisioned since its origins. Even though, due to external pressures, a final resolution was not achieved. Initially, the three mediators in a protocol in Bratislava decided to set the base for regulating the Pridnestrovian issue. The documents pushed for a united federal Moldovan state even though many aspects were not clear in these first proposals envisioned during 2002.

Afterwards, in 2003, the Joint Constitutional Commission was formed and brought the arrival of the Kozak Memorandum. Before that, President Voronin invited Pridnestrovia to co-author a new Moldovan constitution. The Commission headed by both polities included also the three guarantors as well as the Council of Europe and the EU. By then, the EU and the United States supported Moldova's earlier sanctions imposing a travel ban on 17 Pridnestrovian leaders. It was supposed that the sanctions would encourage the Pridnestrovian leadership to comply to find a final political solution. Negotiations continued slowly and by November 2003, Moscow proposed a detailed memorandum with the basis of a new state. The name Kozak came from Dmitri Kozak who was part of Putin's staff. The plan envisaged a Federal Republic of Moldova with two subjects of the Federation, the PMR and Gagauzia and a federal territory that would include the rest of Moldova. Vahl and Emerson explain the proposal in this sense:

> The term 'asymmetric federation' is being used to describe the proposal since the federal territory and the two subjects would not have equal status. The federal government would be responsible for both the federation's competences and government of the federal territory.[1070]

There would be a division of competences between the Federation, the subjects and joint competences. There would be a lower house elected by proportional representations while the laws would need the assent of the senate in which there would be 13 senators elected by the federal lower house, 9 by Pridnestrovia and 4 by Gagauzia. It also included a transitional period until 2015 in which organic laws

---

[1070] Idem, page 171.

would need a three-quarters majority in the senate. The Federal Constitutional Court would have six judges appointed by the lower house, four by Pridnestrovia and one by Gagauzia.[1071]

Moreover, the voting rules differentiated between organic laws and ordinary laws. A two-thirds majority in the lower house could override the vetoes by the senate of ordinary laws but vetoes in organic laws could not be overridden. Finally, changes to the constitution required a four-fifths majority in the senate. Altogether, it is important to note that the proposal guaranteed the PMR the capacity to block legislation that could assure, for instance, a change in foreign policy or any future integration ambition by the Republic of Moldova as noted by Vahl and Emerson.[1072]

Consequently, President Smirnov agreed with a document that gave no military guarantees. Nevertheless, he wanted Russian military deployment for 30 years. The document was first posted in the Pridnestrovian Ministry of Foreign Affairs.[1073] The Moldovan opposition parties rejected the proposal. In that sense, both the EU and the United States also opposed the document and different opinions were present in the OSCE. Originally, President Voronin had supported the document but apparently, he changed his decision due to the pressure of Western countries. Vladimir Putin had already planned a trip to Chisinau to sign what would be the final solution of the Pridnestrovian conflict but it had to be cancelled after Voronin's refusal.[1074]

The document proposed by Russia was a pragmatic attempt to solve the issue, a realist approach by Moscow blocked by Western interests. It was, by then, the only feasible way to create one single polity that would include both Moldova and Pridnestrovia. Instead, Moldova would have to sacrifice any European integration expectations and to deny expectations of becoming a NATO member. Moldova had the opportunity to decide the issue in virtue of what was

---

[1071] Idem, page 172.
[1072] Idem.
[1073] The complete version of the document can still be found on the website. 'Memorandum on basic principles of the state system of the united state,' November 15, 2003, accessed on March 3, 2016. http://mfa-pmr.org/en/archive/all/2003
[1074] Vahl and Emerson, Op. Cit., pages 173–174.

achievable and instead, the territory again became hostage of geopolitics. It means the United States and the EU were the ones to decide regarding their interest while blocking the only viable solution.

As long as Russia will have influence over Pridnestrovia, the goal will be to block the adherence of Moldova (with Pridnestrovia included) to the EU, and mostly to NATO. Therefore, if Moldovan authorities wanted as a goal to retake control of Pridnestrovia under a single polity, the Kozak memorandum was the only way to achieve it. Instead, if Moldova pretends to give priority to European integration (achievable or not), it seems impossible by now, considering the current political forces, to include in that effort the territory of Pridnestrovia. Instead, it would be simpler to let Pridnestrovia go as a separate entity.

By 2005, the European Union and Ukraine under President Yushchenko started to be more active to solve the Pridnestrovian conflict. In fact, the enlargement of 2007 that included Romania and Bulgaria meant that Moldova was already in the border of the EU, therefore compelling the EU authorities to look for a possible solution with its new neighbour. In that sense, since September 2005, the EU and the United States started to be directly involved in the negotiation process as observers, thus expanding the format to the current '5+2'.

The format gave no new results. Chisinau insisted on the adoption of a special status for Pridnestrovia respecting the territorial integrity of the Republic of Moldova, while Tiraspol advocated for normalizing the relations between both polities considering the existing realities, which in practice recognized the Pridnestrovian statehood.[1075] Instead, Tiraspol pushed more for a '1+1' format or with Moscow included while only the '5+2' for consultations.

Altogether, the status quo has since then prevailed. After the failed attempt by the Georgian Army to recover South Ossetia in 2008, the Russian Government tried again to convince the Moldovan authorities to consider without success the Kozak Memorandum. A meeting between Voronin, Smirnov and President Medvedev on 18 March 2009, in Moscow pretended to relaunch the

---

[1075] Stavila, Ion, 'Evolution in settlement of the Transnistrian conflict,' in *The Foreign Policy of the Republic of Moldova (1998–2008)*, Friedirch Ebert Stiftung, Chisinau, Cartdidact, 2010, page 213.

negotiation process beyond the '5+2' format but it did not obtain further results. The meeting intended to put the Republic of Moldova and Pridnestrovia in equal negotiating circumstances.[1076] Still, at the end, it only could conclude that the only acceptable mechanism was the prevailing '5+2'.[1077] In the meantime, the Moldovan political elite started to rely much on the support of the EU and the US to overcome the difficulties in the negotiation process. This brought a halt to the negotiation process, while depicting it as part of the broader political and geopolitical struggle present between Russia, the United States, the EU and some of its members, a struggle that includes several issues and not only Moldova and Pridnestrovia.

There have been even other proposals to solve the conflict like the 'Belkovski plan' by Russian political analyst Stanislav Belkovski, who called for a 'civilization break' to provide opportunity to Moldova to unite with Romania.[1078] Instead, another proposal even suggested decoupling Pridnestrovia of the Moldovan borders for a certain period while it would fall under a protectorate mandate with international guaranties.[1079] All these political speculations at the end would have to consider the political reality. Russia has around 1,200 stationed troops in Pridnestrovia, and is not willing to accept a deal in which the geopolitical orientation of the area would be opposed to Moscow. Therefore, if the Moldovan political elite would like to keep Pridnestrovia they should take this into account. Instead, if Western offers seem more persuading for Chisinau, it does not seem foreseeable to find a solution in the meantime accepted by all parts.

And what about Ukraine?
The Pridnestrovian Moldovan Republic also considers in its official foreign policy the relation with Ukraine as one of its priorities. In-

---

[1076] Idem, page 216.
[1077] The Common Declaration can be consulted in 'ПЕРЕГОВОРНЫЙ ПРОЦЕСС МЕЖДУ МОЛДАВСКОЙ РЕСПУБЛИКОЙ И РЕСПУВЛИКОЙ МОЛДОВА В ДОКУМЕНТАХ,' Ministry of Foreign Affairs of the Pridnestrovian Moldovan Republic, Poligrafist, 2011, page 153.
[1078] Stavila, Idem, page 218.
[1079] Idem, page 218.

stead, Ukrainian position regarding Pridnestrovia has changed notably during the last two decades, depending on who is in the presidency. In that sense, Ukraine's inner political fragility has also reflected in the relations and events regarding its neighbours, and it is not clear until what point the government has pursued a sort of national interest or one of foreign powers. At the end, the settlement in Pridnestrovia should be related also to a matter of Ukrainian national security, considering the territory lies at its borders.

Nevertheless, a border treaty between Moldova and Ukraine was signed on 18 August 1999, while some works regarding border delimitation would be followed between both countries.[1080] Instead, the most important issue for the Moldovan side was the fact that they lacked customs control on the border between Pridnestrovia and Ukraine. For instance, when Moldova joined the WTO, Chisinau introduced new customs stamps and annulled the old ones. This action forbade in practice import and exports from Pridnestrovia, which carried since 1990 operations with the older stamps. At the beginning, Ukraine recognized old stamps as valid for two years but on 15 May 2003, a new protocol between Moldova and Ukraine was signed and it included that all transportation of cargo would be only with documents issued by Chisinau.[1081]

Ukraine, as mentioned, became under Kuchma a mediator and guarantor of the process of a peaceful settlement together with Russia and OSCE. The Ukrainian Government participated in the proposal of July 2002 together with the other mediators to settle the conflict, the same proposal that was later rejected. Besides, when Moldovan authorities refused to give customs clearance for the products from Pridnestrovia, alleging smuggling on the Ukrainian customs, it was only after the EU intervened with a Border Assistance Mission between both countries, and following the protocol both signed on 15 May 2003,[1082] that the crossing of goods restarted in the borders with Pridnestrovia.

[1080] Some minor border changes were agreed between both countries. For further details, see: Boian, Victoria, 'Relations of the Republic of Moldova with Ukraine,' in *The Foreign Policy of the Republic of Moldova (1998–2008)*, Friedirch Ebert Stiftung, Chisinau, Cartdidact, 2010, pages 51–53.
[1081] Idem, page 55.
[1082] Idem, page 57.

Until this point, Ukraine's participation in the conflict had been mostly regarding border and customs issues and without deeper proposals. By then, Ukraine had not only recognized the territorial integrity of the Republic of Moldova but had avoided to seek for any further territorial gains regarding Pridnestrovia, even without considering that almost 29% of the Pridnestrovian population are ethnic Ukrainians[1083] and many of them also have a Ukrainian passport. Besides, the denunciation of the Molotov-Ribbentrop Pact, left open the possibility that the territory at the left bank of the Dniester, which did not belong to the former Bessarabia, could be considered then part of the former Ukrainian SSR. Therefore, giving a potential legal argument to Ukraine to pursue territorial gain in the area. Instead, possibly fearing that in Ukrainian territory, there were Romanian and Hungarian-speaking minorities, that could be used consequently by Moldova or Romania for further territorial gains, Ukrainian authorities never mentioned the issue. Besides, it is important to consider also that during the first decade after the Soviet fall, the situation in Crimea was not completely settled. Therefore, even if there could be a hypothetical geopolitical interest to obtain more territorial gains in the Pridnestrovia area, it was not realistic for Kiev to pursue it, until other issues in the relation with Russia were settled.

The arrival of Yushchenko as explained signified a new pro-US foreign policy that among other things tried to revive Ukraine's participation to solve the conflict in the area. Yushchenko presented his plan during the GUAM Summit in Chisinau in May 2005 with the goal of weakening the Russian position. It proposed a conflict settlement in three phases. The 'Yushchenko plan' included a 'democratization' and demilitarization of the region.[1084] In that sense, demilitarization meant to assure the departure of the Russian troops while democratization would mean an electoral process recognized by the EU and the US. During his term, there were also other proposals like the one from Poroshenko, who by then was Head of the

---

[1083] 'Country overview,' Ministry of Foreign Affairs of Pridnestrovian Moldovan Republic, accessed on March 3, 2016. http://mfa-pmr.org/en/about_republic
[1084] Stavila, Op. Cit., page 210.

National Security and Defense Council. From that post, he attempted also to pursue foreign policy and devised a plan to settle the conflict with Pridnestrovia, a plan initially accepted by Moldova.[1085]

Altogether, Yushchenko's effort was in line with US interest of weakening the Russian position in the area and his plan. The Pridnestrovian leader Igor Smirnov initially considered it, but later rejected it when a new protocol between Moldova and Ukraine established that access for goods could be provided only based on the legal customs requisites. This action affected directly the economy of Pridnestrovia and brought consequently a refusal by the PMR authorities to accept Yushchenko's plan arguing they were making Pridnestrovia subject of an economy blockade. Besides, the Kremlin's answer then was the already mentioned Russian Federation ban on imports of Moldovan wines on the Russian market.

Under Yanukovych's regime, afterwards, the status quo prevailed and it was only after the Ukrainian crisis and Yanukovych's fall that Pridnestrovia regained its strategic importance. Volunteers came from Pridnestrovia to sustain pro-Russian protests in neighbouring Odessa or other regions while even some went to combat with the rebels in the Donbass. Instead, the nomination of a highly controversial personality as governor of Odessa, like Mikhail Saakashvili, shows how Ukrainian authorities still perceive the region as a pro-Russian stronghold that needs to be blocked. Moreover, the fact that the current Ukrainian Government decided to block the access[1086] of Russian troops to Pridnestrovia shows that it intends clearly not only to lock the Russian supply, but also to provoke a stronger Russian reaction, which consequently would be completely detrimental to the already fragile Ukrainian polity, as it is obvious that the Russian Armed Forces do not intend to risk the provisioning of its troops in the area.

That raises the question if Ukraine were to be a sovereign state, what should be its position regarding Pridnestrovia? What would be

---

[1085] Wilson, Andrew, *Ukraine's Orange Revolution*, Op. Cit., page 164.
[1086] 'Pro-Russian "republic" Transnistria calls up reservists as East-West tensions flare,' *The Telegraph*, July 22, 2015, accessed on July 23, 2015. http://www.telegraph.co.uk/news/worldnews/europe/moldova/11753765/Pro-Russian-republic-Transnistria-calls-up-reservists-as-East-West-tensions-flare.html

the Ukrainian national interest in that sense? A multi-ethnic and multilingual Ukraine could be more suitable for Pridnestrovia rather than a union with Moldova? Would it need to receive a kind of republic status with certain autonomy like the one Crimea used to have until 2014? The subject could be used to bargain with Russia after the events in Crimea. Even though, this blurry hypothesis became less plausible when the pro-US Saakashvili became governor in Odessa. Besides, the strong Russian media influence in Pridnestrovia together with how the local population perceives the Ukrainian conflict would not make it suitable in any sense to consider this proposal in the present conditions or any further approach with the authorities in Kiev.

At the end, policies adopted by Yushchenko and by Poroshenko responded not to a supposed Ukrainian national interest but to a US interest to weaken the Pridnestrovian regime without regarding the devastating local effects it would bring in the long term to the already damaged relation between Russia and Ukraine. Therefore, it not only reduces the possibility of a solution to the conflict and increases the strategic meaning of the area in the global geopolitical struggle between the dominant actors. Therefore, Ukrainian's role in the conflict has struggled between being an actor and playing the role of a US emissary. Meanwhile, Kiev is not able to define a solution to the de facto division between the two polities around the Dniester. Thus, it all goes back to geopolitics.

3.5 The geopolitical role of the region

To conclude this chapter, Moldova and Pridnestrovia remain part of the numerous unsolved political and territorial issues consequence of the mishandled disappearance of the Soviet Union. The rush in which USSR's dissolution occurred did not consider the potential risks due to the political and ethnolinguistic divisions present. In this case, the most important fact that forbids a solution between Moldova and Pridnestrovia lies in the fact that both polities and local elites depend notably on foreign support. Meanwhile, they have no possibilities to complete by themselves the desired state-building process each would like for their respective territories.

Therefore, local identities have not been able to produce itself a political force that could push for recognition or a solution accepted in the international scene. At the end, the situation is quite simple. On one side, the United States, the EU and some of its members like Germany, Poland and obviously Romania would like to include Moldova into their sphere of influence, even if the how and until what point are not clear. In that sense, the inclusion of Moldova in this area should also include the territory of Pridnestrovia as having an unrecognized state between Moldova and Ukraine would be quite uncomfortable considering the potential influence Russia could have. Some voices, as mentioned, consider that only as part of Romania could Moldova aspire to join the EU or even NATO. To achieve this goal, there have been different actions. The ones with a general perspective like the Association agreement between Moldova and the EU, and more concrete and specific ones like the visa-free regime given by the EU, to try to seduce the local population of the potential benefits of a pro-Western orientation.

On the other hand, Russia would like Moldova to remain as a 'neutral' country, neutrality interpreted as not being anti-Russian. Moscow has some advantages in that sense. First, the peacekeeping troops in the region, although not a lot in number, are enough as a symbolic presence to forbid a military solution and any kind of settlement without Moscow's agreement. Besides, the existing economic bonds Moldova has with Moscow, mostly in the energetic sphere in which gas provisions come mostly from Gazprom, weigh together with the fact that Pridnestrovia receives some sort of non-unofficial subsidies in that sphere.

Moreover, there is the sympathy of a 'common *ethos*' shared as part of a post-Soviet society that includes several cultural and social links where the Russian language plays a considerable role. The image of the Patriarch of Moscow which 'protects' his patriarchy against the 'damaging' Western influence is not an element to be neglected with ease. People from Pridnestrovia and the local political elite have shown the will to establish a different polity even if they are all englobed in the same Soviet heritage. The prospect of European integration and the 'visa-free travel' do not seduce the same way in Pridnestrovia[1087] as in Moldova. The 'menace' of a Westernization and the 'decadence' product of Western values are

---

[1087] 'Приднестровье евроинтегрироваться не спешит,' September 10, 2015, accessed on September 10, 2015. http://www.pnp.ru/news/detail/96907

common conceptions among the local population. It is even common to find comments (among people with university degrees!) that consider issues like same-sex marriage as part of a plot organized by the West to destroy orthodox society.

It is important to remind ourself that the existing divisions, as shown by Kuchler,[1088] are not ethnic but political. Understanding the origin of these political divisions would allow finding a solution. Moreover, Moldova and Pridnestrovia do not have the same strategic value as other countries like Ukraine, Georgia or even Azerbaijan for the West. Therefore, foreign involvement is less and could become part of a whole bargain ordeal. The ongoing political situation in Ukraine has a bigger value for both the United States and Russia and, consequently, the solution of the Pridnestrovian conflict receives a lower priority. Instead, from a strategic point of view, if the geopolitical interest from the West is to weaken Moscow, as Liddell Hart would sustain, strategy would advise an 'indirect approach'.[1089] In this case, it would mean put pressure on Pridnestrovian issues while Russia gives more attention to Ukraine and the Donbass. Perhaps, this could explain the decision by Ukrainian authorities to forbid the arrival of supplies for Russian troops in Pridnestrovia or the Moldovan negative to allow the circulation of cars with Pridnestrovian plates[1090] for instance.

Instead, the status quo is quite functional for Moscow. It blocks any possible Moldovan integration into the EU and gives the Kremlin advantage with the influence it has in Gagauzia and Taraclia. For the Pridnestrovian authorities, it allows them to have no official international obligations, while they continue to decide their inner affairs in a kind of autonomous way. Therefore, it allows to wait until

---

[1088] Kuchler, op. cit.
[1089] Liddel Hart considers that direct attacks on firm defensive positions usually do not obtain positive results while it is better to disrupt the enemy's equilibrium by searching always for the weakest and unexpected point. The indirect approach theory, even if applied for the military analysis, can be certainly applied to politics and geopolitics. At the end, as Clausewitz would say, the war is an extension of politics. For a deepening on Liddel Hart's theory, it is possible to consult, Liddel, Hart B.H., 'Strategy,' New York, Meridian, 1991.
[1090] 'Nina, Shtanski': 'New sanctions of Moldova against Pridnestrovian car owners are "an own goal",' August 27, 2015, accessed on March 3, 2016. Ministry of Foreign Affairs of Pridnestrovian Moldavian Republic. http://mfa-pmr.org/en/BMt

conditions are conducive for a settlement similar to the Kozar Memorandum that guaranteed Pridnestrovia a considerable autonomy and capacity to block Moldovan aspirations to join the EU or NATO.

Altogether, if the EU and the United States would like to keep Moldova under their area of influence, it should be noted that in the present conditions it would be impossible to do it with the inclusion of the Pridnestrovian territory. That leaves two possible solutions, either Moldova leaves Pridnestrovia and decides its own destiny with Russia, with Ukraine or independently or instead a new sort of federal or confederal state is agreed on the already mentioned basis, guaranteeing the neutrality and recognizing the multi-ethnic base of the country.

Overall, it seems unlikely that the future events will be decided locally. Moldova and Pridnestrovia have a geopolitical role and either future European or Eurasian integration for these polities will likely respond to the correlation of forces in the global scenario among the United States, Germany and Russia. In that sense, local elites are weaker than in Ukraine and therefore less capable to influence and decide their own destiny, leaving the vicissitudes of the future events in a considerable way on how the relations will evolve between the main global actors.

4 Conclusions

4.1 Future clashes between Russia and the West

4.1.1 The evolution of the relation between the United States and Russia

This research showed the great influence of geopolitical processes over the studied polities. Therefore, before answering if Ukraine, Moldova and Pridnestrovia can eventually build a sovereign polity, it would be necessary to point out some remarks about where the relation between Russia and the West and more specifically with the United States is heading.

As of January 2016, the relation between Western powers and Russia continues to be based mostly on the tone of the relation between Washington and Moscow. To that extent, the Ukrainian crisis showed different positions by some EU members and the United States but also portrayed the inability of the former to achieve any sustainable political goals by themselves. US agenda is very clear, to expand its area of influence among Europe, incorporating as much as possible former members of the Soviet Union into that area. There were different options in the United States on how to do it, as shown between the realist positions of Kissinger and Brzezinski or the neoconservative approach of one sector of the Republican Party, though the goal would be the same, attempting to diminish Russia's position in the international scene and weaken its alliance with China.

Meanwhile, US hegemonic position in the global scene allows Washington to risk more than EU members in the Ukrainian arena. To that extent, the military conflict in the Donbass with its peak during 2014–2015 was quite functional for the United States. On one side, Russian support to the rebels had a high political cost internationally;[1091] meanwhile for the EU it meant that they had a mil-

---

[1091] The actions in Crimea and the conflict in Ukraine highly increased Vladimir Putin's popularity among the Russian population.

itary conflict in its borders together with the potential influx of refugees. Instead, the United States far away from any serious repercussions could showcase itself as the only guarantor of stability.

The sanctions imposed against Russia by the Obama administration in different rounds since March 2014 have targeted different personalities, Russian companies, businessmen related to the Kremlin, former Ukrainian officials, Crimean officials, and it became the largest set of sanctions applied against Russia since the fall of the Soviet Union. They were followed up by similar or lesser sanctions by the EU and countries like Canada,[1092] Australia and even Albany, Iceland and Montenegro. The sanctions led by the United States intended to revert or at least diminish Russian actions on the rest of the Ukrainian territory as happened in Crimea. The second round of sanctions imposed by the United States on 28 April 2014, included a ban on business transactions on 7 Russian officials and 17 Russian companies. This follow-up measure proved useless to the US intentions; meanwhile the insurgency in East Ukraine increased. A third round of sanctions came on 17 July 2014, affecting Russian energy firms like Rosneft and Novatek and banks like Gazprombank and Vneshekonombank.[1093] The sanctions were accompanied to a different degree by the EU set of sanctions. Finally, in December 2015 a final list of restrictions on 34 individuals intended to reinforce the existing punitive measures.[1094]

Altogether, by January 2016, it was clear that the sanctions had not obtained the desired effect by the United States. Even if Russia suffered the effects of a harsh economic crisis during 2015, in no way the Kremlin showed any intention of changing its foreign policy, or to put it in other terms, they continued to act sovereignly in the areas that touched Moscow's strategic interests.

In that sense, Russia's national security strategy for 2016 acknowledged clearly and from a different position the policy of the

---

[1092] The sanctions by Canada and Australia also raise the question of how the 'sovereign' interests of those countries mix on the Ukrainian crisis, or if they have any real foreign policy of their own. Note of the author.

[1093] 'Third wave of sanctions slams Russian stocks,' *The Moscow Times*, July 17, 2014, accessed on March 3, 2016. http://www.themoscowtimes.com/business/article/new-sanctions-wave-hits-russian-stocks/503604.html

[1094] 'US imposes financial restrictions to reinforce Ukraine sanctions,' December 22, 2015, accessed on March 3, 2016. http://www.theguardian.com/us-news/2015/dec/22/us-financial-restrictions-ukraine-sanctions-russia

Conclusions 429

United States. It perceives as a grave risk the promotion of colour revolutions as one of the main threats against Russia in its areas of interests. The document also more clearly recognizes the rivalry with the United States while explaining it this way: 'Russia's independent foreign and domestic policy has been met with counteraction by the United States and its allies, seeking to maintain its dominance in world affairs.'[1095]

To that extent, Moscow perceives NATO expansion as a threat to their national security and therefore planned its defence strategy accordingly. The Russian Government also is aware of the importance of political factors that govern the main economic processes in the world.[1096] Meanwhile, Russia will continue to perceive Ukraine as strategic and does not intend to modify its policies due to the ongoing sanctions.

On the other side, during the State of the Union Speech given by Barack Obama, on 12 January 2016, he recognized Ukraine and Syria as 'client-states'.[1097] Obama, with that speech, intentionally or not, was recognizing both polities as part of a geopolitical struggle and as entities without their own sovereignty, therefore implicating that the outcome of the Ukrainian conflict could be related with negotiations in different fronts.

To that extent, Russian's role is also strategic considering scenarios like in the negotiation about Iran's nuclear programme, or the same way it would be very difficult to find a solution to other issues like North Korea's nuclear arsenal without a Chinese and Russian intervention. Hence, in Russia they know that the Ukrainian front, even if very important from a geostrategic point of view for them, is not the only area of concurrency with the United States.

In that sense, the Kremlin understood perfectly the meaning of the geopolitical move that meant the military action by the Russian forces in Syria. It opened a completely new front for bargaining with

---

[1095] 'Russia's national security strategy for 2016 in 9 key points,' Klimentyev Michael, Sputnik, December 31, 2015, accessed on March 3, 2016. https://www.rt.com/news/327608-russia-national-security-strategy/
[1096] Idem.
[1097] Obama, Barack, 'The transcript of President Obama's final State of the Union: What he said, and what it meant,' *Washington Post*, January 12, 2016, accessed on January 12, 2016. https://www.washingtonpost.com/news/the-fix/wp/2016/01/12/what-obama-said-in-his-state-of-the-union-address-and-what-it-meant/

the West. The Russian Air Force's operations to sustain the Assad regime in Syria allowed the opportunity to put into use some of the most modern military technology in possession of the Russian Armed Forces. The cruise missiles launched from the Caspian Sea, together with the opportunity to use the most modern strike fighter, the Su-34, or to give its first combat use to one of the Cold War icons like the bomber Tu-95, intended to show the efficiency and capabilities of the military arsenal present in the Russian Federation.[1098] It also helped give a clear boost to Bashar-al-Assad's regime in Syria to make it clear that Russian's presence in the area is considered strategic for the Kremlin.

Besides, the bombings against the Syrian opposition and against members of the so-called Islamic State made the United States and its allies rethink the relation with Moscow as ISIS carried a greater threat than Russian actions in Ukraine. In that sense, a contradictory position became visible in which Russia and the United States coordinated partially their own air military operations in Syria against a 'common enemy'; meanwhile the United States continued to apply sanctions against Russia. Altogether, Moscow's main goal remains to keep Syria as an allied territory while carrying out bombings against ISIS positions but also against other rebel groups. These actions gave renewed support to Assad and made him even more dependable on Moscow to remain in power. Therefore, Syria became a solid bargaining chip while the further terrorist attacks in Paris during November 2015 transformed for the Western powers Assad's position into the 'least of the evils', compared with ISIS risk. It became necessary again to deal with Russia.

Consequently, in this switching relation between the United States and Russia, it is difficult that the future US administration that will take over Barack Obama from 2017 will change notably its foreign policy regarding Ukraine and Russia. Donald Trump, for example, has suggested he will 'get along fine' with Vladimir Putin,[1099]

[1098] Axe, David, 'Russia pounds ISIS with biggest bomber raid in decades,' November 17, 2015, accessed on November 17, 2015. http://www.theda ilybeast.com/articles/2015/11/17/russia-pounds-isis-with-biggest-bomber-r aid-in-decades.html

[1099] 'Donald Trump says he'll "get along fine" with Russian president Vladimir Putin,' *ABC News*, December 20, 2015, accessed on December 20, 2015.

while the Russian president has also expressed positively about his candidature. On the other hand, Hillary Clinton was one of the promoters of the famous 'restart' between Russia-US relations while she was secretary of state. Either way, it seems Realpolitik will prevail.

Other aspects will certainly influence the relation. The United States has the upper hand in the Middle East and in Europe and has the support of allies like Turkey. For instance, the shooting down[1100] of a Russian Su-24 by the Turkish Air Force on 24 November 2015, in what represented the first shooting down of a Russian or Soviet plane by a NATO member since the Korean War represented a shocking event for the Russian Air Force that until then had enjoyed air supremacy in the area. It changed completely the tone of the relation between Russia and Turkey and brought a new set of sanctions against the Turkish Government together with the deployment of the S-400, the most modern anti-aircraft missile system in the world.

In that sense, the Russian-US geopolitical tussle remains in a stalemate, which considering the more advantageous position by

---

http://abcnews.go.com/Politics/donald-trump-hell-fine-russian-president-vladimir-putin/story?id=35872623

[1100] Ankara claimed the event came as a response to numerous violations of the Turkish air space by Russian military planes. They sustained that they gave 10 warnings by radio to the plane in five minutes. Also, the Turkish government recognized that the Russian plane was only 17 seconds in Turkish air space. Therefore, Ankara's position became contradictory; meanwhile, an operation of that kind would require that the F-16 fighters that shoot the Russian plane to take off in advance from an air base retired from that area. Not enough timing for the acknowledged 17 seconds. At the opposite, the argument that the mission could be a sort of provocation by the Russian Air Force to identify possible Turkish reactions, even if plausible in other contexts, is not sustainable in this case. In that sense, for that kind of operation the Russian Air Force counted on better and more equipped airplanes in the scenario like the SU-30MK or the SU-34 that would be able of defending themselves and recognize risks easier. Altogether, the event, besides remaining as the first attack by a NATO member against the Russian Federation, certainly had a political intention on the Turkish side. The immediate reaction by Ankara to call for a NATO meeting instead of discussing the event with its Russian counterpart could show the event as part of a Turkish strategy to step up the tone against the Russian presence in the area. Until what point the United States knew or instigated the mission will remain unknown. Note of the author.

the United States could be considered a minor or even pyrrhic success for the Kremlin. Moreover, Putin is aware that economically, Russia is behind. The Eurasian Economic Union and its members are far from becoming a serious economic competitor to other economic areas like the EU, or more intricate projects, like the Trans-Pacific Trade Partnership (TPP).[1101] This last project, planned by the United States, includes strategically located countries in the Pacific and surrounding China. To this extent, the words from Barack Obama in his last State of the Union address are eloquent:

> That's how we forged a trans pacific partnership to open markets, and protect workers and the environment, and advance American leadership in Asia. It cuts 18,000 taxes on products made in America which will then support more good jobs here in America. With TPP, China does not set the rules in that region, we do.[1102]

Altogether, this agreement, even if more addressed against China, puts Russia also in a more difficult situation, forcing Moscow to make the alliance with Beijing stronger.

As seen, the strategy of the United States in the global scenario includes different local approaches. The ones regarding Europe and Russia will certainly have an influence on the local political events in Ukraine, Moldova and Pridnestrovia, though they are not the only ones. The European Union could also have more political weight, even if its inner struggles have complicated the prospect of influencing certain matters more. To that extent, it remains a challenge for the EU to determine what kind of relation they need and want with Russia, and, second, to define the possibility of an independent position from the United States.

4.1.2 Could the EU develop an independent stance from the United States?

The tone of the relation between the United States and Russia is clear amidst all the variables present around the globe and the other actors involved. The intentions towards Ukraine, Moldova and Pridnestrovia are also visible from both sides. Instead, the position

---

[1101] The Draft of the TPP, which has not yet signed, would represent a 'free trade' area between twelve members: Brunei, Chile, New Zealand, Singapore, Australia, Canada, Japan, Malaysia, Mexico, Peru, United States and Vietnam.
[1102] Obama, Op. Cit.

of the European Union appears complex and changing while the possibility of really counting as a geopolitical actor fades away, as the EU seems to prefer just to follow the policies pursued by the United States.

The EU and its members have failed to enforce any kind of pan-European solutions to the cumulous recent issues that appeared on its territory. Not only a single EU position would guarantee a stronger and more agile response in the national scene, it could allow the EU to be considered as a geopolitical force, something that by now is far from reality.

For example, the lack of a European migration policy, which could handle easier and more effectively the present refugee crisis, is only one case. National governments, curiously from the countries that receive lesser amounts of migrants, are blocking with a populist and sometimes xenophobic approach a unified European position to handle the issue and establish specific quotas to the countries to receive a determined number of refugees by year. This single issue portrays the capacity of governments with a low economic weight in the EU like Poland or Hungary to block strategic goals that would allow from a European perspective to solve the biggest migratory crisis in the history of the EU.

Besides, not only in this case the EU has failed. Austerity policies imposed on Greece and the failure to achieve a simple and European solution for the debt crisis with the lack of will to create the Eurobonds[1103] would be another example. A strong negative reaction from the German side that did not want to carry the biggest weight of a 'European' debt meant that the proposal has been frozen until now. Meanwhile, austerity policies become each day more unpopular, while they create a stronger division among EU members. It also allows the emergence of populist movements with an anti-

---

[1103] The Eurobonds are proposed government bonds by the 19 members of the Eurozone. There have been different mechanisms proposed to create this debt investment mechanism from a European perspective that could allow to affront the debt from the single members of the Eurozone. To check details about the proposal submitted by the European commission, see: 'European Commission Green Paper on the feasibility of introducing stability bonds,' MEMO 11//820, November 23, 2011, accessed on January 20, 2016. http://europa.eu/rapid/press-release_MEMO-11-820_en.htm

European stance while the EU tends to be more perceived as a technocratic entity not capable of solving or diminishing the effects of increasing social differences among its citizens.

In this context, neither the lack of a migratory policy or the absence of the Eurobonds is the biggest risk. The lack of a European foreign policy that would allow handling from a European perspective strategic and immediate issues relating to security especially in the nearby borders is still a big issue.

Regarding the relation with Russia, the role of the EU has been diminished by its real capabilities but mostly by the lack of will to have an independent role. To this extent, it is worth reminding that EU representatives had already negotiated a deal that allowed the exit of Victor Yanukovych with Russia in February 2014 and that could have avoided the following events in the Donbass and Crimea. Instead, the ousting of Yanukovych and the rapid recognition of the new Ukrainian authorities by the United States, followed by the EU, meant for Moscow a refusal of the former agreements. Later on, after the ordeal in Crimea, the consequences, detailed in the former pages, forced the EU to follow up with sanctions against Russia promoted by the United States, but that became notably counterproductive for the European side.

In that sense, Russia applied countermeasures also in August 2014. They included a ban on products from the EU and the United States, like fruits, vegetables, meat, fish, milk and dairy imports. Several EU members[1104] like the Czech Republic, Slovakia, Cyprus, Greece and Hungary expressed their reluctance to the sanctions, but did not oppose the vote. The effect was devastating, as the food exports from the EU to Russia had meant 11.8 billion Euros in 2013.[1105] It was not the only case, though, in which the EU in practice simply auto inflicted damage on itself. The EU pressured[1106] to

---

[1104] 'Четыре страны ЕС не поддержали расширение санкций против России,' August 31, 2014, accessed on August 31, 2014. http://finance.bigmir.net/n ews/economics/50251-Chetyre-strany-ES-ne-podderzhali-rasshirenie-sankc ij-protiv-Rossii?utm_source=exchange&utm_medium=banner&utm_campa ign=crosspromo

[1105] 'Russia hits west with food import ban in sanctions row,' August 7, 2014, accessed on August 7, 2014. http://www.bbc.com/news/world-europe-28687172

[1106] 'Еврокомиссия давит на участников South Stream,' June 19, 2014, accessed on August 31, 2014. http://www.kommersant.ru/doc/2494070

suspend the construction of the South Stream gas pipe that would have seriously diminished Ukrainian strategic role as transit country and guaranteed gas provisions for EU members like Bulgaria, Greece, Italy, Austria and Hungary among others. The complaints from the affected countries were not considered. Instead, the United States' interest again prevailed to block a strategic Russian project that in this case was also fundamental for the European gas supply and could guarantee the arrival of gas independently from the vicissitudes in Ukraine. No single EU member could be benefited by the suspension of the South Stream gas pipe, still it took place. Therefore, a hypothetical EU interest was never conceived and without a glimpse of a European interest it is impossible to have a subsequent EU foreign policy.

Even single members openly sacrificed to follow up on the sanctions. In the French case, for instance, the military industry that has a considerable role in local economy also participated in the arms embargo. The French Government cancelled the order to deliver to Russia two Mistral-class warships in a deal that was worth 1.2 billion euro. Even the minister of foreign affairs, Laurent Fabius, acknowledged that the loss of contracts would have a negative effect on the French economy.[1107]

The following up of the sanctions raises the following question: What the EU has obtained until now from them? The answer is clear, nothing. The only difference with the United States is that the EU and its members have lesser margin to negotiate with Russia. To that extent, the attempts to design a genuine European or EU interest and push for a European position against Russia have been weak. First, because still some EU members, mostly the Baltic countries and Poland but also the United Kingdom, clearly give preference to attaching themselves to the US position before attempting to define or defend a unified European one. In countries like Lithuania and Poland sometimes this extreme pro-US stance reached the point of ridicule like the occasion in which the minister of foreign

---

[1107] 'France may scrap Russian warship deal over Ukraine crisis,' March 18, 2014, accessed on March 18, 2014. http://sputniknews.com/russia/20140318/188536562/France-May-Scrap-Russian-Warship-Deal-over-Ukraine-Crisis.html

affairs, Radoslaw Sikorski, after a meeting with John Kerry was quoted as saying:

> You know that the Polish-U.S. alliance isn't worth anything ... It is downright harmful, because it creates a false sense of security ... Complete bullshit. We'll get in conflict with the Germans, Russians and we'll think that everything is super, because we gave the Americans a blow job. Losers. Complete losers.[1108]

In this context, it is quite difficult for the EU to attempt to design an own solution for the Ukrainian crisis, though Angela Merkel in a certain way tried it, when she pushed to organize the second round of the Minsk agreements. After long discussions with Vladimir Putin and with Obama's approval, the second round of the Minsk agreements intended with the French-German guidance to push for a resolution that would be convenient for Ukraine and Russia with EU's support.

The way these agreements were negotiated evidenced two factors regarding the role of the EU. First, the complete absence of Federica Mogherini, who as the High Representative of the Union for Foreign Affairs and Security Policy, would need to have a notable role if there is any kind of pretension to at least formally show the political role of the EU in the search of a solution to the conflict. The second is that again, as Carlo Jean considered, the only possibility now to the EU to have any role is through Germany. As mentioned in the first pages of this work, a 'Germanized-Europe' is better than the 'No-Europe'. It was a genuine attempt to solve an ongoing conflict during the winter of 2014–2015 that was affecting directly the EU in many senses. A good political intention was not enough, mostly because the EU had no real way to enforce the agreements. They would be hanging on the 'good will' of Vladimir Putin and Petro Poroshenko. The former with his clearly own agenda and the second quite dependable and influenced by the United States and the IMF. Therefore, the second round of the Minsk agreements served at least to stop the large-scale bloodbath in the Donbass but still did not envisage the possibility of achieving a final settlement of the conflict.

[1108] "'We gave the Americans a blow job," got nothing, says polish foreign minister,' June 22, 2014, accessed on January 25, 2016. http://www.new sweek.com/we-gave-americans-blow-job-got-nothing-says-polish-foreign-m inister-255863

To that extent, the EU relation towards Russia passed from an anti-Putin Hysteria in media to the 'Mon cher Vladimir'[1109] of Françoise Hollande to Putin. That meeting meant also subsequent agreements between France and Russia to coordinate operations in Syria and a notable change of tone, but showed a clear absence of policy towards Russia.

The EU has a more complex position regarding Russia; therefore, it is imperative to rethink the relation independently not to say sovereignly if possible. There is an interdependence in the energy sector while there are common borders and conflicts not only in Ukraine but in other European scenarios in which both actors have political interests at stake. In that sense, it is more than ever needed to consider Carlo Jean's words when he says that in the history of humankind there have never existed civil powers.

> Ma, nella storia, non sono mai esistite potenze solo civili. Se vuole essere un attore geopolitico globale, l'Europa non può limitarsi ad essere una grande Svizzera, né a escludersi dalle turbolenze del mondo.[1110]

If the EU wants to count, they need to have a European Defence Policy not submitted and dependable on the United States. It needs to create mechanisms that allow it to enforce measures and to be respected at the international scene. Instead, this is a very peculiar case in which the EU prefers being 'protected' by the United States without acknowledging that the EU is the biggest economy in the world and could have respectable armed forces on its own. Therefore, this is a case in which, contrary to other countries 'attempting-to-be' world powers, here there is no lack of means, but instead a lack of will, something that could appear quite disturbing for many Europeanists.

In that sense, Angela Merkel would need to understand what all her former German predecessors understood perfectly, but it seems she has not. Germany can only have a bigger role in world politics

---

[1109] This way Hollande referred to Putin when they met in the Kremlin on November 26, 2015, after the terrorist attacks in Paris. 'Russia imposes sanctions on Turkey over downed plane,' *The Guardian*, November 26, 2015, accessed on November 26, 2015. http://www.theguardian.com/world/2015/nov/26/hollandes-anti-isis-talks-with-putin-complicated-by-downing-of-russian-jet

[1110] Jean, Carlo, *Geopolitica del mondo contemporaneo*, Op. Cit., page 40.

through the EU and precisely by enforcing a European position. In that sense, sovereignty needs to be ceded to Brussels so it can count more. It is not, then, by imposing austerity measures or closing borders to migrants that the Kantian dream of the Perpetual Peace[1111] could be achieved.

Scholars like Simms understood also perfectly the importance of German role throughout the history of European integration:

> The Cold War started and ended there. Today, the question of whether Europe will go forward into a closer union or will remain a confederation of nation states will primarily be decided in and by Germany.[1112]

Simms also raised questions regarding the need for a more decisive and unified stance in many issues on which the future of the EU could depend.

> Above all, will the European Union become a more cohesive international actor, particularly in the military sphere. Will its army and navy serve as the 'school of the Union'? Or will Europeans duck these challenges, retreat into themselves and even split apart? If that happens, history will judge the European Union an expensive youthful prank which the continent played in its dotage, marking the completion rather than the starting point of a great-power project.[1113]

Altogether, the EU is at a crucial point. Either it manages to get out stronger after the serious issues it faces, or it crumbles. At the end, either Europe becomes Europe as a geopolitical actor or remains, as Brzezinski said, a sort of US protectorate where foreign policy will be subdued to Washington that in exchange would guarantee security with its own conditions.

Consequently, what will happen in Europe and the EU will have also a deep influence on the events in Ukraine, Moldova and Pridnestrovia, making these post-Soviet polities not only dependent on the state of the relation between the United States and Russia. It could also open the possibility to these territories to set the bases

---

[1111] The essay by Kant was from a liberal perspective a genuine attempt to set the bases for a durable peace in Europe. It also envisioned the idea of a confederation as a way to sustain a more sustainable peace settlement in the continent. Some scholars would even consider the confederation he proposed set the idea of what would become more than 150 years later of the European Union. Kant, Immanuel, *To Perpetual Peace: A Philosophical Sketch*, Hacket Publishing, 2003.
[1112] Simms, Op. Cit., page 531.
[1113] Simms, Op. Cit., page 534.

for establishing a different role in which it is always better to be a 'buffer state' rather than just a geopolitical goal.

4.2 Buffer states or failed states?

After acknowledging the evolution of the geopolitical struggle between Russia, the United States and the EU, it is important to consider what kind of scenarios could allow an arrangement to determine the future role of these polities and if they have a real opportunity to advance their own state-building processes.

Ukraine, Moldova and Pridnestrovia will not stop being considered as geopolitical targets. In those conditions, it would be plausible to look for a sort of arrangement between the actors involved. In that sense, the EU could define more clearly the goals of the Eastern Partnership and obtain an agreement with Russia for these three territories as part of a settlement in which both actors concede.

The deferral of the provisional implementation of the Association Agreement, between Ukraine and the EU, by one year, after trilateral talks between Russia, the EU and Ukraine in September 2014, signalled a possible agreement with Russia. Even though, the Agreement's final implementation was for a while hanging on the balance due to a referendum[1114] in the Netherlands. Needless to say, the failure to implement the agreement would have been a total embarrassment for the EU while the campaign in the Netherlands intended mostly to give assurances to the local population that Ukraine would not become a candidate member for future adhesion.[1115]

Altogether, a sort of pact between the EU and Russia would need assurances on both sides and guarantees for the involved polities

---

[1114] A group of citizens gather more than 427,000 valid requests in the Netherlands to organize a referendum in which the question asked will be: 'Are you for or against the Approval Act of the Association Agreement between the European Union and Ukraine?' Even if the poll would be not binding, and it does not obligate the Dutch government to act on it, numerous members of the parliament have signalled that they would be willing to follow the decision expressed by the population in the vote. In that sense, it creates the possibility that the controversial Association Agreement could eventually not be ratified. Note of the author.

[1115] 'Голландцев успокоили, что Украина не вступает в ЕС,' January 8, 2016, accessed on January 8, 2016. http://korrespondent.net/world/3612593-hollandtsev-uspokoyly-chto-ukrayna-ne-vstupaet-v-es

regarding their territorial integrity in exchange of assuring their neutrality, which means not entering NATO. It is true that Russia and the Eurasian Economic Union cannot compete in the same way with the EU at the economic sphere but instead Brussels cannot give security certainties at least now, without the United States or without an agreement with Moscow. Therefore, an arrangement is needed to ensure Moscow that these territories will not be part of the Atlantic alliance, while giving both actors the possibility to keep an eye on their economic interests in the area, considering that until now the involved polities are more integrated economically with Russia rather than with the EU. This kind of agreement would allow Ukraine, Moldova and Pridnestrovia the possibility of functioning as a sort of 'buffer polity'.

An arrangement among the geopolitical actors involved leaves meanwhile numerous inner issues to be solved. Local political elites from the three studied polities have also to acknowledge two important facts, if they pretend to achieve one day the building of a sovereign state in which its population feels adequately part of it. First, the strong position Russia has in the region, considering that any confrontation against Moscow could break the polity as happened in Ukraine and divide more the multi-ethnic and multilingual population present. Second, an anti-Russian stance if taken would depend on the encouragement of Western allies that pursue their own agenda without considering any kind of state building but instead expect the submission of any sovereignty to their own geopolitical projects.

The bases for a possible settlement depend also on the achievement or failure by the locals to build a solid state in which the population feels identified, while recognizing the multi-ethnic and multilingual characteristics of the social tissue becomes fundamental to avoid giving Moscow the 'right' to defend the Russian-speaking populations in the Near Abroad. Only then it becomes possible to define and defend a genuine state interest and to have at least in a reduced way the capacity to take independent decisions in matters regarding the survival of the polity. It is in this way the studied polities risk confirming themselves in the route of becoming failed states.

Nevertheless, before analysing the specifics of each polity, some words should be written precisely about the terminology 'failed state'. This term became notorious for its use by the US think-tank 'Fund for peace' in 2005. That institution has used diverse social, economic, political and military indicators to classify the level of failed or fragile states.[1116] The use of 12 different indicators individually or combined helps to determine if a country could be considered as a failed state. It should be said that the name 'failed state' and more precisely the classification used by the institute are not independent of political and geopolitical use. For instance, the same annual classification goes curiously in line with the strategic vision from the United States, as Avalos Tenorio noted, and could be useful to justify 'humanitarian interventions' or to condition financial aid from central countries to the peripheral ones.[1117] To that extent, he adds:

> Esta lejos de ser una casualidad que ningun pais del centro del sistema mundial sea considerado como 'Estado fallido', ni que, correlativamerite, todos los Estados asi considerados sean de la periferia. En un sentido mas especifico, la calificacion tambien puede ser usada por diversos grupos internos de cada pais, a fin de desacreditar al grupo o partido gobernante, o a la 'clase política', por su corrupcion e ineficiencia. En fin, el uso politico de la expresión 'Estado fallido' es includable.[1118]

Altogether, for the matter of this research, the parameters mentioned (more than the classification) by the institute are worth mentioning, even if the nodal point remains related mainly to the concept of sovereignty, in Schmittian terms, as stated in the first pages of this work. In this sense, it becomes possible to conclude on a case-by-case basis where the course of action is taking Ukraine, Moldova and Pridnestrovia.

4.2.1 Ukraine

Ukraine's seize and strategic position puts it in a double jeopardy. On one side, it has more strategic advantages but also portrays the

---

[1116] 'The indicators,' http://fsi.fundforpeace.org/indicators, consulted on June 27, 2016.
[1117] Avalos, Tenorio, 'El colapso del Estado Mexicano' in 'No nos alcanzan las palabras. Sociedad, Estado y violencia en México,' Itaca, UAM-X, 2014, page 58.
[1118] Idem.

biggest risks to pursue a successful state-building process in the current context, considering it attracts more attention from foreign political actors. As its name means, 'borderland', it reflects the complexity of the vicissitudes the local population has confronted for centuries.

This territory passed through a historical journey with fundamental moments that defined some of the main characteristics of the current Ukrainian polity. The Pereyaslav Treaty in 1654 signalled the incorporation of Ukraine into Tsarist Russia, and from then on, the territory suffered the heritage of opposed political developments. Most of current Ukraine was under Russian control; meanwhile, Western Ukraine remained under Polish and Austro-Hungarian rule.

In that sense, most of the Ukrainians had a strong interaction at all levels with Russia. Western Ukrainians, instead, during the XVIII developed a different 'Ukrainian' identity, separated from Russia, and to a certain extent anti-Russian identity. Therefore, these West Ukrainians generally misperceive how identity evolved in the rest of the Ukrainian population. These antagonistic visions were evident during World War II but also during the aftermath of the war. In that sense, while in West Ukraine with 20% of the Ukrainian territory, Ukrainian language was a lot more prevalent, the rest, even with a notable amount of Ukrainian speakers, became more used to the bilingual logic and adapted to the stipulated model proper of the attempts to create a Soviet identity.

These remarks relate also that differences appeared with Russia through history have been above all political rather than ethnic or religious origins. Historical examples are notable. Cossacks, for instance, asked the Czar for protection and seemed delighted at being incorporated into the Orthodox rule of Moscow. The only condition was to be allowed to keep the autonomy they enjoyed and that represented a fundamental characteristic of the Cossack way of life. This privileged autonomy, which years later was retired by the autocratic logic of Czarism, was a clear political difference but not ethnic. The same way, years later under Stalin, when the peasants refused to participate in the collectivization, it was a political difference between the peasants and the Stalinized Soviet elite that caused them to refuse to acknowledge any group that did not submit fully to the Politburo and Stalin's will.

Afterwards, during the crumbling process of the Soviet Union, Kravchuk, as leader of the Ukrainian SSR, initially did not take sides for independence and only later sided in the struggle between Yeltsin and Gorbachev when the latter's political decline was evident. Only then, he made an alliance with the nationalists from Western Ukraine but never allowing them considerable participation in the government. Therefore, during the first years of the new Ukrainian republic, there were no intentions to push for an ethnonational identity as happened in other former Soviet republics.

Altogether, the relation between Ukraine and Russia has included several political differences among all the ethnic, cultural, religious and linguistic similitudes present. Thus, for most of Ukrainians, the relation with Russia was conceived until the crisis of 2013–2014, as Anatoly Lieven named it, a 'fraternal rivalry'. This influential relation at different levels complicates until now defining in many cases the cultural border between what is Ukrainian, what is Russian and what is Soviet. Moreover, this complex identity does not diminish two factors. Firstly, the territory always enjoyed a multi-ethnic population, where precisely there was a notable Russian and Russian-speaking component but where different ethnic groups were also found such as Tatars in Crimea, Hungarians and Romanians. Secondly, the increasing social mobility of the late Soviet years also allowed many other ethnic groups to establish themselves in the Ukrainian SSR. Therefore, the Soviet attempt to mould a new kind of identity had a partial success in some regions but enough to leave a certain heritage. To this extent, only the local elites from Western Ukraine understood it differently.

Meanwhile, the multi-ethnic and multifaceted social tissue always present in the territory has become also hostage of the geopolitical factors, and precisely those geopolitical factors have been correspondingly crucial in all the attempts to pursue a state-building process in the area. Geopolitics did not allow the appearance of an independent Ukraine in the different attempts after the Russian Revolution, and it was geopolitics also that caused George Bush to advise Ukrainians against independence from the Soviet Union.

The same geopolitical motives left Ukraine in a complex situation battling to choose between an assertive Russia, with its own geopolitical project, and a strong historical heritage in the area, or the increasing push by the United States and the EU to pursue its own plans.

In that context, there are some facts needed to be remarked about after the political crisis occurred in 2013–2014. The inner political framework remained the same, only with a different geopolitical orientation, which does not mean a different way on how local politics evolve. That means, the oligarchs reorganized themselves and continued to control all the relevant aspects of the political life. In that sense, it was interesting how during the recent war, Ukrainian media, mostly held precisely by oligarchs, pursued a strong 'patriotic' campaign while ignoring instead several serious problems present in the country. Besides, oligarchs' support to Yanukovych was forgotten together with their part in the daily political and economic life.

This 'nationalist' campaign allowed one sole change in the streets in Kiev: the presence of Ukrainian flags everywhere. This nationalist promotion allowed coercing or amalgamating one sector of the Ukrainian society against the 'Russian enemy' while attempting to forge a new sort of Ukrainian identity. In that sense, the same kind of propaganda that Ukrainian media complained was used on a daily basis by Russia to 'denigrate Ukraine'; it was the same style of the propagandist messages that carried a patriotic narration against the 'evil Putin'. At the end, this is another factor that shows more a similitude than a difference among both countries as heritage of the Soviet style of making politics. Meanwhile, the war in the Donbas enjoyed a defined role in media, as Raffestin, the Swiss geographer, once wrote:

> Présentée comme un jeu sur de grandes tables ou de grandes cartes à grand renfort de modelés réduits, la guerre a été apprivoisée pour que la société civile ne s'y oppose pas, davantage même, pour qu'elle y adhère et la regarde comme un spectacle nécessaire.[1119]

[1119] Raffestin, Claude, *Geopolitique et histoire*, Paris, Histoire Payot, 1995, page 308. Quoted in Coutau-Bügarie, Hervé, *Traité de Stratégie*, 4e edition, Paris, Economica, 2003, page 737.

Meanwhile, the intention by the government to be perceived as more pro-Western has arrived even to some ridicule cases. For example, the decision to consider December 25th, a national holiday for Christmas,[1120] instead of January 7th as done in most Orthodox societies, has produced a mixture of laugh and outrage among many. There were even hilarious pretensions like the possibility to forbid on TV a famous Soviet comedy, *The irony of fate*, a film traditionally shown on New Year's Eve in either Russia and Ukraine, only because one of the actors of this 1976 production had supported Russian actions in Crimea.[1121]

Other examples in that sense include the changing of the festivities related to the end of World War II, from May 9 as in Russia and the post-Soviet world to May 8 as in Western Europe. The outlaw of the use of Soviet symbols and the intention to rewrite a new conception in history create also huge contradictions not only among Ukrainian scholars and teachers but also in a daily day life. For instance, it is funny, though, how the same peddlers and street vendors that used to sell Soviet memorabilia and souvenirs in Kiev until 2013 now instead sell anti-Putin propaganda, Ukrainian flags or even insignias or magnets related to the extreme right movement Pravyi Sektor.

Altogether, this patriotic campaign carried out by the government and the oligarchs attempted to allow the authorities to advance with the political reforms intended by the United States and the IMF. But, the push of this patriotic impulse started to get weaker mostly because after two years Yanukovych was ousted from the political scene, the local population has only witnessed a notable deterioration in the living standard. A recent poll showed that more than three-fourths of the Ukrainians considered that their life standard got worse during 2015.[1122] Meanwhile, perceivable corruption level

---

[1120] 'Ukraine may get two Christmases as national identity debate begins,' December 31, 2015, accessed on December 31, 2015. http://www.theguardian.com/world/2015/dec/31/ukraine-two-christmases-orthodox-church-russia

[1121] 'Ukrainian holiday tradition under threat as popular Soviet film faces ban,' December 24, 2015, accessed on December 24, 2015. http://www.theguardian.com/world/2015/dec/24/ukrainian-holiday-tradition-soviet-film-irony-of-fate-faces-ban

[1122] 'Три четверти украинцев стали жить хуже – опрос,' January 13, 2016, accessed on January 13, 2016. http://korrespondent.net/ukraine/3614660-try-chetverty-ukrayntsev-staly-zhyt-khuzhe-opros

remains the same besides demagogic campaigns like the one by the former Georgian president Saakashvili, now Odessa's governor.

Furthermore, the 2015–2016 winter was the first that Ukraine did not buy Russian gas even though the measure traduced itself in a 30% increase in the price for the local consumers.[1123] Altogether, high inflation, the lowest salaries in Europe and no real labour protection leaves future generations only with the expectancy of looking for less harsh conditions in Kiev, migrating to Russia or to expect any opportunity to migrate legally or not to the EU, the United States or Canada.

Ukraine was already by 2013 one of the top 10 countries in the world where people emigrate more.[1124] That explains why Poroshenko has given a great importance to obtain a visa-free regime with the EU, which would allow for Ukrainians a chance to enter the Schengen area more easily. Moreover, even if it would not mean directly a job permit in the EU, it creates a subterfuge for allowing for many the possibility to seek for different options to get any kind of economic benefit from the EU at a medium term and to increase the remittances sent to Ukraine, which in 2015 represented $6.2 billion. By severing banking ties with Moscow, the arrival of remittances sent by the Ukrainian workers in Russia became more complicated, even if they represented three times more the amount of foreign direct investment in Ukraine in 2014.[1125]

Meanwhile, Ukraine today has become completely dependant on Western aid. It diminished even more the possibility to have any kind of economic sovereignty or a proper foreign policy. US involvement is notable at all levels, as, for instance, demanding cabinet changes like the recent US condition for a $1 billion transfer in exchange of the removal of Victor Shorikin as General Prosecutor.[1126]

[1123] Petro, Nicolai, 'Why Ukraine needs Russia more than ever,' *The Guardian*, March 9, 2016, consulted on March 12, 2016. http://www.theguardian.com/world/2016/mar/09/ukraine-needs-russia-nicolai-petro

[1124] 'Migration and remittances Factbook 2016,' World Bank Group, accessed on January 21, 2016. http://siteresources.worldbank.org/INTPROSPECTS/Resources/334934-1199807908806/4549025-1450455807487/Factbookpart1.pdf

[1125] Idem.

[1126] 'США даст Киеву миллиард в обмен на отставку Шокина – СМИ,' January 21, 2016, accessed on January 21, 2016. http://korrespondent.net/ukra

In that same tone, US Vice President Joe Biden arrived to the point of declaring that he talks more often with Poroshenko than with his own wife.[1127] The already mentioned US-born investment banker and then Minister of Finance Natalie Jaresko demonstrates even more the influence the United States has on designing economic policy. That position allows Washington to have complete influence on the economic transformations done together with the effect they have on Prime Minister Yatsenyuk.

Moreover, the fragile government coalition between Poroshenko and Yatsenyuk subsisted mainly due to support from Washington, which tries to avoid the repetition of the Yushchenko failure, when the divisions between Timoshenko and the former made the country ungovernable for five years. In that sense, huge tensions are visible among cabinet and government members that reflect also the divisions among the oligarchs and the US-related technocrats making Poroshenko remain as a relatively weak character.[1128]

The United States has been cautious not to give lethal military support to Ukraine; at least not officially, acknowledging the risks it could carry in the global relation with Russia and considering the possible and logic Russian military reprisals, in which at least in the military sense, Moscow still has the strategic advantage in that area.[1129] Instead, Washington has preferred to advance on the economic transformations in Ukraine that could give them a future lev-

---

ine/politics/3618420-ssha-dast-kyevu-myllyard-v-obmen-na-otstavku-shokyna-smy

[1127] 'Байден: Говорю с Порошенко чаще, чем с женой,' December 12, 2015, accessed on December 12, 2015. http://korrespondent.net/ukraine/3599762-baiden-hovorui-s-poroshenko-chasche-chem-s-zhenoi

[1128] A discussion in a Cabinet meeting in which the Minister of Interior Arsen Avakov was continuously interrupted by Odessa's governor, the Georgian Mikhail Saakashvili, turned almost into a brawl when the former threw him a plastic bottle. Avakov even shouted to Saakashvili complaining that he is not even Ukrainian. All this exchange happened during the meeting while the president and the prime minister just silently observed the scene and seemed powerless. 'Ukrainian minister throws water in Odessa governor's face,' December 15, 2015, accessed on March 3, 2016. http://www.theguardian.com/world/2015/dec/15/ukrainian-minister-throws-water-in-odessa-governors-face

[1129] 'Генерал США объяснил, почему Киеву не дают Javelin,' December 12, 2015, accessed on December 12, 2015. http://korrespondent.net/world/3601980-heneral-ssha-obiasnyl-pochemu-kyevu-ne-dauit-Javelin

erage while pushing to increase the game of sanctions and countersanctions against Russia by the Yatsenyuk Government. The sanctions have affected notably more the Ukrainian side in trade, arms sales and other areas while there remains also the impossibility from the Ukrainian side to pay a debt to Russia of more than $3 billion lent by Moscow when Yanukovych was in power and forced Kiev to default in relation with that payment.

Internally, those sanctions[1130] function also as local propaganda but do not bring closer any possibility of a settlement for the conflict in the Donbass and in the relations with Russia. Instead, the reprisals taken by Moscow against Ukraine do not bother in any sense the United States but deteriorate even more the fragile Ukrainian economic position. Besides, the entering into force of the Association Agreement[1131] with the EU created many expectations. It also has produced a loss of the Russian market for Ukrainian exports, while the EU did not show any intentions of compensating for the damage.[1132]

Altogether, to continue making the relation with Moscow more tense can only have Ukraine in the losing side. To begin with, if the sanctions by the United States and the EU were not able to diminish or change notably the Russian position regarding Crimea and the Donbas, the sanctions carried out by Ukraine in practical terms hurt notably more the local population that it is already obliged to suffer harsh economic measures.

About Crimea, regardless of Poroshenko's rhetoric, in which he assures that Ukraine will recover the territory, the peninsula by 2016 functions in daily life as part of Russia. Crimeans receive the same treatment as any other citizen in the Russian Federation,

---

[1130] The Ukrainian sanctions besides targeting individuals the same as the ones from the United States and the EU included also forbidding Russian commercial planes of using the Ukrainian air space and an embargo on different products. The Russian measures instead also banned the import of several Ukrainian goods. Besides, the military cooperation between both countries practically is suspended, which meant a significant blow to the Ukrainian economy as 70% of the Ukrainian arms sales went to Russia. Note of the author.

[1131] Even though still pending, the definite entry into force is subject to the referendum in the Netherlands.

[1132] 'EU won't compensate Ukraine for losing Russian market from January 1 – EU commissioner,' November 19, 2015, accessed on January 21, 2016. http://tass.ru/en/economy/837849

while sanctions remain. The ban on the operation of ATM from foreign banks which affects mostly foreigners and the impossibility for locals to obtain a US or Schengen visa function as reminders of the peculiar status of the territory. Meanwhile, there was a notable increase in the amount of local pensions and wages while adjusting them to Russian standards.[1133] Besides, there was also a perceivable raise in the public and private investments in different areas, mostly related to tourism and infrastructure. In addition, while asking the local population in the summer of 2015 about their new status, the most common answer given by locals was that they felt 'more protected'. In addition, a road-rail bridge started its construction in 2015 and is expected to be finished by 2019. The project, measuring around 4.5 kilometres, intends to connect the Kerch peninsula in Crimea and the Taman peninsula in the Krasnodar area, leaving then Crimea connected to mainland Russia.

Meanwhile, an electricity crisis left almost all of the Crimean territory without power for several days since 20 November 2015, after a series of explosions by 'unknown saboteurs' blew up power lines in the Ukrainian region of Kherson, which stopped the supply to the peninsula.[1134] It forced Moscow to build improvised new lines but also in a medium term will guarantee full supply from Russia finishing with Ukrainian dependency in that area.[1135] The cut in the energy supply, done or not without governmental support, evidences also the weak position of the Ukrainian authorities in this subject. This event was not a surprise considering that since September 20, activists from the Pravyi Sektor and some Crimean Tatars had organized an economic blockade for freight transport from Ukraine to Crimea. These actions only ratify the weakness of Poroshenko and Yatsenyuk's government that allow activists to organize a blockade and impose what in practice becomes policy without

---

[1133] Russian wages and pensions are not at all high for Western standards but Ukrainian ones are extremely low, making the differences sometimes of 3 to 1 related to what they used to perceive before. Note of the author.
[1134] 'Crimea declares state of emergency after power lines attacked,' November 22, 2015, accessed on January 22, 2016. http://www.theguardian.com/world/2015/nov/22/crimea-state-of-emergency-power-lines-attacked
[1135] 'Путин пустил электричество в Крым,' December 2, 2015, accessed on December 2, 2015. http://korrespondent.net/ukraine/3597884-putyn-pustyl-elektrychestvo-v-krym

a serious response and not even comment on the issue.[1136] Above all, these actions evidence the lack of an alternative approach to settle the Crimean question. In fact, it is certainly not by leaving the population in Crimea without electricity or blocking them the access of basic goods that Crimeans would opt to go back to Ukraine.

To that extent, without denying the questionable legal process in which the incorporation of Crimea in the Russian Federation took place, from the political point of view there is no foreseeable possibility of forcing Moscow to step back in the decision. Former Ukrainian president Kravchuk precisely complained how the current government deceived the Ukrainian population of a future Crimean recovery. He openly conceded that there is no way that the Crimean population would decide to go back to Ukraine.[1137]

The last point regarding Crimea would relate to the Tatar community. An ethnic group that has outlived several tragedies throughout the years appears divided in the new context. Different attitudes are found among them while Moscow was careful of playing a strategy of carrots and sticks that included as one Crimean Tatar interviewed by *The Guardian* said:

> In the incomplete year of 2014, Russia spent as much as Ukraine did in the previous seven years on issues of housing and support for Crimean Tatars.[1138]

Meanwhile, the FSB also keeps an eye on potential Tatar leaders not favourable to the new context.[1139]

Altogether, Ukraine would need to seek for a rational political solution that starts aiming for a settlement in the Donbas, allowing Kiev to retake control over the territory in that area. Obviously, any

---

[1136] 'Почему Порошенко молчит о блокаде Крыма – СМИ,' December 3, 2015, accessed on December 3, 2015. http://korrespondent.net/ukraine/3598301-pochemu-poroshenko-molchyt-o-blokade-kryma-smy

[1137] Kravchuk, Leonid, quoted in 'ЦИТАТА ДНЯ,' January 11, 2016, accessed on January 11, 2016. http://korrespondent.net/quotation/6777-ya-kohda-sly shu-kak-nashy-lydery-hovoriat-da-my-vernem-krym-nash-nu-dlia-cheho-ob manyvat-samykh-sebia-y-ukraynskyi-narod-ne-vernem-cherez-luchshuui-zh yzn-v-ukrayne-ne-budet-nykohda-toho-chtoby-krym-skazal-my-poidem-na zad-v-ukraynu

[1138] 'Crimean Tatars divided between Russian and Ukrainian promises,' March 17, 2015, accessed on March, 17 2015. http://www.theguardian.com/world/20 15/mar/17/crimean-tatars-divided-between-russian-and-ukrainian-promises

[1139] Idem.

kind of agreement would need Moscow's approval and to that extent, numerous elements would have to be considered. A possible solution for the Donetsk and Lugansk would need to agree on a certain kind of economic autonomy together with a political reform in Ukraine to allow it. A settlement would also need to stabilize the relation with Moscow, as this would be the sole way to guarantee what remains of Ukrainian territorial integrity.

The idea of a Consociation Swiss kind of proposal for Ukraine could function but to that extent, it would be imperative that Ukraine guarantees itself as a neutral country as it was until 2014. Pretending to have an aggressive stance against Russia in the current context in which Kiev hardly controls its militias or armed forces could be suicidal to the survival of Ukraine. It already cost the loss of Crimea. At the end, for the Russian position, it is very suitable to have the present status quo in Donetsk and Lugansk while those areas remain in a sort of legal limbo.

It is as a matter of logic that when a stronger neighbour exists the conditions to develop foreign relations must consider present asymmetries. One example could be Mexico, after the Mexican Revolution, and more specifically since 1930 until 1988, considering the continuous US involvement in the American continent, that the only possible way to develop a sovereign foreign policy was through the Doctrine Estrada. This doctrine claimed that no country should judge positively or negatively the governments or the changes in them as this action would imply not respecting state sovereignty. This policy in practice meant the guarantee of none involvement in any countries' affairs. It was the only realpolitik solution that allowed to remain sovereign, while having a northern neighbour that had already invaded and taken half of Mexican territory in the nineteenth century.

Altogether, many issues remained to be settled in Ukraine. For instance, the big number of refugees after the conflict that account for certainly more than a million, which migrated internally or to Russia. Until now, it is not clear in which conditions they could come back while many of them intend to pursue their lives in Kiev or in other cities.

In another issue, after initial attempts to modify the law of regional languages, it still remains in force, and it is not clear until what point, the pro-western stance by the current government would go ahead to modify one of the few linguistic balances in the legal system in exchange for a more ethnonational position. To push more an ethnic basis in the reforms would certainly give more arguments to the Russian-speaking areas of Donetsk and Lugansk to reject a hypothetic real reincorporation into Ukraine.

Meanwhile, it is not clear how long the government can continue to use the excuse of the war and the 'patriotic struggle' against Russia or to recur to populist goals like the recovery of Crimea or the visa-free regime with the EU to recover any sort of legitimacy. At the end, the oligarchs are always in the hegemonic position[1140] while the effect of the crisis, the countersanctions and the economic measures together with the deteriorating state of the Ukrainian economy continue to affect the local population, which could again opt to protest.

At this point, the biggest failure of the *Maidan* is perceived. It was not able to produce a political force capable of seizing power. It turned out only in a revolt in which the same political class recycled itself for survival. Therefore, the challenge remains in place for the Ukrainian society, after it was unable to produce a genuine political force independent from the oligarchs.

Also, the protests in the *Maidan* neither meant an opportunity to democratize institutions. It neither brought a serious investigation of the obscure privatizations processes of the last years, and it did not follow up on the possibility of pursuing a genuine process of state building, or punishing the several abuses of power that allowed the oligarchs to build fortunes at the expense of the resources of the Ukrainian population.

As a matter of fact, Ukraine, as the whole world, is immersed in the same globalized capitalist context, but in this case without the existence of a sovereign state. In Schmitt's terms, there is no possibility of establishing the friend-enemy link based on an own 'raison

---

[1140] To that extent, it is worth reminding that, for example, during the last presidential campaign, one of the campaign promises by the oligarch and current president Petro Poroshenko was that once in power, he would sell the assets of his main company ROSHEN so there would be no conflict of interests with his position as president. More than one year and a half after the election he still refuses to comply. Note of the author.

d'état'. Instead, the country has no opportunity to resist, oppose or even moderate the reforms wanted by the global order.

Moreover, there is no perspective for the political situation to settle. Nor is Ukraine as a polity in the position to solve by itself the ongoing situation in the Donbas or improve the tone of the relation with Russia. The way the Minsk agreements were negotiated clearly showed that the Ukrainian part was not the one to decide. It was a matter of what Russia wanted to accept and how much the United States was willing to push Moscow together with a timid attempt by the French-German tandem to push for a European solution that would not upset the United States.

Altogether, the loss on the monopoly of the use of violence in a Weberian way could be considered only as one of the symptoms of a failed state which then traduces itself in different levels of violence as Avalos wrote.[1141] To that extent, adding the lack of economic sovereignty, no control over the borders, the fact that not all the current population feels identified with the Ukrainian polity together with the clear US and Russian intervention at different levels, leaves Ukraine as an existing failed state.

It would be coarse and unprecise to simply say that Ukraine, after the events in 2013–2014, passed from being a Russian protectorate into a sort of US colony, but the fact is that after more than two decades of the fall of the Soviet Union, Ukrainians were not capable of building a sovereign state. Certainly, external factors played a role, but also the Ukrainian society did not manage to become an actor.

This reality brings more questions. What would happen if a new *Maidan* occurred? What would happen if a new *Maidan* delegitimized the current political class? What would happen if a new *Maidan* targeted the oligarchs? What if a new *Maidan* did not intend to give its avail to the measures imposed by the IMF? Would the West support a real democratic uprising in that sense? It does not seem plausible in the near future.

Besides, a new *Maidan* would hardly count on Western support if the geopolitical alliance is not guaranteed as it is with current Ukrainian authorities. Therefore, it would have little possibilities to

---

[1141] Avalos, Op. Cit., page 59.

succeed. Numerous examples in recent history show similar trends in which genuine and strong political expressions of outrage against local governments did not receive Western sympathy because they did not guarantee a geopolitical alliance. The protests in Mexico in 2006 against the electoral fraud or the events in Tahrir Square in Egypt during 2011 are only some cases in which legitimate expressions against established governments were not capable of consolidating itself in part due to the lack of support or at least foreign recognition. In fact, the logic of capital as explained in the first pages of this research prevails always, but also the geopolitical interest. In the mentioned Mexican case, the United States could not risk then to allow having a moderate social democratic president in Mexico in a period in which several Latin American presidents were challenging US hegemonic role in the area. In the Egyptian case, instead, any democratic outburst could risk disrupting the status quo in the relation with Israel, therefore, in both cases, unbalancing US interests.

The attempts to unbalance even if lightly the logic of Capital[1142] have nowadays little possibilities of success. In that sense, if the Greek Party SYRIZA was not able to oppose the austerity measures imposed by the Troika, the Ukrainian population is in a more fragile position to resist or to oppose politically all the external forces that have influenced the recent processes. The logic of Capital on one side, together with the ways in which it structures itself politically with the United States, the EU and Russia as peaks of different projects, makes it impossible by now to Ukraine to develop sovereignly.

To that extent, it will be noteworthy otherwise to watch the evolution of the events after 2016, but also in the southwestern neighbour, Moldova, where the risk of political uprising started while these lines were being written.

4.2.2 Moldova

The Moldovan case shows up a very different situation. There is less intensity in the geopolitical confrontation for the territory between the Prut and the Dniester. The country has lesser strategic value and fewer strengths to negotiate from a position of force against surrounding countries, especially when it is so dependant on foreign

---

[1142] Capital as described in the first pages of the Introduction.

support and the living standards are together with Ukraine of the lowest in Europe.

Moldova's history is rather different. Moreover, the idea of Moldavia or Moldova grew for many years also in relation to the notion of building a Romanian nation. Therefore, it became complicated and even baffling the Soviet attempts to design a Soviet Moldovan identity first in the Moldovan ASSR and then as a SSR and even afterwards as an independent Republic of Moldova. The contradicting case of the national language and the discussion of using the nominative Romanian or 'Moldovan' reflect precisely the difficulty to project a separate Moldovan 'ethos' from the Romanian one. Besides, beyond this difficulty remains in Moldova also the composition of a multi-ethnic society. To this extent, minorities like the Gagauz or the Bulgarians accommodate in a certain way the Soviet idea of 'дружба народов' (Friendship of the Peoples), which reflected precisely the ideal community in which all ethnic groups were included. In that sense, a semi-Russified society allows especially the two mentioned minorities (considering the Pridnestrovian case different) to prefer also Russian language against the fear of being subdued by a hypothetical Romanization, with Romanian being the most spoken language in the republic.

This leaves Moldova besides others as a polity in which the most important differences that appeared during the last century in relation with Romania were above all political. A political difference emerged after the Russian Revolution when Bessarabia opted to incorporate itself into Romania but with the precondition that the agrarian reform would take place. In a similar way, just as how Ukraine decided to incorporate itself to Russia with the conditionality of preserving certain autonomy, the Bessarabian political elite expected also from Bucharest not only the mentioned land reform that would entitle peasants their own land but also to preserve a certain degree of autonomy or at least a formal regional recognition.

The lack of political vision by Romanian authorities, which did not acknowledge the already multi-ethnic composition of the territory, together with the denial to proceed to compel with the reforms in the terms stipulated, as explained in the third chapter, had a profound effect. The final dissolution of the Sfatul Tarii signalled that there was no intention to accept the different social tissue formed in Bessarabia under Russian rule for around one century until 1918. This lack of understanding, as Basciani[1143] explained, brought a profound political effect afterwards.

In that sense, the retake by Soviet authorities, as a response of a previous geopolitical agreement with Nazi Germany, allowed a 'smooth' Soviet integration and even more after the vicissitudes suffered by the local population during World War II. It also left the tracks of a deep Sovietization of the local population that simply 'adjusted' itself to the Soviet multi-ethnic logic in a sort of passive acceptance.

The emergence of the Moldovan Soviet Socialist Republic acknowledged at least formally[1144] something the Kingdom of Romania had not done, the existence of a different political identity in the region between the Prut and the Dniester. The only difference being that the new entity in this case opted to include also a small strip of territory at the left bank of the Dniester on today's Pridnestrovia. The Soviet authorities kept one small portion of the former Moldovan ASSR into the new Moldovan SSR. This action intended perhaps to give a sense of ethnic rationality to the existence of the former ASSR[1145] instead of being a bridgehead to push for the Soviet geopolitical goal of recovering Bessarabia from Romanian hands. Altogether, after World War II, the Soviet period brought also to the region the arrival of a new kind of local identity, a sort of 'Sovietized Romanians' that became diverse from the Romanian ones.

To that extent, the nationalist revival brought by the Perestroika, the same as in Ukraine, had an encountered effect. There was a national revival by one sector of the population but it also generated an encounter against the different minorities to which a Russified

---

[1143] Basciani, Op. Cit.
[1144] It is clear that it is a mere formal recognition considering the logic of the centralist Soviet political system but still it was important in the sense that it gave a 'place' to the Moldovan political elite, Sovietized indeed, while also perceived as equal to the other 14 Soviet republics. Besides, the last SSR to be created, allowed even the possibility to build a career in the Soviet political life to different personalities as was the case of Leonid Brezhnev who as mentioned held the post of first secretary of the Moldovan Communist Party. Note of the author.
[1145] The Moldovan ASSR existed from 1924 to 1940.

Sovietization suited more against the fear of a hypothetical 'Romanization'. Besides, Moldova appeared to the international scene in the middle of a civil war and without any national army. Therefore, it became completely dependent on the actions of stronger actors capable of enforcing a political settlement. The result obtained in 1992 was completely adverse to the pretensions of building a sovereign state in this former Soviet territory. It also had to deal with Russian peacekeepers in Pridnestrovia as the sole guarantors of stability in the region, therefore allowing Moscow to determine any kind of settlement to the newly appeared division between Moldova and the newly proclaimed Pridnestrovian Moldovan Republic.

During the next two decades, the pretension by one sector of the political elite to proceed for a union with Romania clashed with two political realities. First, the de facto division on the territory that meant the appearance of the Pridnestrovian polity but also the fact that another sector of the Moldovan political elite did not intend to pursue the idea of a future incorporation, something that for a moment seemed for granted after the Soviet collapse.

Therefore, Moldova appeared to the international scene in a much more complex position than the rest of the former Soviet republics. It had to struggle with the intention of recovering control over Pridnestrovia while having an extremely weak economy and with a great energetic and economic dependence with Russia. To that extent, the development of the local political life reflected these dissimilar alternatives. Initially, the support of a pan-Romanian position or a closer approach to the West or to Moscow were part of the 'alternatives' that in fact reflected more the will of the foreign dominant political goals. There was no national choice; there was the choice wanted by the Western powers and the option wanted by Moscow.

Moreover, the nationalistic and pan-Romanian enthusiasm lost force mainly because the 'Sovietized Moldovan elite' did not want to lose its position of privilege with the incorporation into Romania. Besides, Bucharest had nothing really to offer that could tempt the Moldovan elites to accept.

Moldova was one of the few post-Soviet countries that adopted a parliamentary system instead of a presidential one, while the president had mostly a ceremonial role. In this case, the party that stayed for a longer period in a leading role has been the Party of Communists of the Republic of Moldova which received the biggest number of votes in all the elections from 1998 to 2010, even though, not in all cases it was able to form a government. Its leader, Vladimir Voronin, for instance, at the end, was also hostage of opposed geopolitical intentions. First, he intended to form a close relation with Moscow and then, after the rejection of the Kozak Memorandum in 2003, which was the only realistic opportunity until now to settle the Pridnestrovian question, he transformed his government into a 'pro-western' one.

During the next years, again, Moldova intended a strong pro-West foreign policy but without settling the Pridnestrovian question where Moscow's role remains basic to any possible solution. In that sense, the next governments until now reflected different stances that still did not improve in any sense the situation of the local population while strongly pursuing a closer integration in the EU's area of influence and also allowing the consolidation of local oligarchs.

The EU signed the Association Agreement with Moldova and gave a visa-free regime to Moldovan citizens, different to what happened in Ukraine by then. This action was mostly considering that Moldova has a population of less than 3 million, reducing the migratory risk that the no-visa regime would carry. Meanwhile, it is noteworthy that the lack of opportunities for the local population together with the low salaries confirm Moldova as one of the poorest countries in Europe and very dependant on foreign remittances, which accounted for 26% of the GDP in 2014.[1146]

Altogether, even if Moldova has not taken the same anti-Russian approach in foreign politics that Ukraine pretends, and even if NATO is not officially in the Moldovan agenda, a closer integration to the EU looks complicated without the solution of the Pridnestrovian question.

It is true that the EU could take the same approach[1147] they had on Cyprus, that is, to pursue European integration and to leave the

---

[1146] 'Migration and remittances Factbook 2016,' World Bank Group, accessed on February 21, 2016. http://siteresources.worldbank.org/INTPROSPECTS/Resources/334934-1199807908806/4549025-1450455807487/Factbookpart1.pdf

[1147] This idea was suggested by Moldovan scholar Victor Chirila during an interview in Chisinau.

current division on the island to be solved later on.[1148] From a practical point of view, it can be true but there are also some differences. First, Moldova does not have the same economic and geostrategic interest that Cyprus has; second, Cyprus is smaller and has an important bank system while Moldova is a poor territory, besides, to incorporate it even more in the European area of influence will necessary imply a negotiation with Moscow. Instead, with Cyprus, the geopolitical struggle is against Turkey. For the EU and members, it is always preferable and easier to negotiate with Ankara than with Moscow. There is simply more leverage.

Besides, it is worth noticing the events that occurred in January 2016, when numerous demonstrations took place in Moldova after the formation of a new government. The notably numerous rallies against the nomination of Pavel Filip and his cabinet regarding his relation to the recent cases of corruption complicate the political situation.[1149] In this case, the rallies are against a pro-western government; therefore, they are in route to receive less attention by the EU and not even significant media support internationally. In that sense, the current uprising did not count with western support and, instead, risks to become Moscow's prey in the region, used to counterbalance the pro-western tendency that predisposed Chisinau in the last years.

Altogether, this case and the mentioned robbery in May 2015 of $1 billion from Moldovan banks show, clearer than the Ukrainian case, that in Moldova state building has been a complete failure. The country enjoys no control over its borders; there is a strong lack of national identity, in which Gagauz and Bulgarians identify first with their ethnic group of belonging while there is even no consensus on how to name the national language and where endemic corruption and a tendency to migrate by the population makes the outcome complicated.

[1148] Cyprus became a EU member in 2004, member of the Eurozone in 2008 and participates fully in every aspect of the EU except on the Schengen area. The entry into force of the agreement would take place once the division of the island is solved or to be more precise a geopolitical arrangement is obtained with Turkey and the Turkish population at the northern part of the island. Note of the author.

[1149] 'Майдан в Молдове. К чему приведут протесты,' January 22, 2016, accessed on January 22, 2016. http://korrespondent.net/world/3618810-maidan-v-moldove-k-chemu-pryvedut-protesty

In that sense, suitable pragmatic solutions if the intention is to pursue a further integration with the EU would include to let go Pridnestrovia, and seek a further integration with Romania that would have to guarantee a certain autonomy to the Gagauz and Bulgarian minorities and some sort of negotiation with Moscow. Otherwise, if Moldova would like separately to approach the EU, the scenario seems complicated. For Brussels, it is more comfortable to have the territory as part of the Eastern Partnership and as a buffer zone while not committing to give Moldova all the benefits that a full membership would include. Instead, the state of the Moldovan polity, the way it exists today, seems in no condition to avoid being another failed state in the post-Soviet space.

4.2.3 Pridnestrovia

The Pridnestrovian case is rather peculiar. Its origins could be traced almost as an accident, or a consequence of the minor political, administrative and geographic adjustment that meant the inclusion of one section of the former Moldovan ASSR into the newly formed Moldovan SSR in 1940. It meant that the territory of Bessarabia would include, then, a small strip of land at the east of the Dniester. This territory plus some reduced adjacent territories at the opposite side of the river would then become the Pridnestrovian Moldovan Republic after the fall of the Soviet Union. This small precedent became important as soon as political differences emerged between the industrial and political elite at the east of the Dnieper against the authorities in Chisinau once the shell that sustained the Soviet Union started to crack.

This polity with half a million inhabitants, on one side, developed a more rooted multi-ethnic Soviet- and Russian-speaking identity which intended to distinguish itself from the Romanian-speaking population at the other side of the Dniester. Meanwhile, the fragility of the new Moldovan polity forbade a suitable political settlement while allowing the authorities of the newly formed PMR to establish a separate polity from Moldova, but, mostly thanks to the support of the Russian 14th Army that 'settled' the civil war between Pridnestrovian and Moldovan forces in 1992.

In that sense, Pridnestrovia appeared to the international scene without foreign recognition but with a de facto political existence that allowed it to build a peculiar stability compared to its surrounding neighbours Ukraine and Moldova. Moreover, the denunciation of the Molotov-Ribbentrop Pact would allow precisely a legal cadre to justify the existence of this new polity, which was born as a political opposition to the Chisinau political elite and regrouped in a sort of Soviet-multi-ethnic identity. The PMR intended at least from the legal point of view to recognize the multi-ethnic characteristic of its society while acknowledging the existence of three official languages. This was opposed to the view of Chisinau, where only Romanian (or Moldovan) was an official language.

More than two decades, the lack of international recognition and Moscow's support allowed a rather different political evolution in the territory. In that sense, Pridnestrovia enjoyed under Russian protection first, the long rule of Igor Smirnov as president of the PMR, but it also carried on with its own non-recognized elections that even brought opposition parties to win and allow a peaceful transition, something not quite common in the post-Soviet space. Since 2011, Yevgeny Shevchuk has been the president and the last parliamentary elections that took place on 29 November 2015, saw again his party 'Renewal' to keep its status as a majority after winning 33 out of 43 seats of the Supreme Council.[1150]

Altogether, the PMR functions with a certain political constancy. Meanwhile, without official recognition, Moldovan authorities are obliged to solve several daily issues with the PMR authorities, giving them a tacit acknowledgement. Besides, the non-recognition has become quite functional, both for Moscow and for Tiraspol. It denies Pridnestrovia any international obligations, including foreign debt, which officially becomes Moldovan debt. Instead, for Russian authorities, the fact that they do not officially recognize the country allows threatening with a possible recognition as happened in South Ossetia and Abkhazia and using meanwhile symbolic and indirect means of support for Tiraspol.

The PMR functions in practice as a sort of Russian protectorate where inner affairs are handled by local authorities while recogniz-

---

[1150] 'Первое заседание Верховного совета ПМР нового созыва состоитс я в средуSputnik Молдова,' December 22, 2015, accessed on December 22, 2015. http://ru.sputnik.md/moldova/20151222/3808962.html

ing Moscow's main role in any hypothetical settlement of the conflict. Meanwhile, the Russian peace troopers in Pridnestrovia, even if reduced in number to represent a real military threat, are enough considering the weak status of the Moldovan Armed Forces. Their symbolic presence is enough, besides, to make it known that any aggression against Russian troops could bring a similar response as in Georgia in 2008, where Saakashvili erroneously thought that an attack against a reduced Russian garrison would not bring a full response by Moscow.

Altogether, a possible settlement of the Pridnestrovian question does not seem visible in the next years. On one side, it depends mainly on the state of the relation between Russia and the West, where, for instance, this polity serves Moscow precisely to remind Moldova that a strong anti-Russian stance could mean the loss of the territory.

The '5+2' format that includes Moldova, Russia, Ukraine, the PMR and the OSCE has shown also to have its limitations. It simply portrays that any real solution of the conflict would need to look for Russian interests in the area. This format as mentioned gives voice directly to the Pridnestrovian side, leaving the United States and the EU as observers while daily issues force a direct exchange between Chisinau and Tiraspol.

At the end, Pridnestrovia has a geopolitical role for Moscow, therefore, its future status will be inserted in the logic of how the Russian foreign policy operates in the region. It seems under the present conditions any arrangement that could allow Chisinau to recover control over the territory would need to concede serious strategic advantages to Moscow, including a sort of veto power for Pridnestrovian authorities in any legislation or foreign policy stance perceived as anti-Russian. It was precisely this logic that influenced the Kozak Memorandum already explained, which after more than two decades of the appearance of Pridnestrovia, has been the closest possibility to solve the issue.

Meanwhile, the status quo is also very comfortable either for Pridnestrovians, which mostly have also Ukrainian, Russian or

Moldovan citizenship[1151] or even combine two or more of those nationalities. Instead, it does not allow Moldova to pursue a further integration with the West while the country does not have control over its own internationally recognized borders.

Altogether, the evolution of the Pridnestrovian polity since 1992, shows some significant features. Even if the outcome of the political status will not depend on Tiraspol, the local population has built a different political identity as opposed to Chisinau. This diverse distinctiveness has created roots also in the locals, with kids in school studying about the 1992 war against Moldova and visiting museums and monuments that mix Soviet memories with the remembrance of those fallen in what is presented by Pridnestrovian historiography as a war of liberation against Moldova. In that sense, Hobsbawm's idea of the invention of a tradition[1152] perfectly fits this case in which Soviet and post-Soviet elements mix, and allow the creation of a sort of 'post-Soviet ethos' for the local population.

This new ethos does not deny locals their status as ethnic Russians, Ukrainians or Romanians but uses the former elements plus an idealistic vision of 'Great Motherland Russia' reinforced by local media increased the sustain of a different political identity and complicate even more an hypothetic reunification of the territory with Moldova. Therefore, even if international recognition does not seem feasible for the PMR by now, Pridnestrovia has managed to be acknowledged as a political 'other', while its 'sovereignty' is attached to Moscow. Meanwhile, remains a social imaginary or local awareness that needs to be considered for any possible political solution to the status of this polity.

4.3 Is it possible to build a state in the middle of a geopolitical struggle?

The question reflects the essence of this work. Is it possible in the current context the appearance of a sovereign polity when surrounded by stronger political actors? Is it necessary to take sides with one of the two interested geopolitical forces? Is it possible to

---

[1151] Russian diplomatic sources claimed around 170,000 citizens of the Russian Federation lived in Pridnestrovia in 2013. 'Весеннее обострение' Abril 21, 2013, accessed on April 21, 2013. http://profvesti.org/2013/04/21/10490/
[1152] Hobsbawm, Op. Cit.

stay neutral or is it an obligation when the intention is to maintain a certain degree of sovereignty? Altogether, those questions do not have an absolute answer.

Besides, a recurring paradigm surrounding state building regards the possibility of establishing states without nations or considering if each nation should enjoy the right to have its own state. The dilemma could have an ethical answer from political philosophy but would need also a geopolitical reply. In that sense, each of the Catalan people or the Palestinians should enjoy, as being part of a constituted nation, the right to have their own state. Even though, geopolitics or to be more precise the geopolitics of other sovereign states would not allow it so easily. Therefore, in a pragmatic stance, state building should consider these variables to answer how the correlation of forces would allow in a determined context the emergence of a new state.

State building requires an inner struggle to reaffirm its establishment but also it must overcome the external limitations that may appear in the process. It could be a civil war or a revolution. In that sense, the Civil War in the United States from 1861 to 1865 was the real political foundation of the United States as a state. The Italian unification, the Reform War in Mexico or Bismarck's quest to unite Germany during the nineteenth century, are only some examples of armed conflicts that brought the foundation of a polity that intended to reaffirm itself as a state.

Moreover, another question commonly present in Europe and in other areas of the world is how to build a state in a multi-ethnic territory. The Polish exception in which practically all the population is Polish with no notable minorities present goes far away from the complexity of the multilingual logic of the heritage left in Europe by the Austro-Hungarian empires, the Russian Tsarism or the Soviet Union.

Therefore, state building has also become a response to incorporate different ethnic groups, languages and nations and creates a new political identity. At the end, the state is a political act. It is 'the political act'.[1153] The outcome of the social process in which a society

---

[1153] A political act again in Schmttian terms as explained during the Introduction.

organizes itself politically and juridically. This process goes precisely beyond the idea of solely a nation or an ethnic group. It is precisely the political meaning, the international recognition and the geopolitical use of a polity, which goes in the current global reality over the will of many ethnic groups to build a state.

Agamben referred that 'States without a nation' like Kuwait are defended by foreign powers; meanwhile, nations without a state like Kurds, Palestinians or others can be exterminated or oppressed. To that extent Agamben wrote that 'il concetto di popolo ha senso soltanto se ricodificato in quello di cittadinanza',[1154] referring that citizenship as a political right goes beyond the ethnic group of origin.

Therefore, social and political processes depend on many factors that influence the events. It is not an absolute possibility to build or not a sovereign polity in the middle of a geopolitical struggle. In that sense, it would be interesting to notice some examples around the globe.

Switzerland, for instance, could be a sort of example. It uses neutrality as a pillar of their sovereignty. The country has a solid economy based on the full Swiss immersion in the international banking system and with a 'neutral' bank secrecy as an attractive feature, allowing the Swiss polity to survive all the European turbulences of the last two centuries. Neutrality was a big factor but not the only one that allowed the country to survive in the international scene with a strong position. It has a population with one of the highest living standards in the world. Besides, Switzerland acknowledges the heterogeneous social and linguistic tissue present. The country has four official languages. Even Romansch language[1155] with a population of less than 60,000 speakers enjoys the same status as German, French or Italian. This small detail could serve as an example in Ukraine or Moldova to show that precisely a state can exist in a multi-ethnic and multinational territory and not only around mono-ethnic proposals.

[1154] Agamben, Giorgio, *Mezzi senza fine*, Torino, Note sulla Politica, Bollati Boringhieri, 1996, page 57.
[1155] Romansh is mostly speaking in the Swiss Grissons canton by around 60,000 people including nearly 36,000 that use it as mother tongue.

It is important to acknowledge that the period of the classic European sovereign states as perceived during the nineteenth century does not exist anymore. States had to deal with several changes in the last decades mostly regarding how the new capitalist order influenced the political processes while the same logic of Capital has conditioned the pretension to build new states in the current global context. Therefore, the recently mentioned examples were part of a specific historical and political context that allowed them to appear; hence, it would be a mistake to universalize these processes rather than use them as a simple reference.

In the case of undeveloped countries, and especially when they are located near stronger neighbours, neutrality should be an issue. As mentioned, Mexico had for many years the Doctrine Estrada as pillar of its foreign policy and became an example in Latin America. The presence of the United States as northern neighbour turned complex for the Mexicans the possibility to develop an own foreign policy that could risk of being anti-US and bringing immediate repercussions. Instead, never intervening in other countries' affairs allowed international recognition and to pursue own national interests. As an example, Mexico was the first country that recognized the Cuban regime after the Cuban revolution in 1959 and that fact did not diminish or endanger their relation with the United States. Besides, the only country that did not suffer a military coup in Latin America after World War II was precisely Mexico.[1156]

In a different case in the same region, neutrality was not an option. For instance, Cuba was first part of a geopolitical dispute between Spain and the United States, and then, it was solely under the US influence and it was only after the Cuban revolution and the continuous aggressions by the United States that the Soviet Union became the only viable ally in the context of the Cold War. Cuba also had a multi-ethnic population and as in many ex-Spanish colonies, a new political identity emerged. In that context, Cuba preserved only some autonomy but surrendered to the Soviet Union in issues like the right to have an independent foreign policy.

[1156] Mexico was ruled from 1929 to 2000 and since 2012, by the same party, the Institutional Revolutionary Party (PRI), and even if it has mostly based its rule in authoritarian and repressive measures at different levels, it would be far from being considered a military dictatorship. Note of the author.

Conclusions 467

History shows also opposed cases of nations, which obtained a state only due to geopolitics, like Romania or Mongolia. Others instead were mere geopolitical inventions like Uruguay and Panama that acquired independence only due to foreign support. Altogether, these rather different cases have subsisted until now in the international scene although in different contexts. The question of until what point these countries are really sovereign would remain an argument for further discussion.

In the post-Soviet world, state building took different directions. In the Russian case, Yeltsin bombing the parliament and the First War in Chechnya were unsuccessful attempts to pursue this process. Instead, Putin's second war in Chechnya and its struggle against the oligarchs took the opposite direction. Both events aided the arrival, as explained in the first chapter, of a renewed sovereign Russian state.

In the rest of the former USSR, the roads were diverse. In many cases, civil wars erupted that had to count as in Armenia, Azerbaijan, Tajikistan, Moldova or Georgia with the presence of what remained of the Red Army to establish its own order and leaving the new polities already in a conditioned and dependable position with Moscow.

Overall, the conditions in Ukraine, Moldova and Pridnestrovia were rather complex. Contrary to Ukraine, where it is clear the existence of a Ukrainian nation (even if as explained, includes mix elements of Soviet and Russian culture), it would be arguable if there is a truly Moldovan or Pridnestrovian national identity. Geopolitics allowed both to appear in the international scene, the former recognized and the latter with a tacit (no) recognition.[1157] Afterwards, the possibilities of the local elites for political survival became completely attached with the motivations of the geopolitical projects to which they were related.

Altogether, two significant factors have notably influenced the studied polities. First, the social degradation suffered by most of the

---

[1157] Besides the legal argument and the implications carried in the international system, at the end, there is a tacit recognition of the PMR. Internationally, it is acknowledged as a 'problem'; it is acknowledged that Moldova has no control over Pridnestrovia and attempting not to be tautological, it is recognized that Pridnestrovia is not recognized, therefore recognizing the existence of the PMR. Note of the author.

population after the disappearance of the Soviet Union. Second, the transformation from a society controlled by a vertical and corrupt bureaucratic elite into a 'no man's land' while the same local corrupt bureaucracy adapted itself to remain in charge, but with no obligation to compel anymore with a Soviet authority or to any real notion of state and national development. Meanwhile, locals were deprived of their resources and the emerging social differences deepened.

To make it worse, the political and economical transformations required by the logic of Capital have no ways of being opposed. Therefore, austerity measures required by the IMF and the large set of reforms including privatizations and social transformations that go in that sense are not even questioned by the local population or are conceived as part of a 'necessary process' as a way of achieving some sort of 'modernity'. Instead, those same reforms do not challenge seriously the political control by the local oligarchs who can easily adapt to remain in charge.

Besides, the few attempts to pursue genuine democratic political projects in Ukraine or Moldova until now had to deal with the break imposed again by geopolitics. The same political elite against whom many citizens attempted to struggle, for example, silenced the thousands of independents and autonomous participants in the *Maidan*. The activists were 'helped' when they supported a geopolitical goal but were never allowed to become a political force on its own.

At the end, maybe the major tragedy of decades of Soviet rule was that it created a feeling of disenchantment with politics and blocked for decades the possibility for a real social and political mobilization. The *Maidan* partially revived this desire by one sector of the locals but in most cases was quickly co-opted.

In that sense, it remains to the local population the goal of establishing political forces able to achieve a genuine state-building process. Even though this aim seems out of reach by now. The studied region still enjoys one of the lowest living standards in Europe, and most of the population has an everyday struggle to survive with decrepit salaries, shaming labour conditions. For them remains only the increasing expectation to migrate somewhere else to improve their quality of life. To that extent, the fact that these territories are also a prey of a geopolitical struggle leaves them without an appealing scenario to achieve state building at least by now.

Bibliography

Agamben, Giorgio, *Mezzi senza fine*, Torino, Note sulla Politica, Bollati Boringhieri, 1996.

Agnew, John, *Geopolitics: Re-visioning World Politics*, New York, Routledge, 2nd edition, 2003.

'Аргументы и факты', Number 4, 1996.

Arjakovsky, Antoien, *De la Guerre a la paix ?* Paris, Parole et silence, 2014.

'ASMAE, Affari Politici, 1919–1930.' Romania. Envelope 1508, report from colonel Baffigi.

Avalos, Tenorio Gerardo, 'El colapso del Estado Mexicano' in *No nos alcanzan las palabras. Sociedad, Estado y violencia en México*, Itaca, UAM-X, 2014.

Avalos, Tenorio Gerardo, *El Monarca, El ciudadano y el excluido*, México, D.F. UAM-X, CSH, 2006.

Avalos, Tenorio Gerardo and Hirsch, Joachim, *La política del capital*, México, UAM-X, 2007.

Babilunga, N.V., *Повторение пройдённого: феодализм как светлое будущее Республики Молдова*, Tiraspol, Bendery, 2012.

Basciani, Alberto, *La difficile Unione, La Bessarabia e la Grande Romania 1918–1940*, Roma, Aracne, 2007.

Becket, Ian, *The Great War*, Great Britain, Pearson Longman, 2007.

Belostecinic, *Analiza Barometrului de Opinie Publica 1998, 2000, 2001*, Chisinau, Institutul de Politici Publice, 2001.

Bogomolov, Oleg, 'Resta la speranza', Moskovskoe Novosti, 1992, quoted in Medvedev, Roj, *La Russia post-sovietica, Un viaggio nell'era Eltsin*, Torino, Giulio Enaudi Editori, 2000.

Boian, Victoria, 'Relations of the Republic of Moldova with Ukraine', in *The Foreign Policy of the Republic of Moldova (1998–2008)*, Chisinau, Cartdidact, Friedirch Ebert Stiftung, 2010.

Bomeshko, B.G., *Создание, становление и защита приднестровском государственности 1990–1992 гг.*, Bendery, Poligrafist, 2010.

Bomeshko, B.G., 'Законодательная власть в системе приднестровском государственности и её развитие', in *Государственность Приднестровья: история и современность*, Bendery, Poligrafist, 2007.

Boyko, Natalia, 'Eglises orthodoxies et identité nationale en Ukraine postsoviétique', in *L'Ukraine dans la Nouvelle Europe*, edited by Lepesan, Gilles, Paris, Espaces Milieux, CNRS Editions, 2005.

Brzezinski, Zbigniew, *Russia and the Commonwealth of Independent States: Documents, Data and Analysis*, Armonk, ME Sharp Inc., 1997.

Brzezinski, Zbigniew, *Strategic Vision: America and the Crisis of Global Power*, New York, Basic Books, 2012.

Brzezinski, Zbigniew, *The Grand Chessboard: American Strategy and Its Geostrategic Imperatives*, New York, Basic Books, 1997.

Carrère d'Encausse Héléne, *La Russie entre deux mondes*, Paris, Fayard, 2010.

Chirila, Victor, 'Cooperation of the Republic of Moldova within GUAM', in *The Foreign Policy of the Republic of Moldova (1998–2008)*, Chisinau, Friedrich Ebert Stiftung, Cartdidact, 2010.

Chirila, Victor, 'Relations of the Republic of Moldova with the European Union', in *The Foreign Policy of the Republic of Moldova (1998–2008)*, Chisinau, Friedrich Ebert Stiftung, Cartdidact, 2010.

Chirila, Victor, 'Republic of Moldova relations with Romania' in *The Foreign Policy of the Republic of Moldova (1998–2008)*, Chisinau, Friedrich Ebert Stiftung, Cartdidact, 2010.

Clowes, Edith W., *Russia on the Edge*, Ithaca, Cornell University Press, 2011.

Conea, Ion, *L'Unità Geopolitica dello stato romeno*, Bucharest, Amicizia Italo-Romena, 1940.

Conquest, Robert, *The Harvest of Sorrow. Soviet Collectivization and the Terror-Famine*, New York, Oxford University Press, 1986.

Coutau-Bégarie, Hervé, *Traité de Stratégie*, Paris, Economica, 2003.

Danero Iglesias, Julien, *Nationalisme et pouvoir en République de Moldavie*, Bruxelles, Editions de l'Université de Bruxelles, 2014,

Davies, R.W. and Wheatcroft, S.G., *The Years of Hunger: Soviet Agriculture, 1931–33*, New York, McMillan, 2004.

De Bonis, Mauro, *Le mani sul Polo*, Limes, Rivista italiana di Geopolitica, March 2010.

Delovoj, Vtornik, Delovoy 'Mir', 3 February 1996 quoted in Medvedev Roj, *La Russia post-sovietica, Un viaggio nell'era Eltsin*, Torino, Giulio Enaudi Editori, 2000.

Demirdirek, Hulya, 'In the Minority: (Dis) Empowerment through Territorial Conflict', in *Europe's Last Frontier? Belarus, Moldova and Ukraine between Russia and the European Union*, edited by Schmidtke, Oliver and Yekelchyk, Serhy, Basingstoke, Palgrave McMillan, 2008.

Dodds, Klaus, *Geopolitics: A Very Short Introduction*, Oxford, OUP, 2007.

Doroshko, M.С., 'Геополітичні інтереси та зовнішня політика держав', Dubrova Irina, Kharismatiki у Ortodoksy, Novoe vremia, 26 July, 1999. '*пострадянського простору*', Nika Centre, Kiev, 2011.

Dromundo, Rolando, 'Ucraina: Un conflitto geopolitico fra la Russia e Occidente' ,Thesis to obtain the Master's Degree in International Relations, EU-Latin America at the Bologna University, Italy, 2007.

Eberhard, Adam, *'The paradoxes of Moldovan Sports'*, *Point of View*, Centre for Eastern Studies, November 2011.

Ellman, Michael, 'Soviet repression statistics: Some comments', *Europe-Asia Studies*, Vol. 54, No. 7 (2002), pages 1151–1172.

Gallina, Nicole, 'Ukraine Knocking at the Door? The Ukraine-EU Relationship after the Orange Revolution', in *Ukraine on Its Meandering Path Between East and West*, edited by Lushnycky, Andrej N. and Riabchuk, Michola, Peter Lang AG, Bern, 2009.

Gangloff, Camile, *L'import-export de la démocratie : Serbie, Géorgie, Ukraine, Kirghizstan*, Paris, L'Harmattan, 2008.

Garnett, Sherman W., 'The integrationist temptation', *The Washington Quarterly*, Vol. 18, No. 2 (Spring 1995), page 40, quoted in Kuzio Taras, Ukraine Back from the Brink, European Security Study No. 2, Institute for European Defence and Strategic Studies, MCP Litho Ltd., 1995.

Garrad, John and Newell, James L., *Scandals in Past and Contemporary Politics*, Manchester, Manchester University Press, 2006.

Gogol, N.V., 'Sobranie sochinenii', in *Vol. 10—Collected Letters*, Moscow, Russkaia kniga, 1994.

Gogol, Nicolai, *Taras Bulba e gli altri racconti di Mirgorod*, Milano, Garzanti, Grandi libri, 2012.

Goldman, Marshall I., *Petrostate: Putin, Power and the New Russia*, Oxford, Oxford University Press, 2008.

Graziosi, Andrea, *L'Unione Sovietica 1914–1991*, Bologna, Il Mulino, 2011.

Graziosi, Andrea, *L'URSS dal trionfo al degrado, Storia dell'Unione Sovietica. 1945–1991*, Il Mulino, Bologna 2008.

Gressova, Maria, 'Ukraine—Possible New Member State of the EU with post-Transition economy—and the EU' in Collection of papers from the 1st PhD Students' International Conference 'my PhD', Friedrich Ebert Stiftung, Slovakia, 2007, page 115.

Heuser, Beatrice, 'Clausewitz ideas of strategy and victory', in *Clausewitz in the Twenty-First Century*, edited by Strachen, Hew and Herbrer-Rothe, Andras, Oxford, OUP, 2007.

Hill, Christopher, Ed. *The Actors in Europe's Foreign Policy*, London, Routledge, 1996.

Hirsch, Joachim, *Globalización, Capital y Estado*, México, UAM Xochimilco, 1996.

Hirsch, Joachim, 'Globalization of capital, nation states and democracy', *Studies in Political Economy*, Vol. 54, University of Toronto, 1997.

Hensel, Stuart and Gudim, Anatol, 'Moldov'as economic transition: Slow and contradictory' in *The EU & Moldova*, edited by Lewis, Ann, London, The Federal Trust, 2004.

Hobsbawn, Eric, 'Inventing traditions', in *The Invention of Tradition*, edited by Hobsbawm, Eric and Ranger, Terence, Cambridge, Cambridge University Press, 1983.

Horowitoz, Shale, *From Ethnic Conflict to Stillborn Reform*, The Former Soviet Union and Yugoslavia, College Station, Texas A & M University Press, 2005.

Izvestiya, 21 March 1995.

Jean, Carlo, *Geopolitica*, Bari, Editori Laterza, 1996.

Jean, Carlo, *Geopolitica del mondo contemporaneo*, Bari, Editori Laterza, 2012.

Judt, Tony, *Postwar: A History of Europe since 1945*, New York, Penguin Press, 2005.

Kant, Immanuel, *To Perpetual Peace: A Philosophical Sketch*, Indianapolis, Hacket Publishing, 2003.

Katchanovski, Ivan, *Cleft Countries, Regional Political Divisions and Cultures in Post-Soviet Ukraine and Moldova*, Stuttgart, Ibidem, 2006,

Khmelko, В.Е., *ЛІНГВО-ЕТНІЧНА СТРУКТУРА УКРАЇНИ: РЕГІОНАЛЬНІ ОСОБЛИВОСТІ ТА ТЕНДЕНЦІЇ ЗМІН ЗА РОКИ НЕЗАЛЕЖНОСТІ*, Kiev International Institute of Sociology, 2003.

King, Charles, *The Moldovans: Romania, Russia, and the Politics of Culture*, Stanford, Hoover Institution Press, Stanford University, 2000.

Kolodziejczyk, Dariusz, 'The Crimean Khanate and Poland-Lithuania, International diplomacy on the European Periphery (15th–18th century)' A study of peace treaties followed by annotated documents, Boston, Brill, 2011.

Kortunov, Vladimir, Nezavisimaya Gazeta, December 5, 1996.

Kozelsky, Mara, *Christianizing Crimea, Shaping sacred space in the Russian Empire and beyond*, DeKalb, Northern Illinois University Press, 2010.

Kryshtanovskaya, Olga and White, Stephen, 'The sovietization of Russian politics', *Post-Soviet Affairs*, 25, No. 4 (2009), page 287.

Kuchler, Florian, *The Role of the European Union in Moldova's Transnistria Conflict*, Stuttgart, Ibidem, 2006,

'Куда идет страна, 5 главных вопросов и ответов по поводу текущих событий в Украине', Вести, 2 December 2013, pages 4–5.

Kuzio, Taras, 'Ukraine back from the brink', European Security Study No. 2, Institute for European Defence and Strategic Studies, MCP Litho Ltd., 1995.

Lacoste, Yves, *D'autres geopolitiques,* Herodote, 2ᵉ trimester, 1982.

Laitin, David D., *Identity in Formation*, Ithaca, Cornell University Press, 1998.

Lieven, Anatoly, *Ukraine & Russia, A Fraternal Rivalry*, Washington, D.C., United States Institute of Peace Press, 1999.

Limes, Rivista italiana di Geopolitica, 3/2009.

Lo, Bobo, *Vladimir Putin and the Evolution of Russian Foreign Policy*, The Royal Institute of International Affairs, Russia and Eurasia Programme, Oxford, Blackwell Publishers, 2003.

Liddell, Hart, *Strategy*, New York, Meridian, 1991.

Lunt, Horace, 'The Language of the Rus' in the eleventh century: Some observations about facts and theories', *Harvard Ukrainian Studies*, Vol. 12–13 (1988–1989), pages 276–313, referred in Wilson, Andrew, *The Ukrainians Unexpected Nation*, Yale University Press, 2002.

Luttwak, Edward, *Coup d'Etat, A Practical Handbook—A Brilliant Guide to Taking Over a Nation*, New York, Fawcett Publications, 1968.

Luttwatk, Edward N., *Strategy, The Logic of War and Peace*, Cambridge, The Belknap Press of Harvard University Press, 2001.

Mackinder, H.J., *Democratic Ideas and Reality*, New York, NDU Press, 1942, Page xviii.

Magocsi, Paul Robert, 'A history of Ukraine', University of Toronto Press incorporated, Canada, 1996.

Magosci, Paul, *The Roots of Ukrainian Nationalism, Galicia as Ukraine's Piedmont*, Toronto, University of Toronto Press, 2002.

Maric, A., *Les faiseurs de revolutions, Politique International*, No. 106, hiver, 2004–2005.

Martin, Terry, *The Affirmative Action Empire, Nations and Nationalism in the Soviet Union: 1923–1939*, Ithaca, Cornell University Press, 2001.

Marx, Karl, *El Capital*, Vol. 1, Mexico, D.F., Fondo de Cultura Economica, 1995.

Medvedev, Roj, *La Russia post-sovietica, Un viaggio nell'era Eltsin*, Torino, Giulio Enaudi Editori, 2000.

'МЕМОРАНДУМ об основах нормализации отношений между Республики Молдова и Приднестровье' in *ПЕРЕГОВОРНЫЙ ПРОЦЕСС МЕЖДУ МОЛДАВСКОЙ РЕСПУБЛИКОЙ И РЕСПУВЛИКОЙ МОЛДОВА В ДОКУМЕНТАХ*, Ministry of Foreign Affairs of the Pridnestrovian Moldovan Republic, Poligrafist, 2011.

Mini, Fabio, 'La strana coppia Russia-Cina, figlia delle manipolazioni e degli errori di Obama', Limes, *Rivista italiana di Geopolitica*, August 2014.

Montanari, Arianna, 'Un caso di nazionalismo normativo: l'Estonia', in *La fine del Sistema Sovietico e i Paesi Baltici, Il caso dell'Estonia*, edited by Pirzio Ammassari, Gloria and Montanari, Arianna, Milan, Francoangeli, 2003.

Morozov, Kostiantin, *Above and Beyond, From Soviet General to Ukrainian State Builder*, Harvard, Harvard Ukrainian Research Institute Publications, 2001.

Nahaylo, Bodan, *The Ukrainian Resurgence*, Toronto, C. Hurst & Co. Publishers, 1999.

Neukirch, Claus, 'Moldova's Eastern dimension', in *The EU & Moldova, On a Fault Line of Europe*, edited by Lewis, Ann, London, The Federal Trust, 2004.

Nohlen, D, Grotz, F., and Hartmann, C., *Elections in Asia: A Data Handbook*, Vol. I, Oxford University Press, 2001.

Nohlen, D. and Stöver, P., *Elections in Europe: A Data Handbook*, Baden-Baden, Germany, Nomos, 2010.

Orlando, Cristiano, *La partita eurasiatica, Geopolitica della Sicurezza tra occidente e Russia*, Roma, Archivio Disarmo, 2009.

Ozhiganov, Edward, 'The Republic of Moldova: Transdniester and the 14th Army', in *Managing Conflict in the Former Soviet Union: Russian and American Perspectives*, edited by Arbatov, Alexei et al., Cambridge, MIT Press, 1997

'ПЕРЕГОВОРНЫЙ ПРОЦЕСС МЕЖДУ МОЛДАВСКОЙ РЕСПУБЛИКОЙ И РЕСПУВЛИКОЙ МОЛДОВА В ДОКУМЕНТАХ', Ministry of Foreign Affairs of the Pridnestrovian Moldovan Republic, Poligrafist, 2011.

Perepelytsia, G.M. Ed., *Foreign Policy of Ukraine*, Annual Strategic Review 2008, Stylos Publishing House, 2009.

Perepelytsia, G.M., 'Ukraine's relations with the USA and Canada' in *Foreign Policy of Ukraine Annual Strategic Review 2009/10*, Kiev, Stylos Publishing House, 2011.

Pleines, Heiko, *From* 'Competitive authoritarianism to defective democracy: Political regimes in Ukraine before and after the Orange Revolution', in *Presidents, Oligarchs and Bureaucrats, Forms of Rule in the Post-Soviet Space*, edited by Stewart, Susan, Klein, Margarete, Schmitz, Andrea and Schroder, Hans-Henning, Presidents, oligarchs and Bureaucrats, Ashgate, Burlington, 2012.

Pleines, Heiko, 'The political role of the Oligarchs', in *Ukraine on Its Way to Europe, Interim Results of the Orange Revolution*, edited by Besters-Dilger, Juliane, Peter Lang, New York, Frankfurt am Main, 2009.

Primakov, Evgeniy, *Мир без России?*, Moscow, Российская газета, 2010.

Pritsak, O., *The Origin of Rus'*, Cambridge, Harvard Ukrainian Research Institute, 1981.

Pukhov, Ruslan, Ed., 'The Tanks of August', Centre for Analysis of Strategies and Technologies, Moscow, Russia, 2010.

Qualls, Karl D., *From Ruins to Reconstruction, Urban Identity in Soviet Sevastopol After World War II*, Ithaca, Cornell University Press, US, 2009.

Raffestin, Claude, *Geopolitique et histoire*, Paris, Histoire Payot, 1995.

Rakickaya, Galina, Nezavisimaya Gazeta, January 5, 1996.

Rees, E.A. *Iron Lazar: A Political Biography of Lazar Kaganovich*, London, Anthem Press, 2012.

Rossiskaya Gazeta, 24 January 1995.

'RUSSIAN FEDERATION: WHAT JUSTICE FOR CHECHNYA'S DISAPPEARED', AI Index, EUR, 46/015/2007, Amnesty International, May 2007.

Rutland, Peter, *The Challenge of Integration, Annual Survey of Eastern Europe and the Former Soviet Union*, New York, East West Institute, 1998.

Ruzé, Alain, *La Moldova entre la Roumanie et la Russie*, Paris, L'Harmattan, 1997.

Sasse, Gwendolyn, *The Crimea Question: Identity, Transition, and Conflict*, Cambridge, Ukrainian Research Institute, Harvard University, 2007.

Schmid, Alex P., 'The definition of terrorism', in *The Routledge Handbook of Terrorism Research*, edited by Schmid, Alex P., New York, Routledge, 2011.

Schmitt, Carl, *Il nomos della terra*, Milano, Adelphi Edizioni S.P.A., 1991.

Schmitt, Carl, *La Notion de Politique*, Paris, Calmann-Levy, 1972.

Schrad, Mark Lawrence, *Vodka Politics, Alcohol Autocracy, and the Secret History of the Russian State*, Oxford, Oxford University Press, 2014.

Serebrian, Oleg, '"Good Brothers", Bad neighbours: Romanian/Moldovan relations', in *The EU & Moldova, On a Fault Line of Europe*, edited by Lewis, Ann, London, The Federal Trust, 2004.

Simms B., *Europe, The Struggle for Supremacy, From 1453 to the Present*, New York, Basic Books, 2013.

Skalnes, Lars S., 'Geopolitics and the Eastern enlargement of the European Union', in *The Politics of European Union Enlargement, Theoretical Approaches*, edited by Schimmelfennig, Frank and Sedelmeier, Ulrich, New York, Routledge, 2005.

'СОГЛАШЕНИЕ О ПРИНЦИПИПАХ МИРНОГО УРЕГУЛИРОВАНИЯ ВООРУЖЁННОГО КОНФЛИКТА В ПРИДНЕСТРОВСКОМ РЕГИОНЕ РЕСПУБЛИКИ МОЛДОВА' in *ПЕРЕГОВОРНЫЙ ПРОЦЕСС МЕЖДУ МОЛДАВСКОЙ РЕСПУБЛИКОЙ И РЕСПУВЛИКОЙ МОЛДОВА В ДОКУМЕНТАХ*, Ministry of Foreign Affairs of the Pridnestrovian Moldovan Republic, Poligrafist, 2011.

Spanu, Vlad, 'Why is Moldova poor and economically volatile?', in *The EU & Moldova*, edited by Lewis, Ann, London, The Federal Trust, 2004.

Stavila, Ion, 'Evolution in settlement of the Transnistrian conflict', in *The Foreign Policy of the Republic of Moldova (1998–2008)*, Chisinau, Cartdidact, Friedirch Ebert Stiftung, 2010.

Subtelny, Orest, 'The ambiguities of national identity: The case of Ukraine', in *Ukraine: The Search for a National Identity*, edited by Wolchik, Sharon L., and Zviglyanich, Volodymir, Lanham, Rowman & Littlefield, 2000.

Subtelny, Orest, *Ukraine a History*, Canada, University of Toronto, 2000.

Taubman, William, *Khrushchev: The Man and His Era*, New York, W.W. Norton & Co., 2003.

Taccani, Matteo, *Ucraina, La Danza degli oligarchi*, Limes Oggi, 20 May 2014.

'TOP 100', Korrespondent, Kiev, Number 32(221). 17 August 2006.

Tuathail, Ó, *Critical Geopolitics: The Politics of Writing Global Space*, Routledge, London, 1996

Trotsky, Leon, *The History of the Russian Revolution*, Chicago, Haymarket Books, 2008.

'Uomini Verdi, Uomini Neri, Ominicchi e Quaquaraquà', Editoriale, Limes, Rivista italiana di Geopolitica, December 2014

'US assistance to Eurasia', fiscal years 2000–2004, SEED Act implementation report 2002–2004

Vahl, Marius and Emerson, Michael, 'Moldova and the Transnistrian conflict', in *Europeanization and Conflict Resolution Case Studies* from the European Periphery, Gent, Academia Press, 2004.

Vernochet, Jean-Michel, 'Ukraine l'escalade ', Chronique ukrainiennes Saison 2, Sigest. Mai/Novembre 2014.

Vitale, Alessandro e Romeo Giuseppe, *La Russia post imperiale, la tentazione di potenza*, 2013. Rubbettino, Italia, 2009.

Von Clausewitz, Carl, *Della Guerra*, Torino, Giulio Enaude Editore s.p.a., 2002.

Vrabie, Radu, 'Relationships of the Republic of Moldova with the Russian Federation', in *The Foreign Policy of the Republic of Moldova* (1998–2008), Chisinau, Friedrich Ebert Stiftung, Cartdidact, 2010.

Wallerstein, Immanuel, *Geopolitics and Geoculture*, Cambridge University Press, 1991.

Williamson, Jon, 'What washing means by policy reform' in *Latin American Adjustment: How Much Has Happened?*, edited by Williamson, Jon, Washington, D.C., Peterson Institute for International Economics, April 1990.

Wilson, Andrew, *Ukraine's Orange Revolution*, London, Yale University Press, 2005.

Wilson, Andrew, *The Ukrainians: Unexpected Nation*, New Haven, Yale University Press, 2002.

Wolczuk, Roman, *Ukraine's Foreign and Security Policy*, 1991–2000, Routledge, Curzon, 2003.

Wood, Ellen Meiksins, *Empire of Capital*, London, Verso, 2007.

Yafimava, Katja, *The Transit Dimension of EU Energy Security*, Oxford, Oxford University Press, 2011.

Zaborsky, Victor, *Crimea and the Black Sea Fleet in Russian-Ukrainian Relations*, Discussion paper 95–11, Center for Science and International Affairs, September 1995.

Zafesova, Anna, *e da Mosca è tutto, storie Della Russia che cambia e che non cambia*, Torino, UTET, 2005.

Zaporjoran-Pirgari, Angelina, 'Minority rights in Moldova: Consolidating a multiethnic society', in *The EU & Moldova, On a Fault Line of Europe*, edited by Lewis, Ann, London, The Federal Trust, 2004.

Zaslavsky, Victor, *Dopo L'Unione Sovietica, La perestroika e il problema delle nazionalità*, Bologna, Il Mulino 1991.

Electronic Sources

'A brief primer on Vladimir Putin's Eurasian dream', February 18, 2014. http://www.theguardian.com/world/shortcuts/2014/feb/18/brief-primer-vladimir-putin-eurasian-union-trade

'A Kiev, l'opposition dépassée par la colère des manifestants', 20 January 2014, accessed on 20 January 2014. http://www.lemonde.fr/europe/article/2014/01/20/a-kiev-l-opposition-en-passe-d-etre-depassee-par-la-colere-des-manifestants_4350966_3214.html

'Афганистан и Сербия стали наблюдателями при ПА ОДКБ', accessed on 5 November 2014. http://www.odkbcsto.org/news/detail.php?ELEMENT_ID=1779&SECTION_ID=92&sphrase_id=8903

'After the parliamentary elections in Ukraine: a tough victory for the party of regions', 7 November 2012, accessed on 7 November 2012. http://www.osw.waw.pl/en/publikacje/analyses/2012-11-07/after-parliamentary-elections-ukraine-a-tough-victory-party-regions

'Agreement on the Settlement of the Crisis in Ukraine-full text', *The Guardian*, 21 February 2014. http://www.theguardian.com/world/2014/feb/21/agreement-on-the-settlement-of-crisis-in-ukraine-full-text

'Ахметов поддержал Евромайдан и призвал стороны конфликта сесть за стол переговоров', 13 December 2013, accessed on 13 December 2013. http://korrespondent.net/business/economics/3276964-akhmetov-podderzhal-evromaidan-y-pryzval-storony-konflykta-sest-za-stol-perehovorov

'Alegerile parlamentare Republicii Moldova din 30 noiembrie 2014',Accessed on 1 July 2015. http://www.cec.md/r/r/

Allison, Graham T., and Matthew Lantz. 'Assessing Russia's Democratic Presidential Election'. http://belfercenter.ksg.harvard.edu/publication/2362/assessing_russias_democratic_presidential_election.html

'АЛМА-АТИНСКАЯ ДЕКЛАРАЦИЯ', 21 December 1991, Archive Egor Gaidar, accessed on 22 February 2016. http://gaidar-arc.ru/file/bulletin-1/DEFAULT/org.stretto.plugins.bulletin.core.Article/file/2880

'Ангела Меркель сочла высказывания Нуланд 'недостойными'', 8 February 2014, accessed on 8 February 2014. http://korrespondent.net/world/3302950-anhela-merkel-sochla-vyskaz yvanyia-nuland-nedostoinymy

'Антимайдан» Одессы объявил о создании Одесской республики', 14 April 2014, accessed on 14 April 2014. http://www.sinoptik.md/ru/news/695?utm_campaign=Informer&utm_medium=referral&utm_source=Kommersant

Appointments of regional governors and cabinet by President Yushchenko compiled by the Action Ukraine Report Monitoring Service on 4 February 2005. Accessed on 29 February 2016. http://www.europarl.europa.eu/meetdocs/2004_2009/documents/fd/ua_20050223_04_/ua_20050223_04_en.pdf

ASSESSMENT REPORT OF DIRECTIVE 2004/67/EC ON SECURITY OF GAS SUPPLY, Commission Staff Working Document, Brussels, SEC, (2009) 978 final, 16/7/2009. http://eurlex.europa.eu/LexUriServ/LexUriServ.do?uri=SEC:2009:0978:FIN:EN:PDF

'Austria pleads for South Stream pipeline', 24 June 2014. http://www.euractiv.com/sections/energy/austria-pleads-south-stream-pipeline-303010

Axe, David, 'Russia pounds ISIS with biggest bomber raid in decades', 17 November 2015, accessed on 17 November 2015. http://www.thedailybeast.com/articles/2015/11/17/russia-pounds-isis-with-biggest-bomber-raid-in-decades.html

'Байден: Говорю с Порошенко чаще, чем с женой', 12 December 2015, accessed on 12 December 2015. http://korrespondent.net/ukraine/3599762-baiden-hovorui-s-poroshenko-chasche-chem-s-zhenoi

Barinova, Maria, 'Проект Россия', 22 November 2004, accessed on 17 February 2015. http://www.profile.ru/archive/item/45597

'Berezovsky's funded revolution', 12 November 2005, *The Independent.* http://www.independent.co.uk/news/world/europe/berezovsky-funded-revolution-514948.html

Berkut units were dissolved on 25 February 2014, but unofficially remained operational in Crimea. 'Head of Ukrainian Interior Ministry signs order to dissolve "Berkut,"' 26 February 2014, accessed on 26 February 2014. http://sputniknews.com/voiceofrussia/news/2014_02_26/Head-of-Ukrainian-Interior-Ministry-signs-order-to-dissolve-Berkut-3065/

'Beyond 2010: The Critical Core of Europe's Security', accessed on 23 February 2016. http://www.rusolub.ocatch.com/pages/library/Grand/150dpi/image018.jpg

'Без вмешательства ЕС и России решить конфликт в Украине уже не получится—политолог', 28 January 2014, accessed on 28 January 2014. http://korrespondent.net/ukraine/politics/3297944-bez-vmeshatelstva-es-y-rossyy-reshyt-konflykt-v-ukrayne-uzhe-ne-poluchytsia-polytoloh

'Bill on Taraclia Status approved in First Reading', 6 April 2015, accessed on 5 September 2015. http://www.infotag.md/politics-en/201882/

'Biographie: La Consolidation du regime', http://www.charles-de-gaulle.org/pages/l-homme/accueil/biographie/1962-1968-la-consolidation-du-regime.php?id_article=375

'Бойцы батальонов МВД начали переходить в армию', 5 September 2014, accessed on 1 March 2016. http://korrespondent.net/ukraine/3414884-boitsy-batalonov-mvd-nachaly-perekhodyt-v-armyui

'Больше трех не собираются', Газета 'Коммерсантъ Украина', №172 (1875), 24 November 2013, accessed on 24 November 2013. http://www.kommersant.ru/doc/2326962

Bullough, Oliver, 'Welcome to the most corrupt nation in Europe', The Guardian, 4 February 2015, accessed on 1 March 2016. http://www.theguardian.com/news/2015/feb/04/welcome-to-the-most-corrupt-nation-in-europe-ukraine#comments

Buzina, Oles. 'Истории от Олеся Бузины: Тарас Шевченко – эталон двуязычия', 10 October 2010. Accessed on 22 August 2016. http://www.buzina.org/povtorenie/2204-taras-shevchenko-etalon-bilengvizma.html

'Central Asia: Widespread Rights Abuse, Repression', 31 January 2013. http://www.hrw.org/news/2013/01/31/central-asia-widespread-rights-abuse-repression

'CIS leaders sign free trade deal', 18 November 2011. http://sputniknews.com/russia/20111018/167833875.html

Champion Mark, 'U.S. Ally proves volatile amid dispute with Russia', 30 August 2008. http://online.wsj.com/news/articles/SB122006041734285393?mod=hpp_us_whats_news&mg=reno64-wsj&url=http%3A%2F%2Fonline.wsj.com%2Fartcle%2FSB122006041734285393.html%3Fmod%3Dhpp_us_whats_news

'Changes in Turkey in Europe 1856 to 1878,' accessed on 1 March 2016. https://upload.wikimedia.org/wikipedia/commons/f/fd/Balkans_1878.png

Chantal Beaucourt, 'L'Union soviétique et la Roumanie', in Jean-Baptiste, Duroselle, *Les frontières européennes de l'URSS*, Paris, Colin, 1975.

Chiesa, Giuletto, I congiurati dell'Operazione Kosovo, La Stampa (Torino), 13 June 1999, page 3. http://www.archiviolastampa.it/component/option,com_lastampa/task,search/mod,avanzata/action,viewer/Itemid,3/page,1/articleid,0494_01_1999_0160_0001_13626651/anews,true/

'Citizenship rows divide Latvia', 25 March 2005, accessed on 23 February 2016. http://news.bbc.co.uk/2/hi/europe/4371345.stm

Cohen, Roger, 'Who really bought down Milosevic?', 26 November 2000. http://www.nytimes.com/library/magazine/home/20001126mag-serbia.html

'Commissioner Malmström on visa-free travel for the citizens of the Republic of Moldova', European Commission Statement, 27 April 2014, accessed on 17 March 2015. http://europa.eu/rapid/press-release_STATEMENT-14-137_en.htm?locale=en

'Con Poroshenko in Ucraina viene eletto il Gattopardo', 27 May 2014, accessed on 27 May 2014. http://temi.repubblica.it/limes/con-poroshenko-in-ucraina-viene-eletto-il-gattopardo/62419

'Confidence in Democracy and Capitalism wanes in Former Soviet Union', 5 December 2011. http://www.pewglobal.org/2011/12/05/confidence-in-democracy-and-capitalism-wanes-in-former-soviet-union/

Cordsman, Anthony H., 'Russia and the color revolution, Center for Strategic and International Studies', 28 May 2014. http://csis.org/publication/russia-and-color-revolution

'CONSTITUŢIA REPUBLICII MOLDOVA', accessed on 5 September 2015. http://lex.justice.md/document_rom.php?id=44B9F30E:7AC17731

'Countries and Regions: Russia.' Last updated 27 October 2015, accessed on 23 February 2016. http://ec.europa.eu/trade/policy/countries-and-regions/countries/russia/

'Country overview', Ministry of Foreign Affairs of Pridnestrovian Moldovan Republic, accessed on 3 March 2016. http://mfa-pmr.org/en/about_republic

'Courte défaite des communistes en Moldavie', 31 July 2010, accessed on 9 March 2015. http://www.lemonde.fr/europe/article/2009/07/31/courte-defaite-des-communistes-en-moldavie_1224620_3214.html

'Creation of Eurasian Parliament deemed possible', 20 November 2013. http://itar-tass.com/en/russia/708233

'Crimea declares state of emergency after power lines attacked', 22 November 2015, accessed on 22 January 2016. http://www.theguardian.com/world/2015/nov/22/crimea-state-of-emergency-power-lines-attacked

'Crimean Tatars divided between Russian and Ukrainian promises', 17 March 2015, accessed on 17 March 2015. http://www.theguardian.com/world/2015/mar/17/crimean-tatars-divided-between-russian-and-ukrainian-promises

'CSTO tightens foreign bases norms', 20 December 2011. http://www.thehindu.com/todays-paper/tp-international/article2736607.ece

'Cum a devenit Vladimir Plahotniuc milionar în euro', 27 January 2011, accessed on 10 August 2015. http://adevarul.ro/moldova/actualitate/cum-devenit-vladimir-plahotniuc-milionar-euro-1_50ad70757c42d5a663952dc5/index.html

'Customs Union, Eurasian Union no threat to Kazakhstan's sovereignty council', 27 August 2014. http://itar-tass.com/en/world/746905

'Четыре страны ЕС не поддержали расширение санкций против России', 31 August 2014, accessed on 31 August 2014. http://finance.bigmir.net/news/economics/50251-Chetyre-strany-ES-ne-podderzhali-rasshirenie-sankcij-protiv-Rossii?utm_source=exchange&utm_medium=banner&utm_campaign=crosspromo

'Что и говорить', Газета 'Коммерсантъ Украина', №207 (1910), 12 December 2013, accessed on 12 December 2013. http://www.kommersant.ua/doc/2365723

'Dancing with the Bear: Merkel Seeks a Hardline on Putin', 24 March 2014, accessed on 15 March 2015. http://www.spiegel.de/international/germany/merkel-and-europe-search-for-an-adequate-response-to-putin-a-960378.html

'Declaration of independence of the Republic of Moldova', 27 August 1991, accessed on 1 March 2016. http://www.presedinte.md/eng/declaration

'Депутаты приняли закон о блокировке сайтов, продаже SIM-карт по паспорту и наказании за «экстремизм» в соцсетях', 16 January 2014, accessed on January 16, 2014. http://ain.ua/2014/01/16/508940?utm_source=ain&utm_medium=fb&utm_campaign=social

'Decision making processes of the Eurasian Customs Union and Single Economic Space.' http://en.wikipedia.org/wiki/Eurasian_Economic_Union#mediaviewer/File:Decision_making_process_of_the_Eurasian_Customs_Union_and_the_Single_Economic_Space.jpg

'Договор Януковича и Медведева о базировании флота до 2042 года. Текст документа', Украинская правда, 22 April 2010, accessed on February 29, 2016. http://www.pravda.com.ua/rus/articles/2010/04/22/4956018/

'Donald Trump Says He'll 'Get Along Fine' with Russian President Vladimir Putin', ABC News, 20 December 2015, accessed on 20 December 2015. http://abcnews.go.com/Politics/donald-trump-hell-fine-russian-president-vladimir-putin/story?id=35872623

'Донецк патрулируют отряды казаков и ветеранов-афганцев', 26 January 2014, accessed on 26 January 2014. http://korrespondent.net/ukraine/politics/3297360-donetsk-patruly-ruuit-otriady-kazakov-y-veteranov-afhantsev

Dromundo Rolando, 'La Geopolítica de la Eurocopa Polonia-Ucrania 2012', El Internacionalista, 19 April 2012, accessed on 25 February 2015. http://elinternacionalista.com/2012/04/19/la-geopolitica-de-la-eurocopa-polonia-ucrania-2012/

Eckel, Mike, 'Putin calls Soviet collapse a 'Geopolitical Catastrophe', Associated Press, 26-IV-2005. http://www.utsandiego.com/uniontrib/20050426/news_1n26russia.html

Eke, Steven, 'Profile: Aslan Asabidze', 4 May 2004. http://news.bbc.co.uk/2/hi/europe/3683629.stm

'Elections of people's deputies of Ukraine', accessed on 29 February 2016. http://www.cvk.gov.ua/pls/vd2002/webproc0e

'Elections 31.10.2004', accessed on 23 April 2015. http://www.cvk.gov.ua/pls/vp2004/wp0011e

'Elections 21.11.2004', accessed on 23 April 2015. http://www.cvk.gov.ua/pls/vp2004/wp0011e

'Elections 26.12.2004', accessed on 26 April 2015. http://www.cvk.gov.ua/pls/vp2004/wp0011e

Elliot, Larry, 'Stakes are high as US plays the oil card against Iran and Russia', *The Guardian*, 9 November 2014. http://www.theguardian.com/business/economics-blog/2014/nov/09/us-iran-russia-oil-prices-shale

'En Ukraine, le premier ministre a démissionné', 28 January 2014, accessed on 28 January 2014. http://www.lemonde.fr/europe/article/2014/01/28/en-ukraine-le-premier-ministre-a-demissionne_4355497_3214.html

'Enlargement of NATO', accessed on 23 February 2016. http://en.wikipedia.org/wiki/Enlargement_of_NATO#mediaviewer/File:History_of_NATO_enlargement.svg

'Эштон перед встречей с Януковичем побывала на Майдане', 10 December 2013, accessed on 10 December 2013. http://korrespondent.net/ukraine/politics/3276159-eshton-pered-vstrechei-s-yanukovychem-pobyvala-na-maidane

'Ethno-linguistic map of Austria-Hungary', 1910. Accessed on 4 February 2015. http://en.wikipedia.org/wiki/Austria-Hungary#mediaviewer/File:Austria_Hungary_ethnic.svg

'EU accused over Kosovo mission failings', 6 November 2014. http://www.theguardian.com/world/2014/nov/06/eu-accused-over-kosovo-mission-failings

'EU-backed Nabucco project 'over' after rival pipeline wins Azeri gas bid', 27 June 2013. http://www.euractiv.com/energy/eu-favoured-nabucco-project-hist-news-528919

'EU pact challenges Russian influence in the East.' 7 May 2009. http://www.theguardian.com/world/2009/may/07/russia-eu-europe-partnership-deal

'EU-Ukraine Summits: 16 Years of Wheel-Spinning', 28 February 2013, accessed on 29 February 2016. http://ukrainianweek.com/Politics/73494

'EU won't compensate Ukraine for losing Russian market from January 1 — EU commissioner', 19 November 2015, accessed on 21 January 2016. http://tass.ru/en/economy/837849

'European Commission Green Paper on the feasibility of introducing Stability Bonds', MEMO 11//820, 23 November 2011, accessed on 20 January 2016. http://europa.eu/rapid/press-release_MEMO-11-820_en.htm

'European Union spending and contributions 2010', 26 January 2012. http://www.theguardian.com/news/datablog/2012/jan/26/eu-budget-european-union-spending#data

Evangelista, Joshua, 'Ucraina, la milizia nazionalista con dentro nazi ed ebrei', 10 December, 2014. Accessed on 1 March 2016. http://temi.repubblica.it/micromega-online/ucraina-la-milizia-nazionalista-con-dentro-nazi-ed-ebrei/?printpage=undefined

'ЕВРАЗИЙСКОЕ ЭКОНОМИЧЕСКОЕ СООБЩЕСТВО', http://evrazes.com/en/about/

'Евросоюз не расслышал предложения Украины', 26 November 2013, accessed on 26 November 2013. http://www.kommersant.ua/doc/2352676

'Еврокомиссия давит на участников South Stream', 19 June 2014, accessed on 31 August 2014. http://www.kommersant.ru/doc/2494070

'Facts and figures', Eurasian Development bank. http://www.eabr.org/e/about/figures-facts/

'FM Kozhara tells US, EU ambassadors Rada's laws meet democratic standards', 17 January 2014, accessed on 17 January 2014. http://www.ukrinform.ua/eng/news/fm_kozhara_tells_us_eu_ambassadors_radas_laws_meet_democratic_standards_316142

'France may scrap Russian warship deal over Ukraine crisis', 18 March 2014, accessed on 18 March 2014. http://sputniknews.com/russia/20140318/188536562/France-May-Scrap-Russian-Warship-Deal-over-Ukraine-Crisis.html

Freedom Support Act, Enrolled Bill as passed through the Senate and the House of Representatives, S.2532 1992, accessed on 5 November 2014. http://thomas.loc.gov/cgi-bin/query/F?c102:1:./temp/~c102yFQjHe:e926

'Гагаузия и Тараклия вслед за Приднестровьем станут зоной особого внимания России', 4 January 2014, accessed on 4 January 2014. http://www.kommersant.md/node/24239

'Gas per il dragone', LIMES. http://temi.repubblica.it/UserFiles/limes/Image/altro3/RU-CINA_gas%20per%20il%20dragone_big.jpg

'GDP at Market Prices', World Bank. Accessed on 23 November, 2014. http://data.worldbank.org/indicator/NY.GDP.MKTP.CD/countries/EU?display=graph

'Генерал США объяснил, почему Киеву не дают Javelin', 12 December 2015, accessed on 12 December 2015. http://korrespondent.net/world/3601980-heneral-ssha-obiasnyl-pochemu-kyevu-ne-dauit-Javelin

'Генпрокуратура назвала незаконной передачу Крыма УССР', 27 June 2015, accessed on 27 June 2015. https://news.mail.ru/inregions/crimea/110/politics/22484922/?from-mail=1

'Филат признал, что Европейский союз не хочет интеграции Молдовы', 4 November 2013, accessed on 4 November 2013. http://point.md/ru/novosti/politika/filat-priznal-chto-evropejskij-soyuz-ne-hochet-integracii-moldovi

'Georgia in the foreign press', 27 November 2004, accessed on 29 February 2016. http://www.kvali.com/kvali/index.asp?obiektivi=show&n=195

'Глазами Беркута. МВД обнародовало свое видео, снятое на Грушевского', 21 January 2014, accessed on 21 January 2014. http://korrespondent.net/ukraine/events/3287130-hlazamy-berkuta-mvd-obnarodovalo-svoe-vydeo-sniatoe-na-hrushevskoho

'Голландцев успокоили, что Украина не вступает в ЕС', 8 January 2016, accessed on 8 January 2016. http://korrespondent.net/world/3612593-hollandtsev-uspokoyly-chto-ukrayna-ne-vstupaet-v-es

Gorbachev, Mikhail, quoted in Blomfield Adrian and Smith Mike, 'Gorbachev: US could start a new cold war', 6 May 2008. http://www.telegraph.co.uk/news/worldnews/europe/russia/1933223/Gorbachev-US-could-start-new-Cold-War.html

Gordon, Michael R., 'U.S. and Russia Reach Deal to Destroy Syria's Chemical Arms', 14 September 2013. http://www.nytimes.com/2013/09/15/world/middleeast/syria-talks.html?pagewanted=all&_r=1&

Gorenburg Dmitry, 'Countering Color Revolutions, Russia's New Security Strategy and Its implications for U.S. Policy', PONARS Eurasia Policy Memo No. 342, 15 September 2014, CAN, Harvard University. http://russiamil.wordpress.com/2014/09/15/countering-color-revolutions-russias-new-security-strategy-and-its-implications-for-u-s-policy/

'GUAM Leaders Hail Chisinau Summit', 22 April 2005, accessed on 26 February 2015. http://www.civil.ge/eng/article.php?id=9677

'GUAM Organization for Democracy and Economic Development', accessed on 27February 2015. http://en.wikipedia.org/wiki/GUAM_Organization_for_Democracy_and_Economic_Development#/media/File:Europe_location_GUAM.png

'GUAM organizational structure', accessed on 29 February 2016. http://guam-organization.org/en/node/269

'GUAM-USA Framework programm', accessed on 29 February 2016. http://guam-organization.org/en/node/291

'Half Ukrainian fighters killed by poor kit and friendly fire', 22 February 2015, accessed on 22 February 2015. http://www.thesundaytimes.co.uk/sto/news/world_news/Ukraine/article1522268.ece

'Harper accused of Exaggerating Ukrainian Genocide Death Toll', Kiev Ukraine News Blog, 30 October 2010, accessed on 10 February 2015. http://news.kievukraine.info/2010/10/harper-accused-of-exaggerating.html

'Henry, A. Kissinger looks back on the Cold War.' 4 November 2014. Accessed 23 February, 2016. http://www.cfr.org/united-states/henry-kissinger-looks-back-cold-war/p33741

'Imas Sondaj la Nivel national', Moldova, November 2014, accessed on 2 March 2016. http://ipn.md/infoprim/UserFiles/Image/PDF/Raport_IPN_perspective_alegeri_22.11.2014.pdf

'How to buy an EU citizenship', 13 September 2012, accessed on 1 March 2016. http://www.balkaninsight.com/en/article/how-to-buy-an-eu-citizenship

'How William Hague Deceived the House of Commons on Ukraine', 10 March 2014, accessed on 28 February 2016. http://www.huffingtonpost.co.uk/david-morrison/ukraine-willliam-hague_b_4933177.html

'Is western media coverage of the Ukraine crisis anti-Russian?', 4 August 2014, 1 March 2016. http://www.theguardian.com/world/2014/aug/04/western-media-coverage-ukraine-crisis-russia

'It's not Russia that's pushed Ukraine to the brink of war', 30 April 2014, 1 March 2016. http://www.theguardian.com/commentisfree/2014/apr/30/russia-ukraine-war-kiev-conflict

Jacoby, J.R. and Charles, H., 'Statement of General Charles H. Jacoby, JR. United States Army Commander, United States Army Commander, United States Northern Command and North American Aerospace Defense Command before the Senate Armed Services Committee', March 13,2014. http://www.northcom.mil/Portals/28/Documents/2014%20NC%20SASC%20Posture%20Statement.pdf

'Кабмин предлагает сократить расходы на образование и науку на 28%', 25 December 2014, accessed on January 29, 2015. http://news.mail.ru/inworld/ukraina/politics/20578890/

'Как они делят Украину', Published on 4 February 2014, accessed on 4 February 2014. https://www.youtube.com/watch?v=kOjrACdTQE8

Kapitonenko, Mykola, 'Resolving Post-Soviet "Frozen Conflicts": Is regional integration Helpful?' *Caucasian Review of International Affairs*, Vol. 3, No. 1 (2009). Accessed on 26 February 2015. http://www.cria-online.org/6_4.html

Kasyanenko, Mikita, 'On the 15th Anniversary of the ARC', ICC News Digest No.4 (Winter 2006), A Review of the 15th Anniversary of the Founding of the Autonomous Republic of Crimea (ARC). Accessed on 28 June 2016. http://www.iccrimea.org/news/newsdigest4.html

'Киевляне стали чаще жаловаться на Евромайдан – КГГА', 6 January 2014, accessed on 6 January 2014. http://korrespondent.net/kyiv/3282855-kyevliane-staly-chasche-zhalovatsia-na-evromaidan-khha

'Кличко исключил участие УДАРа в 'правительстве Януковича'14February 2014, accessed on 14 February 2014. http://news.liga.net/news/politics/979991-klichko_isklyuchil_uchastie_udara_v_pravitelstve_yanukovicha.htm

Kissinger, Henry A., 'Henry Kissinger: To settle the Ukrainian crisis, start at the end', 5 March 2014. https://www.washingtonpost.com/opinions/henry-kissinger-to-settle-the-ukraine-crisis-start-at-the-end/2014/03/05/46dad868-a496-11e3-8466-d34c451760b9_story.html

'Кличко открестился от Бандеры и его 'героизма", 2 January 2014, accessed on 2 January 2014. http://news.mail.ru/politics/16349438/

'Коаліція офіційно всохлася до 238 депутатів', 6 April 2007, accessed on 29 February 2016. http://www.unian.ua/politics/40758-koalitsiya-ofitsiyno-vsohlasya-do-238-deputativ.html

Korduban, Pavel, 'Were Ukrainian arms supplies to Georgia Illegal?', *Eurasia Daily Monitor*, Vol. 5, No. 22, 19 November 2008, accessed on 27 February 2015. http://www.jamestown.org/single/?no_cache=1&tx_ttnews%5Btt_news%5D=34145#.VVCoZCHtmko

Kranish, Michael, 'Bush says Ukraine should accept loose union with USSR', *The Boston Globe*, 2 August 1991, accessed on 28 February 2016. http://highbeam.com/doc/1P2-7671451.html

Kravets, David, 'Former Ukrainian PM sentenced for fraud', *The Associated Press*, 25 August, 2006, accessed on 16 February 2015. http://www.washingtonpost.com/wp-dyn/content/article/2006/08/25/AR2006082500897.html

Kucera, Joshua, 'U.S. formally closes its Kyrgyzstan Air Base', 3 June 2014, accessed on 23 February 2016. http://www.eurasianet.org/node/68430

Kuzio, Taras, 'Oligarchs wield power in Ukrainian politics', *Eurasia Daily Monitor*, Vol. 5, No. 125, 1 July 2008. Accessed on 25 February 2015. http://www.jamestown.org/single/?no_cache=1&tx_ttnews%5Btt_news%5D=33765#.VRl1Q_msWZw

Kuzio, Taras, 'Strident, Ambiguous and Duplicitous, Ukraine and the 2008 Russia-Georgia War', accessed on 1 March 2015. http://www.taraskuzio.net/International%20Relations_files/Kuzio_Georgia_Demok.pdf

Kuzio, Taras, 'The Rusyn question in Ukraine: Sorting out fact from fiction', *Canadian Review of Studies in Nationalism*, XXXII, 2005. http://www.taraskuzio.net/Nation%20and%20State%20Building_files/national-rusyns.pdf

Kuzio, Taras, 'Yushchenko and Yanukovych forge an electoral alliance', 5 January 2010, *Eurasia Daily Monitor*, Vol. 7, No. 2, accessed on 29 February 2016. http://www.jamestown.org/single/?tx_ttnews%5Btt_news%5D=35871&no_cache=1#.VVTDnvntmko

Kravchuk, Leonid, quoted in 'ЦИТАТА ДНЯ', 11 January 2016, accessed on 11 January 2016. http://korrespondent.net/quotation/6777-ya-kohda-slyshu-kak-nashy-lydery-hovoriat-da-my-vernem-krym-nash-nu-dlia-cheho-obmanyvat-samykh-sebia-y-ukraynskyi-narod-ne-vernem-cherez-luchshuui-zhyzn-v-ukrayne-ne-budet-nykohda-toho-chtoby-krym-skazal-my-poidem-nazad-v-ukraynu

'Кремль: США используют Украину как таран', 29 January 2015, accessed on 29 January 2015. http://korrespondent.net/world/russia/3472625-kreml-ssha-yspolzuuit-ukraynu-kak-taran

'Квасьневский рассказал о ненависти Януковича к Тимошенко', 19 November 2013, accessed on 19 November 2013. https://news.mail.ru/inworld/ukraine/politics/15706634/

'La défiance croissante des habitants de l'Est ukrainien envers l'armée de Kiev', 8 September 2014, accessed on 8 September 2014. http://www.lemonde.fr/international/article/2014/0 9/08/la-defiance-croissante-des-habitants-de-l-est-ukrainien -envers-l-armee-de-kiev_4483511_3210.html

'La Russie avance ses pions en Moldavie', *Le Monde*, 22 April 2015, accessed on 22 April 2015. http://www.lemonde.fr/decryptag es/article/2015/04/22/la-russie-avance-ses-pions-en-molda vie_4620603_1668393.html

'L'héroïne gangrène la Russie', *Le Monde*, 14 October 2010, http://www.lemonde.fr/europe/article/2010/10/14/l-heroin e-gangrene-la-russie_1426158_3214.html

'Le nouveau président ukrainien forme une coalition pour sortir le pays de la crise', 12 March 2010, accessed on 1 March 2015. http://www.lemonde.fr/europe/article/2010/03/12/le-nouv eau-president-ukrainien-forme-une-coalition-pour-sortir-le-pays-de-la-crise_1318204_3214.html

'Легионеры 'Азова': Как иностранцы воюют на Донбассе', 9 October 2014, accessed on 1 March 2016. http://korre spondent.net/ukraine/politics/3429499-lehyonery-azova-ka k-ynostrantsy-vouiuit-na-donbasse,

'Les cinq leçons du ' fuck the EU !' d'une diplomate américaine', *Le Monde*, 9 February 2014, accessed on 9 February 2014. http://www.lemonde.fr/europe/article/2014/02/09/les-cinq -lecons-du-fuck-the-eu-d-une-diplomate-americaine_436301 7_3214.html

Lieven, Anatol, 'Ukraine—The way out', 5 June 2014, accessed on 1 March 2016. http://www.nybooks.com/articles/archives/2 014/jun/05/ukraine-way-out/

Lomsadze, Giorgii, 'Georgia: Political crisis prompts speculation about Ivanishvili's political role', *Eurasianet*, 13 November 2014, accessed on 22 February 2015. http://www.eurasi anet.org/node/70911?utm_

'L'Ukraine met en garde Berlin contre un 'boycott politique' de l'Euro 2012', 30 April 2012, accessed on 30 April 2012. http://www.lemonde.fr/sport/article/2012/04/30/l-ukrain e-met-en-garde-berlin-contre-un-boycott-politique-de-l-euro -2012_1693037_3242.html

Lynch, Allen C., 'The Realism of Russia's Foreign Policy', *Europe-Asia Studies*, Vol. 53, No. 1, January, 2001, pages 7–31, Published by Taylor & Francis, Ltd. http://www.jstor.org/stable/826237, accessed on 17 October 2014, 11:48.

'L'Ukraine, cette guerre que les Européens ne veulent pas voir en face', 26 June 2015, accessed on 26 June 2015. http://www.letemps.ch/Page/Uuid/45671aec-1b5e-11e5-9d4e-1dfb5906ea79/LUkraine_cette_guerre_que_les_Europ%C3%A9ens_ne_veulent_pas_voir_en_face

'L'Ukraine renonce à s'associer avec l'UE, Ioulia Timochenko reste en prison', *Le Monde*, 21 November 2013, accessed on 21 November 2013. http://www.lemonde.fr/europe/article/2013/11/21/ioulia-timochenko-reste-en-ukraine_3518120_3214.html

'Майдан в Молдове. К чему приведут протесты', 22 January 2016, accessed on 22 January 2016. http://korrespondent.net/world/3618810-maidan-v-moldove-k-chemu-pryvedut-protesty

Major Russian pipelines. http://en.wikipedia.org/wiki/Nord_Stream#mediaviewer/File:Major_russian_gas_pipelines_to_europe.png

'Manifestation contre 1 milliard de dollars ' envolé ' en Moldavie', 4 May 2015, accessed on 4 May 2015. http://www.lemonde.fr/europe/article/2015/05/04/manifestation-contre-un-milliard-de-dollars-envole-en-moldavie_4626663_3214.html

'Map of the Tradnestrian Region', accessed on 4 September 2015. https://upload.wikimedia.org/wikipedia/commons/9/90/TransnistrianRegionMap.png

'Map of the War in Donbass', Situation on February 2015. Accessed on 30 July 2015. https://commons.wikimedia.org/wiki/File%3AMap_of_the_war_in_Donbass.svg

'Massimo d'Azeglio', accessed on 28 February 2016. http://it.wikiquote.org/wiki/Massimo_d%27Azeglio

'Медведев: Отношение ЕС к Украине похоже на неоколониализм', 12 December 2014, accessed on 29 January 2015. http://korrespondent.net/ukraine/3455983-medvedev-otnoshenye-es-k-ukrayne-pokhozhe-na-neokolonyalyzm

'Member State General Situation According to Significance of Impact' ,Memo 09/3, Brussels, 9 January 2009, accessed on 26 February 2015. http://europa.eu/rapid/press-release_MEMO-09-3_en.htm

'Memorandum on basic principles of the state system of the United States', 15 November 2003. Accessed on 3 March 2016. http://mfa-pmr.org/en/archive/all/2003

'Memorandum on security assurances in connection with Ukraine's accession to the treaty on the NPT', 19 December 1994. Published on 6 February 2014, accessed 29 February 2016. https://www.msz.gov.pl/en/p/wiedenobwe_at_s_en/news/memorandum_on_security_assurances_in_connection_with_ukraine_s_accession_to_the_treaty_on_the_npt

'MEPs Oppose South Stream, Seek Sanctions against Russian Energy Firms', 17 April 2014. http://www.novinite.com/articles/159923/MEPs+Oppose+South+Stream,+Seek+Sanctions+against+Russian+Energy+Firms

'Мэр Славянска подтвердила присутствие российских военных в городе', April 16 2014, accessed on 16 April 2014. http://korrespondent.net/ukraine/politics/3350468-mer-slavianska-podtverdyla-prysutstvye-rossyiskykh-voennykh-v-horode

'Меркель намерена поговорить с Путиным об Украине и Восточном партнерстве', 23November 2013, accessed on 23 November 2013. http://www.kommersant.ua/news/2351686

'Меркель: Нельзя ставить Украину перед выбором между Россией и ЕС', 18 December 2014, accessed on 18 December 2014. http://korrespondent.net/world/worldabus/3278376-merkel-nelzia-stavyt-ukraynu-pered-vyborom-mezhdu-rossyei-y-es

'Меркель – Путину: Мир в Украине – в обмен на ЗСТ с Евросоюзом', 23 January 2015. http://korrespondent.net/ukraine/politics/3470382-merkel-putynu-myr-v-ukrayne-v-obmen-na-zst-s-evrosouizom

Meyer, Herbert E., 'Why is the world so dangerous?' Memorandum for the Director of Central Intelligence, 30 November 1983. http://www.foia.cia.gov/sites/default/files/document_conversions/89801/DOC_0000028820.pdf

'Migration and remittances Factbook 2016', World Bank Group, accessed on 21 January 2016. http://siteresources.worldbank.org/INTPROSPECTS/Resources/334934-1199807908086/4549025-1450455807487/Factbookpart1.pdf

'Михаил Саакашвили стал губернатором Одесской области', 30 May 2015, accessed on 30 May 2015. Подробнее: http://www.kommersant.ru/doc/2738605

'Милиция не использовала огнестрельное оружие во время "освобождения улиц Киева" – МВД', 19 February 2014, accessed on 19 February 2014. http://korrespondent.net/ukraine/politics/3307616-mylytsyia-ne-yspolzovala-ohnestrelnoe-oruzhye-vo-vremia-osvobozhdenyia-ulyts-kyeva-mvd

'Минобороны Украины: ополченцы не могли захватить украинский "Бук"', 20 October 2014, accessed on 20 October 2014. http://news.mail.ru/politics/19885487/?frommail=1

'Minsk Agreement on the Ukrainian Crisis: Text in Full', 12 February 2015, accessed on 27 July 2015. http://www.telegraph.co.uk/news/worldnews/europe/ukraine/11408266/Minsk-agreement-on-Ukraine-crisis-text-in-full.html

'Minsk Protocol' by Goran tek-en. Licensed under CC BY-SA 4.0 via Wikimedia Commons – Accessed on 23 July 2015. https://commons.wikimedia.org/wiki/File:Minsk_Protocol.svg#/media/File:Minsk_Protocol.svg

'Министр иностранных дел Германии Гидо Вестервелле посетил митингующих на Евромайдане в центре Киева.' 3 December 2013, accessed on 3 December 2013. http://korrespondent.net/ukraine/politics/3274431-hlava-myd-hermanyy-posetyl-evromaidan-v-kyeve

'Moldavia and the Modern boundaries', accessed on 1 March 2016. https://en.wikipedia.org/wiki/History_of_Moldova#/media/File:MoldavianPrincipalityPhysical.jpg

'Moldova recount "confirms result,"' 17 April 2009. Accessed on 9 March 2015. http://news.bbc.co.uk/2/hi/europe/8004603.stm

'Moldova weighs up implications of overtures from EU and Russia', 30 April 2013, accessed on 2 March 2016. http://www.theguardian.com/world/2013/apr/30/moldova-implications-overtures-eu-russia

'Молдаване за год израсходовали на взятки более 62 млн евро — опрос', 3 November 2012, accessed on 5 August 2015. http://news.mail.ru/inworld/moldova/society/10823906/?frommail=1

'Молдовагаз» сегодня', accessed on 27 August 2015. http://www.moldovagaz.md/menu/ru/about-company/mg-today

'Molotov-Ribbentrop Pact', Moscow, 24 August 1939. Accessed on September 1st 2015: https://en.wikisource.org/wiki/Molotov%E2%80%93Ribbentrop_Pact

'Most censored countries', 2 May 2006. http://cpj.org/reports/2006/05/10-most-censored-countries.php

'Moscow respects will expressed by population of Donetsk and Luhansk regions of Ukraine', TASS, 12 May 2014, accessed on 12 May 2014. http://tass.ru/en/world/731214

'Московский комсомолец',: 'Хочешь мира, готовься... Страны ОДКБ провели успешные маневры в Кыргызстане', 7 August 2014. http://www.odkb-csto.org/news/detail.php?ELEMENT_ID=3594&SECTION_ID=92

Muller, Andrew, *The Guardian*, 3 December 2005 http://www.theguardian.com/media/2005/dec/03/tvandradio.russia

'На Евромайдане происходит внутренний конфликт – социолог', 23 December 2013, http://korrespondent.net/ukraine/politics/3279399-na-evromaidane-proyskhodyt-vnutrennyi-konflykt-sotsyoloh,

'На каких условиях Россия профинансировала Украину', Forbes Ukraine, 17 December 2013, accessed on 17 December 2013. http://forbes.ua/business/1362429-na-kakih-usloviyah-rossiya-profinansirovala-ukrainu?utm_source=korrespondent.net&utm_medium=picstrip&utm_campaign=KorrMain

'Natural Gas Proved Reserves', The World Factbook, accessed on 22 February 2015. https://www.cia.gov/library/publications/the-world-factbook/rankorder/2253rank.html

Nato-Russia Council Statement, 28 May 2002. http://archives.nato.int/nato-russia-council-statement-28-may-2002-rome-italy;isad

'Не менее 30 регионалов готовы пойти против Януковича – Шевченко', 9 February, 2014, accessed on 9 February 2014. http://news.liga.net/news/politics/976974-v_partii_regiono v_poyavilas_gruppa_gotovaya_idti_protiv_yanukovicha.htm

'НГ: В Украине может полыхнуть с новой силой', 20 December 2013, accessed on 20December 2013. http://korrespond ent.net/world/worldabus/3278895-nh-v-ukrayne-mozhet-po lykhnut-s-novoi-syloi

'Никто же ни фига не читает! Читать умеете?' Путин о Соглашении Украины с ЕС, 18 December 2013, accessed on 18 December 2013. http://korrespondent.net/business/eco nomics/3278646-nykto-zhe-ny-fyha-ne-chytaet-chytat-umee te-putyn-o-sohlashenyy-ukrayny-s-es

'Nina Shtanski: "New sanctions" of Moldova against Pridnestrovian car owners are "an own goal"', 27 August 2015, accessed on 3 March 2016. Ministry of Foreign Affairs of Pridnestrovian Moldavian Republic, http://mfa-pmr.org/en/BMt

'Nordstream', accessed on 26 February 2015. http://en.wiki pedia.org/wiki/Nord_Stream#/media/File:Nordstream.png

'Об Университете, информация о деятельности вуза', accessed on 1 March 2016. http://tdu-tar.md/ru/about

Obama, Barack, 'The transcript of President Obama's final State of the Union: What he said, and what it meant', *Washington Post*, 12 January 2016, accessed on 12 January 2016. https://www.washingtonpost.com/news/the-fix/wp/2016/0 1/12/what-obama-said-in-his-state-of-the-union-address-an d-what-it-meant/

'О ГАРАНТИЯХ ПРЕЗИДЕНТУ РОССИЙСКОЙ ФЕДЕРАЦИИ, ПРЕКРАТИВШЕМУ ИСПОЛНЕНИЕ СВОИХ ПОЛНОМОЧИЙ, И ЧЛЕНАМ ЕГО СЕМЬИ', Rossiskaya Gazeta, 31 December 1999, http://www.rg.ru/oficial/doc /ykazi/1763.htm

'О Заявлении Президиума Верховного Совета Крымской АССР', Органы власти АРК, Президиум ВР АРК; Постановление, Заявление от 01.10.1991 № 136-1, accessed on 1 March 2016. http://zakon4.rada.gov.ua/krym/show/rb0136003-91

'Operation Iraqi Freedom', accessed on 15 February 2015. http://c21.maxwell.af.mil/iraq.htm#willing

'Оппозиция уже не в состоянии контролировать радикалов – Захарченко', 25January 2014, accessed on 25 January 2014. http://korrespondent.net/ukraine/politics/3297085-oppozy tsyia-uzhe-ne-v-sostoianyy-kontrolyrovat-radykalov-zakharc henko

'Организация договора о коллективной безопасности', accessed on February 22,2016. http://www.odkb-csto.org/

'Ответственность за поджог Дома профсоюзов лежит на 'Правом секторе' – МВД', 19 February 2014, accessed on 19 February 2014. http://korrespondent.net/ukraine/politics/3 307613-otvetstvennost-za-podzhoh-doma-profsouizov-lezhyt -na-pravom-sektore-mvd

'Пан Березовский вершит историю Украины', 15 September 2005, accessed on 29 February 2016. http://lenta.ru/artic les/2005/09/15/money/

Parfitt, Tom, 'Document proclaiming death of Soviet Union missing', 7 February 2013. http://www.telegraph.co.uk/news /worldnews/europe/russia/9854619/Document-proclaiming -death-of-Soviet-Union-missing.html

Paul, Robert. 'The Rusyn language question revisited', in *Of the Making of Nationalities There Is No End*, edited by Magocsi, Paul Robert, Vol. I. New York, Columbia University Press/East European Monographs, 1999, pages 86–111, accessed on 4 January 2015. http://www.rusyn.org/images/4.%20Rusyn% 20Language%20Question%20Revisted.pdf

'Парламент Крыма призывает Януковича жестко навести порядок в стране', 20 January 2014, accessed on 20 January 2014. http://korrespondent.net/ukraine/politics/3286979- parlament-kryma-pryzyvaet-yanukovycha-zhestko-navesty- poriadok-v-strane

'Parliament passes law on parliamentary elections', 17 November 2011, accessed on 29 February 2016. http://www.kyivpost.co m/content/politics/parliament-passes-law-on-parliamentary -elections-117151.html

'Partitions of Poland.' Accessed on 45 February 2015. http://e n.wikipedia.org/wiki/Partitions_of_Poland#me- diaviewer/File:Rzeczpospolita_Rozbiory_3.png

'Periods of the Foreign Policy of Ukraine', Pak-Ukraine Trade and Culture information centre, accessed on 28February 2016. http://pakukrainecentre.com/fpou.htm

'Первое заседание Верховного совета ПМР нового созыва состоится в среду Sputnik Молдова', 22 December 2015, accessed on 22December 2015. http://ru.sputnik.md/moldova/20151222/3808962.html

'Первым заместителем министра юстиции назначили грузина', 14 January 2015, accessed on 14 January 2015. http://korrespondent.net/ukraine/politics/3466575-pervym-zamestytelem-mynystra-yustytsyy-naznachyly-hruzyna

Petro, Nicolai, 'Why Ukraine needs Russia more than ever', *The Guardian*, 9 March 2016, Consulted on 12 March 2016. http://www.theguardian.com/world/2016/mar/09/ukraine-needs-russia-nicolai-petro

'Президент Румынии напомнил, что стремится к объединению страны с Молдовой', 13 August 2013, accessed on 13 August 2013. http://korrespondent.net/world/1591893-prezident-rumynii-napomnil-chto-stremitsya-k-obedineniyu-strany-s-moldovoj

'Police implicate, link Klitschko brothers, other opposition members to Chornovol beating suspects', 27December 2013, accessed on 27 December 2013. http://www.kyivpost.com/content/ukraine/police-implicate-link-klitschko-brothers-other-opposition-members-to-chornovol-beating-suspects-334343.html

'Polish plumber' beckons French', 21June 2005, accessed on 23 February 2016. http://news.bbc.co.uk/2/hi/europe/4115164.stm

'Политическая карма Виктора Я', 10 June 2005, accessed on 29 February 2016. http://www.from-ua.com/articles/7569-politicheskaya-karma-viktora-ya.html

'Політичні партії України у взаємодії зі структурами влади', accessed on 16 February 2015. http://analitik.org.ua/ukr/publications/joint/3dd12dea/3dd13f15/

'Population Census 2004', Republic of Moldova. Accessed on 1 March 2016. http://www.statistica.md/pageview.php?l=en&idc=263&id=2208

'Post-Soviet integration process to benefit Moscow-Tashkent relations', 10 December 2014. http://itar-tass.com/en/economy/766223

'ПОЗАЧЕРГОВІ ВИБОРИ ПРЕЗИДЕНТА УКРАЇНИ', 25 May 2014, accessed on 25 May 2014. http://www.cvk.gov.ua/info/protokol_zvo_28.05.2014.pdf

'Патриарх помолился за экономику Приднестровья', 9 September 2013, accessed on 17 September 2013. http://www.kommersant.md/node/20462

'Правительство Молдовы подтверждает, что будет осуществлять пограничный контроль на Днестре', 22 November 2013, accessed on 22 November 2013. http://novostipmr.com/ru/news/13-10-22/pravitelstvo-moldovy-podtverzhdaet-chto-budet-osushchestvlyat

'Предложение Януковича занять пост премьера повергло Яценюка в шок—СМИ', 25 January 2014, accessed on 25 January 2014. http://korrespondent.net/ukraine/politics/3297200-predlozhenye-yanukovycha-zaniat-post-premera-poverhlo-yatsenuika-v-shok-smy

'Приднестровье евроинтегрироваться не спешит', 10 September 2015, accessed on 10 September 2015. http://www.pnp.ru/news/detail/96907

'PRELIMINARY FINDINGS ON THE EVENTS IN ANDIJAN, UZBEKISTAN 13 MAY 2005', 20 June 2005, accessed on 23 February 2016. http://www.osce.org/odihr/15653?download=true

'Премьер Грузии объявил Саакашвили врагом народа', 26 December 2014, accessed on 22 February 2016. http://korrespondent.net/world/3461040-premer-hruzyy-obiavyl-saakashvyly-vrahom-naroda

'Президент Приднестровья рассказал за чей счет летает на чартерных рейсах', 24 April 2015, accessed on 24 April 2015. http://www.kp.md/daily/26371/3252519/

'President's office ex-official blows Yushchenko-Yanukovych secret deal', 8 January 2010, accessed on 5 March 2015. http://zik.com.ua/en/news/2010/01/08/211289

'При Януковиче было больше свободы слова, чем при Порошенко – Ляшко', 18 February 2015, accessed on 18 February 2015. http://korrespondent.net/ukraine/politics/3480836-pry-yanukovyche-bylo-bolshe-svobody-slova-chem-pry-poroshenko-liashko

'Приднестровье нарастило внешний товарооборот в первом квартале 2014 года', 16 April, 2014, accessed on 16 April 2014. http://www.kommersant.md/node/28572

'Principalities of the Kievan Rus'.' Accessed on 28 February 2016. http://en.wikipedia.org/wiki/Kievan_Rus%27#mediaviewer/File:Principalities_of_Kievan_Rus%27_(1054-1132).jpg

'Pro-Russian "republic" Transnistria calls up reservists as East-West tensions flare', *The Telegraph*, 22 July 2015, accessed on 23 July 2015. http://www.telegraph.co.uk/news/worldnews/europe/moldova/11753765/Pro-Russian-republic-Transnistria-calls-up-reservists-as-East-West-tensions-flare.html

'Proclamation 4311', 8 September 1974. http://en.wikisource.org/wiki/Proclamation_4311

Profile Mikhail Prokhorov on Forbes List as April 2014. http://www.forbes.com/profile/mikhail-prokhorov/

'Proiectul legii cu privire la denunțarea Acordului de constituire a Comunității Statelor Independente nr.40-XII din 08.04.1994', 25March 2014. http://www.parlament.md/ProcesulLegislativ/Proiectedeactelegislative/tabid/61/LegislativId/2230/language/ro-RO/Default.aspx

'Почему Порошенко молчит о блокаде Крыма – СМИ', 3 December 2015, accessed on 3 December 2015. http://korrespondent.net/ukraine/3598301-pochemu-poroshenko-molchyt-o-blokade-kryma-smy

'Проект Постанови про питання участі України в Співдружності Незалежних Держав', 27 November 2014. http://w1.c1.rada.gov.ua/pls/zweb2/webproc4_1?pf3511=52424

'Протокол Центральної виборчої комісії', 30 September 2007, accessed on 28 February 2016. http://www.cvk.gov.ua/info/protokol_cvk_2007.pdf

'Протокол Центральної виборчої комісії про результати голосування у день виборів Президента України', published on 25 January 2010, accessed on 4 March 2015. http://www.cvk.gov.ua/info/protokol_cvk_17012010.pdf

'Протокол Центральної виборчої комісії про результати повторного голосування з виборів Президента України', published on 14February 2010, accessed on 4 March 2015. http://www.cvk.gov.ua/info/protokol_cvk_07022010.pdf

'ПРОТОКОЛ ЦЕНТРАЛЬНОЇ ВИБОРЧОЇ КОМІСІЇ ПРО РЕЗУЛЬТАТИ ВИБОРІВ НАРОДНИХ ДЕПУТАТІВ УКРАЇНИ У ЗАГАЛЬНОДЕРЖАВНОМУ БАГАТОМАНДАТНОМУ ВИБОРЧОМУ ОКРУЗІ', 10 November 2012, accessed on 5 March 2015. http://www.cvk.gov.ua/info/zbvo_2012.pdf

'Putin: Kyrgyzstan signs deal to join Eurasian Economic Union', 23December 2014. http://sputniknews.com/business/201412 23/1016151391.html

'Путин назвал условие сохранения территориальной целостности Украины', 10 February 2014, accessed on 10 February 2014. http://korrespondent.net/ukraine/politics/3 426731-putyn-nazval-uslovye-sokhranenyia-terrytoryalnoi-ts elostnosty-ukrayny

'Путин предложил создать зону свободной торговли с Евросоюзом', 28 January 2014, accessed on 28 January 2014. http://news.liga.net/news/politics/969816-putin_predlozhi l_sozdat_zonu_svobodnoy_torgovli_s_evrosoyuzom.htm

'Путин пустил электричество в Крым', 2 December 2015, accessed on 2 December 2015. http://korrespondent.net/uk raine/3597884-putyn-pustyl-elektrychestvo-v-krym

'Putin wants NATO to let Russia join', 18 July 2001. http://www.de seretnews.com/article/853851/Putin-wants-NATO-to-let-Ru ssia-join.html?pg=all

'R&B poll: 17% of Ukrainians would vote "against everybody" during elections', 11November 2012, accessed on 11 November 2012. http://en.interfax.com.ua/news/general/128943.html

Rasmussen, Sun Engel, 'NATO ends combat operations in Afghanistan', 28 December 2014. http://www.theguardian.co m/world/2014/dec/28/nato-ends-afghanistan-combat-oper ations-after-13-years

'Разгона Майдана не будет – Захарченко', 11 December 2013, accessed on 11 December 2013. http://korrespondent.net/ukraine/politics/3276258-razghona-maidana-ne-budet-zakharchenko

'Regions and territories: Ajaria', 22 November 2011. http://news.bbc.co.uk/2/hi/europe/country_profiles/3520322.stm

Rodriguez Araujo Octavio, 'México y el ejemplo de Ucrania', *La Jornada*, July 27, 2006. Accessed on 29 February 2016. http://www.jornada.unam.mx/2006/07/27/index.php?section=politica&article=032a1pol

'Рогозин: Россия не выведет миротворцев из Приднестровья', 18 May 2013, accessed on 18 May 2013. http://news.mail.ru/inworld/moldova/politics/13139361/?frommail=1

'Romanian becomes regional language in Bila Tserkva in Zakarpattia region', 24 September 2012, accessed on 29 February 2016. http://www.kyivpost.com/content/ukraine/romanian-becomes-regional-language-in-bila-tserkva-in-zakarpattia-region-313373.html

'Россия останавливает строительство Южного потока', 2 December 2014. http://korrespondent.net/business/economics/3450548-rossyia-ostanavlyvaet-stroytelstvo-yuzhnoho-potoka

'Россия развязала торговую войну с еще одним западным соседом', 10 September 2013, accessed on 10 September 2013. http://korrespondent.net/business/economics/1601882-rossiya-razvyazala-torgovuyu-vojnu-s-eshche-odnim-zapadnym-sosedom

'Россия считает новые власти Украины нелегитимными—МИД РФ', 24 February 2014, accessed on 24 February 2014. http://korrespondent.net/world/russia/3310699-rossyia-schytaet-novye-vlasty-ukrayny-nelehytymnymy-myd-rf

'Round Two: EU Grooming Klitschko to Lead Ukraine', 10 December 2013, accessed on 39 February 2016. http://www.spiegel.de/international/europe/eu-grooms-boxer-vitali-klitschko-to-lead-ukraine-opposition-a-938079.html

'Румыния объявила тендер на строительство газопровода Яссы-Унгены', 5 May 2013, accessed on 5 May 2013. http://news.mail.ru/inworld/moldova/economics/12970816/?frommail=1

'Russia "blackmailed Ukraine to ditch EU pact"' The Guardian, 22 November 2013, accessed on 22 November 2013. http://www.theguardian.com/world/2013/nov/22/russia-ukraine-eu-pact-lithuania

'Russia does not rule out future NATO membership', 1 April 2009. http://euobserver.com/defence/27890

'Russia has more right to Crimea than Britain to Falkands, says Russian MP', 23 March 2015, accessed on March 1st. 2016. http://www.theguardian.com/world/2015/mar/23/russia-has-more-right-to-crimea-than-britain-to-falkands-says-russian-mp

'Russia hits West with food import ban in sanctions row', 7 August 2014, accessed on 7 August 2014. http://www.bbc.com/news/world-europe-28687172

'Russia hopes to open consulate in Tiraspol', 12 September 2012. Accessed on 12 September 2012. http://www.allmoldova.com/en/moldova-news/1249054177.html

'Russia imposes sanctions on Turkey over downed plane', The Guardian, 26 November 2015, accessed on 26 November 2015. http://www.theguardian.com/world/2015/nov/26/hollandes-anti-isis-talks-with-putin-complicated-by-downing-of-russian-jet

'Russia suspicious of GUAM motives', 20 June 2007, accessed on 22 February 2015. http://www.isn.ethz.ch/Digital-Library/Articles/Detail/?lang=en&id=53439

'Russia tells Ukraine to stay out of NATO', 8 June 2006, The Guardian, accessed on 24 February 2015. http://www.theguardian.com/world/2006/jun/08/russia.nickpatonwalsh

'Russia to boost Artic research', 23-IX-2009. http://blogs.nature.com/news/2010/09/russia_to_boost_arctic_researc.html

'Russia to charge Greenpeace activists with piracy over oil rig protest', The Guardian, 24 September 2013. http://www.theguardian.com/environment/2013/sep/24/russia-greenpeace-piracy-oil-rig-protest

'Russia's claim under Polar irks Americans', 19 February 2008. http://www.nytimes.com/2008/02/19/world/europe/19arctic.html?adxnnl=1&adxnnlx=1311810481-IXSrMDBjzhfGopGmYcf6tw&_r=0

'Russia's national security strategy for 2016 in 9 key points', Klimentyev Michael, Sputnik, 31 December 2015, accessed on 3 March 2016. https://www.rt.com/news/327608-russia-national-security-strategy/

'SA-17 Grizzly 9A317E BUK-M2 air defense missile system', accessed on 1 March 2016. http://www.armyrecognition.com/russia_russian_missile_system_vehicle_uk/sa-17_grizzly_buk-m2_9a317e_missile_technical_data_sheet_specifications_description_pictures.html

'Саакашвили запрещен въезд в Украину по требованию нардепа Царева—Ъ', 24 December 2013, accessed on 24 December 2013. http://korrespondent.net/ukraine/politics/3279907-saakashvyly-zapreschen-vezd-v-ukraynu-po-trebovanyui-nardepa-tsareva

'Schematic map of Gagauzia', accessed on 1 March 2016. https://en.wikipedia.org/wiki/Gagauzia#/media/File:Gagauzja.png

'Schuman declaration', 9 May 1950. http://www.schuman.info/9May1950.htm

Shekhovstov, Anton and Umland, Andreas, 'Ukraine's radical right', *Journal of Democracy*, Vol. 25, No. 3 (July 2014), accessed on 27 February 2015. http://muse.jhu.edu/journals/journal_of_democracy/v025/25.3.shekhovtsov.html

'США даст Киеву миллиард в обмен на отставку Шокина – СМИ', 21 January 2016, accessed on 21 January 2016. http://korrespondent.net/ukraine/politics/3618420-ssha-dast-kyevu-myllyard-v-obmen-na-otstavku-shokyna-smy

'Симоненко больше не поддерживает Януковича', 26 January 2014, accessed on 26 January 2014. http://delo.ua/ukraine/simonenko-bolshe-ne-podderzhivaet-janukovicha-225502/?supdated_new=1390867181

'Single European Act, 1986', accessed on 23 February 2016. http://en.wikisource.org/wiki/Single_European_Act

Snyder, Timothy, 'Holocaust: The ignored reality', *Eurozine*, 26 June 2005, accessed on 28 February 2016. http://www.eurozine.com/articles/2009-06-25-snyder-en.html

Socor, Vladimir, 'Moldovan Government chickens out of Historical Assessment of Communism', *Eurasia Daily Monitor*, Vol. 7, No. 126, 30 June 2010. Accessed on 5 April 2015. http://www.jamestown.org/programs/edm/single/?tx_ttnews%5Btt_news%5D=36552&tx_ttnews%5BbackPid%5D=484&no_cache=1#.VcYl9fntmko

South Stream pipeline, accessed on 2 March 2014. http://en.wikipedia.org/wiki/South_Stream#mediaviewer/File:South_Stream_map.png

'Soviet Union Administrative Divisions', 1989. http://en.wikipedia.org/wiki/History_of_the_Soviet_Union_(1982%E2%80%9391)#mediaviewer/File:Soviet_Union_Administrative_Divisions_1989.jpg

'США профинансируют команду Саакашвили', 6 July 2015, accessed on 1 March 2016. https://news.mail.ru/politics/22574674/?frommail=1

'США требуют от Ахметова и Клюева поднять партийный бунт против Януковича. Иначе – санкции', 13 December 2013, accessed on 13 December 2013. http://censor.net.ua/news/263364/ssha_trebuyut_ot_ahmetova_i_klyueva_podnyat_partiyinyyi_bunt_protiv_yanukovicha_inache_sanktsii

'США вводят санкции против ряда граждан', Украины, 22 January 2014, accessed 22 January 2014. http://korrespondent.net/ukraine/politics/3287579-ssha-vvodiat-sanktsyy-protyv-riada-hrazhdan-ukrayny

'Sheremeta explains his resignation as being due to uncoordinated appointment of trade representative', 21 August 2014, accessed on 21 August 2014. http://en.interfax.com.ua/news/economic/219334.html

'Statement by EU High Representative Catherine Ashton on Ukraine', Brussels, 21 November 2013, 131121/04. www.eeas.europa.eu

'Status of world nuclear forces.' Accessed on 23 February 2016. http://fas.org/issues/nuclear-weapons/status-world-nuclear-forces/

Stroophants Jean Paul, 'L'UE divisée sur un éventuel boycott de l'Euro 2012 en Ukraine', *Le Monde*, 14 May 2012, accessed on 14 May 2012. http://www.lemonde.fr/europe/article/2012/0 5/14/l-union-europeenne-divisee-sur-un-eventuel-boycott-d e-l-euro-2012-en-ukraine_1701148_3214.html

'Суркис Григорий Михайлович', 14 April 2015, accessed on 28 February 2016. http://file.liga.net/person/284-grigorii-syr kis.html

'Survival of the fittest', 16 May 1999, TIME http://content.tim e.com/time/magazine/article/0,9171,24834-2,00.html

'Таможенный союзник Гагаузия хочет к России, Белоруссии и Казахстану', 3 February 2014, accessed on 20 February 2014. http://www.kommersant.md/node/25241

'Taraclia District', accessed on 5 September 2015. https://en.wi kipedia.org/wiki/Taraclia_District#/media/File:Taraclia_di strict,_MDA.svg

'The indicators', http://fsi.fundforpeace.org/indicators, consulted on 27 June 2016.

'Third Wave of Sanctions Slams Russian Stocks', *The Moscow Times*, 17 July 2014, accessed on 3 March 2016. http://www.t hemoscowtimes.com/business/article/new-sanctions-wave-h its-russian-stocks/503604.html

'Трагедия в Одессе: у каждой из сторон своя версия', 5 May 2014, accessed on 5 May 2014. http://news.mail.ru/politi cs/18081380/?frommail=1

'Transnistriche Moldawische Republik (Moldawien), 17. September 2006: Unabhängigkeitskurs und Beitritt zu Russland', acces sed on 18 March 2015. http://www.sudd.ch/event.php ?lang=en&id=md012006

'Transnistriche Moldawische Republik (Moldawien), 17. September 2006: Verzicht auf Unabhängigkeit', accessed on 18 March 2015. http://www.sudd.ch/event.php?lang=en&id=md022006

'The Constitution of the Russian Federation', Chapter 3 The Federal Structure. http://www.constitution.ru/en/10003000-04.htm

'The Foreign Policy Concept of the Pridnestrovian Moldovan Re public', 20 November 2012, accessed on 22 November 2012. http://mfa-pmr.org/en/yGL

'The Great Soviet Encyclopedia', 3rd Edition. S.v. 'Slovo i Delo Gosudarevo', accessed on 4 February 2015. http://encycloped ia2.thefreedictionary.com/Slovo+i+Delo+Gosudarevo

'The Khadija project', accessed on 23 February 2016. http://occrp.org/free-khadija-ismayilova/

'The not-very-nice things U.S. officials used to say about Ukraine's new president', 29 May 2014, accessed on 29 May 2014. http://www.washingtonpost.com/blogs/worldviews/wp/201 4/05/29/the-not-very-nice-things-u-s-officials-used-to-say-about-ukraines-new-president/

'The Old Guard wins in Transdniestria', 19 September 2006, accessed on 18 March 2014. http://www.kommersant.com /p705753/r_1/The_Old_Guard_Wins_in_Transdniestria/

'The Polish-Lithuanian Commonwealth in 1569.' Accessed on 4 January 2015. http://en.wikipedia.org/wiki/Union_of_Lub lin#mediaviewer/File:Irp1569.jpg

'Theses on the National Question.' Accessed on 6 February 2015. https://www.marxists.org/archive/lenin/works/1913/jun/30 .htm#fwV19E085

'Тирасполь подчеркнул сырьезность ситуации', 31 January 2014, accessed on 2 February 2014. http://www.kommers ant.md/node/25186

'Траян Бэсеску: Молдове нужно присоединиться к Румынии во имя евроинтеграции', 6 January 2014, accessed on 6 January 2014. http://www.kommersant.md/node/24263

'Treaty on European Union/ Title V: Provisions on a Common Foreign and Security Policy', http://en.wikisource.org/wiki/T reaty_on_European_Union/Title_V:_Provisions_on_a_Co mmon_Foreign_and_Security_Policy

'Treaty on the Eurasian Economic Union', 29 May 2014. https://translate.google.com/translate?hl=en&sl=ru&tl=en& u=http%3A%2F%2Fwww.alta.ru%2Fshow_orders.php%3Fa ction%3Dview%26filename%3D14bn0044&sandbox=1

'Три четверти украинцев стали жить хуже – опрос', 13 January 2016, accessed on 13 January 2016. http://korrespondent.net /ukraine/3614660-try-chetverty-ukrayntsev-staly-zhyt-khuz he-opros

'Турчинов отказался подписать решение Рады об отмене закона о языках', 2 March 2014, accessed on 28 February 2016. http://korrespondent.net/ukraine/politics/3314338-turchynov-otkazalsia-podpysat-reshenye-rady-ob-otmene-zakona-o-yazykakh

Турчинов опроверг описанные сепаратистами чудеса явки на 'референдум', 12 May 2014, accessed on 12 May 2014. http://www.pravda.com.ua/rus/news/2014/05/12/7025064/

'Угода між Україною і Російською Федерацією про статус та умови перебування Чорноморського флоту Російської Федерації на території України', 28 May 1997. Accessed on 29 February 2016. http://zakon4.rada.gov.ua/laws/show/643_076

'Участники Народного вече приняли резолюцию и выбрали сопредседателей гражданского объединения Майдан', 22 December 2013, accessed on 22 December 2013. http://korrespondent.net/ukraine/politics/3279454-uchastnyky-narodnoho-veche-prynialy-rezoluitsyui-y-vybraly-sopredsedatelei-hrazhdanskoho-obedynenyia-maidan

'Учение КСОР ОДКБ 'Взаимодействие-2014' началось в Казахстане', 8 August 2014, accessed on 22 February 2016. http://www.odkb-csto.org/news/detail.php?ELEMENT_ID=3600&SECTION_ID=91

'УКАЗ ПРЕЗИДЕНТА УКРАИНЫ № 127/2013', 12 March 2013, accessed on 27 February 2015. http://www.president.gov.ua/ru/documents/15520.html

'Украина под угрозой раскола по языковому признаку – ООН', 16 April 2014, accessed on 20 April 2014. http://korrespondent.net/ukraine/politics/3350493-ukrayna-pod-uhrozoi-raskola-po-yazykovomu-pryznaku-oon

'Ukraine crisis: Oligarchs are Yanukovych's weakest link', 20 February 2014, accessed on 20 February 2014. http://www.bbc.com/news/world-europe-26277970

'Ukraine Crisis: Putin adviser accused US of meddling', 6 February 2014, accessed on 6 February 2014. http://www.bbc.com/news/world-europe-26068994

'Ukraine : des enregistrements clandestins embarrassent les Etats-Unis', http://www.lemonde.fr/international/article/2014/02/07/ukraine-quand-une-diplomate-americaine-s-emporte-contre-l-ue_4361896_3210.html

'Ukraine faces critical East-West Tug of war over Association Agreement', *The Guardian*, 20 November 2013, accessed on 20 November 2013. http://www.theguardian.com/world/2013/nov/20/ukraine-eu-association-agreement-europe-russia

'Ukraine forces 'helpless' to stop pro-Russia takeover in east', *The Guardian*, April 30,2014, accessed on 1 March 2016. http://www.theguardian.com/world/2014/apr/30/ukraine-forces-helpless-stop-pro-russia-takeover-east

'Ukrainian holiday tradition under threat as popular Soviet film faces ban', 24 December 2015, accessed on 24 December 2015. http://www.theguardian.com/world/2015/dec/24/ukrainian-holiday-tradition-soviet-film-irony-of-fate-faces-ban

'Ukraine may get two Christmases as national identity debate begins', 31 December 2015, accessed on 31 December 2015. http://www.theguardian.com/world/2015/dec/31/ukraine-two-christmases-orthodox-church-russia

'Ukraine leader sacks government', *BBC News*, 8 September 2005. Accessed on 29 February 2016. http://news.bbc.co.uk/2/hi/europe/4225566.stm

'Ukraine: Les partisans de l'UE dispersés', Le Monde, 30 November 2013, accessed on 30 November 2013. http://www.lemonde.fr/europe/article/2013/11/30/ukraine-la-police-disperse-les-partisans-de-l-europe_3523130_3214.html

'Ukraine: l'opposant Timoshenko cessera sa grève de la faim mercredi', *Le Monde*, 8 May 2012, accessed on 8 May 2012. http://www.lemonde.fr/europe/article/2012/05/08/affaire-timochenko-l-ukraine-boycottee-annule-un-sommet-international_1697787_3214.html

'Ukrainian minister throws water in Odessa governor's face', 15 December 2015, accessed on 3 March 2016. http://www.theguardian.com/world/2015/dec/15/ukrainian-minister-throws-water-in-odessa-governors-face

'Ukraine "stealing Europe's gas"', 2 January 2006, accessed on 25 February 2015. http://news.bbc.co.uk/2/hi/europe/4574630.stm

'Ukraine suggests setting up GUAM peacekeeping unit', 31 May 2006, accessed on 26 February 2016. http://today.az/news/politics/26721.html

'Ukraine presidential election 1994 Second round', accessed on 28 February 2016. http://upload.wikimedia.org/wikipedia/commons/f/fe/Ukraine_presidential_elections_1994%2C_second_round.png

'Ukraine's EU trade deal will be catastrophic, says Russia', *The Guardian*, 22 September 2013, accessed on 22 September 2013. http://www.theguardian.com/world/2013/sep/22/ukraine-european-union-trade-russia

'Ukraine's Secret Weapon: Feisty Oligarch Ihor Kolomoisky', 27 June 2014, accessed on March 1st. 2016. http://www.wsj.com/articles/ukraines-secret-weapon-feisty-oligarch-ihor-kolomoisky-1403886665

'Ukrainian parliamentary election 2002', accessed on 29 February 2016. http://en.wikipedia.org/wiki/Ukrainian_parliamentary_election,_2002

'Украинская диаспора в 20 городах мира присоединяется к Маршу миллиона', 8 December 2013, accessed on 8 December 2013. http://korrespondent.net/ukraine/politics/3275314-ukraynskaia-dyaspora-v-20-horodakh-myra-prysoedyniaetsia-k-marshu-myllyona

'Ultimate betrayal: Ukraine retreats to a Dark past', 18 October 2011. Accessed on 25 February 2015. http://www.spiegel.de/international/europe/ultimate-betrayal-ukraine-retreats-to-a-dark-past-a-792458-2.html

'Ультимативная нота советского правительства румынскому правительству', 26 June 1940, accessed on 1 September 2015. http://ru.convdocs.org/docs/index-23045.html

'Unified Combatant Comands', accessed on 22 February 2016. http://upload.wikimedia.org/wikipedia/commons/e/e6/Unified_Combatant_Commands_map.png

'Union of Kreva', accessed on 4 January 2015. http://polishkingdom.co.uk/unionkreva.html

'Up in flames, Humanitarian Law Violations and Civilian Victims in the conflict over South Ossetia.' Humans Right Watch, 23 January 2009, Page 10. http://www.hrw.org/en/node/79681/section/10

'US imposes financial restrictions to reinforce Ukraine sanctions', December 22 2015, accessed on 3 March 2016. http://www.theguardian.com/us-news/2015/dec/22/us-financial-restrictions-ukraine-sanctions-russia

'В беспорядках в Киеве пострадали уже 254 правоохранителя – МВД', 23 January 2014, accessed on 23 January 2014. http://korrespondent.net/ukraine/3296288-v-besporiadkakh-v-kyeve-postradaly-uzhe-254-pravookhranytelia-mvd

'В Кабмине будет три министра-иностранца — Луценко', 2 December 2014, accessed on 2 December 2014. http://news.mail.ru/inworld/ukraina/politics/20329100/?frommail=1

'В киевском Евромайдане принимают участие грузинские оппозиционеры', 3 December 2013, accessed on 3December 2013. http://korrespondent.net/world/3273941-v-kyevskom-evromaidane-prynymauit-uchastye-hruzynskye-oppozytsyonery

'В Молдове румынский признали государственным языком', 5 December 2013, accessed on 2 September 2015. http://korrespondent.net/world/3274646-v-moldove-rumynskyi-pryznaly-hosudarstvennym-yazykom

'В Севастополе заявили о возможности создания государства Малороссия', 26 January 2014, accessed on 26 January 2014. http://korrespondent.net/ukraine/politics/3297354-v-sevastopole-zaiavyly-o-vozmozhnosty-sozdanyia-hosudarstva-malorossyia

'В столкновениях в Киеве погибли 25 человек – Минздрав', 19 February 2014, accessed on 19 February 2014. http://korrespondent.net/ukraine/politics/3307609-v-stolknovenyiakh-v-kyeve-pohybly-25-chelovek-mynzdrav

'В Тбилиси начался суд по делу против Саакашвили', 9 July 2015, accessed on 1 March 2016. http://korrespondent.net/world/3537567-v-tbylysy-nachalsia-sud-po-delu-protyv-saakashvyly

'В Узбекистане прошли парле выборы без оппозиции', 21 December 2014. http://korrespondent.net/world/3458976-v-uzbekystane-proshly-parlamentskye-vybory-bez-oppozytsyy

Vasilyeva, Nataliya, 'Conviction of Putin's foe sets off protest in Moscow', 30 December 2014, http://news.yahoo.com/putin-foe-arrives-court-hear-verdict-061609972.html

'Весь бизнес Порошенко. Журналисты составили список активов президента-олигарха', 30 May 2014, accessed on 30 May 2014, http://korrespondent.net/ukraine/politics/3371259-ves-byznes-poroshenko-zhurnalysty-sostavyly-spysok-aktyvov-prezydenta-olyharkha

'Весеннее обострение', 21 April 2013, accessed on 21 April 2013. http://profvesti.org/2013/04/21/10490/

'ВИБОРИ НАРОДНИХ ДЕПУТАТІВ УКРАЇНИ 26 березня 2006 року П Р О Т О К О Л ЦЕНТРАЛЬНОЇ ВИБОРЧОЇ КОМІСІЇ ПРО РЕЗУЛЬТАТИ ВИБОРІВ НАРОДНИХ ДЕПУТАТІВ УКРАЇНИ', accessed on 29 February 2016. http://www.cvk.gov.ua/info/protokol_cvk_2006.pdf

'Вибори-99: Кучма і КПУ — знову разом!' 15 May 1999. Accessed on 28 February 2016. https://web.archive.org/web/20140923002907/http://www.day.kiev.ua/uk/article/podrobici/vibori-99-kuchma-i-kpu-znovu-razom

'Виктор Янукович не отпустил Сергея Левочкина в отставку', Kommersant Ukraine online, 2 December 2013. Accessed on 2 December 2013. http://www.kommersant.ua/doc/2358759

'Военная доктрина Российской Федерации', 5 February 2010. http://kremlin.ru/supplement/461

'Wahlkreise Ukraine', 2006 eng, accessed on 29 February 2016. http://en.wikipedia.org/wiki/Ukrainian_parliamentary_election,_2006#/media/File:Wahlkreise_ukraine_2006_eng.png

'"We Gave the Americans a Blow Job," Got Nothing, Says Polish Foreign Minister', 22 June 2014, accessed on 25 January 2016. http://www.newsweek.com/we-gave-americans-blow-job-got-nothing-says-polish-foreign-minister-255863

Wilson Andrew, 'Yatseniuk loses fresh-face label, popularity after his financial backers exposed', *Kyiv Post*, 22 October 2009, accessed on 2 March 2015. http://www.kyivpost.com/o pinion/op-ed/yatseniuk-loses-fresh-face-label-popularity-aft er--51159.html

'World publics say governments should be more responsive to the will of the people', 12 May 2008, accessed on 29 February 2016. http://www.worldpublicopinion.org/pipa/articles/gove rnance_bt/482.php?lb=btgov&pnt=482&nid=&id=

'Why does Latvia still honour the Waffen-SS?' 16 March 2012. Accessed on 28 February 2016. http://www.newstatesman.co m/blogs/the-staggers/2012/03/latvia-riga-waffen-european

'World proven oil reserves by country', OPEC, 31 December 2013. http://www.opec.org/library/Annual%20Statistical%20Bul letin/interactive/current/FileZ/XL/T31.HTM

'World's ten most corrupt leaders', accessed on 29 February 2016. http://www.infoplease.com/ipa/A0921295.html

'Yanukovych has yet to secure ruling majority in parliament', 25 February 2010, accessed on 29 February 2016. https://ww w.kyivpost.com/content/ukraine/yanukovych-has-yet-to-sec ure-ruling-majority-in-pa-60468.html?flavour=mobile

'Янукович подписал закон об амнистии арестованных активистов Евромайдана', 23 December 2013, accessed on 23 December 2013. http://www.kommersant.ua/news/237 5677

'Yanukovych signs language bill into law', 8 August 2012, accessed on 29 February 2016. http://www.kyivpost.com/content/uk raine/yanukovych-signs-language-bill-into-law-311230.html

'Янукович заявил, что не собирался разгонять Майдан', 24 December 2014. Accessed on 24 December 2014. http://kor respondent.net/ukraine/politics/3460021-yanukovych-zaiav yl-chto-ne-sobyralsia-razghoniat-maidan

'Яценюк согласовывает министров с США? В сети появилось письмо премьеру', 5 July 2015, accessed on 5 July 2015. http://korrespondent.net/ukraine/3535860-yatsenuik-sohla sovyvaet-mynystrov-s-ssha-v-sety-poiavylos-pysmo-premeru

'Юлия Тимошенко нажила врагов в Швейцарии', 20 November 2013, accessed on 20 November 2013. http://www.kommersant.ua/doc/2347889

'Yulia Timoshenko will not challenge the results in Supreme Court', 20 February 2010, accessed on 5 March 2015. http://www.tymoshenko.ua/en/article/vu8az6s6

Yushchenko, Victor, 'Georgia and the stakes for Ukraine', *The Washing Post*, 12 August 2008, accessed on 28 February 2015. http://www.washingtonpost.com/wp-dyn/content/article/2008/08/24/AR2008082401856.html

'Yushchenko pushes for official recognition of OUN-UPA combatants', 10 January 2008, accessed on 23 February 2015. http://zik.com.ua/en/news/2008/01/11/121551

'Yushchenko to back Yanukovych in runoffs', 10 November 2009, accessed on 29 February 2016. http://zik.com.ua/en/news/2009/11/10/204057

Zaitchik, Alex and Ames, Mark, 'How the West helped invent Russia's election fraud: OCSE's whistle-blower exposes 1996 whitewash', 9 December 2011. http://exiledonline.com/how-the-west-helped-invent-russias-election-fraud-osce-whistleblower-exposes-1996-whitewash/

'Заявление Яценюка о финансовой помощи ЕС безосновательны – политолог', 3 February 2014, accessed on 3 February 2014. http://korrespondent.net/ukraine/politics/3300787-zaiavlenye-yatsenuika-o-fynansovoi-pomoschyes-bezosnovatelny-polytoloh

Zizek, Slavoj, 'Who can control the post-superpower capitalist order', *The Guardian*, 6 May 2014. http://www.theguardian.com/commentisfree/2014/may/06/superpower-capitalist-world-order-ukraine

'1861. L'Italia unita fanalino di coda rispetto all'Europa', 10 March 2011, accessed on 28 February 2016. http://www.corriere.it/unita-italia-150/11_marzo_10/de-cesare-italia-unita-fanalino-coda_13e7441c-4b22-11e0-9e9a-b429a0ac9415.shtml

2012 Georgian parliamentary election results. http://www.results.cec.gov.ge/index.html

Videos

'Best of Drunk Boris Yeltsin', Published on 7 April 2014. Accessed on 2 October 2014. http://www.youtube.com/watch?v=v9YnDirqwT4

'Bringing down a dictator', accessed on 27 October 2014. https://www.youtube.com/watch?v=UBvzsDUh8eY

Fabry Mikulas, 'Unrecognized States and National Identity', Geopolitical Conference, Prague, 13 November 2015, Published on 27 November 2015, accessed on 1 March 2016. https://www.youtube.com/watch?v=qAIgjCnDs5c

'House of Cards', Season 2 Episode 12. Written by Beau Willimon, Directed by James Foley. Netflix, 2014.

'La politica estera europea, tra mediterraneo, primavere arabe e crisi ucraina', Panzieri Antonio e Dromundo Rolando, Conference organized by the Partito Democratico at Iseo, Lombardy, Italy, 20 March 2014. Accessed on 23 February 2016. https://www.youtube.com/watch?v=EeBgkT8dJuE

'Марионетки майдана—puppets of the Maidan', Published on 6 January 2014. https://www.youtube.com/watch?v=YBWP48O_5Mo

'Putin: "Collapse of the Soviet Union was a major geopolitical disaster of the century"', Published on 12 January 2014. http://www.youtube.com/watch?v=nTvswwU5Eco

'Russian Godfathers', Published on 20 August 2012. http://www.youtube.com/watch?v=w_LE77YFnGk

'Поединок: Жириновский VS Прохоров', Published on 5 February 2012. https://www.youtube.com/watch?v=6B0LR7mn7-k

Ukraine, 'Appel intercepté Catherine Ashton/Urmas Paet (26/02/14) VOSTFR', Published on 16 March 2014. https://www.youtube.com/watch?v=equgXlRLePs

'Владимир Путин: "Люди в Приднестровье должны сами решать свою судьбу"', Published 17 April 2014, accessed on 2 March 2016. https://www.youtube.com/watch?v=o06hVmxkcWA

ibidem.eu